ISBN 978-0-282-76809-6
PIBN 10864137

1 MONTH OF
FREE
READING

at
www.ForgottenBooks.com

By purchasing this book you are eligible for one month membership to ForgottenBooks.com, giving you unlimited access to our entire collection of over 700,000 titles via our web site and mobile apps.

To claim your free month visit:
www.forgottenbooks.com/free864137

English
Français
Deutsche
Italiano
Español
Português

www.forgottenbooks.com

Mythology Photography **Fiction**
Fishing Christianity **Art** Cooking
Essays Buddhism Freemasonry
Medicine **Biology** Music **Ancient
Egypt** Evolution Carpentry Physics
Dance Geology **Mathematics** Fitness
Shakespeare **Folklore** Yoga Marketing
Confidence Immortality Biographies
Poetry **Psychology** Witchcraft
Electronics Chemistry History **Law**
Accounting **Philosophy** Anthropology
Alchemy Drama Quantum Mechanics
Atheism Sexual Health **Ancient History**
Entrepreneurship Languages Sport
Paleontology Needlework Islam
Metaphysics Investment Archaeology
Parenting Statistics Criminology
Motivational

HAKSPERE'S HOLINSHED

THE CHRONICLE
AND THE HISTORICAL PLAYS COMPARED

BY

W. G. BOSWELL-STONE

LONDON

LAWRENCE AND BULLEN, Ltd.
16 HENRIETTA STREET, COVENT GARDEN, W.C.

RICHARD CLAY & SONS, LIMITED,
LONDON & BUNGAY.

LIBRUM HUNC
QUEM SI APUD NOS HODIE VERSARETUR
IPSIS MANIBUS ACCIPERE DEBUIT
IN MEMORIAM MATRIS OPTIMAE
QUOD RESTAT, DEDICO.

CONTENTS.

	PAGE
PREFACE	ix
AUTHORITIES REFERRED TO IN THIS BOOK	xvii
CORRECTIONS AND ADDITIONS	xxiii

	PAGE		PAGE		PAGE
Lear . I. i. . . . 1		1 *Hen. IV.* II. iii. . . . 136		*Hen. V.* IV. viii. . . . 195
„ . „ iii., II. iv. . 4		„ „ iv. . . . „		„ V. Chorus . . 197
„ . IV. vii.—V. iii. 5		„ III. i. . . . 137		„ „ ii. . . . 199
Cymbeline III. i. . . . 7		„ „ ii. . . . 139		1 *Hen. VI.* I. i. . . . 205
„ V. iii. . . . 15		„ IV. i. . . . 142		„ „ ii. . . . 209
Macbeth L i. 18		„ „ ii. . . . 143		„ „ iii. . . . 212
„ „ iii.—II. iii. 22		„ „ iii. . . . „		„ „ iv. . . . 213
„ II. iv. . . . 31		„ V. i. . . . „		„ „ v.—vi. . . 215
„ III. iii. . . . 33		„ „ ii.—iv. . . 144		„ II. i. . . . 216
„ IV. i. . . . 35		„ „ v. . . . 147		„ „ ii. . . . 217
„ „ ii. . . . 36		2 *Hen. IV.* I. i. . . . 148		„ „ iii. . . . 218
„ „ iii. . . . 37		„ „ iii. . . . „		„ „ iv. . . . „
„ V. ii.—viii. . 40		„ II. iii. . . . 149		„ „ v. . . . 219
John . I. i. . . . 45		„ III. i. . . . 150		„ III. i. . . . 220
„ . II.—III. . . . 51		„ IV. i.—ii. . . „		„ „ ii. . . . 224
„ . IV. 59		„ „ iii. . . . 155		„ „ iii. . . . 226
„ . V. i. . . . 63		„ „ iv. . . . 156		„ „ iv. . . . 228
„ . „ ii. . . . 68		„ „ v. . . . 158		„ IV. i. . . . „
„ . „ iii. . . . 71		„ V. ii. . . . 161		„ „ ii.—vii. . . 230
„ . „ iv. . . . 72		„ „ v. . . . 164		„ V. i. . . . 234
„ . V. v.—vii. . . 73		*Hen. V.* I. Prol. . . . 165		„ „ ii. . . . 236
Rich. II. I. i. . . . 77		„ „ i. . . . 167		„ „ iii. . . . 237
„ „ ii. . . . 84		„ „ ii. . . . 168		„ „ iv. . . . 238
„ „ iii. . . . 86		„ II. Chorus . . 173		„ „ v. . . . 241
„ „ iv. . . . 89		„ „ ii. . . . „		2 *Hen. VI.* I. i. . . . 242
„ II. i. . . . 91		„ II. iv. . . . 177		„ „ ii. . . . 248
„ „ ii. . . . 97		„ III. Chorus . . 179		„ „ iii. . . . „
„ „ iii. . . . 100		„ „ i. . . . „		„ „ iv. . . . 252
„ „ iv. . . . 102		„ „ ii. . . . 180		„ II. i. . . . 253
„ III. i. . . . 104		„ „ iii. . . . 182		„ „ ii. . . . 255
„ „ ii. . . . 106		„ „ v. . . . „		„ „ iii. . . . 258
„ „ iii. . . . 107		„ „ vi. . . . 183		„ „ iv. . . . 261
„ „ iv. . . . 110		„ „ vii. . . . 185		„ III. i. . . . 262
„ IV. i. . . . „		„ IV. Chorus . . 186		„ „ ii. . . . 266
„ V. i. . . . 120		„ „ i. . . . 187		„ „ iii. . . . 269
„ „ ii.—iii. . . „		„ „ ii. . . . 188		„ IV. i. . . . 270
„ „ iv.—v. . . 124		„ „ iii. . . . 189		„ „ ii. . . . 271
„ „ vi. . . . 126		„ „ iv. . . . 191		„ „ iii. . . . 272
1 *Hen. IV.* I. i. . . . 130		„ „ vi. . . . 192		„ „ iv. . . . 273
„ „ iii. . . . 133		„ „ vii. . . . „		„ „ v. . . . 275

	PAGE		PAGE		PAGE
2 *Hen. VI.* IV. vi. . . .	275	3 *Hen. VI.* IV. viii. . . .	332	*Rich. III.* IV. iii. . . .	394
" " vii. . . .	276	" V. i. . . .	333	" " iv. . . .	397
" " viii. . . .	279	" " ii. . . .	337	" " v. . . .	406
" " ix. . . .	281	" " iii. . . .	,,	" V. i. . . .	409
" " x. . . .	283	" " iv. . . .	338	" " ii. . . .	410
" V. i. . . .	284	" " v. . . .	,,	" " iii. . . .	,,
" " ii.—iii. . .	288	" " vi. . . .	340	" " iv. . . .	418
3 *Hen. VI.* I. i. . . .	289	" " vii. . . .	341	*Hen. VIII.* I. i. . . .	424
" " ii. . . .	295	*Rich. III.* I. i. . . .	343	" " ii. . . .	431
" " iii. . . .	297	" " ii. . . .	345	" " iii. . . .	439
" " iv. . . .	298	" " iii. . . .	346	" " iv. . . .	440
" II. i. . . .	300	" " iv. . . .	348	" II. i. . . .	446
" " ii. . . .	303	" II. i. . . .	,,	" " ii. . . .	454
" " iii. . . .	305	" " ii. . . .	350	" " iii. . . .	455
" " v. . . .	306	" " iii. . . .	353	" " iv. . . .	,,
" " vi. . . .	307	" " iv. . . .	,,	" III. i. . . .	466
" III. i. . . .	308	" III. i. . . .	356	" " ii. . . .	469
" " ii. . . .	309	" " ii. . . .	362	" IV. i. . . .	482
" " iii. . . .	312	" " iii. . . .	368	" " ii. . . .	487
" IV. i. . . .	318	" " iv. . . .	,,	" V. i. . . .	493
" " ii.—iii. . .	322	" " v. . . .	373	" " ii. . . .	498
" " iv. . . .	324	" " vi. . . .	376	" " iii. . . .	499
" " v. . . .	,,	" " vii. . . .	377	" " v. . . .	505
" " vi. . . .	326	" IV. i. . . .	386		
" " vii. . . .	330	" " ii. . . .	387		

PREFACE.

ABOUT the compiler of the chronicles whence most of the historical excerpts in this book have been taken, we know nothing save what his will reveals. He there described himself as "Raphael Hollynshed of Bromecote [Bramcott] in the County of Warr[wick]"; and bequeathed all his property to "Thomas Burdett of Bromecote aforesaid Esq.," whom he calls "my Master." The will was made on October 1, 1578, and proved on April 24, 1582.[1]

The first edition of Holinshed's *Chronicles* appeared in 1577. John Hooker *alias* Vowell, Abraham Fleming, Francis Thynne, and others, produced a second edition, bringing down the English annals to January, 1587. In this second edition the text was altered or modernized,[2] and many new passages were added.

The historical authority used for some of the plays (when other works were not consulted) was apparently the second edition of Holinshed. In the subjoined parallel columns certain different readings of the two editions are collated, and a few enlargements of the second edition are noted. The left-hand column's references indicate the pages of this book, where the later readings or fresh matter will be found. The right-hand column gives references to the plays which have readings identical with or like the readings presented by the text of the second edition, or which embody matter added to that edition.

---

[1] Camden's *Annals*, I. cxlix, cl. For conjectures touching Holinshed's kindred, see the *Dictionary of National Biography*, under his name.

[2] In the story of Lear more than a dozen textual changes were made. I give two examples: *that you haue alwaies borne towards me*] ed. 2 (p. 3 below). *that towards me you haue alway borne* ed. 1.—*scarslie*] ed. 2 (p. 4 below). *vnneth* ed. 1.

HOLINSHED, ed. 2.	HOLINSHED, ed. 1.	PLAY.
wild] p. 23.	*ferly*	*wilde*] Mach. I. iii. 40.
In this yeare ... vnknowne euent] p. 103.	Not in ed. 1.	Rich. II., II. iv. 8.
pickthanks] p. 140.	::	1 Hen. IV., III. ii. 25.
In this yeare ... to be seene.] p. 158.	,,	2 Hen. IV., IV. iv. 125.
alledge euer against the kings of England in barre of their iust title] p. 169.	*alledge to defeate the Kyngs of England of their iust ... title*	*There is no barre To make against your Highnesse claime*] Hen. V., I. ii. 34, 35.
dishonest] p. 169.	*vnhonest*	*dishonest*] Hen. V., I. ii. 49.
who veurped] p. 170.	*which veurped*	*who veurpt*] Hen. V., I. ii. 69.
Numbers] p. 171.	*Numeri*	*Numbers*] Hen. V., I. ii. 98.
should shake the walles of the best court in France, p. 173.	*shoulde breake and batter downe the roofes of his houses about hys eares.*	*That all the Courts of France will be disturb'd*] Hen. V., I. ii. 265.
desolation] p. 177.	*destruction*	*desolation*] Hen. V., II. ii. 173.
offenses] p. 177.	Not in ed. 1.	*offenses*] Hen. V., II. ii. 181.
die your tawnie ground with your red bloud.] p. 185.	*make red your tawny ground with the effusion of christian bloud.*	*We shall your tawny ground with your red blood Discolour: ...*] Hen. V., III. vi. 170, 171.
In time of this siege ... hereafter followeth.] pp. 210–212.	Not in ed. 1.	1 Hen. VI., I. ii.
for hir pranks ... and witches.] pp. 238, 239.	,,	1 Hen. VI., V. iv.
Edward the third ... his grandsire ; ...] p. 256.	,,	2 Hen. VI., II. ii. 10-20.
Lionell the third ... died without issue.] p. 257.	,,	2 Hen. VI., II. ii. 34-38.
And the said ... same king Edward.] p. 258.	,,	2 Hen. VI., II. ii. 44-52.
a taper in hir hand.] p. 261.	,,	2 Hen. VI., II. iv. 16 (S. D.).
created the lord Thomas...saint Edwards chamber.] p. 347.	,,	Rich. III., I. iii. 255, 256.
wishing and ... casting away.] p. 410.	,,	Rich. III., V. ii. 20, 21.
The oration ... his armie.] p. 414.	,,	Rich. III., V. iii. 236 (S. D.).
The oration ... his armie.] p. 416.	,,	Rich. III., V. iii. 313 (S. D. in Qq.).
moothers meanes, ...] p. 417.	*brothers meanes*	*Mothers cost f*] Rich. III., V. iii. 324.

The second edition of Holinshed must have been employed for those parts of *Henry VIII.* which are based on Cavendish's *Life of Wolsey;* if the dramatist did not resort directly to Stow, in whose *Chronicles of England* (1580) selections from this biography were first published.

With regard to the wider question of sources, the reader will find that, in *Lear, Cymbeline,* and the historical plays preceding 1 *Henry VI.*, most of the borrowed action and dialogue can be illustrated by excerpts from Holinshed. Passages in the following plays—not traceable to Holinshed—are compared with other likely sources at the references given below: *John* (pp. 48-51); *Richard II.* (p. 118); 1 *Hen. IV.* (pp.

139 n. 2, 141 n. 2); 2 *Hen. IV.* (p. 163); *Hen. V.* (pp. 172, 173 n. 1, 185 n. 3, 186, 188).

As most of the quotations from Holinshed, illustrating the three Parts of *Henry VI.*, are paraphrases of Halle, it is generally impossible to determine which of these authorities was used, and I have therefore in such cases added a reference to the latter chronicler. But, when Halle alone is cited, the reader will understand that the subsequent excerpt is not paraphrased or copied in the second edition of Holinshed.[1] It is clear that the dramatist of *The First Part of Henry VI.* availed himself of accounts of Jeanne Darc, given by Holinshed (see pp. 210-212, 238, 239), which are not in Halle; and we may conjecture that Holinshed's paraphrase of Halle was the source of 1 *Hen. VI.*, V. i. 5, 6. In the passage illustrating these lines (p. 234 below), both editions of Holinshed read *peace* for *concorde.* Holinshed has : " exhorting them . . . to conforme themselues to reason, . . . so that, in concluding a godlie *peace*, they might receiue profit and quietnesse heere in this world," &c. The equivalent words of Halle are : " exhorting . . . them, . . . that they would . . . conforme themselfes to reason, and to Godly *concorde*, by the whiche they should receaue honor, profite, and continuall quietnesse in the worlde," &c. Ll. 83 and 95, 96, Act III. sc. ii. (pp. 225, 226), were probably derived from Holinshed. Fabyan may have yielded some details in Act I. sc. iii. (p. 213), Act III. sc. i. (p. 221), and Act III. sc. ii. (P. 225). Ll. 61-71, Act IV. sc. vii. (p. 233), were copied from an epitaph published by Crompton and Brooke in 1599 and 1619, respectively.[2]

The reviser who turned *The Contention* into *The Second Part of Henry VI.* was indebted to Holinshed or Stow for York's full pedigree [3] (pp. 256-258). Amalgamated with the dramatic version of Cade's revolt are many particulars—recorded by these chroniclers—of the villeins' outbreak in the reign of Richard II. (pp. 271, 272, 272 n. 2, 273 n. 4, 277, 278). Recourse to Holinshed (p. 251) is indicated by ll. 163, 164, Act I. sc. iii. ; and a hint for the Entry at Act II. sc. iv. l. 16, was probably taken from his chronicle (p. 261). The excerpts from Holinshed (pp. 246-249, 281), and from Stow (pp. 253, 261), may be regarded as possible sources of the play both in its

---

[1] *Halle,* 256 ("This deadly," &c., p. 306), the last clause of *Halle,* 293 (p. 334),—including the words "periured duke,"—and *Halle,* 300 (p. 338), are in the first edition of Holinshed. *Halle,* 296 (p. 337) and 295 (p. 338, n. 2), are slightly changed in *Hol.* ed. 1.

[2] Slight verbal resemblances suggest that the text of the inscription given by Brooke was the immediate source of these lines. See p. 233, n. 1, below.

[3] The pedigree in *The Contention* (1594) is very erroneous and defective. In *The Whole Contention* (1619) some mistakes were corrected, but York's descent from Philippa, daughter of Lionel Duke of Clarence, was not traced.

original and enlarged form. The same may be said of the quotations from Fabyan,[1] at pp. 246, 268, 276, and 286 ; though, in I. i. 114, the reviser uses a phrase—not, however, an uncommon one—which occurs *verbatim* in that chronicler (p. 245). A doubtful instance of resort to Hardyng will be found at p. 262. Neither Halle nor Holinshed gives Sir Thomas More's story of the sham miracle at St. Albans (pp. 253-255) ; dramatized in both forms of the play.

The Third Part of Henry VI. is, as a rule, based on Halle or on his paraphraser Holinshed ; but the dramatist appears to have profited also by Stow and parts of Holinshed's compilation which were not drawn from Halle. See pp. 291 n. 3, 293, 295, 296, 299, 302, 309.

Holinshed was the chief historical source of *Richard III.* Halle and Grafton contain the story mentioned in III. v. 76-79 (p. 374). In an Entry at III. vii. 94 (p. 383) Halle or Grafton's continuation of Hardyng was turned to account.

The primary authorities dramatized in *Henry VIII.* are Halle, Stow, Polydore Vergil, Foxe, and Cavendish. These materials—Foxe excepted—are brought together in the second edition of Holinshed. Most of the Fifth Act and some other portions of the play were derived from Foxe.

Valuable as Holinshed's *Chronicles* were as a store-house of our national history, the method pursued by the editors was uncritical. Thus, Raphael and his successors interwove the late and mostly fictitious *Historia Britonum* with authentic notices of British affairs, taken from Roman writers. (See pp. 7-13 below.) A few meagre facts recorded by Marianus Scottus, Tighernac, the *Ulster Annals*, and the *Saxon Chronicle* embrace nearly all that we know about the real Macbeth, but Holinshed presented to the reader a circumstantial romance composed by Hector Boece. From the scant genuine particulars extant, we may, I think, conjecture that Macbeth was not regarded as "an vntitled Tyrant" (*Macb.* IV. iii. 104) among his own Gaelic countrymen dwelling north of Edinburgh, though, in the Anglicized region of Lothian, his rival Malcolm—who had adopted the customs of strangers—was doubtless preferred.[2] It is certain at least that

---

[1] *Halle* (246, n. 2) is a more likely source of I. i. 159 than *Fab.*, whom I have quoted in the text (246). From *Halle* (247, n. 2) also, perhaps, rather than from *Hol.'s* reprint of *Stow* (247), came I. i. 191-193.

[2] These facts, recorded in the *Saxon Chronicle* (ed. Ingram, p. 307), are significant : Malcolm III., and Margaret, his English wife, died in 1093. Disregarding the claim of their sons, "the Scots [the Gael] then chose Dufenal [Donalbain] to king, Melcolm's brother, and drove out all the English that formerly were with the king Melcolm."

Macbeth ruled for fourteen years;[1] from the time when young[2] Duncan was murdered to the day when Siward triumphed. Three of the stories commonly associated with Macbeth—the weird sisters' predictions, Birnam Wood coming to Dunsinane, and his death at the hand of a foe not born of woman—were first narrated by Andrew Wyntoun, Prior of St. Serf, who finished his *Cronykil of Scotland* about 1424. According to Wyntoun, Macbeth saw the weird sisters in a dream (p. 24, n. 1, below), and was slain by a "knycht," whose name is not given. Subjected to the fancy of Boece, the dream became an apparition; and the nameless knight assumed definite shape as Macduff, Thane of Fife. Fordun,—who was writing in the last quarter of the fourteenth century,—and Wyntoun, first make mention of Macduff. Banquo and Fleance were, I suppose, creatures of Boece's imagination. Of Gruoch, Macbeth's wife, there is one contemporary memorial. It is a copy of a charter whereby "Machbet filius finlach . . . & gruoch filia bodhe rex *et* regina Scotorum" gave Kyrkenes to the Culdees of St. Serf's monastery on Loch Leven; free of all obligations save the duty of praying for the donors.[3]

The purpose of this book does not include a detailed examination of the evidence which a dramatist found in the printed chronicles of his times, and I therefore say no more anent the materials used by Holinshed. I warn the reader (if a caution be needed) to take with a large grain of salt what Holinshed, Halle, and others relate concerning the youthful follies of Henry V., the evil life and death of Cardinal Beaufort, and the crimes of Cardinal Wolsey. The shameful charges against Jeanne Darc need, of course, no comment. Before, however, closing these prefatory words, I shall briefly notice two cases in which treatment of character has far exceeded such historical warrant as was easily accessible. Margaret of

---

Duncan II.—a son of Malcolm by a prior union—assembled an Anglo-Norman army, and deposed Donalbain. "But the Scots afterwards gathered some force together, and slew full nigh all his men; and he himself with a few made his escape. Afterwards they were reconciled, on the condition that he never again brought into the land English or French." See pp. 41, 42 below.

[1] In 1046, according to *Ann. Dunelm.* (*Pertz*, xix. 506), Siward dethroned Macbeth, who, however, was speedily reinstated. A revolt seems to have broken out on behalf of Duncan's sons, for under the year 1045 we find the following entry: "Battle between the Albanich on both sides, in which Crinan, abbot of Dunkeld [Duncan's father], was slain, and many with him, viz. nine times twenty heroes."—*Tighernac* (*Skene*), 78.

[2] Dreaming of Duncan's murder, Lady Macbeth says: "yet who would haue thought the olde man to haue had so much blood in him" (V. i. 43-45). The historical Duncan I. was slain "immatura etate."—*Tighernac* (*Skene*), 78.

[3] *Liber Cartarum Prioratus Sancti Andree in Scotia* (Bannatyne Club), ed. T. Thomson, 1841, p. 114.

Anjou's guilty love for Suffolk is sheer fiction; or was perhaps inferred from expressions which describe him as a minister whom she trusted. "By the queenes meanes," we are told, Suffolk was "aduanced so in authoritie, that he ruled the king at his pleasure" (*Hol.* iii. 626/1/43. *Halle*, 207). She is said also to have "intierlie loued the duke" (*Hol.* iii. 632/1/9. *Halle*, 218). Moreover, Halle (219, om. *Hol.*) employed a phrase capable of injurious construction when he called Suffolk "the Quenes dearlynge." There can be little doubt that Richard III. was unscrupulous in gratifying his ambition, but he was not a flawless villain, who loved evil for its own sake, apart from its results. Just before the armies joined battle at Bosworth he is alleged to have thus disclosed to his followers remorse for his nephews' murder: "And although in the adeption and obteigning of the garland, I, being seduced and prouoked by sinister counsell and diabolicall temptation, did commit a wicked and detestable act, yet I haue with streict penance and salt tears (as I trust) expiated & cleerelie purged the same offense: which abominable crime I require you of frendship as cleerelie to forget, as I dailie remember to deplore and lament the same" (*Hol.* iii. 756/1/18. *Halle*, 415). Other parts of his speech were worked into the play (pp. 416, 417 below), but this passage was ignored, and some prelusive words,[1] well becoming the superhuman impiety of the dramatic Richard, were invented. Still, he was false to himself once, and a parallel of this passage is, perhaps, to be found in the confession (V. iii. 193-200) wrung from him by the dreams of his last night.

The plan of *Shakspere's Holinshed* requires brief explanation. The historical excerpts are arranged in the dramatic order, and the action of the play which they illustrate is briefly described. I quote the second edition (1587) of Holinshed's *Chronicles.* Each excerpt is preceded by a bracketed reference to the volume, page, column, and first line of the quotation, as it stands in that edition. The three volumes of Holinshed are cited as *Hol.* i. *H. E.* (Holinshed, vol. i., *Historie of England*), *Hol.* ii. *H. S.* (Holinshed, vol. ii., *Historie of Scotland*), and *Hol.* iii. (Holinshed, vol. iii.). The line-numbers of the *Globe Shakespeare* (1891) are followed

---

[1] "Let not our babling Dreames affright our soules:
Conscience is but a word that Cowards vse,
Deuis'd at first to keepe the strong in awe:
Our strong armes be our Conscience, Swords our Law!
March on, ioyne branely, let vs to't pell mell;
If not to heauen, then hand in hand to Hell!"
                    (V. iii. 308-313. Q. reading of l. 309.)

AUTHORITIES REFERRED TO IN THIS BOOK.

An asterisk (*) indicates that an authority is contemporaneous or nearly contemporaneous with the event related below. A dash (—) precedes the last date of an authority, when the first year is not given.

* *Ann. Burton.* Annales de Burton. 1004—1263. H. R. Luard. (Chronicles and Memorials of Great Britain and Ireland during the Middle Ages. Annales Monastici. Vol. 1.)

* *Ann. Dunelm.* Annales Dunelmenses. 995—1199. G. H. Pertz. (Monumenta Germaniae Historica. Vol. 19.)

* *Ann. Marg.* Annales de Margan. 1066—1232. H. R. Luard. (Chron. and Mem. Annales Monastici. Vol. 1.)

* *Ann. R. II.—H. IV.* Annales Ricardi Secundi et Henrici Quarti. 1392—1406. H. T. Riley. (Chron. and Mem. Chronica Monasterii S. Albani. Vol. 4.)

* *Ann. Theok.* Annales de Theokesberia. 1066—1263. H. R. Luard. (Chron. and Mem. Annales Monastici. Vol. 1.)

* *Ann. Waverl.* Annales de ¿Waverleia. 1—1291. H. R. Luard. (Chron. and Mem. Annales Monastici. Vol. 2.)

Anselme. Anselme de la Vierge Marie [P. de Gibours]. Histoire généalogique et chronologique de la Maison Royale de France, &c., continuée par M. Du Fourny. 1726—1733.

Archaeol. Archaeologia; or, Miscellaneous Tracts relating to Antiquity, published by the Society of Antiquaries of London. Vol. 20.

Arnold. Chronicle of the Customs of London. R. Arnold. (?) 1502. F. Douce. 1811.

* *Arrival.* Historie of the Arrivall of Edward IV. in England and the finall recouerye of his kingdomes from Henry VI. A.D. M.CCCC.LXXI. J. Bruce. (Camden Society, No. 1.)

* *A.-S. Chron.* (*M. H. B.*). The Anglo-Saxon Chronicle. 1—1154. H. Petrie and J. Sharpe. (Monumenta Historica Britannica.—1066.)

* *Avesbury.* Roberti de Avesbury Historia de Mirabilibus Gestis Edwardi III. 1308—1356. T. Hearne. 1720.

Bacon's Henry VII. The History of the Reign of King Henry the Seventh. F. Bacon. 1622. J. R. Lumby. 1889. (Cambridge University Press.) Cited by page and first line.

Bartholomew. Gazetteer of the British Isles. J. Bartholomew. 1887.

* *Beckington's Embassy.* Journal of Bishop Beckington's Embassy in 1442. N. H. Nicolas. 1828.

* *Benedict.* Gesta Regis Henrici Secundi Benedicti Abbatis. 1169—1192. W. Stubbs. (Chron. and Mem.)

Boece. Scotorum Historiae. —1460. H. Boece. 1575. Continued by Giovanni Ferrerio, in this 2nd ed., to the year 1488.

Brewer. The Reign of Henry VIII. J. S. Brewer. 1884.

* *Calendar (Hen. VIII.).* Calendar of State Papers of the Reign of Henry VIII. J. S. Brewer and J. Gairdner. (Chron. and Mem.) Cited by volume, part, and numbered document. When *p.* precedes numerals, the reference is to the page.

* *Calend. RR. PP.* Calendarium Rotulorum Patentium. 1201—1483. (Record Commissioners' Publications.)

Camden's Annals. Guilielmi Camdeni Annales Rerum Anglicarum et Hibernicarum regnante Elizabetha. T. Hearne. 1717.

* *Cavendish.* The Life of Cardinal Wolsey. G. Cavendish. S. W. Singer. 1825. Cavendish was Wolsey's gentleman usher.

* *Chron. Auct. Ign.* Chronicon Rerum Gestarum in Monasterio S. Albani, (A.D. 1422—1431,) a quodam auctore ignoto compilatum. R. T. Riley. (Chron. and Mem. Annales Monasterii S. Albani, a Johanne Amundesham, Monacho, ut videtur, conscripti. Vol. 1.)

* *Chron. de la Pucelle.* Chronique de la Pucelle. 1422—1429. G. Cousinot de Montreuil. J. A. Buchon. (Collection des Chroniques Nationales Françoises.)

* *Chron. Giles.* Incerti Scriptoris Chronicon Angliae. 1399—1455. J. A. Giles. 1848. Cited by paginal references to the three Parts, which contain the respective reigns of Henry IV., V., and VI.

* *Chron. Lond.* A Chronicle of London. 1089—1483. N. H. Nicolas. 1827.

* *Chron. Normande.* Chronique de la Pucelle . . . suivie de la Chronique Normande de P. Cochon. 1403—1430. Vallet de Viriville. 1859.

* *Chron. Rich. II.—Hen. VI.* A Chronicle of the Reigns of Richard II., Henry IV., V., and VI. 1377—1461. J. S. Davies. (Camden Society, No. 64.)

* *Coggeshall.* Radulphi de Coggeshall Chronicon Anglicanum. 1066—1225. J. Stevenson. (Chron. and Mem.) The last event recorded by Coggeshall (the banishment of Fawkes de Breauté) took place in 1225.—*M. Paris (Wendover),* iii. 94.

Collins. The Peerage of England. A. Collins. 1714.

* *Cont. Croyl.* Alia Historiae Croylandensis Continuatio. 1459—1485. T. Gale and W. Fulman. 1684. (Scriptores Rerum Anglicarum. Vol. 1.)

Contention. The First part of the Contention betwixt the two famous Houses of Yorke and Lancaster. 1594. F. J. Furnivall. 1889. (Shakspere Quarto Fac-similes.)

* *Creton. (Archaeol.).* 1399—1401. *Archaeologia,* vol. xx. (references to French text and translation), contains the narrative of Creton, a Frenchman, who accompanied Richard II. to Ireland in 1399, and returned with him. Creton gives an account (from hearsay) of Isabelle's return to France in 1401.—*Archaeol.* xx. 226 ; 416.

D. K. Rep. 3. Third Report of the Deputy Keeper of the Records.

* *De Coussy.* Chroniques de Mathieu de Coussy (d'Escouchy). 1444—1461. J. A. Buchon. (Collection des Chroniques Nationales Françoises.)

* *Diceto.* Radulphi de Diceto Decani Lundoniensis Opera Historica. Ymagines Historiarum. 1148—1202. W. Stubbs. (Chron. and Mem.)

Doyle. The Official Baronage of England. J. E. Doyle. 1886.

* *Du Clercq.* Mémoires de Jacques du Clercq. 1448—1467. J. A. Buchon. (Collection des Chroniques Nationales Françoises.)

Dugdale. The Baronage of England. W. Dugdale. 1675—1676.

Iohn Hardyng left, &c. 1461—1543. R. Grafton. 1543. H. Ellis. 1812. (Read with the continuation of "The chronicle of Iohn Hardyng in metre," &c.)

Henr. Hunt. (*M. H. B.*). Henrici Archidiaconi Huntendunensis Historiae Anglorum Libri Octo. —1154. (Monumenta Historica Britannica.—1066.)

Hist. Britt. Galfredi Monumetensis Historia Britonum. J. A. Giles. (Caxton Society.) Geoffrey's dedication of *Hist. Britt.* was written before 1147.

* *Howeden.* Chronica Magistri Rogeri de Houedene. 732—1201. W. Stubbs. (Chron. and Mem.)

* *Itinerarium.* Itineraria Symonis Simeonis et Willelmi de Worcester. J. Nasmith. 1778.

* *Itinerary.* Itinerary of King John. T. D. Hardy. 1835. (With Hardy's Description of the Patent Rolls, one of the Record Commissioners' Publications.)

. * *Jean de Troyes.* Chronique de Jean de Troyes. 1460—1483. C. B. Petitot. (Collection Complète des Mémoires relatifs a l'Histoire de France. Première Série. Tome 14.)

* *Journal.* Journal d'un Bourgeois de Paris. 1409—1449. J. A. Buchon. (Collection des Chronique Nationales Françoises.)

* *Juv.* Histoire de Charles VI. 1380—1422. Jean Juvenal des Ursins. D. Godefroy. 1653.

. *Lewis.* A Topographical Dictionary of England. S. Lewis. 1833.

* *Livius.* Titi Livii Foro-Juliensis Vita Henrici Quinti, Regis Angliae. 1388—1422. T. Hearne. 1716. The closing words of this life (95) show that Livius wrote after Gloucester's resignation of the Protectorate in 1429, and before the Duke's death in 1447.

Lords' Journals. Calendar of the Journals of the House of Lords.

M. H. B. Monumenta Historica Britannica. H. Petrie and J. Sharpe. 1848.

* *M. Paris* (*Wendover*). Matthaei Parisiensis, Monachi Sancti Albani, Chronica Majora. Vol. II. 1067—1216. H. R. Luard. (Chron. and Mem.) Roger of Wendover's chronicles were revised and augmented by Matthew Paris, and continued by the latter from 1235 to 1259.

* *M. Scottus* (*Pertz*). Mariani Scotti Chronicon. 1—1082. G. Waitz. (Monumenta Germaniae Historica. Vol. 5. G. H. Pertz was the general editor of *M. G. H.*) Marianus Scottus was born in 1028 and died in 1082.

* *Mons.* Chroniques d'Enguerrand de Monstrelet. 1400—1444. J. A. Buchon. (Collection des Chroniques Nationales Françoises.)

More. The history of King Richard the Thirde. T. More. 1513. J. R. Lumby. 1883. (Cambridge University Press.) Cited by page and first line in the ed. of 1883. Read with the text printed in More's Workes, 1557. From the title we learn that More wrote this book about 1513, but its authorship has been attributed to Cardinal Morton, who died in 1500.

* *Ott.* Duo Rerum Anglicarum Scriptores Veteres, viz. Thomas Otterbourne et Johannes Whethamstede. *Ott.* —1420. * *Wheth.* 1455—1461. T. Hearne. 1732.

* *Page.* Poem on the siege of Rouen. J. Page. Historical Collections of a Citizen of London in the Fifteenth Century. J. Gairdner. (Camden Society, N. S. No. 17.) Page was present at the siege (1).

* *Paston.* The Paston Letters. 1422—1509. J. Gairdner. 1872—1875. (Arber's Annotated Reprints.)

* *Pol. Poems.* Political Poems and Songs relating to English History. T. Wright. (Chron. and Mem.)

Polyd. Verg. Polydori Vergilii Anglicae Historiae Libri XXVII. (A.C. 55—A.D.

1537.) Basileae. 1555. Cited by page and first line. His first work, *Proverbiorum Libellus*, was published in 1498. He died before 1555.

* *Procès.* Chronique et Procès de la Pucelle d'Orléans. J. A. Buchon. (Collection des Chroniques Nationales Françoises.)

* *Proc. Priv. Co.* Proceedings and Ordinances of the Privy Council of England. N. H. Nicolas. 1834—1837. (Record Commissioners' Publications.)

Quicherat. Procès de Condamnation et de Réhabilitation de Jeanne d'Arc. Jules Quicherat. 1841—1849. (Société de l'Histoire de France.)

Redman. Vita Henrici V. Roberto Redmanno auctore. 1413—1422. C. A. Cole. (Chron. and Mem.) Written between 1536 and 1544.

Reg. Sacr. Angl. Registrum Sacrum Anglicanum. An attempt to exhibit the course of Episcopal Succession in England. W. Stubbs. 1858.

* *Rot. Parl.* Rotuli Parliamentorum. Vols. III.—VI. Cited by page, and column or section. (Record Commissioners' Publications.)

* *Rous.* Joannis Rossi Antiquarii Warwicensis Historia Regum Angliae. —1485. T. Hearne. 1745 (ed. 2). Rous died in 1491.

Rous Rol. The Roll of the Warwick Family. J. Rows. W. Courthope. 1845.

* *Rymer.* Foedera, Conventiones, Literae, et alia Acta Publica inter Reges Angliae et alios Principes. T. Rymer. 1704—1735.

* *St. Denys.* Chronique du Religieux de Saint-Denys. 1380—1422. M. L. Bellaguet. (Collection de Documents Inédits sur l'Histoire de France.)

* *Saint-Remy.* Mémoires de Jean Lefevre, Seigneur de Saint-Remy. 1407—1435. J. A. Buchon. (Collection des Chroniques Nationales Françoises.)

Sandford. A Genealogical History of the Kings and Queens of England, . . . From the Conquest . . . to the year 1707. F. Sandford. S. Stebbins. 1707.

* *Séances du Conseil de Charles VIII.* Procès-Verbaux des séances du Conseil de Régence du Roi Charles VIII. pendant les mois d'août 1484 à janvier 1485. A. Bernier. (Collection de Documents Inédits sur l'Histoire de France.)

Solly-Flood. The Story of Prince Henry of Monmouth and Chief-Justice Gascoign. F. Solly-Flood. 1886. (Transactions of the Royal Historical Society. Vol. 3. Part 1.)

* *Statutes.* The Statutes of the Realm, . . . from Magna Charta to the end of the reign of Queen Anne. 1810—1828.

* *Stevenson.* Letters and Papers illustrative of the Wars of the English in France during the Reign of Henry the Sixth, King of England. J. Stevenson. (Chron. and Mem.)

Stow. The Annales of England . . . vntill this present yeare 1605. J. Stow.

Strype's Cranmer. Memorials of . . . Thomas Cranmer, . . . Archbishop of Canterbury. J. Strype. P. E. Barnes. 1840.

T.-A. Time-Analysis of the Plots of Shakspere's Plays. P. A. Daniel. (The New Shakspere Society's Transactions. 1877—1879.)

* *Three Chronicles.* Three Fifteenth-Century Chronicles. J. Gairdner. (Camden Society, N. S. No. 28.) Two of these chronicles are cited thus: S. E. C. = A Short English Chronicle, and B. L. C. = A Brief Latin Chronicle. The former ends in 1465, the latter embraces the period 1422—1471.

* *Tighernac (Skene).* Annals of Tighernac. —1088. Chronicles of the Picts, . . . and other early Memorials of Scottish History. W. F. Skene. (Chronicles and Memorials of Scotland.)

T. R. The Troublesome Raigne of Iohn King of England. Two Parts. 1591. F. J. Furnivall. 1888. (Shakspere Quarto Fac-similes.)

* *Trois.* Chronique de la Traison et la Mort de Richard Deux. 1398—1400. B. Williams. (English Historical Society.) References to French text and translation.

T. T. The True Tragedie of Richard Duke of Yorke, and the death of good King Henrie the Sixt. 1595. T. Tyler. 1891. (Shakspere Quarto Fac-similes.)

*Usk. Chronicon Adae de Usk. 1377—1404. E. M. Thompson. 1876. References to Latin text and translation.

Var. Sh. The Plays and Poems of William Shakspeare. E. Malone and J. Boswell. 1821.

* *Ven. State PP.* Calendar of State Papers relating to English Affairs in the Archives of Venice. Rawdon Brown. (Chron. and Mem.)

Wake. State of the Church and Clergy of England. W. Wake. 1703.

* *Wals.* Thomae Walsingham Historia Anglicana. 1272—1422. H. T. Riley. (Chron. and Mem. Chronica Monasterii S. Albani.)

* *Warkw.* A Chronicle of the first thirteen years of King Edward the Fourth. 1461—1474. J. Warkworth. J. O. Halliwell. (Camden Society, No. 10.)

* *Waurin.* Recueil des Croniques . . . de la Grant Bretaigne, . . . par Iehan de Waurin. —A.D. 1471. W. Hardy and E. L. Hardy. (Chron. and Mem.) Cited by volume, book, and page.

Weever. Ancient Funeral Monuments of Great Britain, Ireland, and the Islands. J. Weever. 1767.

Wheth. See *Ott.*

Whole Contention. The Whole Contention betweene the two Famous Houses, Lancaster and Yorke. Two Parts. Q 3. 1619. F. J. Furnivall. 1886. (Shakspere Quarto Fac-similes.)

Wylie. History of England under Henry the Fourth. J. H. Wylie. 1884—1896.

Wyntown. The Orygynale Cronykil of Scotland. A. Wyntown. —1420. D. Macpherson. 1795.

* *Wyrc.* Wilhelmi Worcestrii Annales Rerum Anglicarum. 1324—1468. T. Hearne. 1774. (Liber Niger Scaccarii, &c. Vol. 2.)

* *York Records.* Extracts from the Municipal Records of the City of York, during the reigns of Edward IV., Edward V., and Richard III. R. Davies. 1843.

CORRECTIONS AND ADDITIONS.

Page 15, line 18, *for* Loncart *read* Loncarty
,,   29, ,, 4 from foot, *for* Loncart *read* Loncarty
,,   41, ,, 2 from foot, *for* 1092 *read* 1093
,,   85, ,, 1, *for* same *read* fame
,,   90, ,, 6, *for* Iohn Bagot *read* William Bagot
,, 118, last line but one. " Richard, King of the Majorcas " (*Majoricarum*)
is unknown in history.   Richard II.'s godfather was James, titular King of
Majorca.—*Froissart*, ed. Buchon (Panthéon Littéraire), i. 521.   This James,
son of James II. King of Majorca, was the third husband of Joanna I., Queen
of Naples.

Page 122, line 3 from foot, *for* Hugh *read* Thomas
,, 135, ,, 20, *for* brother *read* cousin.   See pedigree of Scrope in *Wylie*,
ii. 197.

Page 150, line 3, *for* Dauid lord Fleming *read* Sir Dauid Fleming
,, 159, ,, 17, *delete* as Fabyan asserts.   See his words at 160 *n* 1 below.
,, 176, ,, 3 of note 1, *for* 1584 *read* 1585
,, 182, ,, 19, vnfought withall.   Cp. *Hen. V.* III. v. 2, 12.
,, 186, ,, 2 of note 1, *for* quôd *read* quód
,, 210, ,, 14.   Glansdale.   So F1.   Glasdale may be the right form.   In
a list of captains of Norman towns (dated 1417) occurs the name of " William
Glasdall Esquier."—*Gesta*, 278.

Page 210, last line (also last sidenote, and p. 211, l. 1), *for* Are *read* Arc
,, 213, line 13.   the great chamber.   " y² grene chambre."—*Rot. Parl.*
iv. 298/1.

Page 240, line 4 of note 1, *for* voulsit *read* voulsit
,, 258, ,, 8.   Lord Grey of Ruthin was released on payment of a large
ransom. *Ellis*, II. i. 9.

Page 342, line 9, *for* son *read* grandson
,, 342 ,, 13.   The red rose was not a badge of Henry VI., but we learn
from a grant (dated Nov. 23, 1461) that Edward IV.'s emblem (" Divisam
nostram ") was a white rose.—*Rymer*, xi. 480.   Edward's father bore " by the
Castle of Clyfford . . . a Whyte Roose."—Digby MS. No. 82, Bodleian
(*Archæol.* xvii. 226).

Page 375, note 3.   Collation of " y² rufflyng " (p. 375, l. 14).
,, 377, sidenote 3, *for* Lady *read* Dame
,, 416, note 2, *for* Hol. *read* Q, and *for* Halle *read* F

Page 489, line 1. January 2 was the day of Chapuys's arrival at Kimbolton. —*Calendar (Hen. VIII.)*, X. 28.

Page 499. The late Mr. Watkiss Lloyd showed (*Notes and Queries*, 7th S. vii. 203, 204) that Halle was the source of the following passage in the Lord Chancellor's address to Cranmer (V. iii. 10—15):

>   *we all* are *men*,
> In our owne natures *fraile* and capable
> *Of* our flesh ; few are *Angels :* out of which *frailty*
> *And* want *of wisdome*, you, that best should teach vs,
> *Haue misdemean'd* your *selfe*, and not a little,
> *Toward the King* first, then *his Lawes*, . . .

Parallel phrases exist in a speech made on September 1, 1531, by John Stokesley, Bishop of London (*Halle*, 783), under these circumstances: Soon after Wolsey's death legal proceedings were commenced against the spiritual peers on the ground that the clergy had incurred the penalties of a premunire through supporting the Cardinal's exercise of his legatine powers. Convocation averted a trial of the case by voting Henry £100,000 for his pardon (*Halle*, 774). When soliciting the help of the priests of his diocese in raising the sum, Stokesley said :

My frendes *all*, you knowe well that *wee* bee *men frayle of* condicion and no *Angels*, and by *frayltie and* lacke *of wysedome* wee *haue misdemeaned* our *selfe toward the kyng* our Soueraygne Lord and *his lawes*, so that all wee of the Cleargy were in the Premunire ; . . .

I. KING LEAR.

HOLINSHED'S *Chronicles*, and a play of untraced authorship, entitled *The True Chronicle History of King Leir*, 1605,[1] were the chief and most accessible sources whence Shakspere might have derived the main plot of his drama.[2]

The fountain-head for the story of Lear and his three daughters is the *Historia Britonum*, a chronicle which Geoffrey of Monmouth professed[3] to have translated from a very ancient book written in the British tongue.

Comparison with the subjoined excerpt from Holinshed shows that the madness of the dramatic Lear, and the fate which befell him and his daughter, are important alterations of the original story. No source for these changes of plot has yet been discovered.[4]

[*Hol.* i. *H. E.* 12/2/59.] Leir the sonne of Baldud was admitted ruler ouer the Britaines, in the yeare of the world 3105, at what time Joas reigned in Juda. This Leir was a prince of right noble demeanor, gouerning his land and subiects in great wealth. He

Leir the 10. ruler.

---

[1] Reprinted in Steevens's *Twenty of the Plays of Shakespeare*, &c., 1766, vol. iv., and in Hazlitt's *Shakespeare's Library*, Pt. II. vol. ii. pp. 307-387.

[2] Some other sources are: Fabyan's *Chronicles*, 1516 (ed. Ellis, i. 14-16); William Warner's *Albions England*, 1586 (ed. 1612, pp. 65, 66); *The firste Parte of the Mirour for Magistrates*, 1587 (ed. Haslewood, i. 123-132); *The Faerie Queene*, 1590-96, II. x. 27-32.

[3] See his dedication of the *Historia Britonum* to Robert Earl of Gloucester (ob. Oct. 31, 1147.—*Ann. Marg.*, 14).

[4] Mrs. Lennox (*Shakespeare Illustrated*, vol. iii. p. 302) first drew attention to a ballad entitled "A Lamentable Song of the Death of King Lear and his Three Daughters" (reprinted in Percy's *Reliques*), which makes mention of: (1) Lear's loss of his retinue through Regan's unkindness; (2) his madness, and his death immediately after the battle which restored to him his crown; (3) Cordelia's death in the battle fought for Lear's restoration. Dr. Johnson conjectured that this ballad might have been the source of Shakspere's *Lear* (*Variorum Shakspere*, 1821, x. 291); but later critics believe that the play was the earlier composition. According to Matthew of Westminster, an epithet, impeaching Lear's sanity, was applied to the old king by his daughters. After relating Lear's deposition by his sons-in-law, the chronicler then proceeds (*Flores Historiarum*, ed. 1601, p. 16): "Rex igitur ignarus quid ageret, deliberauit tandem filias adire, quibus regnum deuiserat, vt si fieri posset, sibi dum viueret & 40. militibus suis stipendia ministrarent. Quæ, cum indignatione verbum ex ore ipsius capientes, dixerunt eum senem esse, *delirum*, & mendicum, nec tanta familia dignum. Sed si vellet, relictis cæteris cum solo

B

Mat. West.
Leicester is
builded.

[Leir's three
daughters.

He loved
Cordeilla
best.]

Gal. Mon.

made the towne of Caerleir now called Leicester, which standeth
vpon the riuer of Sore. It is written that he had by his wife
three daughters without other issue, whose names were Gonorilla,
Regan, and Cordeilla,[1] which daughters he greatly loued, but
specially Cordeilla the yoongest farre aboue the two elder. When
this Leir therefore was come to great yeres, & began to waxe
vnweldie through age, he thought to vnderstand the affections of
his daughters towards him, and preferre hir whome he best loued,
to the succession ouer the kingdome.[2] Whervpon he first asked

milite remaneret." The following lines in *The Mirour for Magistrates* (ed.
Haslewood, stanza 21) may lead one to conjecture that John Higgins—who
wrote "Queene Cordila" for the *Mirour*—had seen the above-quoted passage
from Matthew of Westminster:

"Eke at what time hee [Leire] ask'd of them [Albany and Gonorell] to
  haue his gard,
To gard his noble grace where so he went :
They cal'd him doting foole," &c.

Albany and Gonorell had deprived Lear of his seruants, saue one.
   [1] The earliest occurrence of the familiar spelling "Cordelia" is, I believe,
to be found in the *Faerie Queene*, II. x. 29. In the old churchyard at Lee,
Blackheath, there is a monument erected by *Cordell* Lady Hervey, to the
memory of her parents, Bryan Analie, Esq., of Lee (ob. July 10, 1604), and
Awdry his wife (ob. Nov. 25, 1591).—*Notes and Queries*, 6th S. v. 465. The
form "Cordell" occurs in the *Mirour for Magistrates* (ed. Haslewood), stanza
7. "Cordelia" is the spelling in the older *Leir*.
   [2] According to *Hist. Britt.* II. xi. 30, Lear "cogitavit regnum suum ipsis
dividere," and wished to ascertain the measure of each daughter's love for him,
"ut sciret quae illarum majori regni parte dignior esset." Cp. *Lear*, I. i. 38, 39;
49-54 :

"... Know that we haue diuided
In three our Kingdome : ...
Tell me, my daughters, ...
Which of you shall we say doth loue vs most ?
That we our largest bountie may extend
Where Nature doth with merit challenge ?"

So the *Mirour for Magistrates* (i. 125) :

"But minding her that lou'd him best to note,
Because he had no sonne t'enjoy his land,
He thought to guerdon most where fauour most he fand."

The *Faerie Queene* and the old play make Lear propose to divide his kingdom
equally between his three daughters. Percy pointed out (*Var. Sh.* 1821, x. 2)
that Lear's test of his daughters' love, and their answers, are details paralleled
in the following story :
   "Ina, King of West Saxons [688—728], had three daughters, of whom, upon
a time, he demanded whether they did love him, and so would during their
lives, above all others ; the two elder sware deeply they would ; but the youngest,
but the wisest, told her Father, without flattery, 'That albeit she did love,
honour, and reverence him, and so would whilst she lived, as much as duty
and daughterly love at the uttermost could expect, yet she did think that one

Gonorilla the eldest, how well she loued him: who calling hir *A triall of loue.* gods to record, protested that she loued him more than hir owne [The answer of the eldest daughter.] life, which by right and reason should be most deere vnto hir. With which answer the father being well pleased, turned to the second, and demanded of hir how well she loued him: who answered (confirming hir saiengs with great othes) that she loued [The answer of the second daughter.] him more than toong could expresse, and farre aboue all other creatures of the world.

Then called he his yoongest daughter Cordeilla before him, *The answer of the yoongest daughter.* and asked of hir what account she made of him, vnto whome she made this answer as followeth: "Knowing the great loue and "fatherlie zeale that you haue alwaies borne towards me (for the "which I maie not answere you otherwise than I thinke, and as "my conscience leadeth me) I protest vnto you, that I haue loued "you ever, and will continuallie (while I liue) loue you as my "naturall father.   And if you would more vnderstand of the loue "that I beare you, assertaine your selfe, that so much as you "haue, so much you are worth, and so much I loue you, and no "more."   The father being nothing content with this answer, *The two eldest daughters are married. The realme is promised to his two daughters.* married his two eldest daughters, the one vnto Henninus the duke of Cornewall, and the other vnto Maglanus the duke of Albania,[1] betwixt whome he willed and ordeined that his land should be diuided after his death, and the one halfe thereof immediatlie should be assigned to them in hand: but for the third daughter Cordeilla he reserued nothing.

Neuertheless it fortuned that one of the princes of Gallia

day it would come to pass that she should affect another more fervently,' meaning her Husband, 'when she was married, who, being made one flesh with her, as God by commandement had told, and nature had taught her, she was to cleave fast to, forsaking Father and Mother, kiffe and kin.'"—Camden's *Remains concerning Britain*, 1674, under "Wise Speeches" (Library of Old Authors, pp. 254, 255).

[1] "The third and last part of the Iland he [Brute] allotted vnto Albanact his yoongest sonne. . . . This later parcell at the first, tooke the name of Albanactus, who called it Albania.   But now a small portion onelie of the region (being vnder the regiment of a duke) reteineth the said denomination, the rest being called Scotland, of certeine Scots that came ouer from Ireland to inhabit in those quarters.   It is diuided from Lhoegres [England] also by the Solne and the Firth, yet some doo note the Humber; so that Albania (as Brute left it) conteined all the north part of the Iland that is to be found beyond the aforesaid streame, vnto the point of Cathnesse."—Harrison's *Description of Britain* (in *Hol.* l. 116/2/4).

[Aganippus wished to marry Cordeilla. Leir would give her no dower.]
(which now is called France) whose name was Aganippus, hearing of the beautie, womanhood, and good conditions of the said Cordeilla, desired to haue hir in mariage, and sent ouer to hir father, requiring that he might haue hir to wife : to whome answer was made, that he might haue his daughter, but as for anie dower he could haue none, for all was promised and assured to hir other

[Aganippus married her.]
sisters alreadie. Aganippus notwithstanding this answer of deniall to receiue anie thing by way of dower with Cordeilla, tooke hir to wife, onlie moued thereto (I saie) for respect of hir person and

He gouerned the third part of Gallia as Gal. Mon. saith.
amiable vertues. This Aganippus was one of the twelue kings that ruled Gallia in those daies, as in the British historie it is recorded. But to proceed.

[Leir's sons-in-law rebel against him, and assign him a portion to liue on.]
After that Leir was fallen into age, the two dukes that had married his two eldest daughters, thinking it long yer the gouernment of the land did come to their hands, arose against him in armour, and reft from him the gouernance of the land, vpon conditions to be continued for terme of life : by the which he was put to his portion, that is, to liue after a rate assigned to him for the maintenance of his estate, which in processe of time was

[The vnkindnesse of his daughters when he visited them. They scarcely allow him one seruant at last.]
diminished as well by Maglanus as by Henninus. But the greatest griefe that Leir tooke, was to see the vnkindnesse of his daughters, which seemed to thinke that all was too much which their father had, the same being neuer so little : in so much that going from the one to the other, he was brought to that miserie, that scarslie they would allow him one seruant to wait vpon him.[1]

In the end, such was the vnkindnesse, or (as I maie saie) the vnnaturalnesse which he found in his two daughters, notwithstand-

---

[1] We learn from *Hist. Britt.* II. xii. 31 that, after the duke's revolt, Albany maintained Lear and a retinue of sixty knights. But, when two years had elapsed, "indignata est Gonorilla filia *ob multitudinem militum ejus, qui convicia ministris inferebant,* quia eis profusior epinomia non praebebatur" (cp. *Lear,* I. iv. 220-224 ; 262-267). Albany reduced Lear's attendance to thirty knights. Lear then went to live with Cornwall, but strife broke out between the retainers of the several households, and Regan dismissed all saue five of Lear's knights. He returned to Gonorilla, who allowed him one knight. This last wrong caused Lear's departure to France. The *Mirour for Magistrates* mentions the successive reductions of Lear's followers ; but none of the sources which I have enumerated above has aught to say about the dissensions between Lear's knights and his sons-in-laws' households.

ing their faire and pleasant words vttered in time past, that being [He flees to Cordeilla, in Gallia, and is kindly received.] constreined of necessitie, he fled the land, & sailed into Gallia, there to seeke some comfort of his yongest daughter Cordeilla, whom before time he hated. The ladie Cordeilla hearing that he was arriued in poore estate, she first sent to him priuilie a certeine summe of monie to apparell himselfe withall, and to reteine a certeine number of seruants that might attend vpon him in honorable wise, as apperteined to the estate which he had borne : and then so accompanied, she appointed him to come to the court, which he did, and was so ioifullie, honorablie, and louinglie receiued, both by his sonne in law Aganippus, and also by his daughter Cordeilla, that his hart was greatlie comforted : for he was no lesse honored, than if he had beene king of the whole countrie himselfe.

Now when he had informed his sonne in law and his daughter [Aganippus prepared a mighty army and great nauy, wherewith to restore Leir to his kingdom.] in what sort he had beene vsed by his other daughters, Aganippus caused a mightie armie to be put in a readinesse, and likewise a great nauie of ships to be rigged, to passe ouer into Britaine with Leir his father in law, to see him againe restored to his kingdome. It was accorded, that Cordeilla should also go with him to take possession of the land, the which he promised to [Leir makes Cordeilla his sole heiress.] leaue vnto hir, as the rightfull inheritour after his decease, notwithstanding any former grant made to hir sisters or to their husbands in anie maner of wise.

Herevpon, when this armie and nauie of ships were readie, [Leir and Cordeilla fight a battle with his sons-in-law, who are defeated and slain. Leir ruled two years after his restoration, and then died.] Leir and his daughter Cordeilla with hir husband tooke the sea, and arriuing in Britaine, fought with their enimies, and discomfited them in battell, in the which Maglanus and Henninus were slaine : and then was Leir restored to his kingdome, which he ruled after this by the space of two yeeres, and then died, fortie yeeres after he first began to reigne.[1]

---

[1] Shakspere was perhaps indebted to Holinshed for something more than the story of Lear : α There being (according to *Hol.* i. *H. E.* 12/2/55) a "temple of Apollo, which stood in the citie of Troinouant" (London), may explain why Lear swears by that deity (*Lear*, I. i. 162). Holinshed also says (*H. E.* 14/1/37) that Lear's grandson, Cunedag, built a temple "to Apollo in Cornewall." β Lear's comparison of himself to a dragon (*Lear*, I. i. 123, 124) may have been suggested by the fact that a later British king "was surnamed Pendragon, . . . for that Merline the great prophet likened him to a dragons

Cordeilla succeeded Lear, and reigned for five years, during which time her husband died. At the close of this period, the rebellion of Margan the son of Gonorilla and Cunedag the son of Regan ended with her imprisonment by her nephews. Having no hope of release, and being "a woman of a manlie courage," she slew herself.—*Hol.* i. *H. E.* 13/2/45.

II. CYMBELINE.

HOLINSHED's *Chronicles* contain all the historical or pseudo-historical matter which appears in Shakspere's *Tragedie of Cymbeline.*

The historic Cunobelinus, son of Tasciovanus,[1] was a King of the Britons,[2] whose capital was Camulodunum[3] (Colchester). In A.D. 40 Cunobelin's son Adminius, whom he had banished, made a submission to Caligula which the Emperor affected to regard as equivalent to a surrender of the whole island, but nothing was then done to assert the imperial authority.[4] Cunobelin was dead when, in A.D. 43, Aulus Plautius was sent by Claudius to subdue Britain; and the Romans were opposed by the late king's sons Togodumnus and the renowned Caractacus.[5] These are the sole authentic particulars relating to Cunobelin, beside the evidence derived from his coins.

Act III. sc. i.—In the following passages Holinshed has given an untrustworthy account of Cymbeline, mixed with genuine information

head, that at the time of his natiuitie marualoualie appeared in the firmament at the corner of a blasing star, as is reported. But others suppose he was so called of his wisdome and serpentine subtiltie, or for that he gaue the dragons head in his banner " (*Hol.* i. *H. E.* 87/2/7).

[1] In 1844 Mr. Birch communicated a paper to the Numismatic Society (*Num. Chron.* vol. vii. p. 78), showing that the reverse legends of some of Cunobeline's coins should be read : TASCIOVANI. F.; that is, Tasciovani *Filius.* —See Evans's *Coins of the Ancient Britons,* pp. 221, 327. Other reverses read TASC. F., and TASCIIOVANII. F.—*Evans,* pp. 308, 328. Of the latter form it may be necessary to remark that TASCII— is probably equivalent to TASCE— ; the double I being often used, on British coins, for E (*Evans,* pp. 203, 206, 256, 372). The termination —VANII gives a variant nominative Tasciovanius. Mr. Birch compared these legends with AVGVSTVS DIVI F., on coins of Augustus.

[2] So styled by Suetonius, in his biography of Caligula, cap. xliv. Cunobeline's capital was Camulodunum, which we learn from Ptolemy (*Geographia,* lib. II. cap. iii.) was the town (πόλις) of the Trinobantes ; a people who once inhabited Middlesex and Essex. The obverse of a copper coin of Cunobeline bears the legend CVNOBELINVS REX. See Evans's *Coins of the Ancient Britons,* p. 332.

[3] "τὸ Καμουλόδουνον τὸ τοῦ Κυνοβελλίνου βασίλειον."—*Dion Cassius,* ed. Reimar, lx. 21. A copper coin of Cunobelina, found at Colchester, has the obverse legend CAMVL-ODVNO.—Evans's *Coins of the Ancient Britons,* p. 337.

[4] Suet. *Calig.* xliv.

[5] *Dion Cassius,* lx. 20. Claudius followed Plautius, and was present at the capture of Camulodunum by the Romans.

touching the circumstances of the Empire and Britain during the reign of Augustus.

[*Hol.* i. *H. E.* 32/2/3.] Kymbeline or Cimbeline the sonne of Theomantius[1] was of the Britains made king after the deceasse of his father, in the yeare of the world 3944, after the building of Rome 728, and before the birth of our Sauiour 33. This man (as some write) was brought vp at Rome, and there made knight by Augustus Cesar,[2] vnder whome he serued in the warres, and was in such fauour with him, that he was at libertie to pay his tribute or not. . . . Touching the continuance of the yeares of Kymbelines reigne, some writers doo varie, but the best approoued affirme, that he reigned 35 years and then died, & was buried at London, leauing behind him two sonnes, Guiderius and Aruiragus.[3]

¶ But here is to be noted, that although our histories doo affirme, that as well this Kymbeline, as also his father Theomantius liued in quiet with the Romans, and continuallie to them paied the tributes which the Britains had couenanted with Julius Cesar to pay, yet we find in the Romane writers, that after Julius Cesars death, when Augustus had taken vpon him the rule of the empire, the Britains refused to paie that tribute: whereat as *Cornelius Tacitus* reporteth, Augustus (being otherwise occupied) was contented to winke; howbeit, through earnest calling vpon to recouer his right by such as were desirous to see the vttermost of the British kingdome; at length, to wit, in the tenth yeare after the death of Julius Cesar, which was about the thirteenth yeare of the said Theomantius, Augustus made prouision to passe with an armie ouer into Britaine, & was come forward vpon his iournie

Kymbeline.

Fabian out of Guido de Columna. [Cymbeline knighted by Augustus, and not obliged to pay tribute.]

[Cymbeline reigned 35 years, and left two sons, Guiderius and Arviragus.]

[Roman writers say that the Britons refused to pay tribute to Augustus.] *Cor. Tacitus, in vita Iu. Agr.*

[Augustus prepares to invade Britain.]

---

[1] "Tenantius" (the spelling in *Cymb.* I. i. 31) occurs as a variant form in *Hol.* i. *H. E.* 32/1/58 above. Shakspere seems to have adopted *Fab.'s* conjecture (reported in *Hol.* i. *H. E.* 31/2/22) that Cassibelan, Androgeus, and Tenantius were sons of Lud, Cymbeline's grandfather; for Cymbeline is reminded by Lucius that tribute was imposed by Julius Caesar on "Cassibulan, thine Unkle" (*Cymb.* III. i. 5). Holinshed preferred the supposition that Cassibelan was Lud's brother (*Hol.* i. *H. E.* 23/2/12).

[2] Cp. *Cymb.* III. i. 70:

"Thy Cæsar Knighted me; my youth I spent
      Much vnder him"; . . .

[3] We learn from Juvenal (*Sat.* IV. 124-127) that a British prince named Arviragus was a contemporary of Domitian.

into Gallia Celtica: or as we maie saie, into these hither parts of France.

But here receiuing aduertisements that the Pannonians, which inhabited the countrie now called Hungarie, and the Dalmatians whome now we call Slauons had rebelled, he thought it best first to subdue those rebells neere home,[1] rather than to seeke new countries, and leaue such in hazard whereof he had present possession, and so turning his power against the Pannonians and Dalmatians, he left off for a time the warres of Britain. . . .

But whether this controuersie which appeareth to fall forth betwixt the Britans and Augustus, was occasioned by Kymbeline, or some other prince of the Britains, I haue not to auouch: for that by our writers it is reported, that Kymbeline being brought vp in Rome, & knighted in the court of Augustus, ouer shewed himselfe a friend to the Romans, & chieflie was loth to breake with them, because the youth of the Britaine nation should not be depriued of the benefit to be trained and brought vp among the Romans, whereby they might learne both to behaue themselues like ciuill men, and to atteine to the knowledge of feats of warre.[2]

But whether for this respect, or for that it pleased the almightie God so to dispose the minds of men at that present, not onlie the Britains, but in manner all other nations were contented to be obedient to the Romane empire. That this was

---

[1] Cymbeline replies to Lucius (Cymb. III. i. 73-75):

> . . . "I am perfect,
> That the Pannonians and Dalmatians for
> Their Liberties are now in Armes": . . .

[2] Cp. Posthumus's words (Cymb. II. iv. 20-26):

> . . . "Our Countrymen
> Are men more order'd then when Julius Cæsar
> Smil'd at their lacks of skill, but found their courage
> Worthy his frowning at: Their discipline
> (Now mingled [wing-led F] with their courages) will make knowne
> To their Approuers, they are People such
> That mend vpon the world."

As to the military strength of Britain at the time of Cæsar's invasion, Hol. says (ii., The first inhabitation of Ireland, 51/1/14): . . . "the British nation was then vnskilfull, and not trained to feats of war, for the Britons then being onelie vsed to the Picts and Irish enimies, people halfe naked, through lacks of skill easilie gaue place to the Romans force," . . .

true in the Britains, it is euident enough by *Strabos* words, which are in effect as followeth. "At this present (saith he) certeine "princes of Britaine, procuring by ambassadors and dutifull "demeanors the amitie of the emperour Augustus, haue offered "in the capitoll vnto the gods presents or gifts, and haue ordeined "the whole Ile in a manner to be appertinent, proper, and familiar "to the Romans. They are burdened with sore customs which "they paie for wares, either to be sent foorth into Gallia, or "brought from thence, which are commonlie yuorie vessels, "sheeres, ouches, or earerings, and other conceits made of amber "& glasses, and such like manner of merchandize."

Strab. Geog.

[Respect shown to Augustus by the British princes.]

[Luxuries imported by Britain.]

Holinshed (*Hol.* ii. *H. S.* 45/1/55) records an embassy from Augustus to Cymbeline, which may have given Shakspere a hint for the less peaceful mission of Caius Lucius.

[*Hol.* ii. *H. S.* 45/1/55.] About the same time [?25 B.C.] also there came vnto Kimbaline king of the Britains an ambassador from Augustus the emperor, with thanks, for that entring into the gouernement of the British state, he had kept his allegiance toward the Romane empire: exhorting him to keepe his subiects in peace with all their neighbors, sith the whole world, through meanes of the same Augustus, was now in quiet, without all warres or troublesome tumults.

Kimbaline king of the Britains. [An ambassador from Augustus thanks him for his loyalty to the Romans.]

Caius Lucius demands a yearly tribute of three thousand pounds, which had been imposed on Cassibelan and "his Succession"[1] by Julius Caesar, but had been "lately . . . left vntender'd" by Cymbeline, Cassibelan's nephew (*Cymb.* III. i. 2—10). This pretension to tribute arose when Caesar, after defeating Cassibelan,[2] blockaded the residue of the British levies, so that—

[*Hol.* i. *H. E.* 30/2/73.] Cassibellane in the end was forced to fall to a composition, in couenanting to paie a yearlie tribute of three thousand pounds.

[Cassibelan agrees to pay a yearly tribute.] *So saith Campion, but Galfrid Monu. saith fiue thousand.*

¹ Tenantius, whom Cymbeline succeeded, "paid the tribute to the Romans which Cassibellane [Tenantius's immediate predecessor] had granted."—*Hol.* i. *H. E.* 32/1/73.

² Holinshed's authorities are *Hist. Britt.* IV. x. 67, and Matthew of Westminster (ed. 1601, p. 38). According to them this success was the result of a third invasion by Caesar. The authentic account is that the Romans' second invasion of Britain closed with the submission of Cassivellaunus (or Cassibelan); and that Caesar, before leaving Britain for the last time, "obsides imperat, et, quid in annos singulos vectigalis populo Romano Britannia penderet, constituit" (*De Bello Gallico*, V. 22).

Shakspere forsook his authority in making Cymbeline refuse tribute.[1] The refusal came from Guiderius, as the following excerpt shows.

Guiderius.

[*Hol.* i. *H. E.* 33/1/63.] Guiderius the first sonne of Kymbeline (of whom *Harison* saieth nothing) began his reigne in the seuen-tenth yeere after th' incarnation of Christ. This Guiderius being a man of stout courage, gaue occasion of breach of peace betwixt the Britains and Romans, denieng to paie them tribute, and procuring the people to new insurrections, which by one meane or other made open rebellion, as *Gyldas* saith.[2]

[Guiderius refuses tri-bute to the Romans.]

In Holinshed's second volume, Guiderius's rebellion is thus narrated.

Kimbaline king of the Britains dieth.

[*Hol.* ii. *H. S.* 45/2/42.] . . . Kimbaline king of the Britains died, who for that he had beene brought vp in Rome, obserued his promised obedience towards the empire; but Guiderius suc-ceeding, disdained to see the libertie of his countrie oppressed by the Romans, and therefore procuring the Britains to assist him, assembled a power, and inuaded the Romans with such violence, that none escaped with life, but such as saued themselues within castels & fortresses.

Guiderius the British king rebelleth against the Romans.

The next point to be noticed is Cloten's rejection of tribute because "Britaine's a world by it selfe" (*Cymb.* III. i. 12, 13); a view which Shakspere may have gathered from one or all of the following passages.

Unto what portion Britains is referred.

[*Hol.* i. *Description of Britaine,* 2/1/30.] And whereas by Virgil [, who]—speaking of our Iland—saith;

Et penitùs toto diuisos orbe Britannos,[3]

And some other authors not vnwoorthie to be read and perused, it is not certeine vnto which portion of the earth our Ilands, and Thule, with sundrie the like scattered in the north seas should be ascribed, bicause they excluded them (as you see) from the rest of the whole earth: I haue thought good, for facilitie sake

---

[1] In *The Faerie Queene,* II. x. 50, the Romans are said to have made war on Cymbeline because "their tribute he refusd to let be payd." "Soone after" the birth of Christ this war began. In the next stanza Arviragus is spoken of as Cymbeline's brother.

[2] Gildas records Boadicea's revolt (*Historia Gildae,* IV.). His book contains no mention of Guiderius.

[3] *Ecl.* I. 67.

of diuision, to refer them all which lie within the first minute
of longitude, set downe by *Ptolome*, to *Europa*.

[*Hol.* i. *H. E.* 34/1/10.] The souldiers [of Aulus Plautius]
hearing of this voiage [to Britain], were loth to go with him,
as men not willing to make warre in another world.

Holinshed's *Chronicles* include a panegyric by Claudius Mamertínus,
whose congratulations were offered to the Emperor Maximian I., upon
the reunion of Britain to the Empire, after the fall (A.D. 296) of the
British Emperor Allectus, the panegyrist calling to mind how Caesar

[*Hol.* i. *H. E.* 57/2/60.] writ that he had found an other [Caesar
world, supposing it to be so big, that it was not compassed with called Britain another the sea, but that rather by resemblance the great Ocean was world.] compassed with it.

Subsequently Maximian is thus addressed :

[*Hol.* i. *H. E.* 59/2/59.] Glorie you therefore, inuincible [By the con- emperour, for that you haue as it were got an other world, & quest of Britain in restoring to the Romane puissance the glory of conquest by Maximian has gained sea, haue added to the Romane empire an element greater than another all the compasse of the earth, that is, the mightie maine ocean. world.]

Cloten having renounced tribute, the Queen—scornfully appraising
the value of that "kinde of conquest" which "Caesar made heere"—
declares (III. i. 26—29) how

his Shipping
(Poore ignorant baubles !) on our terrible Seas,
Like Egge-shels mou'd vpon their Surges, crack'd
As easily 'gainst our Rockes.

Caesar, when he first invaded Britain, landed without his cavalry ;
the eighteen transports conveying those troops not having, pursuant
to his orders, followed the fleet which bore him and the foot-soldiers.
Failing in their attempt to prevent his disembarkation, the Britons
sued for peace, and complied with his demand for hostages (*De Bello
Gallico*, IV. 23-31).

[*Hol.* i. *H. E.* 25/2/60.] Peace being thus established after [Caesar's 18 the fourth day of the Romans arriuall in Britain, the 18 ships transports are seen off the coast of which (as ye haue heard) were appointed to conuey the horssemen Britain.] ouer, loosed from the further hauen with a soft wind. Which when they approched so neere the shore of Britaine, that the Romans which were in Cesars campe might see them, suddenlie there arose so great a tempest, that none of them was able to

[They are
dispersed by
a tempest.] keepe his course, so that they were not onelie driuen in sunder
(some being caried againe into Gallia, and some westward) but
also the other ships that lay at anchor, and had brought ouer
[The ships at
anchor are
'pitifullie
beaten';
some are
driven out
to sea, and
others are
near sink-
ing.] the armie, were so pitifullie beaten, tossed and shaken, that a
great number of them did not onelie lose their tackle, but also
were caried by force of wind into the high sea; the rest being
likewise so filled with water, that they were in danger by sinking
to perish and to be quite lost.[1]

The same misfortune befell Caesar on his second expedition to
Britain. He landed unopposed, and, marching inland with the bulk
of his forces, drove the Britons from a stronghold where they awaited
his attack (*De Bello Gallico*, V. 8, 9).

[Caesar
hears that his
ships have
been much
bruised by a
tempest, and
dashed on
the shore.] [*Hol.* i. *H. E.* 28/2/2.] The next day, as he had sent foorth
such as should haue pursued the Britains, word came to him from
Quintus Atrius,[2] that his nauie by rigour of a sore and hideous
tempest was greeuouslie molested, and throwne vpon the shore,
so that the cabels and tackle being broken and destroied with
force of the vnmercifull rage of wind, the maisters and mariners
were not able to helpe the matter.

The Queen's assertion (l. 26), that Caesar was "twice beaten" by
the Britons, rests on the authority of chroniclers whose truthfulness
was perhaps doubted even in Shakspere's day, though he found their
narratives quoted along with the *Commentaries upon the Gallic War*.
Caesar's account of his first expedition to these shores having been set
forth by Holinshed, there follows what professes to be the British
version of the events of this campaign.

*Caesar de
bello Gallico,
lib. 4.* [*Hol.* i. *H. E.* 27/1/15.] ¶ Thus writeth Cesar touching his
first iournie made into Britaine. But the British historie (which

---

[1] Below we read that "not hauing other stuffe to repaire his ships, he
[Caesar] caused 12 of those that were vtterlie past recouerie by the hurts
receiued through violence of the tempest, to be broken, wherewith the other
(in which some recouerie was perceiued) might be repaired and amended."—
Hol. i. *H. E.* 26/1/31. (The famous words, "Veni, Vidi, Vici," are translated
"I came, I saw, I ouercame," in the life of Julius Caesar in North's *Plutarch*,
ed. 1579, p. 787.) It is possible that, before writing the Queen's harangue,—
the aim of which is to show how Caesar's prosperity deserted him in Britain,—
Shakspere glanced at Caesar's remark upon the unforeseen lack of cavalry to
pursue the retreating Britons, after the legionaries had effected their landing :
"And this one thing seemed onelie to disappoint the luckie fortune that was
accustomed to follow Cesar in all his other enterprises."—*Hol.* i. *H. E.* 25/2/28
(*B. G.* IV. 26).

[2] Whom Caesar had left in charge of the fleet.

Polydor calleth the new historie) [1] declareth that Cesar in a pitcht field was vanquished at the first encounter, and so withdrew backe into France. [The British history declares that Caesar was beaten in a pitched battle, and withdrew to Gaul.]

Caesar's account of his second invasion was also contradicted, another victory being claimed by the Britons.

[*Hol.* i. *H. E.* 30/2/9.] Thus according to that which Cesar himselfe and other autentike authors haue written, was Britaine made tributarie to the Romans by the conduct of the same Cesar. ¶ But our histor[i]es farre differ from this, affirming that Cesar comming the second time, was by the Britains with valiancie and martiall prowesse beaten and repelled, as he was at the first, and speciallie by meanes that Cassibellane had pight in the Thames great piles of trees piked with yron, through which his ships being entred the riuer, were perished and lost. And after his comming a land, he was vanquished in battell, and constrained to flee into Gallia with those ships that remained. *Gal. Mon. Matt. West.*

[The British history affirms that Caesar's second invasion was repelled, and he fled to Gaul.]

The Queen also says that Cassibelan "was once at point . . . to master Caesars Sword" [2] (*Cymb.* III. i. 30, 31). According to the *Historia Britonum*—referred to below as "The same historie"—Caesar actually lost his sword during the battle in which he met with the first of those defeats whereof the Queen reminds Caius Lucius.

[*Hol.* i. *H. E.* 27/1/40.] The same historie also maketh mention of . . . Nenius brother to Cassibellane, who in fight happened to get Cesars sword fastened in his shield by a blow which Cesar stroke at him. [Caesar loses his sword.]

---

[1] The "new historie," as Polydore Vergil calls it, is, I believe, the *Historia Britonum;* which contains (IV. iii. 58, 59) particulars of the "pitcht field." There is more about this victory, taken from *Boece* (31/40-80), in *Hol.* i. *H. E.* 27/1/73, &c. Posthumus's father Sicilius (*Cymb.* I. i. 29, 30),—

> "who did ioyne his House
> Against the Romanes with Cassibulan"

,—no doubt took part in this battle, where also, as *Hol.* records, Tenantius was present, from whom Sicilius "had his Titles" (l. 31).

[2] The Queen's expression—"*at point to master* Caesar's Sword"—implies that his sword was nearly wrested from him by force, not caught by accident ; and she has, it will be observed, attributed to Cassibelan the honour of this partial success. Caesar's sword was placed by Cassibelan in a sarcophagus, with the body of Nennius, who died fifteen days after the battle from a wound inflicted by this weapon, which was named "Crocea mors, quia nullus evadebat vivus qui eo vulnerabatur" (*Hist. Britt.* IV. iv. 60).

Caesar's second defeat was attended by rejoicings which the Queen connects with the Britons' first victory, when he lost his sword.

[*Hol.* i. *H. E.* 30/2/22.] For ioy of this second victorie (saith *Galfrid*) Cassibellane made a great feast at London, and there did sacrifice to the gods.

The scene of these rejoicings was "Luds-Towne," (*Cymb.* III. i. 32), known as Troinovant until it became the special care of Lud, Cassibelan's elder brother.

[*Hol.* i. *H. E.* 23/1/59.] By reason that king Lud so much esteemed that citie [1] before all other of his realme, inlarging it so greatlie as he did, and continuallie in manner remained there, the name was changed, so that it was called Caerlud, that is to saie, Luds towne: and after by corruption of speech it was named London.

Courteously, but firmly, Cymbeline rejects the Roman demand, and bids Lucius say to Augustus (III. i. 55—62):

> Our Ancestor was that Mulmutius, which
> Ordain'd our Lawes, ...
> Who was the first of Britaine, which did put   60
> His browes within a golden Crowne, and call'd
> Himselfe a king.

Holinshed relates how, after the deaths of Ferrex and Porrex,[2] the last acknowledged descendants of Brutus, Britain was plunged into civil war, then became subject to a pentarchy of kings, and was finally reunited under one sceptre by Mulmucius Dunwallon, son of Cloton King of Cornwall. Among the great deeds of Mulmucius these are recorded:[3]

[*Hol.* i. *H. E.* 15/2/34.] He also made manie good lawes, which were long after vsed, called Mulmucius lawes, turned out

---

[1] Lud built there "a faire temple neere to his . . . palace, which temple (as some take it) was after turned to a church, and at this daie called Paules."—*Hol.* i. *H. E.* 23/1/59. Perhaps the temple in "Luds-Towne,"—assigned by Shakspere to "great Iupiter,"—where Cymbeline ratified peace with the Romans (*Cymb.* V. v. 481-483).

[2] Sons of Gorboduc, King of Britain. Their history is dramatized in our earliest tragedy, written by Thomas Sackville and Thomas Norton, and acted on January 18, 1561.

[3] The chapter containing these passages (bk. III. chap. i. p. 15) is headed: "Of Mulmucius the first king / of Britaine, who was crowned / with a golden crowne, his lawes, / his foundations, with other / his acts and deeds." Mulmucius "began his reigne ouer the whole monarchie of Britaine, in the yeere of the world 3529, after the building of Rome 314, and after the deliuerance of the Israelites out of captiuitie 97, and about the 26 yeere of Darius Artaxerxes Longimanus, the fift king of the Persians."—*Ibid.*

of the British speech into the Latine by *Gildas Priscus*,[1] and long
time after translated out of latine into english by Alfred king *englished by Alfred].* of England, and mingled in his statutes. . . .

After he had established his land, and set his Britains in good *The first king that was* and conuenient order, he ordeined him by the aduise of his lords *crowned with a golden* a crowne of gold, & caused himselfe with great solemnitie to be *crowne.* crowned, according to the custom of the pagan lawes then in vse :
& bicause he was the first that bare a crowne heere in Britaine,
after the opinion of some writers, he is named the first king of
Britaine, and all the other before rehearsed are named rulers,
dukes, or gouernors.

V. iii.—Another part of *Cymbeline* for which Holinshed furnished
matter is the description given by Posthumus (V. iii. 3—58) of the
means whereby victory was transferred from the Romans to the
Britons. The prowess of Belarius, and his adopted children, Guiderius
and Arviragus, has a parallel in an exploit attributed to a Scottish
husbandman named Hay, who, with his two sons' help, routed the
Danes at the battle of Loncart, fought A.D. 976. Before quoting the
passages of Holinshed which relate to this event, I must premise that,
while the issue of the battle was doubtful, the Scots embarrassed
themselves by beheading those Danes who had fallen.[2]

[*Hol.* ii. *H. S.* 155/1/48.] Which maner being noted of the *The two wings of the* Danes, and perceiuing that there was no hope of life but in *Scots fled. [Cp. Cymb.* victorie, they rushed foorth with such violence vpon their aduer- *IV. iii. 5.]* saries, that first the right, and then after the left wing of the
Scots, was constreined to retire and flee backe, the middle-ward
stoutly yet keeping their ground : but the same stood in such
danger, being now left naked on the sides, that the victorie must

---

[1] Generally known as Gildas Sapiens, born about A.D. 516.
[2] Two more possible traces of Shakspere's Holinshed-reading may be
noticed. *a* In *Cymb.* III. v. 23, the king speaks of chariots as a British arm.
Shakspere would find their use in warfare described by *Hol.* (i. *H. E.* 26/2/11),
who took his account from Caesar (*De Bello Gallico*, IV. 33). *β* When Aulus
Plautius was sailing to invade Britain, "the marriners and men of warre"
were encouraged by seeing "a fierie leame [light] to shoot out of the east
toward *the west*, which way their course lay," . . . (*Hol.* i. *H. E.* 34/2/9).
Cp. Philarmonus's answer to Caius Lucius, who asked for the soothsayer's
dream "of this warres purpose" (*Cymb.* IV. ii. 348-352) :

> "I saw Ioues Bird, the Roman Eagle, wing'd
> From the spungy South to this part of *the West*,
> Then vanish'd in the Sun-beames : which portends
> (Vnlesse my sinnes abuse my diuination)
> Successe to th' Roman hoast."

16   II.   CYMBELINE.

needes haue remained with the Danes, had not a renewer of the
battell come in time, by the appointment (as is to be thought)
of almightie God.

Haie with his two sonnes

For as it chanced, there was in the next field at the same time
an husbandman, with two of his sons busie about his worke,
named Haie, a man strong and stiffe in making and shape of
bodie, but indued with a valiant courage. This Haie beholding

[hasted to aid the King. who was fighting in the middle-ward].

the king with the most part of the nobles, fighting with great
valiancie in the middle ward, now destitute of the wings, and in
great danger to be oppressed by the great violence of his enimies,
caught a plow-beame in his hand, and with the same exhorting
his sonnes to doo the like, hasted towards the battell, there to
die rather amongest other in defense of his countrie, than to
remaine aliue after the discomfiture in miserable thraldome and

[Neare the battle-field was a long lane, where the Danes slew the Scots in heaps (cp. Cymb. IV. iii. 6—14).] Haie staied the Scots frō running away ['and spared ... reach.' Cp. Cymb. IV. iii. 25—28].

bondage of the cruell and most vnmercifull enimies. There was
neere to the place of the battell, a long lane fensed on the sides
with ditches and walles made of turfe, through the which the
Scots which fled were beaten downe by the enimies on heapes.

Here Haie with his sonnes, supposing they might best staie
the flight, placed themselues ouerthwart the lane, beat them backe
whome they met fleeing, and spared neither friend nor fo: but

The Scots were driuen to their battell againe.

downe they went all such as came within their reach, wherewith
diuerse hardie personages cried vnto their fellowes to returne
backe vnto the battell, for there was a new power of Scotishmen
come to their succours, by whose aid the victorie might be easilie
obteined of their most cruell aduersaries the Danes: therefore
might they choose whether they would be slaine of their owne
fellowes comming to their aid, or to returne againe to fight with

The Danes fled towards their fellowes in great dis-order.

the enimies. The Danes being here staied in the lane by the
great valiancie of the father and the sonnes, thought verely there
had beene some great succors of Scots come to the aid of their
king, and thervpon ceassing from further pursute, fled backe in
great disorder vnto the other of their fellowes fighting with the
middle ward of the Scots.

The Scots also that before was chased, being incouraged herewith, pursued the Danes vnto the place of the battell right
fiercelie. Wherevpon Kenneth perceiuing his people to be thus

recomforted, and his enimies partlie abashed, called vpon his men *K. Kenneth called vpō his men to remember their duties.* to remember their duties, and now sith their aduersaries hearts began (as they might perceiue) to faint, he willed them to follow vpon them manfully, which if they did, he assured them that the victorie vndoubtedlie should be theirs. The Scots incouraged with the kings words, laid about them so earnestlie, that in the end the Danes were constreined to forsake the field, and the Scots *The Danes forsake the fields.* egerlie pursuing in the chase, made great slaughter of them as they fled. This victorie turned highlie to the praise of the Scotish nobilitie, the which fighting in the middle ward, bare still the brunt of the battell, continuing manfullie therein euen to the end. But Haie, who in such wise (as is before mentioned) staied them *[The victory was won chiefly through Hay's means.]* that fled, causing them to returne againe to the field, deserued immortall fame and commendation: for by his meanes chieflie was the victorie atchiued.

I conclude with a list of personal names found in *Cymbeline*, which Shakspere may have picked up here and there from the pages of Holinshed's *Chronicles.*

CADWALL, pseudonym of Arviragus (*Cymb.* III. iii. 95). CADWALLO King of Britain; began to reign A.D. 635 (*Hol.* i. H. E. 112/1/65).

CLOTEN (*Cymb.* I. ii.). CLOTON,[1] a king of Cornwall, father of Mulmucius Dunwallon (*Hol.* i. H. E. 15/2/21).

CORNELIUS, a physician (*Cymb.* I. v.). The name of CORNELIUS Tacitus, the historian, occurs in *Hol.* i. H. E. 51/1/60, *et passim*.

HELENE or HELEN, Imogen's woman (*Cymb.* II. ii. 1). HELEN, daughter of Coell King of Britain, and mother of Constantine the Great (*Hol.* i. H. E. 62/1/57).

IMOGEN (*Cymb.* I. i). INNOGEN,[2] wife of Brute, first ruler of Britain (*Hol.* i. H. E. 8/2/48).

LUCIUS, ambassador from Augustus (*Cymb.* III. i.). LUCIUS King of Britain, who began to reign A.D. 124 (*Hol.* i. H. E. 51/2/40). Also LUCIUS, a Roman "capteine" in Gaul, vanquished by Arthur King of Britain (*Hol.* i. H. E. 91/1/39).

MORGAN or MERGAN,[3] pseudonym of Belarius (*Cymb.* III. iii. 106; V. v. 332). MARGAN, joint king of Britain, son of Henninus Duke of Cornwall, and Gonorilla eldest daughter of King Leir (*Hol.* i. H. E. 13/2/56).

POLIDORE or PALADOUR (the latter spelling in *Cymb.* III. iii. 86),

---

[1] On the same page his name appears as "Clotenus." As "Clotyn Duke of Cornewall" he is a character in *Gorboduc* (1st ed., 1565).

[2] "Innogen," the wife of Leonatus, is in the first Entry of *Much Ado* (Q1, 1600). *Cymbeline* was probably written about 1610.

[3] Spelt "Morgan" in Holinshed's "second table for the historie of Britaine and England." In the old *Leir*, Ragan's husband is Morgan King of Cambria.

pseudonym of Guiderius.   The name of POLYDOR Virgil, the historian,
occurs in *Hol.* i. *H. E.* 85/1/34, *et passim.*
POSTHUMUS (*Cymb.* I. i.).   POSTHUMUS, a son of Aeneas and Lavinia,
born after his father's death (*Hol.* i. *H. E.* 7/1/40).
SICILLIUS, father of Posthumus (*Cymb.* I. i. 29).   SICILIUS King of
Britain, began to reign B.C. 430 (*Hol.* i. *H. E.* 19/2/46).

III. MACBETH.

THE historic time embraced by *The Tragedie of Macbeth* begins in
1040, when Duncan was slain, and ends with Macbeth's defeat by
Siward on July 27, 1054.   The historic Macbeth, however, escaped
from the battle, and was killed in August, 1057.
   Act I. sc. ii.—The following excerpts contain the materials for this
scene.   Shakspere was perhaps induced to make "the Norweyan lord"
an ally of Macdonwald because Holinshed says that Sueno invaded
Scotland[1] "immediately" after the suppression of the rebellion.
Steevens conjectured that the mere official title (" sergeant at armes ")
of the messenger, who was sent to command the rebels' presence at
Court, gave Shakspere a hint for introducing a sergeant, from whom
Duncan learns the latest news of the revolt (I. ii. 2, 3).

Duncane.
Duncan king
of Scotland

[*Hol.* ii. *H. S.* 168/2/12.]   After Malcolme succeeded his
nephue Duncane the sonne of his daughter Beatrice : for Malcome
had two daughters, the one which was this Beatrice, being giuen
in mariage vnto one Abbanath Crinen, a man of great nobilitie,
and thane of the Iles and west parts of Scotland, bare of that
mariage the foresaid Duncane ; the other called Doada, was

[cousin to
Macbeth].

Makbeth
[valiant, but
somewhat
cruel].

maried vnto Sinell[2] the thane of Glammis, by whom she had issue
one Makbeth a valiant gentleman, and one that if he had not
beene somewhat cruell of nature, might haue beene thought most
woorthie the gouernement of a realme.   On the other part, Duncane

Duncan of
too soft a
nature.

was so soft and gentle of nature,[3] that the people wished the
inclinations and maners of these two cousins to haue beene so
tempered and interchangeablie bestowed betwixt them, that where

---

[1] These fictitious invasions of Sueno and Canute are, I believe, mentioned
by no writer earlier than *Boece*, 247/55 b, &c.
[2] This name is variously spelt.   *Fordun's* spelling is "Finele" (IV. xlix.
233), whence perhaps came *Boece's* "Synel" (246/64 b).
[3] With this description compare Macbeth's epithet, "the *gracious* Duncan"
(III. i. 66).

ıch of clemencie, and the other of crueltie, the
ᴀt these two extremities might haue reigned
ıtion in them both, so should Duncane haue
ɩe king, and Makbeth an excellent capteine.   The
Duncans reigne was verie quiet and peaceable,
notable trouble; but after it was perceiued how
ᴀᴏ was in punishing offendors, manie misruled persons   [Duncan was negligent in
ᴀsion thereof to trouble the peace and quiet state of the   punishing offenders.]
ᴀ-wealth, by seditious commotions which first had their
ınings in this wise.

Banquho the thane of Lochquhaber, of whom the house of the   *Banquho thane of Lochquhaber.*
ewards is descended, the which by order of linage hath now for   *The house of the Stewards.*
ᴀ long time inioied the crowne of Scotland, euen till these our
daies, as he gathered the finances due to the king, and further
punished somewhat sharpelie such as were notorious offendors,
being assailed by a number of rebels inhabiting in that countrie,   *A mutinie amongst the people of Lochquhaber.*
and spoiled of the monie and all other things, had much a doo
to get awaie with life, after he had receiued sundrie grieuous
wounds amongst them.   Yet escaping their hands, after hee was
somewhat recouered of his hurts, and was able to ride, he repaired
to the court, where making his complaint to the king in most
earnest wise, he purchased at length that the offendors were sent
for by a sergeant at armes, to appeare to make answer vnto such
matters as should be laid to their charge: but they augmenting
their mischiefous act with a more wicked deed, after they had
misused the messenger with sundrie kinds of reproches, they   *A sergeant at armes slaine by the rebels.*
finallie slue him also.

Then doubting not but for such contemptuous demeanor
against the kings regall authoritie, they should be inuaded with
all the power the king could make, Makdowald one of great   *Makdowald offereth himselfe to be capteine of the rebels.*
estimation among them, making first a confederacie with his
neerest friends and kinsmen, tooke vpon him to be chiefe capteine
of all such rebels as would stand against the king, in maintenance
of their grieuous offenses latelie committed against him.   Manie
slanderous words also, and railing tants this Makdowald vttered   [He calls Duncan a faint-hearted milksop.]
against his prince, calling him a faint-hearted milkesop, more meet
to gouerne a sort of idle moonks in some cloister, than to haue the

rule of such valiant and hardie men of warre as the Scots were.
He vsed also such subtill persuasions and forged allurements, that
in a small time he had gotten togither a mightie power of men:

for out of the westerne Iles there came vnto him a great multitude
of people, offering themselues to assist him in that rebellious
quarell, and out of Ireland in hope of the spoile came no small
number of Kernes and Galloglasses, offering gladlie to serue vnder
him, whither it should please him to lead them.

Makdowald thus hauing a mightie puissance about him, incountered with such of the kings people as were sent against him into
Lochquhaber, and discomfiting them, by mere force tooke their
capteine Malcolme, and after the end of the battell smote off his
head. This ouerthrow being notified to the king, did put him in

woonderfull feare, by reason of his small skill in warlike affaires.
Calling therefore his nobles to a councell, he asked of them their
best aduise for the subduing of Makdowald & other the rebels.
Here, in sundrie heads (as euer it happeneth) were sundrie
opinions, which they vttered according to euerie man his skill.
At length Makbeth speaking much against the kings softnes, and
ouermuch slacknesse in punishing offendors, whereby they had
such time to assemble togither, he promised notwithstanding, if

the charge were committed vnto him and vnto Banquho, so to
order the matter, that the rebels should be shortly vanquished
& quite put downe, and that not so much as one of them should
be found to make resistance within the countrie.

And euen so it came to passe: for being sent foorth with a new
power, at his entring into Lochquhaber, the fame of his comming
put the enimies in such feare, that a great number of them stale
secretlie awaie from their capteine Makdowald, who neuerthelesse
inforced thereto, gaue battell vnto Makbeth, with the residue
which remained with him: but being ouercome, and fleeing for
refuge into a castell (within the which his wife & children were
inclosed) at length when he saw how he could neither defend the
bold anie longer against his enimies, nor yet vpon surrender be

suffered to depart with life saued, hee first slue his wife and
children, and lastlie himselfe, least if he had yeelded simplie, he
should haue beene executed in most cruell wise for an example

to other. Makbeth entring into the castell by the gates, as then set open, found the carcasse of Makdowald lieng dead there amongst the residue of the slaine bodies, which when he beheld, remitting no peece of his cruell nature with that pitifull sight, he caused the head to be cut off, and set vpon a poles end, and so *Makdowald's head sent to the king.* sent it as a present to the king, who as then laie at Bertha.[1] The *Makbeth's* headlesse trunke he commanded to bee hoong vp vpon an high *crueltie.* paire of gallows. . . . Thus was iustice and law restored againe *Justice &* to the old accustomed course, by the diligent means of Makbeth. *law restored.* Immediatlie wherevpon woord came that Sueno king of Norway *Sueno king* was arriued in Fife with a puissant armie, to subdue the whole *of Norway landed in* realme of Scotland. *Fife.*

The army raised to resist Sueno was divided into three " battels " ; the van and rear being assigned to Macbeth and Banquho respectively, while Duncan commanded the main body. The events of the subsequent campaign—which ended with an overwhelming defeat of the Danes [2]—are not dramatized. Sueno, accompanied by a few survivors of the expedition, escaped to Norway.—*Hol.* ii. *H. S.* 169/2/61—170/2/4.

[*Hol.* ii. *H. S.* 170/2/21.] The Scots hauing woone so notable *Solemne pro* a victorie, after they had gathered & diuided the spoile of the *cessions for victorie* field, caused solemne processions to be made in all places of the *gotten.* realme, and thanks to be giuen to almightie God, that had sent them so faire a day [3] ouer their enimies. But whilest the people were thus at their processions, woord was brought that a new fleet *A power of Danes arriue* of Danes was arriued at Kingcorne,[4] sent thither by Canute king *at Kingcorne* of England, in reuenge of his brother Suenos ouerthrow. To *out of England.*

[1] According to *Boece* (278/45 b) the site of this town was near the modern Parth, founded by William the Lion to replace Bertha, which was destroyed by an inundation in 1210.
[2] The Scots won the victory by drugging the Danes, who incautiously accepted from Duncan a present of ale and bread, compounded with "the iuice of mekilwoort berries."—*Hol.* ii. *H. S.* 170/1/41. In the Clarendon Press ed. of *Macbeth*, it is conjectured that "mekilwoort" is the "insane Root," spoken of by Banquo (I. iii. 84). The following description of the plant called by *Boece* "Solatium amentiale," and here englished as "mekilwoort," was omitted by *Hol.*, and Bellenden, the translator of Boece : "herba est ingentis quantitatis, acinos principio virides, ac mox vbi maturuerint purpureos & ad nigredinem vergentes habens, ad caulem enatos & sub foliis latentes seséque quasi retrahentes, vimque soporiferam, aut in amentiam agendi si affatim sumpseris habentes, magna vbertate in Scotia proueniens."—248/59 b.
[3] Cp. Macbeth's words (I. iii. 37) : "*So* foule and *faire a day* I haue not seene."
[4] Kinghorn, Fife, on the Firth of Forth.

resist these enimies, which were alreadie landed, and busie in
spoiling the countrie, Makbeth and Banquho were sent with the
kings authoritie, who hauing with them a conuenient power,
incountred the enimies, slue part of them, and chased the other
to their ships. They that escaped and got once to their ships,
obteined of Makbeth for a great summe of gold, that such of their
friends as were slaine at this last bickering, might be buried in
saint Colmes Inch.[1]   *Inchcolm ~ Columbus*

Act I. sc. iii.—II. iii.—It is possible that some passages in
Holinshed, describing the bewitchment of Duff King of Scots, were in
Shakspere's mind when he wrote the couplets detailing the First
Witch's projects of revenge upon the sea-captain whose wife had
insulted her (ll. 18—25). Duff could

[*Hol.* ii. *H. S.* 149/2/2.] not sleepe in the night time by anie
prouocations that could be deuised,[2] but still fell into exceeding
sweats, which by no means might be restreined. . . . But about
that present time there was a murmuring amongst the people, how
the king was vexed with no naturall sicknesse, but by sorcerie and
magicall art, practised by a sort of witches dwelling in a towne
of Murrey land, called Fores.[3]

Becoming aware of this rumour, Duff sent certain trustworthy
agents to the castle of Forres, which was held by his lieutenant
Donwald, of whom we shall hear again. It chanced that a soldier
in the garrison of the castle had a mistress by whom he was made
acquainted with the practices and designs of her mother, who was one
of the suspected witches, leagued with others for the destruction of
Duff. Donwald being informed of these revelations, examined the
witch's daughter, who acknowledged that what he had been told
was true.

[*Hol.* ii. *H. S.* 149/2/59.] Wherevpon learning by hir confession in what house in the towne it was where they wrought their

---

[1] Inchcolm (S. Columba's Island), Firth of Forth. Cp. *Macbeth,* I. ii.
62-65 :

> " Sweno, the Norwayes King craues composition ;
> Nor would we deigne him buriall of his men,
> Till he disbursëd, at Saint Colmes ynch,
> Ten thousand dollars to our generall vse."

[2] Cp. *Macbeth,* I. iii. 19, 20 :

> " Sleepe shall neyther Night nor Day
> Hang vpon his Pent-house Lid ; " &c.

[3] Forres is about half way between Elgin and Nairn, and not far from the
Moray Firth.

mischiefous mysterie, he sent foorth souldiers about the middest
of the night, who breaking into the house, found one of the witches
rosting vpon a woodden broch an image of wax at the fier, resem- *An image of wax rosting at the fire.*
bling in each feature the kings person, made and deuised (as is to
be thought) by craft and art of the diuell: an other of them sat
reciting certeine words of inchantment, and still basted the image
with a certeine liquor verie busilie.

The souldiers finding them occupied in this wise, tooke them *The witches were examined.*
togither with the image, and led them into the castell, where
being streictlie examined for what purpose they went about such
manner of inchantment, they answered, to the end to make away *The whole matter is confessed.*
the king: for as the image did waste afore the fire, so did the
bodie of the king breake foorth in sweat. And as for the words *[The spell kept the king from sleeping; as the wax melted, so did his flesh.]*
of the inchantment, they serued to keepe him still waking from
sleepe, so that as the wax euer melted, so did the kings flesh: by
the which meanes it should haue come to passe, that when the
wax was once cleane consumed, the death of the king should
immediatlie follow.

I now resume the thread of Macbeth's fortunes, from the time
when, according to Holinshed (*Hol.* ii. *H. S.* 170/2/45), a perpetual
peace was established with the Danes.

[*Hol.* ii. *H. S.* 170/2/52.] Shortlie after happened a strange and
vncouth woonder, which afterward was the cause of much trouble
in the realme of Scotland, as ye shall after heare. It fortuned
as Makbeth and Banquho iournied towards Fores, where the king *[Macbeth and Banquo meet three women, in strange and wild apparel. Cp. Macb. I. iii. 40.]*
then laie, they went sporting by the waie togither without other
companie, saue onelie themselues, passing thorough the woods and
fields, when suddenlie in the middest of a laund,[1] there met them
three women in strange and wild apparell, resembling creatures
of elder world, whome when they attentiuelie beheld, woondering
much at the sight, the first of them spake and said: "All haile, *The prophesie of three women supposing to be the weird sisters or fairies.*
"Makbeth, thane of Glammis!"[2] (for he had latelie entered into
that dignitie and office by the death of his father Sinell). The
second of them said: "Haile, Makbeth, thane of Cawder!"

[1] "Medio repente campo" (*Boece*, p. 249/42).
[2] Glamis is five and a half miles S.W. of Forfar.—*Bartholomew.*
[3] Cawdor Castle is five and a half miles S.W. of Nairn.—*Bartholomew.*

But the third said: "All haile, Makbeth, that heereafter shalt "be king of Scotland!"[1]

Then Banquho: "What manner of women" (saith he) "are you, "that seeme so little fauourable vnto me, whereas to my fellow "heere, besides high offices, ye assigne also the kingdome, appoint- "ing foorth nothing for me at all?" "Yes" (saith the first of them) "we promise greater benefits vnto thee, than vnto him, for he "shall reigne in deed, but with an vnluckie end: neither shall "he leaue anie issue behind him to succeed in his place, where "contrarilie thou in deed shalt not reigne at all, but of thee those "shall be borne which shall gouerne the Scotish kingdome by long "order of continuall descent." Herewith the foresaid women

A thing to wonder at.

vanished immediatlie out of their sight. This was reputed at the first but some vaine fantasticall illusion by Mackbeth and Banquho, insomuch that Banquho would call Mackbeth in iest,

[Macbeth (in iest) called King of Scotland.]

king of Scotland; and Mackbeth againe would call him in sport

Banquho the father of manie kings.

likewise, the father of manie kings. But afterwards the common opinion was, that these women were either the weird sisters, that

[The women were goddesses of destinie, nymphs, or fairies.]

is (as ye would say) the goddesses of destinie, or else some nymphs or feiries, indued with knowledge of prophesie by their necromanticall science, bicause euerie thing came to passe as they

The thane of Cawder condemned of treason. Macbeth made thane of Cawder.

had spoken. For shortlie after, the thane of Cawder being condemned at Fores of treason against the king committed; his lands, liuings, and offices were giuen of the kings liberalitie to Mackbeth.[2]

---

[1] The following passage in *Wyntoun* (VI. xviii. 13-26) gives the earliest known form of this story (about 1424):

    Á nycht he [Macbeth] thowcht in hys dremyng,
    Dat syttand he wes besyd þe Kyng [Duncan]
    At a Sete in hwntyng; swá   15
    In-til his Leisch had Grewhundys twá.
    He thowcht, quhile he wes swá syttand,
    He sawe thre Wemen by gangand;
    And þái Wemen þan thowcht he
    Thre Werd Systrys mást lyk to be.   20
    De fyrst he hard say gangand by,
    "Lo, yhondyr þe Thayne of Crwmbawchty" [Cromarty].
    De toþir Woman sayd agayne,
    "Of Morave [Moray] yhondyre I se þe Thayne."
    De thryd þan sayd, "I se þe Kyng."   25
    All þis he herd in hys dremyng.

These thanedoms were afterwards conferred upon Macbeth by Duncan (ll. 27, 28).   [2] Cp. *Macbeth*, I. ii. 63-67; iii. 105-116.

The same night after, at supper, Banquho iested with him and
said: "Now Mackbeth thou hast obteined those things which the
"two former sisters prophesied, there remaineth onelie for thee to
"purchase that which the third said should come to passe." Where- *Mackbeth*
vpon Mackbeth reuoluing the thing in his mind, began euen then *deuiseth how*
to deuise how he might atteine to the kingdome: but yet he *atteine the*
thought with himselfe that he must tarie a time, which should *kingdome.*
aduance him thereto (by the diuine prouidence) as it had come
to passe in his former preferment. But shortlie after it chanced *The daughter*
that king Duncane, hauing two sonnes by his wife which was the *earle of*
daughter of Siward earle of Northumberland, he made the elder *Northumber-*
of them, called Malcolme, prince of Cumberland, as it were thereby *Duncane.*
to appoint him his successor in the kingdome, immediatlie after *made Prince*
his deceasse.   Mackbeth sore troubled herewith, for that he saw *Mackbeth's*
by this means his hope sore hindered (where, by the old lawes of *succession*
the realme, the ordinance was, that if he that should succeed were *is thus*
not of able age to take the charge vpon himselfe, he that was next *endangered.]*
of blood vnto him should be admitted) he began to take counsell
how he might vsurpe the kingdome by force, hauing a iust quarell *Mackbeth*
so to doo (as he tooke the matter) for that Duncane did what in *which way he*
him lay to defraud him of all maner of title and claime, which *kingdome by*
he might in time to come, pretend vnto the crowne.[1] *force.*

The woords of the three weird sisters also (of whom before *Prophesies*
ye haue heard) greatlie incouraged him hereunto, but speciallie his *to vnlawfull*
wife lay sore vpon him to attempt the thing, as she that was verie *attempts.*
ambitious, burning in vnquenchable desire to beare the name of *Women de-*
a queene.   At length therefore, communicating his purposed *estate.*
intent with his trustie friends, amongst whome Banquho was the *Mackbeth*
chiefest, vpon confidence of their promised aid, he slue the king *Duncane*
at Enuerns,[2] or (as some say) at Botgosuane, in the sixt yeare of *nivance].*

---

[1] Cp. *Macbeth*, I. iv. 37 ; 48:

> " *King*. . . . We will establish our Estate vpon
> Our eldest, Malcolme ; whom we name hereafter,
> The Prince of Cumberland ": . . .
> . . . *Macb*. [*aside*]. The Prince of Cumberland !—that is a step
> On which I must fall downe, or else o'er-leape,
> For in my way it lyes."

[2] "Enuern[e]s" = Inverness.

Macbeth
vourpeth the
crowne.
his reigne. Then hauing a companie about him of such as he had
made priuie to his enterprise, he caused himselfe to be proclamed
king, and foorthwith went vnto Scone, where (by common consent)
he receiued the inuesture of the kingdome according to the
Duncanes
buriall.
1046. K. B. accustomed maner.[1] The bodie of Duncane was first conueied
vnto Elgine, & there buried in kinglie wise; but afterwards it
was remoued and conueied vnto Colmekill,[2] and there laid in a
sepulture amongst his predecessors, in the yeare after the birth
of our Sauiour, 1046.[3]

On comparing the foregoing passages with the play, the reader will
observe how closely Shakspere agrees with Holinshed in regard to
(1) the weird sisters' apparition and predictions; (2) the effect on
Macbeth's mind of Malcolm's recognition as Prince of Cumberland,
or heir apparent; and (3) Lady Macbeth's urgency in prompting her
husband to attempt Duncan's murder. Shakspere assumed that
Cawdor's treason—the nature of which is not specified by Holinshed—
consisted in secretly aiding the Norwegians. Banquo's fate could not
have moved our pity, if the Chronicles had been followed in making
him know of, perhaps even share, Macbeth's crime; and adherence to
authority in this respect must have caused Macbeth to appear less
sinful by comparison with his old associate, who, as Shakspere represents the matter, strenuously resisted those "cursed thoughts" (II. i. 8)
which the weird sisters' prophecies had suggested.

No particulars of Duncan's murder are given. For these Shakspere
turned to the murder of King Duff by Donwald. Duff (as we have
seen) suffered from the effects of witchcraft. Regaining his former
health after the witches' charm had been broken, he put to death the
instigators of the sorcery practised against him. Among those thus
executed were some kinsmen of Donwald, who, having vainly craved
their pardon,

[*Hol.* ii. *H. S.* 150/1/39.] conceiued such an inward malice towards
the king (though he shewed it not outwardlie at the first) that

---

[1] Cp. *Macbeth*, II. iv. 31, 32:

> "*Rosse.* . . . Then 'tis most like
> The Soueraignty will fall vpon Macbeth.
> *Macd.* He is already nam'd, and gone to Scone
> To be inuested."

[2] Iona. Cp. *Macbeth*, II. iv. 32-35:

> "*Rosse.* Where is Duncan's body?
> *Macd.* Carried to Colmekill,
> The Sacred Store-house of his Predecessors
> And Guardian of their Bones."

[3] H[ector] B[oece's] date is wrong. Duncan was slain in 1040.—*M. Scottus*
(*Pertz*, v. 557).

the same continued still boiling in his stomach, and ceased not, Donwald conceiued hatred against the king.
till through setting on of his wife, and in reuenge of such
vnthankefulnesse, hee found meanes to murther the king within
the foresaid castell of Fores where he vsed to soiourne. For the
king being in that countrie, was accustomed to lie most commonlie
within the same castell, hauing a speciall trust in Donwald, as
a man whom he neuer suspected.

But Donwald, not forgetting the reproch which his linage had
susteined by the execution of those his kinsmen, whome the king
for a spectacle to the people had caused to be hanged, could not
but shew manifest tokens of great griefe at home amongst his
familie: which his wife perceiuing, ceassed not to trauell with Donwalds wife counselled him to murther the king.
him, till she vnderstood what the cause was of his displeasure.
Which at length when she had learned by his owne relation, she
as one that bare no lesse malice in hir heart towards the king, for
the like cause on hir behalfe, than hir husband did for his friends,
counselled him (sith the king oftentimes vsed to lodge in his [She showed Donwald how the king might be slain when lodging at Forres Castle.]
house without anie gard about him, other than the garrison of the
castell, which was wholie at his commandement) to make him
awaie, and shewed him the meanes wherby he might soonest
accomplish it.

Donwald thus being the more kindled in wrath by the words The womans euill counsell is followed.
of his wife, determined to follow hir aduise in the execution of
so heinous an act. Whervpon deuising with himselfe for a while,
which way hee might best accomplish his cursed intent, at length
gat opportunitie, and sped his purpose as followeth. It chanced
that the king vpon the daie before he purposed to depart foorth
of the castell, was long in his oratorie at his praiers, and there [The night before the King was to leave the castle he stayed late at his prayers.]
continued till it was late in the night. At the last, comming
foorth, he called such afore him as had faithfullie serued him
in pursute and apprehension of the rebels, and giuing them heartie
thanks, he bestowed sundrie honorable gifts amongst them, of the The king rewarded his friends.
which number Donwald was one, as he that had beene euer
accounted a most faithfull seruant to the king.

At length, hauing talked with them a long time, be got him The king went to bed.
into his priuie chamber, onelie with two of his chamberlains, who
hauing brought him to bed, came foorth againe, and then fell to

banketting with Donwald and his wife, who had prepared diuerse
delicate dishes, and sundrie sorts of drinks for their reare supper
or collation, wherat they sate vp so long, till they had charged
their stomachs with such full gorges, that their heads were no
sooner got to the pillow, but asleepe they were so fast, that a man
might haue remooued the chamber ouer them, sooner than to haue
awaked them out of their droonken sleepe.

[Instigated
by his wife,
Donwald en-
gages four of
his servants
to commit
the murder.] Then Donwald, though he abhorred the act greatlie in heart,
yet through instigation of his wife hee called foure of his seruants
vnto him (whome he had made priuie to his wicked intent before,
and framed to his purpose with large gifts) and now declaring
vnto them, after what sort they should worke the feat, they gladlie
obeied his instructions, & speedilie going about the murther,
they enter the chamber (in which the king laie) a little before
cocks crow, where they secretlie cut his throte as he lay sleeping,
without anie buskling[1] at all: and immediatlie by a posterne gate
they caried foorth the dead bodie into the fields, and throwing it
vpon an horsse there prouided readie for that purpose, they conuey
it vnto a place, about two miles distant from the castell, where
they staied, and gat certeine labourers to helpe them to turne the
course of a little riuer running through the fields there, and
digging a deepe hole in the chanell, they burie the bodie in the
same, ramming it vp with stones and grauell so closelie, that
setting the water in the right course againe, no man could perceiue
that anie thing had beene newlie digged there. This they did by
order appointed them by Donwald as is reported, for that the
bodie should not be found, & by bleeding (when Donwald should
be present) declare him to be guiltie of the murther. ¶ For such
an opinion men haue, that the dead corps of anie man being
slaine, will bleed abundantlie if the murtherer be present. But
for what consideration soeuer they buried him there, they had no
sooner finished the worke, but that they slue them whose helpe
they vsed herein, and streightwaies therevpon fled into Orknie.

Donwald, about the time that the murther was in dooing, got
him amongst them that kept the watch, and so continued in

[1] Bustling, noise. "Nullo prope strepitu" (*Boece*, 222/40).

companie with them all the residue of the night. But in the morning when the noise was raised in the kings chamber how the king was slaine, his bodie conueied awaie, and the bed all beraied with bloud; he with the watch ran thither, as though he had knowne nothing of the matter, and breaking into the chamber, and finding cakes of bloud in the bed, and on the floore about the sides of it, he foorthwith slue the chamberleins, as guiltie of that heinous murther, and then like a mad man running to and fro, he ransacked euerie corner within the castell, as though it had beene to haue seene if he might haue found either the bodie, or anie of the murtherers hid in anie priuie place: but at length comming to the posterne gate, and finding it open, he burdened the chamberleins, whome he had slaine, with all the fault, they hauing the keies of the gates committed to their keeping all the night, and therefore it could not be otherwise (said he) but that they were of counsell in committing of that most detestable murther.

Donwald a veris dissembler [: he ran-sacked every corner of the castle to find the king's body, and slew the two chamber-lains, as guilty of the murder].

Finallie, such was his ouer earnest diligence in the seuere inquisition and triall of the offendors heerein, that some of the lords began to mislike the matter, and to smell foorth shrewd tokens, that he should not be altogither cleare himselfe. But for so much as they were in that countrie, where he had the whole rule, what by reason of his friends and authoritie togither, they doubted to vtter what they thought, till time and place should better serue therevnto, and heere vpon got them awaie euerie man to his home.

Some wiser than other. The matter suspected.

The circumstances of Duff's murder, related above, have their dramatic parallels in (1) Duncan's presence as a guest in Macbeth's castle; (2) the part taken by Lady Macbeth in urging and planning the murder; (3) the drunken sleep of Duncan's chamberlains on the night of the murder; (4) Macbeth's precautionary slaughter of the chamberlains; (5) the suspicion caused by his over-acted horror when the murder was discovered.

We have seen how, in *Cymbeline*, Shakspere used a tradition of the three Hays' prowess at the battle of Loncart, fought in the reign of Kenneth III., King of Scots. A story told of this Kenneth furnished, it has been conjectured,[1] a hint for some words of Macbeth (II. ii. 35; 41—43), uttered in the first agony of remorse for Duncan's murder:

---

[1] By Dr. Furness. See his variorum *Macbeth*, p. 359.

Me thought I heard a voyce cry, "Sleep no more!" . . .
Still it cry'd "Sleepe no more!" to all the House:
"Glamis hath murther'd Sleepe, and therefore Cawdor
"Shall sleepe no more; Macbeth shall sleepe no more!"

In order to obtain his son's succession Kenneth had secretly
poisoned his nephew Malcolm,—son of the late King Duff,—who, by
Scottish law, was the rightful heir to the throne.   Kenneth ruled well;
and his sole guilty deed remained undiscovered.

The king had a giltie conscience. [*Hol.* ii. *H. S.* 158/1/9.] Thus might he seeme happie to all
man, haning the loue both of his lords and commons: but yet
to himselfe he seemed most vnhappie, as he that could not but
still liue in continuall feare, least his wicked practise concerning
the death of Malcolme Duffe should come to light and knowledge
of the world.   For so commeth it to passe, that such as are
pricked in conscience for anie secret offense committed, haue euer
an vnquiet mind.   And (as the fame goeth) it chanced that a
A voice heard by the king. voice was heard as he was in bed in the night time to take his
rest, vttering vnto him these or the like woords in effect: "Thinke
"not Kenneth that the wicked slaughter of Malcolme Duffe by
"thee contriued, is kept secret from the knowledge of the eternall
"God: thou art he that didst conspire the innocents death, enter-
"prising by traitorous meanes to doo that to thy neighbour, which
"thou wouldest haue reuenged by cruell punishment in anie of
"thy subiects, if it had beene offered to thy selfe.   It shall there-
"fore come to passe, that both thou thy selfe, and thy issue,
"through the iust vengeance of almightie God, shall suffer
"woorthie punishment, to the infamie of thy house and familie
"for euermore.   For euen at this present are there in hand secret
"practises to dispatch both thee and thy issue out of the waie,
"that other maie inioy this kingdome which thou doost indeuour
[After hearing this voice the King passed a sleeplesse night.] "to assure vnto thine issue."
The king with this voice being striken into great dread and
terror, passed that night without anie sleepe comming in his eies.

All now leave the stage except Duncan's sons, Malcolm and
Donalbain, who, after a brief colloquy, resolve to fly from Scotland
(II. iii. 141—152).   Holinshed says that

[*Hol.* ii. *H. S.* 171/1/73.] Malcolme Cammore and Donald

Bane the sons of king Duncane, for feare of their liues (which *Malcolme Cummore and Donald Bane flee into Cumberland. Malcolme Cummore receiued by Edward king of England.* they might well know that Mackbeth would seeke to bring to end for his more sure confirmation in the estate) fled into Cumberland, where Malcolme remained, till time that saint Edward the sonne of Ethelred recouered the dominion of England from the Danish power, the which Edward receiued Malcolme by way of most friendlie enterteinment: but Donald passed ouer into Ireland, where he was tenderlie cherished by the king of that land.[1]

Act II. sc. iv.—Ross and an old man enter and talk of certain portents connected with Duncan's murder (1—20). Similar occurrences attended the murder of Duff, as my next excerpt shows.

[*Hol.* ii. *H. S.* 151/1/12.] For the space of six moneths *Prodigious weather. [No sun or moon seen for six months, great winds, &c.]* togither, after this heinous murther thus committed, there appeered no sunne by day, nor moone by night in anie part of the realme, but still was the skie couered with continuall clouds, and sometimes such outragious winds[2] arose, with lightenings and tempests, that the people were in great feare of present destruction. . . .

[*Hol.* ii. *H. S.* 152/1/9.] Monstrous sights also that were *Horses eate their owne flesh.* seene within the Scotish kingdome that yeere were these: horsses in Louthian, being of singular beautie and swiftnesse, did eate their owne flesh, and would in no wise taste anie other meate. . . . There was a sparhawke also strangled by an *A sparhawke strangled by an owle.* owle. Neither was it anie lesse woonder that the sunne, as before is said, was continuallie couered with clouds for six moneths

---

[1] Malcolm says: " Ile to England." Donalbain determines otherwise:

"To Ireland, I; our seperated fortune
Shall keepe vs both the safer: where we are,
There's daggers in men's Smiles: the neere in blood,
The neerer bloody."

II. iii. 143-147. By "England" and "Ireland" the kings of those countries are, I suppose, meant. Shakspere several times uses "England" in this sense: see, for example, *Macbeth,* IV. iii. 43, and *John,* III. iv. 8.

[2] Compare what Lennox says (II. iii. 59, 60), just before Duncan's murder is discovered:

"The Night ha's been vnruly: where we lay,
Our Chimneys were blowne downe"; . . .

space.   But all men vnderstood that the abhominable murther of
king Duffe was the cause heereof. . . .[1] -

Two months—the utmost dramatic time, including intervals,[2] which
can fairly be assigned to this play—left Shakspere no room to set forth
Duncan's murderer as other than a graceless tyrant, led rapidly on
from crime to crime.   But the following passages witness that ten of
the seventeen years of Macbeth's reign were distinguished by a just
though rigorous government, harmful to none save lawbreakers and
oppressors of the weak.

Mackbeths liberalitie.

[*Hol.* ii. *H. S.* 171/2/9.]   Mackbeth, after the departure thus
of Duncanes sonnes, vsed great liberalitie towards the nobles of
the realme, thereby to win their fauour, and when he saw that no
man went about to trouble him, he set his whole intention to

Mackbeth studieth to aduance iustice.

mainteine iustice, and to punish all enormities and abuses, which
had chanced through the feeble and slouthfull administration of
Duncane. . . .   Mackbeth shewing himselfe thus a most diligent
punisher of all iniuries and wrongs attempted by anie disordered
persons within his realme, was accounted the sure defense and

A kinglie endeuour.

buckler of innocent people; and hereto he also applied his whole
indeuor, to cause yoong men to exercise themselues in vertuous
maners, and men of the church to attend their diuine seruice
according to their vocations. . . .

[If Macbeth had been a lawful king, and if he had not proved a tyrant at last, he might have been accounted one of the best of princes.]

To be briefe, such were the woorthie dooings and princelie acts
of this Mackbeth in the administration of the realme, that if he
had atteined therevnto by rightfull means, and continued in
vprightnesse of iustice as he began, till the end of his reigne,
he might well haue beene numbred amongest the most noble
princes that anie where had reigned.   He made manie holesome
laws and statutes for the publike weale of his subiects. . . .

Makbeths counterfeit zeale and equitie.

These and the like commendable lawes[3] Makbeth caused to
be put as then in vse, gouerning the realme for the space of ten
yeares in equall iustice.

---

[1] An account of the execution of Duff's murderers is followed by these
words: "This dreadfull end had Donwald and his wife, before he saw anie
sunne after the murther was committed, and that by the appointment of the
most righteous God, the creator of that heauenlie planet and all other things,
who suffereth no crime to be vnreuenged."—*Hol.* ii. *H. S.* 151/2/43.   Cp.
Macbeth, II. iv. 5-7.

[2] *T-A.*, 207, 208.

[3] Given in *Hol.* ii. *H. S.* pp. 171, 172, under this heading: "Lawes made
by king Makbeth set / foorth according to Hector / Boetius."

When the guests have retired from the supper to which Banquo
had been invited, Macbeth and Lady Macbeth converse (III. iv.
128-130):

> *Macb.* How say'st thou, that Macduff denies his person
> At our great bidding?
> *Lady M.*   Did you send to him, Sir?
> *Macb.* I heare it by the way; but I will send: . . .

Act III. sc. vi.[1]— Lennox enquires the issue of Macbeth's summons
(ll. 40-43): "Sent he to Macduff?" And the Lord, with whom
Lennox talks, replies:

> He did: and with an absolute "Sir, not I,"
> The clowdy Messenger turnes me his backe,
> And hums, as who should say, "You'l rue the time
> "That clogges me with this Answer."

Macduff's refusal to personally superintend the building of Dunsinane
Castle may be held to stand for the affront which the dramatic
Macbeth receives from the answer brought him by his "clowdy
Messenger." This is the sole point of comparison with the following
excerpt.

[*Hol.* ii. *H. S.* 174/1/26.] But to returne vnto Makbeth, in
continuing the historie, and to begin where I left, ye shall vnder-

[Nothing prospered with Macbeth after Banquo's murder.]

stand that, after the contriued slaughter of Banquho, nothing
prospered with the foresaid Makbeth: for in maner euerie man
began to doubt his owne life, and durst vnneth appeare in the
kings presence; and euen as there were manie that stood in feare

Makbeths dread. His cruellie caused throgh feare.

of him, so likewise stood he in feare of manie, in such sort that he
began to make those awaie by one surmized cauillation or other,
whome he thought most able to worke him anie displeasure.

At length he found such sweetnesse by putting his nobles thus
to death, that his earnest thirst after bloud in this behalfe might
in no wise be satisfied: for ye must consider he wan double profit
(as hee thought) hereby: for first they were rid out of the way
whome he feared, and then againe his coffers were inriched by
their goods which were forfeited to his vse, whereby he might
better mainteine a gard of armed men about him to defend his
person from iniurie of them whom he had in anie suspicion.
Further, to the end he might the more cruellie oppresse his
subiects with all tyrantlike wrongs, he builded a strong castell

---

[1] As to the impossibility of fixing the time of this scene, see *T-A.*, 205.

. Angered by the Thane of Fife's refusal to assist personally at the
building of Dunsinane Castle, Macbeth could not

[*Hol.* ii.-*H. S.* 174/2/4.] afterwards abide to looke vpon the
said Makduffe, either for that he thought his puissance ouer great;

either else for that he had learned of certeine wizzards, in whose
words he put great confidence, (for that the prophesie had happened so right, which the three faries or weird sisters had declared
vnto him,) how that he ought to take heed of Makduffe, who in
time to come should seeke to destroie him.

And suerlie herevpon had he put Makduffe to death, but that
a certeine witch, whome hee had in great trust, had told that he
should neuer be slaine with man borne of anie woman, nor vanquished till the wood of Bernane came to the castell of Dunsinane.
By this prophesie Makbeth put all feare out of his heart, supposing
he might doo what he would, without anie feare to be punished
for the same, for by the one prophesie he beleeued it was vnpossible for anie man to vanquish him, and by the other vnpossible to

slea him. This vaine hope caused him to doo manie outragious
things, to the greeuous oppression of his subiects. At length
Makduffe, to auoid perill of life, purposed with himselfe to passe
into England, to procure Malcolme Cammore to claime the crowne
of Scotland. But this was not so secretlie deuised by Makduffe,
but that Makbeth had knowledge giuen him thereof: for kings (as
is said) haue sharpe sight like vnto Lynx, and long ears like vnto
Midas. For Makbeth had, in euerie noble mans house, one slie
fellow or other in fee with him, to reueale all that was said or
doone within the same, by which slight he oppressed the most part
of the nobles of his realme.[1]

Act IV. sc. ii.—Macduff's flight to England is reported to Lennox
by a Lord, who enters in a previous scene (III. vi. 29-31). As soon as
the witches vanish, Macbeth hears the same news from Lennox, and
thereupon forms this resolve (IV. i. 150-153):

> The Castle of Macduff, I will surprise;
> Seize vpon Fife; giue to th' edge o' th' Sword
> His Wife, his Babes, and all vnfortunate Soules
> That trace him in his Line.

---

[1] Cp. *Macbeth*, III. iv. 131, 132:
"There's not a one of them but in his house
I keepe a Seruant Feed."

On comparing the following passage with Act IV. sc. ii. ll. 80-85,
it will be noticed that Shakspere did not allow Macbeth to personally
direct the slaughter.

[*Hol.* ii. *H. S.* 174/2/37.] Immediatlie then, being aduertised
whereabout Makduffe went, he came hastily with a great power
into Fife, and foorthwith besieged the castell where Makduffe
dwelled, trusting to haue found him therein. They that kept the
house, without anie resistance opened the gates, and suffered him
to enter, mistrusting none euill. But neuerthelesse Makbeth most
cruellie caused the wife and children of Makduffe, with all other
whom he found in that castell, to be slaine. Also he confiscated
the goods of Makduffe, proclamed him traitor, and confined him
out of all the parts of his realme; but Makduffe was alreadie
escaped out of danger, and gotten into England vnto Malcolme
Cammore, to trie what purchase hee might make by means of his
support, to reuenge the slaughter so cruellie executed on his wife,
his children, and other friends.

Act IV. sc. iii.—The dialogue which succeeds the account (quoted
below) of Macduff's meeting with Malcolm is freely paraphrased in this
scene.   In Holinshed the dialogue contains four clauses, namely:
Malcolm's confessions of (1) incontinence, (2) avarice, (3) faithlessness,
—each clause including Macduff's answers,—and (4) Malcolm's dis-
avowal of his self-detraction. With these clauses compare the lines
in Act IV. sc. iii., indicated by the following references: (1) ll. 57-76,
(2) 76-90, (3) 91-114, (4) 114-132.

[*Hol.* ii. *H. S.* 174/2/53.] At his comming vnto Malcolme, he
declared into what great miserie the estate of Scotland was brought,
by the detestable cruelties exercised by the tyrant Makbeth, hauing
committed manie horrible slaughters and murders, both as well of
the nobles as commons; for the which he was hated right mortallie
of all his liege people, desiring nothing more than to be deliuered
of that intollerable and most heauie yoke of thraldome, which they
susteined at such a caitifes hands.

Malcolme, hearing Makduffes woords, which he vttered in verie
lamentable sort, for meere compassion and verie ruth that pearsed
his sorowfull hart, bewailing the miserable state of his countrie, he
fetched a deepe sigh; which Makduffe perceiuing, began to fall
most earnestlie in hand with him, to enterprise the deliuering of

title was
good, and
the people
hated
Macbeth.]
the Scotish people out of the hands of so cruell and bloudie a
tyrant, as Makbeth by too manie plaine experiments did shew
himselfe to be: which was an easie matter for him to bring to
passe, considering not onelie the good title he had, but also the
earnest desire of the people to haue some occasion ministred,
whereby they might be reuenged of those notable iniuries, which
they dailie susteined by the outragious crueltie of Makbeths mis-

[But, though
Malcolm was
sorry for his
countrymen,
he dissem-
bled, fearing
that Macduff
might be an
emissary
from
Macbeth.]
gouernance.   Though Malcolme was verie sorowfull for the oppression of his countriemen the Scots, in maner as Makduffe had
declared; yet doubting whether he were come as one that ment
vnfeinedlie as he spake, or else as sent from Makbeth to betraie
him, he thought to haue some further triall, and therevpon,
dissembling his mind at the first, he answered as followeth:

Malcolme
Commons
his answer.
    "I am trulie verie sorie for the miserie chanced to my countrie
"of Scotland, but though I haue neuer so great affection to relieue
"the same, yet, by reason of certeine incurable vices, which reigne

[His vices:
1. Lust.]
"in me, I am nothing meet thereto.   First, such immoderate lust
"and voluptuous sensualitie (the abhominable founteine of all
"vices) followeth me, that, if I were made king of Scots, I should
"seeke to defloure your maids and matrones, in such wise that
"mine intemperancie should be more importable vnto you, than
"the bloudie tyrannie of Makbeth now is."   Heerevnto Makduffe

Makduffe
answer.
answered: "This suerlie is a verie euill fault, for manie noble
"princes and kings haue lost both liues and kingdomes for the
"same; neuerthelesse there are women enow in Scotland, and
"therefore follow my counsell.   Make thy selfe king, and I shall
"conueie the matter so wiselie, that thou shalt be so satisfied
"at thy pleasure, in such secret wise that no man shall be aware
"thereof."

[Malcolm's
2nd vice:
Avarice.]
    Then said Malcolme, "I am also the most auaritious creature
"on the earth, so that, if I were king, I should seeke so manie
"waies to get lands and goods, that I would slea the most part
"of all the nobles of Scotland by surmized accusations, to the end
"I might inioy their lands, goods, and possessions; . . . There-
"fore" saith Malcolme, "suffer me to remaine where I am, least,
"if I atteine to the regiment of your realme, mine vnquenchable
"auarice may proone such that ye would thinke the displeasures,

"which now grieue you, should seeme easie in respect of the vnmeasur-
"able outrage, which might insue through my comming amongst you."

Makduffe to this made answer, how it was a far woorse fault *[Macduff's answer:] Couetous-nesse the root of all mischiefe.*
than the other : "for auarice is the root of all mischiefe, and for
"that crime the most part of our kings haue beene slaine and
"brought to their finall end.   Yet notwithstanding follow my
"counsell, and take vpon thee the crowne.   There is gold and
"riches inough in Scotland to satisfie thy greedie desire."   Then
said Malcolme againe, "I am furthermore inclined to dissimula- *[Malcolm's vices of] Dissimula-tion and deliting in lies.*
"tion, telling of leasings, and all other kinds of deceit, so that I
"naturallie reioise in nothing so much, as to betraie & deceiue
"such as put anie trust or confidence in my woords.   Then sith
"there is nothing that more becommeth a prince than constancie,
"veritie, truth, and iustice, with the other laudable fellowship of
"those faire and noble vertues which are comprehended onelie in
"soothfastnesse, and that lieng vtterlie ouerthroweth the same ;
"you see how vnable I am to gouerne anie prouince or region :
"and therefore, sith you haue remedies to cloke and hide all the
"rest of my other vices, I praie you find shift to cloke this vice
"amongst the residue."

Then said Makduffe : "This yet is the woorst of all, and there *Makduffes exclamation.*
"I leaue thee, and therefore saie : Oh ye vnhappie and miserable
"Scotishmen, which are thus scourged with so manie and sundrie
"calamities, ech one aboue other !   Ye haue one curssed and
"wicked tyrant that now reigneth ouer you, without anie right or
"title, oppressing you with his most bloudie crueltie.   This other,
"that hath the right to the crowne,[1] is so replet with the inconstant

---

[1] In ll. 108-111, Macduff refers to the saintly parents of Malcolm, who was
"the truest Issue" of the Scottish throne.   Perhaps Shakspere transferred to
Malcolm's father, and to his mother,—of whom we know nothing,—the virtues
which Malcolm himself possessed, and which were shared with him, in larger
measure, by his wife Margaret.   *Hol.* says (ii. *H. S.* 178/2/44) :
... "king Malcolme (speciallie by the good admonishment and exhortation *King Malcolme, through exhortation of his wife, giueth himselfe to deuotion. A godlie strife.*
of his wife queene Margaret, a woman of great zeale vnto the religion of
that time) gaue himselfe in maner altogither vnto much deuotion, and workes
of mercie ; as in dooing of almes deeds, by prouiding for the poore, and such
like godlie exercises : so that in true vertue he was thought to excell all other
princes of his time.   To be brief, herein there seemed to be in maner a certeine strife betwixt him and that vertuous queene his wife, which of them
should be most feruent in the loue of God, so that manie people by the
imitation of them were brought vnto a better life."

"behauiour and manifest vices of Englishmen, that he is nothing "woorthie to inioy it; for by his owne confession he is not onelie "auaritious, and giuen to vnsatiable lust, but so false a traitor "withall, that no trust is to be had vnto anie woord he speaketh. "Adieu, Scotland, for now I account my selfe a banished man for "euer, without comfort or consolation:" and with those woords the brackish teares trickled downe his cheekes verie abundantlie.

At the last, when he was readie to depart, Malcolme tooke him by the sleeue, and said: "Be of good comfort, Makduffe, for I "haue none of these vices before remembred, but haue iested "with thee in this manner, onelie to prooue thy mind; for diuerse "times heeretofore hath Makbeth sought by this manner of "meanes to bring me into his hands, but the more slow I haue "shewed my selfe to condescend to thy motion and request, the "more diligence shall I vse in accomplishing the same." Incontinentlie heerevpon they imbraced ech other, and, promising to be faithfull the one to the other, they fell in consultation how they might prouide for all their businesse, to bring the same to good effect.

For the matter of the loyal digression (IV. iii. 140-159) which precedes Ross's entrance, Shakspere might have turned to Holinshed's first volume, where the subjoined account of Eadward the Confessor's miraculous gifts is to be found.

[*Hol.* i. *H. E.* 195/1/50.] As hath beene thought, he was inspired with the gift of prophesie, and also to haue had the gift of healing infirmities and diseases. He vsed to helpe those that were vexed with the disease, commonlie called the kings euill, and left that vertue as it were a portion of inheritance vnto his successors the kings of this realme.

The latter part of sc. iii., Act IV., from Ross's entrance, is wholly of Shakspere's invention, for, according to Holinshed, the slaughter of Lady Macduff and her children was known to Macduff before he joined Malcolm.

Act V. scc. ii.-viii.—The following excerpts illustrate the last Act of *Macbeth*.

[*Hol.* ii. *H. S.* 175/2/35.] Soone after, Makduffe, repairing to the borders of Scotland, addressed his letters with secret dispatch vnto the nobles of the realme, declaring how Malcolme was con-

federat with him, to come hastilie into Scotland to claime the
crowne, and therefore he required them, sith he was right inheritor
thereto, to assist him with their powers to recouer the same out of
the hands of the wrongfull vsurper.

In the meane time, Malcolme purchased such fauor at king
Edwards hands, that *old Siward* earle of Northumberland was
appointed *with ten thousand men* to go with him into Scotland, to
support him in this enterprise, for recouerie of his right.[1] After
these newes were spread abroad in Scotland, the nobles drew into
two seuerall factions, the one taking part with Makbeth, and the
other with Malcolme.   Heerevpon insued oftentimes sundrie
bickerings, & diuerse light skirmishes; for those that were of
Malcolmes side would not .ieopard to ioine with their enimies in
a pight field, till his comming out of England to their support.
But after that Makbeth perceiued his enimies power to increase,
by such aid as came to them foorth of England with his aduersarie
Malcolme, he recoiled backe into Fife, there purposing to abide in
campe fortified, at the castell of Dunsinane, and to fight with his
enimies, if they ment to pursue him; howbeit some of his friends
aduised him, that it should be best for him, either to make some
agreement with Malcolme, or else to flee with all speed into the
Iles, and to take his treasure with him, to the end he might wage
sundrie great princes of the realme to take his part, & reteine
strangers, in whome he might better trust than in his owne
subiects, which stale dailie from him; but he had such confidence
in his prophesies, that he beleeued he should neuer be vanquished,
till Birnane wood were brought to Dunsinane; nor yet to be slaine
with anie man, that should be or was born of anie woman.

Siward earle of Northumberland [sent, with 10,000 men, to support Malcolm against Macbeth].

The nobles of Scotland divided.

Makbeth recoileth [to Dunsinane Castle].

Makbeth is counselled to flee into the Iles.

Makbeths trust in prophesies.

It has been conjectured that Shakspere was thinking of a later
passage in the Chronicles when he made Macbeth call Malcolm's
English allies " Epicures " (V. iii. 8).   Malcolm III. (Canmore),
Macbeth's successor, offended his Gaelic subjects by his partiality to
English ideas and manners.   On his death, in 1092, his brother
Donalbain—who had lived under very different conditions—came

---

[1] Malcolm tells Macduff (IV. iii. 133-135) :

> . . . "before thy [they F.] heere approach,
> *Old Seyward, with ten thousand* warlike *men,*
> Already at a point, was setting foorth."

forward as the representative of the old Scottish nation, and was chosen king, in exclusion of Malcolm's sons.   To a people of few wants the standard of living adopted by a more luxurious society might appear to be mere sensual indulgence; and Donalbain owed some of his success to this feeling.

[*Hol.* ii. *H. S.* 180/1/61.]   For manie of the people, abhorring the riotous maners and superfluous gormandizing brought in among them by the Englishmen, were willing inough to receiue this Donald for their king, trusting (bicause he had beene brought vp in the Iles with the old customes and maners of their ancient nation, without tast of the English likerous delicats) they should by his seuere order in gouernement recouer againe the former temperance of their old progenitors.

I resume the illustrative excerpts from the point where we are told of Macbeth's trust in a prophecy that he could not be slain by any man who " was borne of anie woman."

[*Hol.* ii. *H. S.* 176/1/1.]   Malcolme, following hastilie after Makbeth, came the night before the battell vnto Birnane wood; and, when his armie had rested a while there to refresh them, he commanded euerie man to get a bough of some tree or other of that wood in his hand, as big as he might beare, and to march foorth therewith in such wise, that on the next morrow they might come closelie and without sight in this manner within view of his enimies.   On the morrow when Makbeth beheld them comming in this sort, he first maruelled what the matter ment, but in the end remembred himselfe that the prophesie which he had heard long before that time, of the comming of Birnane wood to Dunsinane castell, was likelie to be now fulfilled.[1]   Neuerthelesse, he brought his men in order of battell, and exhorted them to doo valiantlie; howbeit his enimies had scarselie cast from them their boughs, when Makbeth, perceiuing their numbers, betooke him streict to flight; whom Makduffe pursued with great hatred euen till he came

---

[1] There are stories, belonging to other times and places, of armies bearing leafy boughs while advancing upon the forces opposed to them.   See Furness's ed. of *Macbeth*, pp. 379-381.   The removal of Birnam Wood seems, however, to have been a tradition in *Wyntown's* age (fourteenth century), for he says (VI. xviii. 379, 380):

"De flyttand Wod þai callyd ay
Dat [Birnam Wood] lang tyme eftyrehend þat day."

vnto Lunfannaine, where Makbeth, perceiuing that Makduffe was [Macbeth cannot (as he tells Macduff) be slain by any one born of a woman.] hard at his backe, leapt beside his horsse, saieng: "Thou traitor, "what meaneth it that thou shouldest thus in vaine follow me "that am not appointed to be slaine by anie creature that is borne "of a woman? come on therefore, and receiue thy reward which "thou hast deserued for thy paines!" and therwithall he lifted vp his swoord, thinking to haue slaine him.

But Makduffe, quicklie auoiding from his horsse, yer he came at him, answered (with his naked swoord in his hand) saieng: "It [Macduff answers that he was not born of his mother, but ripped out of her womb.] "is true, Makbeth, and now shall thine insatiable crueltie haue an "end, for I am euen he that thy wizzards haue told thee of; who "was neuer borne of my mother, but ripped out of her wombe:" therewithall he stept vnto him, and slue him in the place. Then *Makbeth is slaine.* cutting his head from his shoulders, he set it vpon a pole, and brought it vnto Malcolme. This was the end of Makbeth, after he had reigned 17 yeeres ouer the Scotishmen. In the beginning of his reigne he accomplished manie woorthie acts, verie profitable to the common-wealth (as ye haue heard) but afterward, by illusion of the diuell, he defamed the same with most terrible crueltie. He 1057. *Io. M.*[1] was slaine in the yeere of the incarnation, 1057, and in the 16 1061. *H.B.* yeere of king Edwards reigne ouer the Englishmen. S. *H. B.*

When Earl Siward hears of his son's death, he asks: "Had he his hurts before?" And on Ross answering, "I, on the Front," the old warrior exclaims (V. viii. 46-50):

> Why, then Gods Soldier be he!
> Had I as many Sonnes as I haue haires,
> I would not wish them to a fairer death :
> And so, his Knell is knoll'd.

This event was derived from another account of the war with Macbeth, given in Holinshed's first volume.

[*Hol.* i. *H. E.* 192/1/27.] About the thirteenth yeare of king *Matth. West.* 1054 Edward his reigne[2] (as some write) or rather about the nineteenth *Hector Boet.* or twentieth yeare, as should appeare by the Scotish writers,

---

[1] John Mair or Major, a Scottish divine and historian, whose *Historia Gentis Scotorum* appeared in 1521. He died about 1549. His date (1057) for Macbeth's death is confirmed by *M. Scottus* (*Pertz*, v. 558).

[2] Eadward was crowned on Easter Day (April 3), 1043.—*A-S. Chron.* (*M. H. B.*), 434.

[Siward
went into
Scotland
with an
army,
defeated
Macbeth,
and placed
Malcolm on
the Scottish
throne.]
Simon. Dun.
M. West.

Siward the noble earle of Northumberland with a great power of horssemen went into Scotland, and in battell put to flight Mackbeth [1] that had vsurped the crowne of Scotland, and, that doone, placed Malcolme surnamed Camoir, the sonne of Duncane, sometime king of Scotland, in the gouernement of that realme, who afterward slue the said Mackbeth, and then reigned in quiet. . . .

[In this
battle with
Macbeth,
a son of
Siward was
slain, but
Siward re-
joiced when
told that his
son's death-
wound was
in front.]

It is recorded also, that, in the foresaid battell, in which earle Siward vanquished the Scots, one of Siwards sonnes chanced to be slaine, whereof although the father had good cause to be sorowfull, yet, when he heard that he died of a wound which he had receiued in fighting stoutlie, in the forepart of his bodie, and that with his face towards the enimie, he greatlie reioised thereat, to heare that he died so manfullie. But here is to be noted, that

[It is also
reported
that Si-
ward's son
invaded
Scotland
before this
battle, and
was slain,
whereupon
his father
(hearing of
the death-
wound in
front) said
that neither
of them
would wish
any other
kind of
death.]

not now, but a little before (as *Henrie Hunt.* saith) [2] that earle Siward went into Scotland himselfe in person, he sent his sonne with an armie to conquere the land, whose hap was there to be slaine: and when his father heard the newes, he demanded whether he receiued the wound whereof he died, in the forepart of the bodie, or in the hinder part: and when it was told him that he receiued it in the forepart: "I reioise (saith he) euen with all "my heart, for I would not wish either to my sonne nor to my "selfe any other kind of death."

Malcolm's closing speech (V. viii. 60-75) is illustrated by the subsequent passage, which comprises the names of several characters who appear in *Macbeth.*

Malcolme.

[Malcolm
crowned at
Scone.]

[*Hol.* ii. *H. S.* 176/1/47.] Malcolme Cammore thus recouering the relme (as ye haue heard) by support of king Edward, in the 16 yeere of the same Edwards reigne, he was crowned at Scone [3]

---

[1] Macbeth was defeated by Siward on July 27, 1054.—*A-S. Chron.* (*M. H. B.*, 453). Macbeth's escape from the battle is recorded in the Cottonian MS. (Tiberius, B. 1.) of the *A-S. Chron.*

[2] *Henr. Hunt* (*M. H. B.,* 760 B): "Circa hoc tampus [1052] Siwardus Consul fortissimus Nordhum^r^o . . . misit filium suum in Scotiam conquirendam." The passage given in my excerpt from Holinshed ("whose hap was . . . kind of death") is taken from Henry, who proceeds thus: "Siwardus igitur in Scotiam proficiscens, regem bello vicit, regnum totum destruxit, destructum sibi subjugavit."

[3] Cp. the closing lines of *Macbeth:*

"So thankes to all at once, and to each one
Whom we inuite to see vs Crown'd at Scone."

, the 25 day of Aprill, in the yeere of our Lord 1057. Immediatlie ^{A parlement at Forfair.} after his coronation he called a parlement at Forfair, in the which he rewarded them with lands and liuings that had assisted him against Makbeth, aduancing them to fees and offices as he saw cause, & commanded that speciallie those, that bare the surname of anie offices or lands, should haue and inioy the same. He created manie earles, lords, barons, and knights. Manie of them, ^{Thanes changed into earles.} that before were thanes, were at this time made earles, as Fife, Menteth, . . . Leuenox, . . . Cathnes, Rosse, and Angus. These were the first earles that haue beene heard of amongst the Scotishmen [1] (as their histories doo make mention.) Manie new ^{Surnames.} surnames were taken vp at this time amongst them, as Cauder, . . . Seiton, . . . with manie other that had possessions giuen them, which gaue names to the owners for the time.

IV. JOHN.

THE Shaksperian play entitled *The life and death of King Iohn* opens shortly after the King's first coronation, on Ascension Day (May 27), 1199 ; and closes with his death on October 19,[2] 1216. This is also the time embraced by an anonymous writer's *Troublesome Raigne of Iohn King of England*, 1591 ; a play which Shakspere has closely followed, without making any independent use of historical sources. The author of *The Troublesome Raigne* probably derived most of his historical matter from Holinshed ; from whose Chronicles the larger part of the succeeding excerpts is taken.

Act I. sc. i.—I begin with the excerpts which form the sources of the opening scene.

[*Hol.* iii. 157/1/11.] Iohn the yoongest son of Henrie the ^{Anno Reg. 1.} second was proclaimed king of England, beginning his reigne the sixt daie of April,[3] in the yeare of our Lord 1199. . . . This ^{Rog. Houed.}

---

[1] "*Mal.* . . . My Thanes and Kinsmen,
Henceforth be Earles, the first that euer Scotland
In such an Honor nam'd."

[2] Or October 18. The words in *M. Paris* (*Wendover*), ii. 668, are : "Qui [Johannes] postea, in nocte quae diem sancti Lucae Evangelistae proxime secuta est, ex hac vita migravit." *Coggeshale* (184) says that John died about midnight, "in festo Sancti Lucae evangelistae."

[3] The date of Richard I.'s death. But John's regnal years are computed from his coronation on Ascension Day (May 27), 1199.

man, so soone as his brother Richard was deceassed, sent Hubert
archbishop of Canturburie, and William Marshall earle of Striguill
(otherwise called Chepstow) into England, both to proclaime him
king, and also to see his peace kept; togither with Geffrey Fitz
Peter lord cheefe iustice, and diuerse other barons of the realme ;
whilest he himselfe went to Chinon where his brothers treasure

laie, which was foorthwith deliuered vnto him by Robert de
Turneham: and therewithall the castell of Chinon and Sawmer
and diuerse other places, which were in the custodie of the foresaid Robert. But Thomas de Furnes nephue to the said Robert

de Turneham deliuered the citie and castell of Angiers vnto
Arthur duke of Britaine. For, by generall consent of the nobles
and peercs of the countries of Aniou, Maine, and Touraine, Arthur
was receiued as the liege and souereigne lord of the same
countries.

For euen at this present, and so soone as it was knowne that
king Richard was deceased, diuerse cities and townes, on that
side of the sea belonging to the said Richard whilest he liued, fell
at ods among themselues, some of them indeuouring to preferre
king Iohn, other labouring rather to be vnder the gouernance of

Arthur duke of Britaine: considering that he seemed by most
right to be their cheefe lord, forsomuch as he was sonne to Geffrey
elder brother to Iohn. And thus began the broile in those
quarters, whereof in processe of time insued great inconuenience,
and finallie the death of the said Arthur, as shall be shewed
hereafter.

Now whilest king Iohn was thus occupied in recouering his
brothers treasure, and traueling with his subiects to reduce them

to his obedience, queene Elianor his mother, by the helpe of
Hubert archbishop of Canturburie and other of the noble men
and barons of the land, trauelled as diligentlie to procure the
English people to receiue their oth of allegiance to be true to
king Iohn. . . .

[*Hol.* iii. 158/1/42.] And all this was doone cheeflie by
the working of the kings mother, whom the nobilitie much
honoured and loued. For she, being bent to prefer hir sonne
Iohn, left no stone vnturned to establish him in the throne, com-

paring oftentimes the difference of gouernement betweene a king that is a man, and a king that is but a child. For as Iohn was 32 yeares old, so Arthur duke of Britaine was but a babe to speake of. . . . [She urged that John was 32, Arthur but a babe to speak of.]

Surelie queene Elianor the kings mother was sore against hir nephue Arthur, rather mooued thereto by enuie conceiued against his mother, than vpon any iust occasion giuen in the behalfe of the child, for that she saw, if he were king, how his mother Constance would looke to beare most rule within the realme of England, till hir sonne should come to lawfull age, to gouerne of himselfe[1]. . . . [Queene Elianors enuie against Arthur. Constance, dutchesse of Britaine [would rule in England, if Arthur were king].

When this dooing of the queene was signified vnto the said Constance, she, doubting the suertie of hir sonne, committed him to the trust of the French king, who, receiuing him into his tuition, promised to defend him from all his enimies, and foorthwith furnished the holds in Britaine with French souldiers. [Arthur entrusted by Constance to Philip's care.]

There is no historical authority for Chatillon's embassage; nor did Philip demand that England and Ireland should be yielded to Arthur. Immediately after Richard I.'s death, Anjou, Maine, and Touraine acknowledged, as we have seen, Arthur's right, while England passed without question under the dominion of John. Such was the position of affairs at the coronation of John, shortly after which event the action of both plays begins with Chatillon's embassy.

Chatillon having departed, John says (L. i. 48, 49):

> Our Abbies and our Priories shall pay
> This expeditions charge.

Faulconbridge is commissioned to wring from "hoording Abbots" the money needed (III. iii. 6-11), and afterwards we hear that he is in England, "ransacking the Church" (III. iv. 171, 172). Shakspere merely tells us what the older dramatist brings on the stage, in a scene when the Bastard visits a Franciscan friary, to collect money for John. Perhaps Shakspere's precursor embellished a case recorded by Holinshed, which gave the regular clergy special ground to complain of John's harshness. In 1200[2] he ordered that horses and cattle belonging to "the white moonks" (Cistercians), and left by them in his forests after October 13, should be forfeited to him.

---

[1] Eleanor to Constance (II. i. 122, 123):

"Out, insolent! thy bastard shall be King,
That thou maist be a Queen, and checke the world!"

[2] In 1210, after his return from an expedition into Ireland, John extorted £100,000 from the regular clergy and military orders. "The moonks of the Cisteaux order, otherwise called white moonks, were constreined to paie 40 thousand pounds of siluer at this time, all their priuileges to the contrarie notwithstanding."—Hol. iii. 174/2/61 (M. Paris, ii. 530, 531).

[The Cister-
cians would
give John
nothing
towards the
payment of
the £30,000
(30,000
marks.—
Oggeshale,
101, 102)
which he had
promised
Philip.]
[*Hol.* iii. 162/1/44.] The cause that mooued the king to
deale so hardlie with them was, for that they refused to helpe
him with monie, when before his last going ouer into Normandie,
he demanded it of them towards the paiment. of the thirtie
thousand pounds which he had couenanted to pay the French
king.

King John is then required to hear the appeal of Robert Faulconbridge, who claims his paternal inheritance, on the ground that his
elder brother, Philip, is illegitimate. Concerning Philip (or Richard)
Faulconbridge's historic original, Holinshed records that, in the year
1199,

*Philip king
Richards
bastard son
slue the
vicount of
Limoges.*
[*Hol.* iii. 160/2/69.] Philip, bastard sonne to king Richard,[1] to
whome his father had giuen the castell and honor of Coinacke,
killed the vicount of Limoges, in reuenge of his fathers death,
who was slaine (as yee haue heard) in besieging the castell of
Chalus Cheuerell.

Faulconbridge's choice is the chief subject of the scene in which he
is first presented to us, and he is best remembered in connexion with
this supreme moment of his life. A like choice was made by the
renowned Dunois, the Bastard of Orleans, whom we meet with in the
First Part of Henry VI. It is possible that the earlier dramatist
(whose Faulconbridge was inherited by Shakspere) availed himself of
the main situation in Dunois's case; to which more effect was given by
bringing on the stage a legitimate younger brother, who vehemently
urges his right, and is supported by his mother, who is anxious to
conceal her shame. These additions are, as the reader will perceive,
the most important modifications in the following story, which is
narrated by Halle (6th of Hen. VL, pp. 144, 145).

Lewes Duke of Orleance (murthered in Paris[2] by Ihon Duke
of Burgoyne) . . . was owner of the Castle of Coucy, on the
Frontiers of Fraunce toward Arthoys; whereof he made Constable
the lord of Cauni, a man not so wise as his wyfe was fayre; and

---

[1] Mr. Watkiss Lloyd (*Essays on Shakspere*, ed. 1875, p. 196) saw a resemblance both in name and character between Faulconbridge and Falco de
Brenta or Faukes de Breauté, whom *Hol.* calls Foukes de Brent. *Hol.* relates
how Faukes served John in the barons' war (1215-16), and afterwards aided
the royalists in their struggle with Lewis. Another bastard Fauconbridge—"a
man of no lesse corage then audacitie" (see illustration of 3 *Hen. VI.*, I. i. 239),
"a stoute harted manne" (*Hardyng-Grafton*, 459)—was a contemporary of
Edward IV.
[2] In 1407. Lewis Duke of Orleans was brother to Charles VI. John Duke
of Burgundy, their first cousin, is present—but does not speak—in *Henry V.*
III. v.

yet she was not so faire, but she was aswell beloued of the duke
of Orleance, as of her husband.   Betwene the duke and her
husbande (I cannot tell who was father) she conceiued a child,
and brought furth a prety boye called Ihon ; whiche chylde beynge
of the age of one yere, the Duke disceased, and not longe after
the mother and the lorde of Cawny ended their lyues.   The next
of kynne to the lord Cawny chalenged the enheritaunce, which
was worth four thousand crownes a yere, alledgyng that the boye
was a bastard : and the kynred of the mothers syde, for to saue
her honesty, it plainly denyed.   In conclusion, this matter was in
contention before the Presidentes of the parliament of Paris, and
there hanged in controuersie tyll the child came to the age of .viij.
yeres old.   At whiche tyme it was demaunded of him openly
[*p.* 145] whose sonne he was : his frendes of his mothers syde
aduertised him to requyre a day, to be aduised of so great an
answere ; whiche he asked, & to hym it was graunted.   In the
meane season his sayed frendes persuaded him to claime his
inheritaunce, as sonne to the lord of Cawni, which was an
honorable liuinge, and an auncient patrimony ; affirming that, if
he said contrary, he not onely slaundered hys mother, shamed
himself, & stayned hys bloud, but also should haue no lyuyng, nor
any thynge to take to.   The scolemaister, thinking that hys disciple had well learned his lesson, & woulde reherse it according
to hys instruccion, brought hym before the Iudges at the daye
assigned ; and, when the question was repeted to him again, he
boldly answered, " my harte geueth me, and my noble corage
" telleth me, that I am the sonne of the noble Duke of Orleaunce ;
" more glad to be his Bastarde, wyth a meane liuyng, then the
" lawful sonne of that coward cuckolde Cauny, with hys foure
" thousande crounes [a year]."   The iustices muche merueyled
at his bolde answere, and his mothers cosyns detested him for
shamynge of his mother ; and his fathers supposed[1] kinne
reioysed in gayninge the patrimony & possessions.   Charles, Duke
of Orleance, hearynge of thys iudgement, toke hym into his family
and gaue him great offices & fees, which he wel deserued, for

[The wife of
the Lord of
Cauny was
beloued by
Lewis Duke
of Orleans.
She brought
forth a boy,

[whom her
husband's
next of kin
alleged to
be a
bastard.]

[The child's
legitimacy
was debated
before the
Presidents
of the
Parliament
of Paris,
and, when
he was
eight, he
was called
upon by
them to say
whose son
he was.]

[The boy
answered
that he
was not
coward
cuckold
Cauny's
lawful son,
but the
noble Duke's
bastard.]

---

[1] ? supposed father's.

(duryng his [the Duke's] captiuitie)[1] he [Dunois] defended his [the Duke's] landes, expulsed thenglishmen, & in conclusion procured his deliueraunce.

Slow (256) has a similar story :

Morgan, Prouost of Beuerley, brother to K. Iohn, was elected byshop of Durham, but he comming to Rome to be consecrated, returned againe without it, for that he was a bastard, and K. Henry, father to K. Iohn, had begotten him of the wife of one Radulph Blooth ; yet would the Pope haue dispensed with him, if he would
haue called himselfe the son of the knight, and not of the king. But he, using the aduise of one William of Lane his Clarke, aunswered, that, for no worldly promotion, he would deny the kings blood.

King Richard, says the younger Faulconbridge (I. i. 99-101), took advantage of Sir Robert's absence

in an Embassie
To Germany, there, with the Emperor
To treat of high affairs touching that time.

Perhaps Sir Robert Faulconbridge usurped the mission of William Longchamp, Bishop of Ely and Chancellor ; sent by Richard, in 1196, to confer with the Emperor Henry VI., who was anxious to prevent peace being made between the King and Philip of France (*Hol.* iii. 148/1/25). Or we may imagine that Sir Robert was one of the "diuerse noble men" who represented Richard at the coronation of the Emperor Otto IV., in 1198 (*Hol.* iii. 152/2/69). The objection, that neither of these dates is consistent with Faulconbridge's dramatic age, need not trouble us, for Richard—who sent Sir Robert to Germany— began to reign in 1189, and Faulconbridge could not therefore have numbered more than ten historic years at the opening of Act I. in 1199.

The Bastard would not have his mother sorrow for her weakness, because (I. i. 268, 269),

He, that perforce robs Lions of their hearts,
May easily winne a womans.

A reference to a well-known story, which Fabyan thus notices (304) :

It is red of this Rycharde, that, durynge y⁰ tyme of his Inprysone- ment [in Germany], he shuld sle a lyon, & tere y⁰ Harte out of his
body, where through he shuld deserue y⁰ name of Rycharde Cure de Lyon,[2] . . .

_____

[1] In England, from 1415, when he was taken prisoner at Agincourt, to his release in 1440.

[2] *Hol.* (iii. 156/1/60) gives another reason for this name :
"As he was comelie of personage, so was he of stomach more couragious and fierce, so that, not without cause, he obteined the surname of *Cuewr de lion*, that is to saie, 'The lions hart.'"

Acts II.-III.—The historic time of Acts II. and III. extends to nearly three years; beginning at the interview of John and Philip "on the morrow after the feast of the Assumption of our ladie" (August 16), 1199, and ending "on Lammas daie" (August 1), 1202, when Arthur was taken prisoner by John. Since these Acts contain so much warfare for the possession of Angers, I quote here Holinshed's mention of the winning of this place by Eleanor in 1199; and also his account of its capture by John in 1206.

[*Hol.* iii. 158/2/25.] In [1199] . . . his mother queene Elianor, togither with capteine Marchades, entred into Aniou, and wasted the same, bicause they of that countrie had receiued Arthur for their souereigne lord and gouernour. And, amongst other townes and fortresses, they tooke the citie of Angiers, slue manie of the citizens, and committed the rest to prison. *The citie of Angiers taken.*

[*Hol.* iii. 170/1/27.] [In 1206 John] entred into Aniou, and, comming to the citie of Angiers, appointed certeine bands of his footmen, & all his light horssemen to compasse the towne about, whilest he, with the residue of the footmen, & all the men of armes, did go to assault the gates. Which enterprise with fire and sword he so manfullie executed, that the gates being in a moment broken open, the citie was entered and deliuered to the souldiers for a preie. So that of the citizens some were taken, some killed, and the wals of the citie beaten flat to the ground. *Les annals de France. Polydor.* *King Iohn wan the citie of Angiers by assault.*

Holinshed records nothing which warrants Constance's aspersion of Queen Eleanor's fair fame (II. i. 129-131):

My boy a bastard! by my soule, I thinke
His father neuer was so true begot:
It cannot be, and if thou wert his mother.

In 1151 Eleanor was divorced by Lewis VII. of France, and was soon afterwards married to Henry II.,—then Count of Anjou,—"contrary" (says Fabyan) "to the commaundement of his Fader, for he hadde shewed to hym that he had lyen by her, whan he was y⁰ sayd Kynges Steward."—281. According to Stow (213), "she was defamed of adultery with an Infidell, &c."[1]

Provoked by Constance's railing, Eleanor asserts that a will exists which "barres the title" of Arthur (II. i. 192). This will was made by Richard, who

[*Hol.* iii. 155/2/69.] feeling himselfe to wax weaker and weaker, preparing his mind to death, which he perceiued now to

---

[1] Cp. also the ballad entitled "Queen Eleanor's Confession," in Percy's *Reliques.*

be at hand, he ordeined his testament, or rather reformed and added sundrie things vnto the same which he before had made, at the time of his going foorth towards the holie land.

[*p.* 156] Unto his brother Iohn he assigned the crowne of England, and all other his lands and dominions, causing the Nobles there present to sweare fealtie vnto him.

I now resume Holinshed's narrative of the events which followed John's coronation.

[*Hol.* iii. 160/2/4.] king Philip made Arthur duke of Britaine, knight, and receiued of him his homage for Aniou, Poictiers, Maine, Touraine, and Britaine. Also somewhat before the time that the truce should expire; to wit, on the morrow [Aug. 16] after the feast of the Assumption of our ladie, and also the day next following, the two kings talked by commissioners, in a place betwixt the townes of Buteuant and Guleton.[1] Within three daies after, they came togither personallie, and communed at full of the variance depending betweene them. But the French king shewed himselfe stiffe and hard in this treatie, demanding the whole countrie of Veulquessine[2] to be restored vnto him, as that which had beene granted by Geffrey earle of Anion, the father of king Henrie the second, vnto Lewes le Grosse, to haue his aid then against king Stephan. Moreouer, he demanded, that Poictiers, Aniou, Maine, and Touraine, should be deliuered and wholie resigned vnto Arthur duke of Britaine.

But these, & diuerse other requests which he made, king Iohn would not in any wise grant vnto, and so they departed without conclusion of anie agreement.

About two months after this fruitless interview, William des Roches, Arthur's general, stole Arthur away from Philip, and effected a temporary reconciliation between the uncle and nephew. Des Roches also surrendered Le Mans to John, who entered the town and there met Constance and Arthur. But, being warned that John meant to

---

[1] *Boteavant*, near Portmort, Normandy, and *le Goulet*, in the same duchy.
[2] Cp. John's gift to Lewis (II. i. 527-529):

"Then do I giue Volquessen, Toraine, Maine,
Poyctiers, and Aniow, these fiue Prouinces,
With her to thee "; . . .

Shakspere follows *T. R.*, i. 29.

imprison him, Arthur fled with Constance to Angers (Angiers), where she repudiated her second husband Ranulph, Earl of Chester, and married Guy de Thouars. This third marriage took place in the very year (1199) when the dramatic Constance may be supposed to give Austria [1] "a widdows thanks" (II. i. 32) for championing Arthur.— *Hoveden*, iv. 96, 97.

Blanch of Castile was not present at the interview between John and Philip,—which took place in August, 1199,—or at their later meeting described below; and the circumstances of her subsequent betrothal—on May 23, 1200—bore no resemblance to those imagined by the dramatists. What Holinshed says of the later conference between the two kings should be compared with Shakspere's version (II. i. 484-530), which is based on the older play.

[*Hol.* iii. 161/1/53.] Finallie, vpon the Ascension day in *Anno Reg. 2* this second yeare of his reigne, they came eftsoones to a communication betwixt the townes of Vernon and Lisle Dandelie; [2] where finallie they concluded an agreement, with a marriage to *A peace concluded with a marriage.* be had betwixt Lewes the sonne of king Philip, and the ladie Blanch, daughter to Alfonso king of Castile the 8 of that name, & neece to K. Iohn by his sister Elianor.

In consideration whereof, king Iohn, besides the summe of *Matth. Paris.* thirtie thousand markes in siluer, as in respect of dowrie assigned [Blanch's dowry.] to his said neece, resigned his title to the citie of Eureux, and also vnto all those townes which the French king had by warre taken from him, the citie of Angiers onelie excepted, which citie he [Angiers restored to John.] receiued againe by couenants of the same agreement. The French king restored also to king Iohn (as *Rafe Niger* writeth) the citie *Ra. Niger* of Tours, and all the castels and fortresses which he had taken

---

[1] The dramatic "Austria" has not even a nominal historic existence : he is a compound of Leopold Duke of Austria and Widomar Viscount of Limoges. The former—who imprisoned Richard (*Coggeshale*, 56)—died on December 26, 1195 (*Coggeshale*, 66) ; four years prior to the opening of this play. Richard was mortally wounded while besieging Widomar's castle of Chaluz Chabrol (*Coggeshale*, 95), and died on April 6 (*Diceto*, ii. 166) or April 7 (*Coggeshale*, 96), 1199.

[2] In January, 1200, Philip and John "convenerunt ad colloquium inter Andeli et Gwallun" [*Andeli*, Normandy, and *Gaillon*, Vexin], where they made this agreement.—*Hoveden*, iv. 106. On May 22 they met again between Boteavant and le Goulet.—*Hoveden*, iv. 114. (As to *Hoveden's* probable error in naming Midsummer Day for Ascension Day, see Dr. Stubbs's note in his ed. of *Hoveden*, iv. 114.) A third meeting of John and Philip took place at Vernon (Normandy) on May 23, and Arthur then did homage to John for Brittany. On the same day Lewis and Blanch were betrothed at Portmort.—*Hoveden*, iv. 115. (According to *Itinerary*, John was at Butavant on May 16, and at Roche-Andely from May 17 to May 25.)

[John did homage to Philip for Brittany, and received homage for the same from Arthur.]
within Touraine : . . . The king of England likewise did homage vnto the French king for Britaine, and againe (as after you shall heare) receiued homage for the same countrie, and for the countie of Richmont, of his nephue Arthur. . . .

By this conclusion of marriage betwixt the said Lewes and Blanch, the right of king Iohn went awaie ; which he lawfullie before pretended vnto the citie of Eureux, and vnto those townes in the confines of Berrie, Chateau Roux or Raoul, Cressie and Isoldune, and likewise vnto the countrie of Veuxin or Veulquessine, which is a part of the territorie of Gisors : the right of all which lands, townes and countries was released to the

[Territory surrendered by John.] Polydor.
king of France by K. Iohn, who supposed that by his affinitie, and resignation of his right to those places, the peace now made would haue continued for euer. And, in consideration thereof, he pro-cured furthermore, that the foresaid Blanch should be conueied

The king cometh backe againe into England.
into France to hir husband with all speed. That doone he returned into England.

Arthur's homage to John for Brittany—referred to in my last excerpt—was performed on May 23, 1200,[1] when

[*Hol.* iii. 162/1/22.] king Iohn and Philip king of France

Arthur duke of Britaine doth homage to the king of England.
met togither neere the towne of Vernon, where Arthur duke of Britaine (as vassall to his vncle king Iohn) did his homage vnto him for the duchie of Britaine, & those other places which he held of him on this side and beyond the riuer of Loir, and after-ward, still mistrusting his vncles curtesie, he returned backe againe

[Arthur, mistrusting John, re-turned with Philip.]
with the French king, and would not commit himselfe to his said vncle, who (as he supposed) did beare him little good will.

Perhaps this is the ceremony which has received such a liberal expansion in John's promise (II. i. 551-552) :

. . . wee'l create yong Arthur duke of Britaine,
And Earle of Richmond, . . .

When Pandulph enters (III. i. 134) and demands, in Pope Innocent's name, why John continues to

Keepe Stephen Langton, chosen Archbishop
Of Canterbury, from that holy Sea ?

we are transported from the day of Lewis's betrothal (May 23, 1200)

---

[1] See note 2, p. 53.

to the summer of 1211. The dispute which caused Innocent III.'s complaint arose after the death (on July 13, 1205.—*Coggeshale*, 156) of Hubert Archbishop of Canterbury. To fill Hubert's place had been elected Reginald Sub-Prior of the conventual church at Canterbury, and Walter de Grey Bishop of Norwich, John's chaplain and nominee for the vacant archbishopric.

[*Hol.* iii. 170/2/74.] But [*p.* 171] after the pope was fullie informed of the manner of their elections, he disanulled them both, and procured by his papall authoritie the moonks of Cantur-burie (of whome manie were then come to Rome about that matter) to choose one Stephan Langton the cardinall of S. Chrysogon, an Englishman borne, and of good estimation and learning in the court of Rome, to be their archbishop. . . .

Stephan Langton chosen archbishop of Canterburie by ye popes appointment.

The king, sore offended in his mind that the bishop of Norwich was thus put beside that dignitie, to the which he had aduanced him, . . . wrote his letters vnto the pope, giuing him to vnder-stand for answer, that he would neuer consent that Stephan, which had beene brought vp & alwaies conuersant with his enimies the Frenchmen, should now inioy the rule of the bishoprike and dioces of Canturburie. Moreouer, he declared in the same letters, that he maruelled not a little what the pope ment, in that he did not consider how necessarie the freendship of the king of England was to the see of Rome, sith there came more gains to the Romane church out of that kingdome, than out of any other realme on this side the mountaines. He added hereto, that for the liberties of his crowne he would stand to the death, if the matter so required.

King John writeth vnto the pope [, refusing to accept Langton].

How gainfull England was to the court of Rome.

[John would die for the liberties of the crown.]

In 1208 Innocent,

[*Hol.* iii. 171/2/67.] perceiuing that king Iohn continued still in his former mind (which he called obstinacie), sent ouer his bulles into England, directed to William bishop of London, to Eustace bishop of Elie, and to Mauger bishop of Worcester, commanding them that, vnlesse king Iohn would suffer peaceablie the archbishop of Canturburie to occupie his see, and his moonks their abbie, they should put both him and [*p.* 172] his land vnder the sentence of interdiction, denouncing him and his land plainelie accurssed.

1208.

The pope writeth to the bishops [, command-ing them to lay John and his realm under an interdict, if Langton were not suffered to occupy the see of Canterbury]. *Matt. Paris Nic. Trivet.*

The bishops then had an audience of John, whom they warned of the charge which they had received, but he refused to obey Innocent

and dismissed them with threats. The interdict having been imposed,
John foresaw that Innocent might

 [*Hol.* iii. 172/1/65.] proceed further, and absolue all his
subiects of their allegiance which they owght to him, and that his
lords would happilie reuolt and forsake him in this his trouble.

In the summer of the year 1211,[1]

 [*Hol.* iii. 175/1/8.] the pope sent two[2] legats into England, the
one named Pandulph[3] a lawier, and the other Durant a templer,
who, comming vnto king John, exhorted him with manie terrible
words to leaue his stubborne disobedience to the church, and to
reforme his misdooings. The king for his part quietlie heard
them, and, bringing them to Northampton, being not farre distant
from the place where he met them vpon his returne foorth of
Wales, had much conference with them; but at length, when they
perceiued that they could not haue their purpose, neither for
restitution of the goods belonging to preests which he had seized
vpon, neither of those that apperteined to certeine other persons,
which the king had gotten also into his hands, by meanes of the
controuersie betwixt him and the pope, the legats departed,
 leauing him accursed, and the land interdicted, as they found it
at their comming.

The following passages should be compared with two speeches of
Pandulph (III. i. 172-179; 191-194), in which he pronounces a subject
"blessed" who forswears "Allegeance to an heretique"; and exhorts
Philip, if John continue obstinate, to "raise the power of France vpon
his head."

 [*Hol.* iii. 175/2/17.] In the meane time pope Innocent, after
the returne of his legats out of England, perceiuing that king
Iohn would not be ordered by him, determined, with the consent

---

[1] John met the legates at Northampton, on August 30, 1211.—*Ann. Waverl.*,
268 (cp. *Ann. Burton*, 209, and *Itinerary*, an. 13).
[2] *Fab.* says (318): "ye Pope sent ii. Legattys; or, after some wryters, one
Legat, named Pandulphus," . . .
[3] In answer to Pandulph, John, speaking with the mouth of Henry VIII.,
claims spiritual supremacy (III. i. 155-158). Perhaps the parallel speech in
T. R. was an anachronistic development of an opinion held by a contemporary
of John, a theologian named Alexander the Mason, who asserted "that it
apperteined not to the pope, to haue to doo concerning the temporall possessions
of any kings or other potentats touching the rule and gouernment of their
subiects" (*Hol.* iii. 174/1/7).

with the help of two hundred knights (*milites*) supplied him by Philip, was enabled to reduce Poitou, Touraine, and Anjou. Queen Eleanor's narrow escape from the enemies who "assayled" her in John's "Tent," and Arthur's capture (III. ii. 5-7), are dramatic versions illustrated by my next excerpts, which give the issue of Arthur's temporary success.

[*Hol.* iii. 164/2/13.] Queene Elianor, that was regent in those parties, being put in great feare with the newes of this sudden sturre, got hir into Mirabeau, a strong towne situat in the countrie of Aniou, and foorthwith dispatched a messenger with letters vnto king Iohn, requiring him of speedie succour in this hir present danger. In the meane time, Arthur following the victorie, shortlie after followed hir, and woone Mirabeau, where he tooke his grandmother within the same; whom he yet intreated verie honorablie, and with great reuerence (as some haue reported). ¶ But other write far more trulie, that she was not taken, but escaped into a tower, within the which she was straitlie besieged. Thither came also to aid Arthur all the Nobles and men of armes in Poictou, and namelie the . . . earle of March,[1] according to appointment betwixt them : so that by this meanes Arthur had a great armie togither in the field.

King Iohn, in the meane time, hauing receiued his mothers letters, and vnderstanding thereby in what danger she stood, was maruellouslie troubled with the strangenesse of the newes, and with manie bitter words accused the French king as an vntrue prince, and a fraudulent league-breaker ; and in all possible hast speedeth him foorth, continuing his iournie for the most part both day and night to come to the succour of his people. To be briefe, he vsed such diligence, that he was vpon his enimies necks yer they could vnderstand any thing of his comming, or gesse what the matter meant, when they saw such a companie of souldiers as he brought with him to approch so neere the citie. . . .

And hauing . . . put them [the Poitevins] all to flight, they [the English] pursued the chase towards the towne of Mirabeau, into which the enimies made verie great hast to enter ; but such speed was vsed by the English souldiers at that present, that they

Queene Elianor (got hir into Mirabeau, and sent to Iohn for speedy succour].

[Arthur (as some say) took her prisoner.]

Matth. Paris Matth. West [say that she was not taken prisoner].

Polydor.

K. Iohn commeth vpon his enimies not looked for.

[Arthur's soldiers put to flight, and Mirabeau captured.]

---

[1] Hugh le Brun, Count of La Marche. His hostility was caused by John's marriage with Isabella of Angoulême, who had been betrothed to Hugh.— *Coggeshale*, 135.

entred and wan the said towne before their enimies could come
neere to get into it. Great slaughter was made within Mirabeau
it selfe, and Arthur, with the residue of the armie that escaped
with life from the first bickering, was taken; who, being herevpon
committed to prison, first at Falais, and after within the citie of
Rouen, liued not long after, as you shall heare. . . .

Arthur duke of Britaine take prisoner.

Matth. Paris.

[*Hol.* iii. 165/1/31.] The French king, at the same time lieng in
siege before Arques, immediatlie vpon the newes of this ouerthrow,
raised from thence, and returned homewards, destroieng all that
came in his waie, till he was entred into his owne countrie.

[Philip returned to his own country.]

Act IV.—The sources of Act IV. sc. i., and IV. ii., as far as l. 105,
are contained in the following excerpts. The reader will observe how
much the historical Arthur [1] differed from the gentle, unambitious boy
of the play.

[*Hol.* iii. 165/1/35.] It is said that king Iohn caused his
nephue Arthur to be brought before him at Falais, and there went
about to persuade him all that he could to forsake his freendship
and aliance with the French king, and to leane and sticke to him,
being his naturall vncle. But Arthur, like one that wanted good
counsell, and abounding too much in his owne wilfull opinion,
made a presumptuous answer; not onelie denieng so to doo, but
also commanding king Iohn to restore vnto him the realme of
England, with all those other lands and possessions which king
Richard had in his hand at the houre of his death. For, sith the
same apperteined to him by right of inheritance, he assured him,
except restitution were made the sooner, he should not long continue quiet. King Iohn, being sore mooued with such words thus
vttered by his nephue, appointed (as before is said) that he should
be straitlie kept in prison, as first in Falais, and after at Roan
within the new castell there. Thus by means of this good
successe, the countries of Poictou, Touraine, and Anion were
recouered.

Anno Reg. 4. [John tried to draw Arthur away from Philip.]

[Arthur would not listen, but demanded all that had belonged to K. Richard.]

[John ordered that Arthur should be imprisoned.]

Shortlie after, king Iohn, comming ouer into England, caused
himselfe to be crowned againe at Canturburie by the hands of

Matth. Paris. King Iohn (twice) crowned.

---

[1] He was then more than fifteen years old, having been born on March 29,
1187.—*Benedict*, i. 361. The Arthur of *T. R.* was a youth, if one may judge
from his speeches in the scene which is the source of *John*, IV. i.

Hubert the archbishop there, on the fourteenth day of Aprill,[1] and
then went backe againe into Normandie, where, immediatlie vpon

his arriuall, a rumour was spred through all France, of the death
of his nephue Arthur.   True it is that great suit was made to
haue Arthur set at libertie, as well by the French king, as by

William de Riches a valiant baron of Poictou, and diuerse other
Noble men of the Britains, who when they could not prenaile in
their suit, they banded themselues togither, and, ioining in confederacie with Robert earle of Alanson, the vicount Beaumont,
William de Fulgiers, and other, they began to leuie sharpe wars
against king Iohn in diuerse places, insomuch (as it was thought)
that, so long as Arthur liued, there would be no quiet in those
parts : wherevpon it was reported that king Iohn, through persuasion of his councellors, appointed certeine persons to go vnto

Falais, where Arthur was kept in prison, vnder the charge of
Hubert de Burgh, and there to put out the yoong gentlemans eies.

But through such resistance as he made against one of the
tormentors that came to execute the kings commandement (for
the other [2] rather forsooke their prince and countrie, than they
would consent to obeie the kings authoritie heerein) and such
lamentable words as he vttered, Hubert de Burgh did preserue
him from that iniurie ; not doubting but rather to haue thanks than
displeasure at the kings hands, for deliuering him of such infamie
as would haue redounded vnto his highnesse, if the yoong gentleman had beene so cruellie dealt withall.   For he considered, that
king Iohn had resolued vpon this point onelie in his heat and
furie (which moueth men to vndertake manie an inconuenient
enterprise, vnbeseeming the person of a common man, much more
reprochfull to a prince, all men in that mood being meere foolish
and furious, and prone to accomplish the peruerse conceits of their
ill possessed heart ; . . .) and that afterwards, vpon better aduise-

---

[1] This must be the ceremony which John calls his " double Corronation "
(IV. ii. 40).   But we learn from his *Itinerary* that, on April 14, 1202, he was
at Orival near Rouen.   John's second coronation took place on October 8,
1200.—*Houeden*, iv. 139.   On March 25, 1201, he was crowned for the third
and last time.—*Houeden*, iv. 160.

[2] John bade three of his sergeants (" præcepit . . . tribus suis seruienti-
bus ") go to Falaise, and carry out this order.   But two of the men fled his
Court rather than obey him.—*Coggeshale*, 139.

tell what should follow after. And for so much as oftentimes his
saiengs prooued true, great credit was giuen to him as to a verie
prophet : . . . This Peter, about the first of Ianuarie [1] last past, had
told the king that, at the feast of the Ascension, it should come to
passe, that he should be cast out of his kingdome. And (whether,
to the intent that his words should be the better beleeued, or
whether vpon too much trust of his owne cunning) he offered himselfe to suffer death for it, if his prophesie prooued not true.
Herevpon being committed to prison within the castell of Corf,
when the day by him prefixed came, without any other notable
damage vnto king Iohn, he was, by the kings commandement,
drawne from the said castell vnto the towne of Warham, & there
hanged, togither with his sonne.

Having heard Faulconbridge's account of Peter's doings, John bids
Hubert "away with" the prophet to prison. During Hubert's absence
on this business, 1216 becomes again the historic date, but when, at his
return, he speaks of the five moons, time runs back to the year 1200,
for under the latter date Holinshed records that

[*Hol.* iii. 163/1/44.] About the moneth of December, there
were seene in the prouince of Yorke fiue moones, one in the east,
the second in the west, the third in the north, the fourth in the
south, and the fift as it were set in the middest of the other ;
hauing manie stars about it, and went fiue or six times incom-
passing the other, as it were the space of one houre, and shortlie
after vanished awaie.

If speeches referring to the Dauphin be excluded, the rest of Act
IV. may bear the historical date of April, 1203, about which time
Arthur disappeared. Omitting a sentence which does not illustrate the
play, I resume my quotations at the point where, in the last excerpt
relating to Arthur, the bell-ringing "for his funerals" is mentioned
(p. 61 above).

[*Hol.* iii. 165/2/43.] But when the Britains were nothing
pacified, but rather kindled more vehementlie to worke all the

---

[1] "Sub his . . . diebus," in the year 1212, was the time when, according
to *M. Paris*, Peter flourished as a prophet ; "et publice asserebat, quod non
foret [Johannes] rex in die Dominicæ Ascensionis proximo sequentis nec
deinceps ; sed die illa coronam Angliæ ad alium transferri prædixit."—*M.
Paris* (*Wendover*), ii. 535. Peter's prediction must have been made after
Ascension Day (May 3), 1212, and was fulfilled on the Vigil of Ascension
Day (May 22), 1213, on which day John surrendered his crown to Pandulph.

mischeefe they could deuise, in reuenge of their souereignes death, there was no remedie but to signifie abroad againe, that Arthur was as yet liuing and in health. Now when the king heard the truth of all this matter, he was nothing displeased for that his commandement was not executed, sith there were diuerse of his capteins which vttered in plaine words, that he should not find knights to keepe his castels, if he dealt so cruellie with his nephue. For if it chanced any of them to be taken by the king of France or other their aduersaries, they should be sure to tast of the like cup. ¶ But now touching the maner in verie deed of the end of this Arthur, writers make sundrie reports. Neuerthelesse certeine it is, that, in the yeare next insuing, he was remooued from Falais vnto the castell or tower of Rouen, out of the which there was not any that would confesse that euer he saw him go aliue. Some haue written, that, as he assaied to haue escaped out of prison, and prouuing to clime ouer the wals of the castell, he fell into the riuer of Saine, and so was drowned. Other write, that through verie greefe and languor he pined awaie, and died of naturall sicknesse. But some affirme, that king Iohn secretlie caused him to be murthered and made awaie, so as it is not throughlie agreed vpon, in what sort he finished his daies; but verelie king Iohn was had in great suspicion, whether worthilie or not, the lord knoweth.[1]

[The rumour of Arthur's death was contradicted, in order to pacify the Bretons. John was not displeased, because he had been told that his cruelty would preuent knights from keeping his castles.]

[No one knows how Arthur died, but some say that, in attempting to climb the walls of Rouen Castle, he fell into the Seine, and was drowned.]

Act V. sc. i.—Act V. opens on the Vigil of Ascension Day[2] (May 22, 1213). In the preceding year John had been deposed by Innocent, and Pandulph. was commissioned to request Philip's armed help in effecting the dethronement (see p. 57 above). Philip

[*Hol.* iii. 176/2/20.] was easilie persuaded thereto of an inward hatred that he bare vnto our king, and therevpon with all diligence made his prouision of men, ships, munition and vittell, in purpose to passe ouer into England : . . .

The French king prepared to inuade England.

John assembled a large fleet and army, and, in the spring of 1213, he was awaiting the French at Barham Down, Kent.[3]

---

[1] According to *Ann. Marg.* (27) John slew Arthur at Rouen, on April 3, 1203.

[2] This date must be accepted with a reservation of dramatic time, for the words of Pandulph and John (V. i. 22, 25-27 ; cp. IV. ii. 151-157) show that Act V. opens on Ascension Day.

[3] *M. Paris* (*Wendover*), ii. 539. John's preparations must have begun soon

[*Hol.* iii. 176/2/65.] But as he lay thus readie, neere to the coast, to withstand and beat backe his enimies, there arriued

at Douer two Templers, who, comming before the king, declared vnto him that they were sent from Pandulph the popes legat, who for his profit coueted to talke with him; for he had (as they affirmed) meanes to propone, whereby he might be reconciled both to God and his church, although he were adiudged, in the court of Rome, to haue forfeited all the right which he had to his kingdome.

[*p.* 177] The king, vnderstanding the meaning of the messengers, sent them backe againe to bring ouer the legat, who incontinentlie came ouer to Douer; of whose arriuall when the king was aduertised, he went thither, and recciued him with all due honour and reuerence. Now after they had talked togither a little, and courteouslie saluted each other (as the course of humanitie required) the legat (as it is reported) vttered these words following.

I omit "The sawcie speech of proud Pandulph, the popes lewd legat, to king Iohn, in the presumptuous popes behalfe," since it was not used by either dramatist. Matthew Paris, Holinshed's authority here, enumerates four reasons [1] which moved John to submit. One, which probably had much weight, was Pandulph's assertion—in the course of his "sawcie speech"—that Philip

[*Hol.* iii. 177/1/43.] hath (as he sticketh not to protest openlie to the world) a charter made by all the cheefest lords of England touching their fealtie and obedience assured to him.

The result of Pandulph's threats I give in my next excerpt, which should be compared with V. i. 1-4.

[*Hol.* iii. 177/1/60.] These words being thus spoken by the legat, king Iohn, as then vtterlie despairing in his matters, when he saw himselfe constreined to obeie, was in a great perplexitie of mind, and as one full of thought, looked about him with a frowning countenance; waieng with himselfe what counsell

---

after March 3, 1213, when he issued writs for the assembly of a fleet at Portsmouth in Mid-Lent (Mid-Lent Sunday fell on March 24).—*M. Paris* (*Wendover*), ii. 538.

[1] "Quartam vero causam aliis omnibus plus timebat; instabat enim dies Dominicæ Ascensionis, in qua juxta prophetiam Petri heremitæ, . . . cum ipsa vita regnum tam temporale quam æternum amittere verebatur."—*M. Paris* (*Wendover*), ii. 541.

were best for him to follow. At length, oppressed with the burthen of the imminent danger and ruine, against his will, and verie loth so to haue doone, he promised vpon his oth to stand to the popes order and decree. Wherefore shortlie after (in like manner as pope Innocent had commanded) he tooke the crowne from his owne head, and deliuered the same to Pandulph the legat; neither he, nor his heires at anie time thereafter to receiue the same, but at the popes hands.[1] . . .

[*col.* 2] Then Pandulph, keeping the crowne with him for the space of fiue daies in token of possession thereof, at length (as the popes vicar) gaue it him againe.[2]

As Pandulph departs "to make the French lay downe their Armes" (V. i. 24),—an errand denoting that historic time has again advanced to the year 1216,—John remembers Peter's prophecy, now fulfilled. John's reflection upon the manner of its fulfilment, and a hint that the prediction had caused him some uneasiness (V. i. 25-29), are illustrated by the following passage, completing the excerpt which ends with the information that Peter was "hanged, togither with his sonne" (p. 62 above).

[*Hol.* iii. 180/1/67.] The people much blamed king Iohn for this extreame dealing, bicause that the heremit was supposed to be a man of great vertue, and his sonne nothing guiltie of the offense committed by his father (if any were) against the king. Moreouer, some thought that he had much wrong to die, bicause the matter fell out euen as he had prophesied; for, the day before the Ascension day, king Iohn had resigned the superioritie of his kingdome (as they tooke the matter) vnto the pope, and had doone to him homage, so that he was no absolute king indeed, as authors affirme. One cause, and that not the least

Marginal notes:
[John sweares to obey Innocent.]
[K. John deliuereth his crowne vnto Pandulph.]
[Pandulph restoreth the crowne again to the king.]
[People said that Peter was wrongfully put to death, for, on the vigil of Ascension Day, John did homage to Innocent.]

---

[1] John, Pandulph, and the nobles of the realm met at the Templars' house near Dover, "decima quinta die Maii, in vigilia scilicet Dominicae Ascensionis; ubi idem rex juxta quod Romae fuerat sententiatum resignavit coronam suam cum regnis Angliae et Hyberniae in manus domni Papae, cujus tunc vices gerebat Pandulfus memoratus."—*M. Paris* (*Wendover*), ii. 544. The date (May 15) is wrong, for in 1213 the Vigil of the Ascension fell on May 22.

[2] In Act V. sc. i. the redelivery of the crown by Pandulph to John immediately ensues its surrender to the Legate by the King. In *T. R.* there is an interval between a scene which closes before noon on Ascension Day,—when John goes out to surrender his crown,—and the opening of another scene with the redelivery of the crown to him by Pandulph. This interval comprises the meeting of Lewis and the English nobles at St. Edmundsbury, and Falconbridge's journies to and from the same place (see-*T. R.* ii. pp. 12, 15, 19, 20, 24).

[One cause of John's submission to Innocent was fear of Peter's prophecy.] which mooued king Iohn the sooner to agree with the pope, rose through the words of the said heremit, that did put such a feare of some great mishap in his hart, which should grow through the dialoialtie of his people, that it made him yeeld the sooner.

Historic time embraced by the rest of the action ranges from May 1216 to September 1217, if V. i. 38-43,—where Arthur's death is spoken of as a recent occurrence,—be excepted. These dates mark the arrival and departure of Lewis, the latter of which events took place nearly a year after John's decease. At the historic date reached in V. i. 1-4, when John surrenders his crown to Pandulph, the French, as we have seen, were on the eve of invading England. Diverted from his purpose by John's submission, Philip turned his arms against Ferrand Count of Flanders, who had made a treaty with John, and Ferrand's appeal to his ally for help led to a war which closed with Philip's victory over the combined Flemish, German, and English forces, at Bouvines, on July 27, 1214.[1] This blow, and the failure of an attempt to recover Poitou and Brittany, so weakened John that the opportunity was seized by a party of his barons, whose projects for restraining the royal power finally took shape in the Great Charter of June 15, 1215. The "cloked Pilgrimage" (see next excerpt) of these barons to the shrine of Saint Edmund at Bury, on November 20 (?), 1214,[2] was a first step towards their ultimate triumph, but the dramatic turn given to this meeting by the old playwright associates it with Lewis's invasion in 1216, and attributes to the barons, as a chief motive for joining Lewis, their desire to be avenged on John for the murder of Arthur.[3] Amid such complexity of dates and facts a reader must choose what historical time he pleases for sc. ii., Act V., which opens shortly after these "distemper'd Lords" arrive at St. Edmundsbury, whither they are bound when they leave Faulconbridge in IV. iii. 115.

A cloked pilgrimage. [*Hol.* iii. 183/2/45.] The Nobles, supposing that longer delaie therein was not to be suffered, assembled themselues togither at the abbeie of Burie (vnder colour of going thither to doo their deuotions to the bodie of S. Edmund which laie there

---

[1] *M. Paris* (*Wendover*), ii. 581.
[2] John returned to England in October, 1214. (*M. Paris* gives Oct. 19 as the date of the King's return, but it appears from the *Itinerary* that John was at La Rochelle on Oct. 2 and at Dartmouth on Oct. 15.) "Sub eadem tempestate" his earls and barons met at St. Edmundsbury; "quasi orationis gratia, licet in causa aliud fuisset."—*M. Paris* (*Wendover*), ii. 582. Mr. James E. Doyle wrote to me: "Wendover says that the barons assembled at St. Edmundsbury 'as if for religious duties,'—that is, for duties that were well known, and therefore afforded an obvious and perfectly innocent motive for the gathering. Now the feast of the Patron Saint of that church and locality, St. Edmund, King and Martyr, took place on Nov. 20, and furnished the excuse required."
[3] If *The Troublesome Raigne* had been lost, we should have wondered why the Lords expected to meet Lewis at St. Edmundsbury (IV. iii. 11), for Shakspere says nothing about the "cloked Pilgrimage."

inshrined) where they vttered their complaint of the kings tyrannicall manners, . . .

And therfore, being thus assembled in the queere [*p.* 184] of the church of S. Edmund, they receiued a solemne oth vpon the altar there, that, if the king would not grant to the same liberties, with others which he of his owne accord had promised to confirme to them, they would from thenceefoorth make warre vpon him, till they had obteined their purpose, and inforced him to grant, not onelie to all these their petitions, but also yeeld to the confirmation of them vnder his seale, for euer to remaine most stedfast and inuiolable.

[The nobles swore that, if John refused their demands, they would make war on him till he yielded.]

Returning now to the dramatic order of events, my next excerpt illustrates Faulconbridge's announcement (V. i. 30-34) that

All Kent hath yeelded ; nothing there holds out
But Douer Castle : London hath receiu'd,
Like a kinde Host, the Dolphin and his powers :
Your Nobles will not heare you, but are gone
To offer seruice to your enemy, . . .

[*Hol.* iii. 191/2/25.] Lewes, . . . imbarking himselfe with his people, and all necessarie prouisions for such a iournie, tooke the sea, and arriued at a place called Stanchorre in the Ile of Tenet,[1] vpon the 21 day of Maie[2] [1216]; and shortlie after came to Sandwich, & there landed with all his people, where he also incamped vpon the shore by the space of three daies. In which meane time there came vnto him a great number of those lords and gentlemen which had sent for him ; and there euerie one apart and by himselfe sware fealtie and homage vnto him, as if he had beene their true and naturall prince.

He taketh the sea.

He landeth in Kent.

The lords doo homage vnto him.

King Iohn, about the same time that Lewes thus arriued, came to Douer, meaning to fight with his aduersaries by the way as they should come forward towards London. But yet, vpon other aduisement taken, he changed his purpose, bicause he put some doubt in the Flemings and other strangers, of whome the most part of his armie consisted, bicause he knew that they hated the French men no more than they did the English. Therefore, furnishing the castell of Douer, with men, munition, and vittels, he left it in the

Matth. Paris.

---

[1] Stonar, Isle of Thanet.   [2] *M. Paris* (*Wendover*), ii. 653.

[John left
Dover Castle
in charge of
Hubert de
Burgh, and
retired from
Kent.]
keeping of Hubert de Burgh, a man of notable prowesse &
valiancie, and returned himselfe vnto Canturburie, and from thence
tooke the high waie towards Winchester. Lewes, being aduertised
that king Iohn was retired out of Kent, passed through the
countrie without anie incounter, and wan all the castels and holds
as he went, but Douer he could not win. . . .

Lewes
commeth to
London.
[Afterwards] he came to London, and there receiued the
homage of those lords and gentlemen which had not yet doone
their homage to him at Sandwich.

Act V. sc. ii.—The following excerpts—which, in Holinshed,
immediately succeed my last quotation—should be compared with
the Entry and first eight lines of Act V. sc. ii.

[*Hol.* iii. 191/2/60.] On the other part he [Lewis] tooke
an oth to mainteine and performe the old lawes and customes of
the realme, and to restore to euerie man his rightfull heritage and
lands; requiring the barons furthermore to continue faithfull
towards him, assuring them to bring things so to passe, that the
realme of England should recouer the former dignitie, and they
their ancient liberties. Moreouer he vsed them so courteouslie,
gaue them so faire words, and made such large promises, that they
beleeued him with all their harts. . . .

The rumour of this pretended outward courtesie, being once
spred through the realme, caused great numbers of people to come
Noblemen
reuolting
frõ K. Iohn
vnto Lewes.
flocking to him; among [*p.* 192] whome were diuerse of those which
before had taken part with king Iohn, as William earle Warren,
William earle of Arundell, William earle of Salisburie, William
Marshall the yoonger,[1] and diuerse other; supposing verelie that
the French kings sonne should now obteine the kingdome.

Pandulph's speech and Lewis's answer (V. ii. 69-102) take us back
to a time preceding the latter's invasion. John repudiated his grant as
soon as he had collected a mercenary force to levy war on his barons,
and he also appealed from them to Innocent, who annulled the Charter,
and finally excommunicated its supporters. Hard pressed by John's
soldiers, the barons

---

[1] Son of William Marshal, Earl of Pembroke. "Pembroke," in both plays,
is, I suppose, the younger Marshal. He was one of the twenty-five barons
"sworne to see the liberties granted and confirmed by the king [*Magna Charta*
and *Charta de Foresta*] to be in euerie point obserued, but, if he went against
the same, then they should haue authoritie to compell him to the obseruing of
euerie of them."—*Hol.* iii. 186/1/19.

[*Hol.* iii. 190/1/53.] resolued with themselues to seeke for aid *The lords send to the French kings sonne, offering to him the crowne.* at the enimies hands; and therevpon Saer earle of Winchester, and Robert Fitz Walter, with letters vnder their seales, were sent vnto Lewes the sonne of Philip the French king, offering him the crowne of England, and sufficient pledges for performance of the same, and other couenants to be agreed betwixt them; requiring him with all speed to come vnto their succour. This Lewes had married (as before is said) Blanch daughter to Alfonse [Lewis's marriage to Blanch.] king of Castile, neece to king Iohn by his sister Elianor.

Now king Philip, the father of this Lewes, being glad to haue such an occasion to inuade the relme of England, which he neuer looued, promised willinglie that his sonne should come vnto the [The barons' offer accepted.] aid of the said barons with all conuenient speed; (but first he receiued foure and twentie hostages which he placed at Campaine for further assurance of the couenants accorded;) and herewith he prepared an armie, and diuerse ships to transport his sonne and his armie ouer into England. . . .

[*Hol.* iii. 191/1/14.] The pope, desirous to helpe king Iohn *Anno. Reg.* 18. *Cardinall Gualo. Matth. Paris.* all that he might (bicause he was now his vassall), sent his legat Gualo into France, to disswade king Philip from taking anie enterprise in hand against the king of England. But king Philip, *The French kings allegations to the popes legat Gualo.* though he was content to heare what the legat could saie, yet by no meanes would be turned from the execution of his purpose; alledging that king Iohn was not the lawfull king of England, hauing first vsurped and taken it awaie from his nephue Arthur the [John an usurper, and a would-be vassal of the Pope.] *Matth. West.* lawfull inheritour, and that now sithens, as an enimie to his owne roiall dignitie, he had giuen the right of his kingdome awaie to the pope (which he could not doo without consent of his nobles) and therefore through his owne fault he was worthilie depriued of all his kinglie honor. . . .

Lewes, on the morrow following, being the 26 of Aprill[1] [1216], *Matth. Paris. Lewes the Frēch kings sonne mainteineth his pretended title to the crowne of England.* by his fathers procurement, came into the councell chamber, and with frowning looke beheld the legat; where by his procurator he defended the cause that moued him to take vpon him this iournie into England, disprouing not onelie the right which king Iohn had

---

[1] *M. Paris (Wendover)*, ii. 651, 652.

to the crowne, but also alledging his owne interest, not onelie by
his new election of the barons, but also in the title of his wife,
whose mother the queene of Castile remained onelie aliue of all
the brethren and sisters of Henrie the second, late king of England.

In further illustration of V. ii. 69-102 I quote passages relating to
a time not long after Lewis's arrival, and beginning when he and his
English allies hoped to make their cause good through the arguments
of those ambassadors who had been sent "in all hast vnto the court of
Rome."

[Failure of
Lewis's pro-
curators.]
[*Hol.* iii. 192/1/15.]   But this auailed them not, neither
tooke his excuse any such effect as he did hope it should; for
those ambassadors, that king Iohn had sent thither, replied against
their assertions, so that there was hard hold about it in that court:
albeit that the pope would decree nothing till he hard further from
his legat Gualo, who, the same time, (being aduertised of the pro-

*Cardinall
Gualo
commeth
ouer into
England,*
ceedings of Lewes in his iournie,) with all diligence, hasted ouer
into England, and, passing through the middle of his aduersaries,
came vnto king Iohn, then soiourning at Glocester; of whome he
was most ioifullie receiued, for in him king Iohn reposed all his
hope of victorie.

Before Midsummer,[1] 1216,

[*Hol.* iii. 192/1/73.]   letters came also vnto Lewes from his
procurators, whom he had sent to the pope. . . .

*The points
wherewith
king Iohn
was charged
[: Iohn
hauing been
declared by
the French
peers guilty
of Arthur's
death, had
forfeited his
dominions,
to which
Lewis had
succeeded.]*
The cheefest points (as we find) that were laid by Lewes his
procurators against king Iohn were these: that, by the murther
committed in the person of his nephue Arthur, he had beene condemned in the parlement chamber, before the French king, by the
peeres of France; and that, being summoned to appeare, he had
obstinatelie refused so to doo, and therefore had by good right
forfeited not onelie his lands within the precinct of France, but
also the realme of England, which was now due vnto the said
Lewes, as they alledged, in right of the ladie Blanch his wife,
daughter to Elianor queene of Spaine.   But the pope refelled all

---

[1] The letter from Lewis's procurators was written on or about May 10,
1216.—*M. Paris* (*Wendover*), ii. 656, 657.   Lewis, "instante nativitate sancti
Johannis Baptistae" (the next date given), began the siege of Dover Castle.—
M. Paris (*Wendover*), ii. 664.

such allegations as they produced for proofe hereof, & seemed to defend king Iohns cause verie pithilie; but namelie, in that he was vnder the protection of him as supreme lord of England. [Innocent answered that John was under his protection.]

Act V. sc. iii.—"Alarums" may possibly represent the decisive battle of Lincoln, fought on May 20, 1217,[1] when the French and their English allies were defeated by William Marshal Earl of Pembroke, who commanded the army of the boy-king Henry III. If the general disregard of historic time in this play be remembered, such a conjecture is not affected by the qualification that it involves John's entry some seven months after the date which historians fix for his death. Before John leaves the field, a messenger has bidden him (V. iii. 9-11):

> Be of good comfort; for the great *supply*,
> That was expected by the Dolphin heere,
> Are wrack'd three nights ago on Goodwin sands.

Allowing for altered circumstance and antedating, we may suppose this "great supply" to be the reinforcements sent by Philip of France, about three months after the battle of Lincoln. These needful succours never reached Lewis, for

[*Hol.* iii. 201/1/36.] the earle of Penbroke, and other the lords *Matth. Paris.* that tooke part with king Henrie, hauing aduertisement, that a new *supplie* of men was readie to come and aid Lewes, they appointed Philip de Albenie and Iohn Marshall to associat with them the power of the cinque ports, and to watch for the comming [Watch kept for the French fleet.] of the aduersaries, that they might keepe them from landing; who on saint Bartholomews[2] day set forth from Caleis, in purpose to arriue in the Thames, and so to come vp the riuer to London. Howbeit Hubert de Burgh, capiteine of the castell of Douer, togither with the said Philip de Albenie and Iohn Marshall, with other such power as they could get togither of the cinque ports, hauing not yet aboue the number of 40 ships great & small, vpon the discouering of the French fleet, (which consisted of 80 great ships, besides other lesser vessels well appointed and trimmed,) made foorth to the sea. And, first coasting aloofe from them, till *Hubert de Burgh assaileth the French fleet.* they had got the wind on their backs, came finallie with their maine force to assaile the Frenchmen, and, with helpe of their crossebowes and archers at the first ioining, made great slaughter of their enimies; and so, grapling togither, in the end the English-

---

[1] *Coggeshale*, 185.
[2] August 24, 1217.—*M. Paris* (*Wendover*), iii. 26.

The French
fleet is
vanquished. men bare themselues so manfullie, that they vanquished the whole
French fleet, and obteined a famous victorie.

> Act V. sc. iv.—Melun's confession, and its result in detaching the
> English barons from Lewis, form the subject of this scene. The date
> —referred to in the following excerpt by the words "About the same
> time"—is probably August, 1216.[1]

Matth.
Paris. [*Hol.* iii. 193/2/6.] About the same time, or rather in the
yeare last past as some hold, it fortuned that the vicount of
Melune, a French man, fell sicke at London, and, perceiuing that
death was at ʹhand, he called vnto him certeine of the ʹEnglish
barons, which remained in the citie, vpon safegard thereof, and to
The vicount
of Melune
discouereth
the purpose
of Lewes. them made this protestation : "I lament" (saith he) "your destruc-
"tion and desolation at hand, bicause ye are ignorant of the perils
"hanging ouer your heads. For this vnderstand, that Lewes, and
"with him 16 earles and barons of France, haue secretlie sworne
"(if it shall fortune him to conquere this realme of England, & to
"be crowned king) that he will kill, banish, and confine all those
"of the English nobilitie (which now doo serue vnder him, and
"persecute their owne king) as traitours and rebels ; and further-
"more will dispossesse all their linage of such inheritances as they
"now hold in England. And bicause" (saith he) "you shall not
"haue doubt hereof, I, which lie here at the point of death, doo
"now affirme vnto you, and take it on the perill of my soule,
"that I am one of those sixteen that haue sworne to performe
"this thing : wherefore I aduise you to prouide for your owne
"safeties, and your realmes which you now destroie ; and keepe
The vicount
of Melune
dieth. "this thing secret which I haue vttered vnto you." After this
speech was vttered he streightwaies died.

When these words of the lord of Melune were opened vnto the
barons, they were, and not without cause, in great doubt of themselues, for they saw how Lewes had alredie placed and set French-
The English
nobilitie
beginneth to
mislike of the
match which
they had
made with
Lewes. men in most of such castels and townes as he had gotten, the
right whereof indeed belonged to them. And againe, it greeued
them much to vnderstand, how, besides the hatred of their prince,
they were euerie sundaie and holiedaie openlie accursed in euerie

---

    ¹ After recording the homage of Alexander II. King of Scots to Lewis, in
August, 1216, *Wendover* (*M. Paris*, ii. 666) dates Melun's illness as having
happened "hac tempestate."

church, so that manie of them inwardlie relented, and could haue
bin contented to haue returned to king Iohn, if they had thought
that they should thankfullie haue beene receiued.

Subsequently Holinshed observes :

[*Hol.* iii. 197/2/40.] It is reported by writers, that amongst
other things, as there were diuerse, which withdrew the hearts of   [Effect of
Melun's
the Englishmen from Lewes, the consideration of the confession   confession.]
which the * vicount of Melune made at the houre of his death,   * *See pag.*
198, col. 2.
was the principall.

Act V. sec. v.—vii.—With sc. v., Act V., the excerpts given in
relation to sc. iii., Act V., should be compared. The rest of the play
(save V. vii. 82-95 ; 101-118) is illustrated by my next quotations,
which date from October, 1216, when John, according to Holinshed,
was marching northwards, after spoiling Peterborough and Crowland.

[*Hol.* iii. 194/1/45.] Thus, the countrie being wasted on
each hand, the king hasted forward till he came to Wellestreme
sands, where passing the washes he lost a great part of his armie,
with horsses and carriages ; so that it was iudged to be a punish-   *The losse of
the kings*
ment appointed by God, that the spoile, which had beene gotten   *carriages.*
and taken out of churches, abbeies, and other religious houses,
should perish, and be lost by such means togither with the spoilers.
Yet the king himselfe, and a few other, escaped the violence of   *Matth.*
Paris.
the waters, by following a good guide.   But, as some haue written,   *Matth.*
West.
he tooke such greefe for the losse susteined at this passage, that
immediatlie therevpon he fell into an ague ; the force and heat   *King Iohn*
falleth sicke
whereof, togither with his immoderate feeding on rawe peaches,   *of an ague.*
Matth.
and drinking of new sider, so increased his sicknesse, that he was   *Paris.*
not able to ride, but was faine to be carried in a litter presentlie
made of twigs, with a couch of strawe vnder him, without any bed
or pillow, thinking to haue gone to Lincolne ; but the disease still
so raged and grew vpon him, that he was inforced to staie one
night at the .castell of Laford, and, on the next day with great   *Laford.*
Matth.
paine, caused himselfe to be caried vnto Newarke, where, in the   *West.*
Matth.
castell, through anguish of mind, rather than through force of sick- *Paris.*
nesse, he departed this life the night before the nineteenth day of   *King Iohn*
departed this
October, in the yeare of his age fiftie and one, and after he had   *life.*

reigned seauenteene yeares, six moneths, and seauen and twentie
daies.

¶ There be which haue written, that, after he had lost his
armie, he came to the abbeie of Swineshead in Lincolneshire, and,
there vnderstanding the cheapenesse and plentie of corne, shewed
himselfe greatlie displeased therewith, as he that for the hatred
which he bare to the English people, that had so traitorouslie
reuolted from him vnto his aduersarie Lewes, wished all miserie
to light vpon them ; and therevpon said in his anger, that he would
cause all kind of graine to be at a farre higher price, yer manie
daies should passe.   Wherevpon a moonke, that heard him speake
such words, being mooued with zeale for the oppression of his
countrie, gaue the king poison in a cup of ale, wherof he first
tooke the assaie, to cause the king not to suspect the matter, and
so they both died in manner at one time. . . .

The men of warre that serued vnder his ensignes, being for the
more part hired souldiers and strangers, came togither, and marching foorth with his bodie, each man with his armour on his backe,
in warlike order, conueied it vnto Worcester, where he was pompouslie buried in the cathedrall church before the high altar ; not
for that he had so appointed (as some write) but bicause it was
thought to be a place of most suertie for the lords and other of
his freends there to assemble, and to take order in their businesse
now after his deceasse.

Nearly a year elapsed between the accession of Henry III. and the
departure of Lewis, shortly after the royalists' great naval victory in
August, 1217.   Holinshed's account of how the French reinforcements
were destroyed (see p. 71 above) is followed by the ensuing passages,
which bear upon V. vii. 82-95.

[Hol. iii. 201/2/8.]   But Lewes, after he vnderstood of this
mischance happening to his people that came to his aid, began
not a litle to despaire of all other succour to come vnto him at
any time heerafter : wherfore he inclined the sooner vnto peace, so
that at length he tooke such offers of agreement as were put vnto
him, and receiued furthermore a sum of monie for the release of
such hostages as he had in his hands, togither with the title of the

[John said
he would
make corn
dear in
England,
whereupon
a monk
poisoned
him.]
Caxton.

[He was
buried at
Worcester.]

Bernewell.

[After the
loss of his
reinforce-
ments,
Lewis's
hopes fall.]

An accord
betwixt
K. Henrie
& Lewes.

kingdome of England, and the possession of all such castels and holds as he held within the realme. . . .

This peace was concluded on the eleuenth day of September [1] [1217], not farre from Stanes, hard by the riuer of Thames, where Lewes himselfe, the legat Guallo, and diuerse of the spiritualtie, with the earle of Penbroke, lord gouernor of the realme, and others, did meet and talke about this accord. Now, when all things were ordered and finished agreeable to the articles and couenants of the peace, so farre as the time present required, the lords of the realme (when Lewes should depart homeward) attended him to Douer in honorable wise, as apperteined, and there tooke leaue of him, and so he departed out of the realme about the feast of saint Michaell.[2]

The revival of patriotic feeling, which placed Henry III. on the throne, is exhibited when Faulconbridge and Salisbury—the dramatic characters who severally represent the royalist and baronial parties— unite in proffering allegiance to their youthful sovereign (V. vii. 101-107). Holinshed says :

[*Hol.* iii. 197/1/12.] Immediatlie after the death of his father king Iohn, William Marshall earle of Penbroke, generall of his fathers armie, brought this yoong prince with his brother and sisters vnto Glocester, and there called a councell of all such lords as had taken part with king Iohn. Anon, after it was once openlie knowne, that the sonnes and daughters of the late deceassed prince were brought into a place of safetie, a great number of the lords and cheefe barons of the realme hasted thither (I meane not onelie such as had holden with king Iohn, but also diuerse other, which, vpon certeine knowledge had of his death, were newlie reuolted from Lewes) in purpose to aid yoong king Henrie, to whome of right the crowne did apperteine.

[After John's death,] *William Marshall, earle of Penbroke* [, brought Henry to Gloucester].

[Thither came nobles who had held with John, and others lately revolted from Lewis.

In a speech delivered to the assemblage at Gloucester, Pembroke vindicated Henry's title :

[*Hol.* iii. 197/2/17.] When the barons had heard this earles words, after some silence and conference had, they allowed of

---

[1] September 11.—*M. Paris* (*Wendover*), iii. 30.   September 13.—*Ann. Theok.* 63.
[2] Lewis returned to France on September 28, 1217.—*Ann. Theok.* 63.

his saiengs, and immediatlie, with one consent, proclaimed the

yoong gentleman king of England; whome the bishops of Winchester and Bath did crowne and annoint with all due solemnities at
Glocester, vpon the day of the feast of the apostles Simon & Iude,
in presence of the legat.

Holinshed adds to his chronicle of John's reign the following general
remarks on the King's disposition, and dealings with the clergy.

[*Hol.* iii. 196/1/4.] He was comelie of stature, but of looke
and countenance displeasant and angrie; somewhat cruell of nature,
as by the writers of his time he is noted; and not so hardie as
doubtfull in time of perill and danger. But this seemeth to be
an enuious report vttered by those that were giuen to speake no

good of him whome they inwardlie hated. Howbeit some giue
this witnesse of him (as the author of the booke of *Bernewell*
abbeie and other): that he was a great and mightie prince, but yet
not verie fortunate, much like to Marius the noble Romane, tasting
of fortune both waies; bountifull and liberall vnto strangers, but
of his owne people (for their dailie treasons practised towards him)
a great oppressour; so that he trusted more to forreners than to
them, and therfore in the end he was of them vtterlie forsaken.

¶ Verelie, whosoeuer shall consider the course of the historie
written of this prince, he shall find, that he hath beene little
beholden to the writers of that time in which he liued; for
scarselie can they afoord him a good word, except when the trueth

inforceth them to come out with it as it were against their willes.
The occasion whereof (as some thinke) was, for that he was no
great freend to the clergie. . . .   •

Certeinelie it should seeme the man had a princelie heart in
him, and wanted nothing but faithfull subiects to haue assisted
him in reuenging such wrongs as were doone and offered by the
French king and others.

Moreouer, the pride and pretended authoritie of the cleargie
he could not well abide, when they went about to wrest out of his
hands the prerogatiue of his princelie rule and gouernement.
True it is, that to mainteine his warres which he was forced to
take in hand, as well in France as elsewhere, he was constreined

to make all the shift he could deuise to recouer monie, and, bicause he pinched their pursses, they conceiued no small hatred against him ; which when he perceiued, and wanted peraduenture discretion to passe it ouer, he discouered now and then in his rage his immoderate displeasure, as one not able to bridle his affections, (a thing verie hard in a stout stomach,) and thereby missed now and then to compasse that which otherwise he might verie well haue brought to passe.

Pandulph is spoken of as he "who (as before is expressed) did the message so stoutlie from pope Innocent to king Iohn" (*Hol.* iii. 202/1/65). Hubert de Burgh—"a right valiant man of warre as was any where to be found" (*Hol.* iii. 169/2/50) — showed " singular constancie" in defending Dover Castle against Lewis (*Hol.* iii. 193/1/45). The dramatic character is a person of much lower degree than was this historical Hubert, the Justiciar of England, as he is entitled in the treaty of peace between Henry III. and Lewis ; the three names preceding his own in that document being those of the Legate Gualo, the King, and William Marshal.—*Rymer*, i. 222.

V. RICHARD II.

ACT I. sc. i.—The first scene in *The Tragedie of King Richard the second*[1] opens on April 29,[2] 1398, at Windsor, where a day for combat was assigned to Bolingbroke and Mowbray (I. i. 199). On March 12, 1400,[3] a body, officially declared to be Richard II.'s, was exhibited at St. Paul's. The latter historic date marks the close of the action, when Bolingbroke sees his "buried feare" (V. vi. 31) in the coffin which Exton presents to him.

In the first scene King Richard enters, and thus addresses John of Gaunt (I. i. 1-6) :

> Ovld Iohn of Gaunt, time honoured Lancaster,
> Hast thou, according to thy oath and bande,
> Brought hither Henrie Herford thy bolde sonne,
> Here to make good the boistrous late appeale,
> Which then our leysure would not let vs heare,
> Against the Duke of Norfolke, Thomas Moubray !

---

[1] I quote the text of Q1 (1597), from the Shakspere Quarto Facsimile of Mr. Huth's copy. In the Parliament Scene (IV. i. 162-318) the text of F1 is quoted.
[2] *Rot. Parl.*, iii. 383/1.   [3] *Trais.*, 103 ; 261.

Bolingbroke's "late appeale" was made in a Parliament which reassembled at Shrewsbury on January 27, 1398, and was dissolved on January 31.   On January 30, 1398,[1]

The duke of Hereford appealeth the duke of Norfolk of treson.

[*Hol.* iii. 493/2/16.] . . . Henrie, duke of Hereford, accused Thomas Mowbraie, duke of Norfolke, of certeine words which he should vtter in talke had betwixt them, as they rode togither latelie before betwixt London and Brainford; sounding highlie to the kings dishonor.   And for further proofe thereof, he pre-

Thom. Wals.

sented a supplication to the king, wherein he appealed the duke of Norfolke in field of battell, for a traitor, false and disloiall to the king, and enimie vnto the realme.   This supplication was red before both the dukes, in presence of the king; which doone, the duke of Norfolke tooke vpon him to answer it, declaring that

[Bolingbroke's accusation denied by Mowbray.]

whatsoeuer the duke of Hereford had said against him other than well, he lied falselie like an vntrue knight as he was.   And, when the king asked of the duke of Hereford what he said to it, he, taking his hood off his head, said: "My souereigne lord, euen

[The accusation repeated by Bolingbroke.]

"as the supplication which I tooke you importeth, right so I "saie for truth, that Thomas Mowbraie, duke of Norfolke, is a "traitour, false and disloiall to your roiall maiestie, your crowne, "and to all the states of your realme."

Then the duke of Norfolke being asked what he said to this, he answered: "Right deere lord, with your fauour that I make "answer vnto your coosine here, I saie (your reuerence saued)

[and again denied by Mowbray.]

"that Henrie of Lancaster, duke of Hereford, like a false and "disloiall traitor as he is, dooth lie, in that he hath or shall say "of me otherwise than well."   "No more," said the king, "we

The duke of Surrie, marshall, and the duke of Aumarle, constable of England (, and the Dukes of Lancaster and York, become pledges for Bolingbroke's appearance; but Mowbray was

"haue heard inough"; and herewith commanded the duke of Surrie, for that turne marshall of England, to arrest in his name the two dukes: the duke of Lancaster, father to the duke of Hereford, the duke of Yorke, the duke of Aumarle, constable of England, and the duke of Surrie, marshall of the realme, vndertooke as pledges bodie for bodie for the duke of Hereford; but the duke of Northfolke was not suffered to put in pledges, and so vnder arrest was led vnto Windsor castell, and there

---

[1] *Eves.*, 142-145.   Cp. *Rot. Parl.*, iii. 382/1.

garded with keepers that were appointed to see him safelie kept. kept in Windsor Castle.]

Now after the dissoluing of the parlement at Shrewsburie, there was a daie appointed about six weeks after, for the king to come vnto Windsor, to heare and to take some order betwixt the two dukes, which had thus appealed ech other. There was a great scaffold erected within the castell of Windsor [1] for the king to sit with the lords and prelats of his realme; and so, at the daie appointed, he with the said lords & prelats being come thither and set in their places, the duke of Hereford appellant, and the duke of Norfolke defendant, were sent for to come & appeare before the king, sitting there in his seat of iustice. And then began sir Iohn Bushie to speake for the king; declaring to the lords how they should vnderstand, that where the duke of Hereford had presented a supplication to the king, who was there set to minister iustice to all men that would demand the same, as apperteined to his roiall maiestie, he therefore would now heare what the parties could say one against [p. 494] an other : and withall the king commanded the dukes of Aumarle and Surrie, (the one being constable, and the other marshall,) to go vnto the two dukes, appellant and defendant, requiring them, on his behalfe, to grow to some agreement; and, for his part, he would be readie to pardon all that had been said or doone amisse betwixt them, touching anie harm or dishonor to him or his realme; but they answered both assuredlie, that it was not possible to haue anie peace or agreement made betwixt them.

When he heard what they had answered, he commanded that

[A day appointed for the hearing of the appeal.]

The order of the proceeding in this appeale.

[Richard sent to Bolingbroke and Mowbray, desiring them to be reconciled to each other, but they refused his request.]

---

[1] According to *Trais.*—the original authority for this account of the proceedings at Windsor—"le Roy Richart retourna du parlement de Scrembory en lan mil ccc iiij^{xx} et xviij ou moys de Januier et xl jours apres fut la journee a Windesore pour ouir les deux seigneurs lesquelz auoyent appelle lun lautre de traison" (p. 13). *Hol.* seems to have followed the computation of *Trais.*, regarding the "daie appointed" for Richard's presence at Windsor. The disagreement of this date with the date (April 29) given by *Rot. Parl.* for the Windsor assembly, may perbaps be explained by supposing that the writer of *Trais.* counted forty days from March 19, 1398, when Bolingbroke and Mowbray appeared before Richard at Bristol, and it was decided that their cause should be tried conformably to the "Ley de Chivalrie."—*Rot. Parl.*, iii. 383/1. On February 23, 1398, they appeared before Richard at Oswestry, and were then ordered to present themselves before him at Windsor on April 28, 1398. On the next day (April 29) time and place of battle were fixed.—*Ibid.*

[Then he called them before him, and asked them to make peace togither, but Mowbray would not consent to do so.]

they should be brought foorthwith before his presence, to beare what they would say. Herewith an herald in the kings name with lowd voice commanded the dukes to come before the king, either of them to shew his reason, or else to make peace togither without more delaie. When they were come before the king and lords, the king spake himselfe to them, willing them to agree, and make peace togither: "for it is" (said he) "the best waie ye can take." The duke of Norfolke with due reuerence herevnto answered, it could not be so brought to passe, his honor saued.

[Thereupon Richard commanded Bolingbroke to specify Mowbray's offences.]

Then the king asked of the duke of Hereford, what it was that he demanded of the duke of Norfolke, "and what is the matter that "ye can not make peace togither, and become friends?"

[The objection[s] against the duke of Norfolke: [(1) that he embezzled money due to the garrison of Calais; (2) that he had been the prime-mover of all the treason devised in England for the past eighteen years; (3) and that, by evil suggestion and counsel, he caused Glocester's death.]

Then stood foorth a knight, who, asking and obteining licence to speake for the duke of Hereford, said: "Right deare and "souereigne lord, here is Henrie of Lancaster, duke of Hereford "and earle of Derbie, who saith, and I for him likewise say, that "Thomas Mowbraie, duke of Norfolke, is a false and disloiall "traitor to you and your roiall maiestie, and to your whole "realme: and likewise the duke of Hereford saith, and I for him, "that Thomas Mowbraie, duke of Norfolke, hath receiued eight "thousand nobles to pay the souldiers that keepe your towne of "Calis; which he hath not doone as he ought: and furthermore "the said duke of Norfolke hath beene the occasion of all the "treason that hath beene contriued in your realme for the space "of these eighteene yeares, &, by his false suggestions and "malicious counsell, he hath caused to die and to be murdered "your right deere vncle, the duke of Glocester, sonne to king "Edward. Moreouer, the duke of Hereford saith, and I for him, "that he will proue this with his bodie against the bodie of the

[To proue these charges, Bollingbroke demanded battle against Mowbray.]

"said duke of Norfolke within lists." The king herewith waxed angrie, and asked the duke of Hereford, if these were his woords; who answered: "Right deere lord, they are my woords; and "hereof I require right, and the battell against him."

[Mowbray's spokesman answered that Bolingbroke had lied; and

There was a knight also that asked licence to speake for the duke of Norfolke, and, obteining it, began to answer thus: "Right "deere souereigne lord, here is Thomas Mowbraie, duke of "Norfolke, who answereth and saith, and I for him, that all which

"Henrie of Lancaster hath said and declared (sauing the reuerence "due to the king and his councell) is a lie ; and the said Henrie "of Lancaster hath falselie and wickedlie lied as a false and "disloiall knight, and both hath beene, and is, a traitor against "you, your crowne, roiall maiestie, & realme. This will I proue "and defend as becommeth a loiall knight to doo with my bodie "against his : right deere lord, I beseech you therefore, and your "councell, that it maie please you, in your roiall discretion, to "consider and marke, what Henrie of Lancaster, duke of Hereford, "such a one as he is, hath said."

The king then demanded of the duke of Norfolke, if these were his woords, and whether he had anie more to saie. The duke of Norfolke then answered for himselfe : "Right deere sir, "true it is, that I haue receiued so much gold to paie your people "of the towne of Calis ; which I haue doone, and I doo auouch "that your towne of Calis is as well kept at your commandement "as euer it was at anie time before, and that there neuer hath "beene by anie of Calis anie complaint made vnto you of me. "Right deere and my souereigne lord, for the voiage that I made "into France, about your marriage, I neuer receiued either gold "or siluer of you, nor yet for the voiage that the duke of Aumarle "& I made into Almane, where we spent great treasure. Marie, "true it is, that once I laid an ambush to haue slaine the duke of "Lancaster, that there sitteth ; but neuerthelesse he hath par- "doned me thereof, and there was good peace made betwixt vs, "for the which I yeeld him hartie thankes. This is that which "I haue to answer, and I am readie to defend my selfe against "mine aduersarie ; I beseech you therefore of right, and to haue "the battell against him in vpright iudgement."

After this, when the king had communed with his councell a little, he commanded the two dukes to stand foorth, that their answers might be heard. The K. then caused them once againe to be asked, if they would agree and make peace togither, but they both flatlie answered that they would not : and withall the duke of Hereford cast downe his gage, and the duke of Norfolke tooke it vp. The king, perceiuing this demeanor betwixt them, sware by saint Iohn Baptist, that he would neuer seeke to make

sware that
he would
never more
seek to
reconcile
them.]
The combat
appointed to
be doone at
Couentrie.
The French
pamphlet.
John Stow.
Fabian.
peace betwixt them againe. And therfore sir Iohn Bushie in
name of the king & his councell declared, that the king and his
councell had commanded and ordeined, that they should haue a
daie[1] of battell appointed them at Couentrie. ¶ Here writers
disagree about the daie that was appointed: for some saie, it was
vpon a mondaie in August; other vpon saint Lamberts daie,
being the seuenteenth of September; other on the eleuenth of
September: but true it is, that the king assigned them not onelie
the daie, but also appointed them listes and place for the combat,
and therevpon great preparation was made, as to such a matter
apperteined.

To explain these words a reference to some events in the preceding
Nothing in this scene needs further historical illustration except
Mowbray's rather equivocal answer to the charge of having been
Gloucester's murderer (I. i. 132-134):

> For Glocesters death,
> I slewe him not; but (to my owne disgrace)
> Neglected my sworne duety in that case.

To explain these words a reference to some events in the preceding
year is necessary. Towards the end of June, 1397, Gloucester, Derby
(Henry Bolingbroke), Nottingham (Thomas Mowbray), and others, met
at Arundel Castle, and there agreed that, on a day in the following
August, they would seize and imprison the King and his uncles the
Dukes of Lancaster and York, and would put to death the rest of the
King's Council. Nottingham revealed this plot to Richard, and after-
wards, by the King's order, arrested Gloucester and brought him to
Calais.[2] Hearing that Gloucester's guilt was proved Richard

[Richard
ordered
Mowbray to
despatch
Gloucester
secretly.]
[Mowbray
hesitated,
whereupon
Richard
threatened
him with
death.]
[*Hol.* iii. 489/1/64.]   sent vnto Thomas Mowbraie, earle
marshall and of Notingham, to make the duke secretlie awaie.
The earle prolonged time for the executing of the kings commandement, though the king would haue had it doone with all
expedition, wherby the king conceiued no small displeasure, and

---

[1] September 16.—*Rot. Parl.*, iii. 383/1. "The French pamphlet," referred
to, in the sidenote, as an authority for the date, "a mondaie in August," is
Trais. (17 ; 149). It belonged to John Stow. The date in *Eves.*, 148, is St.
Lambert's day. September 11.—*Fab.*, ii. 544. Bolingbroke and Norfolk were
ordered to leave the realm "dedeins le jour de le oeptas de Seint Edward le
Confessour [October 20] prochein venant."—*Rot. Parl.*, iii. 383/2. The burgesses of Lowestoft informed Richard that Norfolk embarked "le Samady
[October 19] proschein apres la fest de Seynt Edward, l'an de vostre regne vynt
& secounde."—*Rot. Parl.*, iii. 384/1. It seems (*Usk*, 35 ; 149) that Bolingbroke
went into exile on the feast (October 13).

[2] In *Trais.* (3 ; 121) there is a full account of this plot to imprison
Richard.

sware that it should cost the earle his life if he quickly obeied not his commandement. The earle thus, as it seemed, in maner inforced, called out the duke at midnight, as if he should haue taken ship to passe ouer into England, and there in the lodging called the princes In, he caused his seruants to cast featherbeds vpon him, and so smoother him to death; or otherwise to strangle him with towels (as some write.) This was the end of that * noble man, fierce of nature, hastie, wilfull, and giuen more to war than to peace: and in this greatlie to be discommended, that he was euer repining against the king in all things, whatsoeuer he wished to haue forward. . . . His bodie was afterwards with all funerall pompe conueied into England, and buried at his owne manor of Plashie within the church there; in a sepulchre which he in his life time had caused to be made, and there erected.

[Gloucester murdered.]

[His character.]
* For he was son to a king, and vncle to a king.

[He was buried at Pleshey.]

In October, 1399, after Richard had been deposed, and Bolingbroke had ascended the throne, Sir William Bagot, one of the late King's favourites, "disclosed manie secrets [1] vnto the which he was priuie; and being brought on a daie to the barre [of the Commons], a bill was read in English which he had made, conteining certeine euill practises of king Richard"; . . . The following clause formed part of Bagot's revelations:

[*Hol.* iii. 511/2/59.] It was further conteined in that bill, that as the same Bagot rode on a daie behind the duke of Norfolke in the Sauoy street toward Westminster, the duke asked him what he knew of the manner of the duke of Glocester his death, and he answered that he knew nothing at all: "but the people" (quoth he) "doo saie that you haue murthered him." Wherevnto the duke sware great othes that it was vntrue, and that he had saued his life contrarie to the will of the king, and certeine other lords, by the space of three weeks, and more; affirming withall, that he was neuer in all his life time more affraid of death, than he was at his comming home againe from Calis at that time, to the kings presence, by reason he had not put the duke to death. "And "then" (said he) "the king appointed one of his owne seruants, "and certeine other that [*p.* 512] were seruants to other lords to "go with him to see the said duke of Glocester put to death;"

[A common fame that Norfolk had murdered Gloucester.]
[Norfolk swore that he had risked his own life to save Gloucester.]

[Richard appointed servants to put Gloucester to death in Norfolk's presence.]

---

[1] See pp. 110, 111 below.

swearing that, as he should answer afore God, it was neuer his
mind that he should haue died in that sort,[1] but onelie for feare
of the king and sauing of his owne life.

Act I. sc. ii.—Gaunt, on his way to Coventry (l. 56), has visited the
Duchess of Gloucester.
As they enter he says to her (ll. 1-3):

> Alas, the part I had in Woodstockes bloud
> Doth more sollicite me than your exclaimes,
> To stirre against the butchers of his life !

In February, 1397, Richard was alarmed and angered by a rough
censure from Gloucester because Brest had been surrendered to John
Duke of Brittany, on the repayment of the money for which the town
was a pledge.

[*Hol.* iii. 488/1/8.] Upon this multiplieng of woords in such
presumptuous maner by the duke against the king, there kindeled
such displeasure betwixt them, that it neuer coassed to increase
into flames, till the duke was brought to his end. . . .

[Afterwards Richard] determined to suppresse both the duke
and other of his complices, and tooke more diligent regard to the
saiengs & dooings of the duke than before he had doone. And as
it commeth to passe that those, which suspect anie euill, doo euer
deeme the worst ; so he tooke euerie thing in euill part, insomuch
that he complained of the duke vnto his brethren the dukes of
Lancaster and Yorke, in that he should stand against him in all
things and seeke his destruction, the death of his counsellors, and
ouerthrow of his realme.

The two dukes of Lancaster and Yorke, to deliuer the kings
mind of suspicion, made answer, that they were not ignorant, how
their brother of Glocester, as a man sometime rash in woords,
would speake oftentimes more than he could or would bring to
effect, and the same proceeded of a faithfull hart, which he bare
towards the king ; for that it grieued him to vnderstand, that
the confines of the English dominions should in anie wise be
diminished : therefore his grace ought not to regard his woords,
sith he should take no hurt thereby. These persuasions quieted
the king for a time, till he was informed of the practise which the

[Richard
complained
to
Gloucester's
brethren of
the duke's
malevo-
lence.]

*The dukes of
Lancaster &
Yorke excuse
the duke of
Glocester to
the king.*

---

[1] *that sort*] Hol. ed. 1. *the fort* Hol. ed. 2.

duke of Glocester had contriued (as the same went among diuerse persons) to imprison the king. For then the duke of Lancaster and Yorke, first reprouing the duke of Glocester for his too liberall talking, . . . and, perceuing that he set nothing by their woords, were in doubt least, if they should remaine in the court still, he would, vpon a presumptuous mind, in trust to be borne out by them, attempt some outragious enterprise. Wherefore they thought best to depart for a time into their countries, that by their absence he might the sooner learne to staie himselfe for doubt of further displeasure. But it came to passe, that their departing from the court was the casting awaie of the duke of Glocester. For after that they were gone, there ceassed not such as bare him euill will, to procure the K. to dispatch him out of the way.

[Gaunt and York reproued Glocester for his rashnes.]

[Fearing that he would be emboldened by their presence, they left the Court.]

[Their departure caused Glocester's ruin.]

The Duchess of Gloucester's reproaches (I. ii. 9-34) have more weight if, as would seem from the following excerpt, Gaunt and York were at first disposed to avenge their brother's death.

[*Hol.* iii. 489/2/68.] The parlement was summoned to begin at Westminster the 17 of September,[1] and writs therevpon directed to euerie of the lords to appeare, and to bring with them a sufficient number of armed men and archers in their best arraie; for it was not knowen how the dukes of Lancaster and Yorke would take the death of their brother, . . . Suerlie the two dukes when they heard that their brother was so suddenlie made awaie, they wist not what to saie to the matter, and began both to be sorowfull for his death, and doubtfull of their owne states: for with they saw how the king (abused by the counsell of euill men) absteined not from such an heinous act, they thought he would afterwards attempt greater misorders from time to time. There-fore they assembled in all hast great numbers of their seruants, freends, and tenants, and, comming to London, were receiued into the citie. For the Londoners were right sorie for the death of the duke of Glocester, who had euer sought their fauour; in so mnch that now they would haue beene contented to haue ioined with the dukes in seeking reuenge of so noble a mans death, . . .

The lords appointed to come in war-like manner to the parle-mnt [at West-minster].

[A doubt as to how Gaunt and York would take their brother's death.] Polydor.

[They grieved for his death, and feared for them-selves.]

The dukes of Lancaster & Yorke assemble their power to resist the kings dealings.

[Glocester beloved by the Londoners.]

---

[1] This Parliament was adjourned on September 29, 1397, and reassembled at Shrewsbury on January 27, 1398.—*Eves.*, 141, 142 ; *Usk*, 17 ; 123.

[The dukes took counsell as to whether they should be avenged of Richard, or of Mowbray and others, but at last they resolved to forgive their brother's death.]
Here the dukes and other fell in counsell, and manie things were proponed. Some would that they should by force reuenge the duke of Glocesters death ; other thought it meet that the earles Marshall and Huntington, and certeine others, as cheefe authours of all the mischeefe, should be pursued and punished for their demerites ; hauing trained vp the king in vice and euill customes, euen from his youth. But the dukes (after their displeasure was somewhat asswaged) determined to couer the stings of their griefes for a time, and, if the king would amend his maners, to forget also the iniuries past.

Act I. sc. iii.—My next excerpt supplied the material for this scene.

Anno Reg. 22.
[At the time appointed, Richard and the dukes came to Coventry, where lists had been erected.]
[Boling-broke took leave of Richard on the Sunday before the combat, and on the morrow (the day ap-pointed for battle) Mowbray also bade the King farewell.]
[Arming of the ap-pellant and defendant.]
[*Hol.* iii. 494/2/41.] At[1] the time appointed the king came to Couentrie, where the two dukes were readie, according to the order prescribed therein ; comming thither in great arraie, accom-panied with the lords and gentlemen of their linages. The king caused a sumptuous scaffold or theater, and roiall listes there to be erected and prepared. The sundaie before they should fight, after dinner, the duke of Hereford came to the king (being lodged about a quarter of a mile without the towne in a tower that belonged to sir William Bagot) to take his leaue of him. The morow after, being the day appointed for the combat, about the spring of the daie, came the duke of Norfolke to the court to take leaue likewise of the king. The duke of Hereford armed him in his tent, that was set vp neere to the lists ; and the duke of Norfolke put on his armor, betwixt the gate & the barrier of the towne, in a beautifull house, hauing a faire perclois of wood towards the gate, that none might see what was doone within the house.

The order of the combat.
[Aumerle and Surrey first entered the lists.]
The duke of Aumarle that daie, being high constable of England, and the duke of Surrie, marshall, placed themselues betwixt them, well armed and appointed ; and, when they saw their time, they first entered into the listes with a great companie of men apparelled in silke sendall, imbrodered with siluer, both richlie and

_____

[1] The original authority for this excerpt is *Trais.*, 17-23 ; 149-158. *Halle* (3-5) added several details to this account (e. g. the apparel of the Dukes), which *Hyl.* copied.

curiouslie, euerie man hauing a tipped staffe to keepe the field in order. About the houre of prime, came to the barriers of the listes the duke of Hereford, mounted on a white courser, barded with greene & blew veluet imbrodered sumptuouslie with swans and antelops of goldsmiths woorke; armed at all points. The constable and marshall came to the barriers, demanding of him what he was. He answered: "I am Henrie of Lancaster, duke of "Hereford, which am come hither to doo mine indeuor against "Thomas Mowbraie, duke of Norfolke, as a traitor vntrue to God, "the king, his realme, and me." Then incontinentlie he sware vpon the holie euangelists, that his quarrell was true and iust, and vpon that point he required to enter the lists. Then he put vp his sword, which before he held naked in his hand, and, putting downe his visor, made a crosse on his horsse; and, with speare in hand, entered into the lists, and descended from his horsse, and set him downe in a chaire of greene veluet, at the one end of the lists, and there reposed himselfe, abiding the comming of his aduersarie.

Soone after him, entred into the field with great triumph king Richard, accompanied with all the peeres of the realme, . . . The king had there aboue ten thousand men in armour, least some fraie or tumult might rise amongst his nobles, by quarelling or partaking. When the king was set in his seat, (which was richlie hanged and adorned,) a king at armes made open proclamation, prohibiting all men in the name of the king, and of the high constable and marshall, to enterprise or attempt to approch or touch any part of the lists vpon paine of death, except such as were appointed to order or marshall the field. The proclamation ended, an other herald cried: "Behold here Henrie of Lancaster, duke of Hereford, "appellant, which is entred into the lists roiall to doo his deuoir "against Thomas Mowbraie, duke of Norfolke, defendant; vpon "paine to be found false and recreant!"

The duke of Norfolke houered on horssebacke at the entrie of the lists, his horsse being barded with crimosen veluet, imbrodered richlie with lions of siluer and mulberie trees; and, when he had made his oth before the constable and marshall that his quarrell was iust and true, he entred the field manfullie, saieng alowd:

[About prime (6—9 a.m.) Bolingbroke rode to the barriers, and Aumerle and Surrey demanded what he was.]

[Bolingbroke's answer.]

[Having taken an oath that his quarrell was iust, he entered the lists, and dismounting, seated himself on a chair, awaiting his advorsary.]

[Then Richard entered the field, accompanied by the peers of the realm.

[Ten thousand armed men to keep the peace.]

[All (except those who were appointed to marshal the field) were forbidden to approach or touch the lists.]

[Bolingbroke's challenge.]

[When Mowbray had been sworne, he entered the lists, crying, "God aid him that hath the right!" and then dismounting, seated himselfe in a chaire.]

[Afterwards their spears were delivered to the combatants, and they were commanded to mount their horses.]

[Bolingbroke set forward six or seven paces, but Mowbray lingered.]

The combat staied by the king.

"God aid him that hath the right!" and then he departed from his horsse, & sate him downe in his chaire, which was of crimosen veluet, courtined about with white and red damaske. The lord marshall viewed their speares, to see that they were of equall length, and deliuered the one speare himselfe to the duke of Hereford, and sent the other vnto the duke of Norfolke by a knight. Then the herald proclamed that the trauerses & chaires of the champions should be remooued; commanding them on the kings behalfe to mount on horssebacke, & addresse themselues to the battell and combat.

The duke of Hereford was quicklie horssed, and closed his bauier, and cast his speare into the rest, and when the trumpet sounded set forward couragiouslie towards his enimie six or seuen pases. The duke of Norfolke was not fullie set forward,[1] when the king cast downe his warder, and the heralds cried, "Ho, ho!" Then the king caused their speares to be taken from them, and commanded them to repaire againe to their chaires, where they remained two long houres, while the king and his councell deliberatlie consulted what order was best to be had in so weightie a cause. Finallie, after they had deuised, and fullie determined what should be doone therein, the heralds cried silence; and sir Iohn Bushie, the kings secretarie, read the sentence and determina-

The king his doome betwixt the two dukes.

Bolingbroke was exiled for ten yeares, and Mowbray for life.]

[Richard was to levy money from Mowbray's lands, to pay the wages of the garrison of Calais.]

tion of the king and his councell, in a long roll, the effect wherof was, that Henrie duke of Hereford should within fifteene daies depart out of the realme, and not to returne before the terme of ten yeares were expired, except by the king he should be repealed againe, and this vpon paine of death; and that Thomas Mowbraie, duke of Norfolke, bicause he had sowen sedition in the relme by his words, should likewise auoid the realme, and neuer to returne againe into England, nor approch the borders or confines thereof vpon paine of death; and that the king would staie the profits of his lands, till he had leuied thereof such summes of monie as the duke had taken vp of the kings treasuror for the wages of the garrison of Calis, which were still vnpaid.

---

[1] "le duc de Noruolt ne se bouga ne ne fist semblant de soy deffendre."—
Trais., 21.

When these iudgements were once read, the king called before him both the parties, and made them to sweare that the one should neuer come in place where the other was, willinglie; nor keepe any company to gither in any forren region; which oth they both receiued humblie, and so went their waies. The duke of Norfolke departed sorowfullie out of the relme into Almanie, and at the last came to Venice, where he for thought and melancholie deceassed: for he was in hope (as writers record) that he should haue beene borne out in the matter by the king, which when it fell out otherwise, it greeued him not a little. The duke of Hereford tooke his leane of the king at Eltham, who there released foure yeares of his banishment: so he tooke his iornie ouer into Calis, and from thence went into France, where he remained.

[Boling-broke and Mowbray were sworn not willingly to meet in any forreign countrey.]

[Mowbray went to Germany, and at last to Venice, where he died. He had hoped that Richard would have favoured him.]

[Boling-broke's exile was reduced to six years. He went to France.]

Act I. sc. iv.—Richard enters with Bagot, Greene, and Aumerle. Bolingbroke's " courtship to the common people " (I. iv. 24, &c.), which Richard has noticed, is not mentioned in the Chronicles, but the following paragraph shows that the Duke left many friends behind him.

[*Hol.* iii. 495/2/25.] A woonder it was to see what number of people ran after him in euerie towne and street where he came, before he tooke the sea ; lamenting and bewailing his departure, as who would saie, that when he departed, the onelie shield, defense, and comfort of the commonwealth was vaded and gone.

The duke of Hereford beloued of the people.

Dismissing all thought of Bolingbroke, Greene advises Richard to take prompt measures for the subjugation of "the rebels which stand out in Ireland" (I. iv. 37-41). Holinshed says :

[*Hol.* iii. 496/2/70.] In this meane time [1] the king being aduertised that the wild Irish dailie wasted and destroied the townes and villages within the English pale, and had slaine manie of the souldiers which laie there in garison for defense of that [*p.* 497] countrie, determined to make eftsoones a voiage thither, & prepared all things necessarie for his passage now against the spring.

Polydor.
[Revolt of the wild Irish.]
[Richard resolved on an expedition to Ireland in the Spring.]

---

[1] Roger fourth Earl of March was slain by the Irish on July 20, 1398.— *Ush*, 19 ; 196. " Cujus morte cognita, Rex statuit vindicare personaliter mortem ejus, Hibernienseeque domare."—*Wals.* ii. 229. Roger was Richard's Lieutenant in Ulster, Connaught, and Meath.— *Calend. R R. P P.*, 19 Ric. II., 230/2/7.

Holinshed mentions the farming of England by Richard (I. iv. 45 ; and cp. II. i. 57-64, 109-113, 256) :

The realme let to farme by the king.

[*Hol.* iii. 496/1/64.] The common brute ran, that the king had set to farme the realme of England vnto sir William Scroope, earle of Wiltshire, and then treasuror of England, to sir Iohn Bushie, sir Iohn Bagot, and sir Henrie Greene, knights.[1]

Of "blanke charters" (I. iv. 48-51) as sources of revenue, we have the following account. In 1398 a reconciliation was effected between Richard and the Londoners,[2] with whom he had been deeply offended.

Blanke charters.

[*Hol.* iii. 496/1/11.] But yet to content the kings mind, manie blanke charters were deuised, and brought into the oitie, which manie of the substantiall and wealthie citizens were faine to seale, to their great charge, as in the end appeared. And the like charters were sent abroad into all shires within the realme, whereby great grudge and murmuring arose among the people : for, when they were so sealed, the kings officers wrote in the same what liked them, as well for charging the parties with paiment of monie, as otherwise.

In April, 1399,[3] large fines were exacted from the inhabitants of seventeen counties, who had aided the Duke of Gloucester in the *coup d'état* of 1387, and a new oath of allegiance was required.

[Blank charters.]

[*Hol.* iii. 496/2/30.] Moreouer, they were compelled to put their hands and seales to certeine blankes,[4] wherof ye haue heard before ; in the which, when it pleased him, he might write what he thought good.

Holinshed does not name the object to which the money thus raised was applied. Shakspere inferred (I. iv. 43-52) that the cost of the Irish war obliged Richard to farm the revenues and issue blank charters. That Richard was accused of extorting money for such a

---

[1] *Fab.* (545), *Hol.'s* authority, says that this rumour was current in the 22nd year of Richard's reign (June 21, 1398—June 20, 1399).
[2] According to *Fab.* (545) this reconciliation was effected after the adjournment of Parliament on September 29, 1397. Richard's ire was moved by the Londoners' opposition to " certeyne actys " of that Parliament.
[3] " cito post Pascha " (March 30).—*Ott.*, 199. Cp. *Wals.*, ii. 230, 231.
[4] It appears from *Ott.*, 200, and *Wals.*, 231, that these blank charters (*albas chartas*) were contemporaneous with the fines imposed upon the counties. But according to *Eves.* (146, 147) these fines and blank charters were in operation about Michaelmas, 1398.

purpose[1] appears from one of the articles exhibited against him in the Parliament by which he was deposed.

[*Hol.* iii. 502/2/56.] 19 Item, the spiritualitie alledged against him, that he, at his going into Ireland, exacted manie notable summes of monie, beside plate and iewels, without law or custome, contrarie to his oth taken at his coronation. *[The clergy forced to. pay for Richard's 'going into Ireland.']*

Act II. sc. i.—While Richard devised means to pay for his Irish expedition he was entreated to visit John of Gaunt, who lay at Ely House, "grieuous sicke" (I. iv. 54-58). Gaunt's death is thus briefly recorded by Holinshed.

[*Hol.* iii. 496/1/22.] In this meane time [Feb. 3, 1399],[2] the duke of Lancaster departed out of this life at the bishop of Elies place in Holborne. *The death of the duke of Lancaster.*

The particulars of Gaunt's death (II. i. 1-138) were imagined by Shakspere, but for the rest of this scene he found some material in Holinshed. The ensuing excerpt illustrates ll. 160-162; 201-208.

[*Hol.* iii. 496/1/26.] The death of this duke gaue occasion of increasing more hatred in the people of this realme toward the king, for he seized into his hands all the goods that belonged to him, and also receiued all the rents and reuenues of his lands which ought to haue descended vnto the duke of Hereford by lawfull inheritance; in reuoking his letters patents, which he had granted to him before, by vertue wherof he might make his attorneis generall to sue liuerie for him, of any maner of inheritances or possessions that might from thenceforth fall vnto him;[3] and that his homage might be respited, with making reasonable fine: whereby it was euident, that the king meant his vtter vndooing. *[The people's hatred of Richard is increased because he confiscated the rents and goods which had belonged to Gaunt, and refused to allow Bollingbroke to sue livery by attorney as Gaunt's heir.] Tho. Walsi.*

Shakspere had Holinshed's authority for York's resentment of such injustice, and consequent departure from Court (II. i. 163-214).

[*Hol.* iii. 496/1/40.] This hard dealing was much misliked of all the nobilitie, and cried out against of the meaner sort; but

---

[1] *Ott.* (197) says that during Lent, 1399, Richard exacted money, &c., for the Irish expedition.
[2] "in crastino Purificationis beatæ Mariæ" (Feb. 3).—*Ott.*, 198. "in crastino Sancti Blasii" (Feb. 4).—*Usk*, 23; 132.
[3] See p. 102 below.

namelie the duke of Yorke was therewith sore mooued ; who, before
this time, had borne things with so patient a mind as he could,
though the same touched him verie neere, as the death of his
brother the duke of Glocester, the banishment of his nephue the
said duke of Hereford, and other mo iniuries in great number ;
which, for the slipperie youth of the king, he passed ouer for the
time, and did forget aswell as he might. But now perceiuing that
neither law, iustice, nor equitie could take place, where the kings
wilfull will was bent vpon any wrongfull purpose, . . . he thought
it the part of a wise man to get him in time to a resting place, . . .

Herevpon he with the duke of Aumarle his sonne went to his
house at Langlie.

One of the wrongs which York had borne patiently was (II. i. 167,
168)
> . . . the preuention of poore Bullingbrooke
> About his mariadge, . . .

What York refers to is thus narrated by Holinshed :

[*Hol.* iii. 495/2/31.] At his [Bolingbroke's]- comming into
France, king Charles [VI.], hearing the cause of his banishment
(which he esteemed to be verie light), receiued him gentlie, and
him honorablie interteined, in so much that he had by fauour
obteined in mariage the onelie daughter of the duke of Berrie,
vncle to the French king, if king Richard had not beene a let in
that matter ; who, being thereof certified, sent the earle of Salisburie[1]
with all speed into France ; both to surmize, by vntrue suggestion,
heinous offences against him, and also to require the French king
that in no wise he would suffer his cousine to be matched in
mariage with him that was so manifest an offendor.

As Richard leaues the stage he announces his intention of sailing
for Ireland ' to morrow next ' ; and appoints York " Lord gouernour
of England " (II. i. 217-220). The " iusts " performed at Windsor
" a little before " Richard's embarkation (*Hol.* iii. 497/1/3) may be
alluded to in II. i. 223 :

---

[1] The date of Salisbury's mission was, perhaps, March, 1399. Soon after
(" assez tôt après ") his return to England, a royal proclamation directed that
a tournament should be held at Windsor. After this tournament Richard
made preparations for going (" ordonna aller ") to Ireland. He left the Queen
at Windsor, and went thence to Bristol (*Frois.*, xiv. 163, 164).

[*Hol.* iii. 497/1/8.] When these iusts were finished, the king The king saileth ouer into Ireland with a great armie. departed toward Bristow, from thence to passe into Ireland; leauing the queene with hir traine still at Windesor: he appointed for his lieutenant generall in his absence his vncle the duke of Fabian. Caxton. Yorke: and so in the moneth of Aprill,[1] as diuerse authors write, The duke of Yorke lieutenant generall of England, the king being in Ireland. he set forward from Windesor, and finallie tooke shipping at Milford, and from thence, with two hundred ships, and a puissant power of men of armes and archers, he sailed into Ireland.

Three passages in Holinshed may have suggested to Shakspere the conversation of Northumberland, Ross, and Willoughby (ll. 241-248), who remain on the stage after Richard's exit. Northumberland seems to glance at (ll. 241-245) an act of the subservient Parliament of 1397; which Holinshed thus records:

[*Hol.* iii. 493/1/40.] Finallie, a generall pardon was granted for all offenses to all the kings subiects (fiftie onelie excepted) [Fifty unnamed nobles excepted from pardon.] whose names he would not by anie meanes expresse, but reserued them to his owne knowledge, that when anie of the nobilitie offended him, he might at his plesure name him to be one of the number excepted, and so keepe them still within his danger. . . .

Manie other things were doone in this parlement, to the displeasure of no small number of people; namelie, for that diuerse rightfull heires were disherited of their lands and liuings, by Rightfull heires disherited. authoritie of the same parlement: with which wrongfull dooings the people were much offended; so that the king, and those that were about him, and cheefe in councell, came into great infamie and slander.

Large grants had been obtained from his Parliaments by Richard II.; and the oppressive poll-tax—to which we may suppose Ross refers —caused the commons' rebellion in 1381. Of that impost Holinshed says:

[*Hol.* iii. 428/2/36.] There was a new and strange subsidie or A greuous subsidie. taske granted to be leuied for the kings vse, and towards the charges of this armie that went ouer into France with the earle of Buckingham; to wit, of euerie preest secular or regular, six

---

[1] "post Pentecosten proximo sequens" [read *sequentem* or understand *festum*].—*Eves.*, 148. "circa festum Pentecostes."—*Ott.*, 200. *Wals.*, 231. In 1399 Whit Sunday fell on May 18. *Fab.* (545)—quoted by *Hol.* in the marginal note—gives "y⁰ moneth of Aprell" as the date.

shillings eight pence, and as much of euerie nunne, and of euerie
man & woman married or not married, being 16 yeares of age,
(beggers certenlie knowne onlie excepted,) foure pence for euerie
one. Great grudging & manie a bitter cursse followed about the
leuieng of this monie, & much mischeefe rose thereof, as after it
appeared.

In illustration of ll. 247, 248, I quote the passage noticed above
(p. 90) concerning the fines levied from seventeen shires.

    [*Hol.* iii. 496/2/9.] Moreouer, this yeare [1399] he caused
seuenteene shires of the realme, by waie of putting them to their
fines, to paie no small summes of monie, for redeeming their
offenses, that they had aided the duke of Glocester, the earles of
Arundell, and Warwike, when they rose in armor against him.
The nobles, gentlemen, and commons of those shires were inforced
also to receiue a new oth to assure the king of their fidelitie in
time to come; and withall certeine prelats and other honorable
personages were sent into the same shires to persuade men to this
paiment, and to see things ordered at the pleasure of the prince:
and suerlie the fines which the nobles, and other the meaner
estates of those shires were constreined to paie, were not small,
but exceeding great, to the offense of manie.

After "blanckes," Willoughby mentions "beneuolences" as one of
the "new exactions" devised by Richard (II. i. 250). A "benevo-
lence" was—in name, at least—the conception of a later king.[1] In
1473 Edward IV. was meditating an expedition to France:

    [*Hol.* iii. 694/1/43.] But bicause he wanted monie, and could
not well charge his commons with a new subsidie, for that he had
receiued the last yeare great summes of monie granted to him by
parlement, he deuised this shift,—to call afore him a great number
of the wealthiest sort of people in his realme; and to them declaring his need, and the requisite causes thereof, he demanded of
euerie of them some portion of monie, which they sticked not to

---

[1] Of those inhabitants of seventeen counties who paid fines to Richard in
1399, *Wals.* says (ii. 230, 231): "coacti sunt Regi concedere . . . importabiles
summas pecuniæ, pro *benevolentia sua* recuperanda." *Ott.* says (199): "Vocab-
antur itaque tales summæ, sic levatæ de singulis comitatibus, *le pleasaunce.*"
Cp. *Hol.'s* sidenote, "The paiment," &c.

giue. And therefore the king, willing to shew that this their
liberalitie was verie acceptable to him, he called this grant of
monie, "A beneuolence": notwithstanding that manie with grudge
gaue great sums toward that new found aid, which of them might
be called, "A maleuolence." [, which Edward IV. called a 'benevo-lence.']

When Willoughby demands what has become of the money thus
exacted by Richard, Northumberland answers (ll. 252-254):

> Wars hath not wasted it, for warrde he hath not,
> But basely yeelded vpon compromise
> That which his *noble* auncestors atchiued with blowes.

Shakspere may have been thinking of Richard's cession of Brest to
John Duke of Brittany (see p. 84 above); a step which was censured
by Gloucester, who bluntly said to the King:

[*Hol.* iii. 487/2/65.] Sir, your grace ought to put your bodie
in paine to win a strong hold or towne by feats of war, yer you
take vpon you to sell or deliuer anie towne or strong hold gotten
with great aduenture by the manhood and policie of your *noble*
progenitours. [You ought to win a stronghold ere you sell what your ancestors gained.]

Northumberland hints that deliverance is near, and, being urged
to speak out, says:

> I haue from le Port Blan
> A Bay in Brittaine receiude intelligence,
> That Harry duke of Herford, Rainold L. Cobham
> That late broke from the Duke of Exeter
> His brother,[1] archbishop late of Canterburie,
> Sir Thomas Erpingham, Sir John Ramston,
> Sir John Norbery, Sir Robert Waterton, and Francis Coines; 284
> All these well furnished by the Duke of Brittaine
> With eight tall shippes, three thousand men of warre,
> Are making hither with all due expedience,
> And shortly meane to touch our Northerne shore: 288
> Perhaps they had ere this, but that they stay
> The first departing of the King for Ireland.

During Richard's sojourn in Ireland,

[*Hol.* iii. 497/2/57.] . . . diuerse of the nobilitie, aswell prelats
as other, and likewise manie of the magistrats and rulers of the
cities, townes, and communaltie, here in England, perceiuing dailie
how the realme drew to vtter ruine, not like to be recouered to the

---

[1] "His brother," *i. e.* Richard Earl of Arundel's brother. Ritson suggested
that the missing line was taken almost literally from *Hol.*, 'and ran thus:
"The son and heir of the late earl of Arundel."—*Var. Sh.* xvi. 65.

The duke of
Lancaster
solicited to
expell king
Richard, and
to take vpon
him the
regiment.
former state of wealth whilest king Richard liued and reigned, (as
they tooke it,) deuised with great deliberation, and considerate
aduise, to send and signifie by letters vnto duke Henrie, whome
they now called (as he was in deed) duke of Lancaster and
Hereford, requiring him with all conuenient speed to conueie
himselfe into England; promising him all their aid, power, and
assistance, if he, expelling K. Richard, as a man not meet for the
office he bare, would take vpon him the scepter, rule, and diademe
of his natiue land and region.

He, therefore, being thus called vpon by messengers and letters
from his freends, and cheeflie through the earnest persuasion of
Thomas Arundell,[1] late archbishop of Canturburie, who . . . had
beene remooued from his see, and banished the realme by king

The duke of
Britaine a
great friend
to the duke
of Lancaster.
Richards means, got him downe to Britaine, togither with the said
archbishop; where he was ioifullie receiued of the duke and
duchesse, and found such freendship at the dukes hands, that
there were certeine ships rigged, and made readie for him, at a

The duke of
Lancaster &
his adherents
saile into
England
[, starting
from Le port
blanc].
place in base Britaine [2] called Le port blanc, as we find in the
chronicles of Britaine; and, when all his prouision was made
readie, he tooke the sea, togither with the said archbishop of
Canturburie, and his nephue Thomas Arundeli, sonne and heire to
the late earle of Arundell, . . . There were also with him,

Additions to
Polychron.
[, giving the
names of
other
adherents].
Reginald lord Cobham, sir Thomas Erpingham, and sir Thomas
Ramston, knights, Iohn Norburie, Robert Waterton, & Francis
Coint, esquires: few else were there, for (as some write) he had

[Various
accounts of
Buling-
broke's
forces.]
not past fifteene lances, as they tearmed them in those daies, that
is to saie, men of armes, furnished and appointed as the vse then

Thom. Wals.
Chron. Brit.
[records that
Bolingbroke
had 3000
men, and 8
ships.]
was. ¶ Yet other write, that the duke of Britaine deliuered vnto
him three thousand men of warre, to attend him, and that he had
eight ships well furnished for the warre, where Froissard yet

Froissard.
speaketh but of three. Moreouer, where Froissard and also the
chronicles of Britaine auouch, that he should land at Plimmouth,
by our English writers it seemeth otherwise: for it appeareth by

Tho.
Walsing.
their assured report, that he, approching to the shore, did not

---

[1] Thomas Arundel (or Fitz-Alan), was exiled on September 24, 1397.—
Eves., 139.
[2] La Basse Bretagne; lower, or western, Brittany.

streight take land, but lay houering aloofe, and shewed himselfe now in this place, and now in that, to see what countenance was made by the people, whether they meant enuioualie to resist him, or freendlie to receiue him.

In my excerpt from the play I retain the line-order and punctuation, as well as the text, of Q1. In none of the original texts of *Richard II.* is mention made of "Thomas Arundell, sonne and heire to the late earle of Arundell." But the following passage shows that Thomas Arundel must have been named in a preceding line as having "late broke from the Duke of Exeter."

[*Hol.* iii. 496/1/68.] About the same time, the earle of Arundels sonne, named Thomas, which was kept in the duke of Exeters house, escaped out of the realme, by meanes of one William Scot, mercer; and went to his vncle Thomas Arundell, late archbishop of Canturburie, as then soiourning at Cullen [1] [Cologne].

The reader will also note that Bolingbroke delayed his landing in order " to see what countenance was made by the people "; not because he awaited, as Northumberland conjectured (II. i. 290),

The first departing of the King for Ireland.

This deviation from his authority accords with Shakspere's annihilation of time in the present, and the preceding, scene. As one day only can be allowed for both scenes,—cp. the opening of the last scene of Act I., with its close, connecting it with the first scene of Act II.,—Bolingbroke could not have left England; yet, at the close of the present scene, we learn that he is returning from exile. Richard's absence from England, which lasted about two months, is ignored. For it is evident that, when this scene ends, Richard had not even embarked; and, moreover, in the next scene—between which and the present one we may admit an interval of a day or two—Greene hopes " the King is not yet shipt for Ireland " (II. ii. 42).[2]

Act II. sc. ii.—The Queen enters with Bushy and Bagot. They are joined by Greene (l. 40), and York (l. 72). When Northumberland had told his news, he, accompanied by Ross and Willoughby, set forth to meet Bolingbroke (II. i. 296-300). Greene announces their flight and Bolingbroke's landing at Ravenspur (ll. 49-55). Scene ii. is, in general, a dramatic version of the useless, though, doubtless, more formal, deliberations of the council to which York summoned Richard's favourites.

[*Hol.* iii. 498/1/36.] When the lord gouernor, Edmund duke of Yorke, was aduertised, that the duke of Lancaster kept still the

---

[1] From *Fab.* 545 (an. 22 Ric. II.).   [2] *T.A.*, 265.

H

[When York heard that Bolingbroke might land anywhere, he called a councell of war, to which the Earl of Wiltshire, Bushy, Bagot, and Greene were summoned.] sea, and was readie to arriue, (but where he ment first to set foot on land, there was not any that vnderstood the certeintie,) he sent for the lord chancellor, Edmund Stafford, bishop of Excester, and for the lord treasuror, William Scroope, earle of Wiltshire, and other of the kings priuie councell, as Iohn Bushie, William Bagot, Henrie Greene, and Iohn Russell, knights: of these he required to know what they thought good to be doone in this matter, concern-

[Their useless advice to collect an army at St. Albans.] ing the duke of Lancaster, being on the seas. Their aduise was, to depart from London vnto S. Albons, and there to gather an armie to resist the duke in his landing; but, to how small purpose their counsell serued, the conclusion thereof plainlie declared, for

The commõs denie to resist the duke of Lancaster. the most part that were called, when they came thither, boldlie protested, that they would not fight against the duke of Lancaster, whome they knew to be euill dealt withall. . . .

The duke of Lancaster, after that he had coasted alongst the shore a certeine time, & had got some intelligence how the peoples

The duke of Lancaster lãdeth [at Ravens-pur] in Yorkshire. Additions to Polychron. minds were affected towards him, landed about the beginning of Iulie [1] in Yorkshire, at a place sometime called Rauenspur, betwixt Hull and Bridlington; and with him not past threescore persons, as some write: but he was so ioifullie receiued of the lords, knights, and gentlemen of those parts, that he found means (by

[Among the first who came to him were Willoughby, Ros, and Beaumont.] their helpe) forthwith to assemble a great number of people, that were willing to take his part. The first that came to him were the lords of Lincolneshire, and other countries adioining; as the lords Willoughbie, Ros, Darcie, and Beaumont.

The defection, or resignation, of the Earl of Worcester, which Greene next announces (ll. 58-61), occurred soon after Richard's return to Wales, late in July, 1399.[2] Holinshed says:

[*Hol.* iii. 499/2/74.] Sir Thomas Persie, earle of Worcester,[3]

---

[1] On June 28, according to *Usk*, 24; 134. "circa festum [June 24] S. Johannis Baptistæ."—*Eves.*, 151. "circa festum [July 4] translationis sancti Martini."—*Ott*, 203.

[2] Richard landed in Wales on July 22, according to *Usk*, 27; 137. *Eves.'s* (149) date is July 25. In *Traïs.* (46; 194) the date assigned to Richard's landing is August 13.

[3] We learn from one chronicle (*Ott.*, 206, 207) that when Richard, soon after landing, withdrew to Flint,—in *Eulog.*, iii. 381, Conway is, with more probability, the place named,—he left his household in Worcester's care. Worcester, weeping most bitterly, broke his staff, and dismissed the royal

lord [*p.* 500] steward of the kings house, either being so com- *The earle of Worcester leaueth the K. and fleeth to the duke.* manded by the king, or else vpon displeasure (as some write) for that the king had proclaimed his brother the earle of Northumber- land, traitor, brake his white staffe, (which is the representing signe and token of his office,) and without delaie went to duke Henrie. When the kings seruants of [the] houshold saw this (for it was doone before them all) they dispersed themselues, some into one countrie, and some into an other.

A servingman enters, and says to York: "My Lord, your son was gone [to Ireland] before I came" (II. ii. 86). When Richard was at Dublin,[1]

[*Hol.* iii. 497/2/29.] the duke of Aumarle, with an hundred *The duke of Aumarle [arrived at Dublin, with reinforcements].* saile, arriued, of whose comming the king was right ioifull; and, although he had vsed no small negligence in that he came no sooner according to order before appointed, yet the king (as he was of a gentle nature) courteouslie accepted his excuse. Whether [His good faith doubted.] he was in fault or not, I haue not to saie; but verelie he was greatlie suspected, that he dealt not well in tarieng so long after his time assigned.

This servingman, whom York would send to Pleshey, to borrow money from the Duchess of Gloucester, answers: "An houre before I came the Dutchesse died" (II. ii. 97). Holinshed (514/2/3) records her death.[2]

"What, are there *no* Posts dispatcht for Ireland?" exclaims York (II. ii. 103). So Q1 (1597). Q2 (1598) reads "*two* Posts," and F1 has "What, are there postes dispatcht for Ireland?" The reading of Q2 is at variance with the following excerpt from Holinshed, which shows that but one opportunity occurred of sending news to Ireland of

<hr>

servants. *Wals.* (ii. 233) says that Worcester was authorized by Richard to release them from their duties till better times should come. *Frois.* (xiv. 167) has a story—to which, I suppose, *Hol.* refers—that Richard, before going to Ireland, published a sentence of banishment against Northumberland and Henry Percy, and thereby angered Worcester; who is not, however, said by *Frois.* to have done anything to revenge the injury. Cp. *Rich. II.*, II. iii. 26-30.

[1] I cannot reconcile the date when, according to Creton (*Archaeol.* xx. 27, 296), the campaign began,—which, after a few days, became a march to Dublin, —with the dates subsequently given by him. *Hol.* (497/2/ sidenote 2), on the authority of *Annales Hiberniae*, a MS. printed in Camden's *Britannia*, ed. 1607, p. 832, gives June 28 as the date of Richard's arrival at Dublin, and Creton says (*Ibid.* 45, 309) that Aumarle arrived on the same day; a date quite irreconcilable with Creton's subsequent scheme of time.

[2] The inscription on her tomb in Westminster Abbey shows that the Duchess died on October 3, 1399.

Bolingbroke's landing. As Busby soon afterwards (l. 123) remarks
that "the winde sits faire for newes to go to Ireland," the reading "*no*
Posts" conveys a rebuke for tardiness.

[*Hol.* iii. 499/1/14.] But here you shall note, that it fortuned
at the same time in which the duke of Hereford or Lancaster
(whether ye list to call him) arriued thus in England, the seas were
so troubled by tempests, and the winds blew so contrarie for anie
passage to come ouer foorth of England to the king, remaining
still in Ireland, that, for the space of six weeks, he receiued no
aduertisements from thence: yet at length, when the seas became
calme, and the wind once turned anie thing fauourable, there came
ouer a ship; whereby the king vnderstood the manner of the dukes
arriuall, and all his proceedings till that daie in which the ship
departed from the coast of England: wherevpon he meant foorthwith to haue returned ouer into England, to make resistance
against the duke; but through persuasion of the duke of Aumarle
(as was thought) he staied, till he might haue all his ships, and
other prouision, fullie readie for his passage.

Out of master Dew French books ((Creton's Deposition of Richard II.)).

[For six weeks no news came to Richard from England.]

[When at last he had tidings of Bolingbroke's invasion, he would have returned to England, but Aumerle persuaded him to wait.]

My next excerpt shows how, after attending the fruitless council
mentioned above (p. 98), Richard's evil counsellors took to flight.
(Cp. II. ii. 135—141.)

[*Hol.* iii. 498/1/56.] The lord treasuror, Bushie, Bagot, and
Greene, perceiuing that the commons would cleaue vnto, and take
part with, the duke, slipped awaie; leauing the lord gouernour of
the realme, and the lord chancellor, to make what shift they could
for themselues. Bagot got him to Chester, and so escaped into
Ireland; the other fled to the castell of Bristow,[1] in hope there to
be in safetie.

[Perceiving the commons' mind, Bagot escaped to Ireland, and Bushy and Greene took refuge in Bristol Castle.]

Act II. sc. iii.—The scene is laid near Berkeley Castle (ll. 51-53);
and, as the excerpt given below proves, can be dated Sunday, July 27,
1399, St. James's Day (July 25) having, in that year, fallen on a
Friday.[2]

[*Hol.* iii. 498/2/3.] At his [Bolingbroke's] comming vnto
Doncaster, the earle of Northumberland, and his sonne, sir Henrie

---

[1] The swift action of the play establishes the Lord Treasurer (Earl of
Wiltshire) in Bristol Castle before Richard's favourites separate. Cp. II. ii.
135, 136.
[2] The authority for this date is *Eves.*, 152.

Persie, wardens of the marches against Scotland, with the earle of
Westmerland, came vnto him; where he sware vnto those lords,
that he would demand no more, but the lands that were to him
descended by inheritance from his father,[1] and in right of his wife.
Moreouer, he vndertooke to cause the paiment of taxes and
tallages to be laid downe, & to bring the king to good gouernment,
& to remooue from him the Cheshire men, which were enuied of
manie; for that the king esteemed of them more than of anie
other; happilie, bicause they were more faithfull to him than
other, readie in all respects to obeie his commandements and
pleasure. From Doncaster, hauing now got a mightie armie about
him, he marched foorth with all speed through the countries,
comming by Euesham vnto Berkelie: within the space of three
daies, all the kings castels in those parts were surrendred vnto
him.

The duke of Yorke, whome king Richard had left as gouernour
of the realme in his absence, hearing that his nephue the duke of
Lancaster was thus arriued, and had gathered an armie, he also
assembled a puissant power of men of armes and archers; (as
before yee haue heard ;) but all was in vaine, for there was not a
man that willinglie would thrust out one arrow against the duke of
Lancaster, or his partakers, or in anie wise offend him or his
freends. The duke of Yorke, therefore, passing foorth towards
Wales to meet the king, at his comming foorth of Ireland, was
receiued into the castell of Berkelie, and there remained, till the
comming thither of the duke of Lancaster, [to] whom (when he
perceiued that he was not able to resist, on the sundaie, after the
feast of saint Iames, which, as that yeare came about, fell vpon the
fridaie) he came foorth into the church that stood without the

*The duke of
Lancaster
oth to the
lords that
aided him
[, that he
would claim
no more
than his
inheritance.
He also
promised
(1) to
reduce
taxation;
(2) to make
Richard
govern
justly;
(3) and to
disband the
Cheshire-
men.]*

*[He marched
from Don-
caster to
Berkeley.]*

*The harts of
the commons
wholie bent
to the duke of
Lancaster
[; and
York's
soldiers
would not
fight with
him.*

*[York at
Berkeley
Castle.]*

---

[1] Cp. Northumberland's words (II. iii. 148, 149):
     " The noble Duke hath sworne his comming is
       But for his owne ; " . . .
Cp. also what Hotspur (1 Hen. IV., IV. iii. 60-65), and Worcester (1 Hen. IV.,
V. i. 41-46), afterwards said about Bolingbroke's oath. The charge of having
transgressed this limitation, ratified by oath at Doncaster, is contained in the
first article of the Percies' " quarell " ; a document presented to Henry IV. on
the day before the battle of Shrewsbury.—Hard., 352. But it appears from
the excerpt quoted in the text that Shakspere wronged Bolingbroke, who
undertook national reformation also.

[Meeting of
Bolingbroke
and York.]
[Names of
those who
were with
York.]
[Names of
those who
were with
Boling-
broke.]

castell, and there communed with the duke of Lancaster. With
the duke of Yorke were the bishop of Norwich, the lord Berkelie,
the lord Seimour, and other; with the duke of Lancaster were
these: Thomas Arundell, archbishop of Canturburie, (that had
beene banished,) the abbat of Leicester, the earles of Northumberland and Westmerland, Thomas Arundell, sonne to Richard, late
earle of Arundell, the baron of Greistoke, the lords Willoughbie
and Ros, with diuerse other lords, knights, and other people, which

[Loue or fear
made people
flock to
Boling-
broke.]

dailie came to him from euerie part of the realme: those that
came not were spoiled of all they had, so as they were neuer able
to recouer themselues againe, for their goods, being then taken
awaie, were neuer restored. And thus, what for loue, and what
for feare of losse, they came flocking vnto him from euerie part.

Justifying his return from banishment, Bolingbroke says to York
(II. iii. 129, &c.) :

> I am denyed to sue my Liuery here,
> And yet my letters pattents giue me leaue: . . .   130
> And I challenge law : Atturnies are denied me ;
> And therefore personally I lay my claime
> To my inheritance of free descent.   136

This complaint formed the subject of an article exhibited against
Richard in the Parliament which deposed him.

[*Hol.* iii. 502/2/16.] 10 Item, before the dukes departure, he

[Boling-
broke denied
attornies to
plead his
causes.]

[Richard] vnder his broad seale licenced him [Bolingbroke] to
make atturnies to prosecute and defend his causes: the said king,
after his departure, would suffer none atturnie to appeare for him,
but did with his at his pleasure.[1]

Act II. sc. iv.—From what follows, Shakspere constructed the
dialogue between Salisbury and "a Welch captaine" (II. iv.), whose
countrymen, after waiting "ten dayes" (l. 1) in arms, have dispersed,
believing Richard to be dead. Richard, as we have seen (p. 100 above),
delayed his return from Ireland "till he might haue all his ships, and
other prouision, fullie readie for his passage."[2]

[*Hol.* iii. 499/1/32.] In the meane time, he sent the earle of

---

[1] See p. 91 above.
[2] Creton says (*Archaeol.*, xx. 55-58, 312, 313) that Aumerle treacherously
gaue Richard this advice ; and also suggested that Salisbury should oppose
Bolingbroke in the field, while the royal preparations for return were being
made.

Salisburie ouer into England, to gather a power togither, by helpe of the kings freends in Wales, and Cheshire, with all speed possible; that they might be readie to assist him against the duke, vpon his arriuall, for he meant himselfe to follow the earle, within six daies after. The earle, passing ouer into Wales, landed at Conwaie, and sent foorth letters to the kings freends, both in Wales and Cheshire, to leauie their people, & to come with all speed to assist the K., whose request, with great desire, & very willing minds, they fulfilled, hoping to haue found the king him- self at Conwaie; insomuch that, within foure daies space, there were to the number of fortie thousand[1] men assembled, readie to march with the king against his enimies, if he had beene there himselfe in person.

But, when they missed the king, there was a brute spred amongst them, that the king was suerlie dead; which wrought such an impression, and euill disposition, in the minds of the Welshmen and others, that, for anie persuasion which the earle of Salisburie might vse, they would not go foorth with him, till they saw the king: onelie they were contented to staie foureteene daies to see if he should come or not; but, when he came not within that tearme, they would no longer abide, but scaled & departed awaie; wheras if the king had come before their breaking vp, no doubt, but they would haue put the duke of Hereford in aduenture of a field: so that the kings lingering of time, before his comming ouer, gaue opportunitie to the duke to bring things to passe as he could haue wished, and tooke from the king all occasion to recouer afterwards anie forces sufficient to resist him.

The Welsh Captain makes partial mention (II. iv. 8) of a portent which may have happened not long before the time of this scene.

[*Hol.* iii. 496/2/66.] In this yeare in a manner throughout all the realme of England, old baie trees withered, and, afterwards,

marginal notes:
[Salisbury was sent to gather an army before Richard's arrival.]

[Forty thousand men assembled.]

[But when Richard came not, a rumour went amongst them that he was dead, so, after waiting for him fourteen days, they dispersed.]

Abr. Fl. out of Thom. Wals. pag. 396.

---

[1] Cp. Richard's words (III. ii. 76, 77) when he hears that the Welshmen have dispersed:

"But now the bloud of 20000. men
Did triumph in my face, and they are fled"; . . .

Salisbury had told him (l. 70) that the Welshmen numbered twelve thousand.

[Bay trees withered.] contrarie to all mens thinking, grew greene againe; a strange sight, and supposed to import some vnknowne euent.

Act III. sc. i.—July 29, 1399,[1] is the historic date on which the Third Act opens. "On the morow after" the day (July 27) when York met Bolingbroke at Berkeley,

The Duke of Lancaster marcheth to Bristow. [*Hol.* iii. 498/2/61.] the forsaid dukes, with their power, went towards Bristow, where (at their comming) they shewed themselues before the towne & castell; being an huge multitude of people. There were inclosed within the castell, the lord William Scroope, earle of Wiltshire and treasuror of England, sir Henrie Greene, and sir Iohn Bushie, knights, who prepared to make resistance; but, when it would not prenaile, they were taken and brought foorth bound as prisoners into the campe, before the duke of Lancaster. On the morow next insuing, they were arraigned before the constable and marshall, and found giltie of treason, for misgouerning the king and realme; and foorthwith had their heads smit off.

At the close of sc. i., Act III., Bolingbroke says :

> Come, Lords, away,
> To fight with Glendor and his *complices :*
> A while to worke, and, after, holiday !

Theobald suspected that the second line of this quotation had been interpolated, because (1) the first and third lines ryme; (2) the second line is, historically, quite out of place. It is true that the earliest recorded foray of Glendower must be dated about a year later than the time with which we are now concerned; but Shakspere was not bound by chronological fetters. Perhaps the following account of Glendower's attack on Lord Grey of Ruthin—in the summer of 1400—is the source of this line, for Holinshed, it will be obserued, applied the term "complices" to those who joined the raid.

The Welsh-men rebell by the setting on of Owen Glendour. [*Hol.* iii. 518/2/53.] In the kings [Henry IV.'s] absence, whilest he was foorth of the realme, in Scotland, against his enimies, the Welshmen tooke occasion to rebell vnder the conduct of their capteine Owen Glendouer; dooing what mischeefe they could

---

[1] According to *Eves.* (153),—whom *Hol.* followa,—Scrope, Bushy, and Greene were arraigned on July 29; and (*Rot. Parl.*, iii. 656/1) condemned to death on the same day. Cp. *Ott.*, 205. But *Usk* (24; 134) says that Bolingbroke did not reach Bristol till July 29. Adam of Usk was at Bristol when Bolingbroke was there in July, 1399 (25; 135).

deuise vnto their English neighbours. This Owen Glendouer *John Stow.*
was sonne to an esquier of Wales, named Griffith Vichan: *Owen Glendour, what he was.*
he dwelled in the parish of Conwaie, within the countie of
Merioneth in Northwales, in a place called Glindourwie, which
is as much to saie in English, as "The vallie by the side of
the water of Dee;" by occasion whereof he was surnamed
Glindour Dew.

He was first set to studie the lawes of the realme, and became [He was admitted to practise without the English bar; and served Richard at Flint Castle. Some say that he was Boling- broke's squire.]
an vtter barrester, or an apprentise of the law, (as they terme him,)
and serued king Richard at Flint castell, when he was taken by
Henrie duke of Lancaster; though other haue written that he
serued this king Henrie the fourth, before he came to atteine the
crowne, in roome of an esquier; and after, by reason of variance
that rose betwixt him and the lord Reginald Greie of Ruthin, *Tho. Walsi.*
about the lands which he [*p.* 519] claimed to be his by right of [Glen- dower's quarrel with Lord Grey of Ruthin.]
inheritance, when he saw that he might not prenaile, finding no
such fauor in his sute as he looked for, he first made warre
against the said lord Greie, wasting his lands and possessions with *The occasion that mooued him to rebell.*
fire and sword, cruellie killing his seruants and tenants. The king,
aduertised of such rebellious exploits,[1] enterprised by the said *The king entreth into Wales, meaning to chastise ye rebels.*
Owen, and his vnrulie *complices*, determined to chastise them, as
disturbers of his peace, and so with an armie entered into Wales;
but the Welshmen with their capteine withdrew into the mounteines
of Snowdon, so to escape the reuenge, which the king meant
towards them. The king therefore did much hurt in the countries
with fire and sword; sleing diuerse that with weapon in hand came
foorth to resist him, and so with a great bootie of beasts and
cattell he returned.[2]

---

[1] Full particulars of Glendower's rebellion reached Henry at Northampton,
about September 12-19, 1400. The campaign began soon or immediately after
September 26, and was over before October 19, 1400.—*Wylie* (i. 146-148),
citing public records.

[2] According to one story Glendower "serued king Richard at Flint castell,
when he was taken by Henrie Duke of Lancaster." I venture to suggest that
Shakspere—assuming from these words that Glendower was personally attached
to the King—turned the border strife with Lord Grey of Ruthin into warfare on
Richard's behalf. The lines which I quote above (III. i. 42-44) might have
introduced this lost or omitted portion of the play, but they are now, I
suspect, imperfect and disarranged: the ryming lines—which should end the
scene—being out of place, and two half lines, at least, having been lost.

Act III. sc. ii.—My next excerpt continues the history of Richard's fortunes, from the time when the Welshmen dispersed.

[*Hol.* iii. 499/1/66.]   At length, about ˙eighteene daies after that the king had sent from him the earle of Salisburie, he tooke the sea, togither with the dukes of Aumarle, Excester, Surrie, and diuerse others of the nobilitie, with the bishops of London, Lincolne, and Carleill. They landed neere the castell of Barclowlie [1]

K. Richard returneth out of Ireland, and landeth in Wales.

in Wales, about the feast of saint Iames the apostle, and staied a while in the same ˙castell, being aduertised of the great forces which the duke of Lancaster had got togither against him ;

Thom. Wals.

wherewith he was maruellouslie amazed, knowing certeinelie that those, which were thus in armes with the duke of Lancaster against him, would rather die than giue place, as well for the hatred as feare which they had conceiued at him. Neuerthe-

[After leaving Barclowlie, he went to Conway.]

lesse he, departing from Barclowlie, hasted with all speed towards Conwaie, where he vnderstoode the earle of Salisburie to be

Additions to Polychron.

still remaining.

He therefore taking with him such Cheshire men as he had with him at that present (in whom all his trust was reposed) he doubted not to reuenge himselfe of his aduersaries, & so at the

[News came of the loss of his castles, the revolt of nobles and commons, and the beheading of his counsellors at Bristol.]

first he passed with a good courage ; but when he vnderstood, as he went thus forward, that all the castels, euen from the borders of Scotland vnto Bristow, were deliuered vnto the duke of Lancaster ; and that likewise the nobles and commons, as well of the south parts, as the north, were fullie bent to take part with the same duke against him ; and further, hearing how his

K. Richard, in vtter despaire, [licenced his soldiers to return to their homes.]

trustie councellors had lost their heads at Bristow, he became so greatlie discomforted, that sorowfullie lamenting his miserable state, he vtterlie despaired of his owne safetie, and calling his armie togither, which was not small, licenced euerie man to depart to his home.

---

[1] "Castrum de Hertlowli in Wallia."—*Eves.*, 149. Williams (*Trais.* 188, note) supposed this place to be Harlech Castle, Merionethshire. According to *Usk* (27 ; 137), and the text of *Trais.* (41 ; 188), Richard landed at Pembroke. The Lebaud and Ambassade MSS. of *Trais.* (*Trais.* 41, note 6), Creton (*Archaeol.* xx. 75 ; 321), and *Ott.* (206) have Milford as Richard's landing-place.

The souldiers, being well bent to fight in his defense, besought him to be of good cheere, promising with an oth to stand with him against the duke, and all his partakers vnto death; but this could not incourage him at all, so that, in the night next insuing, he stole from his armie, and, with the dukes of Excester and Surrie, the bishop of Carleill, and sir Stephan Scroope, and about halfe a score others, be got him to the castell of Conwaie,[1] where he found the earle of Salisburie; determining there to hold himselfe, till he might see the world at some better staie; for what counsell to take to remedie the mischeefe thus pressing vpon him he wist not.

[Though they were readie to fight for him.] K. Richard stealeth awaie from his armie, and taketh the castell of Flint.

Act III. sc. iii.—The scene is laid before Flint Castle. After relating the cause of Richard's departure from Conway, and describing the ambush on the journey (see note 1), Holinshed proceeds:

[*Hol.* iii. 500/2/71.] King Richard being thus come vnto the castell of Flint, on the mondaie, the eighteenth of August, and the duke of Hereford being still aduertised from houre to houre by posts, [*p.* 501] how the earle of Northumberland sped, the morow following being tuesdaie, and the nineteenth of August,[2] he came thither, & mustered his armie before the kings presence; which vndoubtedlie made a passing faire shew, being verie well ordered by the lord Henrie Persie, that was appointed generall, or rather (as we maie call him) master of the campe, vnder the duke, of the whole armie. . . .

[Richard at Flint Castle (Aug. 18, 1399.)]

[Boling-broke mustered his army before the castle, on Aug. 19.]

---

[1] In a sidenote against this passage Richard is said to have withdrawn to "the castell of Flint," after deserting his army ; and at the close of sc. ii., Act III., he exclaims:

"Go to Flint Castle, there Ile pine away ; . . .
    That power I haue, discharge," . . .

We learn from Creton (*Archaeol.* xx. 129-149 ; 349-366), whom *Hol.* sub-sequently follows, that Northumberland decoyed Richard from Conway Castle to a part of the road between Conway and Flint, where an ambush was laid. On reaching this spot the King was obliged to proceed to Flint, which was in the possession of Northumberland's troops. *Trais.* (47-52 ; 196-201) has the same story, with less detail. These authorities place the meeting of Richard and Bolingbroke at Flint Castle. *Usk* (27 ; 138, 139), *Ott.* (207, 208), and *Wals.* (ii. 233, 234), agree that Richard left Conway and met Bolingbroke at Flint Castle. But, according to *Eves.*, Richard, forsaking his army, betook himself to Flint Castle (150), whence, after some negotiation, he departed to Conway Castle, where Bolingbroke met him (154, 155).

[2] This date is derived from *Eves.*, 155.

[Richard
watched
the coming
of the army.] The king . . . was walking aloft on the braies [1] of the wals, to behold the comming of the duke a farre off.

Shakspere altered the time, place, and purpose of Northumberland's mission. That mission had for its object the beguilement of Richard from Conway to Flint, where he would be in Bolingbroke's power. I begin the following excerpt—which contains the outline of III. iii. 31-126—at the time when Northumberland—entrusted with the difficult task of persuading Richard to leave Conway Castle—

[*Hol.* iii. 500/2/14.] came before the towne, and then sending an herald to the king, requested a safe conduct from the king, that he might come and talke with him; which the king granted, and so *The earle of Northumber-
lands mes-
sage to the
king: [if
Richard
would
engage to
summon a
Parliament,
and grant
Bolingbroke
a full
pardon,
Bolingbroke
would
become
Richard's
obedient
subject.]* the earle of Northumberland, passing the water, entred the castell, and comming to the king, declared to him, that, if it might please his grace to vndertake, that there should be a parlement assembled, in the which iustice might be had against such as were enimies to the common-wealth, and had procured the destruction of the duke of Glocester, and other noblemen, and herewith pardon the duke of Hereford of all things wherin he had offended him, the duke would be readie to come to him *on his knees,* [2] to craue of him forgiuenesse, and, as an humble subiect, to obeie him in all dutifull seruices.

The excerpt illustrating the rest of the scene is an account of what happened at Flint, on a later date. When Bolingbroke approached the castle, he

[*Hol.* iii. 501/1/62.] compassed it round about, euen downe to the sea, with his people ranged in good and seemelie order at the [Again
ascending to
the walls,
Richard saw
Boling-
broke's army
encircling
the castle, foot of the mounteins: and then the earle of Northumberland, passing foorth of the castell to the duke, talked with him a while in sight of the king, being againe got vp to the walles, to take better view of the armie, being now aduanced within two bowe

---

[1] Creton—*Hol.*'s authority for this passage—says that Richard "monta sur les murs dudit chastel [of Flint], qui sont grans & larges par dedens" (*Archæol.* xx. 370). Cp. the stage direction (l. 61): "The trumpets sound, *Richard appeareth on the walls.*"

[2] Cp. III. iii. 112, &c.:
    "His comming hither hath no further scope
    Then for his lineall roialties, and to beg
    Infranchisement immediate *on his knees.*"

Act III. sc. iv.—This scene—which is wholly of Shakspere's invention—has been laid by editors at King's Langley (Herts.), the seat of York, to whom Bolingbroke says (III. i. 36): "Vncle, you say the Queene is at your house." The gardener's words (III. iv. 68-70) show that the historic time is shortly before September 30, 1399, the day of Richard's deposition. Queen Isabelle was then, perhaps, at Wallingford Castle, Berks.[1]

Act IV. sc. i.—"Enter Bullingbrooke with the Lords to parliament," is the stage direction which heads the Fourth Act. A Parliament, summoned in Richard's name, met at Westminster on September 30, 1399, deposed the King, elected Bolingbroke as his successor, and dissolved on the same day. On October 13, Henry IV. was crowned, and, on the following day, a new Parliament, summoned in his name, assembled at Westminster.[2] If we regard Act IV., sc. i., ll. 1-90, from a historical point of view, the latter Parliament was sitting when Bolingbroke enters, and, calling for Sir William Bagot, thus addresses him :

> Now, Bagot, freely speake thy mind ;
> What thou doest know of noble Gloucesters death,
> Who wrought it with the King, and who performde   4
> The bloudy office of his timeles end.

We lost sight of Bagot on the eve of his flight to Ireland (II. ii. 141). Thence he had been brought fettered to London, and imprisoned.[3] On Thursday, October 16, 1399, the Commons "rehearsed all the errors of the last parlement holden in the one and twentith yeare of king Richard [1397-98], & namelie in certeine fiue of them." Of these "errors" the third was that "the duke of Glocester was murthered, and after foreiudged" (*Hol.* 511/2/14). On the same day Bagot was placed at the bar of the House, and a statement,[4] drawn up by him, was read, from which I quote two clauses illustrating IV. i. 10-19 ; adding thereto the sources of ll. 33-90.

[*Hol.* iii. 512/1/6.]   . . . there was no man in the realme to whom king Richard was so much beholden, as to the duke of

---

[1] On July 12, 1399, the Queen was at Wallingford Castle, Berks.—*Rymer,* viii. 83. On January 6, 1400, she was at Sonning, Berks.—*Ott.,* 225.

[2] *Eves.,* 156, 157, 160, 161. Parliament was summoned, in Henry's name, to meet on October 6, but no business was done on that day.—*Rot. Parl.,* iii. 415/1-2.

[3] *Usk,* 28 ; 140. *Fab.* (565) says that Bagot was a prisoner in the Tower at this time.

[4] The excerpts relating to Bagot's charges, and the subsequent appeals, are in MS. Bodl. 2376. f. ccvii. b. & seq., translated in *Archaeol.* xx. 275, &c. That part of the MS. which contained the charges themselves is missing, but the portion embracing my excerpt beginning with the words "On the saturdaie," is perfect. Comparison of what is left shows that *Hol.* followed this authority. *Fab.*'s account (565-567) of the Bagot incident, though varying in details, is substantially the same as *Hol.*'s.

Aumarle: for be was the man that, to fulfill his mind, had set him
in hand with all that was doone against the said duke, and the
other lords. . . . There was also conteined in the said bill, that
Bagot had heard the duke of Aumarle say, that he had rather than
twentie thousand pounds that the duke of Hereford were dead; not
for anie feare he had of him, but for the trouble and mischeefe
that he was like to procure within the realme.

The duke of
Aumarle
accused [of
being con-
cerned in
Gloucester's
death;]
[and of
saying that
he had
rather than
20,000
pounds that
Bolingbroke
were dead.]

After that the bill had beene read and heard, the duke of
Aumarle rose vp and said, that as touching the points conteined
in the bill concerning him, they were vtterlie false and vntrue;
which he would proue with his bodie, in what manner soeuer it
should be thought requisit. . . .

The duke of
Aumarle his
answer vnto
Bagots bill.

On the saturdaie next insuing [Oct. 18], sir William Bagot and
the said John Hall[1] were brought both to the barre, and Bagot was
examined of certeine points, and sent againe to prison. The lord
Fitzwater herewith rose vp, and said to the king, that where the
duke of Aumarle excuseth himselfe of the duke of Glocester's
death, "I say" (quoth he) "that he was the verie cause of his
"death"; and so he appealed him of treason, offering by throwing
downe his hood as a gage to proue it with his bodie. There were
twentie other lords also that threw downe their hoods, as pledges
to proue the like matter against the duke of Aumarle. The duke
of Aumarle threw downe his hood to trie it against the lord
Fitzwater, as against him that lied falselie, in that he had charged
him with, by that his appeale. These gages were deliuered to the
constable and marshall of England, and the parties put vnder
arrest.

The lord
Fitzwater
appealeth
the duke of
Aumarle of
treason [, in
conspiring
Gloucester's
death; and
throws down
a gage of
battle.]
[Twenty
other lords
did the
same.
Aumerle
answered
Fitz-
Walter's
challenge by
throwing
down a
gage.]

The duke of Surrie stood vp also against the lord Fitzwater,
auouching that where he had said that the appellants were causers
of the duke of Glocesters death, it was false, for they were constrained to sue the same appeale, in like manner as the said lord
Fitzwater was compelled to giue iudgement against the duke of
Glocester, and the earle of Arundell; so that the suing of the
appeale was doone by constraint, and if he said contrarie he lied:

[Surrey said
that Fitz-
Walter's
charge was
false; and
threw down
a gage.]

---

[1] A former valet of Thomas Mowbray, Duke of Norfolk. Hall was, by his
own confession, present at the murder of Gloucester.—*Rot. Parl.*, iii. 453/1.

and therewith he threw downe his hood. The lord Fitzwater answered herevnto, that he was not present in the parlement house, when iudgement was giuen against them, and all the lords bare witnesse thereof. Moreouer, where it was alledged that the duke of Aumarle should send two of his seruants to Calis, to murther the duke of Glocester, the said duke of Aumarle said, that if the duke of Norfolke affirme it, he lied falselie, and that he would proue with his bodie; throwing downe an other hood which he had borowed. The same was likewise deliuered to the constable and marshall of England,[1] and the king licenced the duke of Norfolke to returne, that he might arraigne his appeale.

[Aumerle threw down a borrowed gage of battle against Norfolk, who accused him of sending two servants to murder Glocester.]
[Norfolk was licensed to return, that he might arraign his appeale.]

In agreement with the last sentence of these excerpts, Shakspere makes Bolingbroke promise that Norfolk shall be recalled from exile, to answer Aumerle's challenge. Carlisle says that Norfolk is dead (IV. i. 86-102). Norfolk's death is thus noticed by Holinshed:[2]

The death of the duke of Norffolke.

[Hol. iii. 514/1/73.] This yeare [1399] Thomas Mowbraie, duke of Norffolke, died in exile at Venice; whose death might haue beene worthilie bewailed of all the realme, if he had not beene consenting to the death of the duke of Glocester.

Holinshed does not tell us that Norfolk joined crusades

Against black Pagans, Turkes, and Saracens;

but Shakspere may have transferred to Bolingbroke's foe the honour, which Bolingbroke had himself acquired through warfare with "miscreants." In 1390 a small corps of Englishmen formed part of an army—commanded by Lewis Duke of Bourbon, uncle of Charles VI.—which besieged Africa, a fortress seventy miles distant from Tunis.

[Polydore Vergil said that Bolingbroke commanded the Englishmen at the siege of Africa.]

[Hol. iii. 473/1/69.] Where, by Polydor Virgil it may seeme, that the lord Henrie of Lancaster, earle of Derbie,[3] should be capteine of the English men, that (as before ye haue heard) went into Barbarie with the Frenchmen, and Genowais. It should

---

[1] Northumberland was Constable.—Dugdale, i. 278/1. The Marshal was Ralph Neville, Earl of Westmoreland.—Dugdale, i. 298/1.
[2] Norfolk died on September 22, 1399.—Inq. p. m. 1 H. IV—71 (O. B.).
[3] Polyd. Verg. has the support of St. Denys (i. 652),—written by a contemporary of Bolingbroke,—which records that a small band of Englishmen went to the siege of Africa "cum comite Delby (sic) anglico, filio ducis Lencastrie." Frois. (xii. 255)—whom Hol. had previously cited—does not mention Bolingbroke's presence, but says that "messire Jean, dit Beaufort, fils bâtard au duc de Lancastre" was at the siege of Africa in 1390.

otherwise appeare by other writers, who affirme that the said earle made a iournie in deed the same time against the miscreants'; not into Barbarie, but into Prutzenland, where he shewed good proofe of his noble and valiant courage :

*Thom. Wals.
The earle of Derbie his exploits in his iournie against the infidels of Pruteen-land.*

The appeals of battle having been adjourned (ll. 104-106), York enters with the news that Richard has abdicated. On August 31 (?), 1399, the day after his arrival in London, Richard was conveyed to the Tower,[1] where

[*Hol.* iii. 503/1/47.] diuerse of the kings seruants, which by licence had accesse to his person, comforted him (being with sorrow almost consumed, and in manner balfe dead) in the best wise they could, exhorting him to regard his health, and saue his life.

And first, they aduised him willinglie to suffer himselfe to be deposed, and to resigne his right of his owne accord, so that the duke of Lancaster might without murther or battell obteine the scepter and diademe, after which (they well perceiued) he gaped : by meane whereof they thought he might be in perfect assurance of his life long to continue. Whether this their persuasion proceeded by the suborning of the duke of Lancaster and his fauourers, or of a sincere affection which they bare to the king, as supposing it most sure in such an extremitie, it is vncerteine ; but yet the effect followed not, howsoeuer their meaning was : notwithstanding, the king, being now in the hands of his enimies, and vtterlie despairing of all comfort, was easilie persuaded to renounce his crowne and princelie preheminence, so that, in hope of life onelie, he agreed to all things that were of him demanded. And so (as it should seeme by the copie of an instrument hereafter following) he renounced and voluntarilie was deposed from his roiall crowne and kinglie dignitie ; the mondaie being the nine and twentith daie of September, and feast of S. Michaell the archangell, in the yeare of our Lord 1399, and in the three and twentith yeare of his reigne.

The king is persuaded to resigne the crowne to the duke.

[Richard abdicated on St. Michael's Day, 1399.]

The news, that Richard has yielded his sceptre to Bolingbroke (ll. 107-110), should be compared with the testimony of witnesses present at the abdication, as to what followed the King's reading aloud of the instrument mentioned in the preceding excerpt.

---

[1] *Eves.*, 155, 156.

[*Hol.* iii. 504/2/39.] Now foorthwith, in our presences and others, he subscribed the same, and after deliuered it vnto the archbishop of Canturburie, saieng that if it were in his power, or at his assignement, he would that the duke of Lancaster there present should be his successour, and king after him . . .: desiring and requiring the archbishop of Yorke, & the bishop of Hereford, to shew and make report vnto the lords of the parlement of his voluntarie resignation, and also of his intent and good mind that he bare towards his cousin the duke of Lancaster, to haue him his successour and their king after him.[1]

[Richard wished to be succeeded by Bolingbroke.]

When York has announced Richard's abdication, Bolingbroke says (l. 112):

In Gods name Ile ascend *the regall throne.*

With reference to these words I quote the following passages, showing how, on September 30, after hearing the sentence of Richard's deposition read, Parliament elected Bolingbroke as his successor.

[*Hol.* iii. 505/2/28.] Immediatlie as the sentence was in this wise passed, and that by reason thereof the realme stood void without head or gouernour for the time, the duke of Lancaster, rising from the place where before he sate, and standing where all those in the house might behold him, in reuerend manner made a signe of the crosse on his forhead, and likewise on his brest, and, after silence by an officer commanded, said vnto the people, there being present, these words following.

[Bolingbroke stood up, and crossed himself.]

The duke of Lancaster laieth challenge
or claime to the crowne.

"In the name of the Father, and of the Sonne, & of the Holie-

---

[1] Richard and the commissioners appointed to receive his abdication met in the forenoon of September 29,—the abdication took place in the afternoon of the same day,—"where was rehearsed vnto the king by the mouth of the foresaid earle of Northumberland, that, before time at Conwaie [? Flint] in Northwales, the king being there at his pleasure and libertie, promised vnto the archbishop of Canterburie, then Thomas Arundell, and vnto the said earle of Northumberland, that he, for insufficiencie which he knew himselfe to be of to occupie so great a charge as to gouerne the realme of England, he would gladlie leaue of and renounce his right and title, as well of that as of his title to the crowne of France, and his maiestie roiall, vnto Henrie Duke of Hereford ; and that to doo in such conuenient wise, as by the learned men of this land it should most sufficientlie be deuised and ordeined."—*Hol.* 503/2/46 (*Rot. Parl.,* iii. 416/2).

"ghost. I Henrie of Lancaster claime the realme of England and
"the crowne, with all the appurtenances, as I that am descended by
"right line of the blood comming from that good lord king Henrie
"the third; and through the right that God of his grace hath sent
"me, with the helpe of my kin, and of my freends, to recouer the
"same, which' was in point to be vndoone for default of good
"gouernance and due iustice."

After these words thus by him vttered, he returned and sate
him downe in the place where before he had sitten. Then the
lords hauing heard and well perceiued this claime thus made by
this noble man, ech of them asked of other what they thought
therein. At length, after a little pausing or staie made, the archbishop of Canturburie, hauing notice of the minds of the lords,
stood vp & asked the commons if they would assent to the lords,
which in their minds thought the claime of the duke made, to be
rightfull and necessarie for the wealth of the realme and them all:
whereto the commons with one voice cried, "Yea, yea, yea!"
After which answer, the said archbishop, going to the duke, and
kneeling downe before him on his knee, addressed to him all his
purpose in few words. The which when he had ended, he rose, &,
taking the duke by the right hand, led him vnto the kings seate,
(the archbishop of Yorke assisting him,) and with great reuerence
set him therein, after that the duke had first vpon his knees made
his praier in deuout manner vnto almightie God.

[Each Lord asked another's opinion of the claim.]

The demand of the archbishop of Canterburie to the commons.

[The commons cried "Yea, yea, yea!"]

Thom. Wals. The duke of Hereford placed in the regall throne. [Cp. l. 112.]

Shakspere has antedated Carlisle's speech,[1] if we assume it to have
been delivered on or about "wednesdaie following" the day (Saturday,
October 18, 1399) on which Aumerle was appealed by Fitz-Walter.

My next excerpt comprises the part of Carlisle's speech paraphrased
by Shakspere (IV. i. 117-135).

[*Hol.* iii. 512/2/29.] On wednesdaie [Oct. 22, 1399] following,

---

[1] The authenticity of this speech is doubtful. According to the writer of
Trais.—the earliest known authority for it—the speech was delivered on
October 1 (70 ; 220) ; if we are to understand "lendemain" as having reference to September 30, the date immediately preceding. But, as Mr. Williams
pointed out (*Trais.*, 221, note), Carlisle's protest seems more apposite if we
suppose that it was made on October 23, when, in a secret committee, Northumberland asked the peers, "what should be done with Richard lately King,
saving his life, which King Henry wished by all means to be held sacred?"—
Rot. Parl., iii. 426/2. The excerpt, "On wednesdaie . . . was granted," is in
Bodl. MS. 2376 (*Archaeol.* xx. 279, 280).

John Stow.
The request
of the
commons.
request was made by the commons, that sith king Richard had
resigned, and was lawfullie deposed from his roiall dignitie, he
might haue iudgement decreed against him, so as the realme were
not troubled by him, and that the causes of his deposing might be
published through the realme for satisfieng of the people: which
demand was granted. Wherevpon the bishop of Carleill, a man
both learned, wise, and stout of stomach, boldlie shewed foorth
his opinion concerning that demand; affirming that there was
none amongst them woorthie or meet to giue iudgement vpon so
noble a prince as king Richard was, whom they had taken for their
souereigne and liege lord, by the space of two & twentie yeares
and more: "And I assure you" (said he) "there is not so ranke a
"traitor, nor so errant a theef, nor yet so cruell a murtherer
"apprehended or deteined in prison for his offense, but he shall be
"brought before the iustice to heare his iudgement; and will ye
"proceed to the iudgement of an anointed king, hearing neither
"his answer nor excuse? I say, that the duke of Lancaster, *whom*
"ye *call king* [Cp. l. 134], hath more trespassed to K. Richard &
"his realme, than king Richard hath doone either to him, or
"vs:" . . . As soone as the bishop had ended this tale, he was
attached by the earle marshall, and committed to ward in the
abbeie of saint Albons.

Holl.
A bold
bishop and
a faithful
[was
Carlisle,
who argued
(1) that
Richard
being their
soveraign,
the Lords
could not
judge him;
(2) it were
unjust to
condemn
him in his
absence].

[When
Carlisle had
ended his
speech, he
was
arrested.]

When Carlisle has been arrested, Bolingbroke says :

> Fetch hither Richard, that in common view
> He may surrender ; so we shall proceede   156
> Without suspition.

Afterwards Northumberland desires Richard to read

> These Accusations, and these grieuous Crymes
> Committed by your Person, and your followers,   224
> Against the State and Profit of this Land ;
> That, by confessing them, the Soules of men
> May deeme that you are worthily depos'd.

The official acts, which have been dramatized in "the Parliament
Sceane," are thus described :

[*Hol.* iii. 504/2/60.] Upon the morrow after, being tuesdaie,
and the last daie of September, all the lords spirituall and
temporall, with the commons of the said parlement, assembled at
Westminster, where, in the presence of them, the archbishop of

Yorke, and the bishop of Hereford, according to the kings request, shewed vnto them the voluntarie renouncing of the king, with the fauour also which he bare to his cousine of Lancaster to haue him his successour. And moreouer shewed them the schedule or bill of renouncement, signed with king Richards owne hand; which they caused to be read first in Latine, as it was written, and after in English. This doone, the question was first asked of the lords, if they would admit and allow that renouncement: the which when it was of them [p. 505] granted and confirmed, the like question was asked of the commons, and of them in like manner confirmed. After this, it was then declared, that, notwithstanding the foresaid renouncing, so by the lords and commons admitted and confirmed, it were necessarie, in auoiding of all suspicions and surmises of euill disposed persons, to haue in writing and registred the manifold crimes and defaults before doone by king Richard, to the end that they might first be openlie declared to the people, and after to remaine of record amongst other of the kings records for euer.

[Richard's abdication, and his wish that Boling-broke might succeed him, announced to Parlia-ment.]

K. Richards resignation confirmed by parlement.

[Articles, setting forth Richard's crimes, were to be drawn up, and publicly read.]

All this was doone accordinglie, for the articles, which before yee haue heard, were drawne and ingrossed vp, and there shewed readie to be read; but, for other causes more needfull as then to be preferred, the reading of those articles at that season was deferred.

Holinshed thus prefaces the "Articles" which Northumberland desires Richard to "reade o're" (l. 243):

[*Hol.* iii. 502/1/8.] . . . manie heinous points of misgouernance and iniurious dealings in the administration of his kinglie office, were laid to the charge of this noble prince king Richard: the which (to the end the commons might be persuaded, that he was an vnprofitable prince to the common-wealth, and worthie to be deposed) were ingrossed vp in 33 solemne articles.

[Richard's crimes were set forth in 33 articles.]

Perhaps Richard's manual surrender of his crown (ll. 181-189) is a dramatic version of a symbolical transfer made by him in the Tower, on September 29, after he had expressed a wish that Bolingbroke—who was present—might be his successour.

[*Hol.* iii. 504/2/45.] And, in token heereof, he tooke a ring of

gold from his finger, being his signet, and put it vpon the said
dukes [Bolingbroke's] finger, . . .

But Froissart (xiv. 222, 223) describes how, in the presence of
"lords, dukes, prelates, erles, barones, and knyghts, and of the notablest
men of london & of other good townes," Richard, "aparelled like a
king in his robes of estate, his sceptre in his hand, & his croun on his
hed," delivered the sceptre to Bolingbroke, and then "toke the crowen
fro his head with both his hands, and set it before him, & sayd: 'Fair
[Richard put
his signet
ring upon
Boling-
broke's
finger.] 'cosyn, Henry duke of Lancaster, I geue and deliuer you this crowne
'wherewyth I was crowned king of England, and therewith all the
'right there to dependynge.'"—Berner's *Froissart*, 1525, vol. ii. fol.
cccxiiii.

On the afternoon of September 29, 1399, Bolingbroke, Northumberland, William, Abbot of Westminster, and other witnesses, met "in
the cheefe chamber of the kings lodging," at the Tower (*Hol.* iii. pp.
503, 504), before whom Richard,

[*Hol.* iii. 504/1/19.] with glad countenance . . . said openlie
that he was readie to renounce and resigne all his kinglie maiestie
in maner and forme as he before had promised. And although he
had and might sufficientlie haue declared his renouncement by the
reading of an other meane person ; yet, for the more suertie of the
matter, and for that the said resignation should haue his full force
and strength, himselfe therefore read the scroll of resignation, in
maner and forme as followeth.

By this official document,—which has a remote general likeness to
his speech in IV. i. 204-215,—Richard absolved his subjects from their
allegiance, resigned his crown and lordships, renounced the style and
honours of a king, and acknowledged that he was justly deposed.

In regard to Richard's words (ll. 255-257),—

I haue no Name, no Title,
No, not that Name was giuen me at the Font,
But tis vsurpt,—

the late Rev. W. A. Harrison pointed out (*Transactions of the New
Shakspere Society*, 1880-82, p. 59*) two passages in *Traïson*, whence it
appears that Richard, after his abdication, was styled "Iehan de
Bordeaulx qui fu nomme Roy Richart Dengleterre" (71, 72), and
"Iehan de Londres lequel fu nomme Richart" (94). After his capture
the Londoners called him a bastard (*Trais.*, 64) ; and Bolingbroke,
conversing with the fallen King in the Tower, before the abdication,
spoke of Richard's illegitimacy as a common rumour (*Frois.*, xiv. 219,
220). We learn from *Ann. R. II.—H. IV.* (237, 238) that Richard,
being in danger of death, was hastily baptized by the name of John,
but afterwards, in compliment to his godfather Richard King of the
Majorcas, "confirmatus fuit per Episcopum, vocatusque 'Ricardus.'"

I have not found this story anent Richard's name in chronicles published before 1608, when the Parliament Scene was first printed. While he is gazing into the mirror (ll. 281-283), Richard says :

> Was this Face the Face
> That euery day, vnder his House-hold Roofe,
> Did keepe ten thousand men ?

Holinshed speaks thus of the King's lavish household expenditure :

[*Hol.* iii. 508/1/5.] He kept the greatest port, and mainteined the most plentifull house, that euer any king in England did either before his time or since. For there resorted dailie to his court aboue ten thousand persons that had meat and drinke there allowed them. *Harding. The noble house-keep-ing of king Richard.*

Shakspere has postdated Richard's committal to the Tower (l. 316). According to Holinshed :

[*Hol.* iii. 501/2/63.] The next day after his comming to London, the king from Westminster was had to the Tower,[1] and there committed to safe custodie. *The king cōmitted to the tower.*

I know not why Bolingbroke should "solemnly set downe" his coronation on "Wednesday next" (ll. 319, 320). He was crowned on Monday, October 13, 1399 ; as appears from Holinshed, who records Bolingbroke's coronation on "saint Edwards daie, and the thirteenth of October" (511/1/24), and says (511/1/71): "The solemnitie of the coronation being ended, the morow after being tuesdaie, the parlement began againe."

The first Parliament of Henry IV. entailed the crown upon him and the heirs of his body. Holinshed relates this settlement, and thus alludes to the impending plot of the Abbot of Westminster, broached at the close of Act IV.

[*Hol.* iii. 514/1/22.] By force of this act king Henrie thought himselfe firmelie set on a sure foundation, not needing to feare any storme of aduerse fortune. But yet shortlie after he was put in danger to haue beene set besides the seat, by a conspiracie begun in the abbat of Westminsters house, which had it not beene hindred, it is doubtfull whether the new king should haue inioied *[The Abbot of West-minster's plot might haue dethroned Boling-broke.*

----

[1] According to *Eves.* (156) Richard reached London on Saturday, August 30, 1399, and was taken to the Tower on the following day. *Ann. R. II.—H. IV.* (251) and *Ott.* (208, 209) give September 1 as the date of his arrival in London, and add that on September 2 he was removed from the palace of Westminster, by water, to the Tower. With hesitation I accept the dates of the monk of Evesham, whose authority concerning the events of Richard's last year deserves great regard.

his roialtie, or the old king (now a prisoner) restored to his principalitie.

Act V. sc. i.—There was no such parting of Richard and Isabelle as is here represented. They never met again after Richard left Windsor ;[1] not long before he sailed for Ireland. Between the two historical events which this scene connects—Richard's transference to Pomfret,[2] and Isabelle's return to France—an interval of more than a year elapsed. Richard's captivity in the Tower is ignored. Northumberland enters, and thus addresses the deposed King (ll. 51, 52):

> My Lord, the minde of Bullingbrooke is changde ;
> You must to Pomfret, not vnto the Tower.

Richard was sent to the Tower on or about August 31, 1399; whence,

[Richard was conveyed to Leeds, and afterwards to Pomfret, where he died.] [*Hol.* iii. 507/2/64.] shortlie after his resignation, he was conueied to the castell of Leeds in Kent, & from thence to Pomfret, where he departed out of this miserable life (as after you shall heare).

Moreover, Northumberland tells the Queen that she "must away to France" (l. 54). She was, however, detained by Bolingbroke; and did not, when returning to France, leave London—where this scene is laid—until June 28, 1401.[3]

Act V. sc. ii., iii.—The description which York gives of Boling-broke's reception by the Londoners (V. ii. 7-17) has full warrant from the following excerpt.

The dukes receiuing into London. [*Hol.* iii. 501/2/44.] As for the duke, he was receiued with all the ioy and pompe that might be of the Londoners, and was lodged in the bishops palace, by Paules church. It was a woonder to see what great concursse of people, & what number of horsses, came to him on the waie as he thus passed the countries, till his

---

[1] When in the Tower, Richard commanded that the Queen might be sent for, to speak to him ; but Bolingbroke, who was present, pleaded the Council's authority as an excuse for disobedience.—*Trais.*, 66 ; 217. Richard married her in 1396 ; and, at the historic date of Act V. sc. i., she was about twelve years of age.—*Chron. R. II.—H. IV.*, 129 (Appendix).

[2] Richard was removed from the Tower on the Morrow of SS. Simon and Jude (Oct. 29, 1399), soon after midnight.—*Ann. R. II.—H. IV.*, 313. *Ott.*, 223. In *Trais.* (75 ; 227) the date given for his removal from the Tower is October 31, 1399. According to *Ann. R. II.—H. IV.* (313) and *Ott.* (223) the place of his subsequent imprisonment was then, at least, a state secret; but the writer of *Chron. Giles* tells us (*Hen. IV.*, 10) that Richard was taken from the Tower to Leeds Castle in Kent, and was thence conveyed to Pomfret Castle.

[3] *Usk*, 61 ; 185. Adam of Usk was an eye-witness of her departure from London.

comming to London, where (vpon his approch to the citie) the maior rode foorth to receiue him, and a great number of other citizens. Also the cleargie met him with procession ; and such ioy appeared in the countenances of the people, vttering the same also with words, as the like [had] not lightlie beene seene. For in euerie towne and village where he passed, children reioised, women clapped their hands, and men cried out for ioy. But to speake of the great numbers of people that flocked togither in the fields and streets of London at his comming, I here omit; neither will I speake of the presents, welcommings, lauds, and gratifications made to him by the citizens and communaltie.

When Richard was removed from Westminster to the Tower (p. 119 above), he narrowly escaped an outbreak of hatred far exceeding what York noticed (V. ii. 5, 6 ; 27-30) on the day before.

[*Hol.* iii. 501/2/66.] Manie euill disposed persons, assembling themselues togither in great numbers, intended to haue met with him, and to haue taken him from such as had the conueieng of him, that they might haue slaine him. But the maior and alder-men gathered to them the worshipfull commoners and graue citizens, by whose policie, and not without much adoo, the other were reuoked from their euill purpose : . . .

As York ends with a firm profession of loyalty to Bolingbroke, the Duchess of York exclaims: "Here comes my sonne[1] Aumerle !" to which the Duke replies (ll. 41-43) :

> Aumerle that was ;
> But that is lost for being Richards friend,
> And, Madam, you must call him Rutland[2] now :

By Parliament sitting on November 3, 1399,

[*Hol.* iii. 513/2/1.] it was finallie enacted, that such as were appellants in the last parlement against the duke of Glocester and other, should in this wise following be ordred. The dukes of Aumarle, Surrie, and Excester, there present, were iudged to loose

---

[1] Aumerle's mother was Isabel, daughter of Pedro the Cruel, King of Castile and Leon. She died in 1394.—*Hol.* 481/1/28 (*Wals.*, ii. 214, 215). York was survived by his second wife, Joan Holland, daughter of Thomas Holland, second Earl of Kent.

[2] Earl of Rutland was his former title. He was created Duke of Albemarle on September 29, 1397 ; on which day the Parliament wherein he appealed Gloucester was prorogued.—*Eves.*, 141.

their names of dukes, togither with the honors, titles, and dignities
therevnto belonging.

The historic date of January 4, 1400,[1]—the day on which York
detected Aumerle's treason,—can be given to such portions of scenes ii.
and iii., Act V., as have for their subject the discovery of the Abbot's
plot. The material for these portions was chiefly furnished by the
closing sentence of the third, and the whole of the fourth, paragraph
quoted below.

[*Hol.* iii. 514/2/10.] But now to speak of the conspiracie,
which was contriued by the abbat of Westminster as cheefe instrument thereof. Ye shall vnderstand, that this abbat (as it is
reported) vpon a time heard king Henrie saie, when he was but
earle of Derbie, and yoong of yeares, that princes had too little,
and religious men too much. He therfore doubting now, least if
the king continued long in the estate, he would remooue the great
beame that then greeued his eies, and pricked his conscience,
became an instrument to search out the minds of the nobilitie, and
to bring them to an assemblie and councell, where they might consult and commen togither, how to bring that to effect, which they
earnestlie wished and desired; that was, the destruction of king
Henrie, and the restoring of king Richard. For there were diuerse
lords that shewed themselues outwardlie to fauor king Henrie,
where they secretlie wished & sought his confusion. The abbat,
after he had felt the minds of sundrie of them, called to his house,
on a day in the terme time,[2] all such lords & other persons which
he either knew or thought to be as affectioned to king Richard, so
enuious to the prosperitie of king Henrie; whose names were:
Iohn Holland earle of Huntington, late duke of Excester; Thomas
Holland earle of Kent, late duke of Surrie; Edward earle of
Rutland, late duke of Aumarle, sonne to the duke of Yorke; Iohn
Montacute earle of Salisburie; Hugh lord Spenser, late earle of
Glocester; Thomas [3] the bishop of Carleill; sir Thomas Blunt; and
Maudelen, a priest, one of king Richards chappell, a man as like

---

[1] Aumerle went to dine with his father "le premier Dimenche de lan"
[1400]; and, having seated himself, laid the letter containing evidence of the
plot on the table.—*Trais.*, 80; 233.
[2] The conspirators met at the Abbot of Westminster's chambers, on
December 17, 1399.—*Trais.*, 77; 229.   [3] *Thomas*] John Hol.

him in stature and proportion in all lineaments of bodie, as vnlike in birth, dignitie, and conditions.

The abbat highlie feasted these lords, his speciall freends, and, when they had well dined, they withdrew into a secret chamber, where they sat downe in councell, and, after much talke & conference had about the bringing of their purpose to passe concerning the destruction of king Henrie, at length by the aduise of the earle of Huntington it was deuised, that they should take vpon them a solemne iusts to be enterprised betweene him and 20 on his part, & the earle of Salisburie and 20 with him, at Oxford; to the which triumph K. Henrie should be desired, &, when he should be most busilie marking the martiall pastime, he suddenlie should be slaine and destroied, and so by that means king Richard, who as yet liued, might be restored to libertie, and haue his former estate & dignitie. It was further appointed, who should assemble the people; the number and persons which should accomplish and put in execution their deuised enterprise. Hervpon was an indenture sextipartite made, sealed with their seales, and signed with their hands, in the which each stood bound to other, to do their whole indeuour for the accomplishing of their purposed exploit. Moreouer, they sware on the holie euangelists to be true and secret each to other, euen to the houre and point of death.

When all things were thus appointed, the earle of Huntington came to the king vnto Windsore, earnestlie requiring him, that he would vouchsafe to be at Oxenford on the daie appointed of their iustes; both to behold the same, and to be the discouerer and indifferent iudge (if anie ambiguitie should rise) of their couragious acts and dooings. The king, being [*p.* 515] thus instantlie required of his brother in law,[1] and nothing lesse imagining than that which was pretended, gentlie granted to fulfill his request. Which thing obteined, all the lords of the conspiracie departed home to their houses, as they noised it, to set armorers on worke about the trimming of their armour against the iusts, and to prepare all other furniture and things readie, as to such an high & solemne

A iusts deuised to be holden at Oxford

[where Bolingbroke was to be slaine, and Richard thus reinstated in the throne.]

An indenture sextipartite.

He is desired to come and see the iusts.

[The conspirators' preparations.]

---

[1] "Our trusty brother in law" (*Rich. II.*, V. iii. 137), John Earl of Huntingdon, married Elizabeth, sister german of Bolingbroke.

triumph apperteined. The earle of Huntington came to his house and raised men on euerie side, and prepared horsse and harnesse for his compassed purpose; and, when he had all things readie, he

departed towards Oxenford, and, at his comming thither, he found all his mates and confederates there, well appointed for their purpose, except the earle of Rutland, by whose follie their practised conspiracie was brought to light and disclosed to king Henrie.

For this earle of Rutland, departing before from Westminster to see his father the duke of Yorke, as he sat at dinner, had his counterpane of the indenture of the confederacie in his bosome.

The father, espieng it, would needs see what it was; and, though the sonne humblie denied to shew it, the father, being more earnest to see it, by force tooke it out of his bosome; and perceiuing the

contents therof, in a great rage caused his horsses to be sadled out of hand, and spitefullie reproouing his sonne of treason, for whome he was become suertie and mainpernour for his good abearing in open parlement,[1] he incontinentlie mounted on horssebacke to ride towards Windsore to the king, to declare vnto him the malicious intent of his complices. The earle of Rutland, seeing in what danger he stood, tooke his horsse,[2] and rode another waie to

Windsore in post, so that he got thither before his father, and, when he was alighted at the castell gate, he caused the gates to be shut, saieng that he must needs deliuer the keies to the king.

When he came before the kings presence, he kneeled downe on his knees, beseeching him of mercie and forgiuenesse, and, declaring

the whole matter vnto him in order as euerie thing had passed, obteined pardon. Therewith came his father, and, being let in, deliuered the indenture, which he had taken from his sonne, vnto the king, who thereby perceiuing his sonnes words to be true, changed his purpose for his going to Oxenford.

Act V. sce. iv. and v.—Scene iv., Act V., and the latter part[3] (ll.

---

[1] Cp. *Rich. II.*, V. ii. 44, 45.

[2] Shakspere has made Aumerle take York's horse; for, according to all the texts of *Rich. II.*, V. ii. 111, the Duchess exclaims: "After, Aumerle! mount the vpon *his* horse."

[3] What a groom, who had once served Richard, says about "Roane Bar-barie" (ll. 76-80), and the fallen King's comment thereon (ll. 84-86), may possibly have been suggested to Shakspere by a story of a greyhound named

95-117) of the next scene, faithfully represent one of the several accounts of Richard's death.

[*Hol.* iii. 517/1/7.] One writer,[1] which seemeth to haue great knowledge of king Richards dooings, saith, that king Henrie, sitting on a daie at his table, sore sighing, said: "Haue I no "faithfull freend which will deliuer me of him, whose life will be "my death, and whose death will be the preseruation of my life?" This saieng was much noted of them which were present, and especiallie of one called sir Piers of Exton. This knight incontinentlie departed from the court, with eight strong persons in his

Sir Piers de Exton, a murtherer of king Richard [, because of words which he heard Bolingbroke say].

Mathe; though the dog's abandonment of his old master was deliberately cruel, while Barbary was, as Richard admits, "created to be awed by man," and "borne to beare."

[Berner's *Froissart*, ed. 1 (1523-25), vol. ii. fol. ccc.xli.] And, as it was enformed me, kynge Richarde had a grayhounde called Mathe, who alwayes wayted vpon the kynge, and wolde knowe no man els. For, whansouer the kyng dyde ryde, he that kept the grayhounde dyde lette hym lose, and he wolde streight rynne to the kynge and fawne vpon hym, and leape with his fore fete vpon the kynges shulders. And as the kynge & the erle of Derby talked togyder in the courte [of Flint Castle], the grayhounde, who was wont to lepe vpon the kyng, left the kynge & came to the erle of Derby, duke of Lancastre, and made to hym the same frendly countinaunce & chere as he was wonte to do to the kyng. The duke, who knewe nat the grayhounde, demaunded of the kyng what the grayhounde wolde do. "Cosyn," quod the kyng, "it is a gret good token to you, and an yuyll "sygne to me." "Sir, howe knowe you that?" quod the duke. "I knowe it well," quod the kyng: "The grayhounde maketh "you chere this day as kynge of Englande: (as ye shalbe, and I "shalbe deposed:) the grayhounde hath this knowledge natur- "ally, therfore take hym to you; he wyll folowe you & forsake "me." The duke vnderstode well those wordes, and cherished the grayhounde, who wolde neuer after folowe kyng Richarde, but folowed the duke of Lancastre.

[Richard had a grayhound called Mathe, who would follow no one else.]

[At Flint Castle, Mathe left Richard, and fawned on Bolingbroke.]

[This was an omen that Bolingbroke should be King of England.]

[Mathe would never after follow Richard.]

Usk says (39, 40; 155) that the dog once belonged to Thomas Holland Earl of Kent, on whose death it came to Richard, whom it had never before seen. After leaving Richard it went to Shrewsbury, and there *Usk* saw it fawn upon Henry.

[1] The writer, I suppose, of *Trais.* (93-96; 248-250). *Hol.* had a MS. of *Trais.*, which he cites as "The French pamphlet" (see p. 82, note 1, above). But Mr. Williams pointed out (*Trais.*, I., note 3) that a MS. of Froissart's fourth book (No. 8323 Regius, Bibliothèque du Roi) has an addition containing the familiar story of Richard's murder by Exton, the writer of which addition says that he was informed of its truth "par homme digne de foy, nommé Creton" (li.). The only important difference between *Hol.*'s version, and the original story as narrated by Creton and the writer of *Trais.* is that, according to the latter authorities, Bolingbroke expressly ordered Exton to slay Richard: the aside which gave Exton his cue ("Haue I no . . . of my life") first occurring, I believe, in *Halle* (20), whose account of Richard's murder agrees in other particulars with what *Hol.* relates.

companie, and came to Pomfret, commanding the esquier, that was
accustomed to sew[1] and take the assaie before king Richard, to doo
so no more, saieng: "Let him eat now, for he shall not long eat."
King Richard sat downe to dinner, and was serued without
courtesie or assaie; wherevpon, much maruelling at the sudden
change, he demanded of the esquier whie he did not his dutie:
"Sir" (said he) "I am otherwise commanded by sir Piers of
"Exton, which is newlie come from K. Henrie." When king
Richard heard that word, he tooke the keruing knife in his hand,
and strake the esquier on the head, saieng: "The diuell take
"Henrie of Lancaster and thee togither!" And with that word,
sir Piers entred the chamber, well armed, with eight tall men
likewise armed, euerie of them hauing a bill in his hand.

King Richard, perceiuing this, put the table from him, &, steping
to the formost man, wrung the bill out of his hands, & so valiantlie
defended himselfe, that he slue foure of those that thus came to
assaile him. Sir Piers, being half dismaied herewith, lept into the
chaire where king Richard was woont to sit, while the other foure
persons fought with him, and chased him about the chamber.
And in conclusion, as king Richard trauersed his ground, from one
side of the chamber to an other, & comming by the chaire, where
sir Piers stood, he was felled with a stroke of a pollax which sir
Piers gaue him vpon the head, and therewith rid him out of life;[2]
without giuing him respit once to call to God for mercie of his
passed offenses. It is said, that sir Piers of Exton, after he had
thus slaine him, wept right bitterlie, as one striken with the
pricke of a giltie conscience, for murthering him, whome he had so
long time obeied as king.

Act V. sc. vi.—This scene is postdated, for the revolt was suppressed before Richard's death. When sc. vi. opens, "the latest
newes" which Bolingbroke has heard is that the rebels have burnt

---

[1] " sew . . . assaie" = serve and remove the dishes, and taste the food in
them.
[2] February 14, 1400, is the usually accepted date of Richard's death (see
Eves., 169) ; but, on January 29, 1400, Charles VI. referred to him as Richard
late King of England, whom God pardon.—*Rymer*, viii. 124. *Wylie* (i. 114,
115) cites documentary evidence from which he infers that Richard was
murdered about the middle of January, 1400.

Cirencester; but whether they had been "tane or slaine" was unknown. As Holinshed's account of the rebellion was not dramatized,
an epitome of the chief facts recorded by contemporary chroniclers
will suffice. The rebel lords marched to Windsor, hoping to surprise Henry. Warned in time, he fled by night (Jan. 4-5) to
London, and raised forces to oppose them. The rebels retreated, and
arrived at Cirencester on January 6. At midnight, the townsmen
attacked them in their lodgings, and, after a struggle which lasted for
many hours, obliged them to surrender. The lords were then confined
in the abbey. About vespers a chaplain attached to them set fire to
some houses in Cirencester, in order that the prisoners might escape
while the townsmen were extinguishing the flames. But the men of
Cirencester, paying no heed to the fire, brought the rebels out of the
abbey, and beheaded the Earls of Salisbury and Kent about sunset, on
January 7, 1400.—*Unk*, 40, 41; 156. *Traïson*, 80-82; 233-235.
Ann. R. II.—H. IV., 323-326.

Holinshed's narration of what befell the other conspirators should
be compared with ll. 7-29.

[*Hol.* iii. 516/2/16.] The lord * Hugh Spenser,[1] otherwise called
earle of Glocester, as he would haue fled into Wales, was taken
and carried to Bristow, where (according to the earnest desires of
the commons) he was beheaded. . . . Manie other that were
priuie to this conspiracie, were taken, and put to death, some at
Oxford, as sir Thomas Blunt, sir Benet Cilie, knight, . . . but sir
Leonard Brokas, and [others] . . . , were drawne, hanged, and
beheaded at London. There were nineteene in all executed in
one place and other, and the heads of the cheefe conspirators were
set on polles ouer London bridge, to the terror of others. Shortlie
after, the abbat of Westminster, in whose house the conspiracie
was begun, (as is said,) gooing betweene his monasterie & mansion,
for thought fell into a sudden palsie, and shortlie after, without
speech, ended his life.[2] The bishop of Carleill was impeached, and
condemned of the same conspiracie; but the king, of his mercifull

Margin notes:
* *Thoma Spenser with Wal. & others.*
[*Spenser beheaded.*]
Hall.
Execution[s of Blunt, Seely, Brocas, and others].
The Waleing. Hall.
[*The chief conspirators' heads set on London Bridge.*]
The abbat of Westminster dieth suddenlie. Thom. Wals.

---

[1] Qq. 1, 2, 3, 4, read: "The heades of *Oxford*, Salisbury, Blunt and Kent"
(V. vi. 8). F1 has: "The heads of Salisbury, *Spencer*, Blunt, and Kent." As
Aubrey de Vere, Earl of Oxford, had no share in the rebellion, the reading of
F1 should be preferred.

[2] William Colchester, Abbot of Westminster, was a prisoner in the Castle
of Reigate on January 25, 1400.—*Claus*: 1 H. IV. pars i. m. 19 (O. B.). He
must have soon regained his freedom.—*Ann. R. II.—H. IV.*, 330; and *Claus*,
1 H. IV. pars ii. m. 6 (O. B.). He was probably the William Abbot of Westminster present at Pisa in 1406.—Martène's *Thesaurus Novus Anecdotorum*, ii.
1395 C. According to Dugdale (*Monasticon*, ed. 1817-30, i. 275, 276) Colchester
was Abbot of Westminster until some date in October, 1420.

The bishop of Carlill dieth through feare, or rather through grief of mind, to see the wicked prosper as he tooke it. Hall. clemencie, pardoned him of that offense ; although he died shortlie after,[1] more through feare than force of sicknesse, as some haue written.

The excerpt quoted above (pp. 125, 126) contains all that Holinshed has recorded touching Exton. From the subjoined description of Richard's funeral, it appears that Bolingbroke paid as much respect to the late King's memory as may warrant the closing lines of this scene.

[*Hol.* iii. 517/1/49.] After he was thus dead, his bodie was imbalmed, and seered, and couered with lead, all saue the face, to the intent that all men might see him, and perceiue that he was *[Richard's body conueyed from Pomfret to London.]* departed this life : for as the corps was conueied from Pomfret to London, in all the townes and places where those that had the conueiance of it did staie with it all night, they caused dirige to be soong in the euening, and masse of *Requiem* in the morning ; and as well after the one seruice as the other, his face discouered, was shewed to all that coueted to behold it.

The dead bodie of K. Richard brought to y' Tower. Thus was the corps first brought to the Tower, and after through the citie, to the cathedrall church of saint Paule, bare faced ; where it laie three daies togither, that all men might behold it. There was a solemne obsequie doone for him, both at Paules, *[Funerall rites at Westminster and St. Paul's.]* and after at Westminster, at which time, both at dirige ouernight, and in the morning at the masse of *Requiem*, the king and the citizens of London were present. When the same was ended, the corps was commanded to be had vnto Langlie, there to be buried in the church of the friers preachers.

The following excerpts bear upon the characters of Richard II., Edmund Duke of York, and Sir John Bushy.

In summing up the general aspect of society in Richard's time, Holinshed says, with regard to the King :

His personage. [*Hol.* iii. 507/2/68.] He was seemelie of shape and fauor, & of nature good inough, if the wickednesse & naughtie demeanor of such as were about him had not altered it.

His chance verelie was greatlie infortunate, which fell into such calamitie, that he tooke it for the best waie he could deuise to renounce his kingdome, for the which mortall men are accustomed

---

[1] He lived several years after this time. See *Wylie* (i. 109, 110) for an account of Carlisle's fortunes subsequent to the rebellion.

to hazard [*p.* 508] all they haue to atteine therevnto. But such misfortune (or the like) oftentimes falleth vnto those princes, which,
when they are aloft, cast no doubt for perils that maie follow. [He was
He was prodigall, ambitious, and much giuen to the pleasure and disso-
of the bodie. . . . lute.]

[*Hol.* iii. 508/1/32.] Furthermore, there reigned abundantlie [He was an
the filthie sinne of leacherie and fornication, with abhominable adulterer,]
adulterie, speciallie in the king.[1]

York, says Holinshed,

[*Hol.* iii. 464/2/49.] being verelie a man of a gentle nature, [York's
wished that the state of the common-wealth might haue beene nature.]
redressed without losse of any mans life, or other cruell dealing.

He

[*Hol.* iii. 485/2/25.] was a man rather coueting to liue in [York was
pleasure, than to deale with much businesse, and the weightie ambitious.]
affaires of the realme.[2]

When John of Gaunt married Katharine Swinford, the Duke of
Gloucester,

[*Hol.* iii. 486/1/20.] being a man of an high mind and stout [Gloucester
stomach, misliked his brothers matching so meanlie, but the duke but York
of Yorke bare it well inough. tolerated,
Gaunt's
match.]

The Speaker of the "Great Parliament" (September, 1397) was

[*Hol.* iii. 490/2/28.] sir Iohn Bushie, a knight of Lincolneshire, *Sir Iohn
accompted to be an exceeding cruell man, ambitious, and couetous speaker.*
beyond measure.

While discharging the office of Speaker at this Parliament,

---

[1] Bolingbroke charges Bushy and Greene with tempting Richard to commit
this sin (III. i. 11-15).
[2] *Hardyng* thus describes him (340, 341):

> . . . Edmonde hyght of Langley of good chere,
> Glad and mery and of his owne ay lyued,
> Without wronge, as chronicles haue breued.
> When all the lordes to councell and parlyament
> Went, he wolde to hunte and also to hawekyng,
> All gentyll disporte as to a lorde appent,
> He vsed aye, and to the pore supportyng
> Where euer he was in any place bidyng,
> Without suppryse, or any extorcyon
> Of the porayle, or any oppressyon.

K

[*Hol.* iii. 490/2/57.]   Sir Iohn Bushie, in all his talke, when he proponed any matter vnto the king, did not attribute to him titles of honour, due and accustomed ; but inuented vnused termes, and such strange names as were rather agreeable to the diuine maiestie of God, than to any earthlie potentate.   The prince, being desirous inough of all honour, and more ambitious than was requisite, seemed to like well of his speech, and gaue good eare to his talke.

Impudent flatterie [of Sir John Bushy liked by Richard].

Richard was very unfortunate in his choice of favourites, for

[*Hol.* iii. 492/2/72.]   such as were cheefe of his councell were esteemed of the commons to be the woorst creatures that might be ; as [*p.* 493] the dukes of Aumarle, Norfolke, and Excester, the earle of Wiltshire, sir Iohn Bushie, sir William Bagot, and sir Henrie [1] Greene : which three last remembred were knights of the Bath, against whom the commons vndoubtedlie bare great and priuie hatred.

[The commons held Aumarle, Norfolk, and Wiltshire, to be the worst of men ; and greatly hated Bushy, Bagot, and Greene (Cp. R. II., II. ii. 127—139.)]

VI. FIRST PART OF KING HENRY THE FOURTH.

ACT I. sc. i.—A more precise date than the year 1402 [2] cannot be assigned to the opening scene in *The Historie of Henry the fourth ;* [3] because, though but " yesternight " (l. 36) a post had brought tidings of Sir Edmund Mortimer's capture by Glendower, on June 22, 1402, [4] Sir Walter Blunt has since arrived with news of the Scots' defeat at Homildon (ll. 67-73) ; which happened on September 14, 1402. [5]   The last historic event of the play is the battle of Shrewsbury ; fought on July 21, 1403. [6]

Of Mortimer's capture Holinshed gives the following account :

[*Hol.* iii. 520/1/64.]   Owen Glendouer, according to his accustomed manner, robbing and spoiling within the English borders, caused all the forces of the shire of Hereford to assemble togither against them, vnder the conduct of Edmund Mortimer, earle of

---

[1] *Henrie*] *Thomas* Hol.

[2] For an excerpt relating to the proposed crusade, of which Henry speaks in this scene (ll. 18-29), see p. 159 below.

[3] I quote the text of Q1 (1598).

[4] *Usk,* 75 ; 200.   [5] *Ott.,* 238.   [6] *Usk,* 80 ; 206.

March.[1] But, comming to trie the matter by battell, whether by The earle of March [Sir Edmund Mortimer] treason or otherwise, so it fortuned, that the English power was discomfited, the earle taken prisoner, and aboue a thousand of his taken prisoner in batell by Owen Glendower. people slaine in the place.   The shamefull villanie[2] vsed by the Welshwomen towards the dead carcasses, was such as honest [The Welsh-women's villany.] eares would be ashamed to heare, and continent toongs to speake thereof.   The dead bodies might not be buried, without great summes of monie giuen for libertie to conueie them awaie.

A Scottish army hauing been defeated on June 22, 1402,[3] while returning from a border foray,

[*Hol.* iii. 520/2/40.] Archembald, earle Dowglas, sore displeased in his mind for this ouerthrow, procured a commission to inuade England, and that to his cost, as ye may likewise read in the Scotish histories.   For, at a place called Homildon, they were so Scots vanquished at Homildon. fiercelie assailed by the Englishmen, vnder the leading of the lord Persie, surnamed Henrie Hotspur,[4] and George earle of March,[5] that with violence of the English shot they were quite vanquished and

---

[1] In 1402, Edmund Mortimer, fifth Earl of March, being a minor, was Henry's ward.—*Usk*, 21 ; 127. Glendower's prisoner was Sir Edmund Mortimer, brother to Roger Mortimer, fourth Earl of March (see p. 134, note 4, below), and uncle to the fifth Earl. *Hol.'s* mistake niisled Shakspere (1 *Hen. IV.*, I. iii. 84). On December 13, 1402, Sir Edmund Mortimer wrote to his tenants, informing them that he had joined in a quarrel raised by Owen Glendower, " of which the object is, if King Richard be alive, to restore him to his Crown, and if not, that my honoured nephew, who is the right heir to the said Crown, shall be King of England (la quelle est tielle, qe si le Roy Richard soit en vie de luy restorer a sa coronne, et sinoun qe mon honore Neuewe q'est droit heir al dit coronne seroit Roy d'Engleterre)."—*Ellis*, II. i. 24.

[2] I shall imitate Shakspere's reticence (I. i. 43-46) in regard to the Welsh-women's " villanie." *Hol.* (528/1/36-48) gives full details.

[3] *Hol.* 520/2/34. They were defeated at Nisbet, Roxburghshire. " Nesbit-more in Marchia."—*Fordun*, ii. 433. *Hol.* does not mention the date of Mortimer's capture, which, as the reader will perceive, coincides with the overthrow of the Scots in the summer of 1402. If it were possible that Shak-spere could have known the former date, we might conjecture that he rolled into one the defeats at Nisbet and Homildon, in order that the post bringing tidings of Glendower's victory should reach London about the same time as Sir Walter Blunt arrived with the consoling news of Scottish disaster.

[4] The Earl of Northumberland had two sons, " the one named Henrie, and the other Rafe ; verie forward and lustie gentlemen. This Henrie, being the elder, was surnamed, for his often pricking, Henrie Hotspur, as one that seldome times rested, if there were anie seruice to be doone abroad."—*Hol. H. S.* 249/1/30. According to *Dugdale* (i. 278/2) Northumberland had three sons, named Henry, Thomas, and Ralph.

[5] Shakspere's " Lord Mortimer of Scotland " (1 *Hen. IV.*, III. ii. 164). See p. 142 below.

put to flight, on the Rood daie in haruest, with a great slaughter *The number slaine.* made by the Englishmen. . . . There were slaine . . . three and twentie knights, besides ten thousand of the commons; and of *Prisoners taken.* prisoners among other were these: Mordacke earle of Fife, son to the gouernour, Archembald earle Dowglas,[1] (whioh in the fight lost one of his eies,) Thomas erle of Murrey, George[2] earle of Angus, and (as some writers haue) the earles of Atholl & Menteith;[3] with fiue hundred other of meaner degrees.

I supplement my last excerpt by quoting from Holinshed's *Historie of Scotland* another account of the battle of Homildon.

Archembald Dowglas inuadeth England. [*Hol.* ii. *H. S.* 254/1/57.] Archembald, earle of Dowglasse, sore displeased, and woonderfullie wroth in his mind for this ouerthrow [at Nisbet], got commission to inuade England with an armie of ten thousand men; and, hauing the same once readie with all things necessarie for his voiage, he set forward, and entering into England, burnt and harried the countrie, not staieng till he came as farre as *The nobles of Scotland in this armie.* Newcastell. In this armie there was with the Dowglasse, Murdocke (eldest sonne to duke Robert) earle of Fife, Thomas erle of Murrey, *Henrie Hotspur and the earle of March assaile the Scots at Homildon.* George earle of Angus; with manie other lords and nobles of Scotland. At the last, when they were returning homewards with a preie of infinit goods and riches, Henrie Hotspur, and George earle of March, with a great power of men, met them, and assailed

---

[1] In the original text of *Hol.* (ed. 2) this sentence stands thus: "Mordacke earle of Fife, son to the gouernour Archembald earle Dowglas"; and in the 1st ed. of *Hol.* also the words "gouernour Archembalde" are unpunctuated. The corresponding lines (70-72) of 1 *Hen. IV.* (ed. 1), I. i. are:

> ". . . . of prisoners, Hotspur tooke
> Mordake [the] Earle of Fife, and eldest sonne
> To beaten Douglas;" . . .

and subsequent editions have the same reading. Steevens believed (*Var. Sh.* xvi. 187) that the omission of a comma after "gouernour" misled Shakspere; because the "gouernour," or Regent, of Scotland was Robert Steward, Duke of Albany, whose eldest son was "Mordacke earle of Fife." But, as in the play Murdach Steward is called "*eldest* sonne," it would seem that Shakspere must have known one or both of the excerpts relating to the battle of Homildon, which I quote from Holinshed's *Historie of Scotland.*

[2] *Georgc*] *Robert* Hol.

[3] *Hol.*'s slip has misled Shakspere (cp. I. i. 73). "Menteith" was another title of Murdoch Steward, who, in *Hol.* (ii. *H. S.* 259/2/65, is called "Mordo Steward earle of Fife and Menteith"; a description confirmed by *Hol.* ii. *H. S.* 262/2/54, and *H. S.* 419/1/32.

them so with such incessant shot of arrowes, that where the earle *The Scots, through* of Dowglas with his armie had the aduantage of an hill, called *force of the Englishmens* Homildon, he was constreined to forsake the same; and, comming *shot, descend the hill.* downe vpon the Englishmen, was neuerthelesse put to the woorsse, the most part of his people being either taken or slaine. . . .

Archembald earle of Dowglas, Murdocke Steward, eldest sonne *Prisoners taken.* to duke Robert the gouernour, George erle of Angus, . . . with the most part of all the barons of Fife and Louthian, *Buch. 1401.* were taken prisoners. This battell was fought on the Rood *1402 H.B.* day in haruest, in the yeere 1403 [1402], vpon a Tuesday.

Act I. sc. iii.—This scene and ll. 91-99, sc. i. Act I., are illustrated by my next excerpts.

[*Hol.* iii. 521/1/l. l.]   Henrie, earle of Northumberland, with *[Northumberland and* his brother Thomas, earle of Worcester, and his sonne the lord *Hotspur were* Henrie Persie, surnamed Hotspur, which were to king Henrie, in *angered because all* the beginning of his reigne, both faithfull freends, and earnest *their Scottish* aiders, began now to enuie his wealth and felicitie; and especiallie *prisoners were claimed* they were greeued, bicause the king demanded of the earle and *by the King, to whom the* his sonne such Scotish prisoners as were taken at Homeldon and *Earl of Fife alone had* Nesbit: for, of all the captiues which were taken in the conflicts *been delivered.]* foughten in those two places, there was deliuered to the kings possession onelie Mordake earle of Fife, the duke of Albanies sonne; though the king did diuers and sundrie times require deliuerance of the residue, and that with great threatnings: wherewith the Persies being sore offended, (for that they claimed them as their owne proper prisoners, and their peculiar preies,) by the counsell of the lord Thomas Persie, earle of Worcester, whose *[Worcester a makebate.]* studie was euer (as some write) to procure malice, and set things in a broile, came to the king vnto Windsore, (vpon a purpose to prooue him,) and there required of him, that either by ransome or *The request of the Persies* otherwise, he would cause to be deliuered out of prison Edmund *[, that Henry would* Mortimer earle of March, their cousine germane,[1] whom (as they *ransom Mortimer].*

---

[1] Henry IV. and Hotspur were cousins, Henry's grandfather, Henry Plantagenet Duke of Lancaster, being brother german to Mary, Hotspur's grandmother. Perhaps *Halle* (*Hol.'s* authority) alluded to the common descent of the two Percies, and Edmund fifth Earl of March, from Henry III.

reported) Owen Glendouer kept in filthie prison, shakled with
irons ; onelie for that he tooke his part, and was to him faithfull
and true.

[Henry's
misgiving
about this
request.] The king began not a little to muse at this request, and not
without cause : for in deed it touched him somewhat neere, sith
this Edmund was sonne to Roger earle of March, sonne to the
ladie Philip, daughter of Lionell duke of Clarence, the third sonne
[The Earl of
March had
been pro-
claimed heir-
apparent by
Richard.] of king Edward the third ; which Edmund, at king Richards going
into Ireland, was proclamed heire apparant to the crowne and
realme ; [1] whose aunt, called Elianor,[2] the lord Henrie Persie had
married ; and therefore king Henrie could not well beare,[3] that
anie man should be earnest about the aduancement of that linage.
[Henry
answered
that he
would not
ransom
Mortimer,
who had
willingly
suffered
himself to
be taken.] The king, when he had studied on the matter, made answer, that
the earle of March was not taken prisoner for his cause, nor in his
seruice, but willinglie suffered himselfe to be taken, bicause he would
not withstand the attempts of Owen Glendouer, and his complices ;
& therefore he would neither ransome him, nor releeue him.[4]

The Persies with this answer and fraudulent excuse were not a
*The raising of
the L. Persie.* little fumed, insomuch that Henrie Hotspur said openlie : " Behold,
" the heire of the relme is robbed of his right, and yet the robber
" with his owne will not redeeme him ! " [5] So in this furie the

---

[1] *Hol.* has, I believe, copied a mistake of *Halle* (27). On August 6, 1385,
Parliament recognized Edmund's father—Roger fourth Earl of March—as
heir-presumptive to the crown.—*Eulog.*, iii. 361.

[2] *Elizabeth.*—*Rymer*, viii. 334. She was the sister of Sir Edmund
Mortimer, and the wife of Hotspur.—*Eulog.*, iii. 396.

[3] *bears*] *hears* Hol. edd. 1, 2.

[4] In the last article of their "quarell" the Persies, addressing Henry IV.,
said that " Edmundus Mortymere, frater Rogeri Mortymere nuper comitis
Marchie et Ultonie, fuit captus per Owinum Glendore in mortali bello cam-
pestri, et in prisona ac vinculis ferreis adhuc crudeliter tentus, in causa tua,
quem tu proclamasti captum ex dolo, et noluisti pati deliberacionem suam per
se nec per nos consanguineos suos et amicos."—*Hardyng*, 353. Cp. p. 131,
n. 1, above, where a letter is quoted in which Edmund Mortimer speaks of his
nephew. As to Roger, fourth Earl of March, and father of Edmund, fifth
Earl, see p. 89, n. 1, above. *Halle's* version of this article (30) has " Edmond
Mortimer earle of Marche and Ulster," to represent " Edmundus Mortymere,
frater Rogeri Mortymere nuper comitis . . . Ultonie."

[5] We learn from *Eulog.* (iii. 395, 396) that, in 1403, Hotspur desired Henry
IV. to ransom Sir Edmund Mortimer. An altercation ensued, and the King
drew his dagger. " ' Non hic,' dixit Henricus [Percy], ' sed in campo.' Et
recessit." This open quarrel can hardly be assigned to an earlier date than
June, for on June 26, 1403, Northumberland wrote a friendly letter to Henry.
—*Proc. Priv. Co.* i. 204.

Persies departed, minding nothing more than to depose king Henrie from the high type of his roialtie, and to place in his seat their cousine Edmund earle of March, whom they did not onelie deliuer out of captiuitie, but also (to the high displeasure of king Henrie) entered in league with the foresaid Owen Glendouer. . . .

The con-spiracies of the Persies with Owen Glendouer.

King Henrie, not knowing of [*p.* 522] this new confederacie, and nothing lesse minding than that which after happened, gathered a great armie to go againe into Wales; whereof the earle of Northumberland and his sonne were aduertised by the earle of Worcester, and with all diligence raised all the power they could make, and sent to the Scots, which before were taken prisoners at Homeldon, for aid of men: promising to the earle of Dowglas the towne of Berwike, and a part of Northumberland, and, to other Scotish lords, great lordships and seigniories, if they obteined the vpper hand.   The Scots, in hope of gaine, and desirous to be reuenged of their old greefes, came to the earle with a great companie well appointed.

[Henry was unaware of the Persies plot.]

The Persies raise their powers.

They craue aid of Scots.

The Persies, to make their part seeme good, deuised certeine articles, by the aduise of Richard Scroope, archbishop of Yorke, brother to the lord Scroope, whome king Henrie had caused to be beheaded at Bristow.

The arch-bishop of Yorke of counsell with the Persies in conspiracie.

The Chronicles contain this notice of the marriage of Sir Edmund Mortimer; whom Shakspere, misled by Holinshed, makes Henry call "that Earle of March" (I. iii. 84):

[*Hol.* iii. 521/1/21.]   Edmund Mortimer, earle of March, prisoner with Owen Glendouer, whether for irkesomnesse of cruell captiuitie, or feare of death, or for what other cause, it is vncerteine, agreed to take part with Owen against the king of England; and tooke to wife the daughter of the said Owen.[1]

The earle of March marieth the daughter of Owen Glendouer.

Believing that Glendower's prisoner was Edmund Earl of March, Holinshed thus comments upon Henry's unwillingness to ransom a dangerous rival (Cp. 1 *Hen. IV.,* I. iii. 158, 159):

[*Hol.* iii. 520/2/5.]   The king was not hastie to purchase the

---

[1] " Eodem anno [1402] Dominus Edmundus Mortimer, . . . circa festum S. Andreae Apostoli [Nov. 30], filiam prædicti Owyni Glyndore desponsavit maxima cum solemnitate, & (sicut vulgariter dicitur) conversus est totaliter ad Wallicos."—*Eves.,* 182.

The suspicion of K. Henrie grounded vpő a guiltie conscience. deliuerance of the earle March, bicause his title to the crowne was well inough knowen, and therefore suffered him to remaine in miserable prison; wishing both the said earle, and all other of his linage, out of this life, with God and his saincts in heauen, so they had beene out of the waie, for then all had beene well inough as be thought.

Act II. sc. iii.—The Lord, whose temporising letter roused Hotspur's scorn (II. iii. 1-38), was, no doubt, one of the "noblemen" or "states of the realme" to whom the Percies' articles were submitted.

Thom. Wals. [*Hol.* iii. 522/1/19.] These articles being shewed to diuerse noblemen, and other states of the realme, mooued them to fauour their purpose, in so much that manie of them did not onelie promise to the Persies aid and succour by words, but also by their writings and scales[1] confirmed the same. Howbeit, when the matter came to triall, the most part of the confederates abandoned them, and at the daie of the conflict left them alone. Thus, after that the conspirators had discouered themselues, the lord Henrie Persie, desirous to proceed in the enterprise, vpon trust to be assisted by Owen Glendouer, the earle of March [*i. e.* Sir Edmund Mortimer], & other, assembled an armie of men of armes and archers foorth of Cheshire and Wales.

[The Percies were abandoned by nobles who promised to aid them.]

Act II. sc. iv.—The Prince of Wales was at a tavern in Eastcheap when Falstaff—reporting to him the news of the rebellion, brought by a nobleman of the Court—says: "Worcester is stolne away to night" (l. 392). We learn from Holinshed that, as soon as Hotspur had made the first move, by assembling "an armie of men of armes and archers,"

The earle of Worcester, gouernour to the prince, slippeth from him. Hall. [*Hol.* iii. 522/1/32.] his vncle Thomas Persie, earle of Worcester, that had the gouernement of the prince of Wales, who as then laie at London, in secret manner conueied[2] himselfe

---

[1] *Harding* tells us (351, prose addition ; 361) that he saw the sealed letters by which these noblemen bound themselues to join the Percies' revolt. The Lord, whose letter is read in II. iii., was "well contented to bee" at the gathering-place, "in respect of the loue" he bore the Percies' house, but what followed was a tacit refusal of help.

[2] "the prince . . . manner conueied." I have altered the punctuation here by placing a comma after "London," and removing a comma which stood after "manner." *Hol.'s* punctuation—which is the same in both editions of his Chronicles—might lead one to infer that the Prince had come to town to enjoy himself clandestinely, and Shakspere perhaps so understood the sentence. Comparison with *Ott.* (240) shows that the words "in secret manner" apply to Worcester.

out of the princes house; and comming to Stafford (where he
met his nephue) they increased their power by all waies and
meanes they could deuise.

Act III. sc. i.—The first scene of Act III. is laid at the Archdeacon
of Bangor's house, where Hotspur, Mortimer, and Glendower have met
to partition between them King Henry's realm.   Before going to
business, Hotspur and Glendower talk of certain portents attending
the latter's nativity (ll. 13-40).   I do not find in Holinshed any birth
recorded which was marked by such signs, but it is possible that a
horrible prodigy associated with Mortimer's entrance into the world
set Shakspere's imagination working to devise marvels suited to the
fairer fortunes of the Welsh prince.

[*Hol.* iii. 521/1/27.]   Strange wonders happened (as men
reported) at the natiuitie of this man, for, the same night he was
borne, all his fathers horsses in the stable were found to stand in
bloud vp to the bellies.[1]

[Prodigy at Mortimer's birth.]

Malone conjectured that Shakspere transferred to the time of
Glendower's birth a portent recorded in the ensuing excerpt:

[*Hol.* iii. 519/2/59.]   In the moneth of March [1402] appeared
a blasing starre, first betweene the east part of the firmament and
the north, flashing foorth fire and flames round about it, and,
lastlie, shooting foorth fierie beams towards the north; foreshewing
(as was thought) the great effusion of bloud that followed, about
the parts of Wales and Northumberland.   For much about the
same time, Owen Glendouer (with his Welshmen) fought with the
lord Greie of Ruthen, comming foorth to defend his possessions,
which the same Owen wasted and destroied; and, as the fortune
of that daies worke. fell out, the lord Greie was taken prisoner,
and manie of his men were slaine.   This hap lifted the Welshmen
into high pride, and increased meruelouslie their wicked and
presumptuous attempts.

1402

A blasing starre [, fore-shewing bloodshed in Wales and Northum-berland].

The lord Greie of Ruthen taken in fight by Owen Glendouer.

---

[1] According to *Eves.* (179), *Chron. Giles* (*Hen. IV.* 11), and *Eulog.* (398),
Mortimer's birth was thus signalized.   But, as in *Hol.*, the paragraph immediately preceding—which records Mortimer's marriage, and is quoted by me at
p. 135 above—ends with the words "the said Owen," "this man" might be
understood to mean Glendower. *Wals.* (ii. 253, 254)—from whom *Hol.* derived
both paragraphs—meant, perhaps, that Glendower was the man at whose
nativity horses "were found to stand in bloud vp to the bellies."

Glendower claims to have thrice sent Henry "weather beaten backe" to England (III. i. 64-67).   The first of these luckless expeditions was made in 1400 (see an account of it at p. 104 above).   Henry's second failure was ascribed to the "art magike," in which Glendower professes to be so deeply skilled (III. i. 46-49).   Holinshed says:

[*Hol.* iii. 520/2/19.]   About mid of August [1402],[1] the king, to chastise the presumptuous attempts of the Welshmen, went with a great power of men into Wales, to pursue the capteine of the Welsh rebels,[2] Owen Glendouer; but in effect he lost his labor, for Owen coueied himselfe out of the waie into his knowen lurking places, and (as was thought) through art magike, he caused such *Intemperat weather [caused by Glendower's sorcery].* foule weather of winds, tempest, raine, snow, and haile to be raised, for the annoiance of the kings armie, that the like had not beene heard of : in such sort, that the king was constreined to returne home, hauing caused his people yet to spoile and burne first a great part of the countrie.

The third expedition has been antedated.   It was undertaken in 1405,[3] after the suppression of Archbishop Scrope's revolt, when Henry

The K. passeth into Wales.   [*Hol.* iii. 530/2/70.]   tooke his iournie directlie into Wales, where he found fortune nothing fauourable vnto him, for all his *He looseth his cariages. He returneth.* attempts had euill successe ; in somuch that, losing fiftie of his cariages through abundance of raine and waters, he returned.

Waiving further discussion of supernatural matters, Glendower draws Hotspur's attention to a map, upon which Mortimer points out the intended partition of England and Wales between the confederates (ll. 70-77).   According to Holinshed, Northumberland, Hotspur, and Glendower,

[*Hol.* iii. 521/2/57.]   by their deputies, in the house of the archdeacon of Bangor, diuided the realme amongst them ; causing *An indenture tripartite.* a tripartite indenture to be made and sealed with their scales, by the couenants whereof, all England from Seuerne and Trent, south *A division of that which they had not.* and eastward, was assigned to the earle of March : all Wales, & the lands beyond Seuerne westward, were appointed to Owen

---

[1] *Wals.* ii. 250.   *Usk,* 76 ; 201.   *Ott.* 235.
[2] *rebels*] Hol. ed. 1.   *rebell* Hol. ed. 2.
[3] *Wals.* ii. 271.

Glendouer: aud all the remnant from Trent northward, to the lord
Persie.[1]

Hotspur scoffs at a prophecy (ll. 149-155) which seems to have had
much weight; for Holinshed, speaking of the partition described in my
last excerpt, says:

[*Hol.* iii. 521/2/67.]   This was doone (as some haue said)
through a foolish credit giuen to a vaine prophesie,[2] as though king   *A vaine*
Henrie was *the moldwarpe,* curssed of Gods owne mouth, and they   *prophesie.*
three were the *dragon,* the *lion,* and the woolfe, which should diuide
this realme betweene them.

Act III. sc. ii.—In this scene Prince Henry is reproached by his
father for devotion to ignoble pleasures and base associates. The
Prince answers (ll. 18-28):

> So please your Maiestie, I would I could
> Quit all offences with as clear excuse,
> As well as (I am doubtlesse) I can purge   20
> My selfe of many I am chargd withall:
> Yet such extenuation let me beg,
> As, in reproofe of many tales deuisde
> (Which oft the eare of greatnes needs must heare) 24
> By smiling *pickthanks,* and base newesmongers,
> I may, for some things true, wherein my youth
> Hath faulty wandred and irregular,
> Find pardon on my true submissiön.   28

---

[1] This alliance was made after Hotspur's death.   On February 28, 1405,
"Henricus, comes Northumbriae, fecit legiam et confoederationem et amicitiam
cum Owino Glendore, et Edmundo de Mortuomari, filio quondam Edmundi
comitis Marchiae [the third Earl], in certis articulis continentibus formam quae
sequitur et tenorem."—*Chron. Giles (Hen. IV.* 39).   In the following pages
of *Chron. Giles* (40, 41) the tripartite division of England and Wales is set
forth.

[2] This prophecy is in MSS. Bodl. 1787 (printed in *Archaeol.,* xx. 258). The
"talpa ore Dei maledicta" was to suffer for her past misdeeds; and "terra rever-
tetur ad asinum [Richard II.], vel aprum, vel draconem, vel leonem." Hotspur
was angered by hearing from Glendower

> " . . . of *the Moldwarp* and the Ant,
> Of the dreamer *Merlin* and his prophecies, . . .
> And of a *Dragon* . . .
> A couching *Lion,* &c."

Halle says (28): "a certayne writer writeth that this earle of Marche, the
Lorde Percy and Owen Glendor wer vnwysely made beleue by a Welsh Pro-
phecier, that king Henry was the Moldwarpe, . . . by the deuiacion and not
deuinacion of that mawmet *Merlyn.*"   A clause in the indenture between
Northumberland, Mortimer and Glendower runs thus: "Item, si disponente
Deo, appareat praefatis dominis ex processu temporis, quod ipsi sint eaedem
personae, de quibus propheta loquitur, inter quos regimen Britanniae majoris
dividi debeat et partiri, tunc ipsi laborabunt, et quilibet ipsorum laborabit juxta
posse, quod id ad effectum efficaciter perducatur."—*Chron. Giles (Hen. IV.,* 40).

The Prince's reference to the slanders of certain "pickthanks," who accused him of a more serious transgression than that of keeping loose company, seems to anticipate a misunderstanding which arose between the father and son towards the end of Henry IV.'s reign. In 1412, the

The prince of Wales accused to his father.

[*Hol.* iii. 539/1/1.] lord Henrie, prince of Wales, eldest sonne to king Henrie, got knowledge that certeine of his fathers seruants were busie to giue informations against him, whereby discord

Iohn Stow.

might arise betwixt him and his father: for they put into the kings head, not onelie what euill rule (according to the course of youth) the prince kept to the offense of manie, but also what great resort of people came to his house; so that the court was nothing furnished with such a traine as dailie followed the prince.

The suspicious gelousie of the king toward his son.

These tales brought no small suspicion into the kings head, least his sonne would presume to vsurpe the crowne, he being yet aliue; through which suspicious gelousie, it was perceiued that he fauoured not his sonne, as in times past he had doone.

The Prince (sore offended with such persons as, by slanderous reports, sought not onelie to spot his good name abrode in the realme, but to sowe discord also betwixt him and his father) wrote his letters into euerie part of the realme, to reprooue all such slanderous deuises of those that sought his discredit. And to cleare himselfe the better, (that the world might vnderstand what wrong he had to be slandered in such wise,) about the feast of

The prince goeth to the court with a great traine.

Peter and Paule, to wit, the nine and twentith daie of June, he came to the court with such a number of noble men and other his freends that wished him well, as the like traine had beene sildome seene repairing to the court at any one time in those daies.

At Westminster Prince Henry made his peace with the King, by whom "he was dismissed with great loue and signes of fatherlie affection." I give the passage following these words, because it contains the epithet "pickthanks," which occurs in the lines quoted above; and also elucidates the Prince's avowal that "some things" were "true," wherein his youth had "faulty wandred."

["Pick-thanks" sowed division between the King and Prince Henry.]

[*Hol.* iii. 539/2/28.] Thus were the father and the sonne reconciled, betwixt whom the said *pickthanks* had sowne diuision, insomuch that the sonne, vpon a vehement conceit of vnkindnesse sproong in the father, was in the waie to be worne out of fauour.

Which was the more likelie to come to passe, by their informations that priuilie charged him with riot[1] and other vnciuill demeanor vnseemelie for a prince.   Indeed he was youthfullie giuen, growne to audacitie, and had chosen him companions agreeable to his age ; with whome he spent the time in such recreations,[2] exercises, and delights as he fansied.   But yet (it should seeme by the report of some writers) that his behauiour was not offensiue or at least tending to the damage of anie bodie ; sith he had a care to auoid dooing of wrong, and to tedder his affections within the tract of vertue ; whereby he opened vnto himselfe a redie passage of good liking among the prudent sort, and was beloued of such as could discerne his disposition, which was in no degree so excessiue, as that he deserued in such vehement maner to be suspected.

[Prince Henry's behaviour.] Abr. Fl. out of Angl. prœlia. [Note against "Thus . . ; diuision" in orig.]

Continuing to rebuke his son, the King says (ll. 32, 33) :

> Thy place in counsell thou hast rudely lost,
> Which by thy yonger brother is supplide.

Holinshed briefly mentions the well-known story[3] that Prince Henry once struck Chief-Justice Gascoign ; and adds :

[*Hol.* iii. 543/2/17.]   The king after expelled him out of his priuie councell, banisht him the court, and made the duke of Clarence (his yoonger brother) president of councell in his steed.

[Clarence made president of the Council instead of Prince Henry.]

---

[1] I find nothing to warrant this charge, but it is said that Eastcheap—the Shaksperian Prince Hal's old haunt—was once disturbed by a riot in connexion with which Prince John—Falstaff's "yong sober blouded boy" (2 *Hen. IV.*, IV. iii. 94)—is mentioned.   Under 1410, *Stow* writes (550) : "Vpon the eeuen of Saint Iohn Baptist [June 23], Thomas and Iohn, the kings sonnes, being in East-cheap at London, at supper, after midnight, a great debate hapned betweene their men, and men of the court, lasting an houre, till the Maior and Sheriffes with other Citizens ceased the same."   The riot is thus chronicled by *Greg.* (106) : "And the same tyme [1410] was the hurlynge in Estechepe by the lorde Thomas and the lorde John, the kyngys sone, &c."

[2] One of these "recreations" is thus described by *Stow* (557) : 'He [Prince Henry] liued somewhat insolently, insomuch that, whilest his father liued, being accompanied with some of his yong Lords and gentlemen, he would waite in disguised aray for his owne receiuers, and distresse them of their money ; and sometimes at such enterprises both he and his company were surely beaten : and when his receiuers made to him their complaints how they were robbed in their comming vnto him, *hee would giue them discharge of so much money as they had lost ; and, besides that, they should not depart from him without great rewards for their trouble and vexation ;* especially they should be rewarded that best had resisted him and his company, and of whom he had receiued the greatest and most strokes.'   With the words italicized cp. what Prince Henry says in regard to the booty taken from the travellers on Gadshill : "The money shall bee paid backe againe with aduantage " (1 *Hen. IV.*, II. iv. 599).   [3] See p. 161, below.

Shakspere has used a dramatist's freedom in making Henry IV. speak of Hotspur as "being no more in debt to yeares" than the Prince (l. 103). Whether Shakspere was ignorant of, or chose to disregard, the chronological aspect of this matter, I know not, but from a comparison of two passages in his authority (*Hol.* ii. *H. S.* 249/ 2/7, &c., and iii. 511/2/9, &c.) he could have learnt that in 1388 Harry Percy was old enough to command the English forces at Otterburne, while in 1399 Harry Monmouth was only twelve years of age. Indeed it is probable that Hotspur was older than the King. Henry IV. was born on April 3, 1367 (*Compotus Hugonis de Waterton*, cited in *Notes & Queries*, 4th S. xi. 162) ; and Walsingham tells us (i. 388) that, on November 25, 1378, Hotspur displayed his pennon for the first time ("primo . . . suum vexillum displicuit") at the siege of Berwick Castle.

When the Prince has succeeded in gaining his father's confidence, and has been promised a command in the royal army, Sir Walter Blunt enters and announces that news of the rebels' gathering at Shrewsbury has been sent by "Lord Mortimer of Scotland" (l. 164). In the following excerpt George of Dunbar, Earl of the March of Scotland,[1] is called "the Scot, the earle of March" ; an appellation which might have led Shakspere to believe that the Scottish Earls of March were akin to the English Mortimers, Earls of March.

[*Hol.* iii. 522/2/39.] King Henrie, aduertised of the proceedings of the Persies, foorthwith gathered about him such power as he might make, and, being earnestlie called vpon by the Scot, the earle of March, to make hast and giue battell to his enimies, before their power by delaieng of time should still too much increase, he

The kings speedie diligence.

passed forward with such speed, that he was in sight of his enimies, lieng in campe neere to Shrewesburie, before they were in doubt of anie such thing ; for the Persies thought that he would haue staied at Burton vpon Trent, till his councell had come thither to him to giue their aduise what he were best to doo. But herein the enimie was deceiued of his expectation, sith the king had great regard of expedition and making speed for the safetie of his owne person ; whervnto the earle of March incited him, considering that in delaie is danger, & losse in lingering.

Act IV. sc. i.—A messenger brings Hotspur news that Northumberland "is grieuous sicke" (l. 16), and delivers a letter containing the Earl's excuses for not coming himself or sending the expected reinforcements. After speaking of the efforts made by Hotspur and Worcester to increase their strength (p. 137 above), Holinshed says:

---

[1] He is called "George de Dunbarre, Erle of the Marche of Scotland," in the indenture (dated July 25, 1400) by which he engages to transfer his allegiance from Robert III. to Henry IV.—*Rymer*, viii. 153.

[*Hol.* iii. 522/1/39.] The earle of Northumberland himselfe was not with them, but, being sicke, had promised vpon his amendement to repaire vnto them (as some write) with all conuenient speed.

Act IV. sc. ii.—If, in Shakspere's day, there were some captains who "misused the kinges presse damnablie" (l. 13), contemporaries of Sir John Falstaff had also enriched themselves by a like practice. In 1387, Richard Earl of Arundel,—to whom the command of an English fleet had been given,—

[*Hol.* iii. 454/1/53.] vnderstanding that the duke of Glocester, and manie other noblemen would see the muster of his men, vsed all diligence, and spared for no costs, to haue the most choisest and pikedst fellowes that might be gotten ; not following the euill example of others in times past, which receiued tag and rag to fill vp their numbers, whom they hired for small wages, and reserued the residue to their pursses.

A great abuse in choise of souldiers.

Act IV. sc. iii.—Shakspere assigned to Sir Thomas Blunt the mission (ll. 41-51) which, as my next excerpt shows, was entrusted to the Abbot of Shrewsbury and a clerk of the Privy Seal.

[*Hol.* iii. 523/1/35.] The next daie in the morning earlie, being the euen of Marie Magdalene [July 21, 1403], they set their battels in order on both sides, and now, whilest the warriors looked when the token of battell should be giuen, the abbat of Shrewesburie, and one of the clearks of the priuie seale, were sent from the king vnto the Persies, to offer them pardon, if they would come to any reasonable agreement. By their persuasions, the lord Henrie Persie began to giue eare vnto the kings offers, & so sent with them his vncle the earle of Worcester, to declare vnto the king the causes of those troubles, and to require some effectuall reformation in the same.

The king offereth to pardon his aduersaries.

Act V. sc. i.—Holinshed's epitome of the Percies' charges is interwoven with the speeches of Hotspur (IV. iii. 60-62 ; 90-96) and Worcester (V. i. 41-58). I have transposed the order of the passages in Holinshed concerning the Abbot of Shrewsbury's mission, and the delivery of the Percies' articles to Henry. "The next daie"—when, as appears from the preceding excerpt, the Abbot offered Henry's terms to the rebels—was the day after that on which Hotspur's esquires were sent to the royal camp with these articles.

[*Hol.* iii. 523/1/8.] Now when the two armies were incamped,

The Persies sent their articles to the king. the one against the other, the earle of Worcester and the lord Persie with their complices sent the articles (whereof I spake before), by Thomas Caiton, and Roger [1] Saluain, esquiers, to king *King Henrie charged with periurie.* Henrie, vnder their hands and seales ; which articles in effect charged him with manifest periurie, in that (contrarie to his oth receiued vpon the euangelists at Doncaster, when he first entred the realme after his exile) he had taken vpon him the crowne and roiall dignitie, imprisoned king Richard, caused him to resigne his title, and finallie to be murthered. Diuerse other matters they laid to his charge, as leuieng of taxes and tallages, contrarie to his promise, infringing of lawes & customes of the realme, and suffering the earle of March to remaine in prison, without trauelling to haue *Procurors & protectors of the common-wealth.* him deliuered.[2] All which things they, as procurors & protectors of the common-wealth, tooke vpon them to prooue against him, as they protested vnto the whole world.

King Henrie, after he had read their articles, with the defiance *The kings answer to the messengers that brought the articles.* which they annexed to the same, answered the esquiers, that he was readie with dint of sword and fierce battell to prooue their quarrell false, and nothing else than a forged matter ; not doubting, but that God would aid and assist him in his righteous cause, against the disloiall and false forsworne traitors.

Act V. sc. ii.—On the day of battle (July 21), Hotspur, after hearing Henry's proposals, sent back their bearer, the Abbot of Shrewsbury, accompanied by Worcester, to the King (see p. 143 above). Holinshed left Worcester's treacherie unexplained, but Shakspere has supplied a motive for it (ll. 4-23).

[*Hol.* iii. 523/1/48.] It was reported for a truth, that now

---

[1] *Roger*] *Thomas* Hol.
[2] All these charges are made in Hotspur's or Worcester's speech. (They are contained in the Percies' " quarell," cited at p. 134, n. 4, above.) Hotspur says that Henry " taskt the whole state " (IV. iii. 92), and reformed " certaine edicts " and " streight decrees " (IV. iii. 79) ; words which embody the accusations of having levied " taxes and tallages," and infringed " lawes and customes of the realme." Worcester's complaint that they were in danger of their lives from Henry's jealousy (V. i. 59-64)—cp. what Hotspur says (IV. iii. 98)— occurs in some letters which, besides the articles, were sent abroad by the Percies, wherein they affirmed that " where through the slanderous reports of their enimies, the king had taken a greeuous displeasure with them, they durst not appeare personallie in the kings presence, vntill the prelats and barons of the realme had obteined of the king licence for them to come and purge themselues before him, by lawfull triall of their peeres, whose iudgement (as they pretended) they would in no wise refuse."—*Hol.* iii. 522/1/52.

when the king had condescended vnto all that was resonable at
his hands to be required, and seemed to humble himselfe more
than was meet for his estate, the earle of Worcester (vpon his
returne to his nephue) made relation cleane contrarie to that the
king had said, in such sort that he set his nephues hart more in
displeasure towards the king, than euer it was before ; driuing him
by that meanes to fight whether he would or not.

The earle of Worcesters double dealing in wrong reporting the kings words.

The armies are on the point of joining battle when Hotspur thus
encourages his followers (V. ii. 82-89) :

> O Gentlemen, the time of life is short !
> To spend that shortnesse basely were too long,
> If life did ride vpon a dials point,   84
> Still ending at the arriual of an houre.
> And if we liue, we liue to tread on kings,
> If die, braue death, when princes die with vs !
> Now, for our consciences, the armes are faire,   88
> When the intent of bearing them is iust.

The ensuing excerpt contains a speech attributed to Hotspur, which
has less martial ardour than is displayed in these lines.
Henry's rapid advance obliged the rebels to desist

The Persies troubled with the kings sudden comming.

[*Hol.* iii. 522/2/60.]   from assaulting the towne of Shrewesburie,
which enterprise they were readie at that instant to haue taken in
hand ; and foorthwith the lord Persie (as a capteine of high
courage) began to exhort the capteines and souldiers to prepare
themselues to battell, sith the matter was growen to that point,
that by no meanes it could be auoided, "so that" (said he) "this
"daie shall either bring vs all to aduancement & honor, or else, if
"it shall chance vs to be ouercome, shall deliuer vs from the kings
"spitefull malice and cruell disdaine : for plaieng the men (as we
"ought to doo), better it is to die in battell for the common-
"wealths cause, than through cowardlike feare to prolong life,
"which after shall be taken from vs, by sentence of the enimie."

The lord Persie exhorteth his complices to stick to their tackle.

Act V. sc. ii. ll. 97-101 ; sc. iii. ll. 1-29 ; sc. iv. ll. 1-86.—Hotspur,
deceived by Worcester's false report of Henry's words, resolves to
fight :

[*Hol.* iii. 523/1/57.]   then suddenlie blew the trumpets, the
kings part crieng, "S. George ! vpon them !" the aduersaries cried,
"*Esperance ! Persie !*" and so the two armies furiouslie ioined. The
archers on both sides shot for the best game, laieng on such load

with arrowes, that manie died, and were driuen downe that never rose againe.

Hall.
The Scots.

The Scots (as some write), which had the fore ward on the Persies side, intending to be reuenged of their old displeasures doone to them by the English nation, set so fiercelie on the kings fore ward, led by the earle of Stafford, that they made the same draw backe, and had almost broken their aduersaries arraie. The

The Welsh-
men come to
aid the
Persies.

Welshmen also, which before had laine lurking in the woods, mounteines, and marishes, hearing of this battell toward, came to the aid of the Persies, and refreshed the wearied people with new succours. The king perceiuing that his men were thus put to distresse, what with the violent impression of the Scots, and the tempestuous stormes of arrowes, that his aduersaries discharged freely against him and his people,—it was no need to will him to stirre : for suddenlie, with his fresh battell, he approched and relieued his men ; so that the battell began more fierce than

[Valour of
Hotspur and
Douglas.]

before. Here the lord Henrie Persie, and the earle Dowglas, a right stout and hardie capteine, not regarding the shot of the kings battell, nor the close order of the ranks, pressing forward togither, bent their whole forces towards the kings person ; comming vpon

The earle of
March
[withdrew
Henry from
the side of
the field
where Hot-
spur and
Douglas
fought].

him with speares and swords so fiercelie, that the earle of March, the Scot, perceiuing their purpose, withdrew the king from that side of the field (as some write) for his great benefit and safegard (as it appeared)` ; for they gaue such a violent onset vpon them that

Tho. Walsi.
[Sir Walter
Blunt and
the Earl of
Stafford
slain.]

stood about the kings standard, that, slaieng his standard-bearer sir Walter Blunt, and ouerthrowing the standard, they made slaughter of all those that stood about it ; as the earle of Stafford, that daie made by the king constable of the realme, and diuerse other.

Hall.
The valiance
of the yoong
prince [, who
would not
retire
though
he was
wounded.]

The prince that daie holpe his father like a lustie yoong gentle-man ; for although he was hurt in the face with an arrow, so that diuerse noble men, that were about him, would haue conueied him foorth of the field, yet he would not suffer them so to doo, least his departure from amongst his men might happilie haue striken some feare into their harts : and so, without regard of his hurt, he continued with his men, & neuer ceassed either to fight where the battell was most hot, or to incourage his men where it seemed most need.   This battell lasted three long houres, with indifferent *A sore battell & well maintained.* fortune on both parts, till at length, the king, crieng, "saint "George! victorie!" brake the arraie of his enimies ; and aduen- tured so farre, that (as some write) the earle Dowglas strake him *The valiant dooings of the earle Dowglas.* downe, & at that instant slue sir Walter Blunt, and three other, apparelled in the kings sute and clothing, saieng: "I maruell to *[He slew Blunt and three others who wore the King's coat.]* "see so many kings thus suddenlie arise one in the necke of an "other."   The king, in deed, was raised, & did that daie manie a noble feat of armes, for, as it is written, he slue that daie with his *The high manhood of the king.* owne hands six and thirtie persons of his enimies.   The other on his part, incouraged by his dooings, fought valiantlie, and slue the *The lord Persie slaine.* lord Persie, called sir Henrie Hotspurre.[1]

Act V. sc. v.—Touching the numbers slain (ll. 6-10), and the fates of Worcester and Vernon (l. 14), Holinshed says :

[*Hol.* iii. 523/2/52.]   There was also taken the earle of *The earle of Worcester taken.* Worcester, the procuror and setter foorth of all this mischeefe, sir Richard Vernon, and . . . diuerse other.   There were slaine vpon *Knights slaine on the kings part.* the kings part, beside the earle of Stafford, . . . sir Hugh Shorlie, sir Iohn Clifton, . . . sir Robert[2] Gausell, sir Walter Blunt,[3] . . . There died in all vpon the kings side sixteene hundred, and foure thousand were greeuouslie wounded.   On the contrarie side were slaine, besides the lord Persie, the most part of the knights and esquiers of the countie of Chester, to the number of two hundred, *The slaughter of Cheshire men at this battell.* besides yeomen and footmen : in all there died of those that fought on the Persies side, about fiue thousand.   This battell was fought on Marie Magdalene euen, being saturdaie.   Upon the mondaie folowing, the earle of Worcester, . . . and sir Richard Vernon . . . *The earle of Worcester and others beheaded.* were condemned and beheaded. [*p.* 524]   The earles head was sent to London, there to be set on the bridge.

Douglas is then released, "ransomlesse and free" (ll. 27-31). Holinshed thus ends his account of the battle:

---

[1] "Inter quos [the slain] Henricus Percy corruit interemptus, dubium cujus manu, suis, ignorantibus ejus casum, putantibus, ipsum regem captasse vel occidisse.   Quamobrem se cohortantes, clamabant ingementes, 'Henry Percy Kinge.'   Quorum clamores rex intelligens, ne vana spe deducti certarent ulterius, . . . clamavit et ipse voce qua valuit, 'Mortuus est Henricus Percy.'" —*Ott.*, 243.   [2] *Robert*] *Nicholas* Hol.
[3] "Sherly, Stafford, Blunt" (V. iv. 41).   "Sir Nicholas Gawsey . . . Clifton" (V. iv. 45, 46).

[*Hol.* iii. 523/2/46.] To conclude, the kings enimies were vanquished, and put to flight; in which flight, the earle of Dowglas, for hast, falling from the crag of an hie mounteine, brake one of his cullions, and was taken, and for his valiantnesse, of the king frankelie and freelie deliuered.

VII. THE SECOND PART OF KING HENRY IV.

The Second part of Henrie the fourth is separated from the preceding play by a historic interval of nearly two years, which elapsed between the battle of Shrewsbury (July 21, 1403) and Archbishop Scrope's rebellion (May—June, 1405).   Dramatic action pauses while Morton is speeding to the Earl of Northumberland with the news of Hotspur's defeat and death.   The historic period dramatized in the two Parts of *Henry IV.* closes with Henry V.'s coronation on April 9, 1413.

Act I. sc. i.—For the brief space of time filled by Morton's warning —that a "speedy power" (l. 133) has been sent against Northumberland—historic and dramatic dates coincide.   Though Sir Robert Waterton—not Prince John—was Westmoreland's colleague, we may fairly identify the "power" spoken of by Morton with the "armie" which, as the ensuing passage shows, was 'got on foot' to meet Northumberland.

[*Hol.* iii. 524/1/3.] The earle of Northumberland was now marching forward with great power, which he had got thither, either to aid his sonne and brother (as was thought) or at the least towards the king, to procure a peace; but the earle of Westmerland, and sir Robert Waterton, knight, had got an armie on foot, and meant to meet him.   The earle of Northumberland, taking neither of them to be his freend, turned suddenlie backe, and withdrew himselfe into Warkewoorth castell.

Northumberland's submission, however, averted a battle, and peace was restored until he gave countenance to Archbishop Scrope's revolt in 1405.

Act I. sc. iii.—Archbishop Scrope and his fellow-conspirators discuss their chances of success, and resolve to move at once, without waiting for Northumberland.   Nothing in this scene admits of historical comment except Hasting's report (ll. 70-73) that the King's

> . . . diuisions, as the times do brawle,
> Are in three heads : one power against the French,
> And one against Glendower ; perforce a third
> Must take vp vs : . . .

The third power is commanded by Prince John [1] and Westmoreland, the King and Prince Henry will encounter the Welsh, but "no certaine notice" has been obtained of the leader who will oppose the French (ll. 82-85).

Shakspere seems to have antedated some assistance rendered by the French to Glendower in the summer of 1405, after Archbishop Scrope's revolt had been suppressed.   About this time [2]

[*Hol.* iii. 531/1/8.]   the French king had appointed one of the marshals of France, called Montmerancie, and the master of his crosbowes, with twelue thousand men, to saile into Wales to aid Owen Glendouer.   They tooke shipping at Brest, and, hauing the wind prosperous, landed at Milford hauen, with an hundred and fourtie ships, as *Thomas Walsingham* saith ; though *Enguerant de Monstrellet* maketh mention but of an hundred and twentie.

*Hall.
The marshall
Môtmerdcie
sent to aid
Owen
Glendouer.*

Failing to capture Haverfordwest,

[*Hol.* iii. 531/1/37.]   they departed towards the towne of Denbigh, where they found Owen Glendouer abiding for their comming, with ten thousand of his Welshmen.   Here were the Frenchmen ioifullie receiued of the Welsh rebels, and so, when all things were prepared, they passed by Glamorganshire towards Worcester, and there burnt the suburbes : but, hearing of the kings approch, they suddenlie returned towards Wales.

*[They met
Glendower
at Denbigh.]*

*The suburbs
of Worcester
burnt.*

*[The French
and Welsh
retreated
when Henry
approached.*

Act II. sc. iii.—Moved by the prayers of his wife and daughter-in-law the Earl of Northumberland determines to seek refuge for a while in Scotland, though he would fain "go to meete the Archbishop" (l. 65).   But the historical fact is that Scrope was executed before Henry marched against Northumberland, who,

[*Hol.* iii. 530/2/35.]   hearing that his counsell was bewraied, and his confederats brought to confusion, through too much hast of the archbishop of Yorke, with three hundred horsse got him to Berwike.   The king comming forward quickelie, wan the castell of

---

[1] Wrongly styled "Duke of Lancaster" (l. 82) by Shakspere. This title was borne by Henry Prince of Wales.—*Rot. Parl.*, iii. 425/1.

[2] In a writ addressed to the Sheriff of Hereford, and dated from Pomfret Castle, "vii die Augusti" [1405], Henry says that the arrival of the French at Milford Haven "ad nostrum jam noviter pervenit intellectum."—*Rymer*, viii. 405. The French embarked about the end of July, 1405. When the wind favoured them, they set sail, and landed at Milford Haven.—*St. Denys*, iii. 328. According to *Chron. Normande* (370), they sailed on July 22, 1405, and remainèd in Wales until November 1 next following.

The earle of
Northumber-
land (and
Lord
Berdolph
fled to
Scotland.)
Warkewoorth. Wherevpon the earle of Northumberland, not
thinking himselfe in suertie at Berwike, fled with the lord Berdolfe
into Scotland, where they were receiued of Dauid lord Fleming.[1]

Act III. sc. i.—A note of time occurs at l. 60, which, if we could
ignore historic and dramatic contradictions, would enable us to say
that the Third Act opens in 1407. Henry calls to mind how "eight
yeares since,"—that is, in 1399,—Northumberland had been his
trustiest friend. Yet this memory presents itself in the historical year
1405, before the end of Archbishop Scrope's rebellion was known. We
need not, however, concern ourselves about years, for but a few dramatic days have elapsed since the battle of Shrewsbury.[2] Chronology
being thus travestied, the news that "Glendour is dead" (l. 103) is not
liable to question because he survived Henry; nor is anything gained
if we accept the erroneous date[3] given in the following excerpt :

Owen
Glendower
endeth his
life in great
miserie.
[Hol. iii. 536/1/1.] The Welsh rebell Owen Glendouer made
an end of his wretched life in this tenth yeare [1408-9] of king
Henrie his reigne; being driuen now in his latter time (as we find
recorded) to such miserie, that, in manner despairing of all comfort,
he fled into desert places and solitarie caues; where, being destitute
of all releefe and succour, dreading to shew his face to anie
creature, and finallie lacking meat to susteine nature, for meere
hunger and lacke of food, [he] miserablie pined awaie and died.

Act IV. scc. i.-ii.—From the ensuing passages were derived the
scenes in which the suppression of Archbishop Scrope's revolt is
dramatized. Before the rebellion broke out "the king was minded to
haue gone into Wales against the Welsh rebels, that, vnder their
cheefteine Owen Glendouer, ceassed not to doo much mischeefe still
against the English subiects" (Hol. iii. 529/1/51).

---

[1] Northumberland sealed a letter written at Berwick-upon-Tweed on June
11, 1405.—Rot. Parl., iii. 605/1. Before his flight he delivered Berwick to the
Scots.—Ott., 257. In the same month of June, ere Henry reached Berwick,
the Scots burnt the town and retreated.—Rot. Parl., iii. 605/2. Ott., 257.

[2] T.-A., 285.

[3] Pennant says, without citing any authority, that Glendower died on
September 20, 1415.—Tour in Wales, 1778, p. 368. But in the following year
Sir Gilbert Talbot was licensed to receive Glendower's submission. On
February 24, 1416, powers were granted by Henry V. "ad Communicandum
& Tractandum cum Meredith ap Owyn, Filio Owyni de Glendourdy, de &
super certis Materiis, praefato Gilberto per Nos injunctis & declaratis, Et tam
ad praedictum Owinum, quàm alios Rebelles nostros Wallenses, ad Obedientiam
& Gratias nostras, si se ad eas petendum optulerint, nomine nostro Admitten-
dum & Recipiendum," . . . Rymer, ix. 330, 331. Mr. Gairdner wrote to me :
"But his [Glendower's] obit was no doubt observed in some churches in Wales,
by which the day of his death would have been long preserved, while the year,
I take it, was a mere false inference on Pennant's part."

[*Hol.* iii. 529/1/56.]   But at the same time, to his further dis- *A new conspiracie against king Henrie by the earle of Northumberland & others.*
quieting, there was a conspiracie put in practise against him at
home by the earle of Northumberland, who had conspired with
Richard Scroope, archbishop of Yorke, Thomas Mowbraie, earle
marshall, sonne to Thomas duke of Norfolke, (who for the quarrell
betwixt him and king Henrie had beene banished, as ye haue
heard,) the lords Hastings, Fauconbridge,[1] Berdolfe, and diuerse
others. It was appointed that they should meet altogither with
their whole power, vpon Yorkeswold, at a daie assigned, and that
the earle of Northumberland should be cheefteine ; promising to [*Northumberland promised to ioin them with a number of Scots. Scrope deuised articles setting forth the grieuances of the nobility and commons.*]
bring with him a great number of Scots. The archbishop, accom-
panied with the earle marshall, deuised certeine articles of such
matters, as it was supposed that not onelie the commonaltie of the
Realme, but also the nobilitie found themselues greeued with :
which articles they shewed first vnto such of their adherents as
were neere about them, & after sent them abroad to their freends
further off; assuring them that, for redresse of such oppressions,
they would shed the *last* drop of blood in their bodies,[2] if need
were.

The archbishop, not meaning to staie after he saw himselfe *The archbishop of Yorke one of the cheefe conspirators.*
accompanied with a great number of men, that came flocking to
Yorke to take his part in this quarrell, foorthwith discouered his
enterprise ; causing the articles aforesaid to be set vp in the publike
streets of the citie of Yorke, and vpon the gates of the monasteries,
that ech man might vnderstand the cause that mooued him to rise
in armes against the king : the reforming whereof did not yet
apperteine vnto him.[3]   Herevpon, knights, esquiers, gentlemen,
yeomen, and other of the commons, as well of the citie townes
and countries about, being allured either for desire of change, or

---

[1] In *Rot. Parl.*, iii. 604/1, John " Fauconberge," Ralph Hastings, and John
" Colvyle de Dale," are styled " Chivalers."

[2] With "they would shed the *last* drop of blood in their bodies," cp.
Mowbray's threat (IV. ii. 43, 44) that, if the articles were rejected,

> " . . . we ready are to trie our fortunes,
> To the *last* man."

[3] Westmoreland, addressing the Archbishop, denies the "neede of any such
redresse " as Scrope speaks of, and adds (IV. i. 98) : " Or if there were, *it not
belongs to you.*"

else for desire to see a reformation in such things as were
mentioned in the articles, assembled togither in great numbers;
and the archbishop, comming foorth amongst them clad in armor,[1]
incouraged, exhorted, and (by all meanes he could) pricked them
foorth to take the enterprise in hand, and manfullie to continue in
their begun purpose; promising forgiuenesse of sinnes to all them,
whose hap it was to die in the quarrell: and thus not onelie all
the citizens of Yorke, but all other in the countries about, that
were able to beare weapon, came to the archbishop, and the earle
marshall. In deed, the respect that men had to the archbishop
caused them to like the better of the cause, since the grauitie of
his age, his integritie of life, and incomparable learning, with the
reuerend aspect of his amiable personage, mooued all men to haue
him in no small estimation.

The king, aduertised of these matters, meaning to preuent
them, left his iournie into Wales, and marched with all speed
towards the north parts. Also Rafe Neuill, earle of Westmerland,
that was not farre off, togither with the lord Iohn of Lancaster the
kings sonne, being informed of this rebellious attempt, assembled
togither such power as they might make, and, togither with those
which were appointed to attend on the said lord Iohn to defend
the borders against the Scots, (as the lord Henrie Fitzhugh, the
lord Rafe Eeuers, the lord Robert Umfreuill, & others,) made forward against the rebels; and, comming into a plaine within the
forrest of Galtree,[2] caused their standards to be pitched downe in
like sort as the archbishop had pitched his, ouer against them,
being farre stronger in number of people than the other; for (as
some write) there were of the rebels at the least twentie thousand
men.

When the earle of Westmerland perceiued the force of the
aduersaries, and that they laie still and attempted not to come

The arch-
bishop in
armor.

The estima-
tion which
men had of
the arch-
bishop of
Yorke.

The earle of
Westmer-
land and the
lord Iohn of
Lancaster
the kings
sonne pre-
pare them-
selues to
resist the
kings
enimies.

The forest of
Galtree.

---

[1] Prince John reproues the Archbishop for appearing "here, an *yron man*"
(IV. ii. 8). With the Prince's complimentary words (ll. 16-22), cp. what is
said of Scrope in the last passage of this paragraph, "In deed, the respect," &c.

[2] The two armies met on May 29, 1405, at "Shupton [Shipton] sur le More,
bien pres la Citee d'Everwyk."—*Rot. Parl.*, iii. 605/1. Galtres Forest formerly
reached from York to Aldborough.—*Bartholomew, s.v.*

forward vpon him, he subtillie deuised how to quaile their purpose; The subtill policie of the earle of Westmerland.
and foorthwith dispatched messengers vnto the archbishop to
vnderstand the cause as it were of that great assemblie, and for
what cause (contrarie to the kings peace) they came so in a[r]mour.
The archbishop answered, that he tooke nothing in hand *against*
the kings *peace*,[1] but that whatsoeuer he did, tended rather to The archbishops protestation why he had on him armes.
aduance the peace and quiet of the common-wealth, than other-
wise; and where he and his companie were in armes, it was for
feare of the king, to whom he could haue no free accesse, by reason
of such a multitude of flatterers as were about him; and therefore
he mainteined that his purpose to be good & profitable, as well for
the king himselfe, as for the realme, if men were willing to vnder-
stand a truth: & herewith he shewed foorth a scroll, in which the [Scrope sent Westmoreland a scroll containing the articles.]
articles were written wherof before ye haue heard.

The messengers, returning to the earle of Westmerland, shewed
him what they had heard & brought from the archbishop.   When
he had read the articles, [*p.* 530] he shewed in word and countenance
outwardly that he *liked*[2] of the archbishops holie and vertuous [Westmoreland affected to like them.]
intent and purpose; promising that he and his would prosecute the
same in assisting the archbishop, who, reioising hereat, gaue credit
to the earle, and persuaded the earle marshall (against his will as
it were) to go with him to a place appointed for them to commune [Mowbray was persuaded by Scrope to confer with Westmoreland.]
togither.   Here, when they were met with like number on either
part, the articles were read ouer, and, without anie more adoo,
the earle of Westmerland and those that were with him agreed
to doo their best, to see that a reformation might be had, according
to the same.

The earle of Westmerland, vsing more policie than the rest: The earle of Westmerldds politike dealing.
"Well" (said he) "then our trauell is come to the wished end;
"and where our people haue beene long in armour, let them depart
"home to their woonted trades and occupations: in the meane [He proposed that they should drink
"time *let vs drinke togither*[3] in signe of agreement, that the people

---

[1] The Archbishop says to Prince John (IV. ii. 31): "I am not here *against* your fathers *peace*."

[2] Prince John says of the articles (IV. ii. 54): "I *like* them all, and do allow them well."

[3] Cp. Prince John's words (IV. ii. 63): "*Lets drinke together* friendly, and embrace."

together in
sight of the
two armies.]
"on both sides maie see it, and know that it is true, that we be

[Meanwhile
a message
was sent to
the rebels
that they
might
depart, for
peace was
concluded.]
"light at a point." They had no sooner shaken hands togither,
but that a knight was sent streight waies from the archbishop, to
bring word to the people that there was peace concluded; commanding ech man to laie aside his armes, and to resort home to
their houses. The people, beholding such tokens of peace, as
shaking of hands, and drinking togither of the lords in louing
manner, they being alreadie wearied with the vnaccustomed trauell

They
accordingly
left the
field, but
Westmore-
land's forces
increased.]
of warre, brake vp their field and returned homewards; but, in the
meane time, whilest the people of the archbishops side withdrew
awaie, the number of the contrarie part increased, according to
order giuen by the earle of Westmerland; and yet the archbishop

The arch-
bishop of
Yorke and
the earle
marshall
arrested,
perceiued not that he was déceiued, vntill the earle of Westmerland arrested both him and the earle marshall, with diuerse other.
Thus saith *Walsingham.*

I quote another account which Holinshed gives, because two details
were taken from it by Shakspere; namely, that the conference of the
royal officers with Scrope and Mowbray was held—as Westmoreland
proposes—" *iust* distance tweene our *armies* " (IV. i. 226); and that
the rebels submitted to Prince John.

Bison.
[Another
account is
that, in a
conference
midway
between the
armies,
Westmore-
land per-
suaded
Scrope and
Mowbray to
trust the
king's mercy
by submis-
sion to
Prince
John.]
[*Hol.* iii. 530/1/38.] But others write somwhat otherwise of
this matter; affirming that the earle of Westmerland, in deed, and
the lord Rafe Eeuers, procured the archbishop and the earle
marshall, to come to a communication with them, vpon a ground
iust in the midwaie betwixt both the *armies;* where the earle of
Westmerland in talke declared to them how perilous an enterprise
they had taken in hand, so to raise the people, and to mooue
warre against the king; aduising them therefore to submit themselues without further delaie vnto the kings mercie, and his sonne
the lord Iohn, who was present there in the field with banners
spred, redie to trie the matter by dint of sword, if they refused
this counsell: and therefore he willed them to remember themselues well; &, if they would not yeeld and craue the kings pardon,
he bad them doo their best to defend themselues.

Herevpon as well the archbishop as the earle marshall submitted themselues vnto the king, and to his sonne the lord Iohn
that was there present, and returned not to their armie. Where-

vpon their troops scaled and fled their waies; but, being pursued, [The rebels dispersed because Scrope and Mowbray did not return to them.] manie were taken, manie slaine, and manie spoiled of that that they had about them, & so permitted to go their waies.   Howsoeuer the matter was handled, true it is that the archbishop, and the earle marshall were brought to Pomfret to the king, who in this meane while was aduanced thither with his power; and from thence he went to Yorke, whither the prisoners were also brought, The archbishop of Yorke, the earle marshall, & others put to death. Abr. Fl. out of Thom. Walsin. Hypod. pag. 168. and there beheaded the morrow after Whitsundaie [June 8, 1405] in a place without the citie : that is to vnderstand, the archbishop himselfe, the earle marshall, sir Iohn Lampleie, and sir William[1] Plumpton.   ¶ Unto all which persons, though indemnitie were promised, yet was the same to none of them at anie hand performed.

Act IV. sc. iii.—The surrender of Sir John Colevile of the Dale[2] to Falstaff is a comic incident which appears to have been suggested by the mere record of Colevile's execution at Durham, when Henry was marching against Northumberland.

[*Hol.* iii. 530/2/31.]   At his [Henry's] comming to Durham, the The lords [—and Sir John Colevile of the Dale—] executed. lord Hastings, the lord Fauconbridge, sir Iohn Colleuill of the Dale, and sir Iohn Griffith, being conuicted of the conspiracie, were there beheaded.

Whether the historic time of this scene be 1405[3] or 1412 is doubtful, for, shortly before leaving the stage, Prince John says (l. 83) :

I heare the King my father is sore sick.

---

[1] *William*] *Robert* Hol.

[2] It appears that in the month of May,—but before the Archbishop and Earl Marshal were arrested,—the rebels under Sir John Fauconberg, Sir Ralph Hastings, and Sir John Colvyle de Dale, were embattled near Topcliff, until ("tan que") Prince John and Westmoreland "eux fesoit voider le champ, & eux myst a fuyte & sur lour fuier feurent pris." On May 29 the troops of Prince John and Westmoreland were ranged in order of battle upon Shipton on the Moor, confronting the forces of Scrope and Mowbray, "armes & arraies a faire de guerre, . . . & en tiel arraie les ditz Richard [Scrope] & Thomas [Mowbray] & autres lour complices feuront pris mesme le jour sur le dit More."—*Rot. Parl.*, iii. 604/2 ; 605/1.

[3] *Halle* (35) makes contemptuous mention of a story that "at the howre of the execucion of" Archbishop Scrope, "the kyng at the same tyme syttyng at dyner . . . was incontinently striken with a leprey," and (45) denies that the "sore sodayn disease" which caused Henry's death was a "Lepry stryken by the handes of God as folysh Friers before declared" (see p. 160 below). According to *Eulog.* (408) the king, immediately after Scrope's execution (June 8, 1405), "quasi leprosus apparere cepit." Another account is that, in 1408, Henry, after his return from York, where he had been occupied with punishing Northumberland's accomplices, "decidit in languorem et extasim consequenter, ita ut mortuus putaretur apud Mortlake."—*Ott.*, 263.

Under the latter date Holinshed first makes mention of the sickness which eventually proved fatal to Henry.

[*Hol.* iii. 540/2/72.]   He [Henry] held his Christmas this yeare at Eltham, being sore vexed with sicknesse, so that it was thought sometime, [*p.* 541] that he had beene dead: notwithstanding it pleased God that he somwhat recouered his strength againe, and so passed that Christmasse with as much ioy as he might.

Act IV. sc. iv.—Henry died on March 20, 1413 (*Wals.*, ii. 289), about which time we might suppose this scene to open, if dramatic chronology were reconcilable with historic dates.   Soon after entering the King says to Clarence (ll. 20-26):

> How chance thou art not with the prince thy brother ?   20
> He loues thee, and thou dost neglect him, Thomas ;
> Thou hast a better place in his affection
> Then all thy brothers : cherrish it, my boy ;
> And noble offices thou maist effect   24
> Of mediation, after I am dead,
> Between his greatnesse and thy other brethren.

It is just possible that a hint for these lines was taken from part of a long speech addressed by Henry IV. to his eldest son (*Stow*, 554-556), in which the King—who was then on his deathbed—expressed a fear lest Clarence's ambition and the Prince's haughtiness might cause strife between the two brothers.

The King advises Clarence to refrain from chiding Prince Henry for faults,

> Till that his passions, like a whale on ground,
> Confound themselues with working.

Perhaps the source of this metaphor was the following account of a stranded whale :

[*Hol.* iii. 1259/2/32.]   The ninth of Iulie [1574.   1573 according to Harrison's *Chronologie* (*Shakspere's England*, ed. F. J. Furnivall, App. I. lvi.)], at six of the clocke at night, in the Ile

of Thanet besid[e]s Ramesgate, in the parish of saint Peter vnder the cliffe, a monstrous fish or whale of the sea did shoot himselfe on shore ; where, for want of water, beating himselfe on the sands, he died about six of the clocke on the next morning, before which time he roared, and was heard more than a mile on the land.

As Westmoreland announces Prince John's success (ll. 83-87), time recedes until 1405 is again the historic date, but, when Harcourt brings tidings that Northumberland and Bardolph, "*with a great power of English and of Scots*," have been overthrown by the Sheriff of Yorkshire (ll. 97-99), we are transported to the historical year 1408. Northumberland's defeat is thus described :

[*Hol.* iii. 534/1/20.] The earle of Northumberland, and the *1408*
lord Bardolfe, after they had beene in Wales, in France, and
Flanders, to purchase aid against king Henrie, were returned
backe into Scotland, and had remained there now for the space of
a whole yeare: and, as their euill fortune would, whilest the king
held a councell of the nobilitie at London, the said earle of North- *The earle of*
umberland and lord Bardolfe, in a dismall houre, *with a great* *the lord*
power of Scots, returned into England; recouering diuerse of the earls *Bardolfe*
castels and seigniories, for the people in great numbers resorted *England.*
vnto them. Heerevpon, incouraged with hope of good successe,
they entred into Yorkeshire, & there began to destroie the
countrie. At their comming to Threske, they published a proclamation, signifieng that they were come in comfort of the English
nation, as to releeue the common-wealth; willing all such as loued
the libertie of their countrie, to repaire vnto them, with their
armor on their backes, and in defensible wise to assist them.

The king, aduertised hereof, caused a great armie to be
assembled, and came forward with the same towards his enimies;
but, yer the king came to Notingham, sir Thomas, or (as other
copies haue) Rafe Rokesbie, shiriffe of Yorkeshire, assembled the *The shiriffe*
forces of the countrie to resist the earle and his power; comming *(assembled*
to Grimbaut brigs, beside Knaresbourgh, there to stop them the *the forces of*
passage; but they, returning aside, got to Weatherbie, and so to *them).*
Tadcaster, and finallie came forward vnto Bramham more, neere
to Haizelwood, where they chose their ground meet to fight vpon.
The shiriffe was as readie to giue battell as the earle to receiue it, *His hard*
and so, with a standard of S. George spred, set fiercelie vpon the *fight.*
earle, who, vnder a standard of his owne armes, incountred his
aduersaries with great manhood. There was a sore incounter and
cruell conflict betwixt the parties, but in the end the victorie fell to
the shiriffe. The lord Bardolfe was taken, but sore wounded, so *[Lord*
that he shortlie after died of the hurts. ¶ As for the earle of *taken.]*
Northumberland, he was slaine outright: . . . This battell was *The earle of*
fought the ninteenth day of Februarie [1408]. *land slaine.*

Hardly has the news of Northumberland's defeat been uttered ere
the King swoons, and historic time is again as it was when the scene
opened.

While the King is unconscious, Clarence mentions a portent [1] (l. 125):

The riuer hath thrice flowed, *no ebbe between.*

Holinshed says:

Abr. Fl. out of Fabian pag. 566. Three floods without ebbing between.

[*Hol.* iii. 540/1/45.] In this yeare [1411], and vpon the twelfth day of October, were three flouds in the Thames, the one following vpon the other, & *no ebbing betweene:* which thing no man then liuing could remember the like to be scene.

Act IV. sc. v.—My next excerpt is the well-known story which is dramatized in the "Crown Scene."

Hall.

[*Hol.* iii. 541/1/22.] During this his [Henry IV.'s] last sick-nesse, he caused his crowne (as some write) to be set on a pillow *[Henry IV. swooned, and was left for dead, with his crown on his pillow.]* at his beds head; [2] and suddenlie his pangs so sore troubled him, that he laie as though all his vitall spirits had beene from him departed. Such as were about him, thinking verelie that he had beene departed, couered his face with a linnen cloth.

The prince taketh awaie the crowne before his father was dead.

The prince, his sonne, being hereof aduertised, entered into the chamber, tooke awaie the crowne, and departed. The father, being suddenlie reuiued out of that trance, quicklie perceiued the lacke of his crowne; and, hauing knowledge that the prince his sonne *He is blamed of the king.* had taken it awaie, caused him to come before his presence, requiring of him what he meant so to misuse himselfe. The *His answer.* prince, with a good audacitie, answered: "Sir, to mine and all "mens iudgements you seemed dead in this world; wherefore I, as "your next heire apparant, tooke that as mine owne, and not as *A guiltie conscience in extremitie of sickness pincheth sore.* "yours." "Well, faire sonne" (said the king with a great sigh), "what right I had to it, God knoweth." "Well" (said the prince), "if you die king, I will haue the garland, and trust to keepe it "with the sword against all mine enimies, as you haue doone."

---

[1] Recorded by *Fab.* (576) under the 13th year of Henry IV. Clarence speaks of a threefold tide which occurred "a little time before" Edward III.'s death, and Gloucester is alarmed by "vnfather'd beires, and lothly births of nature" (IV. iv. 121-128), lately observed. I find no records of these latter portents. There may be an allusion to the wet summer of 1594—cp. *Mids. N. D.,* II. i. 82-114—in Gloucester's remark that "the seasons change their manners," &c. (ll. 123, 124).

[2] *Mons.* (ii. 435), who was, I suppose, *Halle's* authority for the following story, says that, "comme il est accoutumé de faire au pays," the crown was placed "sur une couche assez près de lui" [Henry].

Then said the king, "I commit all to God, and remember you to
"doo well." With that he turned himselfe in his bed, and shortlie *The death of Henrie the*
after departed to God in a chamber of the abbats of Westminster *fourth.*
called Ierusalem, the twentith daie of March, in the yeare 1413,
and in the yeare of his age 46 : when he had reigned thirteene
yeares, fiue moneths, and od daies, in great perplexitie and little
pleasure. . . .

The King's "very latest counsaile" (l. 183) to Prince Henry is
illustrated by two passages from Holinshed.   Advising engagement in
"forraine quarrells" as an expedient for occupying the "giddie
mindes" of unfaithful subjects, Henry says (ll. 210-213) that he

> had a purpose now
> To leade out manie to the Holy Land,
> Lest rest and lying stil might make them looke   212
> Too neare vnto my state.

Holinshed thus describes the warlike preparations which were made
—as Fabyan asserts[1]—with the design of reconquering Jerusalem :

[*Hol.* iii. 540/2/60.]   In this fourteenth and last yeare of king *Fabian.*
Henries reigne, a councell was holden in the white friers in London ; *The k. meant to haue made a iournie against the Infidels.*
at the which, among other things, order was taken for ships and
gallies to be builded and made readie, and all other things necessarie to be prouided for a voiage which he meant to make into the
holie land, there to recouer the citie of Ierusalem from the
Infidels. . . .

[*Hol.* iii. 541/1/5.]   The morrow after Candlemas daie began a *1413*
parlement, which he had called at London, but he departed this *A parlement.*
life before the same parlement was ended : for now that his prouisions were readie, and that he was furnished with sufficient
treasure, soldiers, capteins, vittels, munitions, tall ships, strong
gallies, and all things necessarie for such a roiall iournie as he

---

[1] These preparations have perhaps been postdated, and their object (an
expedition against France) misunderstood.   On April 18, 1412, a patent
(*Rymer*, viii. 730) was issued to press sailors "ad Deserviendum nobis in
quodam Viagio supra Mare infra breve faciendo"; and on July 12, 1412,
Henry acknowledges the loan of a thousand marks from the Archbishop of
Canterbury, for the expenses which "Nos, pro communi Commodo, circa
Prosecutionem & Adeptionem Juris nostri (Deo dante) in partibus Aquitanniæ,
ac alibi, in partibus Transmarinis, infra breve facere oportebit."—*Rymer*, viii.
760.   In August, 1412, the Duke of Clarence was sent with a strong force
("manu valida") to the assistance of the Armagnac faction.—*Wals.* ii. 288.
On August 10 he landed at la Hogue-Saint-Vast.—*Chron. Normande*, 418.

The K. sick
of an
apoplexie.
Hall.
pretended to take into the holie land, he was eftsoones taken with
a sore sicknesse, which was not a leprosie, striken by the hand of
God (saith maister *Hall*) as foolish friers imagined; but a verie
apoplexie, of the which he languished till his appointed houre, and
had none other greefe nor maladie.

As the scene ends Henry recognizes the fulfilment of a prophecy
that he "should not die but in Jerusalem" (l. 238). Holinshed relates
how this prediction was accomplished:

Fabian.
[*Hol.* iii. 541/1/63.] We find, that he was taken with his last
sickenesse, while he was making his praiers at saint Edwards
shrine, there as it were to take his leaue, and so to proceed foorth
[Henry
swooned
while pray-
ing at the
shrine of
Edward the
Confessor.]
on his iournie: he was so suddenlie and greeuouslie taken, that
such as were about him, feared lest he would haue died presentlie;
wherfore to releeue him (if it were possible) they bare him into a
chamber that was next at hand, belonging to the abbat of Westminster, where they laid him on a pallet before the fire, and vsed
all remedies to reuiue him. At length, he recouered his speech,
and, vnderstanding and perceiuing himselfe in a strange place
which he knew not, he willed to know if the chamber had anie
particular name; wherevnto answer was made, that it was called
Ierusalem. Then said the king: "Lauds be giuen to the father of
[A prophecy
that Henry
should
depart this
life in Jeru-
salem.]
"heauen, for now I know that I shall die heere in this chamber;
"according to the prophesie of me declared, that I should depart
"this life in Ierusalem." [1]

---

[1] *Fab.* (576) says that, by a council held at White Friars on November 20,
1412, it was "concluded, that for the kynges great Iournaye that he entendyd
to take, in vysytynge of the holy Sepulcre of our Lord, certayne Galeys of warre
shuld be made, & other purueaunce concernynge the same Iournay." *Fab.*
then tells the story—which I quote from *Hol.*—of Henry's death in the Jerusalem Chamber. There can hardly be a doubt, however, that Henry accomplished a pilgrimage to Jerusalem before he ascended the throne. On November
18, 1392, the Venetian Senate granted the request of "Lord Henry of Lancaster,
Earl of Derby, Hereford, and Northampton, . . . the eldest son of the Duke
of Aquitaine" [John of Gaunt], that he might have "the hull of a galley, with
all necessary tackle, to visit the holy places."—*Ven. State PP.*, i. 33/107. On
November 30, 1392, the Senate decreed the expenditure of a sum of public
money to honour the Earl of Derby, the eldest son of the Duke of Lancaster,
"the intimate friend of our Signory, on this his coming to Venice, bound for
the Holy Sepulchre."—*Ibid.*, 33/108. And on March 31, 1393, the Grand
Council ordained that one hundred golden ducats of public money should be
expended to "honour the Earl of Derby, son of the Duke of Lancaster, on this
his return."—*Ibid.*, 34/110.

Act V. sc. ii.—The new King hears a vindicatory speech of the Lord Chief-Justice (ll. 73-101), by whom, in time past, he had been committed to prison for a gross act of lawlessness. I have mentioned above (p. 141) an insult offered by Prince Henry to the Chief-Justice, and I here quote the account which Holinshed gives of this matter. After his coronation Henry V. is said to have dismissed his unworthy associates,

[*Hol.* iii. 543/2/10.] and in their places he chose men of grauitie, wit, and high policie, by whose wise counsell he might at all times rule to his honour and dignitie; calling to mind how once, to his offense of the king his father, he had with his fist striken[1] the cheefe iustice for sending one of his minions (vpon desert) to prison: when the iustice stoutlie commanded himselfe also streict to ward, & he (then prince) obeied.

[When Henry V. came to the throne he chose wise counsellors.

[Once, when he was Prince, he struck the Chief-Justice.]

In his answer to the Chief-Justice the King repeats Henry IV.'s words (ll. 108-112):

> Happie am I that haue a man so bold,
> That dares do iustice on my proper sonne;
> And no lesse happie, hauing such a sonne,
> That would deliuer vp his greatnesse so,
> Into the hands of Iustice!

The story of Prince Henry's rudeness to the Chief-Justice made its earliest known appearance in Sir Thomas Elyot's *Gouernour*, 1531[2] (ff. 122-123 verso). Stow copied Elyot (557, 558). I quote *The Gouernour* because it contains the remark attributed to Henry IV., which Holinshed omitted.

---

[1] The following passage in *Redman* (11) is the earliest known authority for the blow given by Prince Henry to the Chief-Justice, and the consequent supersession of the Prince in the Council by the Duke of Clarence: "Senatu movebatur, nec in curiam aditus ei patebat; et illius fama hæsit ad metas, quod summum judicem, litibus dirimendis et causarum cognitionibus præpositum, manu percuteret, cum is unum in custodiam tradidisset ex cujus familiaritate voluptatem mirificam Henricus perciperet. Eam dignitatem, quam is amisit, Thomas illius frater, Dux Clarensis, est consecutus." Mr. Cole proves that Redman's *Vita Hen. V.* was "composed between 1536 . . . and 1544."—*Ibid.*, pp. ix., x.

[2] Sir N. H. Nicolas pointed out (*Placitorum Abbreviatio*, pp. 256, 257) a likely source for this fiction; and in an exhaustive paper entitled "The Story of Prince Henry of Monmouth and Chief-Justice Gascoign," Mr. F. Solly-Flood has given details from which it appears that, on account of a judgment delivered towards the close of Edward I.'s reign, in the case of Roger de Hengham *versus* William de Brews, the Chief-Justice of the King's Bench was reviled in open court by the defendant. The record (Rot. coram Rege, m. 33, 34 Ed. I., m. 75) of the Court's judgment against De Brews for his misbehaviour contains the following passage: "Quæ quidem, videlicet *contemptus et inobedientia* [cp. the words—"contempt and disobedience"—attributed by Elyot to the Chief-Justice] tam ministris ipsius Domini Regis quam sibi ipsi aut curiæ suæ facta valde sunt odiosa et hoc nuper apparuit cum idem Dominus Rex filium suum primogenitum et carissimum Edwardum Principem Walliæ

The moste renomed prince kinge Henry the fifte, late kynge of
Englande, durynge the life of his father was noted to be fierce [*fol.*
122 *verso*] and of wanton courage : it hapned that one of his
seruantes, whom he well fauored, for felony by hym committed
was arrayned at the Kynges benche, wherof he being aduertised,
and incensed by light persones aboute hym, in furious rage came
hastily to the barre, where his seruant stode as a prisoner, and
commaunded hym to be vngyued and sette at libertie ; where at
all men were abasshed, reserued the chiefe iustice, who humbly
exhorted the prince to be contented that his seruaunt mought be
ordred accordyng to the auncient lawes of this realme, or, if he
wolde haue hym saued from the rigour of the lawes, that he shuld
optaine, if he moughte, of the kynge his father his gracious
pardon, wherby no lawe or iustice sbulde be derogate.   With
whiche answere the prince nothynge appeased, but rather more
inflamed, endeuored hym selfe to take away his seruaunt.   The
iuge (consideringe the perilous example and inconuenience that
moughte therby ensue) with a valiant spirite and courage commaunded the prince, vpon his alegeance, to leue the prisoner and
departe his way.   With whiche commandement the prince being
set all in a fury, all chafed & in a terrible maner, came vp to the
place of [*fol.* 123] iugement ; (men thinkyng that he wolde haue
slayne the iuge or haue done to hym some damage ;) but the
iuge, sittyng styll without mouynge, declarynge the maiestie of
the kynges place of iugement, and with an assured and bolde
countenance, hadde to the prince these wordes folowyng :

"Sir, remembre your selfe : I kepe here the place of the king

pro eo quod quædam verba grossa et acerba cuidam ministro suo dixerat et
hospicio suo fere per dimidium annum amovit nec ipsum filium suum in con-
spectu suo venire permisit quousque predicto ministro de predicta transgres-
sione satisfecerat."—*Solly-Flood*, 106.   Here we have evidence of verbal abuse
bestowed on a royal officer by the first Prince of Wales, whose punishment
resembles that which, according to Redman, Prince Henry suffered for striking
the Chief-Justice. (Cp. "nec in curiam aditus ei patebat," p. 161, note 1,
above.) Mr. Solly-Flood informs us that the Rotuli coram Rege and the Con-
trolment rolls embrace every commitment by the King's Bench either *ad
respondendum* or *in penam*.   He carefully examined all the entries made
during the reign of Henry IV. on these rolls,—which are perfect throughout
this reign,—and found no record of Prince Henry's commitment for any
offence, or of the commitment of any one during Henry IV.'s reign for the
offences attributed to the Prince by Elyot and Redman.—*Solly-Flood*, 102.

[One of
Prince
Henry's
servants was
arraigned at
the King's
Bench for
felony.]

[The Prince
came to the
bar and
demanded
the release
of his
servant.]

[The Chief-
Justice
admonished
the Prince
to let the
law take its
course, or
obtain a
pardon from
the King.]

[The Prince
endeavoured
to take away
his servant,

[and, being
commanded
to desist,

[went up to
the Chief-
Justice in a
menacing
manner.]

[But the
Chief-
Justice,
without
blenching,
asserted his
authority
as the
King's
represent-
ative,

"your soueraigne lorde and father,[1] to whom ye owe double
"obedience; wherfore eftsones in his name I charge you desiste
"of your wilfulnes and vnlaufull entreprise, & from hensforth gyue
"good example to those whiche hereafter shall be your propre [and bade the Prince go to the prison of the King's Bench.]
"subiects. And nowe for your contempt and disobedience go you
"to the prisone of the kynges benche, where vnto I committe you;
"and remayne ye there prisoner vntill the pleasure of the kyng
"your father be further knowen."

With whiche wordes beinge abasshed, and also wondrynge at [The Prince obeyed; whereat his servants, being indignant, laid the whole matter before the King. King Henry answered that [he was happy to have a judge who ministered justice fearlessly, and a son who obeyed justice.]
the meruailous grauitie of that worshipful Iustice, the noble prince,
layinge his waipon aparte, doinge reuerence, departed, and wente
to the kynges benche as he was commaunded. Wherat his
seruantes, disdainyng, came and shewed to the kynge all the hole
affaire. Whereat he a whiles studienge, after, as a man all
rauisshed with [*fol.* 123 *verso*] gladnesse, holdyng his eien and
handes vp towarde heuen, abrayded, sayinge with a loude voice:

"O mercifull god, how moche am I, aboue all other men,
"bounde to your infinite goodnes! specially for that ye haue
"gyuen me a iuge who feareth nat to ministre iustice, and also
"a sonne who can suffre semblably and obey iustice!"

Before leaving the stage Henry says (l. 134; 141, 142):
 Now call we our high court of parliament: . . .
 Our coronation done, we wil accite
 (As I before remembred) all our state.
Holinshed briefly notices the first Parliament of Henry V.

[*Hol.* iii. 543/2/44.] Immediatlie after Easter he called a *A parlement [called by Henry V.].*
parlement, in which diuerse good statutes, and wholesome ordin-

---

[1]
 I then did vse the person of your father;
 The image of his power lay then in me: . . .
 Your Highnesse pleased to forget my place,
 The maiestie and power of law and iustice,
 The image of the King whom I presented,
 And strooke me in my very seate of iudgement; . . . 80
The writer of *The Famous Victories of Henry the fifth*, 1598, made the Judge—
to whom Prince Henry had given "a boxe on the eare"—say (sc. iv. ll. 99-102,
p. 14): "in striking me in this place, you greatly abuse me, and not me onely,
but also your father: whose liuely person here in this place I doo represent."
This assertion has—accidentally, no doubt—the same scope as the doctrine laid
down by the Court of King's Bench in regard to William de Brews's contempt:
"Et quia sicut honor et reuerentia qui ministris ipsius Domini Regis ratione
officii sui [fiunt] ipsi Regi attribuuntur, sic dedecus et contemptus ministris suis
facta eidem Regi attribuuntur."—*Solly-Flood*, 106.

ances, for the preseruation and aduancement of the common-
wealth were deuised and established.

Act V. sc. v.—Falstaff interrupts the royal procession on its return
after Henry's coronation, and is sent by the King into banishment
with Henry's other "misleaders"; all of whom have been forbidden to
come within "*ten mile*" of 'our person'; though they are to receive
pensions now for "competence of life," and "aduancement" in future,
if they reform themselves (ll. 67-74). Holinshed thus records Henry's
coronation and altered behaviour :

*The day of
king Henries
coronation
a very
tempestuous
day.*

[*Hol.* iii. 543/1/54.] He was crowned the ninth of Aprill,
being Passion sundaie, which was a sore, ruggie, and tempestuous
day, with wind, snow, and sleet; that men greatlie maruelled
thereat, making diuerse interpretations what the same might
signifie. But this king euen at first appointing with himselfe, to
shew that in his person princelie honors should change publike
manners, he determined to put on him the shape of a new man.

*A notable
example of
a woorthie
prince
[, who, when
he became
King,
banished his
unruly
mates].*

For whereas aforetime he had made himselfe a companion vnto
misrulie mates of dissolute order and life, he now banished them
all from his presence (but not vnrewarded, or else vnpreferred);
inhibiting them vpon a great paine, not once to approch, lodge, or
soiourne within *ten miles* of his court or presence : . . .

The following sketch of Henry IV.'s character and circumstances
may have afforded Shakspere some hints.

His stature.

[*Hol.* iii. 541/2/20.] This king was of a meane stature, well
proportioned, and formallie compact; quicke and liuelie, and of a

*[His
character.]*

stout courage. In his latter daies he shewed himselfe so gentle,
that he gat more loue amongst the nobles and people of this
realme, than he had purchased malice and euill will in the
beginning.

But yet to speake a truth, by his proceedings, after he had
atteined to the crowne, what with such taxes, tallages, subsidies,
and exactions as he was constreined to charge the people with;
and what by punishing such as, mooued with disdeine to see him
vsurpe the crowne (contrarie to the oth taken at his entring into
this land, vpon his returne from exile), did at sundrie times rebell
against him; he wan himselfe more hatred, than in all his life time
(if it had beene longer by manie yeares than it was) had beene
possible for him to haue weeded out & remooued.

VIII. HENRY V.

HENRY V. appears to have received the Dauphin Lewis's [1] gift of tennis-balls in Lent, 1414.[2] This date marks the commencement of historic time in *The Life of Henry the Fift;* and the play ends with Katharine of Valois's betrothal in May, 1420.

Act I. Prologue.—

O for a Muse of Fire, that would ascend
    The brightest Heauen of Inuentiön,
A Kingdome for a Stage, Princes to Act,
And Monarchs to behold the swelling Scene!
Then should the Warlike Harry, like himselfe,
Assume the Port of Mars; and at his heeles
(Leasht in, like.Hounds) should Famine, Sword, and Fire
Crouch for employment.   8

A speech [3] attributed to the "Warlike Harry" contains a parable which may have suggested the picture of these crouching hounds of Famine, Sword, and Fire. On January 2, 1419, Rouen, despairing of succour, after five months' siege,[4] yielded to the pressure of famine so far as to open communication with Henry through ambassadors.

[*Hol.* iii. 567/1/39.] One of them, seene in the ciuill lawes, was appointed to declare the message in all their names; who, shewing himselfe more rash than wise, more arrogant than learned, first tooke vpon him to shew wherin the glorie of victorie consisted; aduising the king not to shew his manhood in famishing a multi-

A presumptuous orator.

---

[1] Lewis was a contemporary of the events dramatized in *Hen. V.*, Acts I.-IV. He died on December 18, 1415.—*Mons.*, iii. 366; *Journal*, xv. 210. His brother, the Dauphin John, died on April 3 (*Journal*, 216) or 4 (*Mons.*, iii. 408), 1417. During the historic time embraced by Act V. the Dauphin was Charles, who afterwards reigned as Charles VII., and is a character in 1 *Hen. VI.*

[2] "Eodem anno [1414] in Quadragesima rege existente apud Kenilworth, Karolus [*sc.* Ludovicus], regis Francorum filius, Dalphinus vocatus, misit pilas Parisianas ad ludendum cum pueris."—*Ott.*, 274. In 1414 Ash Wednesday fell on February 21.

[3] A speech, similar in outline, is attributed to Henry by *Redman* (55). I quote from it a passage which has some resemblance to that in which Henry takes credit to himself for employing the "meekest maid" to punish Rouen: "Benigne et clementer omnia me administrare nemo est qui non intelligat, cum fame potius quam flamma, ferro, aut sanguine, Rotomagum ad deditionem perpello."

[4] The forces blockading Rouen were ordered to take up their positions on August 1, 1418.—*Page*, 6. On January 2, 1419, Henry gave audience to the ambassadors from Rouen.—*Page*, 26-28. Rouen opened her gates on January 19, 1419.—*Page*, 41, 42. Page was present at the siege.—*Page*, 1.

[Henry
should allow
the people
without the
walls to
pass through
his lines,
and then
assault
Rouen.]
tude of poore, simple, and innocent people, but rather suffer such
miserable wretches, as laie betwixt the wals of the citie and the
trenches of his siege, to passe through the campe, that they might
get their liuing in other places; and then, if he durst manfullie
assault the citie, and by force subdue it, he should win both
worldlie fame, and merit great meed at the hands of almightie
God, for hauing compassion of the poore, needie, and indigent
people.

When this orator had said, the king, who no request lesse
suspected, than that which was thus desired, began a while to
muse; and, after he had well considered the craftie cautell of his
*The kings
answer to
this proud
message.*
enimies, with a fierce countenance, and bold spirit, he reprooued
them; both for their subtill dealing with him, and their malapert
presumption, in that they should seeme to go about to teach him
what belonged to the dutie of a conquerour.   And therefore, since
it appeared that the same was vnknowne vnto them, he declared
that the goddesse of battell, called *Bellona*, had three handmaidens, euer of necessitie attending vpon hir, as blood, fire, and
[He has
chosen
Famine—
the meekest
of Bellona's
handmaids—
to punish
Rouen.]
famine.   And whereas it laie in his choise to vse them all three,
(yea, two or one of them, at his pleasure,) he had appointed onelie
the meekest maid of those three damsels to punish them of that
citie, till they were brought to reason.

And whereas the gaine of a capteine, atteined by anie of the
said three handmaidens, was both glorious, honourable, and
woorthie of triumph: yet, of all the three, the yoongest maid,
which he meant to vse at that time, was most profitable and
[If the
people with-
out the
walls die,
those who
expelled
them from
Rouen must
bear the
blame.]
commodious.   And as for the poore people lieng in the ditches,
if they died through famine, the fault was theirs, that like cruell
tyrants had put them out of the towne, to the intent he should
slaie them; and yet had he saued their liues, so that, if anie
lacke of charitie was, it rested in them, and not in him.   But to
their cloked request, he meant not to gratifie them within so
much; but they should keepe them still to helpe to spend their
vittels.   And as 'to assault the towne, he told them that he
[He will
take his own
course to
win the
city.]
would they should know, he was both able and willing thereto,
as he should see occasion: but the choise was in his hand, to
tame them either with blood, fire, or famine, or with them all;

whereof he would take the choise at his pleasure, and not at theirs.

Act I. sc. i.—Henry Chichele Archbishop of Canterbury tells John Fordham Bishop of Ely [1] that a bill for disendowing the Church, which nearly passed in the eleventh year of Henry IV.'s reign, has been revived. If this bill were carried, the clergy must lose "the better halfe" of their "Possession":

> For all *the Temporall Lands,* which men deuout
> By Testament haue *giuen* to the Church,
> Would they strip from vs; being valu'd thus:
> As much as would *maintaine, to the* Kings *honor,*   12
> Full *fifteene Earles,* and *fifteene hundred Knights,*
> *Six thousand and two hundred good Esquires;*
> And, to *reliefe of* Lazars, and weake age
> Of indigent faint Soules, past corporall toyle,   16
> *A hundred Almes-houses,* right well supply'd;
> *And to* the *Coffers* of *the King,* beside,
> A *thousand pounds* by th'yeere. Thus runs the Bill.

Holinshed took from Halle (49) the following account of the renewal of this bill:

[*Hol.* iii. 545/2/6.] In the second yeare of his reigne, king *Anno Reg. 2.* Henrie called his high court of parlement, the last daie of Aprill, 1414 in the towne of Leicester; in which parlement manie profitable [Parliament at Leicester. lawes were concluded, and manie petitions mooued were for that time deferred. Amongst which, one was, that a bill exhibited in the parlement holden at Westminster, in the eleuenth yeare of king Henrie the fourth (which by reason the king was then troubled with ciuill discord, came to none effect), might now with good deliberation be pondered, and brought to some good conclusion. The effect of which supplication was, that *the temporall lands* *A bill* (deuoutlie *giuen,* and disordinatlie spent by religious, and other *exhibited to the parlemēt against the* spirituall persons) should be seized into the kings hands; sith the *clergie.* same might suffice to *mainteine, to the honor* of the king, and defense of the realme, *fifteene earles, fifteene hundred knights, six thousand and two hundred esquiers,* and *a hundred almesse-houses,* for *reliefe* onelie *of* the poore, impotent, and needie persons; *and the king* to haue cleerelie *to* his *coffers* twentie *thousand pounds:* with manie other prouisions and values of religious houses, which I passe ouer.

---

[1] Bishop of Ely from 1388 to 1425.—*Godwin,* 274.

My next excerpt shows how the danger was averted:

[*Hol.* iii. 545/2/29.] This bill was much noted, and more feared, among the religious sort, whom suerlie it touched verie neere; and therefore to find remedie against it, they determined to assaie all waies to put by and ouerthrow this bill: wherein they thought best to trie if they might mooue the kings mood with some sharpe inuention, that he should not regard the importunate petitions of the commons.[1]   Wherevpon, on a daie in the parlement, Henrie Chichelie archbishop of Canturburie made a pithie oration, wherein he declared, how not onelie the duchies of Normandie and Aqui-taine, with the counties of Anion and Maine, and the countrie of Gascoigne, were by vndoubted title apperteining to the king, as to the lawfull and onelie heire of the same; but also the whole realme of France, as heire to his great grandfather king Edward the third.[2]

Act I. sc. ii.—In presence of the assembled English peers, Henry calls upon Chichele to show whether the Salic law " or should or should not " bar the King's claim to France.   I exhibit in parallel columns Holinshed's version[3] of the Archbishop's speech and Shakspere's paraphrase of it.   Chichele inveighed

[The clergy resolved to divert Henry's attention from the disendowment bill.]

The archbishop of Canturburie oration in the parliament house.

---

[1] And this yere [1414] the kyng helde his Parlyament at Leyceter, where, amonge other thynges, the foresayd Bylle [*Fab.*, 575, 576] put vp by the Commons of the lande, for the Temporalties beynge in the Churche, as it is before [towchid in the xi yere of the iiiith Henry], was agayne mynded. In fere wherof, lest the kynge wolde therunto gyue any Comfortable Audyence, as testyfye some wryters, certayne Bysshoppes and other hede men of the Churche put y⁰ kyng in mynde to clayme his ryght in Fraunce; & for the exployte therof they offrede vnto hym great & notable summes.   By reason whereof y⁰ sayd byll was agayne put by, and the kynge sette his mynde for the Recouery of the same ; . . .—*Fab.*, 578.

When I said (*Henry V.*, revised ed., New Sh. Soc., p. viii) that " Hall seems to be the sole authority for the revival of the confiscation scheme in Henry the Fifth's reign," this passage in *Fab.* was unknown to me.

[2] There is not so much as an allusion to these claims of Henry in the accounts of the Leicester Parliament's proceedings given by *Rot. Parl.* and *Elmham* (cap. xvii.).   When Parliament met at Westminster, on November 19, 1414, the Chancellor (Henry Beaufort) opened the session by a sermon in which he announced that the King had determined to resort to war with France, and therefore needed a large subsidy.—*Rot. Parl.*, iv. 34.   It does not appear from *Rot. Parl.* (iv. 16/1) that Chichele was one of the triers of petitions in the Leicester Parliament, but we learn from the same authority (*Rot. Parl.* iv. 35/1) that he held the office of trier in the Parliament of West-minster.   He was translated from S. David's to Canterbury.—*Godwin*, 512. The Pope's confirmation of Chichele's election was requested by Henry in a letter dated on March 23, 1414.—*Rymer*, ix. 119.   The temporalities were restored on May 30, 1414.—*Ibid.* 131.

[3] *Hol.* abridged and turned into the third person a speech which *Halls*

[*Hol.* iii. 545/2/46.] against the surmised and false fained law Salike, which the Frenchmen alledge euer *against* the kings of England in *barre* of their iust title *to* the crowne of *France.* The verie words of that supposed law are these : ' *In terram Salicam* ' *mulieres ne succedant ;* ' that is to saie, ' *Into* the *Salike land* let ' *not women succeed.' Which the French* glossers expound *to be the realme of France, and that this law* was made by king *Pharamond ;* whereas *yet their owne authors affirme, that the land Salike is in Germanie, betweene the* riuers *of Elbe and Sala ;* and that when *Charles the great* had ouercome *the Saxons,* he placed there *certeine Frenchmen,* which hauing *in disdeine the dishonest maners of the Germane women,* made a *law,* that the *females should* not succeed to any inheritance *within that land, which at this daie is called Meisen :* so that, if this be true, this *law was not* made *for the realme of France, nor the Frenchmen possessed the land Salike, till foure hundred* and *one and twentie yeares after* the death *of Pharamond,* the *supposed* maker *of this* Salike *law ;* for this Pharamond deceassed *in*

There is no *barre*
To make *against* your Highnesse   36
Clayme *to France,*
But this, which they produce from
Pharamond :
" *In terram Salicam Mulieres ne succedant,*"
" No Woman shall *succeed in Salike Land :* "
Which Salike Land, *the French*   40
vniustly gloze
To be the Realme of France, and Pharamond
The founder of *this Law,* and
Female Barre.
Yet their owne Authors faithfully
affirme,
That the Land Salike is in   44
Germanie,
Betweene the Flouds *of Sala and of Elue ;*
Where *Charles the Great,* hauing
subdu'd *the Saxons,*
There left behind, and settled
certaine French,
Who (holding *in disdaine the*   48
German Women,
For some *dishonest manners of* their
life)
Establisht then this *Law ;* to wit,
" No *Female*
" *Should* be Inheritrix *in* Salike
Land : "
Which Salike, (as I said,) 'twixt   52
Elue and Sala,
Is at this day in Germanie *call'd Meisen.*
Then doth it well appeare, the
Salike *Law*
Was not deuisëd *for the Realme of France ;*
Nor did *the French possesse the*   56
Salike Land
Vntill foure hundred one and twentie yeeres
After defunction *of King Phara-mond,*
(Idly *suppos'd* the founder *of this Law,*)

The Salike law.

[Though the French say that Pharamond made the law for France, the Salic land is in Germany, where Charles the Great placed certain Frenchmen, long after Pharamond's death.]

Mesina [Misena, Meissen].

---

assigns to Chichele (50-52). On his deathbed Henry protested that neither ambition nor the desire of fame prompted him to undertake war with France ; " but onelie that, in prosecuting his iust title [to the French crown, through Edward III.], he might in the end atteine to a perfect peace, and come to enioie those peeces of his inheritance [from Henry II.], which to him of right belonged : and that, before the beginning of the same warres, he was fullie persuaded by men both wise and of great holinesse of life, that vpon such intent he might and ought both begin the same warres, and follow them," &c. This last clause has the following sidenote : " Cheeflie Chichelie archb. of Cantur. for dashing y⁰ bill against the cleargie," &c. Cp. Henry's appeal to Chichele (I. ii 13-32 ; 96).

the yeare 426, and Charles the great subdued the Saxons, and placed the Frenchmen in those parts beyond the riuer of Sala, in the yeare 805.

Moreouer, it appeareth by their owne writers, that king Pepine, which deposed Childerike, claimed the crowne of France, as heire generall, for that he was descended of Blithild, daughter to king Clothair [p. 546] the first. Hugh Capet also, (who vsurped the crowne vpon Charles duke of Loraine, the sole heire male of the line and stocke of Charles the great,) to make his title seeme true, and appeare good, (though in deed it was starke naught,) conueied himselfe as heire to the ladie Lingard, daughter to king Charlemaine, sonne to Lewes the emperour, that was son to Charles the great. King Lewes also, the tenth,¹ (otherwise called saint Lewes,) being verie heire to the said vsurper Hugh Capet, could neuer be satisfied in his conscience how he might iustlie keepe and possesse the crowne of France, till he was persuaded and fullie instructed, that queene Isabell his grandmother was linealie descended of the ladie Ermengard, daughter and heire to the aboue named Charles duke of Loraine; by the which marriage, the bloud and line of Charles the great was againe vnited and restored to the crowne & scepter of France: so that more cleere than the sunne it openlie appeareth, that the title of king

[Pippin traced his title to the French crown through the female line, and so also did Hugh Capet.]

[Therefore the king of England cannot be barred from claiming France

Who died within the yeere of our 60
  Redemption
Foure hundred twentie six; and
  Charles the Great
Subdu'd the Saxons, and did seat
  the French
Beyond the Riuer Sala, in the yeere
Eight hundred fiue. Besides, their 64
  Writers say,
King Pepin, which deposed Chil-
  derike,
Did, as Heire Generall, (being
  descended
Of Blithild, which was Daughter to
  King Clothair,)
Make Clayme and Title to the 68
  Crownes of France.
Hugh Capet also, (who vsurpt the
  Crowne
Of Charles the Duke of Loraine, sole
  Heire male
Of the true Line and Stock of Charles
  the Great,)
To find his Title with some shewes 72
  of truth,
(Though, in pure truth, it was
  corrupt and naught,)
Conuey'd himselfe as th'Heire to th'
  Lady Lingare,
Daughter to Charlemaine, who was
  the Sonne
To Lewes the Emperour, and Lewes, 76
  the Sonne
Of Charles the Great. Also King
  Lewes the Tenth,
Who was sole Heire to the Vsurper
  Capet,
Could not keepe quiet in his
  conscience,
Wearing the Crowne of France, 'till 80
  satisfied
That faire Queene Isabel, his Grand-
  mother,
Was Lineall of the Lady Ermengare,
Daughter to Charles the foresaid
  Duke of Loraine:
By the which Marriage, the Lyne of 84
  Charles the Great
Was re-vnited to the Crownes of
  France.
So that, as cleare as is the Summers
  Sunne,
King Pepins Title, and Hugh Capets
  Clayme,
King Lewes his satisfaction, all 88
  appeares
To hold in Right and Title of the
  Female:

---

¹ *Hol.'s* slip misled Shakspere. *Halle* has: "Kyng Lewes also the ninth " (51).

Pepin, the *claime* of *Hugh Capet*,
the possession of *Lewes;* yea, and
the French *kings to this daie*, are
deriued and conueied from *the*
heire *femals;* though *they would*,
vnder the colour of such a fained
law, *barre* the kings and princes
of this realme of England of their
right and lawfull inheritance.

The archbishop further alledged
out of *the bookes of Numbers* this
saieng : ' When a man *dieth* with-
' out a sonne, *let the inheritance*
' *descend to* his *daughter*.'

So doe the Kings of France vnto *this*
    day;
Howbeit *they would* hold vp this
    Salique *Law*
To *barre* your Highnesse clayming 92
    from the Female ;
And rather chuse to hide them in a
    Net,
Then amply to imbarre their
    crooked Titles
Vsurpt from you and your Pro-
    genitors.
  King. May I, with right and 96
    conscience, make this claim ?
  Cant. The sinne vpon my head,
    dread Souëraigne !
For in *the Bookes of Numbers* is it
    writ,
" *When* the *man dyes*, *let the In-
    heritance*
" *Descend vnto* the *Daughter*."   100

through
the same
line of
descent.]

[The book of
Numbers.]

Chichele then reminds Henry how Edward III., " *on a Hill*,
stood"; watching the Black Prince defeat "the full Power of France,"
with but half of the English army (I. ii. 105-110). Holinshed records
(iii. 372/2/27) how a knight, sent to ask Edward for reinforcements,
came "where" the King "*stood* aloft *on a* windmill *hill*," surveying
the battle.[1]

When Westmoreland says that the hearts of the English nobles are
in France, Chichele exclaims :

> O let their bodyes follow, my deare Liege,
> With *Blood* and *Sword* and *Fire*, to win your *Right !*
> In ayde whereof, we *of the Spiritualtie*   132
> Will rayse your *Highnesse such a* mightie *Summe*,
> *As neuer* did the Clergie at one time
> Bring in to any of your Ancestors.

Chichele,

[*Hol*. iii. 546/1/30.] hauing said sufficientlie for the proofe of
the kings iust and lawfull title to the crowne of France, he
exhorted him to aduance foorth his banner to fight for his *right*, to
conquer his inheritance, to spare neither *bloud*, *sword*, nor *fire ;* sith
his warre was iust, his cause good, and his claime true. And to
the intent his louing chapleins and obedient subiects *of the
spiritualtie* might shew themselues willing and desirous to aid his
maiestie, for the recouerie of his ancient right and true inheritance,
the archbishop declared that, in their spirituall conuocation, they

[Chichele
urged Henry
to make
war, and
promised
him a larger
sum of
money than
the clergy
had ever
paid to any
prince.]

---

[1] An incident which Charles VI. reminds his nobles of (*Hen. V.*, II. iv.
53-62).

had granted to his *highnesse such a summe* of monie, *as neuer* by no
spirituall persons was to any prince before those daies giuen or
aduanced.[1]

Chichele answers Henry's fear, that the Scot might pour down upon
defenceless England, by recalling the day (October 17, 1346) when
David II. was vanquished and taken prisoner, during Edward III.'s
absence in France.—*Avesbury*, 145, 146. For the unhistorical assertion
that David was sent to France (l. 161), Shakspere was perhaps indebted
to the play of *King Edward III.*, where (Act IV. sc. ii. p. 53) we find
Edward resolving to summon Copeland, David's captor,

> hither out of hand,
> And with him he shall bring his prisoner king.

In the last scene (Act V. sc. i. p. 71), which is laid at Calais, Copeland
enters, "and King David."

To Chichele's instance Westmoreland replies (ll. 166-168) :

> But there's a saying very old and true :
> "If that you *will France win*,
> "Then *with Scotland first begin.*"

After recording Chichele's speech, and offer of a subsidy, Holinshed
adds :

The earle of Westmerland persuadeth y king to the conquest of Scotland.
[*Hol.* iii. 546/1/44.] When the archbishop had ended his prepared tale, Rafe Neuill, earle of Westmerland, and as then lord
Warden of the marches against Scotland, vnderstanding that the
king, vpon a couragious desire to recouer his right in France, would
suerlie take the wars in hand, thought good to mooue the king to
begin first with Scotland; and therevpon declared how easie a
matter it should be to make a conquest there, and how greatlie
the same should further his wished purpose for the subduing of
the Frenchmen; concluding the summe of his tale with this old
saieng: that, "Who so *will France win*, must *with Scotland first*
"*begin.*"

War with France being resolved on, audience is given to ambassadors from the Dauphin. They present to the King a "Tun [2] of

---

[1] The Convocation of Canterbury met on October 1, 1414, and broke up on
October 20, 1414, after granting Henry two whole tenths.—*Wake*, 350, 351.
This convocation was summoned for the settlement of matters relating to
church discipline, as the mandate (*Wake*, Appendix, 87) shows.

[2] Perhaps "Tunne" = a *cup*. Higins (*Nomenclator*, 1585, p. 233, col. 1)
defined "Ooscyphium" as "a *tun*, or nut to drinke in." In *The Famous
Victories*, sc. ix., p. 29, the ambassador's action is described by this stage
direction: "He deliuereth a Tunne of Tennis Balles." Henry says: "What, a
guilded Tunne? I pray you, my Lord of Yorke, looke what is in it." York
answers: "Here is a Carpet and a Tunne of Tennis balles."

Treasure" (l. 255), containing tennis-balls (l. 258) ; a gift which their
master deems "meeter for" Henry's "spirit" than French dukedoms.
Of this incident Holinshed gives the following account:

[*Hol.* iii. 545/1/1.]   Whilest in the Lent season the king laie at
Killingworth, there came to him from Charles [*sc.* Lewis] Dolphin
of France certeine ambassadors, that brought with them a barrell
of Paris balles; which from their maister they presented to him for
a token that was taken in verie ill part, as sent in scorne, to
signifie, that it was more meet for the king to passe the time with
such childish exercise, than to attempt any worthie exploit.

Eiton.
A disdaine-
full
ambassage.
[The
Dauphin's
'Paris
balles.']

Part of Henry's answer (ll. 264-266) to the ambassadors—

    Tell him, "he hath made a match with such a Wrangler,
    "That all *the Courts* of *France* will be disturb'd
    "With Chaces"

—may be derived from the concluding portion of this excerpt :

[*Hol.* iii. 545/1/9.]   Wherfore the K. wrote to him, that yer
ought long, he would tosse him some London balles that perchance
should shake the walles of *the* best *court* in *France.*[1]

[Henry's
'London
balles.']

Act II. Chorus.—When Shakspere wrote ll. 8-10,—

    For now sits Expectation in the Ayre ;
    And hides a Sword, from Hilts vnto the Point,
    With Crownes Imperiall, Crownes, and Coronets

,—he may have been thinking of a woodcut-portrait of Edward III.,[2]—
engraved on page 174,—which appeared in the first edition of Holinshed
(1577, vol. iii. p. 885).

Act II. sc. ii.—This scene is laid at Southampton, in August, 1415.[3]

---

[1] Cp. the rest of the passage in *Ott.* (cited above, p. 165) : "Cui rex
Anglorum rescripsit, dicens, se in brevi pilas missurum Londoniarum quibus
terreret [tereret] & confunderet sua tecta." Henry's threat that the Dauphin's
balls shall become "Gun-stones" (I. ii. 282) may be Shakspere's reminiscence
of Caxton (*Chronicle*, ed. 1482, sign. t. 5), who says that Henry "lete make
tenys balles for the dolphyn in al the hast that they myȝt be made, and they
were grete *gonne stones* for the Dolphyn to playe with all." But a cannon-
shot was called a gunstone in Shakspere's time. See examples in the revised
ed. of *Henry V.* (New Sh. Soc.), p. 162. In a contemporary poem, ascribed to
Lydgate, Henry speaks of a "game at tynes" which his guns "shall play with
Harflete."—*Chron. Lond.,* 220.

[2] In Rastell's *Pastyme of People,* 1529, Edward III. is portrayed at full
length, holding a sword encircled by two crowns. For a comparison with II.,
Chorus, l. 6,—where Henry is styled "the Mirror of all Christian Kings,"—
see p. 205, note 2, below.

[3] The treason of Cambridge, Scrope, and Grey was "publisshid and openli
knowe" at Southampton, on August 1, 1415.—*Chron. R. II.—H. VI.,* 40. On
August 2, a jury found the conspirators guilty (*Rot. Parl.* iv. 65), and, on
August 5, Clarence was commissioned to pass sentence on Cambridge and
Scrope (*Rymer,* ix. 300).

All the historic negotiation which preceded Henry's departure for
France was passed over or postdated, and the event placed next to the
tennis-balls' incident is the conspiracy of Cambridge, Scrope, and Grey.

[*Hol.* iii. 548/1/66.]   When king Henrie had fullie furnished
his nauie with men, munition, & other prouisions, [he,] perceiuing
that his capteines misliked nothing so much as delaie, determined
his souldiors to go a ship-boord and awaie.   But see the hap! the
night before the daie appointed for their departure, he was crediblie
informed, that Richard earle of Cambridge, brother to Edward
duke of Yorke, and Henrie lord Scroope of Masham, lord treasuror,
with Thomas Graie, a knight of Northumberland, being confederat
togither, had conspired his death : wherefore he caused them to be
apprehended.

*The earle of
Cambridge &
other lords
apprehended
for treason*

Neither Holinshed nor, I believe, any chronicler published in Shakspere's day [1] relates that the conspirators were led on by Henry to doom
themselves (ll. 39-51).   The speech (ll. 79-144) in which Henry upbraids

---

[1] *Saint-Remy*—whose *Mémoires*, from 1407 to 1422, were first published
in 1663—says—as do other chroniclers—that the conspirators sought to make
the Earl of March an accomplice by offering to place him on the throne, but
that he revealed their design to Henry.   *Saint-Remy* adds (vii. 488-489) that
the King thereupon called a council of his nobles, and after telling them that
he had heard, though he could not believe, that some of his subjects were
engaged in a plot to deprive him of his crown, asked, if the report were true,
what should be done to these traitors.   The question was put to each lord in
succession, and the conspirators answered that such traitors ought to suffer a
death so cruel as to be a warning to others.   Every one present having given
his opinion, Henry confronted March with the guilty men, who owned their
treasonable project.   *Waurin* (V. i. 177-179) gives the same account of the
conspirators' detection.

the traitors was wholly Shakspere's work, except that part of it where
Scrope's dissimulation and ingratitude is denounced (ll. 93-142). The
germ of these lines lay in the following passage :

[*Hol.* iii. 548/2/3.] The said lord Scroope was in such fauour
with the king, that he admitted him sometime to be his bedfellow;
in whose fidelitie the king reposed such trust, that, when anie *Thom. Wals.*
priuat or publike councell was in hand, this lord had much in the [Henry's
determination of it.   For he represented so great grauitie in his Lord
countenance, such modestie in behauiour, and so vertuous zeale to Scrope.]
all godlinesse in his talke, that whatsoeuer he said was thought for
the most part necessarie to be doone and followed.   Also the
said sir Thomas Graie (as some write) was of the kings priuie
councell.

The formal words used by Exeter in arresting Cambridge seem to
have been taken from Holinshed : "I arrest thee of High Treason, *by
the name of Richard Earle of Cambridge.*" Holinshed says (iii. 549/
1/26) : "indicted he was *by the name of Richard earle of Cambridge* of
Connesburgh in the countie of Yorke, knight."
Cambridge qualifies his guilt (ll. 155-157) :

> For me : the Gold of France did not seduce ;
> Although I did admit it as a motiue,
> The sooner to effect what I intended.

The motive which is supposed to have really influenced him was of
a different sort.

[*Hol.* iii. 548/2/72.] Diuerse write that Richard earle of
Cambridge did not conspire with the lord Scroope & Thomas
Graie for the murthering of king Henrie to [*p.* 549] please the
French king withall, but onelie to the intent to exalt to the crowne [Cambridge
his brother in law Edmund earle of March as heire to Lionell duke feigned to be
of Clarence : after the death of which earle of March, (for diuerse French
secret impediments, not able to haue issue,) the earle of Cambridge interest, but
was sure that the crowne should come to him by his wife, and to object was
his children, of hir begotten.   And therefore (as was thought) he the crown
rather confessed himselfe for need of monie to be corrupted by the whom he
French king, than he would declare his inward mind, and open his succeed.]
verie intent and secret purpose, which if it were espied, he saw
plainlie that the earle of March should haue tasted of the same
cuppe that he had drunken, and what should haue come to his
owne children he much doubted.   Therefore destitute of comfort

& in despaire of life to saue his children, he feined that tale;
desiring rather to saue his succession than himselfe, which he did
in deed; for his sonne Richard duke of Yorke not priuilie but
openlie claimed the crowne, and Edward his sonne both claimed
it, & gained it, as after it shall appeare.

Having heard Grey's [1] confession (ll. 161-165), Henry dooms the
traitors:

> *K.* God quit you in his mercy!   Hear your sentence!
> You haue *conspir'd* against Our Royall person,
> Ioyn'd with an enemy proclaim'd, and from his Coffers   168
> Receyu'd the Golden Earnest of Our death;
> Wherein you would haue sold your King to slaughter,
> His Princes and his Peeres to seruitude,
> His Subiects to oppression and contempt,   172
> And his whole Kingdome into *desolation.*
> *Touching* our *person, seeke* we no *reuenge;*
> But we our Kingdomes safety must so tender,
> Whose ruine you haue [2] sought, that to her Lawes   176
> We do deliuer you.   *Get* you *therefore hence,*
> (*Poore miserable wretches!*) to *your* death!
> The taste whereof, *God, of his mercy, giue*
> *You* patience to indure, *and* true *Repentance*   180
> *Of* all *your* deare *offences!*—Beare them hence!

These lines should be compared with the following speech, taken by
Holinshed from Halle:

Hall.

[*Hol.* iii. 548/2/15.] These prisoners, vpon their examination,
confessed, that for a great summe of monie which they had
receiued of the French king, they intended verelie either to haue
deliuered the king aliue into the hands of his enimies, or else to
haue murthered him before he should arriue in the duchie of
Normandie.   When king Henrie had heard all things opened,
which he desired to know, he caused all his nobilitie to come
before his presence; before whome he caused to be brought the
offendors also, and to them said: "Hauing thus *conspired* the

---

[1] Johnson pointed out (*Var. Sh.*, xvii. 314) a resemblance between Grey's
words (l. 165),—"My *fault,* but not my *body,* pardon, Soueraigne,"—and an
expression of Dr. William Parry, executed on March 2, 1584, for plotting the
death of Elizabeth.   In a letter addressed to the Queen, Parry said: "I haue
no more to saie at this time, but that with my hart & soule I doo now honour
& loue you, am inwardlie sorie for mine offense, and readie to make you
amends by my death and patience.   Discharge me *A culpa* but not *A poena,*
good ladie."—*Hol.* iii. 1387/1/57.
[2] *you haue*] Qq. *you three* F2.   *you* F1.

"death and destruction of me, which am the head of the realme *King Henries words to the traitours.*
"and gouernour of the people, it maie be (no doubt) but that you
"likewise haue sworne the confusion of all that are here with me,
"and also the *desolation* of your owne countrie.   To what horror
"(O lord!) for any true English hart to consider, that such an
"execrable iniquitie should euer so bewrap you, as for pleasing of
"a forren enimie to imbrue your hands in your bloud, and to ruine
"your owne natiue soile.   *Reuenge* herein *touching* my *person,*
"though I *seeke* not; yet for the safegard of you my deere freends,
"& for due preseruation of all sorts, I am by office to cause
"example to be shewed.   *Get* ye *hence therefore,* ye *poore miserable*
"*wretches,* to the receiuing of *your* iust reward; wherein *Gods* *The earle of Cambridge and the other traitors executed.*
"maiestie *giue you* grace *of his mercie, and repentance of your*
"heinous *offenses.*"   And so immediatlie they were had to
execution.

The general purport of Henry's final speech (ll. 182-193) is the same
as the " words few " which he is said to have spoken after the traitors
" were had to execution."

[*Hol.* iii. 548/2/43.]   This doone, the king, calling his lords
againe afore him, said in words few and with good grace.   Of his *[Henry's address to his lords, after the traitors were had to execution.]*
enterprises he recounted the honor and glorie, whereof they with
him were to be partakers; the great confidence he had in their
noble minds, which could not but remember them of the famous
feats that their ancestors aforetime in France had atchiued, whereof
the due report for euer recorded remained yet in register.   The
great mercie of God that had so gratiouslie reuealed vnto him the
treason at hand, whereby the true harts of those afore him [were]
made so eminent & apparant in his eie, as they might be right sure
he would neuer forget it.   The doubt of danger to be nothing in
respect of the certeintie of honor that they should acquire; wherein
himselfe (as they saw) in person would be lord and leader through
Gods grace.   To whose maiestie, as cheeflie was knowne the equitie
of his demand, euen so to his mercie, did he onelie recommend
the successe of his trauels.

Act II. sc. iv.—A dramatic date should perhaps be given to the
council over which Charles VI. is presiding when the English ambassadors crave admittance (ll. 65-66).   Henry—who, we learn, " is footed

in this Land already " (l. 143)—disembarked near Harfleur on August 14, 1415.[1]   In February, 1415, Exeter was an ambassador to the French Court, associated with others in negotiating a marriage between Henry and Katharine.[2] But the message here delivered by Exeter (ll. 77-109) substantially, and, to some slight extent, literally, repro-duces the terms of a despatch addressed to Charles VI., which must have been received about the time of the invasion, for, before putting to sea, Henry,

[Before sailing from Southamp-ton, Henry despatched letters to Charles VI.] [*Hol.* iii. 548/1/44.] first princelie appointing to aduertise the French king of his comming, therefore dispatched Antelope his purseuant at armes with letters to him for restitution of that which he wrongfully withheld ; contrarie to the lawes of God and man : the king further declaring how sorie he was that he should be thus compelled for repeating of his right and iust title of inheritance, to make warre to the destruction of christian people ; but sithens he had offered peace which could not be receiued, now, for fault of iustice, he was forced to take armes.   Neuerthelesse exhorted the French king, *in the bowels of* Iesu Christ,[3] to render him that which was his owne; whereby effusion of Christian bloud might be auoided.   These letters, cheeflie to this effect and purpose, were written and dated from Hampton the fift of August.   When the same were presented to the French king, and by his councell well perused, answer was made, that he would take aduise, and prouide therein as time and place should be conuenient: so the messenger [was] licenced to depart at his pleasure.

Two passages may have served as authorities for the talk concerning defensive measures which precedes Exeter's entrance (ll. 1-49).   When news of Henry's preparations for invasion reached France,

[*Hol.* iii. 547/2/7.] the Dolphin, who had the gouernance of the realme, bicause his father was fallen into his old disease of

---

[1] *Gesta*, 14.   " Kidecaws "—Henry's landing-place—is about three miles distant from Harfleur.—*Ibid.*, 13.
[2] Their powers are dated December 5, 1414.—*Rymer*, ix. 184, 185. They had not concluded their mission on February 17, 1415.—*Ibid.*, 201. An account of this embassy—taken from *Halle* (57)—was given by *Hol.* (iii. 546/2/37). Cp. *Mons.*, iii. 273, 274, 289.
[3] Henry bids Charles (II. iv. 102, 103),

" . . . *in the Bowels of* the Lord,
Deliver vp the Crowne," . . .

frensie, sent for the dukes of Berríe [1] and Alanson, and all the other [The Dauphin summoned the Duke of Berri and other lords of the Council, who gave advice for the defence of France.]
lords of the councell of France: by whose aduise it was deter-
mined, that they should not onelie prepare a sufficient armie to
resist the king of England, when so euer he arriued to inuade
France, but also to stuffe and furnish the townes on the frontiers
and sea coasts with conuenient garrisons of men: . . .

At a later date:

[*Hol.* iii. 549/2/55.] The French king, being aduertised that [The Constable and other lords provided for the defence of France.]
king Henrie was arriued on that coast, sent in all hast the lord de
la Breth constable of France, the seneshall of France, the lord
Bouciqualt marshall of France, the seneshall of Henault, the lord
Lignie, with other; which fortified townes with men, victuals, and
artillerie, on all those frontiers towards the sea.

Act III.   Chorus.—Shakspere thus sums up the answer which
Exeter—"th'Embassador from the French"—brings to Henry (ll.
29-31):

That the King doth offer him
Katherine his Daughter, and with her, to Dowrie,
Some petty and vnprofitable Dukedomes.

This offer was made by William Bouratier, Archbishop of Bourges,
the spokesman of an embassy charged with the answer of the French to
Henry's demands.   At Winchester,[2]

[*Hol.* iii. 547/2/34.] before the kings presence, sitting in his
throne imperiall, the archbishop of Burges made an eloquent and
a long oration, dissuading warre, and praising peace; offering to
the king of England a great summe of monie, with diuerse
countries, being in verie deéd but base and poore, as a dowrie with
the ladie Catharine in mariage; so that he would dissolue his [The Princess Katharine and a dowry offered to Henry.]
armie, and dismisse his soldiers, which he had gathered and put in
a readinesse.

Act III. sc. i.—Henry encourages a storming-party, which has been
repulsed, to mount again a breach in the walls of Harfleur. Holinshed's

---

[1] John Duke of Berri is present, and the Constable speaks (see next
excerpt), in sc. iv., Act II. At this council it was resolved that the Archbishop of Bourges should be sent to Henry (*Hol.* iii. 547/2/17). See next
note.

[2] The ambassadors left France on June 17, 1415.—*St. Denys*, v. 512. On
July 26, 1415, they reported, in Charles's presence, the ill success of their
mission.—*St. Denys*, v. 530.

words (iii. 549/2/69), " And dailie was the towne assaulted," may have suggested to Shakspere the King's speech (ll. 1-34).

Act III. sc. ii.—Gower bids Fluellen " come presently to the Mynes ; the Duke of Gloucester would speake with you " (ll. 58-60). Fluellen answers that "the Mynes is not according to the disciplines of the Warre : [1] . . . th'athuersarie . . . is digt himselfe foure yard vnder the Countermines." Holinshed says that

[Gloucester's mines.]

[*Hol.* iii. 549/2/70.] the duke of Glocester, to whome the order of the siege was committed, made three mines vnder the ground ; and, approching to the wals with his engins and ordinance, would not suffer them within to take anie rest.

[The French counter-mines.]

[*p.* 550] For although they with their countermining somwhat disappointed the Englishmen, & came to fight with them hand to hand within the mines, so that they went no further forward with that worke ; yet they were so inclosed on ech side, as well by water as land, that succour they saw could none come to them.

Titus Liuius.

Act III. sc. iii.—In the last scene a parley [2] was sounded from Harfleur (III. ii. 148). Now King Henry enters and summons the Governor to yield "to our best mercy " (l. 3). On September 18, 1415,[3] the besieged made a conditional offer of submission.

[*Hol.* iii. 550/1/38.] The king, aduertised hereof, sent them word, that, except they would surrender the towne to him the morow next insuing, without anie condition, they should spend no more time in talke about the matter. But yet at length through the earnest sute of the French lords, the king was contented to grant them truce vntill nine of the clocke the next sundaie, being the two and twentith of September ; with condition, that, if in the meane time no rescue came, they should yeeld the towne at that houre, with their bodies and goods to stand at the kings pleasure.

[An unconditional surrender of Harfleur demanded.]

[A fiue daies respit.]

We may suppose that this scene opens on September 22,—the day fixed for yielding Harfleur, if no relief came,—and therefore the Governor thus answers King Henry's summons (ll. 44-47) :

---

[1] It seems that "the disciplines of the Warre" really were violated, for, contrary to the prohibition of Ægidius Romanus, the mines were begun in sight of the besieged, who of course countermined them.—*Gesta,* 24, 25. Ægidius Romanus wrote for Philip the Bold, Duke of Burgundy (1363-1404), *De Regimine Principum,* a part of which is entitled " De re militari veterum." —*Gesta,* p. 16, note 2.

[2] *Hol.'s* account of the first overture for surrender has this sidenote : "The seuenteenth of September they within Harflue praie *parlee.*"

[3] The truce was ratified on September 18.—*Gesta,* 30. The besieged asked for a parley " about midnight," September 17.—*Hol.* iii. 550/1/23.

> Our expectation hath this day an end:
> The Dolphin, whom of Succours we entreated,
> Returnes vs " *that* his *Powers* are *yet not* ready
> " *To rayse so great a Siege.*"

During the truce,

[*Hol.* iii. 550/1/68.]   the lord Bacqueuill was sent vnto the French king, to declare in what point the towne stood.   To whome the Dolphin answered, *that* the kings *power* was *not yet* assembled, in such number as was conuenient *to raise so great a siege.*   This answer being brought vnto the capteins within the towne, they rendered it vp to the king of England, after that the third daie was expired; which was on the daie of saint Maurice, being the seuen and thirtith daie after the siege was first laid.   The souldiors were ransomed, and the towne sacked, to the great gaine of the Englishmen. [Succour refused by the Dauphin.] *Harflue yeelded and sacked.*

Henry then commands Exeter (ll. 52, 53) to enter Harfleur;
> there remaine,
> And fortifie it strongly 'gainst the French : [1] . . .

On September 22,

[*Hol.* iii. 550/2/30.]   the king ordeined capteine to the towne his vncle the duke of Excester, who established his lieutenant there, one sir Iohn Fastolfe; with fifteene hundred men, or (as some haue) two thousand, and thirtie six knights. [Exeter made Captain of Harfleur.]

Harfleur being disposed of, Henry says (ll. 54-56) :
> For vs, deare Vnckle,
> (The Winter comming on, and Sicknesse growing
> Vpon our Souldiers,) we will retyre to Calis.

Holinshed names several Englishmen of rank who died during the siege, or were licensed to return home on account of sickness; and adds :

[*Hol.* iii. 550/2/44.]   King Henrie, after the winning of Harflue, determined to haue proceeded further in the winning of other townes and fortresses; but, bicause the dead time of the winter approched, it was determined by aduise of his councell, that he should in all conuenient speed set forward, and march through the countrie towards Calis by land, least his returne as then home- [A march to Calais resolved on.]

---

[1] In making Henry say to Exeter, "Vse mercy to them all" (l. 54), Shakspere ignored *Hol.*'s report (iii. 550/2/5) that the King expelled from Harfleur " parents with their children, yoong maids and old folke," and filled their places with English immigrants.   Higden's *Polychronicon* (edd. Babington and Lumby, viii. 550) is *Hol.*'s authority.

wards should of slanderous toongs be named a running awaie;
and yet that iournie was adiudged perillous, by reason that the
number of his people was much minished by the flix and other
feuers, which sore vexed and brought to death aboue fifteene
hundred persons of the armie: and this was the cause that his
returne was the sooner appointed and concluded.

*Great death
in the host
by the flix.*

Act III. sc. v.—Henry left Harfleur on October 8,[1] and crossed the
Somme on October 19.[2] The following excerpt illustrates this scene,
which opens after Charles VI. has received sure tidings that Henry
"hath past the Riuer Some" (l. 1):

*The French
king consult-
eth how to
deale with
y* English-
men.*

[*Hol.* iii. 552/1/42.] The French king, being at Rone, and
hearing that king Henrie was passed the riuer of Some, was
much displeased therewith, and, assembling his councell[3] to the
number of fiue and thirtie, asked their aduise what was to be
doone. There was amongst these fiue and thirtie, his sonne the
Dolphin, calling himselfe king of Sicill;[4] the dukes of Berrie and
Britaine, the earle of Pontieu the kings yoongest sonne, and other
high estates. At length thirtie of them agreed, that the Englishmen should not depart vnfought withall, and fiue were of a
contrarie opinion, but the greater number ruled the matter: and
so Montioy king at armes was sent to the king of England to
defie him as the enimie of France, and to tell him that he should
shortlie haue battell.

*Dolphin
king of
Sicill.*

*The French
K. sendeth
defiance to
king Henrie.*

Charles commands the French princes to "goe downe vpon" (l. 53)
Harry England;

> And in a Chariot, Captiue into Roan,[5]
> Bring him our Prisoner!

Touching the assurance of victory which the French had on the
night before their defeat at Agincourt, Holinshed says:

A chariot.]

[*Hol.* iii. 554/1/7.] The noble men had deuised a chariot,
wherein they might triumphantlie conueie the king captiue to the

---

¹ *Gesta*, 36 (cp. note 4).   ² *Gesta*, 43.

³ To reconcile a subsequent date (see p. 184, n. 2, below) we must suppose
that this council was held on October 19, not, as *Mons.* says (iii. 330), on
October 20.

⁴ *Hol.* has been misled by *Halle* (64). *Mons.* (iii. 330) does not mention
the presence of the Dauphin at this council, but says that "le roi Louis" was
there. Lewis was titular King of Sicily. He was the son of Lewis Duke of
Anjou, Charles VI.'s eldest uncle; and father of Réné, whose daughter Margaret
married our Henry VI.

⁵ *Chariot, Captiue*]P. A. Daniel conj. *And in a Captiue Chariot into Roan* Fi.

citie of Paris ; crieng to their soldiers : "Haste you to the spoile,
"glorie and honor!" little weening (God wot) how soone their
brags should be blowne awaie.

The Dauphin's presence at Agincourt (III. vii.), despite his father's
injunction to remain at Rouen (III. v. 64), is unhistorical.[1]

[*Hol.* iii. 552/1/72.] The Dolphin sore desired to haue beene
at the battell, but he was prohibited by his father. [The Dauphin not at the battle.]

Act III. sc. vi.—Gower is told by Fluellen that "the Duke of
Exeter . . . keepes the Bridge most valiantly, with excellent discipline"
(ll. 6-12). The fighting of which Fluellen speaks occurred at the
Ternoise, and is thus described by Holinshed :

[*Hol.* iii. 552/2/3.] The king of England, (hearing that the
Frenchmen approched, and that there was an other riuer for him
to passe with his armie by a bridge, and doubting least, if the
same bridge should be broken, it would be greatlie to his hinderance,) appointed certeine capteins with their bands, to go thither
with all speed before him, and to take possession thereof, and so
to keepe it, till his comming thither.

Those that were sent, finding the Frenchmen busie to breake
downe their bridge, assailed them so vigorouslie, that they discomfited them, and tooke and slue them ; and so the bridge was
preserued till the king came, and passed the riuer by the same
with his whole armie. This was on the two and twentith day of
October.[2] [The French defeated in an attempt to break down the bridge over the Ternoise.]

Pistol then enters and asks Fluellen to intercede with Exeter for
Bardolph, whom the Duke has sentenced to be hung for stealing a
"Pax[3] of little price" (ll. 42-51). During Henry's march there was no

---

[1] In the Q. version of *Henry V*. "Burbon" has the part in Act III. sc. vii.
and Act IV. sc. v. which F. assigns to the Dauphin. As to this matter, and
also Johnes's conjecture that Shakspere confounded Sir Guichard Dauphin (see
p. 196 below) with the Dauphin of France, see Mr. Daniel's Introduction to the
Parallel Texts of Henry V. (New Sh. Soc.), p. xiii.

[2] *Livius* (15) gives the date October 22, wrongly adding that it was the day
of S. Romanus, Confessor. This saint's day is kept on October 23. *Elmham*
says (56) that Henry crossed the Ternoise on the morrow of S. Romanus (Oct.
24). On October 23, according to another authority, Henry was marching
towards the Ternoise, which he crossed on October 24.—*Gesta*, 46. We may,
I think, fairly infer that the bridge was seized on the day before Henry's
transit.

[3] *Elmham* (53), *Livius* (13), and *Gesta* (41), agree that a pyx was stolen.
D'Arnis's *Lexicon Manuale*, 1866, has these definitions : "Pax—Instrumentum
quod inter Missarum solemnia populo osculandum praebetur ; *instrument que*

Justice in
warre [, for
the theft of
a pyx].
[*Hol.* iii. 552/1/33.] outrage or offense doone by the Englishmen, except one, which was, that a souldiour took a pix out of
a church, for which he was apprehended, & the king not once
remooued till the box was restored, and the offendor strangled.

Hearing from Fluellen of Bardolph's sentence, Henry says (ll. 113-
117): "Wee would haue all such offendors so cut off: and we giue
expresse charge that, in our Marches through the Countrey, there be
nothing compell'd from the Villages; nothing taken but pay'd for."
At some time between August 14—the date of Henry's landing near
Harfleur—and August 17,[1] the King

Titus
Liuius.
A charitable
proclama-
tion.
[*Hol.* iii. 549/2/28.] caused proclamation to be made, that no
person should be so hardie, on paine of death, either to take anie
thing out of anie church that belonged to the same; or to hurt or
doo anie violence either to priests, women, or anie such as should
be found without weapon or armor, and not readie to make
resistance: . . .

One hardship of the march from Harfleur was lack of victuals:

[Everything
paid for.]
[*Hol.* iii. 552/1/30.] Yet in this great necessitie, the poore
people of the countrie were not spoiled, nor anie thing taken of
them without paiment, . . .

>   Turne thee back,   148
> And tell thy King, *I* doe *not seeke* him now,
> . . . .
> Goe, bid thy Master well aduise himselfe   168
> If we may passe, we will; if we be hindred,
> We shall *your tawnie ground with your red blood*
> Discolour: . . .

I have quoted above parts of Henry's answer to Montjoy[2] (ll. 148,

---

le prêtre présente à baiser; ol[im] *paix.*" "Pyxis—Vas in quo reponuntur
hostiæ consecratæ ad viaticum; *pyxis, boîte à hosties.*" For more information
on this point see *Var. Sh.,* 1821, xvii. 362, 363; Nares's *Glossary,* s. vv. "Pax"
and "Pix"; Dyce's *Glossary,* s. v. "Pax"; and *French,* 106-110. According
to *Gesta* (41) the thief "suspensus interiit" on October 17.
    [1] *Gesta,* 14, 15.
    [2] On October 20, Henry was informed by three French heralds that the
Dukes of Orleans and Bourbon would give him battle before he reached Calais.
—*Gesta,* 44, 45. According to *Elmham* (54) the three heralds who delivered
this message were sent from the Constable, the Dukes of Orleans, Brabant,
Bourbon, Alençon, and Bar. Perhaps Montjoy—whom *Halle* makes the sole
bearer of the French challenge—was one of these heralds. We learn from
Mons. (iii. 331, 332) that, during the interval which elapsed between the
decision of the council and the battle (Oct. 25), the Constable sent Montjoy to
Aire, a place not far distant from Agincourt.

149; 168-171); italicizing words found in Holinshed's paraphrase of the speech attributed to the King by Halle (64).

[*Hol.* iii. 552/1/56.] King Henrie aduisedlie answered: "Mine *K. Henries answer to the defiance.* "intent is to doo as it pleaseth God: *I* will *not seeke* your maister "at this time; but, if he or his seeke me, I will meet with them, "God willing. If anie of your nation attempt once to stop me in "my iournie now towards Calis, at their ieopardie be it; and yet "wish I not anie of you so vnaduised, as to be the occasion that "I die *your tawnie ground with your red bloud.*"

When he had thus answered the herald, he gaue him a princelie reward,[1] and licence to depart.

Act III. sc. vii.—Two of the French leaders named below—the Constable and Rambures—take part in the dialogue which may have been suggested to Shakspere by the closing words of my next excerpt.

[*Hol.* iii. 552/2/50.] The cheefe leaders of the French host [The French leaders.] were these: the constable of France, the marshall, the admerall,[2] the lord Rambures, maister of the crosbowes, and other of the French nobilitie; which came and pitched downe their standards and banners in the countie of saint Paule, within the territorie of Agincourt, . . .

They were lodged euen in the waie by the which the Englishmen must needs passe towards Calis; and all that night, after their comming thither, made great cheare, and were verie merie, pleasant, [The French were "full of game."] and full of game.[3]

Midnight is past when a messenger enters and says (ll. 135, 136): "My Lord high Constable, the English lye within fifteene hundred paces of your Tents." According to Holinshed, the French were

---

[1] "There's for thy labour, Mountioy. . . . Thankes to your Highnesse" (ll. 167, 176).
[2] Marshal Boucicaut, and the Admiral Jacques de Châtillon.
[3] The Constable says that the English will "fight like Deuils," if they have "great Meales of Beefe." Orleans observes: "I, but these English are shrowdly out of Beefe." The Constable rejoins: "Then shall we finde to morrow, they haue only stomackes to eate, and none to fight."—ll. 161-166. *Halle* (66) makes the Constable encourage the French captains—when they were awaiting a signal to join battle—by laying down this maxim: "For you must vnderstand, yᵗ kepe an Englishman one moneth from hys warme bed, fat *befe*, and stale drynke, and let him that season tast colde and suffre hunger, you then shall se his courage abated, hys bodye waxe leane and bare, and euer desirous to returne into hys own conntrey." Cp. *Famous Victories*, xiii. 39; 1 *Hen. VI.*, I. ii. 9; and *Edward III.*, III. iii. pp. 43, 44.

[*Hol.* iii. 552/2/48.] incamped not past two hundred and fiftie pases distant from the English.

Act IV. Chorus.—In describing the two camps as they appeared by night, the Chorus bids us observe how (ll. 8, 9)

> Fire answers fire, and through their paly flames
> Each Battaile sees the others vmber'd face.

When the English encamped,

[*Hol.* iii. 552/2/47.] fiers were made to giue light on euerie side, as there likewise were in the French host, . . .

> The confident and ouer-lustie French   18
> Doe the low-rated English play at Dice; . . .

The French,

[*Hol.* iii. 554/1/3.] as though they had beene sure of victorie, made great triumph ; for the capteins had determined before how
to diuide the spoile, and the soldiers the night before had plaid the Englishmen at dice.[1]

In the other camp (ll. 22-28) :

> .   The poore condemnèd English,
> Like Sacrifices, by their watchfull Fires
> Sit patiently, and inly ruminate   24
> The Mornings danger ; and their gesture sad,
> Inuesting lanke-leane Cheekes, and Warre-worne Coats,
> Presenteth[2] them vnto the gazing Moone
> So many horride Ghosts.   28

Steevens compared these lines with Tacitus's description (*Ann.* I. lxv.) of the night before a battle between the Romans and the Germans, in A.D. 15, when Arminius was endeavouring to prevent Caecina from reaching the Rhine. The different aspect of the hostile camps is thus portrayed in Grenewey's translation (ed. 1598, p. 26) of this passage :

The night was vnquiet for diuers respects : the barbarous enimie, in feasting and banketting, songs of ioie and hideous outcries, filled the valleies and woods, which redoubled the sounde
againe. The Romans had small fires, broken voices, laie neere the trenches, went from tent to tent ; rather disquieted, and not able to sleepe, then watchfull.

---

[1] This is mentioned in the *Gesta* (49) as a report: "Et ut dicebatur tam securos se reputabant de nobis, quòd regem nostrum et nobiles suos nocte illâ sub jactu aleæ posuerunt." Rambures asks (III. vii. 93, 94): "Who will goe to Hazard with me for twentie Prisoners?"

[2] 27. *Presenteth*] Hanmer. *Presented* F.

Holinshed gives a somewhat brighter picture :

[*Hol.* iii. 552/2/63.]   The Englishmen also for their parts were of good comfort, and nothing abashed of the matter ; and yet they were both hungrie, wearie, sore trauelled, and vexed with manie cold diseases.   Howbeit, reconciling themselues with God by hoossell and shrift, requiring assistance at his hands that is the onelie giuer of victorie, they determined rather to die, than to yeeld, or flee. *[Demeanour of the English.]*

Act IV. sc. i.—Henry and Gloucester enter, and are soon joined by Bedford and Sir Thomas Erpingham.   In the third scene of this Act, Exeter, Westmoreland, and Salisbury take parts, and Warwick has a short speech (l. 20) in the eighth scene.   Gloucester[1] and Exeter[2] were at Agincourt.   Erpingham had the honour of beginning the battle.[3] Bedford and Westmoreland were not at Agincourt.   Westmoreland was a member of a council assigned to Bedford,[4] who was appointed "Custos" of England during Henry's absence.[5]   The presence of Salisbury and Warwick at Agincourt is not, I believe, mentioned by any chronicler.   I do not know an authority for the association of "Talbot"—doubtless the celebrated soldier of that name is meant— with those whom Henry speaks of (IV. iii. 51-55) as sharers in the fame of the coming battle.

Gower calls out "Captaine Fluellen!" (l. 64), and, being reproved by the Welshman, promises to "speake lower" (l. 82). On the previous day (October 24), Henry, after crossing the Ternoise, beheld the French approaching.[6]   Expecting an attack, he disposed his troops for battle. Subsequently the English continued their march until they reached a village in which they encamped.[7]

[*Hol.* iii. 552/2/41.]   Order was taken by commandement from the king, after the armie was first set in battell arraie, that no noise or clamor should be made in the host ; so that, in marching foorth to this village, euerie man kept himselfe quiet : . . . *[The English kept silence.]*

The hour of battle is drawing near when Henry prays (ll. 309-312) :

> Not to day, O Lord,
> O not to day, thinke not vpon the fault
> My Father made in compassing the Crowne !
> I Richards body haue interrèd new ; . . .

Soon after ascending the throne, Henry

---

[1] *Gesta*, 58, 59. *Mons.*, iii. 341.   [2] *Mons.*, iii. 341.
[3] The English attacked ; "before whome there went an old knight, sir Thomas Erpingham (a man of great experience in the warre) with a warder in his hand" (*Hol.* iii. 554/1/53).
[4] *Rymer*, ix. 223.   [5] *Rymer*, ix. 305.
[6] *Gesta*, 46. *Elmham*, 57.   [7] *Gesta*, 46-48. *Elmham*, 57-59.

[*Hol.* iii. 543/2/58.]   caused the bodie of [*p.* 544] king Richard
to be remooued with all funerall dignitie conuenient for his estate,
from Langlie to Westminster; where he was honorablie interred
with queene Anne his first wife, in a solemne toome erected and
set vp at the charges of this king.

[Richard's body removed from Langley to Westminster.]

Henry also pleads (ll. 315-319) :

> Fiue hundred poore I haue in yeerely pay,
> Who twice a day their wither'd hands hold vp
> Toward Heauen, to pardon blood ; and I haue built
> Two Chauntries, where the sad and solemne Priests
> Sing still for Richards Soule.

Fabyan records (577) Henry's prouision that there should be, on
Richard's behalf,

one day in the weke a Solempne Dirige, and vpon the morowe a
Masse of Requiem by note ; after which Masse endyd, to be gyuen
wekely vnto pore people. xi. s. viii. d. in pens : & vpon y° day of
his Anniuersary, after y° sayd masse of Requiem is songe, to be
yerely Destrybuted for his soule. xx. li. in .d.

[A weekly mass and alms.]

[A yearly almsgiving.]

Henry founded three [1] houses of religion,

[*Fab.,* 589.]   for asmoche as he knewe well that his Fader had
laboured the meanes to depose the noble Prynce Richarde the
Seconde, and after was consentyng to his deth ; for which offence
his said Fader had sent to Rome, of that great Cryme to be
assayled, and was by y° Pope enioyned, that lyke as he had beraft
hym of his naturall and bodely lyfe for euer in this world, that so,
by contynuel prayer and Suffragies of the Churche, he shuld cause
his Soule to lyue perpetuelly in the Celestyall worlde.

[Henry IV. enjoined by the Pope to haue continual prayer made for Richard's soul.]

Act IV. sc. ii.—" The Sunne is high " (l. 63) when the Constable
exclaims (ll. 60-62) :

> I stay but for my Guard.   On !   To the field ! [2]
> I will the Banner from a Trumpet take,
> And vse it for my haste.

Henry is said to have received a message from the French leaders,
inviting him to fix his ransom (see p. 191 below).

[*Hol.* iii. 554/1/23.]   When the messenger was come backe to
the French host, the men of warre put on their helmets, and

---

[1] One of the houses was dissolved by Henry V.—*Fab.*, 589.
[2] *I . . . Guard: on To . . . take,*] F1.

caused their trumpets to blow to the battell.   They thought themselues so sure of victorie, that diuerse of the noble men made such
hast towards the battell, that they left manie of their seruants and
men of warre behind them, and some of them would not once staie
for their standards: as, amongst other, the duke of Brabant, when
his standard was not come, caused a baner to be taken from a
trumpet and fastened to a speare; the which he commanded to be
borne before him in steed of his standard.

Act IV. sc. iii.—The English leaders converse before each goes to
his charge.   Speaking of the French, Westmoreland says (l. 3) :

> Of fighting men they haue full threescore thousand.

This was Halle's [1] computation, according to whom they had

[*Hol.* iii. 552/2/56.] in their armie (as some write) to the
number of threescore thousand horssemen, besides footmen,
wagoners, and other.

Exeter remarks (l. 4) :

> There's fiue to one ; besides they all are fresh.

Shakspere made large allowance for losses on the march, and
invalided soldiers.   After crossing the Somme, Henry

[*Hol.* iii. 552/1/15.] determined to make haste towards Calis,
and not to seeke for battell, except he were thereto constreined ;
bicause that his armie by sicknesse was sore diminished : in so
much that he had but onelie two thousand horssemen, and
thirteene thousand archers, bilmen, and of all sorts of other
footmen.

When the King enters, Westmoreland cries (ll. 16-18) :

> O that we now had here
> But one ten thousand of those men in England,
> That doe no worke to day !

Henry expresses another view of the matter (ll. 20, 21) :

> If we are markt to dye, we are enow
> To doe our Countrey losse ; . . .

These words comprise all that Shakspere took from a speech

---

[1] Though in the sidenote *Hol.* refers to "Enguerant" (Monstrelet) as an
authority for 60,000, this estimate is really derived from *Halle* (65).   But
Mons.—whom, to judge from the context, *Halle* followed—says (iii. 335) that
"les François fussent bien cent cinquante mille chevaucheurs."

attributed to Henry by Livius[1] (Forojuliensis), and englished by Holinshed. This speech[2] should be contrasted with IV. iii. 21-67.

[*Hol.* iii. 553/2/44.] It is said, that as he heard one[3] of the host vtter his wish to another thus: "I would to God there were "with vs now so manie good soldiers as are at this houre within "England!" the king answered: "I would not wish a man more "here than I haue; we are indeed in comparison to the enimies "but a few, but if God of his clemencie doo fauour vs, and our "inst cause, (as I trust he will,) we shall speed well inough. But "let no man ascribe victorie to our owne strength and might, but "onelie to Gods assistance; to whome I haue no doubt we shall "worthilie haue cause to giue thanks therefore. And if so be that "for our offenses sakes we shall be deliuered into the hands of our "enimies, the lesse number we be, the lesse damage shall the "realme of England susteine; but if we should fight in trust of "multitude of men, and so get the victorie, (our minds being prone "to pride,) we should thervpon peraduenture ascribe the victorie "not so much to the gift of God, as to our owne puissance, and "thereby prouoke his high indignation and displeasure against vs: "and if the enimie get the vpper hand, then should our realme "and countrie suffer more damage and stand in further danger. "But be you of good comfort, and shew your selues valiant! God "and our iust quarrell shall defend vs, and deliuer these our proud "aduersaries with all the multitude of them which you see (or at "the least the most of them) into our hands."

As Henry dismisses the English leaders to their posts, he is

A wish.
A noble courage of a valiant prince.

[If our enemies prevail, the fewer we are the less loss shall England sustain.]

---

[1] *Livius,* 16, 17.

[2] Part of another speech of Henry to his "capteins and soldiers"—epitomized by *Hol.* (553/2/32) from *Halle* (67, 68)—has a more Shaksperian tone: "To conclude, manie words of courage he vttered, to stirre them to doo manfullie, assuring them that England should neuer be charged with his ransome, nor anie Frenchman triumph ouer him as a captiue; for either by famous death or glorious victorie would he (by Gods grace) win honour and fame."

[3] Sir Walter Hungerford. This wish was uttered on October 24, after the English had crossed the Ternoise and were expecting an attack. Henry's chaplain—an ear-witness, as the words I quote indicate—says: "Et inter cætera quæ tunc dicta notaui, quidam dominus Walterus Hungyrford miles imprecabatur ad faciem regis quod habuisset ad illam paucam familiam quam ibi habuit, decem millia de melioribus sagittariis Angliæ, qui secum desiderarent esse. Cui rex, . . . nollem habere etsi possem plures per unum quàm habeo."—*Gesta,* 47.

addressed by Montjoy, whom the Constable has sent with a message (ll. 79-81):

> Once more I come to know of thee, King Harry,
> If for thy Ransome thou wilt now compound,
> Before thy most assuréd Ouerthrow: . . .

In his answer Henry recounts his soldiers' vow that (ll. 116-121)

>   yet ere Night
> They'le be in fresher Robes ; or they will pluck
> The gay new Coats o're the French Souldiers heads,
> And turne them out of seruice. If they doe this,
> (As, if God please, they shall,) my Ransome then
> Will soone be leuyed.

And adds (ll. 122-125):

> Come thou no more for Ransome, gentle Herauld !
> They shall haue none, I sweare, but these my ioynts,
> Which if they haue as I will leaue vm them,
> Shall yeeld them little, tell the Constable !

This incident is based on the following story :

[*Hol.* iii. 554/1/13.] Here we may not forget how the French, thus in their iolitie, sent an herald to king Henrie, to inquire what ransome he would offer. Wherevnto he answered, that within two or three houres he hoped it would so happen, that the Frenchmen should be glad to common rather with the Englishmen for their ransoms, than the English to take thought for their deliuerance ; promising for his owne part, that his dead carcasse should rather be a prize to the Frenchmen, than that his liuing bodie should paie anie ransome.

Hall.
[The French desired Henry to offer them a ransom. He said that ransoms might be required from them, but that they should have nothing save his dead body.]

As the scene closes, York[1] enters and craves a boon (ll. 129, 130) :

> My Lord, most humbly on my knee I begge
> The leading of the Vaward !

Holinshed says that Henry

[*Hol.* iii. 553/1/55.] appointed a vaward, of the which he made capteine, Edward duke of Yorke, who of an haultie courage had desired that office, . . .

[York captain of the vaward.]

Act IV. sc. iv.—That Pistol was able to win a ransom shows how utterly the French were defeated. As some warrant for the possibility of such luck as befel " this roaring diuell i'th olde play " (IV. iv. 75, 76), I quote a passage from Holinshed, who thus describes the result of

---

[1] Aumerle in *Rich. II.* Lydgate tells us that York "fell on kne " to beg this command from Henry.—*Chron. Lond.*, 226.

a threatening movement made by Henry against the French rearward. (The closing words of this excerpt should be noted.)

The French rearward discomfited.

[*Hol.* iii. 554/2/30.] When the Frenchmen perceiued his intent, they were suddenlie amazed and ran awaie like sheepe ; without order or arraie. Which when the king perceiued, he incouraged his men, and followed so quickelie vpon the enimies, that they ran hither and thither, casting awaie their armour : manie on their knees desired to haue their liues saued.

      Act IV. sc. vi.—" Enter the King and his trayne, with Prisoners." Henry says (l. 2) that "all's not done ; yet keepe the French the field." By and bye an alarum is heard, and he exclaims (ll. 35-38) :

> But, hearke ! what new alarum is this same !
> The French haue re-inforc'd their scatter'd men :
> Then euery souldiour kill his Prisoners ;
> Giue the word through !

      Act IV. sc. vii.—We now learn what had happened. Fluellen enters, speaking to Gower (ll. 1-4) : " Kill the poyes and the luggage ! 'Tis expressely against the Law of Armes : 'tis as arrant a peece of knauery, marke you now, as can bee offert : in your Conscience now, is it not ?" Gower answers : " 'Tis certaine there's not a boy left aliue ; and the Cowardly Rascalls that ranne from the battaile ha' done this slaughter : besides, they haue burned and carried away all that was in the Kings Tent ; wherefore the King, most worthily, hath caus'd euery soldiour to cut his prisoners throat."

      When the French van and centre had been overthrown, their rearward put to flight, and

[*Hol.* iii. 554/2/38.] the Englishmen had taken a great number of prisoners, certeine Frenchmen on horssebacke, whereof were capteins Robinet of Borneuill, Rifflart of Clamas, Isambert of Agincourt, and other men of armes, to the number of six hundred horssemen, (which were the first that fled,) hearing that the English tents & pauilions were a good waie distant from the armie, without anie sufficient gard to defend the same, either vpon a couetous meaning to gaine by the spoile, or vpon a desire to be reuenged, *The kings campe robbed [, and the seruants who resisted killed].* entred vpon the kings campe ; and there spoiled the hails, robbed the tents, brake vp chests, and caried awaie caskets, and slue such seruants as they found to make anie resistance. . . .

[The outcry of the lackies and boys who ran away came But when the outcrie of the lackies and boies, which ran awaie for feare of the Frenchmen thus spoiling the campe, came to the kings eares, he, (doubting least his enimies should gather togither

againe, and begin a new field; and mistrusting further that the to Henry's ears.]
prisoners would be an aid to his enimies, or the verie enimies to
their takers in deed if they were suffered to liue,) contrarie to his
accustomed gentlenes, commanded by sound of trumpet, that
euerie man (vpon paine of death) should incontinentlie slaie his All the prisoners slaine.
prisoner.

"Alarum. Enter King Harry with Burbon and prisoners.[1]
Flourish." As sc. v., Act IV., ends, Bourbon and the other French
leaders rush out, hoping to retrieve the day or at least sell their lives
dearly. Entering now with the prisoners taken during this renewal of
the conflict, Henry speaks thus (ll. 58-68) :

> I was not angry since I came to France,
> Vntill this instant.—Take a Trumpet, Herald ;
> Ride thou vnto the Horsemen on yond hill :   60
> If they will fight with vs, bid them come downe,
> Or voyde the field ; they do offend our sight :
> If they'l do neither, we will come to them,
> And make them sker away, as swift as stones   64
> Enforcëd from the old Assyrian slings :
> Besides, wee'l cut the throats of those we haue ;
> And not a man of them that we shall take,
> Shall taste our mercy !   Go and tell them so !

The prisoners spoken of here (l. 66) are evidently those who have
been captured with Bourbon; not those who entered in sc. vi., Act IV.
The existence of an entry showing that a second batch of prisoners was
taken disposes of Johnson's stricture on IV. vii. 66 : "The King
is in a very bloody disposition. He has already cut the throats of his
prisoners, and threatens now to cut them again."[2] Moreover, Shakspere had authority—as the following excerpt shows—for a renewal of
the battle after the prisoners previously taken were massacred.

[*Hol.* iii. 554/2/74.] When this lamentable slaughter was ended,
the [*p.* 555] Englishmen disposed themselues in order of battell,
readie to abide a new field, and also to inuade, and newlie set on,
their enimies: with great force they assailed the earles of Marle A fresh onset.
and Fauconbridge, and the lords of Louraie, and of Thine, with
six hundred men of armes ; who had all that daie kept togither,
but [were] now slaine and beaten downe out of hand.

Immediately after this passage comes Holinshed's account (see next
excerpt) of the means adopted to rid the field of the lingering Frenchmen, whom Shakspere made Henry threaten with the slaughter "of
those" prisoners "we haue" (IV. vii. 66).

---

[1] *Enter . . . prisoners*] *Enter King Harry and Burbon with prisoners.* F1.
[2] *Var. Sh.*, xvii. 440.

[*Hol.* iii. 555/1/7.] Some write, that the king, perceiuing his enimies in one part to assemble togither, as though they meant to giue a new battell for preseruation of the prisoners, sent to them an herald, commanding them either to depart out of his sight, or *A right wise* else to come forward at once, and giue battell: promising herewith, *and valiant* *challenge of* that, if they did offer to fight againe, not onelie those prisoners *the king.* which his people alreadie had taken, but also so manie of them as, in this new conflict, which they thus attempted, should fall into his hands, should die the death without redemption.

The Frenchmen, fearing the sentence of so terrible a decree, without further delaie parted out of the field.

The bearer of Henry's message to the French horsemen goes out, and Montjoy, entering, begs (ll. 74-76),

for charitable License,
That we may wander ore this bloody field,
To booke our dead, and then to bury them ; . . .

Henry is not sure "if the day be ours, or no" (l. 87); and, when Montjoy says, "The day is yours," asks, "What is this Castle call'd that stands hard by ?" Montjoy answers : "They call it Agincourt." Henry replies (l. 93): "Then call we this the field of Agincourt." Shakspere rightly altered the date which my next quotation assigns to Montjoy's replies.[1]

[Montjoy *desired leave* [*Hol.* iii. 555/1/36.] In the morning, Montioie king at armes *to bury the* *dead. Henry* and foure other French heralds came to the K., to know the *asked to* *whom the* number of prisoners, and to desire buriall for the dead. Before *victory* *belonged.]* he made them answer (to vnderstand what they would saie) he demanded of them whie they made to him that request ; considering that he knew not whether the victorie was his or theirs ? When Montioie by true and iust confession had cleered that doubt to the high praise of the king, he desired of Montioie to vnderstand the name of the castell neere adioining: when they had told him that *The battell of* it was called Agincourt, he said, "Then shall this conflict be called *Agincourt.* "the battell of Agincourt."

"Fought on the day of Crispin Crispianus !" adds Henry, when he has named the battle. After telling us how the English behaved on the night of October 24 (see p. 187 above), Holinshed continues:

---

[1] According to *Mons.* (iii. 346) both these replies were given on the day of the battle. He does not say that Montjoy asked leave to bury the dead. The French dead were left unburied till Henry quitted Agincourt, on October 26.—*Mons.*, iii. 357.

[*Hol.* iii. 552/2/70.] The daie following was the fiue and
twentith of October in the yeare 1415; being then fridaie, and the
feast of Crispine and Crispinian: a day faire and fortunate to the
English, but most sorrowfull and vnluckie to the French.

*The battell of
Agincourt,
the 25 of
October,
1415.*

Permission having been granted to register and bury the French
dead, Montjoy departs, accompanied, as Henry directs, by some English
heralds (l. 121). Holinshed relates that Henry

[*Hol.* iii. 555/1/48.] feasted the French officers of armes that
daie, and granted them their request; which busilie sought through
the field for such as were slaine. But the Englishmen suffered
them not to go alone, for they searched with them, & found manie
hurt, but not in ieopardie of their liues; whom they tooke prisoners,
and brought them to their tents.

[The French
heralds not
allowed to
go alone
seeking for
the slain.]

For the accomplishment of a practical joke, Henry gives Fluellen a
glove, saying (ll. 161-163): "when Alanson and my selfe were downe
together, I pluckt this Gloue from his Helme." Reference is here made
to an encounter which Holinshed thus describes:

[*Hol.* 554/2/20.] The king that daie shewed himselfe a valiant
knight, albeit almost felled by the duke of Alanson; yet with
plaine strength he slue two of the dukes companie, and felled the
duke himselfe; whome, when he would haue yelded, the kings gard
(contrarie to his mind) slue out of hand.

*A valiant
king. [His
encounter
with
Alençon.]*

Act IV. sc. viii.—A herald presents to Henry a note containing
"the number of the slaught'red French" (l. 79). From Exeter the
King learns "what Prisoners of good sort" have been taken. I give
below, in parallel columns, Shakspere's metrical roll of the French
prisoners, and of those slain on either side, for comparison with
Holinshed's lists.

[*Hol.* iii. 555/2/30.] There were
taken prisoners: *Charles duke of
Orleance, nephue to the* French
*king; Iohn duke of Burbon; the
lord Bouciqualt,* one of the marshals of France (he after died in
England); with a number *of other
lords, knights, and esquiers,* at the
least *fifteene hundred, besides* the
common people. There were *slaine*
in all of the *French* part to the
number of ten thousand men;
whereof were *princes* and noble

Exe. *Charles Duke of Orleance,
    Nephew to the King;*
Iohn *Duke of Burbon,* and Lord
    Bouchiquald;
Of other Lords and Barons, *Knights
    and Squires,*
Full *fifteene hundred, besides common 84
    men.*
King. This Note doth tell me *of
    ten thousand French,*
That in the field lye *slaine:* of
    Princes, in this number,
And Nobles *bearing Banners,* there
    lye dead
One hundred twentie six: added to 88
    these,

*Noble men
prisoners.*

*The number
slaine on the
French part.*

Englishmen slaine.¹

men *bearing baners one hundred twentie* and *six; to these, of knights, esquiers, and gentlemen,* so manie as made vp the number of *eight thousand and foure hundred (of the which fiue hundred were dubbed knights* the night before the battell): *so as, of the meaner sort, not past sixteene hundred.* Amongst those of the nobilitie that were slaine, these were the cheefest: *Charles lord de la Breth, high constable of France; Iaques of Chatilon, lord of Dampier, admerall of France; the lord Rambures, master of the crossebowes; sir Guischard Dolphin, great master of France; Iohn duke of Alanson; Anthonie duke of Brabant, brother to the duke of Burgognie; Edward duke of Bar;* the earle of Neuers, an other brother to the duke of Burgognie; with the *erles of Marle, Vaudemont, Beaumont, Grandpree, Roussie, Fauconberge, Fois, and Lestrake;* beside a great number of lords and barons of name.

Of Englishmen, there died at this battell, *Edward duke of²* *Yorke; the earle of Suffolke; sir Richard Kikelie; and Dauie Gamms, esquier; and, of all other,* not aboue *fiue and twentie* persons, . . .³

Of Knights, Esquires, and gallant Gentlemen,
Eight thousand and foure hundred; of the which,
Fiue hundred were but yesterday dubb'd Knights:
So that, in these ten thousand they [92] haue lost,
There are but sixteene hundred Mercenaries;
The rest are Princes, Barons, Lords, Knights, Squires,
And Gentlemen of bloud and qualitie.
The Names of those their Nobles [96] that lye dead:
Charles Delabreth, High Constable of France;
Iaques of Chatilion, Admirall of France;
The Master of the Crosse-bowes, Lord Rambures;
Great Master of France, the braue [100] Sir Guichard Dolphin;
Iohn Duke of Alanson; Anthonie Duke of Brabant,
The Brother to the Duke of Burgundie;
And Edward Duke of Barr: of lustie Earles,
Grandpree and Roussie, Fauconbridge [104] and Foyes,
Beaumont and Marle, Vaudemont and Lestrale.
Here was a Royall fellowship of death!
Where is the number of our English dead?—
Edward the Duke of Yorke, the [108] Earle of Suffolke,
Sir Richard Ketly, Dauy Gam, Esquire:
None else of name; and, of all other men,
But fiue and twentie.

The death-rolls read, and solemn acknowledgment made that the victory is due to God alone, Henry says (l. 128):

Let there be sung *Non nobis,* and *Te Deum.*

These thanksgivings are recorded by Holinshed:

[*Hol.* iii. 555/1/21.] And so, about foure of the clocke in the after noone, the king, when he saw no apperance of enimies, caused

---

¹ In *Hol.* the sidenote "Englishmen slaine" is printed twice: here, and also immediately after the sidenote ending "French part."
² *duke of Yorke*] Hol. ed. 1. *duke Yorke* Hol. ed. 2.
³ "as some doo report" (says *Hol.*); "but other writers of greater credit" (Grafton and Livius) raised the numbers of the slain.

the retreit to be blowen ; and, gathering his armie togither, gaue
thanks to almightie God for so happie a victorie ; causing his *Thanks given to God for the victorie.*
prelats and chapleins to sing this psalme : " In exitu Israel de
" Aegypto ; " and commanded euerie man to kneele downe on the
ground at this verse : " *Non nobis*, Domine, non nobis, sed nomini *A woorthie example of a*
" tuo da gloriam." Which doone, he caused *Te Deum*, with certeine *godlie prince.*
anthems to be soong ; giuing laud and praise to God, without
boasting of his owne force or anie humane power.

> Naught remains save the burial of the dead,
>   And then to Callice, and to England then : . . .

The resumption (on October 26 [1]) of Henry's march to Calais is
thus chronicled :

[*Hol.* iii. 555/1/55.] When the king of England had well
refreshed himselfe, and his souldiers, (that had taken the spoile of
such as were slaine,) he, with his prisoners, in good order, returned *[Return to Calais.]*
to his towne of Calis.

Act V. Chorus.—The Chorus plays a historic "interim," beginning
on October 29,[2] 1415, when the audience must imagine Henry at
Calais (ll. 6, 7), and ending on August 1, 1417, the date of his " backe
returne againe to France " [3] (ll. 39-43).   Nothing is said touching his
second campaign, which lasted about four years, and was brought to a
close by the treaty of Troyes, in 1420.
Shakspere's figure of (ll. 11-13)

>   the deep-mouth'd Sea,
>   Which, like a mightie Whiffler 'fore the King,
>   Seemes to prepare his way,

was perhaps suggested by Holinshed's mention of the gale which
Henry's fleet encountered on its return to England.

[*Hol.* iii. 556/1/16.] After that the king of England had *Hall.*
refreshed himselfe, and his people at Calis, . . . the sixt [16th]
daie of Nouember,[4] he with all his prisoners tooke shipping, and
the same daie-landed at Douer, . . . In this passage, the seas *[The seas were rough.*
were so rough and troublous, that two ships belonging to sir Iohn

---

[1] *Gesta*, 60.
[2] The date of Henry's arrival at Calais.—*Gesta*, 60.
[3] He landed near Touque Castle, in Normandy, on August 1, 1417.—
Gesta, 111.
[4] Henry, " die Sabbati post sancti Martini solennia, . . . per portum
Dovoriæ . . . remeavit in Angliam."—*Gesta*, 60.   In 1415 S. Martin's Day
(Nov. 11) fell on a Monday.

Cornewall, lord Fanhope, were driuen into Zeland; howbeit,
nothing was lost, nor any person perisht.

Henry having landed, and "set on to London,"

> You may imagine him vpon Black-Heath,   16
> Where that his Lords desire him to haue borne
> His bruisèd Helmet, and his bendèd Sword,
> Before him, through the Citie: he forbids it,
> Being free from vain-nesse and selfe-glorious pride;   20
> Giuing full Trophee, Signall, and Ostént,
> Quite from himselfe, to God. But now behold,
> In the quick Forge and working-house of Thought,
> How London doth powre out her Citisens!   24
> The Maior and all his Brethren, in best sort,
> (Like to the Senatours of th'antique Rome,
> With the Plebeians swarming at their beeles,)
> Goe forth and fetch their Conqu'ring Cæsar in: . . .   28

Holinshed gives the following account of Henry's reception and
demeanour:

[Henry met
on Black-
heath by the
Mayor and
Aldermen of
London.]
[*Hol.* iii. 556/1/28.] The maior of London, and the aldermen,
apparelled in orient grained scarlet, and foure hundred commoners
clad in beautifull murrie, (well mounted, and trimlie horssed, with
rich collars, & great chaines,) met the king on Blackheath;[1] reioising
at his returne: and the clergie of London, with rich crosses, sumptuous copes, and massie censers, receiued him at saint Thomas of
Waterings with solemne procession.

*Titus
Liuius.*
The king, like a graue and sober personage, and as one remem-
bring from whom all victories are sent, seemed little to regard such
*The great
modestie of
the king.*
[He would
not suffer
his helmet
to be carried
with him.]
vaine pompe and shewes as were in triumphant sort deuised for
his welcomming home from so prosperous a iournie: in so much
that he would not suffer his helmet to be caried with him, whereby
might haue appeared to the people the blowes and dints that were
to be seene in the same; neither would he suffer anie ditties to be
made and soong by minstrels of his glorious victorie, for that he
would wholie haue the praise and thanks altogither giuen to God.

The last occurrence of the Interim is that (ll. 38, 39)

> The Emperour's comming[2] in behalfe of France,
> To order peace betweene them; . . .

---

[1] On November 23.—*Gesta*, 61.
[2] "Emperour's comming" = "Emperour is comming": assuming "As yet
. . . betweene them" (ll. 36-39) to be a parenthesis.

On or about May 1, 1416,[1]

[*Hol.* iii. 556/2/27.] the emperour Sigismund . . . came into England, to the intent that he might make an attonement betweene king Henrie and the French king: . . .

Anno Reg. 4.
The emperor
Sigismund
commeth into
England.

Act V. sc. ii.—This scene ends with Katharine of Valois's betrothal to Henry V. (ll. 376-397), on May 21, 1420. The Duke of Burgundy who speaks in this scene, and who, as appears from my next excerpt, sent "ambassadours . . . to mooue" Henry "to peace," was Philip the Good, son of John the Fearless, whom Charles VI. addresses in III. v. 42.[2] In September (?),[3] 1419, while Henry was at Rouen,

[*Hol.* iii. 572/1/18.] there came to him eftsoones ambassadours from the French king and the duke of Burgognie to mooue him to peace. The king, minding not to be reputed for a destroier of the countrie, which he coueted to preserue, or for a causer of christian bloud still to be spilt in his quarell, began so to incline and giue eare vnto their sute and humble request, that at length, (after often sending to and fro,) and that the bishop of Arras, and other men of honor had beene with him, and likewise the earle of Warwike, and the bishop of Rochester had beene with the duke of Burgognie, they both finallie agreed vpon certeine articles; so that the French king and his commons would thereto assent.

King Henrie
condescend-
eth to a
treatie of
peace.

Now was the French king and the queene with their daughter Katharine at Trois in Champaigne; gouerned and ordered by them, which so much fauoured the duke of Burgognie, that they would not, for anie earthlie good, once hinder or pull backe one iot of such articles as the same duke should seeke to preferre. And therefore what needeth manie words? a truce tripartite was accorded betweene the two kings and the duke, and their countries; and order taken that the king of England should send, in the companie of the duke of Burgognie, his ambassadours vnto Trois in Champaigne; sufficientlie authorised to treat and conclude of so great matter. The king of England, being in good hope that all his affaires should take good successe as he could wish or desire,

A truce
tripartite.

---

[1] According to *Chron. Lond.* (103): "the firste day of Maij, at nyght, he [Sigismund] landed at Dovorr."

[2] Philip was then (October, 1415) Count of Charolois. He is addressed by Charles VI. (III. v. 45).

[3] *Mons.*, iv. 203-207. The murder of John the Fearless, on September 10, 1419 (*Mons.*, iv. 179), caused his son to take this step.

Ambassadors from K. Henrie to the French king. sent to the duke of Burgognie, his vncle the duke of Excester, the earle of Salisburie, the bishop of Elie, the lord Fanhope, the lord Fits Hugh, sir Iohn Robsert, and sir Philip Hall, with diuerse doctors, to the number of fiue hundred horsse; which in the companie of the duke of Burgognie came to the citie of Trois the eleuenth of March. The king, the queene, and the ladie Katharine them receiued, and hartilie welcomed; shewing great signes and tokens of loue and amitie.

The articles of the peace concluded betweene king Henrie and the French king. After a few daies they fell to councell, in which at length it was concluded, that king Henrie of England should come to Trois, and marie the ladie Katharine; and the king hir father after his death should make him heire of his realme, crowne, and dignitie. It was also agreed, that king Henrie, during his father in lawes life, should in his steed haue the whole gouernement of the realme of France, as regent thereof: with manie other couenants and articles, as after shall appeere.

Burgundy begins an appeal for peace by reminding the sovereigns of England and France (ll. 24-28) how he has laboured to bring them

Vnto this Barre and Royall enterview, . . .

Perhaps Shakspere supposed that the same course was taken at Troyes as had been adopted at Meulan, where, on May 29, 1419,[1] Henry, Queen Isabelle, the Princess Katharine, and John Duke of Burgundy, met to hold a personal conference which, it was hoped, might lead to a peace between England and France. Henry then had his ground

[Henry's ground 'barred about.'] [*Hol.* iii. 569/2/2.] barred about and ported, wherin his tents were pight in a princelie maner.

Burgundy winds up his speech by desiring to know "the *Let*" (l. 65) which hinders the return of Peace to France. Henry answers (ll. 68-71):

If, Duke of Burgonie, you would the Peace,
Whose want giues growth to th'imperfections
Which you haue cited, you must buy that Peace
With full accord to *all* our iust demands, . . .

Shakspere may have been thinking of the unsuccessful close of the conference at Meulan, when Henry,

[The 'let' to Henry's desires.] [*Hol.* iii. 569/2/43.] mistrusting that the duke of Burgognie was the verie *let* and stop of his desires, said vnto him before his departure: "Coosine, we will haue your kings daughter, and *all*

---

[1] *Rymer*, ix. 759.

"things that we demand with hir, or we will driue your king and
"you out of his realme."

Charles VI. then retires to scrutinize the treaty of peace ; and is
attended by some members of the English Council, whom Henry thus
names (ll. 83-85) :

> Goe, Vnckle Exeter,
> And Brother Clarence, and you, Brother Gloucester,
> Warwick, and Huntington, goe with the King ; . . .

Henry went to Troyes,

[*Hol.* iii. 572/2/8.] accompanied with his brethren the dukes
of Clarence and Glocester, the earles of Warwike, Salisburie,
Huntington, . . .[1] [The English peers who went with Henry to Troyes.]

A revision of the treaty, after Henry's arrival at Troyes, is noticed
by Holinshed, who says that

[*Hol.* iii. 572/2/32.] the two kings and their councell assembled
togither diuerse daies ; wherein the first concluded agreement was
in diuerse points altered and brought to a certeinetie, according to
the effect aboue mentioned.[2] [The treaty revised.]

Queen Isabelle desires to have a voice in discussing the treaty ;
whereupon Henry asks that the Princess Katharine may remain with
him :

> She is our capitall Demand, compris'd
> Within the fore-ranke of our Articles.—ll. 96, 97.

The first article of the treaty of Troyes runs thus :

[*Hol.* iii. 573/1/61.] 1 First, it is accorded betweene our father
and vs, that forsomuch as by the bond of matrimonie made for the
good of the peace betweene vs and our most deere beloued
Katharine,[3] daughter of our said father, & of our most deere

---

[1] Charles (*St. Denys*, vi. 410), Isabelle, and Clarence (*Juv.*, 480), were at
Troyes when Henry married Katharine. On December 30, 1419, Gloucester
was appointed Warden of England because Bedford had been summoned to
join Henry.—*Rymer*, ix. 830. Gloucester was to hold office during the King's
absence.—*Ibid.* From what Exeter says in a letter written at Troyes, on May
23, 1420, I infer that he was present at the convention and betrothal.—*Rymer*,
ix. 907, 908. On June 4, 1420, Henry resumed his campaign (*Gesta*, 142) ;
and, in July, 1420, he had with him, at the siege of Melun, Clarence, Bedford,
Exeter, Huntingdon, and Warwick.—*Gesta*, 144. *Wals.*, ii. 335.

[2] See excerpt at p. 200 above.

[3] In May, 1419, Katharine was at Meulan (p. 200 above), having been
brought thither " by hir mother onelie to the intent that the king of England,
beholding hir excellent beautie, should be so inflamed and rapt in hir loue,
that he, to obteine hir to his wife, should the sooner agree to a gentle peace

moother Isabell his wife, the same Charles and Isabell beene made
[Filial
reverence
due from
Henry to
Katharine's
parents.]
our father and moother: therefore them as our father and moother
we shall haue and worship, as it fitteth and seemeth so worthie a
prince and princesse to be worshipped, principallie before all other
temporall persons of the world.

Soon after the re-entry of Charles, Isabelle, Burgundy, and the rest,
Exeter points out that an article of the treaty has not yet been
subscribed (ll. 364-370) : " Where your Maiestie demands, ' *That* the
King of France, hauing any occasion to *write* for matter of Graunt,[1]
shall name your Highnesse *in this* forme, and with this addition, *in
French: Nostre trescher fils Henry, Roy d'Angleterre, Heretere de
Fraunce; and thus in Latine: Præclarissimus Filius noster Henricus,
Rex Angliæ, & Heres Franciæ.'* "

This article appears in Holinshed with the same mistranslation of
treschier[2] as is found in Shakspere's text.

[*Hol.* iii. 574/2/69.]   25 Also *that* our said father, during his
life, *shall name*, call, and *write* vs *in French in this* maner: *Nostre*
[Henry to be
styled heir
of France.]
*treschier filz Henry roy d'Engleterre heretere de France. And in
Latine* in this maner: *Præclarissimus filius noster Henricus rex
Angliæ & hæres Franciæ.*

Isabelle having invoked God's blessing on the wedlock which is to
bring with it the union of England and France (ll. 387-396), Henry
says (ll. 398-400):

> Prepare we for our Marriage ! on which day,
> My Lord of Burgundy, wee'le take your Oath,
> And all the Peeres, for suretie of our Leagues.

On reaching Troyes, Henry rested a while, and then

*King Henrie
commeth to
Troie to the
French king.*
[*Hol.* iii. 572/2/26.]   went to visit the French king, the queene,
and the ladie Katharine, whome he found in saint Peters church,
where was a verie ioious meeting betwixt them; (and this was on
*King Henrie
affieth the
French kings
daughter.*
the twentith daie of Maie ;)[3] and there the king of England and the
ladie Katharine were affianced.

---

and louing concord."—*Hol.* iii. 569/2/11.   The conferences at Meulan led to
no result, " same onlie that a certeine sparke of burning loue was kindled in
the kings heart by the sight of the ladie Katharine."—*Hol.* iii. 569/2/38.
[1] By article 23 it is stipulated that, as a rule, "*grants* of offices and gifts
. . . shall be written and proceed vnder the name and seale of " Charles VI.
—*Hol.* 574/2/51.
[2] *Præclarissimus*] Hol. edd. 1 and 2. *Præclarissimus* Halle (ed. 1550).
Præcharissimus Halle (edd. of 1548).
[3] May 21. In a letter written at Troyes on May 22, 1420, and addressed
to the Duke of Gloucester, Warden of England, Henry says: " Upon Moneday,
the xx. day of this present Monath of May, wee arriued in this Towne of

When the terms of the treaty were finally settled,

[*Hol.* iii. 572/2/37.] the kings sware for their parts to obserue all the couenants of this league and agreement. Likewise the duke of Burgognie, and a great number of other princes and nobles which were present, recciued an oth, . . .

I close the excerpts illustrating this play with the panegyric of Henry, which Holinshed deriued from Halle.

[*Hol.* iii. 583/1/59.] This Henric was a king, of life without spot; a prince whome all men loued, and of none disdained; a capteine against whome fortune neuer frowned, nor mischance once spurned; whose people him so seuere a iusticer both loued and obeied, (and so humane withall,) that he left no offense vnpunished, nor freendship vnrewarded; a terrour to rebels, and suppressour of sedition; his vertues notable, his qualities most praise-worthie. *The commendation of king Henrie the fift, as is expressed by maister* Hall [, 112].

In strength and nimblenesse of bodie from his youth few to him comparable; for in wrestling, leaping,[1] and running, no man well able to compare. In casting of great iron barres and heauie stones he excelled commonlie all men; neuer shrinking at cold, nor slothfull for heat; and, when he most laboured, his head commonlie vncouered; no more wearie of harnesse than a light cloake; verie valiantlie abiding at needs both hunger and thirst; so manfull of mind as neuer seene to quinch at a wound, or to smart at the paine; to turne his nose from euil sauour, or to close[2] his eies from smoke or dust; no man more moderate in eating and drinking, with diet not delicate, but rather more meet for men of warre, than *[Henry's strength, agility, and endurance.]*

Troyes; And on the Morowe hadden a Convention betwix our Moder the Queene of France, and our Brother the Duc of Burgoigne (as Commissaire of the King of France our Fader for his Party) and Us in our own Personne, for our Partie: And th' Accorde of the . . . Pees Perpetuell was there Sworne by both the sayde Commissaires, yn name of our foresaid Fader; And semblably by Us in oure owne Name: . . . Also at the saide Convention was Mariage betrowthed betwixt Us and oure Wyf, Doghter of our forsaid Fader the King of France."—*Rymer,* ix. 906, 907. The date of the marriage is given in a private letter written at Sens by "Johan Ofort," on June 6, 1420: "And, as touchyng Tydynges, The Kyng owre Sovereyn Loord was Weddid, with greet Solempnitee, in the Cathedrale Chirche of Treys, abowte Myd day on Trinite Sunday" [June 2].—*Rymer,* ix. 910.

[1] In his wooing of Katharine, Henry says (V. ii. 142-145): "If I could winne a Lady at Leape-frogge, or by vawting into my Saddle with my Armour on my backe, (vnder the correction of bragging be it spoken,) I should quickly leape into a Wife."

[2] *to turne . . . or to close*] *not to turne . . . nor close* Hol.

[Any honest
person
might speak
to him at
mealtimes,
and he
would gladly
hear causes
himself.]
for princes or tender stomachs. Euerie honest person was permitted to come to him, sitting at meale; where either secretlie or
openlie to declare his mind. High and weightie causes, as well
betweene men of warre and other, he would gladlie heare; and
either determined them himselfe, or else for end committed them

[He slept
little, but
very
soundly.]
to others. He slept verie little, but that verie soundlie, in so
much that when his soldiers soong at nights, or minstrels plaied,
he then slept fastest; of courage inuincible, of purpose vnmutable;
so wisehardie alwaies, as feare was banisht from him; at euerie
alarum he first in armor, and formost in ordering. In time of
warre such was his prouidence, bountie and hap, as he had true
intelligence, not onelie what his enimies did, but what they said

[His great
ability in
warfare.]
and intended: of his deuises and purposes, few, before the thing
was at the point to be done, should be made priuie.

He had such knowledge in ordering and guiding an armie, with
such a gift to incourage his people, that the Frenchmen had
constant opinion he could neuer be vanquished in battell. Such
wit, such prudence, and such policie withall, that he neuer enterprised any thing, before he had fullie debated and forecast all the
maine chances that might happen; which doone, with all diligence
and courage, he set his purpose forward. What policie he had in
finding present remedies for sudden mischeeues, and what engines
in sauing himselfe and his people in sharpe distresses, were it not
that by his acts they did plainlie appeare, hard were it by words
to make them credible. Wantonnesse of life and thirst in auarice
had he quite quenched in him[1]; vertues in deed in such an estate

[Freedom
from
wantonness
and
avarice.]
of souereigntie, youth, and power, as verie rare, so right commendable in the highest degree. So staied of mind and countenance

[Equanimity
in good or
evil
fortune.]
beside, that neuer iolie or triumphant for victorie, nor sad or
damped for losse or misfortune. For bountifulnesse and liberalitie,
no man more free, gentle, and franke, in bestowing rewards to all

[Bountiful-
ness.]
persons, according to their deserts: for his saieng was, that he
neuer desired monie to keepe, but to giue and spend.

Although that storie properlie serues not for theme of praise
or dispraise, yet what in breuitie may well be remembred, in truth

---

[1] *Hol.* (ed. 1) and *Halle* read: "he . . . didde continually absteyne . . .
from lasciuious lyuing and blynde auarice."

would not be forgotten by sloth ; were it but onlie to remaine as a spectacle for magnanimitie to haue alwaies in eie, and for incouragement to nobles in honourable enterprises. Knowen be it therefore, of person and forme was this prince rightlie representing his [His person and speech.] heroicall affects ; of stature and proportion tall and manlie, rather leane than grose, somewhat long necked, and blacke haired, of countenance amiable ; eloquent and graue was his speech, and of great grace and power to persuade : for conclusion, a maiestie was he that both liued & died a paterne in princehood, a lode-starre [1] in [A 'lodestarre' and honour, and mirrour [2] of magnificence ; the more highlie exalted in a 'mirrour' to other his life, the more deepelie lamented at his death, and famous to princes.] the world alwaie.

IX. HENRY VI. PART I.

IF the range of *The first Part of Henry the Sixt* [3] were measured by historic dates, not by the order in which occurrences are dramatized, it might be said that the time embraced by the action extended from Henry V.'s funeral, on November 7, 1422,[4] to Talbot's death on July 17, 1453. But the dramatist has made the latter event precede Jeanne Darc's capture in 1430 ; as well as the despatch of Suffolk to Tours in 1444, for the purpose of espousing Margaret and conducting her to England.

Act I. sc. i.—The funeral of Henry V. is disturbed by the entrance of a messenger who announces a series of calamities (ll. 57-61), some of which are fictitious, while others are antedated.[5] Orleans and Poitiers

---

[1] In the Epilogue (*Hen. V.*, l. 6) he is called ' This Starre of England.'

[2] The Chorus of Act II. (l. 6) styles Henry " the Mirror of all Christian Kings." The original, which *Hol.* paraphrased, is " the mirror of Christendome."—*Halle*, 113.

[3] In quoting the three Parts of *Henry VI.*, I follow the text of F1 (1623).

[4] This date is given in *Fab.* (592), and *Wyrc.* (ii. 454). The F. entry is : " Enter the Funerall of King Henry the Fift, attended on by the Duke of Bedford, Regent of France ; the Duke of Gloster, Protector ; the Duke of Exeter, Warwicke, the Bishop of Winchester, and the Duke of Somerset." The corresponding personages in *Hol.* iii. 584/1/19 (*Halle*, 114) are : " Thomas duke of Excester, Richard [Beauchamp] earle of Warwike, . . . the earle of Mortaigne, Edmund Beaufort [afterwards Duke of Somerset], . . . "

[5] The 1st Mess. anticipates the loss of Rheims (l. 60) and Gisors (l. 61). Charles VII. received the keys of the former place in 1429 (*Waurin*, V. iv. 315) ; the latter was surrendered to the French in 1449 (*Stevenson*, II. ii. 622). Paris opened her gates to them in 1436. To the series of calamities Gloucester prophetically adds Rouen (l. 65), which we lost in 1449.

were not in our possession at Henry V.'s death ; and Guienne—the
last left of our continental dominions save Calais—was not lost till
1451. Perhaps the messenger's report is an embellishment of the
succeeding excerpt :[1]

[Charles
VI.'s death
disposed the
French to
revolt.]

[*Hol.* iii. 585/2/13. *Halle,* 15.] And suerlie the death of this
king Charles caused alterations in France. For a great manie of
the nobilitie, which before, either for feare of the English puissance,
or for the loue of this king Charles, (whose authoritie they followed,)
held on the English part, did now reuolt to the Dolphin ; with all
indeuour to driue the English nation out of the French territories.
Whereto they were the more earnestlie bent, and thought it a
thing of greater facilitie, because of king Henries yoong yeares ;
whome (because he was a child) they esteemed not, but with one
consent reuolted from their sworne fealtie : . . .

His assertion, that these reverses were caused by "want of Men
and Money" (l. 69) and "Factions" (l. 71) among the English nobles,
seems to embody a remark of Holinshed on the loss of Paris in 1436.

[Either the
dissension
of the chief
English
peers, or the
Councell's
neglect to
send rein-
forcements,
caused the
loss of
France.]

[*Hol.* iii. 612/2/65. *Halle,* 179.] But heere is one cheefe
point to be noted, that either the disdeine amongest the cheefe
peeres of the realme of England, (as yee haue heard,) or the
negligence of the kings councell, (which did not foresee dangers
to come,) was the losse of the whole dominion of France, betweene
the riuers of Somme[2] and Marne ; and, in especiall, of the noble citie
of Paris. For where before, there were sent ouer thousands for
defense of the holds and fortresses, now were sent hundreds, yea,
and scores ; some rascals, and some not [*p.* 613] able to draw a
bowe, or carrie a bill : . . .

A second messenger brings tidings (l. 92) that

The Dolphin Charles is crownèd King in Rheimes.

---

[1] If so, the dramatist ignores what *Hol.* adds (585/2/30) : "The duke of
Bedford, being greatlie mooued with these sudden changes, fortified his townes
both with garrisons of men, munition, and vittels ; assembled also a great armie
of Englishmen and Normans ; and so effectuouslie exhorted them to continue
faithfull to their liege and lawfull lord yoong king Henrie, that manie of the
French capteins willinglie sware to king Henrie fealtie and obedience ; by
whose example the communaltie did the same. Thus the people quieted, and
the countrie established in order, nothing was minded but warre, and nothing
spoken of but conquest." Their defeat at Verneuil—related by *Hol.*—in 1424
was nearly as disastrous to the French as Agincourt had been ; and the tide of
our success did not turn till we besieged Orleans in 1428-29.

[2] *Somme*] Halla. *Sone* Hol. ed. 2. *Soane* Hol. ed. 1.

This ceremony was not performed till 1429,[1] but, if the second messenger's words be construed freely, the following passage is sufficient warrant for his news :

[*Hol.* iii. 585/2/42.   *Halle*, 115.]   The Dolphin, which lay the same time in the citie of Poitiers, after his fathers deceasse,[2] caused himselfe to be proclamed king of France, by the name of Charles the seuenth; and, in good hope to recouer his patrimonie, with an haultie courage preparing war, assembled a great armie : and first the warre began by light skirmishes, but after it grew into maine battels.

The third messenger's report is noticeable as showing how historic time is dealt with in this play.   The battle which he describes (ll. 110-140) took place at Patay.   On June 18, 1429,[3] about six weeks after the siege of Orleans—dramatized in two subsequent scenes—had been raised, Joan, Alençon, and Dunois, followed by an army numbering

[*Hol.* iii. 601/2/17.   *Halle*, 601.] betweene twentie and three and twentie thousand men,

. . . fought with the lord Talbot (who had with him not past six thousand men) neere vnto a village in Beausse called Pataie : at which battell the charge was giuen by the French so vpon a sudden, that the Englishmen had not leisure to put themselues in araie, after they had put vp their stakes before their archers ; so that there was no remedie but to fight at aduenture.   This battell continued by the space of three long houres ; for the Englishmen, though they were ouerpressed with multitude of their enimies, yet they neuer fled backe one foot, till their capteine the lord Talbot was sore wounded at the backe, and so taken.

Then their hearts began to faint, and they fled ; in which flight were slaine about twelue hundred, and fortie taken, of whome the lord Talbot, the lord Scales,[4] the lord Hungerford, & sir Thomas Rampston were cheefe. . . .   From this battell departed without

Marginal notes:
[The Dauphin proclaimed King of France.]
Nichol. Giles. Fiue thousand, saith Hall.
[The English had not time to form, after stakes had been planted before their archers.]
[Talbot was wounded in the back, and taken.]
Great losse on ye English side. The lords Talbot, Scales, and Hungerford taken.

---

[1] *Hol.* iii. 601/2/74.   Charles VII. was crowned at Poitiers, in 1422 ; "et de ce jour [the day of Charles VI.'s death] en avant, par tous ceux tenant son parti, fut nommé roi de France, comme étoit son père en son vivant."—*Mons.*, v. 10.   Charles VII. was crowned at Rheims on July 17, 1429.—*Waurin*, V. iv. 317.

[2] Charles VI. died on October 21, 1422.—*Mons.*, iv. 415.

[3] *Chron. de la Pucelle*, ix. 334.

[4] Thomas Scales, Lord Scales, a character in 2 *Hen. VI.*, IV. v.

anie stroke striken sir Iohn Fastolfe;[1] the same yeare for his
valiantnesse elected into the order of the garter.

Towards the close of the scene, Exeter says (ll. 162-164) :

> Remember, Lords, your Oathes to Henry sworne :
> Eyther to quell the Dolphin vtterly,
> Or bring him in obedience to your yoake.

When Henry V. lay a-dying at Bois de Vincennes, he was visited by

[*Hol.* iii. 583/1/4. Abridged from *Halle*, 111.] the dukes of
Bedford and Glocester, & the earles of Salisburie and Warwike,
whome the king louinglie welcomed, and seemed glad of their
presence.

Now, when he saw them pensife for his sicknesse and great
danger of life wherein he presentlie laie, he, with manie graue,
courteous, and pithie words, recomforted them the best he could ;
and therewith exhorted them to be trustie and faithfull vnto his
sonne, and to see that he might be well and vertuouslie brought
vp. And, as concerning the rule and gouernance of his realms,
during the minoritie and yoong yeares of his said sonne, he willed
them to ioine togither in freendlie loue and concord, keeping con-
tinnall peace and amitie with the duke of Burgognie ; and neuer to
make treatie with Charles that called himselfe Dolphin of Vienne,
by the which anie part, either of the crowne of France, or of the
duches of Normandie and Guien, may be lessened or diminished ;
and further, that the duke of Orleance and the other princes
should still remaine prisoners, till his sonne came to lawfull age ;
least, returning home againe, they might kindle more fire in one
daie than might be quenched in three.

He further aduised them, that if they thought it necessarie,
that it should be good to haue his brother Humfreie duke of
Glocester to be protector of England, during the nonage of his
sonne, and his brother the duke of Bedford, with the helpe of the
duke of Burgognie, to rule and to be regent of France ;[2] commanding

---

[1] The dramatist was not content with making a messenger relate Fastolfe's
cowardice, but must needs exhibit it in some fictitious skirmish near Rouen
(III. ii. 104-109) ; which one might have suspected to be Patay refought, had
not Sir John, alluding possibly to that disastrous battle, said, " We are like to
haue the ouerthrow againe."

[2] Under the year 1422 : " The duke of Bedford was deputed regent of

him with fire and sword to persecute the Dolphin, till he had charged Bedford (3)
either brought him to reason and obeisance, or else to driue and to bring the Dauphin to
expell him out of the realme of France. . . . obeisance, or to expel

The noble men present promised to obserue his precepts, and him from France.]
to performe his desires; but their hearts were so pensife, and [All promised
replenished with sorrow, that one could not for weeping behold an compliance with these
other. behests.]

Two more speeches call for remark. Exeter had been "ordayn'd"
Henry VI.'s "speciall Gouernor" (l. 171), but my next excerpt shows
that Winchester held a similar post [1] and was therefore not a "lack out
of Office" (l. 175).

[*Hol.* iii. 585/1/28. *Halle*, 115.] The custodie of this yoong [Exeter and Winchester
prince was appointed to Thomas duke of Excester, & to Henrie appointed guardians of
Beauford bishop of Winchester. Henry VI.]

Ere leaving the stage, Winchester expresses an intention to steal
the King from Eltham (ll. 176, 177). About four years after Henry
V.'s funeral, Gloucester charged Winchester with this design.

[*Hol.* iii. 591/2/5. *Halle*, 131.] 2 Item, my said lord of
Winchester, without the aduise and assent of my said lord of
Glocester, or of the kings councell, purposed and disposed him to [Winchester meant to
set hand on the kings person, and to haue remooued him from remove the King from
Eltham, the place that he was in, to Windsor, to the intent to put Eltham.]
him in gouernance as him list.

Act I. sc. ii.—Neither Charles VII. nor René of Anjou was present
at the siege of Orleans, but Dunois (the Bastard of Orleans) commanded
the French garrison, and Alençon—accompanied by Joan—led the
relieving force which rescued the city. The following account of a
sally made by Dunois was perhaps transmuted into the fruitless attempt
of Charles, Alençon, and René, to succour Orleans. (The stage direction after l. 21 is: "Here Alarum; they are beaten back by the English,
with great losse.")

[*Hol.* iii. 599/1/30. *Halle*, 145.] After the siege had continued
full three weekes,[2] the bastard of Orleance issued out of the gate of

France, and the duke of Glocester was ordained protectour of England"; . . . .
—*Hol.* iii. 585/1/30.

[1] According to *Gesta* (159), one of Henry's last instructions was: "Avunculum meum ducem Exoniae et avunculum meum Henricum episcopum
Wintoniae unà cum comite Warwici circa regimen filii mei . . . attendentes
fore volo et decerno." With this agrees *Chron. Giles* (*Hen. VI.*), 3.

[2] *Halle* (145)—*Hol.*'s authority—was mistaken. The bridge-tower was

[Dunois's
sally
repulsed.]
the bridge, and fought with the Englishmen; but they receiued
him with so fierce and terrible strokes, that he was with all his
companie compelled to retire and flee backe into the citie. But
the Englishmen followed so fast, in killing and taking of their
A bulworke
at Orleance
taken [by the
English.]
enimies, that they entered with them. ¶ The bulworke of the
bridge, with a great tower standing at the end of the same, was
taken incontinentlie by the Englishmen, who behaued themselues
right valiantlie vnder the conduct of their couragious capteine, as
at this assault, so in diuerse skirmishes against the French; partlie
to keepe possession of that which Henrie the fift had by his magnanimitie & puissance atchiued, as also to inlarge the same. . . .

In this conflict, manie Frenchmen were taken, but more were
[The bul-
wark and
bridge-tower
entrusted to
William
Glansdale.]
slaine; and the keeping of the tower and bulworke was committed
to William Gla[n]sdale esquier. By the taking of this bridge the
passage was stopped, that neither men nor vittels could go or come
by that waie.

The siege of Orleans, begun by Salisbury on October 12, 1428, was
raised on May 8, 1429;[1] and he was mortally wounded (Act I. sc. iv.)
about four months prior to Joan's first meeting with Charles;[2] the
event which is dramatized in this scene. I quote the account given of
her by Holinshed:

W. P.
Ichå de
Tillet.

Les chronic.
de Bretaigne.

Le Rosier
calleth him
Robert.

Ione de Are
Pucell de
dieu.
[Hol. iii. 600/2/2.] In time of this siege at Orleance (French
stories saie), the first weeke of March 1428[-29], vnto Charles the
Dolphin, at Chinon, as he was in verie great care and studie how
to wrestle against the English nation, by one Robert[3] Ba[u]dricourt,
capteine of Va[u]couleur[s], (made after marshall of France by the
Dolphins creation,[4]) was caried a yoong wench of an eighteene
yeeres old, called Ione Are,[5] by name of hir father (a sorie

captured on October 24, 1428, and the attack was made by the English.—*Chron.*
de la Pucelle, ix. 284. The siege began on October 12, 1428.—*Ibid.,* ix. 281.
    [1] The siege was raised on May 8, 1429.—*Chron. de la Pucelle,* ix. 321.
    [2] Joan reached Chinon on March 6, 1429.—Continuation of Guillaume de
Nangis (*Quicherat,* iv. 313). Her first audience of Charles was deferred until
the third day (March 9) after her arrival.—Letter of De Boulainvilliers to Filippo
Maria Visconti (*Quicherat,* v. 118; cp. iii. 4).   [3] *Robert*] Peter Hol.
    [4] An error. Robert's son (Jean de Baudricourt) was made a marshal of
France by Charles VIII.—*Anselme,* vii. 113.
    [5] The earliest instance of "d'Arc" occurs in 1576.—*Nouvelles recherches*
sur la famille et sur le nom de Jeanne Darc, par M. Vallet de Viriville, p. 30.
M. de Viriville cites letters of ennoblement, dated December, 1429, and addressed
"Puellae Joannae Darc de Dompremeyo."—*Ibid,* p. 16. In this document
her father is called "Jacobum Darc."

sheepheard) Iames of Are, and Isabell hir mother; brought vp poorelie in their trade of keeping cattell; borne at Domprin *In vita Bunduica.* (therefore reported by *Bale*, Ione Domprin) vpon Meuse in Lorraine, within the diocesse of Thoule. Of fauour was she *[Joan's aspect, clairvoyant power, and character.]* counted likesome, of person stronglie made and manlie, of courage great, hardie, and stout withall: an vnderstander of counsels though she were not at them; great semblance of chastitie both of bodie and behauiour; the name of Iesus in hir mouth about all hir businesses; humble, obedient; and fasting diuerse daies in the weeke. A person (as their bookes make hir) raised vp by power diuine, onelie for succour to the French estate then deepelie in distresse; in whome, for planting a credit the rather, first the companie that toward the Dolphin did conduct hir, through places *[Her perilous journey to Charles's Court.]* all dangerous, as holden by the English, (where she neuer was afore,) all the waie and by nightertale safelie did she lead: then at the Dolphins sending by hir assignement, from saint Katharins *[Her sword was found among old iron at St. Katharine's church at Fierbois.]* church of Fierbois in Touraine, (where she neuer had beene and knew not,) in a secret place there among old iron, appointed she *Grand chro. 4.* hir sword to be sought out and brought hir, (that with fiue floure delices was grauen on both sides,[1]) wherewith she fought and did manie slaughters by hir owne hands. On warfar rode she in *[From head to foot [was she clad in armour].* armour *cap a pie & mustered as a man; before hir an ensigne all *[Her ensign.]* white, wherin was Iesus Christ painted with a floure delice in his hand.

Unto the Dolphin into his gallerie when first she was brought; *[Charles made some of his lords stand before him, but she picked him out.]* and he, shadowing himselfe *behind*, setting other gaie lords before him to trie hir cunning, from all the companie, with a salutation, (that indeed marz all the matter,) she pickt him out alone;[2] who *This salutation appeareth after Aaere. [See p. 230, below.]* thereupon had hir to the end of the gallerie, where she held him an houre *in* secret and priuate *talke*, that of his priuie chamber *[His courtiers thought that she held Charles long in talk.]* was thought *veric long*,[3] and therefore would haue broken it off; but he made them a signe to let hir saie on. In which (among *Les grand chronic.* other), as likelie it was, she set out vnto him the singular feats (for sooth) giuen hir to vnderstand by reuelation diuine, that in vertue

---

[1] Cp. 1 *Hen. VI.*, I. ii. 98-101.   [2] Cp. 1 *Hen. VI.*, I. ii. 60-67.
[3] "*Reigneir.* My Lord, me thinkes, is *very long in talke*."—1 *Hen. VI.*, I. ii. 118.

of that sword shee should atchiue ; which were, how with honor and

[She presented to relieve Orleans, and drive the English from France.] victorie shee would raise the siege at Orleance, set him in state of the crowne of France, and driue the English out of the countrie, thereby he to inioie the kingdome alone.   Heerevpon he hartened at full, appointed hir a sufficient armie with absolute power to lead them, and they obedientlie to doo as she bad them.   Then fell she [Charles gave her an army, and she relieved Orleans, and caused him to be crowned at Rheims.] to worke, and first defeated, indeed, the siege at Orleance ; by and by incouraged him to crowne himselfe king of France at Reims, that a little before from the English she had woone.   Thus after pursued she manie bold enterprises to our great displeasure a two yeare togither : for the time she kept in state vntill she were taken and for heresie and witcherie burned ; as in particularities hereafter followeth.

Act I. sc. iii.—I preface this scene by quoting what Holinshed says about the open dissension of Gloucester and Winchester.   In 1425

Dissension betwixt the duke of Glocester and the bishop of Winchester. [*Hol.* iii. 590/2/60. *Halle,* 130.] fell a great diuision in the realme of England ; which of a sparkle was like to haue grown to a great flame.   For whether the bishop of Winchester, called Henrie Beaufort, (sonne to Iohn duke of Lancaster by his third wife,) enuied the authoritie of Humfreie duke of Glocester, protectour of the realme ; or whether the duke disdained at the riches and pompous estate of the bishop ; sure it is that the whole realme was troubled with them and their partakers : . . .

The action was partly developed from the first article in a series of five charges against Winchester, preferred by Gloucester at some time after February 18, and before March 7, 1426.[1]

[*Hol.* iii. 591/1/68. *Halle,* 130.] 1 First, whereas he, being protectour, and defendour of this land, desired the Tower to be [Richard Woodvile (by Winchester's opened to him, and to lodge him therein, Richard Wooduile[2] esquier (hauing at that time the charge of the keeping of the

---

[1] Parliament met at Leicester on February 18, 1426.—*Rot. Parl.,* iv. 295/1. On March 7, 1426, Gloucester and Winchester agreed to submit their differences to the arbitration of a committee of the Upper House.—*Rot. Parl.,* iv. 297/2. Gloucester's five articles are not in *Rot. Parl.,* but Winchester's answers to articles 4 and 5 appear there (298/1-2).

[2] Created Earl Rivers on May 24, 1466.—*Dugdale,* iii. 231/1. Father of Elizabeth Woodvile, who married Sir John Grey, and (secondly) Edward IV. Woodvile's son Anthony is Earl Rivers in *Rich. III.*

Tower) refused his desire ; and kept the same Tower against him vndulie and against reason, by the commandement of my said lord of Winchester ; . . .

Winchester styles Gloucester a "most vsurping Proditor" (l. 31). Gloucester retorts (ll. 33, 34) :

> Stand back, thou manifest Conspirator,
> Thou that contriued'st to murther our dead Lord ; . . .

The fourth article of Gloucester's charges contains this accusation :

[*Hol.* iii. 591/2/33. *Halle,* 131.] 4 Item, my said lord of Glocester saith and affirmeth, that our souereigne lord, his brother, that was king Henrie the fift, told him on a time, (when our souereigne lord, being prince, was lodged in the palace of Westminster, in the great chamber,) by the noise of a spaniell, there was on a night a man spied and taken behind a * tapet of the said chamber ; the which man was deliuered to the earle of Arundell to be examined vpon the cause of his being there at that time ; the which so examined, at that time confessed that he was there by the stirring and procuring of my said lord of Winchester ; ordeined to haue slaine the said prince there in his bed : wherefore the said earle of Arundell let sacke him [1] foorthwith, and drowned him in the Thames.

Obeying their master's command (l. 54), "Glosters men beat out the Cardinalls men, and enter in the hurly-burly the Maior of London and his Officers." The Mayor directs an officer to make "open Proclamation" against rioting, and threatens also to "call for Clubs" (ll. 71, 84). Gloucester and Winchester then retire.

After describing (ii. 595) how, on October 30, 1425, possession of London Bridge was contested by the followers of Gloucester and Winchester, Fabyan says (ii. 596) :

. And lykely it was to haue ensued great Effucyon of blode shortly therupon, ne had ben the discressyon of the Mayre and his Brether, that exorted the people, by all Polytike meane, to kepe the kynges peas.

Act I. sc. iv.—Lords Salisbury, and Talbot, Sir William Glansdale, Sir Thomas Gargrave, and others enter "on the Turrets" of the bridge-tower captured by the English (see p. 210 above), whence, through "a secret Grate," they can "ouer-peere the Citie" (ll. 10, 11). Talbot's narrative of his captivity and ransom (ll. 27-56) contains nothing authentic save the exchange by which he obtained his freedom. But

he was not released until 1433[1] (Holinshed was wrong in saying that
Talbot was ransomed "with out delaie"), and the historic date of this
scene is 1428.   In 1431 an English force defeated some French troops
at Beauvais.[2]   Many of the Frenchmen were taken.

*The lord
Talbot ran-
somed by
exchange.*

[*Hol.* iii. 606/2/34. *Halle*, 164.] Amongst other of the cheefest
prisoners, that valiant capteine, Poton[3] de Santrails, was one; who
without delaie was exchanged for the lord Talbot, before taken
prisoner at the battell of Pataie.

But Talbot's association with Salisbury, in the siege of Orleans, is
unhistorical.   Salisbury was dead, and the battle of Patay—which
deprived Talbot of his liberty—had not been fought, when Bedford

[Talbot at
the siege of
Orleans.]

[*Hol.* iii. 599/2/48. *Halle*, 146.]   appointed the earle of
Suffolke to be his lieutenant and capteine of the siege; and ioined
with him the lord Scales, the lord Talbot,[4] sir Iohn Fastolfe, and
diuerse other right valiant capteins.

The following excerpt shows that the circumstances of Salisbury's
and Gargrave's deaths (ll. 1-22; 60-88) are faithfully presented:

[The English
capteins
used to view
Orleans
from a
grated
window in
the bridge-
tower. The
besieged
pointed a
gun against
this tooting
hole (spy-
hole).]

[One day,
when
Salisbury,
Gargrave
and Glans-
dale were
looking out
at the
window, the
maister-
gunner's son
fired, and
mortally
wounded
Salisbury
and
Gargrave.]

*The earle of
Salisburie*

[*Hol.* iii. 599/2/5.   *Halle*, 145.]   In the tower that was taken
at the bridge end (as before you haue heard) there was an high
chamber, hauing a grate full of barres of iron, by the which a man
might looke all the length of the bridge into the citie; at which
grate manie of the cheefe capteins stood manie times, viewing the
citie, and deuising in what place it was best to giue the assault.
They within the citie well perceiued this tooting hole, and laid a
peece of ordinance directlie against the window.

It so chanced, that the nine and fiftith daie[5] after the siege was
laid, the earle of Salisburie, sir Thomas Gargraue, and William
Gla[n]sdale, with diuerse other went into the said tower, and so into
the high chamber, and looked out at the grate; and, within a short
space, the sonne of the maister-gunner, perceiuing men looking out
at the window, tooke his match, (as his father had taught him; who
was gone downe to dinner,) and fired the gun; the shot whereof
brake and shiuered the iron barres of the grate, so that one of the
same bars strake the earle so violentlie on the head, that it stroke

---

.1 *Rymer*, x. 536.   [2] *Journal*, xv. 427, 428.
[3] *Poton*] *Pouton* Hol.
[4] Talbot and the others left Jargeau for Orleans on December 29, 1428.—
Chron. de la Pucelle, ix. 287.   [5] See p. 209, n. 2, above.

awaie one of his eies, and the side of his cheeke.[1] Sir Thomas [and Sir
Gargraue was likewise striken, and died within two daies. Gargraue]
slaine.

After a messenger brings news that Charles and Joan are coming
to raise the siege (ll. 100-103), and during the two remaining scenes of
Act I., historic time must be supposed to have advanced from October,
1428—its position in sc. iv. ll. 1-97—to April 29-May 8, 1429. When
Joan had received "a sufficient armie" (p. 212 above), she

[*Hol.* iii. 600/2/68. *Halle*, 148.] roade from Poictiers to Blois,
and there found men of warre, vittels, and munition, readie to be
conueied to Orleance.

Heere was it knowne that the Englishmen kept not so diligent
watch as they had been accustomed to doo, and therefore this
maid (with other French capteins) comming forward in the dead
time of the [*p.* 601] night, and in a great raine and. thunder, [Joan enters
[*Cp.* I. iv. 97] entred into the citie [2] with all their vittels, artillerie, Orleans.]
and other necessarie prouisions. The next daie the Englishmen
boldlie assaulted the towne, but the Frenchmen defended the
walles, so as no great feat worthie of memorie chanced that daie [The English
betwixt them, though the Frenchmen were amazed at the valiant assault
attempt of the Englishmen: whervpon the bastard of Orleance Orleans.]
gaue knowledge to the duke of Alanson, in what danger the towne
stood without his present helpe ; who, comming within two leagues

---

[1] *Mons.* (v. 194) says that Salisbury "ainsi blessé, . . . véquit l'espace de
huit jours." He died at Meung, "au bout de huit jours de sadite blessure."—
Ibid. If this limit of time be accepted, we must suppose that Salisbury was
mortally wounded on or about October 27, for it appears from various inquisitions *post mortem* dated in January, 1429,—which were examined by Mr.
Oswald Barron,—that the Earl died on November 3, 1428. The date Nov. 3
agrees with the following record of a contemporary chronicler : " le régent de
France . . . partist de Paris . . . le mercredi, veille de Saint-Martin d'yver
[Nov. 10] mil quatre cent vingt-huit. Et le comte de Salcebry estoit mort la
sepmaine devant."—*Journal*, xv. 379. The date Oct. 27 is not, however,
reconcileable with *Mons.*'s assertion (v. 194) that Salisbury was wounded on
the third day of the siege. According to the more exact *Chron. de la Pucelle*
the siege began on October 12 (ix. 281, 282) ; the bridge-tower was taken by
the English on October 24 (ix. 284, 285) ; and, on October 25, the French
fortified their end of the bridge and planted guns to batter the tower (ix. 285,
286). After October 25 "advint un jour" on which Salisbury was mortally
wounded (ix. 286). It does not necessarily follow that, because *Mons.* gave a
wrong prior date,—the third day of the siege,—he was therefore mistaken in
regard to the length of time during which Salisbury lingered between life and
death. The beginning of the siege is vaguely dated by *Mons.* "environ le
mois d'octobre."—v. 192.

[2] On April 29, 1429.—*Chron. de la Pucelle*, ix. 309.

of the citie, gaue knowledge to them within, that they should be
readie the next daie to receiue him.

[Orleans
relieved.]
This accordinglie was accomplished : . . .

    The relief of Orleans was speedily followed by the recapture of the
tower at the bridge-foot. But, when the French assailed Talbot's
bastile, he "issued foorth against them, and gaue them so sharpe an
incounter, that they, not able to withstand his puissance, fled (like
sheepe before the woolfe) againe into the citie, with great losse of men
and small artillerie."—*Hol.* iii. 601/1/34. This may be represented by
the entry (sc. v.) : " Here an Alarum againe, and Talbot pursueth the
Dolphin, and driueth him"; if we allow for a transposition of the French
victory at the bridge-foot (denoted by "Then enter Ioane de Puzel,
driuing Englishmen before her") and subsequent repulse. After Talbot's
successful defence, the English vainly offered battle on open ground,
and retired "in good order" from Orleans (*Hol.* iii. 601/1/22-53).
Their departure is indicated by "Alarum, Retreat, Flourish"; but the
preceding alarums and skirmish (ll. 26, 32) are mere stage business.

    Act II. sc. i.—Talbot's recapture of Orleans is fictitious, but, on
May 28, 1428,[1] Le Mans was regained under circumstances somewhat
like those dramatized in this scene. We learn that "diuers of the
cheefe rulers" of Le Mans agreed with Charles VII. to admit the French
into their city. The enterprise proved successful, and the English

[*Hol.* iii. 598/1/70. *Halle,* 143.] withdrew without any tarri-
ance into the castell, which standeth at the gate of saint Vincent,
whereof was constable Thomas Gower esquier ; whither also fled
manie Englishmen ; so as for vrging of the enimie, prease of the
[Suffolk
withdrew to
the castle,
and sent a
messenger
to Talbot,
asking for
help.]
number, and lacke of vittels, they could not haue indured long :
wherfore they priuilie sent a messenger to the lord Talbot, which
then laie at Alanson, certifieng him in how hard a case they were.
The lord Talbot, hearing these newes, like a carefull capteine, in all
hast assembled togither about seuen hundred men ; & in the
euening departed from Alanson, so as in the morning he came to a
castell called Guierch, two miles from Mans, and there staied a
* Or rather
Goche.
while, till he had sent out Matthew * Gough,[2] as an espiall, to
vnderstand how the Frenchmen demeaned themselues.

* Goche.
    Matthew * Gough so well sped his businesse, that priuilie in
the night he came into the castell, where he learned that the
Frenchmen verie negligentlie vsed themselues, without taking heed

---

[1] My authority for this date is *Journal,* xv. 374, 375. *Chronique de la
Pucelle* (ix. 272-274) contains details given in my excerpt, and not mentioned
in *Journal*.
[2] Slain by Jack Cade's followers. See the entry of 2 *Hen. VI.,* IV. vii.

to their watch, as though they had beene out of all danger: which
well vnderstood, he returned againe, and within a mile of the citie
met the lord Talbot, and the lord Scales, and opened vnto them
all things, according to his credence. The lords then, to make
hast in the matter, (bicause the daie approched,) with all speed
possible came to the posterne gate; and, alighting from their
horsses, about six of the clocke in the morning, they issued out of
the castell, crieng, "*saint George ! Talbot !*"

*The French*men, being thus suddenlie taken, were sore amazed;
in so much that some of them, being not out of their beds, got vp
in their shirts, and lept *ouer the walles*.[1] Other ran naked out of the
gates to saue their liues, leauing all their apparell, horsses, armour,
and riches behind them : none was hurt but such as resisted.

> The scene closes with the entry of "a Souldier, crying 'a Talbot, a
> Talbot !'" Charles, Joan, Alençon, René, and Dunois, "flye, leauing
> their Clothes behind." The soldier remarks (ll. 78-81):
>
>> Ile be so bold to take what they haue left.
>> The Cry of Talbot serues me for a Sword ;
>> For I haue loaden me with many Spoyles,
>> Vsing no other Weapon but his Name.

Holinshed says that

[*Hol.* iii. 597/2/14. *Halle*, 141.] lord Talbot, being both of
noble birth, and of haultie courage, after his comming into France,
obtained so manie glorious victories of his enimies, that his onelie
name was & yet is dreadfull to the French nation; and much
renowmed amongst all other people.

Act II. sc. ii.—On the tomb which Salisbury is to have in Orleans
shall be engraved, says Talbot, "what a terror he had beene to France"
(l. 17). Salisbury's martial ability was thus extolled by Halle, whose
words Holinshed copied :

[*Hol.* iii. 598/2/58. *Halle*, 144.] This earle was the man at
that time, by whose wit, strength, and policie, the English name
was much fearefull and terrible to the French nation; which of
himselfe might both appoint, command, and doo all things in
manner at his pleasure; in whose power (as it appeared after his

Marginal notes:

[Talbot entered the castle with a relieuing force, and, before the French knew of his coming, issued therefrom and fell upon them. Some of the French leaped over the walls in their shirts.] *Mans recouered.* [Others fled naked, leaving all they possessed behind them.]

The lord Talbot, a valiant capteine.

---

[1] Cp. the stage directions (l. 38) : "Cry : '*S. George !*' 'A *Talbot !*' The
French leape *ore the walles in their shirts*."

death) a great part of the conquest consisted: for, suerlie, he was
a man both painefull, diligent, and readie to withstand all
dangerous chances that were at hand, prompt in counsell, and of
courage inuincible;· so that in no one man, men put more trust;
nor any singular person wan the harts so much of all men.

Act II. sc. iii.—No source for this scene has yet been discovered.
The Countess of Auvergne's surprise at the mean aspect (ll. 19-24) of
"the *Scourge* of France" (l. 15), with whose "Name the Mothers still
their Babes" (l. 17), does not accord with Halle's description of Talbot.

[*Halle*, 230.] This man was to the French people a very *scorge*
and a daily *terror ;*[1] in so muche that as his person was fearfull and
terrible to his aduersaries present, so his name and fame was
spitefull and dreadfull to the common people absent; in so much
that women in Fraunce, to feare their yong children, would crye,
"the Talbot commeth, the Talbot commeth!"

Act II. sc. iv.—No one has pointed out a source for this scene and
its sequel (III. iv. 28-45; IV. i. 78-161). From the next scene we
ascertain (cp. II. v. 45-50, 111-114) that Richard Plantagenet and
"Somerset" must have quarrelled on January 19, 1425, the historic
date of Mortimer's death.[2] John Beaufort, then Earl of Somerset, was
older than Richard, who calls him "Boy" (l. 76); the former being at
that time nearly twenty-one,[3] while the latter was about thirteen.[4]
The subsequent action, however, shows that "Somerset" is John's
brother, Edmund Beaufort, whom Richard, in 1452, openly accused of
treason.[5] Edmund Beaufort was about six years older than Richard.[6]
According to Halle, these nobles were foes in 1436, when Richard, who
had been appointed to the chief command in France, was embarrassed

---

[1] Cp. the address of the French general, summoned by Talbot to surrender
Bordeaux (1 *Hen. VI.*, IV. ii. 15, 16):

"Thou ominous and fearefull Owle of death,
Our Nations *terror*, and their bloody *scourge !*"

[2] Esch. 3 Hen. VI. No. 32 (*Proc. Priv. Co.*, iii. 169, note).
[3] John Beaufort completed his twenty-first year on March 25, 1425.—*Inq.
prob. etatis.* 4 H. VI. No. 53 (O.B.).
[4] On December 12, 1415, Richard Plantagenet was of the age of three years
and upwards.—*Inq. p. m.* 3 H. V. No. 45 (O.B.).
[5] See p. 287 below.
[6] An Inq. p. m., taken at Bedford, shows that John Beaufort Duke of
Somerset died on May 27, 1444.—*Inq. p. m.* 22 H. VI. 19 (O.B.). On that
day—as appears from an Inq. p. m. taken at Whitechapel, Middlesex, on
August 21, 1444—his heir male, Edmund Beaufort Marquis of Dorset, was of
the age of thirty-eight years and upwards.—*Inq. p. m.* 22 H. VI. 19 (O.B.).

by Edmund Beaufort's opposition. Upon this matter Halle made the following comment, the paraphrase of which by Holinshed I quote : [1]

[*Hol.* iii. 612/2/22. *Halle*, 179.] The duke of Yorke, perceiuing his euill will, openlie dissembled that which he inwardlie minded, either of them working things to the others displeasure ; till, through malice and diuision betweene them, at length by mortall warre they were both consumed, with almost all their whole lines and ofspring.

[Enmity of Richard Plantagenet and Edmund Beaufort.]

Act II. sc. v.—The historical Edmund Mortimer, fifth Earl of March, was, in his youth, under the care and control of Henry Prince of Wales.[2] He was not imprisoned when Henry succeeded to the throne,—as was the dramatic Mortimer (ll. 23-25),—but served in France, and bore offices of trust.[3] On April 27, 1423,[4] he was appointed Lieutenant in Ireland, and held that post until his death on January 19, 1425. The " Nestor-like agëd " Mortimer, with "Feet, whose strength-lesse stay is numme " (ll. 6, 13), was taken from a brief obituary notice of him, under the year 1424.

[*Hol.* iii. 589/2/73. *Halle*, 128.] During the same season, Edmund Mortimer, the last earle of March [*p.* 590] of that name, (which long time had beene restreined from his libertie, and finallie waxed lame,[5]) deceased without issue ; whose inheritance descended

[The last Mortimer Earl of March died in prison : his heir was

---

[1] The passage immediately preceding this quotation is given at p. 252 below.

[2] In 1409 the " custodia et gubernatio "—*i. e.* the jailorship, as the context shows—of March was transferred from Sir John Pelham to Henry Prince of Wales.—*Rymer*, viii. 608 ; cp. viii. 639.

[3] The muster-roll of the army which went to France in 1417 shows that March was followed by 93 lances and 302 archers.—*Gesta*, App. 266. In the same year he was captain of Mantes.—*Ibid.*, 277. At Katharine's coronation (February 21, 1421) he was "knelyng on the hye deys on the ryght syde of the quene and held a cepture in hys hond of the quenys."—*Greg.*, 139. To the same effect *Fab.*, 586. During the year 1423 March's presence in the Council is often recorded.—*Proc. Priv. Co.*, iii. 21, *et passim.*

[4] *Proc. Priv. Co.*, iii. 68. His patent is dated May 9, 1423.—*Rymer*, x. 282-285. He died at Trim Castle, Co. Meath.—*Greg.*, 158. March was a dangerous possible rival of the House of Lancaster on account of his inherited title to the throne ; and we find that Henry V. did not suffer him " comitivam regiam excedere." When, therefore, March attended the Parliament of 1423-24 with a very large retinue, the Council had misgivings, and sent him into honourable banishment as Lieutenant of Ireland.—*Chron. Giles (Hen. VI.*), 6. He had been appointed to this post in 1423, but it appears from *Rymer* (x. 319) that ships for his transport to Ireland were not ordered until February 14, 1424.

[5] I suspect that Edmund Mortimer, Earl of March, has been confounded with Sir John Mortimer, who, according to *Halle* (128) was the Earl's cousin. Sir John Mortimer had been imprisoned in the Tower, whence, about April, 1422, he escaped. Having been soon captured, he was committed to Pevensey

to the lord Richard Plantagenet, sonne and heire to Richard earle
of Cambridge, beheaded (as before yee haue heard) at the towne
of Southampton.

Mortimer says to Richard (l. 96) :

> Thou art my *Heire ;* the rest I wish thee gather.

Halle—who was Holinshed's authority for Mortimer's imprisonment
—adds a few words touching Richard's subsequent course:

[*Halle,* 128.] Whiche Richard, within lesse then .xxx. yeres,
as *heirs* to this erle Edmo*n*d, in open parliament claimed the
croune and scepter of this realme, as hereafter shall more
manifestly appere.[1]

Act III. sc. i.—I have quoted above (pp. 209, 212, 213) three of the
articles exhibited against Winchester by Gloucester ; which, in the
opening lines of this scene, the former calls "deepe premeditated
Lines," and "written Pamphlets studiously deuis'd."   Gloucester
brands his rival with sundry vices[2] (ll. 14-20), and then makes a
specific charge (ll. 21-23) :

> And for thy Trecherie, what's more manifest ?
> In that thou layd'st a Trap to take my Life,
> As well at London Bridge as at the Tower.

Winchester, as we have seen (p. 209 above), had been accused in
the second article of a design to remove the King from Eltham ; and
the third article contained the charge in ll. 21-23, arising out of the
purposed abduction of Henry VI.

[*Hol.* iii. 591/2/12. *Halle,* 131.] 3 Item, that where my said

---

Castle, and was afterwards sent again to the Tower.—*Exchequer Issues,* 372,
377, 384, 386. From a petition, addressed by him to the Commons of the
Parliament which assembled at Westminster on Dec. 1, 1421, we learn that he
was heavily ironed during his confinement in the Tower.—*Rot. Parl.,* iv.
160/2. Another petition—conjecturally assigned by Nicolas to the year 1421
—was preferred by his wife Eleanor to the Duke of Bedford and the Council,
"stating that her husband was imprisoned underground in the Tower, where
he had neither light nor air, and could not long exist ; praying that he
might be removed to the prison above-ground, in custody, as he was on
his first committal, whence he would not attempt to escape."—*Proc. Priv.
Co.,* ii., pp. xxxiii., 311, 312. In February, 1424, he was charged with
having asserted "that the erle of Marche shulde be kyng, by ryght of
Enherytaunce, and that he hymselfe was nexte ryghtfull heyre to the sayd
Crowne, after the sayde Erle of Marche ; wherfore, if the sayd Erle wold nat
take vpon hym the Crowne, & rule of the Lande, he sayd that he ellys wolde."
—*Fab.,* ii. 593. On Feb. 26, 1424, judgment was delivered against Sir John.
—*Rot. Parl.,* iv. 202/2. On the same day, apparently, he was beheaded.—
Chron. Auc. Ign., 6, 7. *Halle* records (128) the execution, but says nothing
about the imprisonment, of Sir John Mortimer.
    [1] See p. 255 below.
    [2] Halle's character of Winchester is given in an excerpt illustrating 2 *Hen.
VI.,* III. iii. (p. 269 below).

lord of Glocester, (to whome of all persons that should be in the land, by the waie of nature and birth, it belongeth to see the gouernance of the kings person,) informed of the said vndue purpose of my said lord of Winchester, (declared in the article next abouesaid,) and, in letting thereof, determining to haue gone to Eltham vnto the king to haue prouided as the cause required; my said lord of Winchester, vntrulie, and against the kings peace, to the intent to trouble my said lord of Glocester going to the king, purposing his death, in case that he had gone that waie, set men of armes and archers at the end of London bridge next Suthworke; and, in forebarring of the kings high waie, let draw the chaine of the stoupes there, and set vp pipes and hurdles in manner and forme of bulworks; and set men in chambers, cellars, & windowes, with bowes and arrowes and other weapons, to the intent to bring finall destruction to my said lord of Glocester's person, as well as of those that then should come with him.

[Winchester beset London Bridge with armed men, purposing thereby the death of Gloucester, who was going to Eltham to prevent Henry VI.'s removal.]

While Henry preaches peace to his unruly uncles, a "noyse within, 'Down with the Tawny-Coats!'", is heard; followed by a "noyse againe, 'Stones! Stones!'" The Mayor of London entering announces (ll. 78-83) that

> The Bishop and the Duke of Glosters men,
> Forbidden late to carry any Weapon,
> Haue fill'd their Pockets full of peeble *stones*,   80
> And, banding themselues in contráry parts,
> Doe pelt so fast at one anothers Pate,
> That many haue their giddy braynes knockt out: ...

Fabyan says (596) that the Parliament which witnessed the reconciliation of Gloucester and Winchester

was clepyd of the Comon people the Parlyament of Battes: the cause was, for Proclamacyons were made, that men shulde leue theyr Swerdes & other wepeyns in theyr Innys,[1] the people toke great battes & stauys in theyr neckes, and so folowed theyr lordes and maisters vnto the Parlyament. And whan that wepyn was Inhybyted theym, then they toke *stonys* & plummettes of lede, & trussyd them secretely in theyr sleuys & bosomys.

[When other weapons were forbidden them, retainers at the Parliament of 1426 armed themselves with stones.]

---

[1] When Gloucester's and Winchester's servants "skirmish againe," the Mayor is obliged "to make open Proclamation," whereby they are forbidden "to weare, handle, or vse any Sword, Weapon, or Dagger hence-forward, vpon paine of death."—1 *Hen. VI.*, I. iii. 71, &c. Cp. p. 213 above.

The Mayor complains also that

> Our Windowes are broke downe in euery Street,   84
> And we, *for feare*, compell'd *to shut* our *Shops.*

In 1425, when Gloucester and Winchester were at open strife,

[The
Londoners
obliged to
shut their
shops.]

[*Hol.* iii. 590/2/69. *Halle*, 130.] the citizens of London were faine to keepe dailie and nightlie watches, *and to shut* vp their *shops, for feare* of that which was doubted to haue insued of their [Gloucester's and Winchester's] assembling of people about them.

Several columns of Holinshed are filled with the formal documents [1] pertaining to the reconciliation of Gloucester and Winchester (ll. 106-143). The quarrel was submitted to the arbitration of a committee of the Upper House, which wound up the matter by a decree

[*Hol.* iii. 595/1/64. *Halle*, 137.] that the said lord of Winchester should haue these words that follow vnto my said lord of Glocester : "My lord of Glocester, I haue conceiued to my great "heauinesse, that yee should haue receiued by diuerse reports, "that I should haue purposed and imagined against your person, "honor, and estate, in diuers maners ; for the which yee haue

[Winches-
ter's exculpation.]

"taken against me great displeasure : Sir, I take God to my "witnesse, that what reports so euer haue beene to you of me, "(peraduenture of such as haue had no great affection to me, God "forgiue it them!) I neuer imagined, ne purposed anie thing that "might be hindering or preiudice to your person, honor, or estate ; "and therefore I praie you, that yee be vnto me good lord from "this time foorth : for, by my will, I gaue neuer other occasion, nor "purpose not to doo hereafter, by the grace of God." The which words so by him said, it was decreed by the same arbitrators, that

[Glouces-
ter's
answer.]

my lord of Glocester should answer and saie : "Faire vncle, sith "yee declare you such a man as yee saie, I am right glad that it "is so, and for such a man I take you." And when this was doone, it was decreed by the same arbitrators, that euerie each of

[Then they
were to take
each other
by the
hand.]

my lord of Glocester, and Winchester, should take either other by the hand, in the presence of the king and all the parlement, in signe and token of good loue & accord ; the which was doone, and the parlement adiorned till after Easter.

---

[1] The reconciliation of Gloucester and Winchester took place on March 12, 1426.—*Rot. Parl.*, iv. 297/1.

Gloucester and Winchester having made a truce, Henry wills that "Richard be restorëd to his Blood" (l. 159), and therefore creates him "Princely Duke of Yorke" (l. 173). Passing from the subject of Gloucester's reconciliation with Winchester, Holinshed proceeds thus:

[*Hol.* iii. 595/2/30. *Halle*, 138.] But, when the great fier of this dissention, betweene these two noble personages, was thus by the arbitrators (to their knowledge and iudgement) vtterlie quenched out, and laid vnder boord, all other controuersies betweene other lords, (taking part with the one partie or the other,) were appeased, and brought to concord ; so that for ioy [1] the king caused a solemne fest to be kept on Whitsundaie; on which daie he created Richard Plantagenet, sonne and heire to the erle of Cambridge, (whome his father at Southhampton had put to death, as before yee haue heard,) duke of Yorke ; [2] not foreseeing that this preferment should be his destruction, nor that his seed should of his generation be the extreame end and finall conclusion.

[Richard
Plantagenet
created
Duke of
York.]

Having reinstated Richard Plantagenet, Henry accepts Gloucester's advice "to be Crown'd in France" (l. 180) without delay ; and bears that the ships which form the royal fleet "alreadie are in readinesse" (l. 186). Gloucester and Winchester were reconciled during the session of a Parliament which met at Leicester on February 18, 1426, and Henry was crowned at Paris on December 16, 1431.[3]

All now depart except Exeter, who stays to anticipate the renewal of dissension, and the fulfilment of a "fatall Prophecie" (ll. 195-199),

> Which, in the time of Henry nam'd the Fift,
> Was in the mouth of euery sucking Babe ;
> That *Henry borne at Monmouth* should winne all,
> *And Henry borne at Windsor loose all.*

The prophecy is thus recorded :

[*Hol.* iii. 581/1/68. *Halle*, 108.] This yeare [1421], at Windsore,

---

[1] Henry was then about five years old. The dramatist did not much exceed his authority by making the King mediate so eloquently between Winchester and Gloucester.

[2] That Richard was not created Duke of York at the Parliament of Leicester—which met on February 18, 1426—appears from a patent dated February 26, 1425, whereby the King grants to Queen Katharine a house in London formerly belonging to Edmund Earl of March, "in manibus nostris ratione Minoris ætatis carissimi Consanguinei nostri Ducis Eborum existens, Habendum & Tenendum eidem Matri nostræ Hospitium prædictum, durante Minori state prædicti Ducis," . . . —*Rymer*, x. 342. Rapin suggested (*Hist. Eng.*, ed. Tindal, 1732, vol. i. p. 545, col. 1) that the mistake arose from Richard having been made a knight at Leicester, in May, 1426 (*Rymer*, x. 356 cp. x. 358).   [3] *Journal*, xv. 433, 434.

on the daie of saint Nicholas [Dec. 6], in December, the queene
was deliuered of a sonne named Henrie; whose godfathers were
Iohn duke of Bedford, and Henrie bishop of Winchester, and
Iaquet, or (as the Frenchmen called hir) Iaqueline, of Bauier,
countesse of Holland, was his godmother. The king, being certified
hereof, as he laie at siege before Meaux, gaue God thanks; in that
it had pleased his diuine prouidence to send him a sonne, which
might succeed in his crowne and scepter. But, when he heard
reported the place of his natiuitie, were it that he [had been]
warned by some prophesie, or had some foreknowledge, or else
iudged himselfe of his sonnes fortune, he said vnto the lord Fitz
Hugh, his trustie chamberleine, these words: "My lord, I *Henrie*,
"*borne at Monmouth*, shall small time reigne, & much get; *and*
"*Henrie, borne at Windsore*, shall long reigne, and *all loose:* but, as
"God will, so be it."

Act III. sc. ii.—No date can be assigned to this scene. Chronology
and facts are utterly scorned. Rouen was not surprised and recovered,
but willingly received Charles VII. within its walls on October 19,
1449.[1] Joan, by whom the dramatic capture of Rouen is effected, was
burnt there on May 30, 1431;[2] and on December 16 of the same year
took place the coronation of Henry at Paris, which Talbot proposes
attending (ll. 128, 129). If 1431 be accepted as the time of this
scene,—the real circumstances attending our loss of the Norman capital
being ignored,—Bedford's death at Rouen (ll. 110-114) is antedated,
for that event happened on September 14, 1435.[3]

The fictitious capture of Rouen was, perhaps, an adaptation of a
story told by Holinshed, upon Halle's (197) authority. In 1441[4]

[*Hol.* iii. 619/2/69. *Halle*, 197.] Sir Francis the Arragonois,
hearing of that chance [the loss of Evreux], apparelled six strong
fellowes, like men of the countrie, with sacks and baskets, as cariers
of corne and vittels; and sent them to the castell of Cornill, in the
which diuerse Englishmen were kept as prisoners; and he, [p. 620]
with an ambush of Englishmen, laie in a vallie nigh to the fortresse.

The six counterfet husbandmen entered the castell vnsuspected,

[1] *Journal*, xv. 550.   [2] *Procès*, ix. 186-188.
[3] *Journal*, xv. 465. Or between 2 and 3 a.m. on the 15th.—*Greg.*, 177.
[4] It appears from *Halle* (197) that not much time had elapsed between the
surrender of Evreux to the French and the surprise of this castle by the
English. Evreux was yielded by us on September 14, 1441.—*Journal*,
xv. 518.

and streight came to the chamber of the capteine, & laieng hands
on him, gaue knowledge to them that laie in ambush to come to
their aid. The which suddenlie made foorth, and entered the
castell, slue and tooke all the Frenchmen, and set the Englishmen
at libertie : . . .

Fabyan's account of this stratagem (615) may also have been consulted. He says that Sir Francis

sette a Busshement nere vnto yᵉ sayd Castell, and in the Dawnynge [A castle
of the mornynge arayed .iiii.[1] of his Sowdyours in Husbandemennes surprised by
Aray, and sent theym with Sakkes fylled with dyuers Frutes to offer four soldiers
to sell to the Occupyers of the Castell. The whiche, whan they husband-
were comyn to the Gate, and by the langage taken for Frenshmen, men, carry-
anone withoute Susspicion were taken in, and seynge that fewe and speak-
folkes were stirrynge, helde the Porter muet whyle one gaue the ing French.]
foresayd Busshment knowlege, . . .

An incident of the betrayal of Le Mans to the French (see p. 216
above) may have suggested the means employed by Joan to apprize
Charles that the gates of Rouen were open. Compare, with the closing
words of my next excerpt, the stage direction after l. 25 ("Enter
Pucell on the top, thrusting *out a* Torch *burning*"), and ll. 21-30. The
French

[*Hol*. iii. 598/1/46. *Halle*, 142.] in the night season approched
towards the walles, making a little fire on an hill, in sight of the [A signal
towne, to signifie their comming; which perceiued by the citizens from Le
that neere to the great church were watching for the same, *a* Mans.]
burning cresset was shewed *out* of the steeple; which suddenlie was
put out and quenched.

Talbot swears to recover Rouen or die,

As sure as in this late betrayëd Towne,
Great Cordelions Heart was buryëd (ll. 82, 83).

Richard I.

[*Hol*. iii. 156/1/11.] willed his heart to be conueied vnto *Matth.*
Rouen, and there buried; in testimonie of the loue which he had *Paris.*
euer borne vnto that citie for the stedfast faith and tried loialtie [Richard I.'s
at all times found in the citizens there. heart buried
  at Rouen.]

---

[1] In Act III., sc. ii., Joan enters "with *foure* Souldiers." She answers the
watchman's challenge with a few words spoken in French (l. 13).

Bedford, who has been "brought in sicke in a Chayre" (l. 40), determines to "sit before the Walls of Roan" (l. 91), awaiting the issue of an attempt to regain the city, for he has "read"

> That stout Pendragon, *in* his *Litter, sick,*
> Came to the field, and vanquishĕd his foes :
> Me thinkes I should reuiue the Souldiers hearts
> Because I euer found them as my selfe.—ll. 95-98.

Geoffrey of Monmouth (VIII. xxii. 154, &c.) attributes this heroic deed to Uter Pendragon, but Boece's version (152/49 b, &c.) of the story —which Holinshed followed—is that Pendragon's brother, Aurelius Ambrosius,

[Uter Pendragon's brother carried sick in a litter to battle.]   [*Hol.* ii. *H. S.* 99/1/67.] euen *sicke* as he was, caused himselfe to be caried forth *in* a *litter ;* with whose presence his people were so incouraged, that, incountring with the Saxons, they wan the victorie, . . .

Act III. sc. iii.—In August, 1435, representatives of England and France met at Arras to discuss terms of peace. When this negotiation failed, Burgundy, whose attachment to his English allies had long been cooling, abandoned their cause, and soon afterwards turned his arms against them.[1] September 21, 1435, is the date[2] of the instrument by which he made peace with Charles VII. Joan—who is the dramatic agent of their reconciliation—died on May 30, 1431.[3]

Joan proposes inducing Burgundy to forsake Talbot (ll. 17-20). Charles answers (ll. 21-24) :

> I, marry, Sweeting, if we could doe that,
> France were no place for Henryes Warriors ;
> Nor should that *Nation* boast it so with vs,
> *But* be *extirpĕd* from *our* Prouinces.

Alençon adds :

> For euer should they be *expuls'd* from France, . . .

Perhaps these lines echo part of a speech which Halle—translating Polydore Vergil (485/16-24)—makes Charles address—in or about 1435—to Burgundy, whom the King complimented by saying that now there could be no question

[By Burgundy's help the English shall be expelled from France.]   [*Halle,* 177.] *but* by your helpe and aide, we shall *expell,* cleane *pull vp by the rootes,* and put out, all the Englyshe *nacion,* out of *our* realmes, territories, and dominions.

Joan's appeal to Burgundy's patriotism shakes him, and he yields when she uses the following argument as a proof that the English paid no regard to his interests (ll. 69-73).

---

[1] He besieged Calais in 1436.—*Mons.,* vi. 285-310.
[2] *Mons.,* vi. 221.   [3] See p. 224 above.

Was not the Duke of Orleance thy Foe ?
And was he not in England Prisoner ?
But, when they heard he was thine Enemie,
They set him free without his Ransome pay'd,
In spight of Burgonie and all his friends.

My next excerpt shows that these lines are at variance with historic facts :

[*Hol.* iii. 618/2/11. *Halle*, 192.] Philip, duke of Burgognie, partlie mooued in conscience to make amends to Charles duke of Orleance (as yet prisoner in England) for the death of duke Lewes his father, whome duke Iohn, father to this duke Philip, cruellie murthered in the citie of Paris ; and partlie intending the aduancement of his neece, the ladie Marie, daughter to Adolfe duke of Cleue, (by the which aliance, he trusted, that all old rancor should ceasse,) contriued waies to haue the said duke of Orleance set at libertie, vpon promise by him made to take the said ladie Marie vnto wife. This duke had beene prisoner in England euer since the battell was fought at Agincourt, vpon the daie of Crispine and Crispinian, in the yeare 1415, and was set now at libertie in the moneth of Nouember, in the yeare 1440 ;[1] paieng for his ransome foure hundred thousand crownes, though other saie but three hundred thousand.

The cause whie he was deteined so long in captiuitie, was to pleasure thereby the duke of Burgognie : for, so long as the duke of Burgognie continued faithfull to the king of England, it was not thought necessarie to suffer the duke of Orleance to be ransomed, least vpon his deliuerance he would not ceasse to seeke meanes to be reuenged vpon the duke of Burgognie, for the old grudge and displeasure betwixt their two families ; and therefore such ransome was demanded for him as he was neuer able to pay. But, after the duke of Burgognie had broken his promise, and was turned to the French part, the councell of the king of England deuised how to deliuer the duke of Orleance, that thereby they might displeasure the duke of Burgognie.[2] Which thing the duke of Burgognie per-

Marginal notes:

[Burgundy sought to release Orleans from captivity.]

[Orleans had been prisoner from 1415 ? 1440.]

[He was detained to please Burgundy.]

[To punish Burgundy for his desertion, the English proposed releasing Orleans, so Burgundy paid]

---

[1] Orleans was released from custody on October 28, 1440, at Westminster. —*Rymer*, x. 823. He was out of England (cp. 1 *Hen. VI.*, III. iii. 70) on November 12, 1440.—*Ibid.*, 829.

[2] *Halle*, 194. I know not *Halle's* authority for attributing this design to

Orleans's
ransom.]

ceiuing, doubted what might follow if he were deliuered without
his knowledge, and therefore to his great cost practised his deliuerance, paid his ransome, and ioined with him amitie and aliance by
mariage of his neece.

Act III. sc. iv.—Talbot presents himself before his sovereign, who
rewards his services by creating him Earl of Shrewsbury (ll. 25, 26).
The new Earl is bidden to Henry's coronation (l. 27), though that
ceremony took place in 1431, and Talbot's advancement—recorded in
the passage quoted below—is placed by Holinshed among the events
of 1442.

John lord
Talbot
created earle
of Shrews-
burie.

[*Hol.* iii. 623/2/9. *Halle*, 202.] About this season, Iohn, the
valiant lord Talbot, for his approued prowesse and wisdome, aswell
in England as in France, both in peace & warre so well tried, was
created earle of Shrewesburie;[1] and with a companie of three
thousand men sent againe into Normandie, for the better defense
of the same.

Act IV. sc. i.—"Enter King, Glocester, Winchester, Yorke,
Suffolke, Somerset, Warwicke, Talbot, Exeter, and Gouernor of
Paris."[2] This entry should be compared with the list given by
Holinshed of those present at Henry's coronation in Paris.[3]

[Names of
those
present
when Henry
was crowned
at Paris.]

[*Hol.* iii. 606/1/20. *Halle*, 160.] There were in his companie
of his owne nation, his vncle the cardinall of Winchester, the
cardinall and archbishop of Yorke, the dukes of Bedford, Yorke,
and Norffolke, the earles of Warwike, Salisburie, Oxenford,
Huntington, Ormond, Mortaigne, and Suffolke.

King Henrie
the sixt
crowned in
Paris.

[*Hol.* iii. 606/1/44. *Halle*, 161.] he was crowned king of
France, in our ladie church of Paris, by the cardinall of Winchester:
the bishop of Paris not being contented that the cardinall should
doo such an high ceremonie in his church and iurisdiction.

---

the Council. Burgundy did not discharge Orleans's ransom, but merely
authorized the Duchess of Burgundy to make herself responsible for the payment of 30,000 crowns,—which formed part of the ransom,—if the Dauphin
Lewis failed to become Orleans's pledge for the acquittance of that amount.—
Rymer, x. 788.

  [1] On May 20, 1442.—*Charter-roll*, 1-20 H. VI. (O. B.).
  [2] *Exeter, and Gouernor of Paris.*] and *Gouernor Exeter.* F1.
  [3] Gloucester was in England when Henry was crowned at Paris. He was
appointed Lieutenant of England during the King's absence from the realm.—
Proc. Priv. Co., iv. 40. "Somerset" was Edmund Beaufort, then Earl of
Mortain. Talbot was a prisoner of war in 1431 (see pp. 213, 214 above).
Thomas Beaufort, Duke of Exeter, died about five years before Henry's coron-
tion at Paris (see p. 235 below). The French Governor of Paris (ll. 3-8) is a
fictitious personage.

Opinion was converted into very vigorous action when Talbot tore
the Garter from the leg of "Falstaffe" (so spelt in the entry, l. 8).
Holinshed merely says that, "for doubt of misdealing" at the battle of
Patay (see pp. 207, 208 above), Bedford took from Sir John Fastolfe

[*Hol.* iii. 601/2/50.   *Halle*, 150.]   the image of saint George,   [The Garter
and his garter; though afterward, by meanes of freends, and   restored to
apparant causes of good excuse, the same were to him againe Fastolfe.]
deliuered against the mind of the lord Talbot.[1]

Falstaffe had brought with him a letter from Burgundy; "plaine
and bluntly" addressed "*To the King*," whom the Duke does not call
"his Soueraigne" (ll. 51, 52).   Gloucester reads the letter, which runs
thus (ll. 55-60) :

> I haue, vpon especiall cause,
> Mou'd with compassion of my Countries wracke,
> Together with the pittifull *complaints*
> Of such as your oppression feedes vpon,
> Forsaken your pernitious Factiön,
> And ioyn'd with Charles, the rightfull king of France.

Having made peace with Charles,

[*Hol.* iii. 611/2/55.   *Halle*, 177.]   the duke of Burgognie, to [Toison d'Or
set a veile before the king of Englands eies, sent Thoison Dore his brought
cheefe herald to king Henrie with letters; excusing the matter by Henry a
way of information, that he was constreined to enter in this league containing
with K. Charles, by the dailie outcries, *complaints*, and lamenta- Burgundy's
tions of his people, alledging against him that he was the onlie reasons for
cause of the long continuance of the wars, to the vtter impouerish- making
ing of his owne people, and the whole nation of France. . . . peace with
 Charles.]

. . . The superscription of this letter was thus : "*To the* high and [The super-
"mightie prince, Henrie, by the grace of God, *king* of England, his scription of
"welbeloued cousine."   Neither naming him king of France, nor his the letter.]
souereigne lord, according as (euer before that time) he was accustomed to doo.   This letter was much maruelled at of the councell,
after they had throughlie considered all the contents thereof, & [Dismay and
they could not but be much disquieted ; so far foorth that diuerse anger of
of them stomaked so muche the vntruth[2] of the duke, that Henry's
they could not temper their passions, but openlie called him traitor. Councell.]

---

[1] The restoration of the Garter to Fastolfe caused "grand débat" between him
and Talbot, after the latter's release from captivity in 1433.—*Mons.*, v. 230.
[2] *them stomaked so muche the vntruth*] Hol. ed. 1.   *them offended so much
with the vntruth* Hol. ed. 2.

When the letter has been read, Henry bids Talbot march against
Burgundy "straight," and make him feel "what offence it is to flout
his Friends" (l. 75).   Toison d'Or was sent back to his master with the
verbal message that, "what a new reconciled enimie was in respect of an
old tried freend," Burgundy "might shortlie find" (*Hol.* iii. 612/1/30).

After playing the part of umpire in the strife of the Roses, Henry
says (ll. 162-168) :

> Cosin of Yorke, we institute your Grace
> To be our Regent in these parts of France :
> And, good my Lord of Somerset, vnite
> Your Troopes of horsemen with his Bands of foote ;
>
> . . . .
>
> Go cheerefully together, and digest
> Your angry Choller on your Enemies.

There is some historical warrant for this speech.   In 1443, John
Beaufort, Duke of Somerset, received military commands in France and
Guienne, without prejudice to the authority of York, who was then
Lieutenant-General and Governor of France and Normandy.   An
invasion of Normandy by the French was apprehended, and York was
desired to assist Somerset.[1]   I give excerpts wherein mention is made
of a joint campaign conducted by York and Somerset; premising that
the date (20th of Henry VI.) is too early, and that Halle—whom
Holinshed followed—wrongly attributed to Edmund Beaufort (the
dramatic "Somerset") operations which were carried out by Edmund's
brother, John Beaufort.

[Invasion of Anjou by York and Somerset.]

[*Hol.* iii. 619/1/2. *Halle,* 194.]   In the beginning of this
twentith [xix.—*Halle*] yeare, Richard duke of Yorke, regent of
France, and gouernour of Normandie, determined to inuade the
territories of his enimies both by sundrie armies, and in seuerall
places, and thereupon without delaie of time he sent the lord of
Willoughbie with a great crue of soldiers to destroie the countrie
of Amiens ; and Iohn lord Talbot was appointed to besiege the
towne of Diepe ; and the regent himselfe, accompanied with
Edmund duke of Summerset, set forward into the duchie of
Aniou. . . .

[Anjou and Maine ravaged by York and Somerset.]

The dukes of Yorke and Summerset . . . entered into Aniou
and Maine, and there destroied townes, and spoiled the people, and
with great preies and prisoners repaired againe into Normandie, . . .

Act IV. sec. ii.-vii.—Since the historical time of the last scene
ranges from 1431 to 1443, it is impossible to determine the historic

---

[1] *Proc. Priv. Co.,* v. 255 ; 259-261. Cp. *Cont. Croyl.,* 519.

interval between sc. i., Act IV., and the scenes in which Talbot's
expedition to Guienne is dramatized. The dramatic interval being of
uncertain length, an audience might suppose that, after chastising
Burgundy, as the King bade (see p. 230 above), Talbot rashly undertook
to widen the circle of English conquest by the reduction of Bordeaux.
But Bordeaux had belonged to us for nearly three centuries before it
was annexed by the French in 1451.[1] The leaders of an English
party asked us to return, and, their offer having been accepted, Talbot
was sent to win back Guienne. Bordeaux opened its gates to him: the
larger portion of the Bordelois was speedily recovered, together with
Castillon in Perigord.[2] Talbot was at Bordeaux when he heard that a
French army was besieging Castillon, and on July 17, 1453, he brought
relief to the garrison.[3] At his approach, the French

[*Hol.* iii. 640/2/46. *Halle*, 229.] left the siege, and retired in
good order into the place which they had trenched, diched, and
fortified with ordinance. The earle, aduertised how the siege was
remoued, hasted forward towards his enimies, doubting most least
they would haue beene quite fled and gone before his comming.
But they, fearing the displeasure of the French king (who was not
far off) if they should haue fled, abode the earles comming, and so   *The valiant
receiued him: who though he first with manfull courage, and sore   earle of
fighting wan the entrie of their campe, yet at length they com-   Shrewsburie
passed him about, and shooting him through the thigh with an   and his son
handgun, slue his horsse, and finallie killed him lieng on the   manfullie
ground; whome they durst neuer looke in the face, while he stood   slaine.
on his feet.

Scenes ii.-iv. are imaginary. The story of young Talbot's devotion
to his father—dramatized in scenes v., vi.—is thus related:

[*Hol.* iii. 640/2/61. *Halle*, 229.] It was said, that after he
perceiued there was no remedie, but present losse of the battell,
he counselled his sonne, the lord Lisle, to saue himselfe by flight,
sith the same could not redound to anie great reproch in him, this
being the first iournie in which he had beene present. Manie
words he vsed to persuade him to haue saued his life; but nature   [Talbot's
so wrought in the son, that neither desire of life, nor feare of   son would
                                                                       not desert
                                                                       him.]

---

[1] A campaign which lasted about three months closed with the surrender
of Bayonne to the French in August, 1451.—*Du Clercq*, xii. 89, 112.
[2] *Du Clercq*, xiii. 5-7. *De Coussy*, xi. 2, 3.
[3] This date is confirmed by a letter written two days after the battle.—
Bibliothèque de l'École des Chartes, 2nd series, vol. iii. pp. 246, 247.

death, could either cause him to shrinke, or ccnueie himselfe out
of the danger, and so there manfullie ended his life with his said
father.

A few lines of old Talbot's appeal to his son (Act IV., scc. v., vi.)
have parallels in a speech attributed to the former by Halle (229).

Thou neuer hadst Renowne, nor canst not lose it (v. 40).

And leaue my followers here to fight and dye !
My Age was neuer tainted with such shame (v. 45, 46).

Flye, *to reuenge my death, if I be slaine* (v. 18).

My Deaths Reuenge, thy Youth, and Englands Fame :

All these are sau'd, if thou wilt flye away (vi. 39, 41).

In the quasi-historical speech, Talbot urges that he—" the terror and
scourge of the French people " (cp. p. 218 above)—cannot die " without
great laude," or flee " without perpetuall shame " ; and he then thus
counsels his son :

[Talbot
advised his
son to flee.]

"But because this is thy first iourney and enterprise, neither
"thi flyeng shall redounde to thy shame, nor thy death to thy
"glory ; for as hardy a man wisely flieth as a temerarious person
"folishely abidethe : therfore y° fleyng of me shalbe y° dishonor
"not only of me & my progenie, but also a discomfiture of all my
"company ; thy departure shal saue thy lyfe, and make the able
"another tyme, *if I be slayn, to reuenge my death*, and to do honor
"to thy Prince and profyt to his Realme."

Dunois would hew to pieces the bodies, and hack asunder the bones,
of Talbot and young John (vii. 47).   Charles's dissent from this savage
proposal,

Oh, no, forbeare ! For that which we haue fled
During the life, let vs not wrong it dead,

resembles an answer made by Lewis XI. to " certeine vndiscreet
persons " who advised the defacement of Bedford's tomb at Rouen.

*A worthy
saising of a
wise prince.*

[*Hol.* iii. 612/1/54. *Halle*, 178.] " What honour shall it be to
" vs, or to you, to breake this monument, and to pull out of the
" ground the dead bones of him, whome in his life neither my
" father nor your progenitours, with all their power, puissance, and
" freends were once able to make flee one foot backward ; but by
" his strength, wit, and policie, kept them all out of the principall

"dominions of the realme of France, and out of this noble and
"famous duchie of Normandie? Wherefore I saie, first, God haue
"his soule! and let his bodie now lie in rest; which, when he was
"aliue, would haue disquieted the proudest of vs all."

The "silly stately stile"—as Joan calls it—of Talbot's dignities,
enumerated by Sir William Lucy when asking for "the great Alcides
of the field," agrees almost literally with an epitaph on Talbot in
Richard Crompton's *Mansion of Magnanimitie*, 1599, sign. E 4.[1] I
give the epitaph and ll. 60-71 in parallel columns.

Here lieth the right noble knight, / Iohn *Talbott Earle of Shrewsbury,* / *Washford, Waterford, and Valence,* / *Lord Talbot of Goodrige, and* / *Vrchengfield, Lord Strange of the* / *blacks Meere, Lord Verdon of* / *Alton, Lord Crumwell of Wing-* / *field,* Lord Louetoft of Worsop, / Lord *Furniuall of Sheffield, Lord* / *Faulconbri[d]ge, knight of the most* / *noble order of S. George, S. Michaell,* / *and the Golden fleece, Great Mar-* / *shall to* king *Henry the sixt of his* / *realms of France:* who died in the / battell of Burdeaux in the yeare / of our Lord 1453.

But where's the great Alcides of the / field,   60 / Valiant Lord *Talbot, Earls of Shrews-* / *bury!* / Created, for his rare successe in / Armes, / Great Earle of *Washford, Waterford,* / *and Valence;* / *Lord Talbot of Goodrig and Vrchin-*   64 / *field,* / *Lord Strange of Blackmere, Lord* / *Verdon of Alton,* / *Lord Cromwell of Wingfield, Lord* / *Furniuall of Sheffild,* / The thrice victorious *Lord* of *Falcon-* / *bridge;* / *Knight of the Noble Order of S.*   68 / *George,* / Worthy *S. Michael, and the Golden* / *Fleece;* / *Great Marshall to Henry the sixt* / *Of* all *his* Warres within the *Realme* / *of France!*

Inscription on the tomb of Iohn first Earle of Shrewsbury.

---

[1] In his *Catalogus and Succession of the Kings, Princes, Dukes, Marquesses, Earles, and Viscounts of this Realme of England,* ed. 1619, p. 196, Ralph Brooke says of Talbot: "This Iohn being slaine . . . his body was buried in a Toombe at Roane in Normandy, whereon this Epitaphe is written." The epitaph which these words preface is the same as that given by Crompton; with three slight exceptions. After "Earle of Shrewsbury" Brooke has "*Earle of* Washford, Waterford and Valence." Brooke also omits "the" before "Blakmere," and "most" before "Noble Order of S. George." From Leland (*Itinerary,* ed. Hearne, 1744, vol. iv., pt. 1, p. 23, fol. 40) we learn the following particulars concerning the first interment of Talbot's body, and its subsequent removal to England: "This John [3rd Earl of Shrewsbury] had emong his Brethern one caullid Gilbert Talbot, after a Knight of Fame, the which buried the Erle his Grandfathers Bones browght out of Fraunce at Whitechirche in a fair Chapelle, wher he is also buried hymself." Leland adds (*Itin.,* vol. vii., pt. 1, p. 8, fol. 15): "Talbot Erle of Shrobbesbyri and his Sonne Lord Léale slayne in Fraunce. This Erles Bones were browght out of Normandy to Whitchurche in Shrobbeshire." On April 9, 1874, the bones of Talbot were discovered by some workmen engaged in repairing his monument at Whitchurch. These remains were solemnly re-interred on April 17, 1874. —*Notes & Queries,* 5th S. I. 399; cp. 258. Crompton is the earliest known authority for the epitaph I have quoted in my text. He cites in a preceding

Act V. sc. i.—Letters have arrived from the Pope (Eugenius IV.)
and the Emperor (Sigismund), whereby Henry is entreated (ll. 5, 6):

> To haue *a godly peace* concluded of
> Betweene the Realmes of England and of France.

In 1435, during the session of the Council of Basle,

[The Emperor and other Christian Princes desired mediation between England and France.]
[*Hol.* iii. 611/1/7. *Halle*, 174.] motion was made among Sigismund the emperour and other christen kings . . . that, sith such
horror of bloudshed betweene the two nations continuallie so lament-
ablie raged in France, some mediation might be made for accord: . . .

The impiety of war between "Professors of one Faith" (l. 14) is expressed in a speech which forms my next quotation; and this speech also
contains the words "a godlie peace," occurring in the lines quoted above.

The English, French, and Burgundian plenipotentiaries having met
at Arras in August, 1435,[1] "the cardinall of S. Crosse," who represented
Eugenius IV.,

[The Cardinal's exhortation to "a godlie peace."]
[*Hol.* iii. 611/1/40. *Halle*, 175.] declared to the three parties
the innumerable mischeefes, that had followed to the whole state
of the christiän common-wealth by their continuall dissention and
dailie discord; exhorting them, for the honour of God, & for the
loue which they ought to beare towards the aduancement of his
faith and true religion, to conforme themselues to reason, and to
laie aside all rancor, malice and displeasure; so that, in concluding
a godlie peace, they might receiue profit and quietnesse heere in
this world, and of God an euerlasting reward in heauen.

Gloucester informs Henry that, "the sooner to effect and surer
binde" a peace between England and France, the Earl of Armagnac

> Proffers his onely daughter to your Grace
> In marriage, with a large and sumptuous Dowrie.—ll. 19, 20.

The proffer here announced was made in 1442,[2]—not 1435, our last

---

marginal note "Camden 462." The reference shows that he used the ed. of
Camden's *Britannia* which was published in 1594, because no previous ed.
contains any mention of Talbot at p. 462, and the next ed. did not appear till
1600. But at p. 462 of the ed. of 1594 Camden merely notices Talbot's tomb
at Whitchurch, and does not even quote another epitaph on Talbot once exist-
ing at Whitchurch, and having much less resemblance to the lines in 1 *Henry
VI.* than is displayed by the Rouen inscription.

[1] *Mons.*, vi. 178. *Mons.* says (vi. 161): "de par notre Saint-Père le pape,
le cardinal de Saint-Croix."

[2] On May 28, 1442, Robert Roos, Knight, Master Thomas Bekyngton, and
Edward Hull, Gentleman, were empowered to choose one of the daughters of
the Count of Armagnac, and espouse her to Henry.—*Rymer*, xi. 7. Bekyngton
and the other ambassadors embarked at Plymouth on July 10, 1442.—*Beckington's Embassy*, 10. He returned in the following year; landing at Falmouth
on February 10, 1443.—*Beckington's Embassy*, 89.

historical date,—and John Count of Armagnac had, as the following excerpt shows, a very different motive for desiring an alliance with Henry.[1]

[*Hol.* iii. 623/2/57. *Halle*, 202.] In this yeare[2] died in Guien the countesse of Comings, to whome the French king and also the earle of Arminacke pretended to be heire, in so much that the earle entred into all the lands of the said ladie. And bicause he knew the French king would not take the matter well, to haue a Rouland for an Oliuer he sent solemne ambassadours to the king of England, offering him his daughter in mariage, with promise to be bound (beside great summes of monie, which he would giue with hir) to deliuer into the king of Englands hands all such castels and townes, as he or his ancestors deteined from him within anie part of the duchie of Aquitaine, either by conquest of his progenitors, or by gift and deliuerie of anie French king; and further to aid the same king with monie for the recouerie of other cities, within the same duchie, from the French king; or from anie other person that against king Henrie [*p.* 624] vniustlie kept, and wrongfullie withheld[3] them.

[The Earl of Armagnac offered his daughter in marriage to Henry, with a large dower, and contingent advantages.]

This offer seemed so profitable and also honorable to king Henrie and the realme, that the ambassadours were well heard, honourablie receiued, and with rewards sent home into their countrie. After whome were sent, for the conclusion of the mariage, into Guien, sir Edward Hull, sir Robert Ros, and Iohn Grafton,[4] deane of S. Seuerines; the which (as all the chronographers agree) both concluded the mariage, and by proxie affied the yoong ladie.

The earle of Arminacke daughter affied vnto king Henrie.

Though Winchester was a Cardinal when sc. iii., Act I., was before the audience, Exeter is surprised at finding him "install'd" in that dignity, and recollects a prophecy of Henry V. about the Bishop (ll. 32, 33):

> If once he come to be a Cardinall,
> Hee'l make his cap coequall with the Crowne.

Exeter died in 1426 (*Hol.* iii. 595/2/73), but Winchester was not made a Cardinal until 1427.[5] "Whyche degree," says Halle (139),

---

[1] But what *Halle* says about Armagnac's proffer is inaccurate See *Beckington's Embassy*, pp. xxxvii-xli.
[2] The Countess of Cominges died in 1443.—*Anselme*, ii. 637.
[3] *withheld*] *withholden* Hol.
[4] *Grafton*] Halle. *Gralton* Hol.
[5] He received his hat on March 25, 1427.—*Chron. Lond.*, 115.

[Henry V.
would not
suffer
Cardinals'
hats to be
equal with
Princes'.]

Kynge Henry the fifth, knowynge the haute corage, and the
ambicious mynde of the man [Winchester], prohibited hym on hys
allegeaunce once either to sue for or to take; meanynge that
Cardinalles Hattes shoulde not presume to bee *egall with* Princes.[1]

Holinshed copied from Halle a second series of articles containing
charges against Winchester, which were preferred by Gloucester in
1440.[2] The first article was:

[Henry V.
would not
allow
Winchester
to be made a
Cardinal.]

[*Hol.* iii. 620/1/62. *Halle,* 197.] 2 First, the cardinall, then
being bishop of Winchester, tooke vpon him the state of cardinall,
which was naied and denaied him by the king of most noble
memorie, my lord your father (whome God assoile); saieng that he
had as leefe set his crowne beside him, as see him weare a cardinals
hat, he being a cardinall. For he knew full well, the pride and
ambition that was in his person, then being but a bishop, should
haue so greatlie extolled him into more intollerable pride, when
that he were a cardinall: . . .

There is, I believe, no authority for representing Winchester as
having obtained a cardinalate by bribing the Pope (ll. 51-54); but
perhaps the Bishop's subsequent wealth led to the inference that a large
sum must have been asked for the

*The bishop of
Winchester
made a
cardinall.
W. P.*

[*Hol.* iii. 596/2/1. *Halle,* 139.] habit, hat, and dignitie of a
cardinall, with all ceremonies to it apperteining: which promotion,
the late K. (right deeplie persing into the vnrestrainable ambitious
mind of the man, that euen from his youth was euer [wont] to checke
at the highest; and [having] also right well asserteined with what
intollerable pride his head should soone be swollen vnder such a
hat) did therefore all his life long keepe this prelat backe from that
presumptuous estate. But now, the king being yoong and the
regent his freend, he obteined his purpose, to his great profit, and

[Winchester
gathered
treasure by
a bull
legatine.]

the impouerishing of the spiritualtie of this realme. For by a bull
legatine [3], which he purchased from Rome, he gathered so much
treasure, that no man in maner had monie but he: so that he was
called the rich cardinall of Winchester.

Act V. sc. ii.—Charles has heard that "the stout Parisians do

---

[1] Henry "would not that Cardinals hats shoulde in anye wise presume to
bee *equall with* regall crownes."—*Hol.* ed. 1.

[2] *Arnold* (279-286) contains the earliest printed text of these articles.

[3] *legatine] legantine* Hol.

reuolt" (l. 2) ; and Alençon thereupon advises a march to Paris. Paris was lost by the English before the play began (I. i. 61), but the Fourth Act opened with Henry's coronation there. A sentence which concludes Holinshed's account of the loss of the city in 1436 may be compared with Charles's words.

[*Hol.* iii. 613/1/73. *Halle,* 180.] Thus was the citie of Paris brought into possession of Charles the French king,[1] through the vntrue demeanour of the citizens, who, contrarie to their oths, and promised allegiance, like false and inconstant people, so reuolted from the English. *[The Parisians revolted from the English.]*

Act V. sc. iii.—The action of this scene passes in Anjou (l. 147), near the "Castle walles" of René (l. 129), assumed by editors to be those girdling Angers. May 23, 1430, is the historic date of Joan's capture. On that day she accompanied a sally from Compiégne,—then besieged by the English and Burgundians,—and was taken before she could re-enter the town.[2] Bedford was "Regent" (l. 1) at the time, but the dramatist killed him in Act III. sc. ii. York—whose prisoner she becomes in this scene—held no such post until 1436, when he received the chief command in France.[3]

Suffolk's proxy-wooing of Margaret (ll. 45-186) is, of course, fictitious, but he arranged the marriage between her and Henry. In 1444,

[*Hol.* iii. 624/1/61. *Halle,* 203.] England was vnquieted, . . . and France by spoile, slaughter, and burning sore defaced ; (a mischeefe in all places much lamented;) therefore, to agree the two puissant kings, all the princes of christendome trauelled so effectuouslie by their oratours and ambassadours, that a diet was appointed to be kept at the citie of Tours in Touraine ; where for the king of England appeared William de la Poole earle of Suffolke, . . . *The diet at Tours for a peace to be had betweene England and France.*

---

[1] On April 13, 1436.—*Journal,* xv. 471.

[2] In a letter to Henry VI., the Duke of Burgundy announces her capture on May 23.—*Chron. Lond.,* 170.

[3] In the address of a letter from Henry, dated on May 12 (1436, wrongly placed under 1438), York is styled "oure lieutenant of oure reume of France and duchie of Normandie."—*Stevenson,* II., part 1, lxxiii. In this letter York is urged to assume his government without longer delay. The issue roll (cited in Ramsay's *York and Lancaster,* i. 484, note 5) shows that he must have sailed soon after May 24, 1436. On April 7, 1437, the indentures, by which York agreed to undertake the lieutenancy of France and Normandy, had nearly expired, but he was asked to remain at his post until a successor should be appointed.—*Proc. Priv. Co.,* v. 6, 7. The appointment of his successor, Richard Beauchamp, Earl of Warwick, is dated July 16, 1437.—*Rymer,* x. 674. Warwick died in office on April 30, 1439 (*Chron. Lond.,* 124); and, on July 2, 1440, York was made Lieutenant-General and Governor of France, Normandy, &c., for a term of five years ending at Michaelmas, 1445.—*Rymer,* x. 786.

Failing to agree upon the terms of a peace, the commissioners
negotiated a truce.

[*Hol.* iii. 624/2/18. *Halle*, 203.] In treating of this truce, the
earle of Suffolke, aduenturing somewhat vpon his commission, without the assent of his associats, imagined that the next waie to

[Suffolk
arranged a
marriage
between
Margaret
and Henry.]
come to a perfect peace was to contriue a mariage betweene the
French kings kinsewoman,[1] the ladie Margaret, daughter to Reiner
duke of Aniou, and his souereigne lord king Henrie.

Act V. sc. iv.—Entering fully into the spirit of the following
passages, the dramatist was not satisfied to avail himself of the worst
charges which they contain, but taxed his invention to make Joan deny
her father (ll. 2-33). About five months after her capture, she was
delivered to the English,[2] and

[*Hol.* iii. 604/2/23.] for hir pranks so vncouth and suspicious,
the lord regent, by Peter Chauchon bishop of Beauuois, (in whose
diocesse she was taken,) caused hir life and beleefe, after order of

[Joan
examined,
found guilty
of witch-
craft, and
condemned
to perpetual
imprison-
ment.]
law, to be inquired vpon and examined. Wherein found though a
virgin, yet first, shamefullie reiecting hir sex abominablie in acts
and apparell, to haue counterfeit mankind, and then, all damnablie
faithlesse, to be a pernicious instrument to hostilitie and bloudshed
in diuelish witchcraft and sorcerie,[3] sentence accordinglie was pronounced against hir. Howbeit, vpon humble confession of hir
iniquities with a counterfeit contrition pretending a carefull sorow
for the same, execution spared and all mollified into this, that
from thencefoorth she should cast off hir vnnaturall wearing of
mans abilliments, and keepe hir to garments of hir owne kind,
abiure hir pernicious practises of sorcerie and witcherie, and haue
life and leasure in perpetuall prison to bewaile hir misdeeds.
Which to performe (according to the maner of abiuration) a
solemne oth verie gladlie she tooke.

But herein (God helpe vs!) she fullie afore possest of the feend,

---

[1] Niece to Mary of Anjou, Queen of France, who was René's sister.

[2] *Procès* (Dissertation), ix. 217, *n* 1.

[3] In 1434, Bedford, defending his conduct as Regent of France, said that
the loss of territory, which befel the English after Salisbury was slain at the
siege of Orleans, was "causedde in greete partye as I trowe of lak of sadde be
leve and of unlieful doubte þat þei hadde of a disciple and leme of þᵉ fende
calledde þᵉ Pucelle þat usedde fals enchantementes and sorcerie."—*Proc. Priv.
Co.*, iv. 223.

not able to hold her in anie towardnesse of grace, falling streight *Polydo. 23, in H. 6.*
waie into hir former abominations, (and yet seeking to eetch out [Having relapsed, she
life as long as she might,) stake not (though the shift were shame- sought to prolong life
full) to confesse hir selfe a strumpet, and (vnmaried as she was) to by declaring herself to be
be with child.[1] For triall, the lord regents lenitie gaue hir nine with child.]
moneths staie, at the end wherof she (found herein as false as
wicked in the rest, an eight daies after, vpon a further definitiue
sentence declared against hir to be relapse and a renouncer of hir
oth and repentance) was therevpon[2] deliuered ouer to secular [After due respite, she
power, and so executed by consumption of fire in the old market was burnt at Rouen.]
place at Rone, in the selfe same steed where now saint Michaels *Les grand chron.*
church stands: hir ashes afterward without the towne wals shaken
into the wind. Now recounting altogither, hir pastorall bringing vp,
rude, without any vertuous instruction, hir campestrall conuersation *Les grandes chronic. le 4.*
with wicked spirits,[3] whome, in hir first salutation to Charles the Dol- *lieur.*
phin, she vttered to be our Ladie, saint Katharine, and saint Anne, [Wicked spirits gave
that in this behalfe came and gaue hir commandements from her com- mands while
God hir maker, as she kept hir fathers lambs in the fields[4] . . . she kept her father's lambs.]

[*p.* 605, *col.* 1.] These matters may verie rightfullie denounce
vnto all the world hir execrable abhominations, and well iustifie
the iudgement she had, and the execution she was put to for the
same. A thing yet (God wot) verie smallie shadowed and losse [Charles—a Christian
holpen by the verie trauell of the Dolphin, whose dignitie abroad King avalled him-
[was] foulie spotted in this point, that, contrarie to the holie degree self of her sorceries.]
of a right christen prince (as he called himselfe), for maintenance
of his quarels in warre would not reuerence to prophane his sacred *Christian- issimus rex.*
estate, as dealing in diuelish practises with misbeleeuers and witches.

When Joan has been led out to execution, Winchester enters and
greets York (l. 95)

---

[1] This lie was the source of 1 *Hen. VI.*, V. iv. 60-85.
[2] *was therevpon*] *was she therevpon* Hol.
[3] This sentence may have given the dramatist a hint for V. iii. 1-23, where
his Joan entreats the help of certain " Fiends," whom she has summoned.
[4] Cp. I. ii. 76, &c.:

> " Loe, whilest I wayted on my tender Lambes, . . .
> Gods Mother deignĕd to appeare to me,
> And, in a Vision full of Maiestie,
> Will'd me to leaue my base Vocation,
> And free my Countrey from Calamitie."

With Letters of Commission from the King ;

which embody those "conditions of a friendly peace" between England and France, drawn up by Henry's order (v. i. 37-40), in response to an appeal from "the States of Christendome" (V. iv. 96-99). Charles then enters, accompanied by his lords, and says (ll. 116-119) :

> Since, Lords of England, it is thus agreed
> That peacefull truce shall be proclaim'd in France,
> We come to be informëd by your selues,
> What the conditions of that league must be.

Winchester answers (ll. 123-132) :

> Charles, and the rest, it is enacted thus :
> That, in regard King Henry giues consent,   124
> Of meere compassion and of lenity,
> To ease your Countrie of distressefull Warre,
> And suffer you to breath in fruitfull peace,
> You shall become true Liegemen to his Crowne :   128
> And, Charles, vpon condition thou wilt sweare
> To pay him tribute, and submit thy selfe,
> Thou shalt be plac'd as Viceroy vnder him,
> And still enioy thy Regall dignity.   132

The terms of peace here announced were, according to Halle, Holinshed's authority, offered at the conference of Arras, in 1435.

[The
English
terms.]
[*Hol.* iii. 611/1/55.   *Halle*, 175.]   The Englishmen would that king Charles should haue nothing but what it pleased the king of England, and that not as dutie, but as a benefit[1] by him of his
[The French
terms.].
meere liberalitie giuen and distributed.   The Frenchmen, on the other part, would that K. Charles should haue the kingdome franklie and freelie, and that the king of England should leaue the name, armes, and title of the king of France, and to be content with the dukedomes of Aquitaine and Normandie, and to forsake Paris, and all the townes which they possessed in France, betweene the riuers of Some and Loire ; being no parcell of the duchie of Normandie.   To be breefe, the demands of all parts were betweene them so farre out of square, as hope of concord there was none at all.

---

[1] If "benefit" = *beneficium*, fief, the English terms were as extravagant as those dictated by Winchester to Charles (V. iv. 124-132).   But *Mons.*—whom *Halle* seems to have had before him—gives the French terms alone, which were that "le roi Henri d'Angleterre se voulsit déporter et désister de lui nommer roi de France, moyennant que, par certaines conditions, lui seroient accordées les seigneuries de Guienne et Normandie ; laquelle chose les Anglois ne voulurent point accorder."—vi. 180.

Act V. sc. v.—The opposite views of Suffolk and Gloucester touching Henry's marriage are here brought forward. After a truce between England and France had been arranged (see p. 238 above),

[*Hol.* iii. 624/2/45. *Halle*, 204.] the earle of Suffolke with his companie returned into England, where he forgat not to declare what an honourable truce he had taken, out of the which there was a great hope that a finall peace might grow the sooner for that honorable mariage, which he had concluded ; omitting nothing that might extoll and set foorth the personage of the ladie, or the nobilitie of hir kinred.

[Suffolk extolled the marriage which he had made.]

But although this mariage pleased the king and diuerse of his conncell, yet Humfrie duke of Glocester protector of the realme was much against it ;[1] alledging that it should be both contrarie to the lawes of God, and dishonorable to the prince, if he should breake that promise and contract of mariage, made by ambassadours sufficientlie thereto instructed, with the daughter of the earle of Arminacke, vpon conditions both to him and his realme, as much profitable as honorable.   But the dukes words could not be heard, for the earles dooings were onelie liked and allowed.

The protector misliked this second motion of the kings marriage.

[But Suffolk's advice prevailed.]

Having urged that (l. 34)

> A poore Earles daughter is vnequall oddes

for Henry, Suffolk thus answers Gloucester's objection that Margaret's " Father is no better than an Earle " :

> Yes, my Lord, her Father is a King,
> The *King of Naples and Ierusalem* ; . . .   40

Holinshed says :

[*Hol.* iii. 624/2/24. *Halle*, 204.] This Reiner duke of Aniou named himselfe king of Sicill, Naples, and Ierusalem ; hauing onlie

[René's kingly style.]

---

[1] Gloucester might have disliked this marriage, but he expressed a formal approval of it.   On June 4, 1445, the Speaker of the Commons recommended Suffolk to Henry's " good Grace," for having—besides rendering other services to the State—concluded a marriage between Henry and Margaret ; wherefore the Commons " desyred the said declarations, laboures, and demenyng of my said Lord of Suff', to be enacted in thys present Parlement, to his true acquitail and discharge, and honour of hym in tyme to come ; uppon the whiche request thus made to the Kyng our Soueraigne Lorde, and to the Lordes Spirituell and Temporell, by the Communes, my Lorde of Gloucestr', and many other Lordys Spirituell and Temporell abovesaid, arose of their setis, and besoghtyn humbly the Kyng of the same as they wer prayed be the said Communes, to pray and to beseche his Highnesse to do " ; . . .—*Rot. Parl.*, v. 73.

R

the name and stile of those realmes, without anie penie, profit, or
foot of possession.

Suffolk's praise (ll. 70, 71) of Margaret's

> . . . valiant *courage* and vndaunted spirit,
> More then in women commonly is seene,

may be compared with Halle's description of her (p. 208; abridged in
Hol. iii. 626/2/44):

[Character
of Queen
Margaret.]

But on the other parte, the Quene his [Henry's] wyfe was a
woman of a great witte, and yet of no greater wytte then of haute
stomacke ["a ladie of great wit, and no lesse *courage.*"—Hol.];
desirous of glory and couetous of honor; and of reason, pollicye,
counsaill, and other giftes and talentes of nature belongyng to a
man, full and flowyng : of witte and wilinesse she lacked nothyng,
nor of diligence, studie, and businesse she was not vnexperte ; but
yet she had one poynt of a very woman, for, often tyme, when she
was vehement & fully bente in a matter, she was sodainly, lyke a
wethercocke, mutable and turnyng.

Compare also a remark upon her, copied by Holinshed from Halle
(205) :

[Margaret's
manly
courage.]

[*Hol.* iii. 625/1/34.] This ladie excelled all other, as well in
beautie and fanour, as in wit and policie ; and was of stomach and
courage more like to a man than a woman.

X. HENRY VI. PART II.

HISTORIC time in *The Second Part of Henry the Sixt* commences
shortly before Margaret's coronation (I. i. 74) on May 30, 1445, and
ends on May 22, 1455, when the battle of St. Albans [1] was fought. As
this Second Part of *Henry VI.* is a recast of *The First part of the
Contention betwixt the two famous houses of Yorke and Lancaster*, my
excerpts are really illustrations of the latter drama.

Act I. sc. i.—During the interval which divides the First and
Second Parts of this play, Suffolk has escorted Margaret to England
(cp. 1 *Hen. VI.*, V. v. 87-91). He now presents her to Henry, whom
he thus addresses (ll. 1-9) :

---

[1] Called the first battle of St. Albans. A second battle was fought there on
February 17, 1461.

As by your high Imperiall Maiesty
I had in charge at my depart for France,
As Procurator to your Excellence,
To marry Princes Margaret for your Grace;
So, in the Famous Ancient City Toures,
(In presence of the Kings of France, and Sicill,
The Dukes of Orleance, Calaber, Britaigne, and Alanson,
Seuen Earles, twelue Barons, & twenty reuerend Bishops,) 8
I haue perform'd my Taske, and was espous'd : . . .

In November, 1444,[1] Suffolk and a splendid retinue

[*Hol.* iii. 625/1/18. *Halle*, 205.] came to the citie of Tours *Anno Reg.*
in Touraine, where they were honorablie receiued both of the   *22.*
                                                                         1445
French king and of the king of Sicill. The marquesse of Suffolke, [Margaret
as procurator to king Henrie, espoused the said ladie in the church espoused by
                                                                      Suffolk,
of saint Martins. At the which mariage were present the father   Henry's
                                                                     'procura-
and mother of the bride; the French king himselfe, which was   tor.']
vncle to the husband; and the French queene also, which was
aunt to the wife. There were also the dukes of Orleance, of
Calabre, of Alanson, and of Britaine, seauen earles, twelue barons,
twentie bishops, beside knights and gentlemen. When the feast,
triumph, bankets and iusts were ended, the ladie was deliuered to
the marquesse, who in great estate conueied hir through Normandie [She is
                                                                      conveyed by
vnto Diepe, and so transported hir into England, where she landed Suffolk to
                                                                      England.]
at Portesmouth in the moneth of Aprill.

Suffolk hands to Gloucester

the Articles of contracted peace,
Betweene our Soueraigne and the French King Charles,
For eighteene moneths concluded by consent.—ll. 40-42.

Suffolk's mission, in February, 1444,[2] was to establish peace between
England and France,

[*Hol.* iii. 624/2/11. *Halle*, 203.] but, in conclusion, by reason
of manie doubts which rose on both parties, no full concord could
be agreed vpon; but, in hope to come to a peace, a certeine truce,
as well by sea as by land, was concluded by the commissioners for *A truce for*
eighteene moneths; which afterward againe was prolonged to the   *18 moneths.*
yeare of our Lord, 1449.

---

[1] Suffolk left England on November 5, 1444, and returned on April 11,
1445, having been absent 157 days.—Issue Roll, Easter, 23 Hen. VI., 20th July
(cited in *Chron. Rich. II.—Hen. VI.*, 192).

[2] He was appointed ambassador on February 11, 1444.—*Rymer*, xi. 60.

It is provided by the first article (ll. 46-50) that "Henry shal espouse the Lady Margaret, daughter vnto Reignier King of Naples, Sicillia, and Ierusalem ; and Crowne her Queene of England, ere the thirtieth of May next ensuing." Holinshed says :

[*Hol.* iii. 625/1/58. *Halle*, 205.] Upon the thirtith of Maie next following, she was crowned queene of this realme of England at Westminster, with all the solemnitie thereto apperteining.

Another article is read by Cardinal Beaufort (ll. 57-62) : "It is further agreed betweene them, That the Dutchesse [Duchies] of Aniou and Maine shall be released and deliuered ouer to the King her Father, and shee sent ouer of the King of Englands owne proper Cost and Charges, without hauing any Dowry." Suffolk's project for effecting a peace through Margaret's marriage to Henry was coldly received by the French ;

[*Hol.* iii. 624/2/29. *Halle*, 204.] and one thing seemed to be a great hinderance to it ; which was, bicause the king of England occupied a great part of the duchie of Aniou, and the whole countie of Maine, apperteining (as was alledged) to king Reiner.

The earle of Suffolke (I cannot saie), either corrupted with bribes, or too much affectioned to this vnprofitable mariage, con-

descended, that the duchie of Aniou and the countie of Maine should be deliuered to the king the brides father ; [1] demanding for hir mariage neither penie nor farthing : as who would saie, that this new affinitie passed all riches, and excelled both gold and pretious stones.

Henry then (May, 1445) creates his procurator "the first Duke of Suffolke " (l. 64). Three historical years,[2] however, were yet to elapse before

[*Hol.* iii. 627/2/34. *Halle*, 210.] the marquesse of Suffolke, by great fauour of the king, & more desire of the queene, was erected to the title and dignitie of duke of Suffolke, which he a short time inioied.

Addressing York, Henry says (ll. 66-68) :

We heere discharge your Grace from being Regent
I'th parts of France, till terme of eighteene Moneths
Be full expyr'd.

---

[1] "Should *be released and deliuered to the kyng her father*" (Halle, 204). "Shall *be released and deliuered* ouer *to the King her Father*" (2 Hen. VI., I. i. 59, 60).

[2] He was created Duke of Suffolk on June 2, 1448.—*Pat : 26* H. VI. p. ii. m. 14. (H.S.)

This "terme" was, perhaps, the eighteen months' truce (p. 243 above). Compare the next passage (*Hol.* iii. 625/2/29), quoted at pp. 250, 251 below.

[*Hol.* iii. 625/2/25. *Halls*, 205.] During the time of the truce, **[York returned to England during the truce.]** Richard duke of Yorke and diuerse other capteins repaired into England; both to visit their wiues, children, and freends, and also to consult what should be doone, if the truce ended.

Gloucester censures Suffolk for giving Anjou and Maine

> Vnto the poore King Reignier, whose large style
> Agrees not with the leannesse of his purse.—ll. 111, 112.

Suffolk,

[*Hol.* iii. 625/1/9. *Halls*, 205.] with his wife and manie honorable personages of men and women richlie adorned both with apparell & iewels, hauing with them manie costlie chariots and gorgeous horslitters, sailed into France, for the conueiance of the nominated queene into the realme of England. For King Reiner **[René's long style and short purse.]** hir father, for all his long stile, had too short a pursse to send his daughter honorablie to the king hir spouse.

Richard Neville, Earl of Salisbury,[1] cries out against the surrender of Anjou and Maine, because (l. 114)

> These Counties were *the Keyes of Normandie.*

Compare Fabyan (617):

And for that Maryage to brynge aboute, to the . . . kynge of **[Anjou and Maine " the keyes of Normandy."]** Cecyle was delyuered the Duchye of Angeou & Erledome of Mayne, whiche are called *the keyes of Normandy.*[2]

It is "a proper iest," says Gloucester,

> That Suffolke should demand a whole Fifteenth
> For Costs and Charges in transporting her!—ll. 132-134.

---

[1] The revived Earldom of Salisbury was bestowed on Richard Neville in 1429.—*Doyle*, iii. 243. *Hol.* (641/2/71), copying *Halle* (231), says that Richard Neville Earl of Salisbury "was second son [*i. e.* son by a second marriage] to Rafe Neuill earle of Westmerland, whose daughter the duke of Yorke had maried, and the said Richard was espoused to ladie Alice, the onelie child and sole heire of Thomas Montacute earle of Salisburie, slaine at the siege of Orleance (as before is declared), of which woman he begat Richard, Iohn [afterwards Marquesse Montague], and George [afterwards Archbishop of York]. Richard the eldest sonne espoused Anne, the sister and heire of the entire bloud to lord Henrie Beauchamp, earle and after duke of Warwike, in whose right and title he was created and named earle of Warwike." Regarding York's political alliance with the Nevilles, see pp. 283, 288 below.

[2] *Hol.* (625/1/69) verbally repeats *Halle's* similes (205) for Anjou and Maine (205): "which countries were the verie staies and backestands to the duchie of Normandie." Neither of these similes occurs in the *Contention* or *Whole Contention*.

One reason, which caused "manie" to deem Henry's marriage to
Margaret "both infortunate and vnprofitable to the realme of England,"
was that

An ominous
marriage.
(Suffolk
demanded a
fifteenth.) .

[*Hol.* iii. 625/1/64. *Halle,* 205.] the king had not one penie
with hir ; and, for the fetching of hir, the marquesse of Suffolke
demanded a whole fifteenth[1] in open parlement.

Gloucester goes out, whereupon Cardinal Beaufort impugns the
Protector's loyalty ;

> . . . though the common people fauour him,
> Calling him " Humfrey, *the good Duke of Gloster,* . . ."[2]—ll. 158, 159.

According to Fabyan (619) :

["The good
Duke of
Glouces-
ter."]

This [man] for his honourable & lyberall demeanure was surnamed y' *Good duke of Gloucester.*

In Holinshed Gloucester's character is thus summed up :

[Glouces-
ter's
character.]

[He was
beloved of
the
commons.]

[*Hol.* iii. 627/2/9.] But to conclude of this noble duke: he
was an vpright and politike gouernour, bending all his indeuours
to the aduancement of the common-wealth, verie louing to the
poore commons, and so beloued of them againe ; learned, wise,
full of courtesie ; void of pride and ambition : (a vertue rare in
personages of such high estate, but, where it is, most commendable).

Humphrey Stafford Duke of Buckingham,[3] Edmund Beaufort Duke
of Somerset, and Cardinal Beaufort now make an alliance for the
purpose of driving Gloucester from power ; and the Cardinal departs to
inform Suffolk of their cabal (ll. 167-171). Under the years 1446-47,
Holinshed, on Halle's authority, relates that, by Queen Margaret's
" procurement,[4] diuerse noble men conspired against " Gloucester.

[Suffolk,
Bucking-
ham,
Cardinal
Beaufort,
and
Archbishop
Kempe
conspire
against
Gloucester.]

[*Hol.* iii. 626/2/74. *Halle,* 209.] Of the which diuerse writers
[*p.* 627] affirme the marquesse of Suffolke, and the duke of
Buckingham to be the cheefe ; not vnprocured by the cardinall
of Winchester, and the archbishop of Yorke.

---

[1] On April 9, 1446, the Commons gaue Henry a fifteenth and a tenth (*Rot.
Parl.,* v. 69/1) ; but, in specifying the purposes to which these grants were to
be applied, they did not mention the "costs and charges" of bringing Margaret
to England or any other expenses connected with her marriage.

[2] "called the good duke of Gloucester."—*Halle,* 209. Not in *Hol.*

[3] Created Duke of Buckingham in 1444.—*Doyle,* i. 254. His father was
Edmund Earl of Stafford, slain at the battle of Shrewsbury, on July 21, 1403.
See p. 146 above. Edmund Beaufort was created Duke of Somerset in 1448.—
Dugdale, ii. 123/2.

[4] Halle's corresponding words are (209) : "so that, by her permission and
fauor, diuerse noble men," . . .

Buckingham and Somerset having departed, Salisbury, his son Warwick,[1]—the future "Kingmaker,"—and York, are left on the stage. In proposing that they three should form a counter-league against Suffolk, Cardinal Beaufort, Somerset, and Buckingham, Salisbury encourages Warwick by reminding him that (ll. 191-193)

> Thy deeds, thy plainnesse, and thy house-keeping,[2]
> Hath wonne the greatest fauour of the Commons,
> Excepting none but good Duke Humfrey.

At a later time of his life than the date of this scene, Warwick was

[*Hol.* iii. 678/1/33.] one to whom the common-wealth was much bounden and euer had in great fauour of the commons of this land, by reason of the exceeding houshold which he dailie kept in all countries where euer he soiourned or laie: and when he came to London, he hold such an house, that six oxen were eaten at a breakefast, and euerie tauerne was full of his meat, for who that had anie acquaintance in that house, he should haue had as much sod and rost as he might carrie vpon a long dagger. . . .

Abr. Fl. ex l. 8. pag. 722, 723. The earle of Warwike his housekeeping. Fabian.

Addressing the Duke, Salisbury says (ll. 194-198):

> And, Brother Yorke, thy Acts in Ireland,
> In bringing them to ciuill Discipline,
> .   .   .   .
> Haue made thee fear'd and honor'd of the people : . . .

---

[1] Richard Neville, born on November 22, 1428 (*Rows Rol.*, 57), was made Earl of Warwick in 1449 (*Dugdale*, i. 304/1). What the dramatic Warwick says touching his share in the French war (L. i. 119, 120 ; iii. 176, 177) shows that—so far as these allusions apply—he is for a moment confounded with Richard Beauchamp, who was appointed Lieutenant-General and Governor of France, &c., on July 16, 1437 (*Rymer*, x. 674, 675) ; and died at Rouen on April 30, 1439 (*Chron. Lond.*, 124). But, despite this fleeting identification with Richard Beauchamp, we can hardly doubt that the "Warwicke" who takes Richard Plantagenet's part in the Temple Garden scene (1 *Hen. VI.*, II. iv.) is the same Warwick who is a character in the 2nd and 3rd Parts of *Henry VI.* ("Warwick's" assertion that he conquered Anjou and Maine is a dramatic embellishment).

[2] Warwick's other virtues are recorded by *Halle* (231, 232): "This Rycharde was not onely a man of maruelous qualities, and facundious facions, but also from his youth, by a certayn practise or naturall inclinacion, so set them forward, with witte and gentle demeanour, to all persones of high and of lowe degre, that emong all sortes of people he obteyned great loue, muche fauour, and more credence : whiche thinges daily more increased by his abundant liberalitie and plentyfull house kepynge, then by hys ryches, aucthoritie, or hygh parentage. By reason of whiche doynges he was in suche fauour and estimacion emongest the common people, that they iudged hym able to do all thinges, and that, without hym, nothing to be well done. For whiche causes his aucthoritie shortly so fast increased that whiche waie he bowed, that waye ranne the streame, and what part he auaunced, that syde gat the superioritie."

Salisbury, speaking in the historical year 1445, anticipates York's successful administration of Ireland in 1448-50.[1] Afterwards (Act III., sc. i., ll. 282-284) "a Poste" announces the rebellion which caused the government of Ireland to be conferred on York. Holinshed records that, about the year 1448,

A rebellion in Ireland [appeased by York].

[*Hol.* iii. 629/2/26. *Halle*, 213.] began a new rebellion in Ireland; but Richard duke of Yorke, being sent thither to appease the same, so asswaged the furie of the wild and sauage people there, that he wan him such fauour amongst them, as could neuer be separated from him and his linage; which in the sequele of this historie may more plainelie appeare.[2]

Act I. sc. ii.—We here find that Eleanor Cobham, Gloucester's second wife, looks forward to a day when she and her husband shall reign instead of Henry and Margaret. The historic Queen Margaret was not troubled by any ambitious hopes which the Duchess may have cherished; for Eleanor Cobham did penance in November, 1441, and Margaret was, as we have seen, crowned on May 30, 1445.

Act I. sc. iii.—The Queen enters with Suffolk. Peter, an "Armorers Man," presents a petition (ll. 28, 30) against his "Master, Thomas Horner, for saying, That the Duke of Yorke was rightfull Heire to the Crowne." Holinshed merely records that, in 1446,

[The armourer's servant.]

[*Hol.* iii. 626/2/19.] a certeine armourer was appeached of treason by a seruant of his owne.[3]

The petitioners having retired, Margaret tells Suffolk (ll. 53-57) that, when he ran a tilt at Tours in honour of her love,—doubtless a reminiscence of those "iusts" which Holinshed says (iii. 625/1/30) were held to celebrate her proxy-marriage,—she thought her husband had resembled her champion. But all King Henry's mind

is bent to Holinesse,
To number Aue-Maries on his Beades;
His Champions are the Prophets and Apostles,
His Weapons holy Sawes of sacred Writ,
His Studie is his Tilt-yard, and his Loues
Are brazen Images of Canonized Saints.—ll. 58-63.

---

[1] According to *Halle* (213), *Hol.*'s authority, York went to Ireland in the 27th year of Henry VI. (Sept. 1, 1448—Aug. 31, 1449). A warrant,—dated February 10, 1449,—for the payment of York's salary as Lieutenant in Ireland, shows that his ten years' term of office was to begin on September 29, 1447.—*Stevenson*, I. 487, 488. He returned to England in 1450. See p. 282 below.

[2] See p. 282, n. 1, and p. 296 (below).

[3] *Stow* (635) gives these particulars: "Iohn Dauid [Davy] appeached his master William [John] Catur, an armorer dwelling in S. Dunstons parish in Fleetstreet, of treason." The year was 1447. Cp. *Exchequer Issues*, 458, 459. The dramatic servant's name is Peter Thumpe (*2 Hen. VI.*, II. iii. 82-84). The surname of one of the sheriffs of the year (25 Hen. VI., 1446-47) was Horne.—*Fab.*, 618.

Henry is thus described by Holinshed :

[*Hol.* iii. 691/1/69.] He was plaine, vpright, farre from fraud, [Henry's character.] wholie ginen to praier, reading of scriptures, and almesdeeds ; . . .

Halle (303) says :

Kyng Henry was of stature goodly, of body slender, to which [The description of kyng Henry the vi.] proporcion al other members wer correspondent : his face beautiful, in y* which continually was resydent the bountie of mynde wyth [His bodily aspect.] whych he was inwardly endued. He dyd abhorre of hys owne [Holiness.] nature al the vices, as wel of the body as of the soule ; and, from hys verye infancye, he was of honest conuersacion and pure integritie ; no knower of euil, and a keper of all goodnes ; a dispiser of al thynges whych were wonte to cause the myndes of mortall menne to slyde, or appaire. Besyde thys, pacyence was so [Patience.] radicate in his harte that of all the iniuries to him commytted (which were no smal nombre) he neuer asked vengeaunce nor punishement, but for that rendered to almightie God, his creator, hartie thankes, thinking that by this trouble and aduersitie his sinnes wer to him forgotten and forgeuen.

Henry and his Court enter, debating whether York or Somerset shall be appointed Regent of France ; a question which gives Margaret, and the four nobles who made an alliance in Act I., sc. i., an opportunity of attacking Gloucester. Cardinal Beaufort accuses him of having "rackt" the "Commons" (l. 131) ; and Somerset adds (ll. 133, 134) that the Protector's "sumptuous Buildings" and "Wiues Attyre"

Haue cost a masse of publique Treasurie.

In 1446-47, according to Halle (208, 209), Gloucester's enemies

perswaded, incensed, and exhorted the Quene, to loke wel vpon the expenses and reuenues of the realme, and thereof to call an accompt : affirmyng playnly that she should euidently perceiue that the Duke of Gloucester had not so muche aduanced & pre- [Gloucester accused of ferred the commonwealth and publique vtilitie as his awne priuate misapplying public thinges & peculiar estate. money.]

Buckingham thus assails Gloucester (ll. 135, 136 ; cp. III. i. 58, 59 ; 121-123) :

Thy Crueltie in execution
Vpon Offendors hath exceeded Law, . . .

Under the same date (1446-47) we find that Gloucester was charged with this transgression.

The joint
quarrell
picked to the
duke of
Gloucester.

[Illegal
execution of
criminals.]

[*Hol.* iii. 627/1/4. *Halle*, 209.] Diuerse articles were laid against him in open councell, and in especiall one:[1] That he had caused men, adiudged to die, to be put to other execution, than the law of the land assigned. Suerlie the duke, verie well learned in the law ciuill, detesting malefactors, and punishing offenses in seueritie of iustice, gat him hatred of such as feared condign reward[2] for their wicked dooings.

Lastly, Margaret imputes to him (l. 138) the "sale of Offices and Townes in France."

Perhaps Gloucester has been made to change places with Cardinal Beaufort, whom, in 1440, be accused of this misconduct. A long series of criminatory articles (referred to above, p. 236) were then exhibited by Gloucester against Beaufort. In the 22nd article Henry was asked

[Cardinal
Beaufort's
sale of
offices.]

[*Hol.* iii. 622/2/17. *Halle*, 201.] to consider the . . . lucre of the . . . cardinall, and the great deceipts that you be deceiued[3] in by the labour of him & of the archbishop [of York, John Kempe], aswell in this your realme as in your realme of France and duchie of Normandie, where neither office, liuelode, nor capteine may be had, without too great good giuen vnto him; wherby a great part of all the losse that is lost, they haue beene the causers of; for who that would giue most, his was the price, not considering the merits, seruice, nor sufficance of persons.

Making no reply to his adversaries, Gloucester withdraws a while, and, on his return, delivers his opinion in regard to the Regency (ll. 163, 164):

> I say, my Soueraigne, *Yorke* is *meetest man*
> To be your *Regent* in the Realme *of France*.

Suffolk—who had previously (I. iii. 36-39) sent for Horner—now seizes a chance of opposing Gloucester and thwarting York through the accusation of treason brought against the armourer. Holinshed copied from Halle (206) a passage which records that, in 1446,

Anno Reg.
24.
1446

[*Hol.* iii. 625/2/29.] a parlement[4] was called, in the which it was especiallie concluded, that by good foresight Normandie might be so furnished for defense before the end of the truce, that the

---

[1] *in especiall one*] Halle. *in especially one* Hol.

[2] In *2 Hen. VI.*, III. i. 128-130, Gloucester says that he never gave 'condigne punishment' to any one, saue a murderer or a highway robber.

[3] *deceiued*] Halle. *received* Hol.

[4] This must have been the Parliament which began on February 25, 1445 (*Rot. Parl.*, v. 66/1); and was sitting on June 4, 1445, and April 9, 1446 (see p. 241, n. 1, and p. 246, n. 1, above).

French king should take no aduantage through want of timelie prouision: for it was knowne, that, if a peace were not concluded, the French king did prepare to imploie his whole puissance to make open warre. Heerevpon monie was granted, an armie leuied, and the duke of Summerset appointed to be regent of Normandie,[1] and the duke of Yorke thereof discharged.

The duke of Summerset made regent of Normandie, and the duke of Yorke discharged.

From a chronicler[2] who wrote in Henry VI.'s reign, Holinshed derived the information that Suffolk aided Somerset to obtain the Regency.

[*Hol.* iii. 625/2/41.] I haue seene in a register booke belonging sometime to the abbeie of saint Albons, that the duke of York was established regent of France, after the deceasse of the duke of Bedford, to continue in that office for the tearme of fiue yeares; which being expired, he returned home, and was ioifullie receiued of the king with thanks for his good seruice, as he had full well deserued in time of that his gouernement: and, further, that now, when a new regent was to be chosen and sent ouer, to abide vpon safegard of the countries beyond the seas as yet subiect to the English dominion, the said duke of *Yorke* was eftsoones (as a *man most meet* to supplie that roome) appointed to go ouer againe, as *regent of France*, with all his former allowances.

[York Regent of France for fiue years.]

The duke of Yorke appointed to y charge againe.*

But the duke of Summerset, still maligning the duke of Yorkes aduancement, as he had sought to hinder his dispatch at the first when he was sent ouer to be regent, (as before yee haue heard,[3]) he likewise now wrought so, that the king reuoked his grant made to the duke of Yorke for enioieng of that office the terme of other fiue yeeres, and, with helpe of William marquesse of Suffolke, obteined that grant for himselfe.

[Somerset caused York's appointment to be revoked.] The appointmt also appointed, and pointed to [also] the marquesse of Suffolke.

---

[1] On November 12, 1446, the government of France and Normandy was in commission, York being absent.—*Report on Foedera,* App. D. 523. On November 11, 1447, he is styled Lieutenant-General and Governor of France and Normandy.—*Ibid.,* 535. By December 20, 1447, Somerset had been appointed "to goo oure lieutenaunt into oure duchie of Normandie."—*Stevenson,* I. 477, 478. On January 31, 1448, he is styled "oure lievetenaunt in our reame of Fraunce, duchees of Normandie and Guyenne."—*Stevenson,* I. 479, 480. The latter appointment should be regarded as the historical parallel of Gloucester's "doome" on the dramatic second day: "Let Somerset be Regent o're the French."—*2 Hen. VI.,* I. iii. 209.

[2] John de Whethamstede (ed. Hearne, pp. 345, 346).

[3] See next page.

York says (ll. 170-175) :

> . . . if I be appointed for the Place,
> My Lord of Somerset will keepe me here,
> Without Discharge, Money, or Furniture,
> Till France be wonne into the Dolphins hands :
> Last time, I danc't attendance on his will
> Till Paris was besieg'd, famisht, and lost.

Holinshed, paraphrasing Halle (179), illustrates this complaint of
Edmund Beaufort's malice in 1436, when York was appointed to
succeed Bedford (see p. 219 above).

[*Hol.* iii. 612/2/14. *Halle*, 179.] Although the duke of Yorke
was worthie (both for birth and courage) of this honor and preferment, yet so disdeined of Edmund duke of Summerset, (being
cousine to the king,) that by all meanes possible he sought his
hinderance, as one glad of his losse, and sorie of his well dooing :
by reason whereof, yer the duke of Yorke could get his dispatch,
Paris and diuerse other of the cheefest places in France were
gotten by the French king.

[*Paris lost
because
Edmund
Beaufort
hindered
York's
despatch.*]

Act I. sc. iv.—In this scene the Duchess of Gloucester causes a
spirit to be raised, from whom she learns the future fates of Henry,
Suffolk, and Somerset.[1]

Examination of the charges brought against Cardinal Beaufort by
Gloucester in 1440 (see pp. 236, 250 above) was committed to Henry's

[*Hol.* iii. 622/2/58. *Halle*, 202.] councell, whereof the more
part were spirituall persons ; so that, what for feare, and what for
fauour, the matter was winked at, and nothing said to it : onelie
faire countenance was made to the duke, as though no malice had
beene conceiued against him. But venem will breake out, &
inward grudge will soone appeare, which was this yeare to all men
apparant : for diuers secret attempts were aduanced forward this
season, against this noble man Humfreie duke of Glocester, a far
off, which, in conclusion, came so neere, that they bereft him both
of life and land ; as shall hereafter more plainelie appeere.

[*Covert
attacks
made upon
Gloucester.*]

For, first, this yeare, dame Eleanor Cobham, wife to the said
duke, was accused of treason ;[2] for that she by sorcerie and inchant-

[*Eleanor
Cobham
accused of
intending*]

---

[1] For the prophecies concerning the deaths of Suffolk and Somerset see
p. 270, n. 2, and p. 289.

[2] She was arrested in the latter part of July, 1441.—*Chron. Rich. II.*—
Hen. VI., 57, 58. *Wyrc.*, 460. The discrepancy of these authorities, and the
inaccuracy of *Chron. Rich. II.—Hen. VI.* with regard to the days of the week,
do not allow a more precise date to be given.

ment intended to destroie the king, to the intent to aduance hir husband vnto the crowne. . . . [*p.* 623, *col.* 1.] At the same season were arrested, arreigned, and adiudged giltie, as aiders to the duchesse, Thomas Southwell priest, and canon of S. Stephans at Westminster, Iohn Hun priest, Roger Bolingbrooke a cunning necromancer (as it was said), and Margerie Iordeine, surnamed the witch of Eie.

to destroy
Henry by
sorcery.]
[Her con-
federates.]
Alias Iohn
Hum.[1]
[A waxen
image of
Henry made
to be
consumed.]

The matter laid against them was, for that they (at the request of the said duchesse) had deuised an image of wax, representing the king, which by their sorcerie by little and little consumed; intending thereby in conclusion to waste and destroie the kings person.

There is not even an allusion in the play to the offence for which, according to Halle, the Duchess and her confederates were arraigned. But Stow (627) says that

[Boling-
broke
employed
by Dame
Eleanor
Cobham to
reveal her
future.]

Roger Bolingbroke was examined before the Kings Counsaile, where he confessed that he wrought the said Negromancie at the stirring and procurement of the said Dame Elianor, to knowe what should befall of hir, and to what estate she should come, . . .

Act II. sc. i.—Sir Thomas More's *dyaloge . . . Wheryn be treatyd dyuers maters as of the veneracyon & worshyp of ymagys & relyques prayng to sayntis & goynge on pylgrymage* (2nd ed.,[2] 1530, bk. I. chap. xiv. leaf 25) contains the earliest account of the sham miracle at St. Albans. The dramatic version of this story presents no important change save that the rogue is made to feign lameness as well as blindness; a variation which leads up to his being whipped off the stage. The following excerpt from More's *Dialogue* should be compared with Act II., sc. i., ll. 60-160:

. . . I remember me that I haue herde my father tell of a begger that, in kynge Henry his dayes the syxte, came wyth hys wyfe to saynt Albonys. And there was walkynge about the towne

---

[1] So in *Halle* (202) and in *The Contention*. Though the name rymes to "Mum" in 2 *Hen. VI.*, I. ii. 88, the spelling is "Hume" throughout scenes ii. and iv., Act I. In *Fab.* (614) and *Stow* (628) the name is spelt "Hum."

[2] "Newly ouersene" by More. More's story of the sham miracle was copied by *Grafton* (i. 630) and *Foxe* (i. 679/2). *Foxe*—I know not on whose authority—says that the cheat was discovered in Henry VI.'s "young dayes," when the King was "yet vnder the gouernaunce of this Duke Humfrey his protector." *Weever* (321, 322) gives an epitaph "penciled" on the wall near Gloucester's tomb in St. Alban's Abbey; recording the Duke's detection of the man who feigned blindness.

[A beggar
and his wife
came to
St. Albans
when Henry
VI. was
expected
there.]

[The beggar
said that he
was born
blind, and,
warned by a
dream, had
journeyed
from
Berwick to
St. Albans.]

[But, not
being
healed, he
was going to
Cologne,
where some
believed
S. Alban's
body lay.]

[When King
Henry
arrived,
the beggar
could see;
and people
supposed
that a
miracle had
been
wrought.]

[Gloucester
exhorted the
beggar to be
humble,

[and asked
him if he
could ever
see anything
before.]

[The beggar
and his wife
answered
"no"; yet,

[when
questioned,
[he could
name all the
colours
shown him.]

[Then
Gloucester
called him
a rogue, and
set him in
the stocks.]

beggyng a fyue or syxe dayes before the kyngys commynge thyther; sayngge that he was borne blynde, and neuer saw in his lyfe. And was warned in his dreame that he shold come out of Berwyke (where he sayd he had euer dwelled) to seke saynt Albon; and that he had ben at his shryne, and had not bene holpen. And therfore he wold go seke hym at some other place; for he had herde some saye, syns he came, that saynt Albonys body sholde be at Colon: and in dede suche a contencyon hath there bene. But of trouth, as I am surely informed, he lyeth here at saynt Albonys; sauyng some relyques of hym, whiche they there shew shryned. But to tell you forth: when the kyng was comen, and the towne full, sodaynly this blynde man, at saynt albonys shryne, had his syght agayne: and a myracle solemply rongen and te deum songen; so that nothynge was talked of in all yᵉ towne but this myracle. So happened it than that duke Humfry of gloucester, a great wyse man and very well lerned, hauynge greate Ioy to se such a myracle, called yᵉ pore man vnto hym. And fyrst shewynge hym selfe Ioyouse of goddys glory, so shewed in the gettynge of his syght; and exortyng hym to mekenes, and to none ascrybyng of any parte the worssyp to hym selfe; nor to be proude of the peoples prayse, whiche wolde call hym a good and a godly man therby. At last he loked wel vpon his eyen, and asked whyther he coulde neuer se nothynge at all in all his lyfe before. And, whan as well his wyfe as hymselfe afformed fastely "no," than he loked aduysedly vpon his eyen agayn, & sayd: "I byleue you very well, for me thynketh "that ye can not se well yet." "Yes, syr," quod he, "I thanke "god and his holy marter, I can se nowe as well as any man." "Ye can," quod the duke, "what colour is my gowne?" Than anone the begger, tolde hym. "What colour," quod he, "is this "maɴnys gowne?" He tolde hym also; and so forth, without any styckynge, he tolde hym the names of all the colours that could be shewed hym.[1] And, whan my lord saw that, he bad [2] hym, "walke, "faytoure!" and made hym be set openly in the stockys. For, though he coulde haue sene sodenly by myracle yᵉ dyfference

---

[1] With "I byleue . . . shewed hym," cp. 2 *Hen. VI.*, II. i. 106-112.
[2] *bad*] ed. 1.   *had* ed. 2.

bytwene dyuers colours, yet coulde he not by y⁰ syght so sodenly
tell the names of all these colours, but yf he hadde known them
before, no more than the names of all the men y¹ he shold sodenly
se. [Lf. xxv. sign. f. i.]

[For, if the beggar had been born blind, he could not have named colours, though he might have distinguished them.]

Act II. sc. ii.—At the close of sc. iv., Act I., after the Duchess of
Gloucester and her confederates had been arrested, York sent Salisbury
and Warwick an invitation to sup with him "to morrow Night";
that is, the night of the day on which Gloucester exposed the sham
miracle. Supper ended, York desires to have his guests' opinion of his
title to "Englands Crowne" (II. ii. 1-5). Warwick says (ll. 7, 8):

> Sweet Yorke, begin: and if thy clayme be good,
> The Neuills are thy Subiects to command.

The dramatic time of sc. ii., Act II., is brought into close relation
with Eleanor Cobham's arrest in 1441, but Holinshed's authority Halle
records (210) among the events of 1447-48 that

[*Hol.* iii. 627/2/37.] Richard, duke of Yorke, (being greatlie
allied by his wife to the chiefe peeres and potentates of the realme,
beside his owne progenie,) perceiuing the king to be no ruler, but
the whole burthen of the realme to rest in direction of the queene,
& the duke of Suffolke, began secretlie to allure his friends of the
nobilitie;[1] and priuilie declared vnto them his title and right to the
crowne, and likewise did he to certeine wise gouernours of diuerse
cities and townes. Which attempt was so politikelie handled, and
so secretlie kept, that prouision to his purpose was readie, before
his purpose was openlie published; and his friends opened themselues, yer the contrarie part could them espie: for in conclusion
all shortlie in mischiefe burst out, as ye may hereafter heare.

The duke of Yorke tempering about his title to the crowne.

On October 16, 1460, "a writyng,[2] conteignyng the clayme and
title of the right" which York laid "unto the Corones of Englond and
of Fraunce, and Lordship of Ireland," was read before the Lords
Spiritual and Temporal assembled in Parliament at Westminster.
This document, or a similar one, was printed by Stow in his *Annales*
(679, 680); and from Stow it was transferred to the pages of Holinshed.[3]
It sets forth York's pedigree. I quote in parallel columns II. ii. 10-20,
and the corresponding passage in Holinshed. York thus prefaces his
claim:

---

[1] For passages in which Salisbury and Warwick are spoken of as York's
friends, see pp. 283, 288 below.

[2] Printed in *Rot. Parl.*, v. 375.

[3] A prefatory sidenote thus describes *Hol.'s* reprint of this document:
"Abr[aham] Fl[eming] ex I.S [John Stow]. pag. 700, 701, &c. in Quart."

[Edward
III.'s sons.]

[*Hol.* iii. 657/2/47.] *Edward
the third* had issue, *Edward prince
of Wales; William of Hatfield,* his
second sonne; *Lionell the third,
duke of Clarence; Iohn of Gant,*
fourth, *duke of Lancaster; Edmund
of Langleie, fift, duke of Yorke;
Thomas of Woodstoke, sixt, duke of
Glocester;* and *William of Windsor,
seauenth.*

The said *Edward* prince of
Wales, which *died* in the life time

[Richard II.]

of *his father,* had issue *Richard,*
which succeeded *Edward the third*
his grandsire; . . .

Edward the third, my Lords, had
seuen Sonnes:
The first, *Edward* the Black-Prince,
Prince of Wales;
The *second, William of Hatfield;* 12
and *the third,*
Lionel Duke of Clarence: next to
whom
Was *Iohn of Gaunt,* the *Duke of
Lancaster;*
The *fift* was *Edmond Langley, Duke
of Yorke;*
The *sixt* was *Thomas of Woodstock,* 16
Duke of Gloster;
William of Windsor was the *seuenth*
and last.
Edward the Black-Prince *dyed* before
his Father,
And left behinde him *Richard,* his
onely [1] Sonne,
Who, after *Edward the third's* death, 20
raign'd as King : . .

I now quote four lines immediately following my last excerpt from
York's statement of his title :

Till Henry Bullingbrooke, *Duke of Lancaster,*
The eldest *Sonne* and Heire of *Iohn of Gaunt,*
Crown'd by the Name of Henry the fourth,
Seiz'd on the *Realme,* depos'd the rightfull King, . . .   24

Though these lines contain matter of common knowledge, they may
have been prompted by the ensuing fragments of a speech which,
according to Halle (245, 246), York delivered from the throne to the
Peers assembled at Westminster in 1460 :

[Richard II.
was a lawful
king.]

[*Hol.* iii. 656/1/1.] Which king Richard, of that name the
second, was lawfullie & iustlie possessed of the crowne and diadem
of this realme and region, *till Henrie* of Derbie *duke of Lancaster*

[Henry duke
of Lancaster
was a
usurper.]

and Hereford, *sonne* to *Iohn of Gant* . . . wrongfullie vsurped
and intruded vpon the roiall power, and high estate of this *realme*
and region; taking vpon him the name, stile, and authoritie of
king and gouernour of the same.

Salisbury interjects (l. 33) :

But *William of Hatfield dyed without* an Heire.

---

[1] The corresponding passage in the 3rd (1619) ed. of *The Contention* stands
thus (23) : "Now Edward the blacke Prince dyed before his Father, leauing
behinde him two sonnes, Edward borne at Angolesme, who died young, and
Richard that was after crowned King," . . . *Hol.* (iii. 397/1/56) says: "In the
nine and thirtith yeere of king Edwards reigne, and in the moneth of Februarie
[1365], in the citie of Angolesme, was borne the first sonne of prince Edward,
and was named after his father, but he departed this life the seuenth yeare of
his age."

In my last quotation from the pedigree printed by Holinshed the line is carried down to Richard II., who "succeeded Edward the third his grandsire." The next words are:

[*Hol.* iii. 657/2/56.] Richard died without issue; *William of Hatfield,* the second sonne of Edward the third, *died without issue;* ... [William of Hatfield.]

The continuation of York's speech (ll. 34-38) I place beside the parallel passage in Holinshed:

[*Hol.* iii. 657/2/58.] Lionell *the third sonne* of Edward the third, *duke of Clarence, had issue Philip* his *daughter* and heire, which was coupled in matrimonie vnto *Edmund Mortimer* [3rd] *earle of March,* and *had issue Roger* Mortimer [4th] *earle of March,* hir sonne and heire; which *Roger had issue Edmund*[1] [5th] erle of March, Roger Mortimer, *Anne, Elianor;* which Edmund, Roger, and Elianor died without issue.	*The third Sonne, Duke of Clarence,* from whose Line I clayme the Crowne, *had Issue, Phillip,* a *Daughter,* Who marryed *Edmond Mortimer,* 36 *Earle of March:* Edmond *had Issue, Roger Earle of March; Roger had Issue, Edmond, Anne,* and *Elianor.*	[York's descent from Lionel duke of Clarence.]

Salisbury again interrupts York (ll. 39, 40):

> This *Edmond,* in the Reigne of Bullingbrooke,
> As I haue read, layd *clayme* vnto the Crowne; ...

The speech from the throne, attributed by Halle to York (see p. 256 above), has the same misstatement.

[*Hol.* iii. 656/1/54.] *Edmund* earle of March, my most welbeloued vncle, in the time of the first vsurper, (in deed, but not by right, called king Henrie the fourth,) by his coosines the earle of Northumberland, & the lord Persie, (he being then in captiuitie with Owen Glendouer the rebell in Wales,) made his title & righteous *claims* to the destruction of both the noble persons. [Edmund 5th Earl of March claimed the crown.]

Salisbury adds (ll. 41, 42) that Edmund,

> ... but for Owen Glendour, had beene King,
> Who *kept him in Captiuitie till he dyed.*

Here the inevitable confusion between Sir Edmund Mortimer and Edmund Mortimer fifth Earl of March[2] is worse confounded. These lines apparently sprang from the dramatist's vague remembrance of Halle (28), who—in a sentence immediately preceding the assertion that Glendower

---

[1] *had issue Edmund*] had issue of Edmund Hol.
[2] See p. 131, n. 1, above.

made warre on lorde Edmond Mortimer erle of Marche, . . . and
toke hym prisoner, and, feteryng hym in chaynes, cast hym in a
depe and miserable dongeon—

[Mortimer's captivity.]

says that Reginald Lord Grey of Ruthin—another prisoner to
Glendower—was promised freedom conditionally upon marrying his
captor's daughter:

But this false father in lawe, this vntrew, vnhonest, and periured persone, *kept hym* with his wyfe still *in captiuitee till he*
dyed.

[Lord Grey's captivity.]

The conclusion of York's speech (ll. 43-52) and his pedigree as given
by Holinshed are here displayed in parallel columns. The fifth Earl of
March's

[York's mother was Anne Mortimer.]

[*Hol.* iii. 657/2/67.] And the
said *Anne* coupled in matrimonie
to *Richard earle of Cambridge,* the
sonne of *Edmund of Langleie,* the
' *fift sonne* of *Edward* [3] *the third,* and
had issue Richard Plantagenet,
commonlie called duke of Yorke;
. . . To the which Richard duke
of Yorke, as sonne to Anne,
daughter *to Roger* Mortimer *earle*
of March, sonne and heire of the
said *Philip, daughter* and heire of
the said *Lionell,* the third sonne of
king Edward the third, the right,
title, dignitie roiall, and estate of
the crownes of the realmes of
England and France, and the lordship of Ireland, perteineth and
belongeth afore anie issue of the
said Iohn of Gant, the fourth
sonne of the same king Edward.

[The issue of Lionel duke of Clarence should succeed before John of Gaunt's issue.]

eldest Sister, *Anne,*
My Mother, being Heire vnto the 44
Crowne,
Marryed *Richard Earle of Cambridge;*
who was son [1]
To *Edmond Langley, Edward the*
thirds fift Sonne. [2]
By her I clayme the Kingdome: she
was Heire
To *Roger Earle of March,* who was 48
the *Sonne*
Of Edmond Mortimer, who marryed
Phillip,
Sole *Daughter* vnto *Lionel* Duke of
Clarence :
So, if the Issue of the elder Sonne
Succeed before the younger, I am 52
King.

Act II. sc. iii.—In the opening lines of this scene Henry passes
sentence on Eleanor Duchess of Gloucester, and her confederates,
Margery Jourdain, Southwell, Hume, and Bolingbroke. To the latter
Henry says (ll. 5-8) :

You foure, from hence to Prison back againe ;
From thence vnto the place of Execution :
The Witch in Smithfield shall be burnt to ashes,
And you three shall be strangled on the Gallowes.

Holinshed gives the following account of what befel them :

---

[1] *son*] Rowe. om. F1.   [2] *Sonne*] Theobald. *Sonnes Sonne* F1.
[3] *Edward the third*] *Henrie the third* Hol.

[*Hol.* iii. 623/1/20. *Halle*, 202.] Margerie Iordeine was burnt in Smithfield, and Roger Bolingbrooke was drawne to Tiborne, and hanged and quartered; taking vpon his death that there was neuer anie such thing by them imagined. Iohn Hun had his pardon,[1] and Southwell died in the Tower the night before his execution: . . .

Henry then addresses the Duchess of Gloucester (ll. 9-13):

> You, Madame, for you are more Nobly borne,
> Despoylèd of your Honor in your Life,
> Shall, after three[2] dayes open Penance done,
> Liue in your Countrey here in Banishment,
> With Sir Iohn Stanly, in the Ile of Man.

The Duchess of Gloucester

[*Hol.* iii. 623/1/1. *Halle*, 202.] was examined in saint Stephans chappell before the bishop of Canturburie, and there by examination conuict, and iudged to doo open penance in three open places within the citie of London. . . . and after that adiudged to perpetuall imprisonment in the Ile of Man, vnder the keeping of sir Thomas Stanlie[3] knight.

Gloucester is about to withdraw, overwhelmed with sorrow for his wife's disgrace, when Henry speaks (ll. 22-24):

> Stay, Humfrey Duke of Gloster : ere thou goe,
> Giue vp thy Staffe ! Henry will to himselfe
> Protector be ; . . .

This dismissal of Gloucester from the office of Protector is a dramatic representation of a political change effected in 1446-47 by Margaret,[4] who,

---

[1] This fact—which is recorded by *Halle* (202), *Fab.* (615), and *Stow* (628) —may account for the dramatic Hume having been represented as a traitor. *Fab.* (614) says that Hume was the Duchess's chaplain.

[2] *two*] Contention. *Fab.* says nothing about the Duchess's penance. *Stow* gives the dates of the *three* days on which it was performed. See p. 261 below.

[3] *Iohn Stanley* Halle (202). *Thomas Stanley* Fab. (614), Stow (628). In 1446 it was ordered that letters under Henry's privy seal should be directed to Sir Thomas Stanley, authorizing him to convey Eleanor Cobham to the Isle of Man.—*Proc. Priv. Co.*, vi. 51. In 1443 she was removed from Chester Castle to Kenilworth Castle.—*Rymer*, xi. 45.

[4] In 1441, according to *Fab.* (614), "began Murder [murmur] and Grudge to brake at large, that before hadde ben kept in mewe, atwene parsones nere aboute the kynge, and his vncle the famous Humfrey duke of Gloucester and Protectour of the lande ; agayne whom dyuers Coniecturis were attempted a farre, whiche after were sette nere to hym, so that they left nat tyll they hadde brought hym vnto his confucion." In the next paragraph *Fab.* narrates the treason of Eleanor Cobham and her accomplices.

Henry was crowned at Westminster on November 6, 1429 (*Rot. Parl.*, iv.

[Margaret
could not
abide
Henry's
submissive-
ness to
Gloucester.]
[*Hol.* iii. 626/2/51. *Halle*, 208, 209.] disdaining that hir
husband should be ruled rather than rule, could not abide that the
duke of Glocester should doo all things concerning the order of
weightie affaires, least it might be said, that she had neither wit
nor stomach, which would permit and suffer hir husband, being of
most perfect age, like a yoong *pupill*,[1] to be gouerned by the direction of an other man. Although this toy entered first into hir

[Gloucester's
enemies
worked
upon her
impatience.]
braine thorough hir owne imagination, yet was she pricked forward
to the matter both by such of hir husbands counsell, as of long
time had borne malice to the duke for his plainnesse vsed in
declaring their vntruth (as partlie ye haue heard), and also by
counsell from king Reiner hir father; aduising that she and the
king should take vpon them the rule of the realme, and not to be
kept vnder, as wards and mastered orphanes.

*The queene
taketh vpon
hir the
gouernment,
and dis-
chargeth the
duke of
Glocester.*
What needeth manie words? The queene, persuaded by these
meanes, first of all excluded the duke of Glocester from all rule
and gouernance, . . .

Soon after Gloucester's exit, Horner and Peter present themselves
in the manner described by the following stage direction : "Enter at
one Doore the Armorer and his Neighbors, drinking to him so much
that hee is drunke ; . . . and at the other Doore his Man, . . . and
Prentices drinking to him."

As Holinshed's account of this judicial combat (*Hol.* iii. 626/2/21)
is not a mere paraphrase of Halle,—the dramatist's chief authority,—
and differs in some respects from what we find in the play, I quote
Halle (207, 208) :

[The
armourer's
friends
brought him
malmsey
and aqua
vitae ;]
At the daie assigned, the frendes of the master brought hym
Malmesey and Aqua vite, to comforte hym with all ; but it was the
cause of his and their discomforte. For he poured in so muche
that, when he came into the place in Smithfielde, where he should

---

337/1), and Gloucester resigned the Protectorate on November 15, 1429.—*Ibid.*
But Henry was nearly 16 when, on November 13, 1437, he assumed the
responsibility of government by appointing the members of a privy counsell
for the transaction of ordinary business ; reserving to himself the power of
deciding weighty questions and also those matters which might cause the
disagreement of half or two-thirds of his council. — *Proc. Priu. Co.*, vi.
312-314.
[1] Cp. Margaret's words (2 *Hen. VI.*, I. iii. 49, 50):

      "What, shall King Henry be a *Pupill* still
      Vnder the surly Glosters Gouernnnce ? "

Cp. also 2 *Hen. VI.*, II. iii. 28, 29.

fyght, bothe his wytte and strength fayled hym : and so he, beyng
a tall and a hardye personage, ouerladed with hote drynkes, was
vanqueshed of his seruaunte, beyng but a cowarde and a wretche ;[1]
whose [the armourer's] body was drawn to Tyborne, & there
hanged and behedded.

    Act II. sc. iv.—Gloucester watches " the comming of " his " punisht
Duchesse" (l. 7). The historic dates of her " three dayes open
Penance" (II. iii. 11) were November 13, 15, and 17, 1441.[2] I quote
the stage direction of 2 *Hen. VI.*, II. iv. 16 : " Enter the Duchesse in
a white Sheet, and a *Taper* burning *in her hand*, with the Sherife and
Officers." [3] None of the particulars given in this stage direction are
mentioned by Halle or Fabyan. In the second edition of Holinshed
the following detail of her penance is recorded (*Hol.* iii. 623/1/5) :

    Polychronicon saith she was inioined to go through Cheapside
with *a taper in hir hand.*

    Stow says (628) :

    On Monday the 13. of Nouember, she came from Westminster,
by water, and landed at the Temple bridge, from whence, with a
taper of waxe of two pound in hir hande, she went through Fleete-
streete, hoodlesse (saue a kerchefe) to Pauls, where she offered hir
taper at the high altar. . . . On Fryday she landed at Queene
Hiue, and so went through Cheape to S. Michaels in Cornehill, in
forme aforesaid : at all which times the Maior, sherifes, and crafts
of London, receiued hir and accompanied hir. This being done
she was committed to the ward of Sir Thomas Stanley, . . . hauing

---

    [1] As to Peter's cowardice and Horner's knowledge of fence,—not mentioned
by *Hol.*,—see 2 *Hen. VI.*, II. iii. 56-58 ; 77-79. *Hol.* (626/2/28) says that the
armourer " was slaine without guilt," and that " the false seruant . . . liued
not long vnpunished ; for being conuict of felonie in court of assise, he was
iudged to be hanged, and so was, at Tiburne." In 2 *Hen. VI.*, II. iii. 96,
Horner confesses treason, and Henry promises to reward Peter, whom Horner
"thought to haue murther'd wrongfully " (II. iii. 107, 108).
    [2] *Stow*, 628. *Greg.*, 184. *Chron. Lond.*, 129. According to one of *Stow's*
authorities (*Chron. Rich. II.—Hen. VI.*, 59, 60) the days of penance were
November 9, 15, and 17.
    [3] The stage direction in *The Contention* (27) runs as follows : " Enter Dame
Elnor Cobham bare-foote, and a white sheete about her, with a waxe candle in
her hand, and verses written on her backe and pind on, and accompanied with
the Sheriffes of London, and Sir Iohn Standly, and Officers, with billes and
holbards." In the Lament of the Duchess of Gloucester—a poem which Wright
belieued to be of contemporary date—she is made to say : " I went bare fote
on my fette."—*Pol. Poems*, ii. 207, and 205 note 2.

[and made
him so
drunk that
he, though
a valiant
man, was
vanquished
by his
cowardly
accuser.]

*Abr. Fl. ex
Polychron.*
[The
Duchess
carried a
taper.]

[The
Duchess of
Gloucester
bore a taper
through
Fleet
Street.]

[On each
day of her
penance she
was accom-
panied by
the Mayor.
Sheriffs and
crafts of
London.]

[She had a pension assigned her, and was committed to Sir Thomas Stanley's ward.]

yeerely 100. markes assigned for hir finding,[1] . . . whose pride, false couetise,[2] and lecherie, were cause of hir confusion.

The Duchess blames Gloucester for not resenting her disgrace (ll. 23-25; 42-47); and he prays her "sort" her "heart to patience" (l. 68). After recording the fates of the Duchess's confederates (p. 259 above), Holinshed says (iii. 623/1/27):

[Gloucester's patience.]

The duke of Glocester bare all these things patientlie, and said little (*Halle*, 202).

Act III. sc. i.—Henry wonders why Gloucester comes not to the Parliamen assembled at Bury St. Edmunds[3] (ll. 1-3). Margaret asks (ll. 4-8): t

> Can you not see! or will ye not obserue
> The strangenesse of his alter'd Countenance!
> With what a Maiestie he beares himselfe,
> How insolent of late he is become,
> How prowd, how peremptorie, and vnlike himselfe!

What Hardyng says (400) about Gloucester's changed demeanour after Eleanor Cobham's trial may possibly be the source of these lines:

[Gloucester resigned the Protector-ate.]

> Then was the kyng come vnto mannes age,
> Wherfore the lordes wolde no protector,
> Wherfore the duke loste his great auauntage
> And was no more then after defensour;
> But then he fell into a greate errour,
> Moued by his wyfe Elianor Cobham;
> To truste her so, men thought he was to blame.

[Eleanor Cobham's condemna-tion made Gloucester cold towards Henry.]

> He waxed then straunge eche day vnto y° kyng,
> For cause she was foriudged for sossery,
> For enchaun[t]mentees, that she was in workyng
> Agayne the churche, and the kyng cursedly,
> By helpe of one mayster Roger Oonly:
> And into Wales he went of frowardnesse
> And to the kyng had greate heuynesse.

While Margaret and her allies are striving to lessen Henry's esteem for Gloucester, Somerset—lately appointed Regent of France[4]—enters and announces that "all is lost" (l. 85).

---

[1] Stanley assures her that she shall be treated "Like to a Duchesse, and Duke Humfreyes Lady" (2 *Hen. VI.*, II. iv. 98).

[2] *fals couetise*] Chron. Rich. II.—Hen. VI., 60. *false, couetise* Stow.

[3] Opened on February 10, 1447.—*Rot. Parl.*, v. 128/1.

[4] A dramatic interval of about two months has elapsed since his appoint-ment in Act I., sc. iii.—*T-A.*, 307-310.

Suffolk's truce, negotiated in 1444, was renewed [1] from time to time until it was broken on our side by the treacherous seizure of Fougères in March, 1449.[2] A subsequent fifteen months' war [3] made the French masters of Normandy; the reconquest of which was achieved at the surrender of Cherbourg on August 12, 1450.[4] When a year later Bordeaux and a few other places in Guienne were added to Charles VII.'s dominions (see p. 231 above), no foreign territory was left us save Calais and the Channel Islands.[5] Somerset's share in the war ended with his surrender of Caen on July 1, 1450.[6] Thence he departed to Calais,[7] and returned to England in October, 1450.[8]

The Regent's blunt announcement causes York to murmur, aside (ll. 87-90):

> Cold Newes for me; for I had hope of France,
> As firmely as I hope for fertile England.
> Thus are my Blossomes blasted in the Bud,
> And Caterpillers eate my Leaues away; . . .

Holinshed paraphrased Halle's assertion (216) that. Somerset's surrender of Caen

[*Hol.* iii. 630/2/18.] kindled so great a rancor in the dukes heart and stomach, that he neuer left persecuting the duke of Summerset, vntill he had brought him to his fatall end & confusion.

The irreconciliable hate betweene the two dukes [caused by the surrender of Caen].

Gloucester now enters the Parliament to which he was summoned in a preceding scene (II. iv. 70, 71), and is immediately arrested by Suffolk for high treason (ll. 95-97). According to Halle (209), Holinshed's authority, Gloucester's exclusion from power in 1446 (see p. 260 above) was virtually a sentence of death.

[*Hol.* iii. 627/1/15.] But, to auoid danger of tumult that might be raised, if a prince so well beloued of the people should be openlie executed, his enimies determined to worke their feats in his destruction, yer he should haue anie warning. For effecting whereof, a parlement was summoned to be kept at Berrie; whither resorted all the peeres of the realme, and amongst them the duke

1447
A parlement at saint Edmundsburie.

---

[1] The renewals are set forth in Rymer's *Foedera*, vol. xi.
[2] *De Coussy*, x. 133.
[3] Reckoning from the surprise of Pont de-l'Arche by the French, on May 16, 1449.—*De Coussy*, x. 141; *Du Clercq*, xii. 10.
[4] *Du Clercq*, xii. 61.
[5] These islands formed part of the Duchy of Normandy.
[6] *Du Clercq*, xii. 73.
[7] *De Coussy*, x. 283, 284.
[8] *Wyrc.*, 473. Somerset's return to England in October was wrongly placed by *Wyrc.* under the year 1449, but the context shows that the year should be 1450.

of Glocester, which on the second daie of the session [1] was by the
lord Beaumont, then high constable of England, (accompanied with
the duke of Buckingham, and others,) arrested, apprehended, and
put in ward, and all his seruants sequestred from him, and thirtie
two of the cheefe of his retinue were sent to diuerse prisons, to
the great admiration of the people.

[Gloucester
arrested.]

As Suffolk has specified no charge which might warrant the arrest,
Gloucester asks, "wherein am I guiltie!" York answers (ll. 104-106):

> 'Tis thought, my Lord, that you tooke Bribes of France,
> And, being Protector, stay'd the Souldiars pay;
> By meanes whereof his Highnesse hath lost France.

This accusation resembles one of the "Articles proponed by the
commons against the Duke of Suffolke," on February 7, 1450.[2]

[Suffolk
took rewards
from Charles
VII. to stay
armies going
to France.]

[*Hol.* iii. 631/2/58. *Halle*, 218.] 9 Item, when armies haue
beene prepared, and souldiers readie waged, to passe ouer the sea,
to deale with the kings enimies: the said duke, corrupted by
rewards of the French king, hath restreined & staied the said
armies to passe anie further.

In a speech condemning his accusers' malice, Gloucester reveals the
hidden motive which prompted one of them (ll. 158-160):

> . . . dogged Yorke, that reaches at the Moone,
> Whose ouer-weening Arme I haue pluckt back,
> By false accuse doth leuell at my Life: . . .

The following reflection upon the consequences of Gloucester's
death may have suggested these lines:

[*Hol.* iii. 627/1/68. *Halle*, 210.] Oft times it hapneth that a
man, in quenching of smoke, burneth his fingers in the fire: so the
queene, in casting how to keepe hir husband in honor, and hir selfe
in authoritie, in making awaie of this noble man, brought that to
passe, which she had most cause to haue feared; which was the
deposing of hir husband, & the decaie of the house of Lancaster,
which of likelihood had not chanced if this duke had liued: for

---

[1] February 11 was the second day of the session (*Rot. Parl.*, v. 129/9); but
according to *Greg.* (188) Gloucester was arrested on February 18. In a con-
temporaneously written memorandum of the Parliament of Bury, Gloucester's
arrest is dated February 18 (*Chron. Rich. II.—Hen. VI.*, 116).
[2] This is *Hol.*'s title. The charges are given in *Rot. Parl.*, v. 177-179,
where the article which I quote from *Hol.* is the 25th. My authority for the
date of Suffolk's impeachment is *Rot. Parl.*, v. 177/1.

then durst not the duke of Yorke haue attempted to set foorth his title to the crowne, as he afterwards did, to the great trouble of the realme, and destruction of king Henrie, and of many other noble men beside. [If Glouces-ter had lived York durst not have claimed the crown.]

Gloucester closes his speech with a recognition that his fate is sealed (ll. 168-171) :

> I shall not want false Witnesse to condemne me,
> Nor store of Treasons to augment my guilt ;
> The ancient Prouerbe will be well effected :
> " A Staffe is quickly found to beat a Dogge."

We have seen (p. 250 above) that "diuerse articles were laid against him in open councell." Defence was useless, for

[*Hol.* iii. 627/1/11. *Halle*, 209.] although the duke sufficientlie answered to all things against him obiected ; yet, because his death was determined, his wisedome and innocencie nothing auailed. [Gloucester's innocency nothing availed.]

A "Poste" from Ireland enters, bringing news "that Rebels there are vp" (ll. 282, 283). The task of subduing them is assigned to York, who thus obtains the armed force which he needs to serve his ambition (ll. 341-347). The dramatist sent York to Ireland, as Lieutenant, before the opening of the *Second Part of Henry the Sixth*, since in Act I., sc. i., Salisbury applies to an imaginary former term of office praise which belongs to the historic administration of 1448-50 ; undertaken by York in this scene. (See p. 248 above.)

All now go out save York, who thereupon unfolds his policy (ll. 348-359 ; 374, 375) :

> Whiles I in Ireland nourish a mightie Band,   348
> I will stirre vp in England some black Storme
> Shall blowe ten thousand Soules to Heauen or Hell :
> And this fell Tempest shall not cease to rage,
> Vntill the Golden Circuit on my Head,   352
> Like to the glorious Sunnes transparant Beames,
> Do calme the furie of this mad-bred Flawe.
> And, for a minister of my intent,
> I haue seduc'd a head-strong Kentishman,   356
> Iohn Cade of Ashford,
> To make Commotion, as full well he can,
> Vnder the title of Iohn Mortimer. . . .
> By this I shall perceiue the Commons minde,   374
> How they affect the House and Clayme of Yorke.

Cade's rebellion broke out at the end of May, 1450.[1] Its origin is thus described :

---

[1] Septima in Pentecoste [*septimana Pentecostes* Hearne conj.] incepit communis insurreccio in Kancia."—*Wyrc.*, 469. In 1450 Whit Sunday fell on May 24.

[*Hol.* iii. 632/1/63. *Halle,* 220.] Those that fauoured the
duke of Yorke, and wished the crowne vpon his head, for that (as
they iudged) he had more right thereto than he that ware it, procured a commotion in Kent on this manner. A certeine yoong
man, of a goodlie stature and right pregnant of wit, was intised to
take vpon him the name of Iohn Mortimer, coosine to the duke of
Yorke ; (although his name was Iohn Cade, or, of some, Iohn
Mend-all, an Irishman, as *Polychronicon* saith ;) and not for a small
policie, thinking by that surname, that those which fauoured the
house of the earle of March would be assistant to him. [Cp. p.
282, n. 2, below.]

*Iacks Cades
rebellion in
Kent.* [To
gain
adherents,
he called
himself
Mortimer.]

Act III. sc. ii.—"Enter two or three running ouer the Stage, from
the Murther of Duke Humfrey." Afterwards (l. 121) : "Noyse within.
Enter Warwicke, [Salisbury], and many Commons." Warwick informs
Henry that, the murder of Gloucester by means of Suffolk and Cardinal
Beaufort having been reported, the Commons demand to "heare the
order" of Duke Humphrey's death. Gloucester's body is therefore
exhibited on the stage, and Warwick points out these signs of murder
(ll. 168-170) :

> But see, his face is blacke and full of blood,
> His eye-balles further out than when he liued,
> Staring full gastly, like a *strangled* man ; . . .

Gloucester's sudden death gave rise to sinister conjectures :

*The duke of
Gloucester
suddenlie
murthered.*

[*Hol.* iii. 627/1/29.] The duke, the night after he was thus
committed to prison [p. 264 above], being the foure and twentith
of Februarie,[1] was found dead in his bed, and his bodie shewed
to the lords and commons,[2] as though he had died of a palsie,
or of an imposteme.

Edw. Hall.
[209.]

But all indifferent persons (as saith *Hall*) might well vnderstand that he died of some violent death. Some iudged him to be
strangled, some affirme that an hot spit was put in at his funda-

---

[1] February 23.—*Greg.,* 188. *Wyrc.,* 464. From the memorandum of the
Bury Parliament (*Chron. Rich. II.—Hen. VI.,* 117) it appears that Gloucester
"deyde sone appon iij on the belle at aftrenone" of February 23. *Hol.* probably followed *Stow* (635) in giving February 24 as the date of Gloucester's
death. *Halle* (209), the dramatist's chief authority, says that Gloucester "the
night after his empryaonment was found dedde in his bed." Hence I conjecture that between scenes i. and ii., Act III., there is not a dramatic interval
of one clear day from midnight to midnight. See *T-A.,* 310.

[2] "And on the Fryday [February 24, 1447] next folewyng [Gloucester's
death], the lordes spirituelle and temporelle, also knyztes of the parlement, and
whosoeuer wolde come, saugh hym [Gloucester] dede."—Memorandum of the
Bury Parliament (*Chron. Rich. II.—Hen. VI.,* 117).

ment, other write that he was smouldered [1] betweene two feather-beds; and some haue affirmed that he died of verie greefe, for that he might not come openlie to his answer.

[Some judged him to be strangled, others write that he was smothered.]

Subsequently an attempt to enter the Upper House is made by the Commons who had remained "within." Salisbury keeps them back, and becomes their spokesman (ll. 243-253):

<blockquote>
Dread Lord, the Commons send you word by me,
Vnlesse Lord Suffolke straight be done to death,   244
Or banishèd faire Englands Territories,
They will by violence teare him from your Pallace,
And torture him with grieuous lingring death.
They say, by him the good Duke Humfrey dy'de;   248
They say, in him they feare your Highnesse death;
And meere instinct of Loue and Loyaltie
(Free from a stubborne opposite intent,
As being thought to contradict your liking)   252
Makes them thus forward in his Banishment.
</blockquote>

The excerpts I quote seem tame beside such a message as this; enforced by a threat from the impatient Commons that they "will all breake in." There are no materials for judging whether Suffolk was innocent or guilty of the crimes laid to his charge, but hatred and mistrust of him were widely spread. In 1449-50 people

[*Hol.* iii. 631/1/16. *Halle*, 217.] began to make exclamation against the duke of Suffolke, charging him to be the onelie cause of the deliuerie of Aniou and Maine, the cheefe procuror of the duke of Glocester's death, the verie occasion of the losse of Normandie, the swallower vp of the kings treasure,[2] the remoouer of good and vertuous councellours from about the prince, and the aduancer of vicious persons, and of such as by their dooings shewed themselues apparant aduersaries to the common-wealth.

The commõs exclame against yᵉ duke of Suffolk.

The queene hereat, doubting not onelie the duke's destruction, but also hir owne confusion, caused the parlement, before begun at the Blackfriers,[3] to be adiourned to Leicester; thinking there, by force and rigor of law, to suppresse and subdue all the malice and

The parlemẽt adiourned frõ London to Leicester, and from thence to Westminster.

---

[1] *The Contention* (35) has the following stage-direction before Suffolk's first speech (2 *Hen. VI.*, III. ii. 6): "Then the Curtaines being drawne, Duke Humphrey is discouered in his bed, and two men lying on his brest and smothering him in his bed. And then enter the Duke of Suffolke to them."

[2] In 2 *Hen. VI.*, IV. i. 73, 74, the "Lieutenant" thus addresses Suffolk:

<blockquote>
"Now will I dam vp this thy yawning mouth,
For swallowing the Treasure of the Realme:" ...
</blockquote>

[3] Parliament met at Westminster on November 6, 1449, and was adjourned to meet at Black Friars on the following day.—*Rot. Parl.*, v. 171/1.

euill will conceiued against the duke & hir.   At which place few
of the nobilitie would appeare: wherefore it was againe adiourned
to Westminster, where was a full appearance.   In the which
session the commons of the nether house put vp to the king and
the lords manie articles of treason, misprision, and euill demeanor,
against the duke of Suffolke: . . .

> I have cited above (p. 264) one of the "Articles proponed by the
> commons against the Duke of Suffolke."   The most important of these
> articles accuse him of treasonable dealings with the French, but in
> none of them is Gloucester even mentioned.[1]   Under the year 1447
> Fabyan relates (619) that

the Grudge and Murmour of y⁰ people ceasid nat agayne the
Marquys of Suffolke, for the deth of the good Duke of Glouceter,
of whose murdre he was specially suspected.

> Henry directs Salisbury to tell the Commons that, if they had not
> urged this matter,

> > Yet did I purpose as they doe entreat;

> and, addressing Suffolk, says (ll. 295-297):

> > If after three dayes space thou here bee'st found,
> > On any ground that I am Ruler of,
> > The World shall not be Ransome for thy Life.

> According to Halle (219), Holinshed's authority,

[*Hol.* iii. 632/1/23.] the parlement was adiourned to Leicester,[2]
whither came the king and queene in great estate, and with them
the duke of Suffolke, as cheefe councellour.   The commons of the
lower house, not forgetting their old grudge, besought the king,
that such persons, as assented to the release of Aniou, and deliuerance of Maine, might be dulie punished. . . .   When the king
perceiued that there was no remedie to appease the peoples furie

---

But in 1451 the Commons assembled at Westminster, after praying Henry
to attaint Suffolk (then dead) for the treasons of which the Duke had been
accused by the Commons in 1450, ended their petition thus: "Youre grete
Wysdome, rightwisnesse, and high discretion considering, that the seid William
de la Pole hath nought only don and commytted the forseid Treasons and
mischevous dedes, but was the cause and laborer of the arrest, emprisonyng,
and fynall destruction of the most noble vaillant true Prince, youre right
Obeissant Uncle the Duke of Gloucestre, whom God pardon," . . . —*Rot.
Parl.*, v. 226.

The Parliament which met first at Westminster on November 6, 1449
(*Rot. Parl.*, v. 171/1) was adjourned to Leicester for April 29, 1450 (*Rot. Parl.*,
v. 172/11).   But Suffolk was banished on March 17, 1450 (see next note).

by anie colourable waies, shortlie to pacifie so long an hatred, he
first sequestred the lord Saie, (being treasuror of England,) and
other the dukes adherents, from their offices and roomes; and after
banished the duke of Suffolke, as the abhorred tode and common
noiance of the whole realme, for tearme of fiue yeares:[1] meaning
by this exile to appease the malice of the people for the time, and
after (when the matter should be forgotten) to reuoke him home
againe.

[Suffolk banished by Henry for five years.]

Act III. sc. iii.—Cardinal Beaufort was "at point of death" in the
last scene (III. ii. 369). He is now visited by Henry, Salisbury, and
Warwick. The dying man does not know his sovereign, and exclaims
(ll. 2-4):

> If thou beest death, Ile giue thee Englands Treasure,
> Enough to purchase such another Island,
> So thou wilt let me liue, and feele no paine!

I quote Halle's summing up (210, 211) of Cardinal Beaufort's life,
which contains a death-bed speech whence these lines were derived.
On April 11, 1447,[2]

Henry Beaufford, byshop of Wynchester, and called the ryche
Cardynall, departed out of this worlde, and was buried at Wynchester. This manne was sonne to Ihon of Gaunte duke of
Lancaster; discended on an honorable lignage, but borne in
Baste; more noble of bloud then notable in learnyng; haut in
stomacke, and hygh in countenaunce; ryche aboue measure of all
men, & to fewe liberal; disdaynfull to his kynne and dreadfull to
his louers; preferrynge money before frendshippe; many thinges
begynning and nothing perfourmyng. His couetise[3] insaciable, and
hope of long lyfe, made hym bothe to forget God, his Prynce, and
hymself, in his latter daies. For doctor Ihon Baker, his pryuie
counsailer and hys chapellayn, wrote that he, lyeng on his death
bed, said these wordes: "Why should I dye, hauing so muche
"ryches [that], if the whole Realme would saue my lyfe, I am able
"either by pollicie to get it, or by ryches to bye it? Fye! wyll
"not death be byered, nor will money do nothyng? When my

[Beaufort was called "the rich cardinal."]

[His lineage and character.]

[Dr. Baker's report of Beaufort's last words.

["Will not Death be hired, nor will money do nothing?

---

[1] On March 17, 1450, Suffolk was banished for a term of five years, beginning on May 1 next ensuing.—*Rot. Parl.*, v. 182/2, 183/1.

[2] *Chron. Rich. II.—Hen. VI.*, 63. *Wyrc.*, 464. On April 15, 1447,
permission to elect Beaufort's successor in the See of Winchester was granted.
Rymer, xi. 162, 163. *Halle* (210) wrongly placed Beaufort's death in 1448.

[3] *couetise*] *couetous* Halle.

When
Gloucester
died, I
thought
myself the
equal of
kings."]

"nephew of Bedford died, I thought my selfe halfe vp the whole ;
"but when I sawe myne other nephew of Gloucester disceased,
"then I thought my selfe able to be equale with kinges, and so
"thought to encrease my treasure in hoope to haue worne a tryple
"Croune. But I se nowe the worlde fayleth me, and so I am
"deceyued : praiyng you all to pray for me."   Of the gettyng of

[Hoping to
obtain the
Papacy,
Beaufort
hoarded
riches which
would have
relieved the
wants of the
common-
wealth.]

thys mannes goodes, both by power legatine [1] or spiritual bryberie,
I wil not speake : but the kepynge of them for his ambicious
purpose, aspyryng to ascend to the papisticall sea, was bothe great
losse to his naturall Prynce, and natyue countrey ; for his hidden
riches might haue wel holpen the kyng, and his secrete treasure
might haue releued the commonaltie, when money was scante, and
importunate charges were dayly imminent.

Act IV. sc. i.—"Alarum. Fight at Sea. Ordnance goes off."
Suffolk enters as a prisoner, and is beheaded ere the scene closes. The
historic date of the latter event was May 2, 1450.[2] Henry had resolved,
when Suffolk's term of banishment expired, "to reuoke him home
againe" (p. 269 above).

Hol. iii. 632/1/45. *Halle,* 219.] But Gods iustice would not
that so vngratious a person should so escape ; for, when he shipped
in Suffolke, intending to transport himselfe ouer into France, he
was incountered with a ship of warre, apperteining to the duke of
Excester, constable of the Tower of London, called the Nicholas
of the Tower.[3] The capteine of that barke with small fight entered

---

[1] *legatine*] *legantye* Halle.

[2] *Wyrc.,* 469. On April 30, 1450, Suffolk was intercepted and obliged to
transfer himself to the Nicholas of the Tower. There he remained until May
2, when "he was drawyn ought of the grete shippe yn to the bote," and
beheaded "by oon of the lewdeste of the shippe."—*Paston,* i. 124, 125.

[3] Suffolk's ransom is assigned by the Lieutenant to one Walter Whitmore
(*Water Whickmore,* Contention, 43). The Duke starts when he hears this name,
and says (ll. 33-35) :

> "Thy name affrights me, in whose sound is death.
> A cunning man did calculate my birth,
> And told me that by Water I should dye" : . . .

(Cp. the Spirit's prediction in *2 Hen. VI.,* I. iv. 36.) It appears that a prophecy of Suffolk's death really met with a like unforeseen fulfilment. On
May 5, 1450, William Lomner wrote thus to John Paston : "Also he [Suffolk]
asked the name of the sheppe, and whanne he knew it, he remembred Stacy
that seid, if he myght eschape the daunger of the Towr, he should be saffe ;
and thanne his herte faylyd hym, for he thowghte he was desseyvyd," . . .
—*Paston,* i. 125. John Stacy, called "Astronomus," was also "magnus
Necromanticus." He was associated with Thomas Burdet, a valet of George
Duke of Clarence, and was executed in 1477.—*Cont. Croyl.,* 561. Suffolk was

into the dukes ship, and, perceiuing his person present, brought The wretched death of the duke of Suffolke.
him to Douer road, and there, on the one side of a cock bote,
caused his head to be striken off, and left his bodie with the head
lieng there on the sands. Which corps, being there found by a
chapleine of his, was conueied to Wingfield college in Suffolke, and
there buried.

Act IV. sc. ii.—The dramatic version of the Kentishmen's rising
in 1450 contains some gleanings from Holinshed's account of the
villeins' revolt in 1381. A proposal to kill all the lawyers (ll. 83, 84)
was not, so far as we know, made at the former date, but in 1381,
when the rebels had gained strength, they

[*Hol.* iii. 430/1/65.] began to shew proofe of those things which Lawiers, iustices & iurors brought to blochham feast by the rebels.
they had before conceiued in their minds, beheading all such men
of law, iustices, and iurors, as they might catch, and laie hands
vpon, without respect of pitie, or remorse of conscience : alledging
that the land could neuer enioy hir natiue and true libertie, till all
those sorts of people were dispatched out of the waie.

Wat Tyler demanded from Richard II.

[*Hol.* iii. 432/1/56.] a commission to put to death all lawiers, The rebels would haue all law abolished.
escheaters, and other which by any office had any thing to doo
with the law; for his meaning was that, hauing made all those
awaie that vnderstood the lawes, all things should then be ordered
according to the will and disposition of the common people.

Some of Cade's men bring forward "the Clarke of Chattam," [1] who
has been taken "setting of boyes Copies" (l. 95). Cade sentences
him to be hung "with his Pen and Inke-horne [2] about his necke."
Holinshed says that in 1381 the rebels obliged

---

committed to the Tower on January 28, 1450 (*Rot. Parl.*, v. 177/1); before
which time he had asked " of on that was an astronomer, what sholde falle of
him, and how he sholde ende his lif; and whanne the said astronomer hadde
labourid therfore in his said craft, he answerde to the duke and said that he
sholde die a shameful deth, and counselid him alwey to be war of the tour;
wherfor be instaunce of lordis that were his frendis, he was sone delyuerid out
of the said tour of Londoun."—*Chron. Rich. II.—Hen. VI.*, 69.

[1] *Chattam*] Q1. *Chartam* F1. Chartham is 2½ miles S.W. of Canterbury.
—*Bartholomew.* A "parishe Clearke" of "Chetham" figures in a legend of
our Lady of Chatham, told in Lambarde's *Perambulation of Kent* (repr. 1826,
p. 324).

[2] *Pen and Inke-horne*] F1. *penny-inckhorne* Q1. Cp. " penner and inke-
horne " in excerpt from *Hol.* In 1381 the rebels, " if they found any to haue
pen and inke, they pulled off his hoode, and all with one voice of crying, ' Hale
him out, and cut off his head.' "—*Stow*, 453.

[Grammar-
teaching
forbidden.]
Anno Reg. 5.
[It was
dangerous
to bear a
pen-case and
inkhorn.]
[*Hol.* iii. 436/1/9.] teachers of children in grammar schooles [1]
to sweare neuer to instruct any in their art. . . . it was dangerous
among them to be knowne for one that was lerned, and more
dangerous, if any men were found with a penner and inkhorne at
his side : for such seldome or neuer escaped from them with life.

Cade thus animates his followers to encounter the Staffords (ll.
193, 194):

> Now shew your selues men, 'tis for Liberty !
> We will not leaue one Lord, one Gentleman : · ·. .

In June, 1381, John Ball exhorted the people assembled at
Blackheath

[*Hol.* iii. 437/1/73.] to consider that now the time was come
appointed to them by God, in which they might (if they would)
cast off the yoke of bondage, & recouer libertie. He counselled
them therefore to remember themselues, and to take good hearts
vnto them, that, after the manner of a good husband that tilleth
his ground, and riddeth out thereof such euill weeds as choke and
[Great lords
and lawyers
should be
destroyed
that equality
might be
secured.]
destroie the good corne, they might destroie first the great lords [2]
of the realme, and after the iudges and lawiers, questmoongers,
and all other whom they vndertooke to be against the commons ;
for so might they procure peace and suertie to themselues in time
to come, if, dispatching out of the waie the great men, there should
be an equalitie in libertie, no difference in degrees of nobilitie, but
a like dignitie and equall authoritie in all things brought in among
them.

Act IV. sc. iii.—" Alarums to the fight, wherein both the Staffords
are slaine.   Enter Cade and the rest."   The historic date of this fight

---

[1] Cade to Lord Say (2 *Hen. VI.*, IV. vii. 35-37): " Thou hast most traiter-
ously corrupted the youth of the Realme, in erecting a Grammar Schoole."
[2] Ball was wont to say : " A, good people, matters go not wel to passe in
England in these dayes, nor shall not do vntill euery thing be common, and
that there be no Villeynes nor gentlemen, . . . We be all come from one
father and one mother, Adam and Eue."—*Grafton*, i. 417, 418.   His theme
when preaching at Blackheath was:

> " When Adam delu'd, and Eue span
> Who was then a gentleman ?"—*Hol.*, iii. 437/1/63.

Cp. John Holland's assertion (2 *Hen. VI.*, IV. ii. 9, 10) : " Well, I may it was
neuer merrie world in England since Gentlemen came vp." Cp. also Cade's
retort to Sir Humphrey Stafford (IV. ii. 142) : " And Adam was a Gardiner."

was June 18, 1450.[1] Cade declined an engagement with a large force which had been collected to oppose him, and retired from Blackheath.[2]

[*Hol.* iii. 634/1/51. *Halle*, 220.] The queene (that bare rule), being of his retrait aduertised, sent sir Humfreie Stafford knight, and William his brother, with manie other gentlemen, to follow the Kentishmen, thinking that they had fled: but they were deceiued, for at the first skirmish both the Staffords were slaine, & all their companie discomfited.

*The Staf-
fords slaine
at Senocke
by Iack
Cade.*

Cade's words—"This Monument of the victory will I beare"[3] (l. 12)—are explained by the ensuing quotation:

[*Hol.* iii. 634/1/69. *Halle*, 220.] Iacke Cade, vpon victorie against the Staffords, apparelled himselfe in sir Humfreies brigan-dine set full of guilt nailes, and so in some glorie returned againe toward London: diuerse idle and vagarant persons, out of Sussex, Surreie and other places, still increasing his number.

[Cade
apparelled
himself in
Sir H.
Stafford's
brigandine.]

Just before the Kentishmen set forth on their march to London, Dick Butcher says (ll. 17, 18): "If we meane to thriue, and do good, breake open the Gaoles, and let out the Prisoners" In July, 1450, after his repulse from London Bridge (see p. 280 below), Cade,

[*Hol.* iii. 635/1/41. *Halle*, 222.] for making him more friends, brake vp the gailes of the kings Bench and Marshalsie;[4] and so were manie mates set at libertie verie meet for his matters in hand.

[Cade broke
open the
gaols.]

Act IV. sc. iv.—As this scene opens the King enters "with a Supplication"; and soon afterwards Buckingham asks (ll. 7, 8): "What answer makes your Grace to the Rebells Supplication?"[5] Early in June, 1450, Cade—who was then encamped on Blackheath—

[*Hol.* iii. 632/2/73. *Halle*, 220.] sent vnto the king an humble supplication, affirming that his comming was not against his grace, [*p.* 633] but against such of his councellours, as were louers of

[Cade's sup-
plication.]

---

[1] The date of Sir Humphrey Stafford's death given in the Inquisition *post mortem*, 28 Hen. VI., No. 7. (*Paston*, I. p. lii. note 3.)

[2] *Wyrc.*, 470. *Greg.*, 191.

[3] *This . . . beare*] 2 Hen. VI. om. Contention.

[4] In 1381 also the rebels "brake vp the prisons of the Marshalsea, & the Kings bench, set the prisoners at libertie, & admitted them into their com-panie."—*Hol.* 430/2/53. "They also brake vp the prisons of newgate, and of both the counters, destroied the books, and set prisoners at libertie."—*Hol.* iii. 431/2/43.

[5] *Enter the King reading of a Letter*] Contention. From it he learns that the Staffords have been slain, and that the rebels are marching to London. The question, "What . . . Supplication," is not in *Contention*.

themselues, and oppressors of the poore commonaltie; flatterers
of the king, and enimies to his honor; suckers of his purse, and
robbers of his subiects; parciall to their freends, and extreame
to their enimies; thorough bribes corrupted, and for indifferencie
dooing nothing.

A messenger announces that Cade is master of Southwark (l. 27).
Buckingham counsels Henry's retirement "to Killingworth," until a
power can be raised for putting down the rebels (ll. 39, 40). As the
scene closes the King goes out to take horse and away thither. The
historical order of events was as follows: disregarding the rebels'
supplication, Henry marched against them. Cade retreated, and, on
the day of Henry's arrival at Blackheath, the Staffords—who had
advanced in pursuit of the rebels—were overthrown. (June 18, see
pp. 272, 273 above.) The King then returned to London, and subsequently went to Kenilworth. His army broke up.[1] On or about
June 29,[2] Cade

[Ambas-
sadors from
Henry sent
to Cade.]
[*Hol.* iii. 634/2/2. *Halle*, 220.] came againe to the plaine of
Blackheath, & there stronglie incamped himselfe; to whome were
sent from the king, the archbishop of Canturburie, and Humfreie
duke of Buckingham, to common with him of his greefes and
requests.

These lords found him sober in talke, wise in reasoning,
[Cade
demanded
a personal
conference
with Henry.]
arrogant in hart, and stiffe in opinion; as who that by no means
would grant to dissolue his armie, except the king in person would
come to him, and assent to the things he would require. The
K., vpon the presumptuous answers & requests of this villanous
rebell, begining asmuch to doubt his owne meniall seruants, as his
vnknowen subiects, (which spared not to speake, that the capteins
cause was profitable for the common-wealth,) departed in all hast
[Henry
retired to
Kenilworth,
leaving Lord
Scales to
defend the
Tower.]
to the castell of Killingworth in Warwikeshire, leauing onlie
behind him the lord Scales to keepe the Tower of London. The
Kentish capteine, being aduertised of the kings absence, came first
[Cade
entered
Southwark,
and lodged
at the White
Hart.]
into Southwarke, and there lodged at the white hart, prohibiting
to all his retinue, murder, rape, and robberie; by which colour of
well meaning he the more allured to him the harts of the common
people.

---

[1] *Fab.*, 622, 623. *Wyrc.*, 470.
[2] "the xxix. daye of Iuny."—*Fab.*, 623. "after seint Petres day."—*Chron.
Lond.*, 136.

staffe on London stone"; and cries: "*Now is Mortimer Lord of this City!*" On July 2 or 3, Cade

[*Hol.* iii. 634/2/25. *Halle,* 221.] entred into London, cut the ropes of the draw bridge, & strooke his sword on London stone; saieng: "*Now is Mortimer lord of this citie!*"

Seated on London Stone, Cade declares (ll. 5-7) that "henceforward it shall be Treason for any that calles me other then Lord Mortimer." Whereupon a soldier enters "running," and crying, "Iacke Cade! Iacke Cade!" Cade says: "Knocke him downe there!" The soldier is killed; and one of the rebels (*Smith* mod. edd.) observes: "If this Fellow be wise, hee'l neuer call yee Iacke Cade more: I thinke he hath a very faire warning." The incident was probably suggested by a tradition that Cade put to death some

[*Hol.* iii. 634/2/59. *Halle,* 221.] of his old acquaintance, lest they should bewraie his base linage, disparaging him for his vsurped surname of Mortimer.

Fabyan gives precise details (624):

And the same tyme [July 4][1] was there also behedyd an other man, called Baylly; the cause of whose dethe was this, as I haue herde some men reporte. This [*Then* ed. 1516] Baylly was of the famylyer & olde acquayntaunce of Iak Cade, wherfore, so soon as he espyed hym commynge to hym warde, he cast in his mynde that he wolde dyscouer his lyuynge & olde maners, and shewe of his vyle kynne and lynage.

Act IV. sc. vii.—"Alarums. Mathew Goffe is slain, and all the rest. Then enter Iacke Cade, with his Company." The dramatic locality of this scene is Smithfield (cp. IV. vi. 13-15). But the historical conflict in which Matthew Gough fell was waged on London Bridge. The citizens, having determined to resist Cade (see p. 275 above),

[*Hol.* iii. 635/1/1. *Halle,* 221.] tooke vpon them in the night to keepe the bridge, and would not suffer the Kentishmen once to approch. The rebels, who neuer soundlie slept for feare of sudden assaults, hearing that the bridge was thus kept, ran with great hast to open that passage, where betweene both parties was a fierce and cruell fight.

---

[1] The date of Lord Say's decapitation (see p. 278, n. 3 below) was also that on which Bayly was beheaded, according to *Wyrc.* (471), *Greg.* (192), and *Fab.* (624).

Matthew *Gough, perceiuing the rebels to stand to their tackling more manfullie than he thought they would haue doone, aduised his companie not to aduance anie further toward South-warke, till the daie appeared ; that they might see where the place of ieopardie rested, and so to prouide for the same : but this little auailed. For the rebels with their multitude draue back the citizens from the stoops at the bridge foot to the draw bridge, & began to set fire in diuerse houses. . . . Yet the capteins, not sparing, fought on the bridge all the night valiantlie : but, in con-clusion, the rebels gat the draw bridge, and drowned manie ; and slue Iohn Sutton alderman, and Robert[1] Heisand, a hardie citizen, with manie other, beside Matthew *Gough, a man of great wit and much experience in feats of chinalrie, the which in continuall warres had spent his time in seruice of the king and his father.

*Or rather
Goche.
The skirmish
betweene the
citizens and
the rebels
vpon London
bridge.

Matthew
Goche,
famous for
his acts
abroad, now
slaine on
Lõdõ bridge.

After Matthew Gough's defeat, Cade says (ll. 1-3): "So, sirs: now go some and pull down the Sauoy ; others to th'Innes of Court ; downe with them all!" Here is a dramatic postdating of what happened in the villeins' revolt. On June 13, 1381,[2] they went to John of Gaunt's

[*Hol.* iii. 431/1/18.] house of the Sauoie, to the which, in beautie and statelinesse of building, with all maner of princelie furniture, there was not any other in the realme comparable ; which, in despite of the duke, (whom they called traitor,) they set on fire, and by all waies and means indeuoured vtterlie to destroie it. . . .

The Sauoie,
the duke of
Lancasters
house, burnt
by the rebels.

Now after that these wicked people had thus destroied the duke of Lancasters house, and done what they could deuise to his reproch, they went to the temple ; and burnt the men of lawes lodgings, with their bookes, writings, and all that they might lay hand vpon.

The lawiers
lodgings in
the temple
burnt by the
rebels.

Addressing Cade, Dick Butcher says (ll. 4 ; 7, 8): "I haue a suite vnto your Lordship. . . . *that the Lawes of England* may *come* out of *your mouth.*" Cade answers : "I haue thought vpon it, it shall bee so. Away, *burne all* the *Records* of the Realme! my mouth shall be the Parliament of England." On June 14, 1381, Wat Tyler, it is alleged,[3] boasted,

---

[1] Roger (*Fab.*, 625). [2] *Wals.*, i. 456. [3] *Wals.*, i. 463/464.

[The laws of England from Wat Tyler's mouth.] [*Hol.* iii. 432/1/63.] putting his hands to his lips, *that* within foure daies all *the lawes of England* should *come* foorth *of* his *mouth.*

To illustrate Cade's order I quote an assertion that, in 1381,

The next way to extinguish light. [All records burnt.] [*Hol.* iii. 430/1/73.] the common vplandish people, . . . purposed to *burne* and destroie *all records*, euidences, court-rolles, and other muniments, that, the remembrance of ancient matters being remooued out of mind, their landlords might not haue whereby to chalenge anie right at their hands.

Touching this policy, Holinshed asks if they could

[Records destroyed and remembrances slain.] [*Hol.* iii. 436/1/11.] haue a more mischeefous meaning, than to burne and destroie all old and ancient monuments, and to murther and dispatch out of the waie all such as were able to commit to memorie, either any new or old records?[1]

A messenger announces the capture of Lord Say (ll. 23-25); " which sold the Townes in France " (l. 23). The Commons in the Parliament of 1450 charged with being principal parties to the cession of Anjou [Lord Say a party to the cession of Anjou and Maine.] and Maine

. [*Hol.* iii. 632/1/31.] the duke of Suffolke, with William[2] bishop of Salisburie, and sir Iames Fines, lord Saie, and diuerse others.

The same messenger also speaks of Lord Say as having " made vs pay one and twenty *Fifteens*, and one shilling to the pound, the last Subsidie." Cade induced the Kentishmen to rebel by pointing out that,

[*Hol.* iii. 632/2/14. *Halle*, 220.] if either by force or policie they might get the king and queene into their hands, he would cause them to be honourablie vsed, and take such order for the [Abolition of Fifteens.] punishing and reforming of the misdemeanours of their bad councellours, that neither *fifteens* should hereafter be demanded, nor once anie impositions or taxes be spoken of.

Lord Say's murder is thus related : on July 4,[3] 1450, Cade

[*Hol.* iii. 634/2/31. *Halle*, 221.] caused sir Iames Fines, lord

---

[1] " at Westminster . . . they brake open the eschequer, and destroied the ancient bookes and other records there, dooing what they could to suppresse law, and by might to beate downe equitie and right."—*Hol.* iii. 431/2/47.

[2] *William*] *Iohn* Hol.

[3] The inscription on Lord Say's gravestone recorded that he died on July 4, 1450.—Register of the Sepulchral Inscriptions in the Church of the Grey Friars, London (Nichols's *Collectanea Topographica et Genealogica*, v. 279).

Saie, and treasuror of England, to be brought to the Guildhall, and there to be arreigned; who, being before the kings iustices put to answer, desired to be tried by his peeres, for the longer delaie of his life. The capteine, perceiuing his dilatorie plee, by force tooke him from the officers, and brought him to the standard in Cheape, and there (before his confession ended) caused his head to be striken off, and pitched it vpon an high pole, which was openlie *borne before* him *thorough the streets.* The lord Saie beheaded at the standard in Cheap.

Cade bids the executioners strike off Lord Say's "head presently; and then breake into his Sonne in Lawes house, Sir Iames Cromer, and strike off his head, and bring them both vppon two poles hither." On the re-entry of "one with the heads," Cade gives a further order (ll. 138-140; 143-145): "Let them kisse one another, for they lou'd well when they were aliue. . . . with these *borne before* vs, in steed of Maces, will we ride *through the streets*, & at euery Corner haue them kisse." Cade afterwards

[*Hol.* iii. 634/2/42. *Halle*, 221.] went to Mile end, and there apprehended sir Iames Cromer, then shiriffe of Kent, and sonne in law to the said lord Saie; causing him likewise (without confession or excuse heard) to be beheaded, and his head to be fixed on a pole; and with these two heads this bloudie wretch entred into the citie againe, and as it were in a spite caused them in euerie street to kisse togither, to the great detestation of all the beholders. [Sir James Cromer beheaded.] [The heads of Lord Say and Sir James Cromer made to kiss.]

Act IV. sc. viii.—The Entry runs thus: "Alarum, and Retreat. Enter againe Cade, and all his rabblement." Cade cries: "Vp Fish-streete! downe Saint Magnes corner! Kill and knocke downe! throw them into Thames!"[1] These orders are succeeded by "a parley," which announces the entrance of Buckingham and old Clifford. Their offer of pardon makes the Kentishmen waver; and, in recalling his followers to obedience, Cade asks (ll. 23-26): "Hath my sword there-fore broke through London gates, that you should leaue me at the White-heart (*sic*) in Southwarke?"[2] Comparison with the next excerpt might warrant a supposition that, when this scene opens, the Londoners

---

[1] In defending London Bridge "many a man was drowned and slayne."—*Fab.*, 625. "many a man was slayne and caste in Temys, harnys, body, and alle."—*Greg.*, 193. According to *Fab.* (625) the battle was confined to a space not much exceeding the northern end of the central draw-bridge and the "Bulwerke at the Brydgefote" (the stoops in Southwark, I presume). That the rebels penetrated to St. Magnus's corner rests on *Halle's* authority (222).

[2] These lines (*Hath . . . Southwarke?*) and the preceding quotation (*Alarum . . . Thames!*) are not in the *Contention*. Cade "lodged at the white hart." See p. 274 above.

are being "beaten backe to Saint Magnus corner"; but that they
have rallied, and driven the rebels "to the stoops in Southwarke,"
before Cade complains of being left at the White Hart. As however
no interval occurs during which the rebels could have been repulsed,
Mr. Daniel's stricture (*T.A.*, 312) that—the combatants "seem to be
on both sides of the river at one time"—is unanswerable. Waiving
this difficulty we may assume that ll. 1-3 dramatize the battle which,
beginning at 10 o'clock in the evening of Sunday, July 5, 1450,[1]

[*Hol.* iii. 635/1/32.   *Halle*, 222.] indured in doubtfull wise on
the bridge, till nine of the clocke in the morning: for somtime, the
Londoners were beaten backe to saint Magnus corner: and suddenlie againe, the rebels were repelled to the stoops in Southwarke, so that both parts being faint and wearie, agreed to leane
off from fighting till the next daie; vpon condition, that neither
Londoners should passe into Southwarke, nor Kentishmen into
London.

[The battle sways from St. Magnus's corner to the stoups in Southwark.]

A stroke by e mort.

Buckingham thus discharges the commission entrusted to him and
old Clifford (ll. 7-10):

> Know, Cade, we come Ambassadors from the King
> Vnto the Commons, whom thou hast misled;
> And heere pronounce free pardon to them all,
> That will forsake thee, and go home in peace.

Holinshed took from Halle (222) the ensuing account of the rebels'
dispersal.

[*Hol.* iii. 635/1/45.] The archbishop of Canturburie,[2] being
chancellor of England, and as then for his suertie lieng within the
Tower, called to him the bishop of Winchester, who for some safegard laie then at Haliwell. These two prelats, seeing the furie of
the Kentish people, by their late repulse, to be somewhat asswaged,
passed by the riuer of Thames from the Tower into Southwarke;
bringing with them, vnder the kings great seale, a generall pardon
vnto all the offendors, and caused the same to be openlie published.

---

[1] On the "evyn" of July 5 "Londyn dyd a rysse and cam owte uppon
hem [the Kentishmen] at x [of] the belle, beyng that tyme hyr captaynys the
goode olde lorde Schalys and Mathewe Goughe. And from that tyme unto
the morowe viij of belle they were ever fyghtynge uppon London Brygge."—
Greg., 193. *Wyrc.* (471), *Fab.* (625), and *Chron. Lond.* (136), agree that the
conflict began on the night of July 5.

[2] John Kempe, then Archbishop of York, was Chancellor in July, 1450.
He received the Great Seal on January 31, 1450 (*Rot. Parl.*, v. 172/1), and
retained it till his death in March, 1454 (*Rot. Parl.*, v. 240/2). The Bishop of
Winchester was William of Waynflete.

The poore people were so glad of this pardon, and so readie to *Proclama-
tió of pardon
dispersed
the rebels.* receiue it, that, without bidding farewell to their capteine, they withdrew themselues the same night euerie man towards his home.

Deserted, and fearing treachery from his former adherents, Cade runs away. Buckingham exclaims (ll. 68-70):

> What, is he fled ! Go some, and follow him ;
> And he that brings his head vnto the King,
> Shall haue a thousand Crownes for his reward !

After relating the dispersal of the rebels,—"euerie man towards his home,"—Holinshed continues :

[*Hol.* iii. 635/1/59.] But Iacke Cade, despairing of succours, *Abr. Fl. as
l. 8 pag.
661, 662, in
Quart.* and fearing the reward of his lewd dealings, put all his pillage and goods that he had robbed into a barge, and sent it to Rochester by water, and himselfe went by land, and would haue entred into the castle of Quinborow with a few men that were left about him ; but he was there let of his purpose : wherefore he, disguised in strange attire, priuilie fled into the wood countrie beside Lewes in [Cade's
flight.] Sussex, hoping so to scape. The capteine & his people being thus departed, not long after proclamations were made in diuerse places of Kent, Sussex, and Southerie, that, whosoeuer could take the foresaid capteine aliue or dead, should haue a thousand markes [1000 marks
offered for
him.] for his trauell.

Act IV. sc. ix.—"Multitudes" of the rebels enter "with Halters about their Neckes." Old Clifford tells Henry that they yield ;

> And humbly thus, with halters on their neckes,
> Expect your Highnesse doome, of life or death.   12

Henry ends a gentle speech to them by saying (ll. 20, 21):

> And so, with thankes and pardon to you all,
> I do dismisse you to your seuerall Countries.

It was not until after Cade's death—dramatized in the next scene—that

[*Hol.* iii. 635/2/71. *Halle*, 222.] the king himselfe came into [Henry sat
in judgment
upon the
rebels.] Kent, and there sat in iudgement vpon the offendors ;[1] and, if he had not mingled his iustice with mercy, more than fiue hundred by rigor of law had beene iustlie put to [*p.* 636] execution. Yet

---

[1] On August 17, 1450, the Archbishop of York and the Duke of Buckingham went to Rochester to try the Kentish rebels.—*Paston,* i. 139.

[Most of them were pardoned.] he, punishing onelie the stubborne heads, & disordered ringleaders, pardoned the ignorant and simple persons, to the great roioising of all his subiects.

A messenger enters, and, addressing Henry, says (ll. 23-30) :

Please it your Grace to be aduértised,
The Duke of Yorke is newly come from Ireland,   24
And, with a puissant and a mighty power
Of Gallow-glasses and stout Kernes,
Is marching hitherward in proud array ;
And still proclaimeth, as he comes along,   28
His Armes are onely to remoue from thee
The Duke of Somerset, whom he tearmes a Traitor.

York did not take up arms for the purpose here announced until some time had elapsed after his return from Ireland. I give the following excerpt as an illustration of the messenger's news ; premising that, by " this yeare," the year 1451 is meant. The date of York's return was September, 1450.[2]

---

[1] In 2 *Hen. VI.*, Act V. opens with this stage direction : " Enter Yorke, and his Army of Irish, with Drum and Colours." *The Contention* has : " Enter the Duke of Yorke with Drum and souldiers " ; preceding l. 1, spoken by York : " In Armes from Ireland comes Yorke amaine." The messenger's speech (IV. ix. 23-30) is not in *Contention*. When, in October, 1450, a temporary Lancastrian success caused York's flight to Ireland, " he was with all ioy and honour gladlie receiued, all the Irish offering to liue and die with him ; as if they had beene his liege subiects, and he their lord and prince naturallie borne."—*Hol.* iii. 650/2/23. This passage may have been the source of York's " Army of Irish " ; composed of " Gallow-glasses " and " Kernes." Cp. also the excerpt at p. 248 above, where his beneficial government of Ireland is recorded.

[2] In the beginning of September (" in Principio mensis Septembris "), 1450, Henry received news of York's sudden arrival in Wales.—*Wyrc.*, 473. *Chron. Lond.* has a notice of the Kentish rebellion and Cade's death, which is succeeded by the following passage (136, 137) : " And after, in the same yere, Richard Plantagenet duke of Yorke came out of Irland unto Westm', with roial people, lowely bisechyng the kyng that justice and execucion of his lawes myght be hadde upon alle such persones about him and in al his realme, frome the highest degree unto the lowist, as were long tyme noisid and detectid of high treason ageinst his persone and the wele of his realme, offring hymself therto, and his service at the kings comaundement, to spend bothe his body and goodes : and yet it might not be perfourmed." The attainder of York by the Lancastrian Parliament which met at Coventry in November 1459 contains this article : " First, he [York] beyng in Irland, by youre graunte youre Lieutenaunt there, at which tyme John Cade, otherwise called Jakke Cade youre grete Traitour, made a grete insurrection ayenst youre Highnes in youre Shire of Kent, to what entent, and for whome it was after confessed by some of hem his adherentes whan they shuld dye, that is to sey, to have exalted the said Duc, ayenst all reason, lawe and trouth, to the estate that God and nature hath ordeyned you and youre succession to be born to. And within short tyme after, he comme oute of Ireland with grete bobaunce and inordinate people, to youre Paleis of Westmynster unto youre presence," . . .—*Rot. Parl.*, v. 346/1. Moreover, we learn from *Rot. Parl.*, v. 211/2 that, on September 22, 1450,

[*Hol.* iii. 637/1/50. *Halle*, 225.] The duke of Yorke, pretending (as yee haue heard) a right to the crowne, as heire to Lionell duke of Clarence, came this yeare out of Ireland vnto London, in the parlement time,[1] there to consult with his speciall freends: as Iohn duke of Northfolke, Richard earle of Salisburie, and the lord Richard, his sonne, (which after was earle of Warwike,) Thomas Courtneie earle of Deuonshire, & Edward Brooke lord Cobham. After long deliberation and aduise taken, it was thought expedient to keepe their cheefe purpose secret; and that the duke should raise an armie of men, vnder a pretext to remooue diuerse councellors about the king, and to reuenge the manifest iniuries doone to the common-wealth by the same rulers. Of the which, as principall, the duke of Summerset was namelie accused, both for that he was greatlie hated of the commons for the losse of Normandie; and for that it was well knowne, that he would be altogither against the duke of Yorke in his chalenge to be made (when time serued) to the crowne ; . . .

The duke of Yorke wisheth claims to the crowne. [He came from Ireland to consult his friends.]

[It was resolved that York should raise an army, under pretext of removing divers counsellors about the King, chief among whom was Somerset.]

Act IV. sc. x.—Cade climbs into a garden belonging to "*Alexander Iden*, an *Esquire of Kent*" (l. 46); whom he challenges to mortal combat, and by whom he is slain. Iden resolves to bear Cade's head "in triumph to the King," leaving the "trunke for Crowes to feed vpon" (ll. 89, 90).

Cade was slain before July 15, 1450.[2] Halle's account[3] (222) is that, when the Kentishmen withdrew to their homes, Cade,

desperate of succors, whiche by the frendes of the duke of Yorke

---

William Tresham, being then at Sywell, Northamptonshire, was "purposyng by the writyng direct vnto hym of the right high and myghty Prince, the Duke of York, to ride on the morowe for to mete and speke with the seid Duke" ; . . .

[1] Parliament was opened at Westminster on November 6, 1450.—*Rot. Parl.*, v. 210/1. York returned before this date. See foregoing note.

[2] The date of an order to pay Iden 1000 marks for Cade's head.—*Rymer*, xi. 275. Cade was slain on July 12 (*Greg.*, 194), or on July 13 (*Three Chronicles*, S. E. C., 68). In *Rot. Parl.* (v. 234/2) the latest date assigned to his movements is July 11.

[3] On comparing the excerpt in my text with *Hol.'s* account—derived from *Stow* (647)—the reader will observe that the latter is less like the dramatic version. After a reward had been offered for Cade, "a gentleman of Kent, named Alexander Eden, awaited so his time, that he tooke the said Cade in a garden in Sussex: so that there he was slaine at Hothfield [Heathfield, Sussex], and brought to London in a cart, where he was quartered ; his head set on London bridge, and his quarters sent to diuers places to be set vp in the shire of Kent."—*Hol.* iii. 635/2/64.

[Cade
betook
himself in
disguise to
Somers.]
[A thousand
marks
offered for
his appre-
hension.]
[He was
found in a
garden, and
slain by
Alexander
Iden.]
The miser-
able ends of
Jacke Cade.

wer to him promised, and seing his company thus without hys knowledge sodainly depart, mistrustyng the sequele of y* matter, departed secretly, in habite disguysed, into Sussex: but all hys metamorphosis or transfiguracion little preuailed. For, after a Proclamacion made that whosoeuer could apprehende the saied Iac Cade should haue for his pain a M. markes, many sought for hym, but few espied hym, til one *Alexander Iden, esquire of Kent*, found hym in a garden, and there in hys defence manfully slewe the caitife Cade, & brought his ded body to London, whose hed was set on London bridge.

Act V. sc. i.—Buckingham and Somerset were present when Henry learnt that York was in arms for the purpose of removing Somerset from the royal counsels. Hoping to disappoint York's enmity, the King said (IV. iv. 36-40):

> I pray thee, Buckingham,[1] go and meete him,
> And aske him what's the reason of these Armes.
> Tell him Ile send Duke Edmund to the Tower;—
> And, Somerset, we will commit thee thither,
> Vntill his Army be dismist from him.

Buckingham now enters, and, in return to York's question (V. i. 16),

> Art thou a Messenger, or come of pleasure?

answers:

> A Messenger from Henry, our dread Liege,
> To know the reason of these Armes in peace; . . .

York explains:

> The cause why I haue brought this Armie hither,
> Is to remoue proud Somerset from the King,   36
> Seditious to his Grace and to the State. . . .

Buckingham replies:

> The King hath yeelded vnto thy demand: 40
> The Duke of Somerset is in the Tower. . . .

York responds:

> Then, Buckingham, I do dismisse my Powres. . . .   44
> And let my Soueraigne, vertuous Henry,   48
> Command my eldest sonne, nay, all my sonnes,
> As pledges of my Fealtie and Loue;
> Ile send them all as willing as I liue:

---

[1] In May, 1455, "the king, when first he heard of the duke of Yorks approch [to St. Albans], sent to him messengers, the duke of Buckingham, and others, to vnderstand what he meant by his comming thus in maner of warre."—*Hol.* iii. 643/1/34.

Lands, Goods, Horse, Armor, any thing I haue,   52
Is his to vse, so Somerset may die.

Though many months had elapsed since York's return from Ireland in September, 1450, Somerset's control of the state was undiminished. York therefore determined to effect a change by force, and soon after February 3, 1452,[1]

[*Hol.* iii. 637/2/5. *Halle*, 225.] he assembled a great hoast, to the number of ten thousand able men, in the marches of Wales; publishing openlie, that the cause of this his gathering of people was for the publike wealth of the realme. The king, much astonied at the matter, by aduise of his councell raised a great power, and marched forward toward the duke. But he, being thereof aduertised, turned out of that way, which by espials he vnderstood that the king held, and made streight toward London; and, hauing knowledge that he might not be suffered to passe through the citie, he crossed ouer the Thames at Kingston bridge, and so kept on towards Kent, where he knew that he had both freends & well-willers, and there on Burnt heath, a mile from Dertford, and twelue miles from London, he imbatelled, and incamped himselfe verie stronglie, inuironing his field with artillerie and trenches. The king hereof aduertised, brought his armie with all diligence vnto Blackeheath, and there pight his tents.

Whilest both these armies laie thus imbattelled, the king sent the bishop of Winchester, and Thomas Bourchier, bishop of Elie, Richard Wooduile, lord Riuers, and Richard Andrew, the keeper of his priuie seale, to the duke: both to know the cause of so great a commotion, and also to make a concord; if the requests of the duke and his companie seemed consonant to reason. The duke, hearing the message of the bishops, answered: that his comming was neither to damnifie the king in honour, nor in person, neither yet anie good man; but his intent was, to remocue from him

Whethamsted.
The duke of Yorke raiseth a power, for recouerie of his right to the crowne.

[York embattled neer Dartford, Henry at Blackheath.]

Whethamsted.
[Henry sent an embassy to ask the cause of York's appearance in arms.]

The dukes answer to the kings message.

---

[1] A letter from York, addressed to the Bailiffs, Burgesses, and Commons of Shrewsbury, and written at Ludlow Castle on February 3, 1452, contains these words: "I signify unto you that . . . I, after long sufferance and delays, [though it be] not my will or intent to displease my sovereign Lord, seeing that the said Duke [of Somerset] ever prevaileth and ruleth about the King's person, that by this means the land is likely to be destroyed, am fully concluded to proceed in all haste against him, with the help of my kinsmen and friends"; . . .—*Ellis*, I. i. 12, 13.

certeine euill disposed persons of his councell, bloud-succours of
the nobilitie, pollers of the cleargie, and oppressours of the poore
people.

Amongst these, he cheeflie named Edmund duke of Summerset,
whome if the king would commit to ward, to answer such articles
as against him in open parlement should be both proponed and
proued, he promised not onelie to dissolue his armie, but also
offered himselfe (like an obedient subiect) to come to the kings
presence, and to doo him true and faithfull seruice, according to
his loiall and bounden dutie.

[York
offered to
disband his
army if
Somerset
were com-
mitted to
ward.]

Henry apparently accepted this condition, and

[*Hol.* iii. 639/1/23. *Halle*, 226.] it was so agreed vpon by
aduise, for the auoiding of bloudshed, and pacifieng of the duke
and his people, that the duke of Summerset was committed to
ward, as some say ; or else commanded to keepe himselfe priuie in
his owne house for a time.

[Somerset
committed
to ward.]

Satisfied with the result he had obtained,

[*Hol.* iii. 639/1/46. *Halle*, 226.] the duke of Yorke, the first
of March, dissolued his armie, [and] brake vp his campe, . . .

[York's
army
dissolved.]

His embassy having been successful, Buckingham says (ll. 54, 55) :

Yorke, I commend this kinde submissïon :
We twaine will go into his Highnesse Tent.

Henry then enters and receives York's excuse, but shortly afterwards Somerset comes forward with Queen Margaret. Her responsibility for Somerset's liberation in 1455 is asserted by Fabyan (628),
from whom we learn that

[Somerset
released by
the Queen.]

all contrary the Kynges promyse, by meanys of the Quene,[1] which
than bare y⁰ cure & charge of the Lande, the Duke of somerset

---

[1] In December, 1453, Somerset was "sent to the Tower of London";
Henry being then in a state of mental imbecility. "But, when the king was
amended againe [Christmas, 1454.—*Paston*, i. 315], and resumed to him his
former gouernement, either of his owne mind, or by the queenes procurement,
the duke of Summerset was set at libertie ; by which doing great enuie and
displeasure grew."—*Hol.* iii. 642/1/19, 41. *Halle*, 232. (Comparison of *Rot.
Parl.*, v. 248/2, *Rymer*, xi. 361, 362, and *Wyrc.*, 477, shows that Somerset was
sent to the Tower in 1453, not in 1454 ; the date under which this proceeding
is recorded by *Halle* and *Hol.*) Somerset was in the Tower for more than a
year and ten weeks prior to Feb. 7, 1455.—*Rymer*, xi. 362.

was set at large, . . . and had as great rule about the Kyng as he
before dayes had ; . . .

Enraged at this treachery, York unbosoms himself (l. 87, &c.):

> How now ! is Somerset at libertie ? . . .
> False King ! why hast thou broken faith with me,
> Knowing how hardly I can brooke abuse ? . . .   92
> Heere is a hand to hold a Sceptre vp
> And with the same to acte controlling Lawes :
> Giue place ! by heauen thou shalt rule no more   104
> O're him whom heauen created for thy Ruler !

Somerset exclaims (ll. 106, 107):

> O monstrous Traitor ! I arrest thee, Yorke,
> Of Capitall Treason 'gainst the King and Crowne : . . .

The historical authority has not been far overstepped here. After
York "brake vp his campe," he

[Hol. iii. 639/1/47. Halle, 226.] came to the kings tent, where *The duke of York accuseth the duke of Somerset.* contrarie to his expectation, & against promise made by the king (as other write) he found the duke of Summerset going at large and set at libertie, whome the duke of Yorke boldlie accused of *A mutual charge between ye two dukes, Yorke and Summerset, of his treason.* treason, briberie, oppression, and manie other crimes. The duke of Summerset not onelie made answer to the dukes obiectiohs, but also accused him of high treason; affirming, that he with his fautors and complices had consulted togither, how to come by the scepter and regall crowne of this realme.

Threatened with arrest by Somerset, York turns to an attendant and says (ll. 111-113):

> Sirrah, call in my sonne[s] to be my bale :
> I know, ere they will haue me go to Ward,
> They'l pawne their swords for [1] my infranchisement.

The message quickly brings Edward and Richard Plantagenet to their father's assistance. The historical Richard was unborn at the date (March 1) [2] of this part of sc. i., Act V.; but there is warrant for Edward's intervention on York's behalf. York found himself a prisoner when his army was disbanded, and, even if his life were not imperilled, he ran some risk of a long and close detention. He was obliged to return with Henry to London, where the government held debate as to what should be done with their formidable captive. [3]

---

[1] *for*] F2. *of* F1.
[2] Richard was born on October 2, 1452.—*Wyrc.*, 477. Edward was born in April, 1442.—*Wyrc.*, 462.
[3] *Fab.*, 627. *Chron. Lond.*, 138.

[A rumour
that Edward
Earl of
March was
coming with
an army to
London.]
[*Hol.* iii. 639/2/17. *Halle*, 227.] Whilest the councell treated of sauing or dispatching of this duke of Yorke, a rumor sprang through London, that Edward earle of March, sonne and heire apparant to the said duke, with a great armie of Marchmen, was comming toward London: which tidings sore appalled the queene and the whole councell.

York therefore was set free, after taking an oath of allegiance to Henry.[1]

In the play York has a more commanding position. His part is taken by his "two braue Beares," Salisbury and Warwick, whom he calls for when Margaret's summons brings the Cliffords to Henry's aid. A sketch of York's policy in the year 1454 records his leaning toward the Nevilles:

*The duke of
Yorke seeks
the destruction
of the duke of
Summerset.*
[*Hol.* iii. 641/2/56. *Halle*, 231.] The duke of Yorke (aboue all things) first sought means how to stir vp the malice of the people against the duke of Summerset; imagining that, he being made awaie, his purpose should the sooner take effect. He also practised to bring the king into the hatred of the people, as that he should not be a man apt to the gouernment of a realme, wanting both wit and stomach sufficient to supplie such a roome. Manie of the high estates, not liking the world, and disalowing the dooings both of the king and his councell, were faine inough of some alteration. Which thing the duke well vnderstanding,
chiefelie sought the fauour of the two Neuils; both named Richard, one earle of Salisburie, the other earle of Warwike, the first being the father, and the second the sonne.

When the Nevilles enter (l. 147), old Clifford tauntingly asks York, "Are these thy Beares?" In an altercation with Clifford, Warwick exclaims (ll. 202, 203):

> Now, by my Fathers badge, old Neuils Crest,
> The rampant Beare chain'd to the ragged staffe, . . .

Warwick assumed, but did not inherit, the badge of the bear and ragged staff. He acquired a claim to it through his marriage with Anne de Beauchamp, sister of Henry de Beauchamp, Duke of Warwick (see p. 245, n. 1 above).

Act V. scc. ii., iii.—The first battle of St. Albans—fought on May

---

[1] The oath is recited in the Act of Attainder passed against York by a Parliament which met at Coventry on November 20, 1459.—*Rot. Parl.*, v. 346/2.

22, 1455 [1]—is dramatized in scenes ii. and iii., Act V. As at Dartford
in 1452, so at St. Albans in 1455, the Dukes of York and Somerset
met to try the fortune of war ; but at St. Albans their rivalry ended
with the defeat and death of Edmund Beaufort. These scenes contain
no historic matter save the bare fact that Somerset and Thomas Lord
Clifford [2] (old Clifford) are killed. The former falls by the sword of
the dramatic Richard, who thus taunts the slain man (ll. 66-69) :

> So, lye thou there ;
> For vnderneath an Ale-house' paltry signe,
> The Castle in S. Albons, Somerset
> Hath made the Wizard famous in his death.

Halle, speaking of the Lancastrian losses at St. Albans, reported a
story (233) which I quote from Holinshed :

[*Hol.* iii. 643/2/9. *Halle*, 233.] For there died vnder the   *The duke of Summerset slaine.*
signe of the castell, Edmund duke of Summerset, who (as hath
beene reported) was warned long before to auoid all castels : [3] . . .

XI. HENRY VI. PART III.

BETWEEN *The third Part of Henry the Sixt*,—a recast of *The true
Tragedie of Richard Duke of Yorke*,—and the Second part, there is a
dramatic interval sufficient for a rapid march from St. Albans to
London, after the battle at the former place. But the historic time of
the Third Part begins on October 24, 1460,—when York was declared
heir apparent,—and closes with the death of Henry VI. on May 21,
1471.

Act I. sc. i.—The Yorkists enter and boast of their victory. "Lord

---

[1] *Paston*, i. 327. A full account of the battle follows.
[2] Among those slain at St. Albans, *Stow* (661) specifies "the olde Lord
Clifforde." ("olde" first appears in the ed. of 1592, p. 651.) Lord Clifford is
not, I believe, called "old" in any other chronicle printed before the date of
this play ; and he is not thus distinguished from his son in the *Contention*. In
2 *Hen. VI.* we find "*old Clifford*" (Entry, IV. viii. 5), and "*Old Clif.*" is prefixed to several speeches in V. i. His son is "young Clifford" in the *Contention* and 2 *Hen. VI.* The son's name does not appear in a contemporary list
(*Paston*, i. 332, 333) of the chief persons present at the battle of St. Albans,
and I do not know of any book or MS. which records that he was there.
[3] "Thys sayde Edmond duke of Somerset had herde a fantastyk prophecy
that he shuld dy vndre a castelle ; wherefore in as meche as in him was, he
lete the kyng that he sholde nat come in the castelle of Wyndsore, dredyng
the seyde prophecy ; but at Seynt Albonys ther was an hostry hauyng the
sygne of a castelle, and before that hostry he was slayne."—*Chron. Rich. II.—
Hen. VI.*, 72.

Clifford [1] and Lord Stafford" charged the Yorkists' "maine Battailes Front," and were slain by "common Souldiers." Buckingham was "either slaine or wounded dangerous" by Edward ; and Warwick's brother, John Neville, afterwards Marquess Montague,[2] shows "the Earle of Wiltshires blood" (ll. 7-15). These particulars are dramatic additions to a simple record that, on the battle-field of St. Albans,

[The slain at St. Albans.]
Thomas lord Clifford, saith Whethamsted.

[Hol. iii. 643/2/12. Halle, 233.] laie Henrie, the second of that name, earle of Northumberland ; Humfrie earle of Stafford, sonne to the duke of Buckingham ; Thomas [3] lord Clifford ; . . .

[Fugitives from St. Albans.]

Humfreie, duke of Buckingham, being wounded, and Iames Butler, earle of Ormond and Wilshire, . . . seeing fortune thus against them, left the king alone, and with a number fled awaie.

Henry's flight after the battle of St. Albans (ll. 1-3) is fictitious. He remained in the town, and there accepted the excuses of York, who, on the following day, escorted him to London.[4] Parliament met at Westminster on July 9, 1455, and, after passing an Act of indemnity for York and his associates, was adjourned until November 12. On November 19, 1455, York was appointed Protector, Henry having during the adjournment again become imbecile. Early in the year 1456 the King recovered, and on February 25 York's Protectorate was cancelled.[5] On March 25, 1458, in pursuance of an award made by Henry, York, Salisbury and Warwick were formally reconciled to the sons of those nobles who had been slain at St. Albans.[6] Some months later the peace was broken by an affray from which Warwick barely escaped unharmed.[7] On July 10, 1460, the Yorkists' victory at North-ampton left Henry their prisoner. He was conveyed to London, and a

---

[1] In 2 Hen. VI., V. ii. 28, he is slain by York.

[2] On May 23, 1461, summoned to Parliament as Baron de Montague.—Doyle, ii. 512. (1460 is the year according to Dugdale, i. 307/2.) Created Marquess Montague in 1470 (Dugdale, i. 308/1).

[3] Thomas] Iohn Hol.

[4] Paston, i. 330, 331, 333.

[5] Parliament opened on July 9.—Rot. Parl., v. 278/1. Act of indemnity. —Ibid., 281, 282. Prorogation of Parliament to November 12, 1455.—Ibid., 283/1-2. In a letter written on October 28, 1455, James Gresham tells John Paston that "summe men ar a ferd that he [the King] is seek ageyn."—Paston, i. 352. By a commission dated November 11, York was authorized to hold the Parliament adjourned to the following day ; because, "propter certas justas & rationabiles causas," Henry could not be present in person.—Rot. Parl., v. 284/2. For York's appointment as Protector see Rot. Parl., v. 288/1 ; for his discharge from that office see Rot. Parl., v. 321/2.

[6] Henry's award, dated March 24, is given in Wheth., 422 sqq. The agree-ment was celebrated, on March 25, 1458, by a procession of the King, Queen, and nobility at St. Paul's.—Fab., 633.

[7] According to Chron. Rich. II.—Hen. VI, 78, this affray happened on November 9, 1458, but Fab. (633) dates it "aboute the feast of Candrlmasse," 1459. July 4, 1459, is the date assigned by the Lancastrian Parliament of Coventry to the Yorkists' first act of rebellion.—Rot. Parl., v. 349.

Parliament assembled at Westminster on October 7, 1460.[1]　Here we rejoin the course of the drama.

York is seated on the throne when Henry enters with the Lancastrian nobles.　Turning to them the King exclaims (ll. 50, 51):

> My Lords, looke where the sturdie Rebell sits,
> Euen in the Chayre of State!

York is said to have made this, or a similar, public demonstration of his right, soon after the assembly of Parliament in October, 1460.[2]

[*Hol.* iii. 655/1/73.]　Maister *Edward Hall* in his chronicle [245] maketh mention of an oration, which the duke of Yorke vttered, sitting in *the regall seat*,[3] there in the chamber of the peeres, either at this his first comming in amongst them, or else at some one time after: the which we haue thought good also to set downe; though *Iohn Whethamsted*, the abbat of saint Albons, who liued in those daies, and by all likelihood was there present at the parlement, maketh no further recitall of anie words, which the duke should vtter at that time in that his booke of records, where he intreateth of this matter.[4]　But for the oration (as maister *Hall* hath written thereof) we find as followeth:　¶ During the time (saith he) of this parlement, the duke of Yorke with a bold countenance entered into the chamber of the peeros, and sat downe in the throne roiall, vnder the cloth of estate, (which is the

[York in "the regall seat."]

Edw. Hall in Hen. 6. fol. clxxvij, &c.

---

[1] *Fab.*, 636.　*Rot. Parl.*, v. 373/1.

[2] The "writyng" which set forth York's title was read before the Peers on October 16, 1460.—*Rot. Parl.*, v. 375/1.

[3] Warwick says (I. i. 25, 26):

> "This is the Pallace of the fearefull King,
> And this *the Regall Seat:* possesse it, York"; . . .

"the regall seat" is *Hol.'s* phrase, not *Halle's.*　York, answering Warwick (l. 29), says: "hither we haue broken in by force." In October, 1460, York "went to the most principall lodging that the king had within all his palace [of Westminster], breaking vp the lockes and doores, and so lodged himselfe therein," . . .—*Hol.* iii. 655/1/63 (from *Wheth.*, 485).　*Halle* has not this passage.

[4] The passage referred to (*Wheth.*, 484) is thus translated in *Hol.* iii. 655/1/37, &c.: "At his [York's] comming to Westminster he entred the palace, and, passing foorth directlie through the great hall, staied not till he came to the chamber where the king and lords vsed to sit in the parlement time, . . . and, being there entred, stept vp vnto the throne roiall, and there, laieng his hand vpon the cloth of estate, seemed as if he meant to take possession of that which was his right, (for he held his hand so vpon that cloth a good pretie while,) and, after withdrawing his hand, turned his face towards the people, beholding their preassing togither, and marking what countenance they made."

[York set
down in the
throne, and
declared his
title.]
kings peculiar seat,) and, in the presence of the nobilitie, as well
spirituall as temporall (after a pause made), he began to declare
his title to the crowne, in this forme and order as insueth. [See
excerpts from York's speech at pp. 256-258 above.]

Northumberland and Clifford wish to "assayle *the Family of
Yorke*"[1] (l. 65), but Henry demurs :

Ah, know you not the Citie fauours them, . . .

This partiality was of service to York in (?) 1456, when Queen
Margaret perceived that

[The
Londoners
favoured
York.]
[*Hol.* iii. 645/2/66. *Halle*, 236.] she could attempt nothing
against him neere to London ;[2] because the duke was in more
estimation there, than either the king hir husband, or hir
selfe : . . .

Henry fails in an attempt to prove his title to the crown,[3] and,
alarmed by the sudden appearance of Yorkist soldiers, proposes a
compromise, which is accepted (ll. 170-175) :

Henry. My Lord of Warwick, heare me but one word :
Let me for this my life time reigne as King.
 Plant. Confirme the Crowne to me and to mine Heires,   172
And thou shalt reigne in quiet while thou liu'st.
 Henry. I am content : Richard Plantagenet,
Enioy the Kingdome after my decease.

On October 16, 1460, York's claim to the crown was, as we have
seen (p. 255 above), brought before Parliament.

*The deter-
mination of
the parlia-
ment cocern-
ing the
intailing of
[the] crowne.*
[*Hol.* iii. 657/1/69. *Halle*, 249.] After long debating of the
matter, and deliberate consultation amongest the peeres, prelats,
and commons ; vpon the vigill of All saints,[4] it was condescended :
for so much as king Henrie had beene taken as king by the space

---

[1] "Thomas Thorpe, second Baron of thexchequer, greate frende to the
house of Lancaster, and extreme enemie to *the Famylie of Yorke*."—*Halle*, 245.
 [2] After the second battle of St. Albans (p. 301 below) Margaret retired to
the north of England ; "hauing little trust in Essex, and lesse in Kent, but
least of all in London."—*Hol.* iii. 661, col. 1, l. 40. *Halle*, 253. As to the
Yorkist feeling in Kent, see p. 296 below.
 [3] Previously Henry said to York (l. 105) : "Thy [*My* F1] Father was, as
thou art, Duke of Yorke." York's father was Richard Earl of Cambridge,
younger son of Edmund of Langley. The Earl of Cambridge was executed
during the lifetime of his elder brother Edward Duke of York.
 [4] Henry accepted the Peers' arbitrament on October 25.—*Rot. Parl.*, v.
377/2. On October 31 York came to the Upper House, and there, in the
presence of Henry and the Peers, took an oath of fidelity to the King.—*Rot.
Parl.*, v. 379. See next page.

of thirtie and eight yeares and more, that he should inioy the [Henry to be King during life, and York to be his heir.]
name and title of king, and haue possession of the realme during
his naturall life.   And, if he either died, or resigned, or forfeited
the same, by breaking or going against anie point of this concord,
then the said crowne & authoritie roiall should immediatlie be
deuoluted and come to the duke of Yorke, if he then liued; or
else to the next heire of his linage.

.   Henry makes a stipulation (ll. 194-200):

> I here entayle
> The Crowne to thee and to thine Heires for euer;
> Conditionally, that heere thou take an Oath   196
> To cease this Ciuill Warre; and, whil'st I liue,
> To honor me as thy King and Soueraigne,
> And neyther by Treason nor Hostilitie
> To seeke to put me downe, and reigne thy selfe.   200

The agreement [1] by which York was declared heir apparent to the
crown contained the following provision:

[*Hol.* iii. 658/1/33.] Item, the said Richard duke of Yorke,
shall promit and bind him by his solemne oth, in maner and forme
as followeth:

"In the name of God, Amen: I, Richard duke of Yorke, promise *The oth of Richard duke of Yorke.*
"and sweare by the faith and truth that I owe to almightie God,
"that I shall neuer consent, procure, or stirre, directlie or indirectlie,
"in priuie or apert, neither (as much as in me is) shall suffer to be
"doone, consented, procured, or stirred, anie thing that may sound
"to the abridgement of the naturall life of king Henrie the sixt, or
"to the hurt or diminishing of his reigne or dignitie roiall, by
"violence, or anie other waie, against his freedome or libertie:" . . .

When all except Henry and Exeter have left the stage, Queen
Margaret enters with her son Edward Prince of Wales.   She upbraids
Henry with his cowardice, and points out its uselessness (ll. 238-241):

> Warwick is Chancelor, and the Lord of Callice;
> Sterne Falconbridge commands the Narrow Seas;
> The Duke is made Protector of the Realme;
> And yet shalt thou be safe!

Halle (233) and Holinshed (iii. 644/2/17) record that, in the
Parliament which met soon after the first battle of St. Albans,

---

[1] The articles of agreement between Henry and York (*Rot. Parl.*, v. 378, 379), containing this oath, are not in *Halle.*   They were taken by *Hol.* from *Stow* (679-683).

Warwick's father—Richard Neville, Earl of Salisbury—was appointed Chancellor, while Warwick himself received the Captaincy of Calais.[1] " Falconbridge " is perhaps a Lancastrian Vice-Admiral of later date ;

[The bastard Falconbridge

[*Halle*, 301.] one Thomas Neuel, bastard sonne to William[2] lord Fauconbridg[e], the valyant capitayne ; a man of no lesse corage then audacitie. . . . This bastard was before this tyme [1471]

[made Vice-admiral of the sea.] appoynted by the erle of Warwycke to be Vyce-admirall of the sea, and had in charge so to kepe the passage betwene Douer and Caleys, that none which either fauoured kinge Edward or his frendes should escape vntaken and vndrouned.[3]

Holinshed, on Halle's authority (249), relates the proclamation of York's third protectorship.[4]

The duke of Yorke pro-claimed heire apparent & protectour of the realme. [*Hol.* iii. 659/1/30.] And vpon the saturdaie [November 8, 1460] next insuing [All Saints' Day], Richard duke of Yorke was by sound of trumpet solemnelie proclaimed heire apparant to the crowne of England, and protectour of the realme.

Margaret tells Henry that the " Northerne Lords " will follow her colours ; and she and her son are about to go—for " our Army is ready "—when the King says (l. 259) :

> Gentle Sonne Edward, thou wilt stay with[5] me ?
> *Queene.* I, to be murther'd by his Enemies.   260
> *Prince.* When I returne with victorie from[6] the field,
> Ile see your Grace : till then, Ile follow her.

My next excerpt shows that, though York had been declared heir apparent, his position was not secure :

[Margaret came but with her son to Henry, but assembled an army.] [*Hol.* iii. 659/1/44. *Halle*, 249.] The duke of Yorke, well knowing that the queene would spurne against all this, caused both hir and hir sonne to be sent for by the king. But she, as woont rather to rule, than to be ruled, and thereto counselled by

---

[1] In the corresponding lines of *T. T.*, Warwick's appointments as Chancellor and " Lord " of Calais are not mentioned. Salisbury's Chancellorship preceded the battle of St. Albans. He received the seals on April 1 (April 2, the date given in my authority, fell on a Tuesday), 1454, and surrendered them on March 7, 1455.—*Proc. Priv. Co.*, vi. 355-359. Warwick was made Captain of Calais on August 4, 1455.—*Rot. Parl.*, v. 309/2.

[2] *William*] *Thomas* Halle.

[3] This appointment must have been made in 1470, after Warwick had broken with Edward IV.

[4] It appears from *Wyrc.* (484) that York became heir apparent and "Regens" by virtue of the same agreement. According to *Chron. Rich. II.—Hen. VI.* (106) and *Chron. Lond.* (141) York was made Protector in 1460.

[5] *with*] (Qq) F2. om. F1.

[6] *from*] (Qq) F2. *to* F1.

the dukes of Excester and Summerset, not onelie denied to come,
but also assembled a great armie; intending to take the king by
fine force out of the lords hands.

Act I. sc. ii.—When York heard that a Lancastrian army was
gathering in the North, he

[*Hol.* iii. 659/1/52. *Halle,* 250.] assigned the duke of Norffolke,
and erle of Warwike, his trustie freends, to be about the king,[1] while
he, with the earles of Salisburie and Rutland, and a conuenient
number, departed out of London the second daie of December,[2]
northward; and appointed the earle of March his eldest sonne to
follow him with all his power. The duke came to his castell of [York at Sandal Castle.]
Sandall beside Wakefield on Christmasse eeuen,[3] & there began
to make muster of his tenants and freends.

The scene opens at Sandal Castle. Richard argues (ll. 22-27) that
Henry, being an usurper, could not lawfully impose an oath upon York.
York is convinced and resolves to "be King or dye." Holinshed—in
a passage derived from Whethamstede (491)—says that many deemed
York's miserable end

[*Hol.* iii. 659/2/58.] a due punishment for breaking his oth of [The Pope set aside York's oath.]
allegiance vnto his soucreigne lord king Henrie: but others held [*A purchase of Gods curses with y⁹ popes blessing.*]
him discharged thereof, bicause he obteined a dispensation from
the pope, by such suggestion as his procurators made vnto him;
whereby the same oth was adiudged void, as that which was
receiued vnaduisedlie, to the preiudice of himselfe, and disheriting
of all his posteritie.

York then takes steps to warn his friends of his intended revolt
(ll. 40-42):

> You, Edward, shall vnto my Lord Cobham,
> With whom the Kentishmen will willingly rise:
> In them I trust; . . .

Edward Brooke, Lord Cobham, was one of York's "speciall freends"
(see p. 283 above). When—about three weeks before the battle of
Northampton—a Yorkist army, commanded by the Earls of March,
Salisbury, and Warwick,[4] was passing

---

[1] "Warwicke, Cobham, and the rest," were left by York, "Protectors of the
King."—3 *Hen. VI.,* I. ii. 56, 57.

[2] *Halle,* 250. December 9.—*Greg.,* 210. "a lytelle before Crystynmas."—
Chron. Rich. II.—Hen. VI., 107.

[3] *Halle,* 250. December 21.—*Wyrc.,* 484.

[4] They landed at Sandwich on June 26, 1460.—*Ellis,* III. i. 91 compared
with 85-88. The battle of Northampton was fought on July 10, 1460.

Whetham-
sted
1460

[*Hol.* iii. 653/2/71. *Halle*, 243.] through Kent, there came to them the lord Cobham, Iohn Gilford, William Pech, Robert Horne, and manie other gentlemen ; . . .

The Yorkist leaders were encouraged to land in Kent, because

Abr. Flem.

[*Hol.* iii. 653/2/43.] the people of that countrie and other parts were altogither bent in their fauor ; and no lesse addicted to doo

[The
Kentishmen
were
Yorkists.]

them seruice both with bodie and goods, than the Irishmen [1] seemed to be at their receiuing of the said duke of Yorke, and his yoonger sonne Edmund earle of Rutland ; whom they so highlie honoured, that they offered to liue and die in their quarrell. . . .

*Abr. Fl. ex
John
Stow),
pag. 697.*

*The men of
Kent sent to
Calis for the
earles.*

But it is to be read in a late writer, that the commons of Kent . . . sent priuilie messengers to Calis to the foresaid erles ; beseeching them in all hast possible to come to their succour. Wherevpon the said earles sent ouer into Kent the lord Fauconbridge, to know if their deeds would accord with their words : [2] so that anon the people of Kent, and the other shires adioining, resorted to the said lord Fauconbridge in great number.

A messenger enters hastily and addresses York (ll. 49-52) :

> The Queene with all the Northerne Earles and Lords
> Intend here to besiege you in your Castle :
> She is hard by with twentie thousand men ;
> And therefore fortifie your Hold, my Lord.

Hearing of York's arrival at Sandal Castle, Margaret

[*Hol.* iii. 659/1/61. *Halle*, 250.] determined to cope with him yer his succour were come.

[Margaret's
army came
before
Sandal, and
offered
battle to
York.]

Now she,[3] hauing in hir companie the prince hir sonne, the dukes of Excester and Summerset, the earle of Deuonshire, the lord Clifford, the lord Ros, and in effect all the lords of the north parts, with eighteene thousand men, or (as some write) two and twentie thousand, marched from Yorke to Wakefield, and bad base to the duke, euen before his castell gates.

York now welcomes his uncles,—Sir John and Sir Hugh Mortimer, —and adds (l. 64) :

---

[1] See p. 282, n. 1 above. "Irishmen . . . quarrell." Not in *Halle*, or in *Hol.* ed. 1.

[2] *words*] Stow. *woods*] Hol.

[3] Queen Margaret was not present at the battle of Wakefield. After the battle she came from Scotland to York.—*Wyrc.*, 485.

named duke of Yorke, sca[r]ce of the age of .xii. yeres,[1] a faire
gentleman and a maydenlike person,) perceiuyng that f[l]ight was

[secretly
conveyed
the Earl
from the
battle-field.]
more sauegard than tariyng bothe for hym and his master, secretly
conueyd therle out of the felde, by the lord Cliffordes bande,
toward the towne ; but, or he coulde entre into a house, he was by

[Clifford
followed and
overtook
them.]
the sayd lord Clifford espied, folowed, and taken, and, by reson of
his apparell, demaunded what he was. The yong gentelman, dis-

[Rutland
implored
mercy,
mayed, had not a word to speake, but kneled on his knees, implor-
yng mercy and desiryng grace, both with holding vp his handes and
making dolorous countinance, for his speache was gone for feare.

[and his
entreaties
were sup-
ported by
Aspall.]
"Saue him," sayde his Chappelein, "for he is a princes sonne, and

[Clifford said
to Rutland :
"Thy father
slew mine,
and so will I
do thee and
all thy
kin."]
"peraduenture may do you good hereafter." With that word, the
lord Clifford marked him and sayde : "by Gods blode! thy father
"slew myne, and so will I do the and all thy kyn!" and, with that
woord, stacke the erle to the hart with his dagger, and bad his
Chappeleyn bere the erles mother & brother worde what he had
done and sayde. In this acte the lord Clyfford was accompted a
tyraunt and no gentelman, for the propertie of the Lyon [2] (which is
a furious and an vnreasonable beaste) is to be cruell to them that
withstande hym, and gentle to such as prostrate or humiliate them
selfes before hym. Yet this cruel Cliffforde, & deadly bloudsupper,

[Clifford a
child-killer.]
[was] not content with this homicyde or chyldkyllyng,[3] . . .

Act I. sc. iv.—York enters and tells his defeat (ll. 1-4):

> The Army of the Queene hath got the field :
> My Vnckles both are slaine in resouing me ;
> And all my followers to the eager foe
> Turne backe, and flye, . . .

The Lancastrian victory of Wakefield was won on December 30,
1460.[4] Though York

---

[1] Edmund Earl of Rutland, York's third son, was born in May, 1443, and
was therefore more than seventeen years of age at this date.—*Wyrc.*, 462.
After the battle he fled, but was overtaken and slain by Clifford on the bridge
at Wakefield.—*Wyrc.*, 485. Rutland was "one the beste dysposyd lorde in
thys londe."—*Greg.*, 210.

[2] Rutland compares Clifford to "the pent-vp Lyon . . . insulting o're his
Prey."—3 *Hen. VI.*, I. iii. 12, &c.

[3] In 3 *Hen. VI.*, II. ii. 112, Richard calls Clifford "that cruell Child-killer."
(After " chyld-kyllyng," Clifford's unworthy treatment of York's dead body is
related. See next page.)

[4] *Rot. Parl.*, v. 466/2. *Wyrc.* (485) gives December 29, and *Chron. Rich.
II.*—*Hen. VI.* (107), December 31, as the date of the battle.

[*Hol.* iii. 659/2/10. *Halle*, 250.] fought manfullie, yet was he
within half an houre slaine and dead, and his whole armie discomfited : with him died of his trustie freends, his two bastard vncles,
sir Iohn and sir Hugh Mortimer, sir Dauie Hall, sir Hugh
Hastings, sir Thomas Neuill, William and Thomas Aparre, both
brethren ; and two thousand and eight hundred others, whereof
manie were yoong gentlemen, and heires of great parentage in the
south parts : whose kin reuenged their deaths within foure moneths
next,[1] as after shall appeare.

The duke of Yorke slaine.

One thousand hundred southrne men saith Whetham-sted.

Being unable to escape, York becomes Queen Margaret's prisoner,
and is subjected by her to indignities. Addressing Clifford and Northumberland, she says (ll. 67 ; 94, 95) :

> Come, make him stand vpon this Mole-hill here, . . .
> A Crowne for Yorke ! and, Lords, bow lowe to him !
> Hold you his hands, whilest I doe set it on.

Of this matter Holinshed gave two versions, both of which I quote.
The former is an abridgment of Halle (251) ; the latter—whence we
learn that York "was taken aliue, and in derision caused to stand vpon
a molehill"—is, in part, a translation from Whethamstede (489).
According to Halle, Clifford, not satisfied with Rutland's murder,

[*Hol.* iii. 659/2/37. *Halle*, 251.] came to the place where the
dead corpse of the duke of Yorke laie, caused his head to be
striken off, and set on it a crowne of paper,[2] fixed it on a pole, and
presented it to the queene, not lieng farre from the field, in great
despite, at which great reioising was shewed : but they laughed
then that shortlie after lamented, and were glad then of other
mens deaths that knew not their owne to be so neere at hand.
¶ Some write that the duke was taken aliue, and in derision
caused to stand vpon a molehill ; on whose head they put a garland
in steed of a crowne, which they had fashioned and made of sedges
or bulrushes ; and, hauing so crowned him with that garland, they
kneeled downe afore him (as the Iewes did vnto Christ) in scorne,
saieng to him : "Haile king without rule ! haile king without

[York's head struck off, crowned with paper, and presented to Margaret.]

Whetham-sted.
[The Lan-castrians made York stand vpon a molehill ; and, crown-ing him with bulrushes, they knelt before him and derided him.]

---

[1] At the battle of Towton.
[2] Richard afterwards reproached Margaret for crowning his father's " Warlike Brows with Paper."—*Rich. III.*, I. iii. 175. The Qq. and F. have no
stage direction against 3 *Hen. VI.*, I. iv. 95. *Wyrc.* (485) says that the dead
bodies of York and his friends were decapitated, and their heads were placed
in different parts of the city of York. The Duke's head was crowned with
paper (*carta*), in contempt. All this was done at the lords' instance.

"heritage! haile duke and prince without people or possessions!"
And at length, hauing thus scorned him with these and diuerse
other the like despitefull words, they stroke off his head, which (as
yee haue heard) they presented to the queene.

York is at last slain by the hands of Clifford and Margaret, whereupon the Queen cries (ll. 179-180):

> Off with his Head, and set it on Yorke Gates;
> So Yorke may ouer-looke the Towne of Yorke!

The following excerpt illustrates these lines:

The prisoners beheaded.

[*Hol.* iii. 659/2/65. *Halle,* 251.] After this victorie by the
queene, the earle of Salisburie and all the prisoners were sent to
Pomfret, and there beheaded; whose heads (togither with the duke
of Yorkes head) were conueied to Yorke, and there set on poles
ouer the gate of the citie, in despite of them and their linage.

Act II. sc. i.—"A March.   Enter Edward, Richard, and their
power." The brothers are talking of their father—of whose fate they
are ignorant—until Richard says (ll. 21, 22):

> See how the Morning opes her golden Gates,
> And takes her farwell of the glorious Sunne! . . .
> *Ed.* Dazle mine eyes, or doe I see three Sunnes!
> *Rich.* Three glorious Sunnes, each one a perfect Sunne;
> Not seperated with the racking Clouds,
> But seuer'd in a pale cleare-shining Skye.   28
> See, see! they ioyne, embrace, and seeme to kisse,
> As if they vow'd some League inuiolable:
> Now are they but one Lampe, one Light, one Sunne.
> In this the Heauen figures some euent.   32

Edward answers (ll. 39, 40):

> What ere it bodes, hence-forward will I beare
> Vpon my Targuet three faire shining Sunnes.

After collecting an army on the borders of Wales, Edward had
begun his march thence when

[*Hol.* iii. 660/1/14. *Halle,* 251.] newes was brought to him,
that Iasper earle of Penbroke, halfe brother to king Henrie, and
Iames Butler, earle of Ormund and Wilshire, had assembled a
great number of Welsh and Irish people to take him: he, herewith

The battell of Mortimers crosse.

quickned, retired backe and met with his enimies in a faire plaine
neere to Mortimers crosse, not far from Hereford east,[1] on Candle

---

[1] "The field of the battle of Mortimer's Cross is in the parish of Kingsland,
five miles north-west by west from Leominster, close to the fifth mile-stone of
the turn-pike road, leading from Leominster to Wigmore and Knighton," . . .
Brooke's *Visits to Fields of Battle,* 1857, p. 74.

masse daie [1] [Feb. 2, 1461] in the morning. At which time the sunne (as some write) appeared to the earle of March like three sunnes, and suddenlie ioined altogither in one. Upon which sight he tooke such courage, that he, fiercelie setting on his enimies, put them to flight: and for this cause men imagined that he gaue the sunne in his full brightnesse for his badge or cognisance.

The cogni-aūce of [the] bright sunne.

The arrival of a messenger, who brings news to Edward of York's death, is soon followed by the entry of Warwick with an army. From Warwick Edward hears of the Yorkist defeat at the second battle of St. Albans, fought on February 17, 1461. [2] As the combined forces of Edward and Warwick reached London on February 26, 1461, [3] their meeting—dramatised in this scene—must have taken place on some historic day between these dates. After Warwick's defeat at St. Albans, the Lancastrians purposed marching to London, but they retired to the north of England when

[*Hol.* iii. 661/1/33. *Halle*, 252.] true report came not onelie to the queene, but also to the citie; that the earle of March, hauing vanquished the earles of Penbroke and Wilshire, had met with the earle of Warwike (after this last battell at saint Albons) at Chipping Norton by Cotsold; and that they with both their powers were comming toward London.

[Meeting of Edward and Warwick.]

Warwick gives an account of what happened after he had received tidings of the conflict at Wakefield (ll. 111-121):

I, then in London, keeper of the King,
Muster'd my Soldiers, gathered flockes of Friends,   112
And, verie well appointed, as I thought, [4]
Marcht toward S. Albons to intercept the Queene,
Bearing the King in my behalfe along ;
For by my Scouts I was aduértiséd,   116
That she was comming with a full intent
To dash our late decree in Parliament,
Touching King Henries Oath, and your Succession.
Short Tale to make, we at S. Albons met,   120
Our Battailes ioyn'd, and both sides fiercely fought : . . .

---

[1] According to *Chron. Rich. II.—Hen. VI.* (110) the three suns were seen about 10 a.m., on February 2, 1461 ; and the battle of Mortimer's Cross was fought on the following day. In *Greg.* (211) and *Three Chronicles* (S. E. C., 77) the battle and the appearance of three suns are dated February 2.

[2] *Rot. Parl.*, v. 476/2.

[3] *Greg.*, 215. *Fab.*, 639. *Three Chronicles* (S. E. C., 77). February 27.— *Three Chronicles* (B. L. C., 172). February 28.—*Chron. Rich. II.—Hen. VI.*, 110. Edward and Warwick met at Chipping Norton, Oxfordshire.— *Wyrc.*, 488.

[4] 113. *And . . . thought*] T. T. Not in 3 Hen. VI.

But the Lancastrians prevailed ;
 So that we fled ; the King vnto the Queene (l. 137) ; . . .

Halle relates (252) that, after the battle of Wakefield, Queen
Margaret

[Margaret
marched
southward,
intending to
annul the
Yorkist
settlement
of the
crown.] still came forwarde with her Northren people, entendyng to sub-
uerte and defaict all conclusions and agrementes enacted and
assented to in the last Parliament. And so after her long iorney
she came to the town of sainct Albons ; wherof the duke of Northfolke, the erle of Warwycke, and other, (whom the duke of Yorke
[The Yorkist
lords had lefte to gouerne the kyng in his absence,) beyng aduertised,
[gathered an
army, and
marched to
St. Albans,
accompanied
by Henry.] by the assent of yͤ kyng, gathered together a great hoste, and set
forward towarde saincte Albons, hauyng the kyng in their company,
as the head and chefetayn of the warre ; and so, not myndyng to
differre the tyme any farther, vpon shrouetuesday, early in the
[Defeated by
Margaret,
they forsook
Henry and
fled.] mornyng, set vpon their enemyes. Fortune that day so fauored
the Quene, that her parte preuayled, & the duke and the erle were
discomfited, and fled, leauing the king . . .

The Yorkist soldiers might (Warwick conjectures) have been
dispirited by
                          the coldnesse of the King,   122
     Who look'd full gently on his warlike Queene, . . .

Holinshed says that, when the soldiers, who had charge of Henry,
fled from the field, the Yorkist

[*Hol.* iii. 660/2/14.] nobles that were about the king, perceiuing
how the game went, and withall saw no comfort in the king, but
[Henry had
good will
to the Lan-
castrians.] rather a good will and affection towards the contrarie part, . . .
withdrew . . . , leauing the king . . .

Now after that the noble men and other were fled, and the
king left in maner alone without anie power of men to gard his
[Henry
advised to
join the
northern
(Lancas-
trian) lords.] person, he was counselled by an esquier called Thomas Hoo, a man
well languaged, and well seene in the lawes, to send some conuenient messenger to the northerne lords, aduertising them, that
he would now gladlie come vnto them, (whome he knew to be his
verie freends, and had assembled themselues togither for his
seruice,) to the end he might remaine with them, as before he had
remained vnder the gouernement of the southerne lords. . . .

[The Lancastrian lords conveyed Henry to Clifford's tent], and

brought the queene and hir sonne prince Edward vnto his
presence, whome he ioifullie receiued, imbracing and kissing them
in most louing wise ; and yeelding hartie thanks to almightie God,
whome it had pleased thus to strengthen the forces of the
northerne men, to restore his deerelie belooued and onelie sonne
againe into his possession.

Warwick tells Edward (ll. 145-147) that George—afterwards Duke
of Clarence—

> was lately sent
> From your kinde Aunt, Dutchesse of Burgundie,
> With ayde of Souldiers to this needfull Warre.

Isabella of Portugal, a grand-daughter of John of Gaunt,[1] and
consequently a distant cousin of Edward, was Duchess of Burgundy
in 1461. A passage derived by Holinshed from Halle (253) shows
that George was not in England during the historic time of sc. i.,
Act II.

[*Hol.* iii. 661/1/45.] The duches of Yorke, seeing hir husband
and sonne slaine, and not knowing what should succeed of hir
eldest sonnes chance, sent hir two yonger sonnes, George and
Richard, ouer the sea, to the citie of Utrecht in Almaine, where
they were of Philip duke of Burgognie well receiued ; and so
remained there, till their brother Edward had got the crowne and
gouernement of the realme.

Act II. sc. ii.—Henry, at Margaret's bidding, knights Prince
Edward (l. 61). The Prince was knighted on an earlier historic date
than that which must be assigned to this scene. After the second
battle of St. Albans Queen Margaret

[*Hol.* iii. 660/2/64. *Halle*, 252.] caused the king to dub hir
sonne prince Edward, knight ; with thirtie other persons, which the
day before fought on hir side against his part.

A messenger now warns the Lancastrians that Edward and
Warwick "are at hand" (l. 72). In the preceding scene Warwick
said that the Lancastrians had gone to London, and he therefore proposed marching thither to give them battle (II. i. 174-185). But before
sc. i. ended he learnt from a messenger sent by Norfolk that

> The Queene is comming with a puissant Hoast ; . . .

---

[1] Daughter of John I., King of Portugal. Her mother Philippa was the
daughter of Blanch of Lancaster, John of Gaunt's first wife. The dramatist
may have been thinking of Edward IV.'s sister, Margaret Duchess of Burgundy,
who assisted the adventurer known as Perkin Warbeck, for the real or ostensible
reason that he was her nephew, Richard Duke of York.

[Meeting of
Henry,
Margaret,
and Prince
Edward.]

[Edward's
brothers,
George and
Richard,
were
received at
Utrecht by
the Duke of
Burgundy.]

Prince
Edward
made knight.

Scene ii. is laid at the gates of York (ll. 1-4, op. I. iv. 179). We
may suppose perhaps that Margaret, being refused an entrance into
London, turned northwards, and, on her march to York, passed near
the Duke of Norfolk's position; which was "some six miles off" the
place where Warwick met Edward (II. i. 144). Advised by Norfolk of
the Queen's change of plan, Edward and Warwick followed her, and
in scene ii. they reach York. The historic facts are that the Lancastrians withdrew to the north, after the second battle of St. Albans,
but Edward and Warwick made for London, where Edward was
elected King. Soon after his election Edward marched northwards
and won the battle of Towton, which established him on the throne.[1]

No sooner has the near approach of Edward and Warwick been
announced than Clifford breaks forth (ll. 73, 74):

> I would your Highnesse would depart the field !
> The Queene hath best successe when you are absent.[2]

Holinshed took from Halle (252) a remark that Queen Margaret was

Edw. Hall
[. 252].
[Henry's
presence
brought
defeat.]

[*Hol.* iii. 660/2/60.] fortunate in hir two battels [Wakefield
and 2nd St. Albans], but vnfortunate was the king in all his enterprises : for where his person was present, the victorie still fled
from him to the contrarie part.

The wrangle which succeeds the entry of Edward, Richard, and
Warwick admits of little illustration from historical sources. A
spirited utterance of the Prince invites Richard's comment (ll. 133, 134):

> Who euer got thee, there thy Mother stands ;
> For, well I vvot, thou hast thy Mothers tongue ;

and Edward suggests that her "Husband may be Menelaus" (l. 147).

When Prince Edward was born, Queen Margaret

[A rumour
that Prince
Edward was
not King
Henry's
son.]

[*Hol.* iii. 641/1/54. *Halle*, 230.] susteined not a little slander
and obloquie of the common people, who had an opinion that the
king was not able to get a child ; and therefore sticked not to saie,
that this was not his sonne, with manie slanderous words, greatlie
sounding to the queenes dishonour; much part perchaunce vntrulie.[3]

---

[1] *Greg.*, 214-216.

[2] While watching the battle of Towton, Henry says (3 *Hen. VI.*, II.
v. 16-18):

> "For Margaret my Queene, and Clifford too,
> Haue chid me from the Battell ; swearing both
> They prosper best of all when I am thence."

[3] *much . . . vntrulie.*] Hol. *which here nede not to be rehersed.*] Halle, 231.
"the common people" said that Prince Edward "was not the naturall sone of
Kynge Henrye, but chaungyd in the cradell."—*Fab.*, 628. Another slanderous
rumour circulated "that he that was called Prince was nat hir [? his, *i.e.*
Henry's] sone, but a bastard goten in avoutry."—*Chron. R. II.*—*Hen.
VI.*, 79.

Act II. sc. iii.—The action of this and the remaining scenes of Act
II. cover the two days' fighting which ended at Towton on March 29,
1461.[1] A preliminary skirmish at Ferrybridge, where Clifford discomfited the Yorkists, has been magnified into the serious reverse lamented
by Edward and George, when this scene opens (ll. 6-13). Richard
enters and cries to Warwick (ll. 14-16):

> Ah, Warwicke! why hast thou withdrawn thy selfe!
> Thy Brothers[2] blood the thirsty earth hath drunk,
> Broach'd with the Steely point of Cliffords Launce; . . .

Warwick responds:

> Then let the earth be drunken with our blood:
> Ile kill my Horse, because I will not flye!

In the conflict at Ferrybridge was slain

[*Hol.* iii. 664/1/60. *Halle*, 255.] the bastard of Salisburie, [A bastard brother of Warwick slain.]
brother to the earle of Warwike, a valiant yoong gentleman, and
of great audacitie.

When the earle of Warwike was informed hereof, like a man
desperat, he mounted on his backnie, and hasted puffing and
blowing to king Edward, saieng: "Sir, I praie God haue mercie of
"their soules, which in the beginning of your enterprise haue lost
"their liues! And bicause I see no succors of the world but in
"God, I remit the vengeance to him our creator and redeemer."
With that he alighted downe, and slue his horse with his sword, [The earle of Warwike slew his own horse].
saieng: "Let him flee that will, for suerlie I will tarrie with him
"that will tarrie with me": and kissed the crosse of his sword as
it were for a vow to the promise.

As Warwick and the three brothers are going forth to renew the
battle, George says (ll. 49-53):

> Yet let vs altogether to our Troopes,
> And giue them leaue to flye that will not stay;
> And call them Pillars that will stand to vs;
> And, if we thriue, promise them such rewards
> As Victors weare at the Olympian Games:[3] . . .

After the slaughter of the horse,

[*Hol.* iii. 664/1/74. *Halle*, 255.] King Edward, perceiuing the

---

[1] The date from *Rot. Parl.*, v. 477/2. The fighting began early on March
28, when Clifford took Ferrybridge from the Yorkists.—*Greg.*, 216; cp. *Halle*,
254, 255.

[2] In the corresponding lines of *T. T.*, Richard announces the death of
Warwick's father, the Earl of Salisbury. Salisbury was put to death after the
battle of Wakefield.—*Wyrc.*, 485.

[3] In *T. T.* George advises that they should "hiely promise to remunerate"
those who stood by them.

A proclama-
tion
[licensing
soldiers to
depart, but
promising
rewards to
those who
stayed.]

courage of his trustie friend the earle of Warwike, made proclamation, that all men which were afraid to fight should depart: and,
to all those that tarried the battell, he promised great rewards;
with addition, that anie souldier which voluntarilie would abide,
and afterwards, either in or before the fight should seeme to flee
or turne his backe, then he that could kill him should haue a
great reward and double wages.

Act II. sc. v.—Viewed from afar the battle appears to King Henry
(ll. 5-12)

> like a Mighty Sea
> Forc'd by the Tide to combat with the Winde; . . .
> Sometime the Flood preuailes, and than the Winde; . . .
> Yet neither Conqueror nor Conquered:[1] . . .   12

The long struggle at Towton is spoken of by Halle (256) in terms
not unlike these:

[Ebb and
flow of
battle at
Towton.]

> This deadly battayle and bloudy conflicte continued .x. houres
> in doubtful victorie, the one parte some tyme flowyng, and
> sometime ebbyng, . . .

There enter (ll. 54, 79) "a Sonne that hath kill'd his Father, . . .
and a Father that hath kill'd his Sonne;" in both cases unwittingly.
Each then recognizes his foeman's face, and laments the cruel chance of
civil war.

Halle says of Towton (256):

[Family and
social ties
broken at
Towton.]

> This conflict was in maner vnnaturall, for in it the sonne fought
> agaynst the father, the brother agaynst the brother, the nephew
> against the vncle, and the tenaunt agaynst his lord, . . .

At the close of this scene Margaret, Prince Edward, and Exeter[2]
rush in from the field where the Lancastrians have been defeated. The
Queen cries to Henry (l. 128):

> Mount you, my Lord! towards Barwicke post amaine!

When the battle of Towton was decided,

King Henrie
withdraweth
to Berwike,
& from
thence into
Scotland

[*Hol.* iii. 665/1/41. *Halle*, 256.] King Henrie, after he heard
of the irrecouerable losse of his armie, departed incontinentlie with
his wife and sonne to the towne of Berwike; and, leauing the duke

---

[1] Not in *T. T.*
[2] "the dukes of Summerset [Henry Beaufort] and Excester [Henry
Holland] fled from the field and saued themselues."—*Hol.* iii. 665/1/31
(*Halle*, 256).

of Summerset there, went into Scotland, and, comming to the king
of Scots, required of him and his councell, aid and comfort.

Act II. sc. vi.—"Enter Clifford wounded, with an arrow in his
necke,"[1] is the opening stage direction of this scene in *The True
Tragedie*. On March 28, 1461,[2] Clifford blocked the passage of the
Aire at Ferrybridge. After the proclamation made by Edward (see p.
306 above), a Yorkist force passed the Aire

[*Hol.* iii. 664/2/12. *Halle*, 255.] at Castelford, three miles
from Ferribridge, intending to haue inuironed the lord Clifford and
his companie. But they, being therof aduertised, departed in great
hast toward king Henries armie ; yet they met with some that they
looked not for, & were so trapt yer they were aware. For the lord
Clifford, either for heat or paine, putting off his gorget, suddenlie
with an arrow (as some saie, without an head) was striken into the   *The lord
Clifford
throte, and immediatlie rendred his spirit ;[3] . . .   slain.*

By order of Warwick,—who enters subsequently (l. 30) with
Edward, George, and Richard,—Clifford's head is to be fixed where the
head of Edward's father "stands" (l. 86). Edward reached York on
March 30,[4]

[*Hol.* iii. 665/1/36. *Halle*, 256.] and first he caused the heads   [The head of
of his father, the earle of Salisburie, and other his freends, to be   Edward's
                                                                        father
taken from the gates, and to be buried with their bodies : and   removed
there he caused the earle of Deuonshire, and three other, to be   from York
                                                                        gate.]
beheaded, and set their heads in the same place.

Clifford's head being provided for, Warwick says to Edward (ll. 87,
88) :

> And now to London with *Triumphant* march,
> There to be *crownèd* Englands Royall *King* : . . .

Edward assents, and thus addresses his brothers (ll. 103, 104) :

> Richard, I will create thee Duke of Gloucester,
> And George, of Clarence : . . .

In June[5] 1461 Edward

[*Hol.* iii. 665/2/9. *Halle*, 257, 258.] returned, after the maner
and fashion of a *triumphant* conquerour, with great pompe vnto

---

[1] *A lowd alarum. Enter Clifford Wounded.*] 3 *Hen. VI.*
[2] *Greg.*, 216. *Halle*, 254, 255 (*Hol.* iii. 664/1/37).
[3] On Palm Sunday (March 29), 1461.—*Inq. p. m.* 4 E. IV. No. 52 (O. B.).
[4] *Paston*, ii. 5.
[5] On June 27 Edward rode from the Tower to Westminster.—*Three
Chronicles* (*B. L. C.*), p. 174.

London; where, according to the old custome of the realme, he
called a great assemblie of persons of all degrees; and the nine &
twentith daie of Iune [1] was at Westminster with solemnitie *crowned*
and annointed *king*. . . .

[Edward crowned.]

Also, after this, he created his two yoonger brethren dukes;
that is to saie, lord George, duke of Clarence, lord Richard, duke
of Glocester; . . .

[George created Duke of Clarence, Richard, Duke of Gloucester.]

Richard is rather loth to accept this title (l. 107):

> For Glosters Dukedome is too ominous.

Holinshed derived from Halle (209) the following remark on
Humphrey Duke of Gloucester's death:

Dukes of Glocester vnfortunate.

[*Hol.* iii. 627/1/52.] Some thinke that the name and title of
Glocester hath beene vnluckie to diuerse, which for their honours
haue beene erected by creation of princes to that stile and dignitie;
as Thomas [2] Spenser, Thomas of Woodstoke, sonne to king Edward
the third, and this duke Humfreie: which three persons by miserable death finished their daies; and after them king Richard the
third also, duke of Glocester, in ciuill warre slaine.

Act III. sc. i.—After l. 12 (3 *Hen. VI.*) the stage direction in *The
True Tragedie* is: " Enter king Henrie *disguised*." [3] Henry begins a
soliloquy by saying:

> From Scotland am I stolne euen of pure loue,
> To greet mine owne Land with my wishfull sight.[4]

He is overheard by two keepers, one of whom whispers to the other
(l. 23):

> This is the quondam King; let's seize vpon him.

Henry asks the Second Keeper (l. 74):

> Where did you dwell when I was K. of England?
> *Hum.* [*Sec. Keep.*]. Heere in this Country, where we now remaine.
> *King.* I was annointed King at nine monthes old;   76
> My Father and my Grandfather were Kings,
> And you were sworne true Subiects vnto me:
> And tell me, then, haue you not broke your Oathes?

" Not long before " Henry's death,

---

[1] Edward was crowned on June 28, 1461.—*Greg.*, 218. Another contemporary chronicle (Cottonian MS., Vitellius, A. xvi.)—cited in *Paston*, ii.
18, note—gives June 28 as the date of Edward's coronation.

[2] *Thomas*] *Hugh* Hol.

[3] *Enter the King with a Prayer booke.*] 3 *Hen. VI.*

[4] *To . . . sight.*] 3 Hen. VI. *And thus disguised to greete my natiue
land.*—T. T.

[*Hol.* iii. 691/2/33. *Stow,* 706.] being demanded whie he had
so long held the crowne of England vniustlie, he replied: "My [Henry VI.'s title.]
"father was king of England, quietlie inioieng the crowne all his
"reigne; and his father, my grandaire, was also king of England;
"and I euen a child in my cradell was proclamed and crowned
"king without anie interruption; and so held it fortie yeares
"well-neere; all the states dooing homage vnto me, as to my
"antecessors."

The keepers arrest him; and, in the next scene, we find that he has
been brought to the "Pallace Gate" of King Edward, who, on receiving
this news, bids the messenger (III. ii. 120)

> See that he be conuey'd vnto the Tower : . . .

About four historical yeares after the battle of Towton,—probably
in July, 1465,[1]—Henry,

[*Hol.* iii. 667/1/26. *Halle,* 261.] whether he was past all feare;
or that hee was not well established in his wits and perfect mind;
or for that he could not long keepe himselfe secret, in *disguised*
at[t]ire boldlie entred into England.

He was no sooner entred, but he was knowne and taken of one *King Henrie taken.*
Cantlow, and brought toward the king; whom the earle of Warwike
met on the way by the kings commandement, and brought him
through London to the Tower, & there he was laid in sure hold.

Act III. sc. ii.—Edward and his brothers enter, accompanied by
Lady Grey, whose business the King thus explains to Richard (ll. 1-7):

> Brother of Gloster, at S. Albons field
> This Ladyes Husband, Sir Richard Grey, was slaine,
> His Land then seiz'd on by the Conqueror:
> Her suit is now to repossesse those Lands;
> Which wee in Iustice cannot well deny,
> Because, in Quarrell of the House of Yorke,
> The worthy Gentleman did lose his Life.

In the next historical drama (*Rich. III.*, I. iii. 127, 128), she is
reminded by Richard that, when he was a zealous servant of Edward,
she and her

> Husband Grey
> Were factious for the House of Lancaster; . . .

And he demands:

---

[1] Henry was arrested about June 29, 1465.—*Three Chron.* (B. L. C.), 180,
181. He was brought to the Tower on July 24.—*Greg.*, 232, 233.

Was not your Husband,
In Margarets Battaile, at Saint Albons, alaine ?

The truth of these taunts appears from the following excerpt.   In
1464 [1] (?)

Dame Elizabeth Greie [was widow of Sir John Grey, who was slain at the 2nd battle of St. Albans.]
[*Hol.* iii. 726/1/20.   *Halle*, 365.]   there came to make a sute
by petition to the king dame Elizabeth Greie, which was after his
queene, at that time a widow, borne of noble bloud [2] by hir mother,
duches of Bedford yer she maried the lord Wooduile, hir father.

Howbeit, this dame Elizabeth hir selfe, being in seruice with
queene Margaret, wife vnto king Henrie the sixt, was maried vnto
one Iohn Greie, an esquier, whome king Henrie made knight
vpon the field that he had on Barnet heath by saint Albons,
against king Edward.   But litle while inioied he that knighthood :
[She asked Edward to restore her jointure.]
for he was at the same field slaine. . . . this poore ladie made
humble sute vnto the king, that she might be restored vnto such
small lands as hir late husband had giuen her in iointure.

Further to illustrate this scene I quote passages describing the
circumstances and result of Lady Grey's petition to Edward.   We are
told that

[*Hol.* iii. 668/1/1.   *Halle*, 264.]   the king, being on hunting in
the forrest of Wichwood besides Stonistratford, came for his
recreation to the manor of Grafton, where the duchesse of Bedford
then soiourned, wife to sir Richard Wooduile lord Riuers ; on
The ladie Elizabeth Greie [had a suit to Edward].
whome was then attendant a daughter of hirs, called the ladie
Elizabeth Graie, widow of sir Iohn Graie knight, slaine at the last
battell of saint Albons, . . .

This widow, hauing a sute to the king for such lands as hir
husband had giuen hir in iointure, so kindled the kings affection
towards hir, that he not onelie fauoured hir sute, but more hir
person ; for she was a woman of a more formall countenance than
of excellent beautie ; and yet both of such beautie and fauour,

---

[1] After "manie a meeting" and "much wooing" (*Hol.* iii. 726/1/46),
Edward was privately married to Lady Grey on May 1, 1464.—*Greg.*, 226.
Workw., 3.
[2] In 3 *Hen. VI.*, IV. i. 69, 70, the Queen, addressing Clarence, Gloucester,
and Montagu, says :

" Doe me but right, and you must all confesse
That I was not ignoble of Descent " ; . . .

that, with hir sober demeanour, sweete looks, and comelie smiling, (neither too wanton, nor too bashfull,) besides hir pleasant toong and trim wit, she so allured and made subiect vnto him her the heart of that great prince, that, after she had denied him to be his paramour, (with so good maner, and words so well set as better could not be deuised,) he finallie resolued with himselfe to marrie hir; not asking counsell of anie man, till they might perceiue it was no bootie to aduise him to the contrarie of that his concluded purpose; . . .

[Edward fell in love with her, and, as she refused to be his paramour, he resolued to make her his wife.]

Other passages supplied fuller material for the dialogue between Edward and Lady Grey (ll. 36-98): compare especially the words "as she wist . . . be his concubine" with ll. 97, 98:

I know I am *too* meane *to be* your Queene,
And yet *too good to be* your *Concubine*.

I resume my quotations at the point where it is related that Edward heard the personal suit of Lady Grey:

[*Hol.* iii. 726/1/36. *Halle*, 365, 366.] Whome when the king beheld, and heard hir speake, as she was both faire and of a goodlie fauour, moderate of stature, well made, and verie wise: he not onelie pitied hir, but also waxed inamoured of hir. And, taking hir afterward secretlie aside, began to enter in talking more familiarlie. Whose appetite when she perceiued, she vertuouslie denied him.

[Edward took Lady Grey aside, and made illicit love to her.]

But that did she so wiselie, and with so good maner, and words so well set, that she rather kindled his desire than quenched it. And, finallie, after manie a meeting, much wooing, and many great promises, she well espied [1] the kings affection toward hir so greatlie increased, that she durst somewhat the more boldlie saie hir mind; as to him whose hart she perceiued more feruentlie set, than to fall off for a word. And, in conclusion, she shewed him plaine, that, as she wist hir selfe *too* simple *to be* his wife, so thought she hir selfe *too good to be* his *concubine*. The king, much maruelling at hir constancie, (as he that had not been woont elsewhere to be so stiffelie said naie,) so much esteemed hir continencie and chastitie, that he set hir vertue in the steed of possession and riches: and

A wise answer of a chast and continent ladie.

---

[1] *espied*] Halle. *espieng* Hol.

thus, taking counsell of his desire, determined in all possible hast
to marie her.

Now after he was thus appointed, and had betweene them
twaine insured hir; then asked he counsell of his other freends,
and that in such maner, as they might then perceiue it booted not
greatlie to say naie.

Edward's final argument (ll. 102-104)—

> Thou art a *Widow, and* thou hast some *Children;*
> And, *by Gods* Mother, *I*, being but a *Batchelor,*
> *Haue* other-some—

was, it is said, his answer to an objection of his mother (Cecily Duchess
of York) that he disparaged himself by marrying a widow instead of a
maid :

[*Hol.* iii. 726/2/68. *Halle,* 367.] That she is a *widow, and*
hath alreadie *children; by Gods* blessed ladie, *I* am a *bacheler,* and
haue some too, and so ech of vs hath a proofe that neither of vs is
like to be barren.

Act III. sc. iii.—Since the close of scene vi., Act II., Queen
Margaret and Prince Edward have repaired to France. In scene iii.,
Act III., they are welcomed by Lewis XI., from whom Margaret craves
help towards her husband's restoration. So much of this scene as
precedes Warwick's entrance (ll. 1-42) may be historically dated about
a year after the battle of Towton; [1] when Henry, being

[*Hol.* iii. 665/1/58. *Halle,* 257.] somwhat setled in the relme
of Scotland, . . . sent his wife and his sonne into France to king
Reiner hir father; trusting by his aid and succour to assemble an
armie, and once againe to recouer his right and dignitie : but he in
the meane time made his aboad in Scotland, to see what waie his
friends in England would studie for his restitution.

The queene, being in France, did obteine of the yoong French
king, then Lewes the eleuenth, that all hir husbands friends, and
those of the Lancastriall band, might safelie and suerlie haue
resort into anie part of the realme of France : prohibiting all other
of the contrarie faction anie accesse or repaire into that countrie.

In Act II., sc. vi., ll. 89, 90, Warwick proposed going to France

---

[1] On April 16, 1462, Margaret arrived in Brittany. After visiting René
at Angers, she betook herself to Lewis with the view of obtaining his assistance.
— *Wyrc.,* 493.

after Edward's coronation (June 28, 1461), for the purpose of arranging
a marriage between his new sovereign and Lady Bona. Entering now,
Warwick offers Lewis "a League of Amitie"; to be confirmed

> With Nuptiall Knot, if thou vouchsafe to graunt
> That vertuous Lady Bona, thy faire Sister,
> To Englands King in lawfull Marriage.—ll. 55-57.

Holinshed derived from Halle (263, 264) the following account of
this negotiation. In 1464, when Edward had brought England

[*Hol.* iii. 667/2/51.] into a good & quiet estate, it was thought
meet by him and those of his councell, that a marriage were prouided for him in some conuenient place; and therefore was the
earle of Warwike sent ouer into France, to demand the ladie Bona,
daughter to Lewes duke of Sauoie, and sister to the ladie Carlot,
then queene of France; which Bona was at that time in the
French court.

The earle of Warwike, comming to the French king, then lieng
at Tours, was of him honourablie receiued, and right courteouslie
interteined. His message was so well liked, and his request
thought so honourable for the aduancement of the ladie Bona, that
hir sister queene Carlot obteined both the good will of the king
hir husband, and also of hir sister the foresaid ladie: so that the
matrimonie on that side was cleerelie assented to, and the erle of
Dampmartine appointed (with others) to saile into England, for
the full finishing of the same.

The earle of Warwike sent into France about a marriage (between Edward and Bona, Lewis XI.'s sister-in-law).

Margaret warns Lewis not to ally himself with an usurper; and
Warwick, on the other hand, asserts her son to be no more a prince
than she is a queen. Whereupon Oxford remarks (ll. 81, 82):

> Then Warwicke disanulls great Iohn of Gaunt,
> Which did subdue the greatest part of Spaine; . . .

Warwick might well have exposed this misrepresentation. John of
Gaunt, Duke of Lancaster, claimed Castile in right of his second wife
Constance, elder daughter of Pedro the Cruel. The Duke, however,
failed to dethrone John I., son of Pedro's bastard brother Henry II.;
and obtained but a few transient successes by his invasion of Spanish
territory.[1]

In the *Third Part of Henry VI.* Oxford wonders how Warwick can

---

[1] Mr. Daniel suggests that popular belief may have magnified these successes; as, on April 11, 1601, Henslowe paid earnest for a play entitled "the
conqueste of spayne by John a Gant."—*Henslowe's Diary* (Old Sh. Soc.), p.
186. The facts concerning John of Gaunt's Spanish expedition might have
been ascertained from Grafton or Holinshed, but the dramatist was not bound
to regard historical authority.

speak against King Henry after "thirtie and six yeeres" of obedience
(ll. 95-97). But in *The True Tragedie* Oxford assumes that Warwick
has been obedient during Henry's "thirtie and eight" regnal years : a
term ending on August 31, 1460. Warwick was attainted by the
Lancastrian Parliament which met at Coventry on November 20, 1459 ;
and his allegiance was merely formal after the attempt made on his
life some eight or ten months previously.[1] In the interval between
the battles of Northampton and St. Albans (July 10, 1460—February
17, 1461) he acted with the supposed sanction of Henry VI., who was
then under Yorkist control.

Warwick bids Oxford "leaue Henry, and call Edward King."
Oxford indignantly replies (101-107) :

> Call him my King by whose iniurious doome
> My elder Brother, the Lord Aubrey Vere,
> Was done to death ! and more then so, my Father,
> Euen in the downe-fall of his mellow'd yeeres,   104
> When Nature brought him to the doore of Death !
> No, Warwicke, no ; while Life vpholds this Arme,
> This Arme vpholds the House of Lancaster !

In February, 1462,[2]

[John Earl of Oxford rebelled because his father and elder brother were executed.]

[*Hol.* iii. 665/2/20. *Halle*, 258.] the earle of Oxford far striken
in age, and his sonne and heire the lord Awbreie Veer, either
through malice of their enimies, or for that they had offended the
king, were both, with diuerse of their councellours, attainted, and
put to execution ; which caused Iohn earle of Oxford euer after to
rebell.[3]

Having requested Queen Margaret, Prince Edward, and Oxford to
stand aside, Lewis demands of Warwick (ll. 114, 115) :

> Is Edward your true King ! for I were loth
> To linke with him that were not lawfull chosen.

In *The True Tragedie* Lewis asks :

> Is Edward lawfull king or no ! for I were loath
> To linke with him that is not lawful heir.

---

[1] I take the date of the Coventry Parliament from *Rot. Parl.*, v. 345/1.
For the date of the attempt on Warwick's life see p. 290, n. 7, above.

[2] *Wyrc.*, 492. *Fab.*, 652.

[3] John de Vere, thirteenth Earl of Oxford (the merchant Philipson in
Anne of Geierstein), did not rebel until 1470. In 1464 he addressed to Parliament a petition wherein he called himself Edward's "true Liegeman"; and
styled Henry IV. the "late Erle of Derby," who "toke uppon hym to reigne
by Usurpation as Kyng of Englond."—*Rot. Parl.*, v. 549/1, 2. Oxford was
arrested on suspicion of treason in November, 1468, but was released.—*Fab.*,
657. About April, 1470, he followed Warwick and Clarence to France,
whence he returned in September, 1470, as an avowed supporter of Henry.
—*Fab.*, 658.

Although Edward claimed the throne as heir of Lionel Duke of
Clarence, his title was strengthened by the people's direct vote. Parliament was not sitting when, soon after the second battle of St. Albans,
Edward summoned a great council of lords spiritual and temporal, who
determined that Henry had forfeited the crown ;

[*Hol.* iii. 661/2/2. *Halle,* 253, 254.] and incontinentlie was   *The earle of March elected king [by a council of the lords spiritual and temporal].*
Edward earle of March, sonne and heire to Richard duke of Yorke,
by the lords in the said councell assembled, named, elected, and
admitted for king and gouernour of the realme.

On which daie, the people of the earles part being in their
muster in S. Iohns field, and a great number of the substantiall
citizens there assembled to behold their order, the lord Faucon-   *The lord Faucon-bridge [asked the people assembled in St. John's Field whether they would have Henry or Edward to be their King].*
bridge, who tooke the musters, wiselie anon declared to the people
the offenses and breaches of the late agreement, committed by
king Henrie the sixt; and demanded of the people, whether they
would haue him to rule and reigne anie longer ouer them? To
whome they with whole voice answered: "Naie, naie !" Then he
asked them, if they would serue, loue, honour, and obeie the erle
of March, as their onlie king and souereigne lord ? To which
question they answered: "Yea, yea !" crieng, "King Edward!"
with manie great showts & clapping of hands in assent and
gladnesse of the same.

The lords were shortlie aduertised of the louing consent which
the commons frankelie and freelie had giuen. Whervpon, inc-nti-   *[The lords informed Edward that they had chosen him to be their King, with the commons' assent.]*
nentlie, they all with a conuenient number of the most substantiall
commons repaired to the erle at Bainards castell ; making iust and
true report of their election and admission, and the louing assent
of the commons. . . .

[*Hol.* iii. 663/1/64. *Halle,* 254.] After that this prince Edward   *Anno Reg. 1.*
earle of March had taken vpon him the gouernement of this
realme of England (as before ye haue heard), the morow next
insuing, being the fourth of March, he rode to the church of
saint Paule, and there offered ; and, after *Te Deum* soong, with   *The earle of March taketh vpon him as king.*
great solemnitie he was conueied to Westminster, and there
set in the hall with the scepter roiall in his hand : whereto people
in great numbers assembled. His claime to the crowne was de-   *His title declared.*
clared to be by two maner of waies ; the first, as sonne and heire to
duke Richard his father, right inheritor to the same ; the second,

by authoritie of parlement, and forfeiture committed by king Henrie.

[The
commons
again assent
to Edward's
election.]
Wherevpon it was againe demanded of the commons, if they would
admit and take the said erle as their prince and souereigne lord;
which all with one voice cried: "Yea, yea!"

Finally Lewis assents to the proposed marriage. But this agreement is soon of no worth, for a "Poste" enters with letters from
which Lewis and Warwick learn that Edward has wedded Lady Grey.
Lewis is deeply angered, and Warwick renounces allegiance to Edward
(ll. 134-194). My next excerpt shows how Edward's breach of faith
was taken:

[Lewis was
displeased
with
Edward's
marriage.]
[Hol. iii. 668/1/50.   Halle, 265.] The French king was not
well pleased to be thus dallied with; but he shortlie (to appease
the greefe of his wife and hir sister the ladie Bona) married the
said ladie Bona to the duke of Millan.

Now when the earle of Warwike had knowledge by letters sent
to him out of England from his trustie friends, that king Edward
The earle of
Warwike
offended with
the kings
marriage.
had gotten him a new wife, he was not a little troubled in his
mind; for that he tooke it his credence thereby was greatlie
minished, and his honour much stained, namelie, in the court of
France: for that it might be iudged he came rather like an espiall,
to mooue a thing neuer minded, and to treat a marriage determined
before not to take effect. Suerlie he thought himselfe euill vsed,
that when he had brought the matter to his purposed intent and
wished conclusion, then to haue it quaile on his part; so as all
men might thinke at the least wise, that his prince made small
account of him, to send him on such a sleeuelesse errand.

All men for the most part agree, that this marriage was the
onlie cause, why the earle of Warwike conceiued an hatred against
king Edward, whome he so much before fauoured.

The discredit brought upon his embassy makes Warwick speak of
another wrong, which he had condoned (l. 188):

Did I let passe th'abuse done to my Neece!

We have seen that Edward's marriage was generally believed to
have alienated Warwick.

[Edward
tried to
violate
Warwick's
daughter or
niece.]
[Hol. iii. 668/1/73.   Halle, 265.] Other affirme other causes,
and one speciallie: for that king Edward did attempt a thing once
in the earles house, which was much against the earles honestie;

meanes of the French king to conclude a league and amitie
betweene them. And first to begin withall, for the sure foundation

of their new intreatie, Edward prince of Wales wedded Anne
second daughter[1] to the earle of Warwike, which ladie came with
hir mother into France. After which mariage, the duke [of
Clarence] and the earles tooke a solemne oth, that they should

neuer leaue the warre, till either king Henrie the sixt, or his
sonne prince Edward, were restored to the crowne : and that the
queene and the prince [*p.* 675] should depute and appoint the
duke and the earle [of Warwick] to be gouernors & conseruators
of the common wealth, till time the prince were come to estate. . . .

The French king lent both ships, men, and monie vnto queene

Margaret, and to hir partakers ; and appointed the bastard of
Burbon,[2] admerall of France, with a great nauie, to defend them
against the nauie of the duke of Burgognie ; which he laid at the
mouth of the riuer Saine, readie to incounter them, being of
greater force than both the French nauie and the English fleet.

Act IV. sc. i.—Edward and his newly-wedded Queen enter. By
his invitation Clarence, Gloucester, and Montagu tell him freely what
they think of his marriage. Montagu regrets the abandonment of an
alliance with France ; but Hastings would have England trust to God
and the "fence impregnable" of her seas,

> And with their helpes onely defend our selues ;
> In them and in our selues our safetie lyes.

Clarence sarcastically comments (ll. 47, 48) :

> For this one speech, Lord Hastings well deserues
> To haue the Heire of the Lord Hungerford.   48
>   *King.* I, what of that ? it was my will and graunt ;
> And, for this once, my Will shall stand for Law.
>   *Rich.* And yet me thinks your Grace hath not done well,
> To giue the Heire and Daughter of Lord Scales   52
> Vnto the Brother of your louing Bride ;
> Shee better would haue fitted me or Clarence :
> But in your Bride you burie Brotherhood.
>   *Clar.* Or else you would not haue bestow'd the Heire   56
> Of the Lord Bonuill on your new Wiues Sonne,
> And leaue your Brothers to goe speede elsewhere.

---

[1] In 3 *H. VI.* (III. iii. 242) and *T. T.* the marriage of Prince Edward
and Warwick's "eldest daughter" is arranged. Isabel, the elder of Warwick's
two daughters, married Clarence.

[2] "Lord Bourbon, our High Admirall."—3 *H. VI.* (III. iii. 252) and *T. T.*

Holinshed, on Halle's authority (271), relates that, in 1468,

[*Hol.* iii. 671/2/48.]   the earle of Warwike, being a far casting prince, perceiued somewhat in the duke of Clarence, whereby he iudged that he bure no great good will towards the king his brother; and therevpon, feeling his minde by such talke as he of purpose ministred, vnderstood how he was bent, and so wan him to his purpose: . . . [Warwick works on Clarence's disaffection to Edward.]

Holinshed did not copy or paraphrase the subjoined passage in Halle (271), containing Clarence's answer to Warwick's murmurs at Edward's ingratitude.

The erle had not halfe tolde his tale, but y͏ᵉ duke in a greate fury answered: "why, my lorde, thynke you to haue hym kynd to "you, that is vnkynd, yea, and vnnatural to me, beyng his awne "brother? thynke you that frendship will make hym kepe promise "where neither nature nor kynred in any wise can prouoke or "moue him to fauor his awne bloud? Thynke you that he will "exalte and promote hys cosin or alie, whiche litle careth for the "fall or confusion of hys awne line and lignage? This you knowe "well enough, that the heire of the Lorde Scales he hath maried "to his wifes brother, the heire also of the lorde Bonuile and "Haryngton he hath geuen to his wifes sonne,[1] and theire of the "lorde Hungerford he hath graunted to the lorde Hastynges:[2] "thre mariages more meter for hys twoo brethren and kynne then "for suche newe foundlynges as he hath bestowed theim on. "But, by swete saincte George, I sweare, if my brother of "Gloucester would ioyne with me, we would make hym knowe "that wee were all three one mannes sonnes, of one mother and "lignage discended, which should be more preferred and promoted "then straungers of his wifes bloud." [How can you expect kindness from him who is unkind to his own brother?] [Edward has married Lord Scales's heiress to his wife's brother, to his wife's son he has given Lord Bonville's heiress, and the heiress of Lord Hungerford has been bestowed on Hastings.] [If Gloucester would join me, we would teach Edward to prefer us rather than straungers.]

The Post—who in Act III., sc. iii., brought letters to Warwick, Lewis, and Margaret—enters and repeats to Edward their verbal answers; ending with the news (l. 117):

---

[1] "hir brother, lord Anthonie, was married to the sole heire of Thomas lord Scales: sir Thomas Graie, sonne to sir Iohn Graie, the queenes first vsband, was created marques Dorset, and married to Cicelie, heire to the lord Bonuille."—*Hol.* iii. 668/1/46. *Halle*, 264.

[2] The heiress of Lord Hungerford married Edward Lord Hastings, son of William Lord Hastings, whom Clarence sneers at (ll. 47, 48).—*Dugdale*, iii. 211/1; cp. *Doyle*, ii. 149, 150.

That yong Prince Edward marryes Warwicks Daughter.
Clarence says :

> Belike the elder ; Clarence will haue the younger.—
> Now, Brother King, farewell, and sit you fast,
> For I will hence to Warwickes other Daughter ; . . .　　　**120**
> You that loue me and Warwicke, follow me !

In the next scene Clarence joins Warwick, who welcomes him and
adds (l. 12) : "my Daughter shall be thine."
On July 11, 1469,[1] the

1469
Anno Reg. 9.
[Clarence married to Warwick's elder daughter.]

[*Hol.* iii. 671/2/70. *Halle*, 272.] duke of Clarence, being come
to Calis with the earle of Warwike, after he had sworne on the
sacrament to keepe his promise and pact made with the said earle
whole and inuiolate, he married the ladie Isabell, eldest daughter
[*p. 672*] to the earle, in our ladies church there.

The challenge—"You that loue me and Warwick, follow me"—is
succeeded by this stage direction : "Exit Clarence, and Somerset
followes." As Clarence's ally has evidently been a subject of Edward,
we may suppose that "Somerset" is Henry Beaufort, the third Duke,
who, about Christmas, 1462, abandoned the Lancastrian party and was
taken into Edward's favour.[2] Henry Beaufort soon rejoined the
Lancastrians, and was beheaded by the Yorkists on May 15, 1464,
after the battle of Hexham. But the historical peer who is called
"Somerset" in 3 *Hen. VI.*, Act V., was Henry's brother Edmund, the
fourth Duke, who was always a staunch Lancastrian. He and his
brother, however, make one dramatic "Somerset" (see p. 335 below).

Holinshed (iii. 666/1/45) or Halle (259) might have supplied the
fact that in 1463—seven years before Clarence's rebellion—Henry
Beaufort "reuolted from King Edward, and fled to King Henrie."[3]

When Clarence and Somerset have departed, Edward gives an order
to resist Warwick's invasion (ll. 130-133) :

> Pembrooke and Stafford, you in our behalfe
> Goe leuie men, and make prepare for Warre ;
> They are alreadie, or quickly will be, landed :　　　**132**
> My selfe in person will straight follow you.

At the historical date on which we may suppose this order to have
been given, there was no open hostility between Edward and Warwick.
Warwick, however, had secretly fomented a rebellion, which broke out
soon after Clarence's marriage to his daughter[4] (July 11, 1469).
Whereupon

---

[1] This date is given in *Collection of Ordinances and Regulations for the Government of the Royal Household* (Society of Antiquaries), 98.

[2] *Wyrc.*, 495. *Greg.*, 219.

[3] In these chronicles Somerset's return to the Lancastrians appears to be antedated by some six months. He deserted Edward 'a-boute Crystymmas,' 1463 (*Greg.*, 223) ; and was beheaded on May 15, 1464 (*Greg.*, 224, 225).

[4] *Warkw.*, 6. Pembroke was defeated at Edgcote, on July 26, 1469.—*Ibid.*

[Two ex-
planations of
Montague's
conduct.] intent to seeme innocent and faultlesse of his brothers dooings.
But other iudge that he did it, for that, contrarie to his promise
made to his brother, he was determined to take part with king
Edward, with whome (as it shall after appeare) he in small space
entered into grace and fanour.[1]

Act IV., sec. ii., iii.[2]—" Enter Warwicke and Oxford in England,
with French Souldiors" (sc. ii.).
Warwick is confident of success (ll. 1, 2) :

> Trust me, my Lord, all hitherto goes well ;
> The common people by numbers swarme to vs.

Though the rest of sc. ii., and parts of sc. iii., dramatize an event
which happened in the Summer of 1469, the historical date of
Warwick's remark must be August or September, 1470 ;[3] when, as
the chronicler notes :

[Soldiers
flocked to
Warwick.] [*Hol.* iii. 675/1/63. *Halle*, 282.]   It is almost not to be
beleeued, how manie thousands men of warre at the first tidings
of the earles landing resorted vnto him.

They are joined by Clarence and Somerset ; the former of whom
Warwick thus addresses (ll. 13-17) :

> And now what rests but, in Nights Couerture,
> Thy Brother being carelessely encamp'd,
> His Souldiors lurking in the Towne about,
> And but attended by a simple Guard,
> Wee may surprize and take him at our pleasure !

In sc. iii. " Warwicke, Clarence, Oxford, Somerset, and French
Souldiors," enter, " silent all " ; put to flight the royal " Guard " ;—
composed of three " Watchmen " ;—and seize Edward, who demurs at

---

[1] In the Spring of 1470, after Warwick's withdrawal to France (see p. 317
above), Edward " began seriously to immagine who were his frendes, and who
were his foes, . . . many, trustyng to the kynges pardon, submitted and yelded
theimself[s] to the Kynges clemencye. Emongest whome Ihon Marques Montacute humbly yelded hymself, and vowed to bee euer true to the kyng (as
he had doen before tyme) ; whom he [Edward] with muche humanitie and faire
wordes did receiue and intertain," . . .—*Halle*, 280. *Hol.* iii. 674/2/48.

[2] *The True Tragedie* has one scene here, opening thus : " Enter Warwike
and Oxford, with souldiers." The talk between three " Watchmen "—with
which scene iii. opens in 3 *Hen. VI.*—is not in the earlier text, nor are they
mentioned in it. The entry of Warwick and the others (sc. iii.), with " French
Souldiors, silent all," is not in T. T.

[3] On August 5 the landing of Clarence and Warwick was expected " evyrye
daye."—*Paston*, ii. 406. August was the month in which, according to John
Hooker (*Hol.* iii. 676/2/63), they landed. Other chroniclers give the following
dates : about September 8 (*Three Chronicles*, B. L. C., 183) ; September 13
(*Stow*, 701) ; " a lytelle before Michaelmesse " (*Warkw.*, 10).

being spoken of by Warwick as "the Duke." The King-maker answers
(ll. 32-34):

> When you disgrac'd me in my Embassade,
> Then I degraded you from being King,
> And come now to create you Duke of Yorke.

After Warwick's landing, in 1470,

[*Hol.* iii. 675/1/58. *Halle*, 282.] he made proclamation in the
name of king Henrie[1] the sixt, vpon high paines commanding and
charging all men able to bear armor, to prepare themselues to
fight against Edward duke of Yorke, which contrarie to right had
vsurped the crowne.

[Warwick
proclaimed
Henry VI.,
and charged
men to fight
against
Edward
Duke of
York.]

"But Henry now shall weare the English Crowne," says Warwick,
taking—according to the stage direction in 3 *Henry VI.*—the crown off
Edward's head. Warwick then provides for his late sovereign's
detention (ll. 51-53):

> My Lord of Somerset, at my request,
> See that forthwith Duke Edward be conuey'd
> Vnto my Brother, Arch-bishop of Yorke.

The Earl has still to fight "with Pembrooke and his fellowes";
though, if historic chronology be worth regarding, the army of which
Warwick speaks was not in the field when Edward was captured. On
July 26, 1469, Pembroke was defeated by the Northern rebels at
Edgcote.[2] After this battle Edward

[*Hol.* iii. 673/1/50. *Halle*, 275.] assembled his power, and
was comming toward the earle, who, being aduertised thereof, sent
to the duke of Clarence, requiring him to come and ioine with
him. The duke, being not farre off, with all speed repaired to the
earle, and so they ioined their powers togither, and vpon secret
knowledge had, that the king (bicause they were entered into
termes by waie of communication to haue a peace) tooke small
heed to himselfe, nothing doubting anie outward attempt of his
enimies.

[The armies
of Warwick
and Clarence
were bear
Edward,
who took
small heed
to himself.]

The earle of Warwike, intending not to leese such opportunitie

---

[1] "Applaud the Name of Henry with your Leader!" is the order addressed
by Warwick to the soldiers, when they are setting forth to surprise Edward
(3 *Hen. VI.*, IV. ii. 27). In 3 *Hen. VI.* this line is followed by the stage
direction: "They all cry 'Henry!'" In *T. T.* the soldiers, unbidden, shout,
"A Warwike, a Warwike!" *Halle* says (283) that when Warwick landed, in
1470, "al the tounes and al the countrey adiacent [Lincolnshire] was in a
great rore, and made fiers and sange songes; criyng, 'king Henry, kyng
Henry! a Warwycke, a Warwycke!'" [2] *Warkw.*, 6.

of aduantage, in the dead of the night, with an elect companie of men of warre, (as secretlie as was possible,) set on the kings field, killing them that kept the watch, and, yer the king was ware, (for he thought of nothing lesse than of that which then hapned,) at a place called Wolnie [? Honiley,[1] Warwickshire], foure miles from Warwike, he was taken prisoner and brought to the castell of Warwike. And, to the intent his friends should not know what was become of him, the earle caused him by secret iournies in the night to be conueied to Middleham castell in Yorkeshire; and there to be kept vnder the custodie of the archbishop of Yorke,[2] and other his freends in those parties.

King Edward taken prisoner [, conueyed to] Middleham castell [, and kept there by the Archbishop of York].

Act IV. sc. iv.—Queen Elizabeth and Rivers enter. More than a historic year has elapsed since Edward's capture, but she has just had news of this mischance. Being with child she resolues to take sanctuary (l. 31). When, in the Autumn of 1470, Edward's flight from England was known, all his

K. Edwards freends take sanctuarie.

Queene Elizabeth deliuered of a prince.

[*Hol.* iii. 677/2/5. *Halle*, 285.] trustie freends went to diuerse sanctuaries, and amongst other his wife queene Elizabeth tooke sanctuarie at Westminster, and there, in great penurie, forsaken of all hir friends, was deliuered of a faire son called Edward.

Act IV. sc. v.—Gloucester discloses to Lord Hastings and Sir William Stanley a plan for rescuing Edward (ll. 4-13):

> you know our King, my Brother,
> Is prisoner to the Bishop here, at whose hands,
> He hath good vsage and great liberty ;
> And, often but attended with weake guard,
> Comes hunting this way to disport himselfe.   8
> I haue aduértis'd him by secret meanes
> That, if about this houre he makes this way,
> Vnder the colour of his vsuall game,
> He shall heere finde his Friends with Horse and Men,   12
> To set him free from his Captiuitie.

In October, 1469, Edward recovered the liberty which he had lost soon after Edgcote field[3] (July 26, 1469). His escape is thus narrated :

[*Hol.* iii. 673/1/73. *Halle*, 275.] King Edward, being thus in

---

[1] *Gent. Mag.*, 1839, ii. 616.

[2] *the archbishop of Yorke*] Hol. *the Archebishop of Yorke hys brother*] Halle, 275.

[3] On September 29, 1469, Edward was at York, and virtually a prisoner.— *Warkw.*, 7 ; cp. *Cont. Croyl.*, 552. On October 13, 1469, he was in London, and free.—*Paston*, ii. 389. (Mr. Gairdner informed me that the privy seal dates show Edward to have been in London as early as October 13.)

captiuitie, spake euer faire to the archbishop, and to his other **[Edward had leaue to hunt.]**
keepers, so that he had leaue diuerse daies to go hunt. . . .

. . . Now, on a daie, vpon a plaine, when he was thus abrode, **Sir William Stanleie.**
there met with him sir William Stanleie, sir Thomas a Borough, **K. Edward is deliuered out of captiuitie.**
and diuers other of his friends, with such a great band of men,
that neither his keepers would, nor once durst, moue him to
returne vnto prison againe.   Some haue thought that his keepers
were corrupted with monie, or faire promises, and therfore suffred
him thus to scape out of danger.

    Edward and a Huntsman enter.   The King's question—"whether
shall we ?"—is answered by Hastings (ll. 20, 21) :

> To Lyn, my Lord,
> And ship from thence to Flanders.

    Edward's escape from the Nevilles' custody (October, 1469), and his
flight after Warwick's landing (September, 1470), are here fused into
one event.   During the historic interval Edward was formally reconciled to Warwick,[1] and in March, 1470, suppressed a revolt which the
Earl had stirred up (see p. 317 above).   On the failure of this attempt,
Warwick and Clarence withdrew to France, whence they invaded
England in September, 1470 (see p. 322 above).   Edward was unable
to oppose them,

[*Hol.* iii. 675/1/73.   *Halle*, 283.]   and therefore, being accom- **[Edward fled with Gloucester and Hastings.]**
panied with the duke of Glocester his brother, the lord Hastings
his chamberlaine, (which had maried the carles [Warwick's] sister,
and yet was euer true to the king his maister,) and the lord Scales,
brother to the queene, he departed into Lincolneshire.   And,
bicause he vnderstood that all the realme was vp against him, and
some part of the earle of Warwiks power was within halfe a daies
iournie of him, following the aduise of his counsell, with all hast
possible, he passed the Washes in great ieopardie, & comming to **King Edward cometh to Lin and taketh ship to passe ouer seas.**
Lin found there an English ship, and two hulkes of Holland,
readie (as fortune would) to make saile.

    Wherevpon he, with his brother the duke of Glocester, the lord **The lord Hastings [told his acquaintance left in England to feign them-selues]**
Scales, and diuerse other his trustie friends, entered into the ship.
The lord Hastings taried a while after, exhorting all his acquaint-
ance, that of necessitie should tarie behind, to shew themselues

---

[1] *Cont. Croyl.*, 552.

friends of King Henry} openlie as friends to king Henrie [1] for their owne safegard, but hartilie required them in secret to continue faithfull to king Edward. This persuasion declared, he entered the ship with the other, and so they departed ;[2] being in number in that one ship and *The number that passed over with King Edward.* two bulkes, about seuen or eight hundred persons, haning no furniture of apparell or other necessarie things with them, sauing apparell for warre.

Act IV. sc. vi.—This scene opens with Henry's deliverance from the Tower. I quote an account of his liberation and reassumption of kingly state. In the beginning of October,[3] 1470, Warwick

King Henrie fetched out of the Tower & restored to his kinglie gouernment. [*Hol.* iii. 677/2/40. *Halle*, 285.] rode to the Tower of London, and there deliuered king Henrie out of the ward, where he before was kept, and brought him to the kings lodging, where he was serued according to his degree.

On the fiue and twentith day of the said moneth, the duke of Clarence, accompanied with the earles of Warwike and Shrewesburie, the lord Strange, and other lords and gentlemen, some for feare, and some for loue, and some onelie to gaze at the wauering world, went to the Tower, and from thense brought king Henrie, apparelled in a long gowne of blew veluet, through London to the

---

[1] When the Mayor hesitates to open the gates of York to Edward, Hastings says (3 *Hen. VI.*, IV. vii. 28): "Open the Gates ; we are King Henries friends." In *Halle* (283) the passage which I quote in my text (*Hol.* iii. 675/2/14, &c.) runs thus : "The lord Chamberlayne taried a while after, exhortyng al his acquaintaunce, that of necessitie should tarye behinde, to shew themselfs openly as frendes to the parte aduerse for their owne sauegard," . . .

[2] On (*Warkw.*, 11) or about (*Cont. Croyl.*, 554) September 29, 1470.

[3] On October 6, according to *Stow* (702), Warwick removed Henry from the Tower to the Bishop of London's palace at St. Pauls. On October 13 Henry "went a procession crowned in Paules Church."—*Ibid. Cont. Croyl.* (554) also gives October 13 as the date of this public function, but the place is not named. *Halle* (285), *Hol.'s* authority, makes October 12 the date on which Warwick removed Henry from a ward in the Tower to the royal lodgings therein ; whence, on October 25, the King was publicly escorted to the Bishop of London's palace. *Fab.* (659) says that, on October 13, Clarence, "accompanyed with the Erlys of Warwyke, of Shrowysbury, and the lord Stanley, rode vnto the Tower, and there with all honour and reuerence set out kynge Henry, and conueyed hym to Paulys, and there lodgyd hym in the Bysshoppes Palays, & so was than admytted and taken for kynge thorugh all the lande." *Stow's* early date—probably derived from *Three Chronicles* (B. L. C.), 183—for Henry's removal from the Tower is to be preferred, because the restored King's writs for the election of coroners were dated on October 9.—*Rymer*, xi. 661.

church of saint Paule; the people on euerie side the streets
reioising and crieng, "God saue the king!" as though ech thing
had succeeded as they would haue had it: and, when he had
offered (as kings vse to doo), he was conueied to the bishops
palace, where he kept his houshold like a king.

[Henry brought through London in royal state to St. Pauls, and afterwards lodged at the Bishop's palace.]

Having resolved to lead a private life, Henry commits the government of England to Warwick and Clarence (l. 41):

I make you both Protectors of this Land, . . .

Halle (286) was Holinshed's authority for representing that Warwick

[*Hol.* iii. 678/1/43.] was made gouernour[1] of the realme, with whom as fellow was associat George duke of Clarence.

The earle of Warwike instituted gouernour of the realme.

Warwick accepts the charge, and says to Clarence (ll. 53-57):

<blockquote>
now then it is more then needfull,
Forthwith that Edward be pronounc'd a Traytor,
And all <i>his</i> Lands and <i>Goods</i> be <i>confiscate</i>.[2]
Clar. What else? and that Succession be determined.   56
Wark. I, therein Clarence shall not want his part.
</blockquote>

The following excerpt forms the source of these lines, which are not in *The True Tragedie:*

[*Hol.* iii. 677/2/71. *Halle*, 286.] When king Henrie had thus readepted and eftsoons gotten his regall power and authoritie, he called his high court of parlement, to begin the six and twentith day of Nouember, at Westminster; in the [*p.* 678] which king Edward was adiudged a traitor to the countrie, and an vsurper of the realme. *His goods* were *confiscat*[3] and forfeited. . . .

A parlement. *K. Edward adiudged an vsurper [, and his goods confiscated].*

Moreouer, . . . the crownes of the realmes of England and France were by authoritie of the same parlement intailed to king Henrie the sixt, and to his heires male; and, for default of such heires, to remaine to George duke of Clarence, & to his heires male: and, further, the said duke was inabled to be next heire to

The crowns intailed [to Henry, with remainder to Clarence].

---

[1] *Polyd. Verg.* (521) was *Halle's* authority for Clarence's association with Warwick in the government of England. "The roll of the parliament which met on the 26th November 1470 is not known to be in existence; probably it was destroyed in 1477, when all the proceedings of that parliament were annulled (*Rot. Parl.*, vi. 191)."—*Arrival*, 41. From the writer of *The Arrival of Edward IV.* (1, 8) we learn that Warwick was appointed by Henry, "Lievetenaunte of England."

[2] *be confiscate*] Malone. *confiscate* 3 Hen. VI.

[3] *al his gooddes were confiscate*] Halle, 286.

his father Richard duke of Yorke, and to take from him all his
landes and dignities, as though he had beene his eldest sonne at
the time of his death.

Henry entreats Warwick and Clarence (ll. 58-61) to rank "with
the first of all" those "chiefe affaires" needing despatch,

> That Margaret your Queene and my Sonne Edward
> Be sent for, to returne from France with speed ; . . .

They had news of the change in England, but their return was
delayed.

[When Margaret heard of the Lancastrians' success she purposed returning to England.] [*Hol.* lii. 678/1/49. *Halle*, 286, 287.] When queene Margaret
vnderstood by hir husbands letters, that the victorie was gotten
by their freends, she with hir sonne prince Edward and hir traine
entered their ships, to take their voiage into England: but the
winter was so sharpe, the weather so stormie, and the wind so
contrarie, that she was faine to take land againe, and to deferre
hir iournie till another season.[1]

Henry then says (ll. 65, 66) :

> My Lord of Somerset, what youth is that,
> Of whom you seeme to haue so tender care !
> *Somers.* My Liege, it is young Henry, Earle of Richmond.

Laying his hand on Richmond's head, Henry predicts that "this
prettie Lad"[2] is

> Likely in time to blesse a Regall Throne.
> Make much of him, my Lords, for this is hee
> Must helpe you more then you are hurt by mee.

A story which Holinshed copied from Halle (287) has here been
dramatized.   In 1471,[3]

Jasper earle of Penbroke (met Henry Tudor). [*Hol.* iii. 678/1/57.] Jasper earle of Penbroke went into Wales,
to visit his lands in Penbrokeshire, where he found lord Henrie,
sonne to his brother Edmund earle of Richmond, hauing not full
ten yeares of age ;[4] he being kept in maner like a captiue, but

---

[1] Lack of "stable wethar to passe with" detained her from March 24 till
April 13, 1471.—*Arrival*, 22.

[2] Henry VII. was "of a woonderfull beautie and faire complexion."—*Hol.*
iii. 797/1/50. *Halle*, 504. He was "so formed and decorated with all gifts
and lineaments of nature that he seemed more an angelicall creature than a
terrestriall personage."—*Hol.* iii. 757/1/53. *Halle*, 416.

[3] Pembroke seems to have gone to Wales about the time when Margaret was
awaiting a passage.—*Halle*, 287. Cp. *Arrival*, 24.

[4] Henry was born in 1457.—*Doyle*, iii. 119.

honorablie brought vp by the ladie Herbert, late wife to William
earle of Penbroke, . . .

The earle of Penbroke tooke this child, being his nephue, out
of the custodie of the ladie Herbert, and at his returne brought
the child with him to London to king Henrie the sixt; whome
when the king had a good while beheld, he said to such princes as *The coming of king Henrie the sixt, of Henrie of Richmond, after king Henrie the seuenth.*
were with him: "Lo, suerlie this is he, to whom both we and our
"aduersaries, leauing the possession of all things, shall hereafter
"giue roome and place." So this holie man shewed before the
chance that should happen, that this earle Henrie, so ordeined by
God, should in time to come (as he did indeed) haue and inioy the
kingdome and whole rule of this realme of England.

The dramatic fusion which made one event of Edward's escape from
his subjects' custody, and his flight from England, has a strange result
when "a Poste" tells Warwick (ll. 78, 79):

> That Edward is escapèd from your Brother,
> And fled (as he heares since) to Burgundie.[1]

Half of this news (l. 78) takes us back to October, 1469; the other
half (l. 79) transports us to September, 1470 (see p. 325 above).

All now go out save Somerset, Richmond, and Oxford. Somerset
fears what may befall Richmond in the conflicts which are sure to
follow Edward's escape:

> Therefore, Lord Oxford, to preuent the worst,
> Forthwith wee'le send him hence to Brittanie,
> Till stormes be past of Ciuill Enmitie.—ll. 96-98.

The battle of Tewkesbury was fought on May 4, 1471.[2] About
four months [3] after this date Jasper Tudor, Earl of Pembroke,

[*Hol.* iii. 693/1/53. *Halle*, 303.] was conueied to Tinbie, *The earle of Penbroke with his nephue the earle of Richmond*
where he got ships, and with his nephue, the lord Henrie earle of
Richmond, sailed into Britaine, where, of the duke, they were

---

[1] The order of events differs in *T. T.* and 3 *Hen. VI.* In the former we
have: Edward's escape (*F.*, IV. v.); Queen Elizabeth's withdrawal to sanctuary
(*F.*, IV. iv.); Edward's return (*F.*, IV. vii.); Henry's release and prophecy
touching Richmond (*F.*, IV. vi.). Immediately after Henry's presageful words
have been uttered, there enters "one with a letter to Warwike." From
this letter Warwick learns that Edward has landed and is marching to London
(*F.*, IV. viii.).

[2] *Arrival*, 28.

[3] Writing on September 28, 1471, Sir John Paston announces a report that
"the Erle of Penbroke is taken on to Brettayn; and men saye that the Kynge
schall have delyvere off hym hastely, and som seye that the Kynge off France
woll se hym saffe, and schall sett hym at lyberte ageyn."—*Paston*, iii. 17.
Richmond is not mentioned in the letter.

*pass over
into
Britaine.* courteouslie interteined; with assurance made, that no creature
should doo them anie wrong or iniurie within his dominions.

Act IV. sc. vii.—" Flourish. Enter Edward, Richard, Hastings,
and Souldiers." In *The True Tragedie* Edward, Richard, and Hastings
enter " with a troope of Hollanders."[1] Edward has " brought desirèd
helpe from Burgundie " (l. 6) ; and has now "arriu'd,"

> From Rauenspurre Hauen, before the Gates of Yorke, . . .

Charles the Bold, Duke of Burgundy,

1471

*He aïdeth
K. Edward
vnder hand
(with money
and ships).* [*Hol.* iii. 678/2/72. *Halle,* 290.] would not consent openlie to
aid king Edward ; but yet secretlie vnder hand by others he lent
vnto him fiftie thousand florens of the [*p.* 679] crosse of S. Andrew,
and further caused foure great ships to be appointed for him in
the hauen of de Veere, otherwise called Camphire in Zeland, which
in those daies was free for all men to come vnto, and the duke
hired for him fourteene ships of the Easterlings well appointed,
& for the more suertie tooke a bond of them to serue him trulie,
till he were landed in England, and fifteene daies after.

On March 14, 1471,[2] Edward landed at Ravenspur, and moved
towards York (*Halle,* 290, 291).

The gates have been " made fast " (l. 10). Hastings knocks "once
more, to summon " the magnates of the city. In response: " Enter,
on the Walls, the Maior of Yorke and his Brethren." A colloquy
succeeds (ll. 17-24) :

> *Maior.* My Lords, we were fore-warnèd of your comming,
> And shut the Gates for safetie of our selues ;
> For now we owe allegeance vnto Henry.
>   *Edw.* But, Master Maior, if Henry be your King,   20
> Yet Edward, at the least, is Duke of Yorke.
>   *Maior.* True, my good Lord, I know you for no lesse.
>   *Edw.* Why, and I challenge nothing but my Dukedome,
> As being well content with that alone.   24

The Mayor accepts Edward's explanation, and the gates are opened.
To illustrate this part of sc. vii., I quote Halle[3] (291, 292) :

Kyng Edward, without any wordes spoken to hym, cam peaceably nere to Yorke [on March 18,[4] 1471], of whose commynge,

---

[1] *Fab.* (660) says that Edward landed at Ravenspur "with a small company of Flemynges and other."

[2] *Arrival,* 2.

[3] The account which *Hol.* gives of Edward's campaign in 1471 was chiefly
taken from *The Arrival of Edw. IV.* This pamphlet contains a great deal
which is not in *Halle,* whom the writer of *The True Tragedie* followed.

[4] *Arrival,* 5.

when the citiezens wer certefied, without delay they armed them-
selfe, and came to defend the gates ; sendyng to hym two of the
chiefest Aldermen [1] of the citie, whych ernestly admonished hym
on their behalfe to come not one foote nerar, nor temerariouslye to
enter in to so great ieopardy; consideringe that they were fully
determined and bent to compell hym to retract with dent of
swourd. Kyng Edward . . . determined to set forward neither
with army nor with weapon, but with lowly wordes & gentel
entreatynges; requyryng moste hartely the messengers that were
sent to declare to the citizens that he came neither to demaund
the realme of England, nor the superiorities of the same, but onely
the duchie of Yorke, his olde enheritance ; the which duchie, if he
might by their meanes readept and recouer, he would neuer let
passe out of hys memorie so great a benifite, and so frendly a
gratuitie to hym exhibited. And so with fayre wordes and flatter-
ynge speche he dismissed the messengers, and with good spede he
and his folowed so quickly after that they were almost at ye gates
as soue as the Ambassadors. The citezens, heryng his good
answere, that he ment nor entended nothynge preiudiciall to kynge
Henry nor his royall authoritie, were much mitigated & cooled, &
began to commen with him from their walles, willyng him to conuey
hym self into some other place without delay, which if he did they
assured hym that he should haue neither hurte nor damage ; but
he, gently speakyng to all men, and especially to suche as were
Aldermen, (whome he called worshipfull, and by their proper
names them saluted,) after many fayre promises to them made,
exhorted & desyred them that by their fauourable frendshyp &
frendly permission he might enter into his awne towne, of the which
he had both his name and title. All the whole daye was consumed
in doutful communication & ernest interlocution. The citiezens,
partely wonne by hys fayre wordes, & partly by hope [p. 292] of
hys large promises, fell to this pact & conuencion, that, yf kyng
Edward woulde swere to entertayne his citiezens of Yorke after a
gentell sorte & fashyon, and here after to be obedient and faythfull

[Two aldermen of York were sent to tell Edward that the citizens would not admit him within their gates.]

[Edward answered that he came not to claim the realm, but his duchy of York.]

[When the aldermen returned to York, Edward followed, and assured the citizens that he meant nothing prejudicial to Henry's authority.]

[The citizens parleyed with Edward from the walls, desiring him to remove elsewhere, but he mildly persisted in asking to enter York.]

[At last they yielded to his request, on condition that he should use them well, and be loyal to Henry.]

---

[1] In 3 *Hen. VI.*, IV. vii. 34, the Mayor opens the gates of York, and enters
below with "two Aldermen." In *T. T.* he enters alone.

to all kyng Henryes commaundementes and preceptes, that then
they woulde receyue hym in to their citie, & ayde and comfort hym
with money. . . .   When kyng Edward had appeased the citizens,
and that their fury was past, he entred in to the citie, &, clerely
forgettinge his othe, he first set a garrison of souldiers in the
towne,[1] to the entent that nothyng should be moued agaynst hym
by the citezens, & after he gathered a great host, by reason of his
money.

*[But when
Edward was
admitted
into York,
he set a
garrison
there.]*

When Edward has taken the keys of York from the Mayor, a march
is heard, and Sir John Montgomery enters "with Drumme and
Souldiers."   Edward's question—"why come you in Armes"—is thus
answered by Sir John (ll. 43, 44):

> To helpe King Edward in his time of storme,
> As euery loyall Subiect ought to doe.　　　　　　　　　**44**
> 　　*Edw.* Thankes, good Mountgomerie; but we now forget
> Our Title to the Crowne, and onely clayme
> Our Dukedome till God please to send the rest.
> 　　*Mount.* Then fare you well, for I will hence again :　　**48**
> I came to serue a King and not a Duke.—
> Drummer, strike vp, and let vs march away !

Edward is soon persuaded to reassume his royal style; whereupon
Hastings cries (ll. 69, 70) :

> Sound Trumpet ! Edward shal be here proclaim'd :
> Come, fellow Souldior, make thou proclamation !
> 　　　　　　　　　　　　　　　　　*[Flourish. Sound.*
> 　　*Soul.* Edward the Fourth, by the Grace of God, King of England
> and France, and Lord of Ireland, &c.

Edward left York on March 19, and arrived at Nottingham a few
days later ;[2] where

Edw. Hall.
*[Sir Thomas
Montgomery
would serve
no man but
a king.]*

[*Hol.* iii. 680/2/49. *Halle,* 292.] there came to him sir Thomas
Burgh, & sir Thomas Montgomerie, with their aids; which caused
him at their first comming to make proclamation in his owne
name, to wit, of K. Edward the fourth : boldlie affirming to him,
that they would serue no man but a king.

Act IV. sc. viii.—King Henry, Warwick, Montague, Clarence,

---

[1] When the Mayor has yielded the keys of York, he is told that "Edward
will defend the Towne and thee."—3 *Hen. VI.,* IV. vii. 38.

[2] *Arrival,* 5, 7. Sir Thomas Montgomery is not mentioned in *Arrival* or
Warkw. According to the former (and better) authority Edward was "receyvyd
as Kynge" at Warwick, on or about April 2 ; "and so made his proclamations
from that tyme forthe wards."—*Arrival,* 9. *Warkw.* (14) agrees with *Halle* in
assigning an earlier date to Edward's proclamation as King, and in making
Nottingham the scene of that step.

Oxford, and Somerset meet to take counsel, since news has come that Edward

> With hastie Germanes, and blunt Hollanders,
> Hath pass'd in safetie through the Narrow Seas,
> And with his troupes doth march amaine to London; . . . 4

Warwick will muster up friends in Warwickshire,[1] while the other Lords do the same in different parts of England. All are to meet at Coventry (l. 32). These arrangements made, they bid Henry farewell, and depart. The scene is carried on, or a new scene begins,[2] with Henry's remark:

> Here at the Pallace [of the Bishop of London] will I rest a while.

His army is already in the field, and he speaks confidently of his subjects' affection for him. Before Exeter—whom Henry has been addressing—can reply, they hear shouts, which are immediately followed by the entrance of Edward, Richard, and Yorkist soldiers. Edward exclaims (ll. 53, 54, 58):

> Seize on the shamefac'd Henry, beare him hence,
> And once againe proclaime vs King of England! . . .
> Hence with him to the Tower; let him not speake!

Edward received a voluntary offer of submission from the Mayor, aldermen, and leading citizens of London.[3]

When, says Halle (294),

the duke of Somerset,[4] and other of kynge Henryes frendes, saw the world thus sodaynly chaunged, euery man fled, and in haste shifted for hym selfe, leuinge kyng Henry alone, as an hoste that shoulde be sacrificed, in the Bishops palace of London adioyninge to Poules churche; not knowyng of whom, nor what, counsayll to aske, as he which wyth troble and aduersitie was clerely dulled and appalled: in whych place he was [, on April 11,[5]] by kyng Edward taken, and agayne committed to prison and captiuitie.

Kyng Henry ye vi. agayne taken and committed to prison.

Act V. sc. i.—At the close of the last scene, after Henry has been led out, Edward declares the next step to be taken (IV. viii. 59, 60):

> And, Lords, towards Coventry bend we our course,
> Where peremptorie Warwicke now remaines: . . .

---

[1] He was in Warwickshire when Edward landed.—*Hol.* iii. 680/1/5; *Halle*, 291. A letter (printed in Oman's *King-maker*, 221, 222) contains a postscript written by the Earl at Warwick, on March 25, 1471.

[2] Mr. Daniel begins another scene here, and allots a separate day to it. —*T-A.*, 320.   [3] *Arrival*, 16.

[4] In April, 1471, Queen Margaret's landing was expected, and, with the design of collecting men to assist her, Somerset left London for the west of England some days before April 11, when Edward entered the city.— *Arrival*, 14, 15.   [5] *Arrival*, 17.

In this scene he appears before Coventry, and summons Warwick
to the walls.   Warwick marvels (v. i. 19, 20):

> Where slept our Scouts, or how are they seduc'd,
> That we could heare no newes of his repayre !

The dramatic action brings Edward from York to London, and
then from London to Coventry; but the latter movement is fictitious.
Edward was bound for London when—on March 29, 1471 [1]—he

[Edward
bade
Warwick
battle in a
plain before
Coventry,
but the Earl
would not
come
forth.]
[*Halle,* 293.] auaunced hys power toward Couentre, & in a
playn by the citie he pytched his felde.   And the next daye after
that he came thither, hys men were set forwarde, and marshalled
in array, & he valiantly bad the erle battayle: which mistrustyng
that he should be deceaued by the duke of Clarence (as he was in
dede) kept hym selfe close within the Walles.

Warwick rejects with bitter scorn Edward's offer of grace, which
Richard presses (ll. 21-52).   According to Halle (293), after Clarence
had been reconciled to Edward,

[After
Clarence's
secession
the three
brethren
determined
to attempt a
reconcilia-
tion with
Warwick.]
was it concluded emongest the .iii. brethren to attempt therle of
Warwicke, if by any fayr means he might be reconciled or by any
promise allured to their parte.   To whom the duke of Clarence
sent diuers of hys secrete frendes, first to excuse him of the act
that he had done, secondarely to require him to take some good
ende now, while he might, with kyng Edward.

[Clarence
excused
himself
to Warwick,
and advised
the Earl's
reconcilia-
tion with
Edward.]

[Warwick
answered
that he was
not like a
perjured
Duke, and
would never
make peace.]
When the erle had hard paciently the dukes message, lorde,
how he detested & accursed him! crienge out on him that he,
contrary to his oth, promise, & fidelitie, had shamefully turned hys
face from his confederates & alies.   But to the dukes messengers
he gaue none other answere but thys: that he had leuer be
alwayes lyke him selfe then lyke a false and a *periured* [2] duke;
and that he was fully determined neuer to leue war, tyll eyther he
had lost hys owne naturall lyfe, or vtterly extinguished & put
vnder hys foes and enemies.

The forces of Oxford, Montague, and Somerset [3] now march into

---

[1] *Arrival,* 9.

[2] When Clarence is welcomed by Edward and Richard, Warwick exclaims
(3 *Hen. VI.,* V. i. 106): "Oh passing Traytor, *periur'd* and vniust !"

[3] Somerset was not at Coventry.   He went westward before Edward
entered London (see p. 333, n. 4, above); met Queen Margaret at Cerne Abbey,
Dorset, on April 15 (*Arrival,* 28); and mustered the forces which marched to
Tewkesbury (*Ibid.*).

Coventry.   Each leader, as he enters the city, cries that he is "for
Lancaster !" (ll. 59-72).

The noblemen, who afterwards fought on Warwick's side at Barnet,
were, as Halle relates (295) :

> Henry[1] duke of Excester, Edmond Erle of Somerset,[2] Ihon erle
> of Oxenford, and Ihon Marques Montacute, whom y⁰ erle his
> brother wel knewe not to be well mynded (but sore agaynste hys
> stomacke) to take part with these lordes ; and therefore stode in a
> doubt whether he at this tyme might trust him or no ; but the
> fraternal loue betwene them washed awaye and diminished all
> suspicion [cp. 3 *Hen. VI.*, V. ii. 33-47].

(In Warwick's army were Exeter, Somerset, Oxford, and Montagu.]

[Montagu was loth to take part with the Lancastrians, but Warwick trusted him.]

As Somerset enters Coventry, Richard observes (ll. 73-75) :

> Two of thy Name, both Dukes of Somerset,
> Haue sold their Liues vnto the House of Yorke ;
> And thou shalt be the third, if this Sword hold.

The dramatist has here remembered that three historical Dukes of
Somerset lost their lives through opposing the House of York : (1)
Edmund Beaufort the elder, slain at the first battle of St. Albans ; (2)
Henry, his son, beheaded after Hexham field ;—a battle which is not
even alluded to in the play ;—and (3) Henry's brother german Edmund,
who met the same fate after the battle of Tewkesbury[3] (see p. 320
above).

Lastly, Clarence, approaching the walls of Coventry with a large
force, repudiates his oath of allegiance to Henry (ll. 89-91), and turns
to Edward and Richard, by whom he is gladly welcomed[4] (ll. 100-105).

Halle (293) relates that Warwick, before shutting himself up in
Coventry, sent hastily

> for the duke of Clarence to ioyne with hym ; which had conscribed
> & assembled together a great host about London.   But when he
> perceiued that the duke lyngered, & dyd al thinges negligently, as
> though he were in doubt of warre or peace, he then began somwhat
> to suspect that the Duke was of hys bretherne corrupted & lately
> chaunged ; . . . yet he had perfect worde that the duke of
> Clarence came forward toward hym with a great army.   Kyng
> Edward, beynge also therof enformed, raysed his campe, & made
> toward y⁰ duke. . . .   When eche host was in sight of other,

[Warwick sent for Clarence, who had assembled a great host.]

[Clarence's delay caused Warwick some misgivings.]

[Clarence approached with an army, and Edward marched towards him.]

---

[1] *Henry*] *Ihon* Halle.

[2] *Hol.*—who copied *Arrival,* 12—does not mention Somerset's presence.

[3] "Three Dukes of Somerset" are counted by Edward among his slain
foemen (3 *Hen. VI.*, V. vii. 5).

[4] Clarence met his brothers near Warwick, in April ; not later than the
4th of that month.—*Arrival,* 11-13.

[When the armies were in sight, Gloucester mediated between Edward and Clarence,
Rychard duke of Gloucester, brother to them both, as though he had bene made arbitrer betwene them, fyrst rode to the duke, and with hym commoned very secretly: from hym he came to kyng Edward, and with lyke secretnes so vsed hym that in conclusion no vnnaturall warre, but a fraternall amitie, was concluded and pro-

[and at last the two brothers meet and embraced.]
claymed; and then, leuyng all armye and weapon a syde, bothe the bretherne louyngly embraced, and familierly commoned together.

Addressing Warwick, Clarence gives a reason for abandoning Henry (ll. 83-85):

> I will not ruinate my Fathers House,
> Who gaue his blood to lyme the stones together,   84
> *And set vp Lancaster.* Why, trowest thou, Warwicke,
> That Clarence is so harsh, so blunt, *vnnaturall,*
> To bend the fatall Instruments of Warre
> *Against* his Brother and his lawfull King?   88

This view had been urged on Clarence when he was a refugee in France, about a year before his desertion of Warwick. A "damosell," who professed to have been sent from England, by Edward, for the purpose of making terms with the Earl of Warwick,

[Clarence was per-swaded that it was un-natural to take part against his own house, and set up the house of Lancaster.]
[*Halle,* 281.] perswaded the duke of Clarence that it was neither *naturall* nor honorable to hym, either to condiscende, or take parte, *against* the house of Yorke, (of which he was lineally descended,) *and to set vp* again the house of *Lancaster,* . . .

After welcoming Clarence, Edward challenges Warwick to "leaue the Towne and fight." Warwick answers (ll. 110, 111):

> I will away towards Barnet presently,
> And bid thee Battaile, Edward, if thou dar'st.
>   *Edw.* Yes, Warwicke, Edward dares, and leads the way.—   112
> Lords, to the field! Saint George and Victorie!
>   [*Exeunt. March. Warwicke and his companie followes.*

On April 5, 1471, Edward again offered Warwick battle before Coventry.[1] As the Earl would not stir,

[Edward marched towards London.]
[*Halle,* 293-295.] kyng Edward, thus beyng [, by Clarence's alliance,] furnished of a strong hoste, went without any maner [*p.* 294] of diffidence or mistrust toward London. . . . Therle of Warwycke, pondering that the gain of the whole battail stode in makyng hast, with al diligence followed his enemies; hopynge (that

---

[1] *Arrival,* 13. Edward entered London on April 11.—*Arrival,* 17. On April 13 he encamped on Barnet field.—*Arrival,* 18

yf they wer neuer let so lytle with any stop or tariyng by y⁰ waye) [Warwick followed Edward, and, failing to overtake him,
to fight with them before thei should come to London [p. 295]. . . .
[After resting awhile at St. Albans] he remoued to a village in the
meane waye betwene London & saynct Albones, called Barnet, [halted at Barnet.]
beyng tenne myle distaunt from bothe the tounes.

Act V. sc. ii.—"Alarum and Excursions. Enter Edward bringing
forth Warwicke wounded." *The True Tragedie* has: "Alarmes, and
then enter Warwike wounded." From the former stage direction,
and the succeeding lines (1-4),—which are not in *The True Tragedie,*—
one may infer that Warwick has been mortally wounded by Edward.
For Warwick's death at Edward's hand I find no authority. Halle
tells us (296) that, towards the close of the battle of Barnet,—fought
on Easter Day, April 14, 1471,[1]—Warwick,

[*Halle,* 296.] beyng a manne of a mynde inuincible, rushed
into the middest of his enemies, whereas he (auentured so farre
from his awne compaignie, to kill & sley his aduersaries, that he [Warwick died fighting in the midst of his enemies.]
could not be rescued) was, in the middes of his enemies, striken
doune & slain. The marques Montacute, thynkynge to succor his [Montague was slain in attempting to rescue him.]
brother whiche he sawe was in greate ieoperdy, & yet in hope
to obtein the victory, was likewise ouerthrowen and slain.

Edward leaves Warwick to die. Soon Oxford and Somerset enter.
They have just had news that (l. 31)

The Queene from France hath brought a puissant power;

and, as the scene ends, Oxford cries:

Away, away, to meet the Queenes great power!

Queen Margaret, having heard of Edward's return,

[*Halle,* 297.] gathered together no small compaignie of hardy [Margaret's passage was delayed for lack of a favorable wind.]
and valiaunt souldiours, determined with all haste and diligence,
with Prince Edwarde her sonne, to saile into Englande; but yet
once again (suche was her destinie) beyng letted for lacke of pros- [She came too late, when at last she reached England.]
perous wynde, & encombered with to[o] muche rigorous tempeste,
"a daie after the faire," (as the common prouerbe saieth,) landed
at the Port of Weymouth, in Dorsetshire [, on April 14, 1471].[2]

Act V. sc. iii.—The historical date of this scene must be April 14,
1471, if we look solely at the fact that the battle of Barnet is just over.

---

[1] *Arrival,* 19.
[2] *Arrival,* 22. *Warkw.,* 17. The battle of Barnet was fought on the same
day.—*Arrival,* 19.

But Edward already knows that Queen Margaret's troops "doe hold their course toward Tewksbury " (l. 19); and he resolves to go thither "straight." We learn from *The Arrivall of King Edward IV.* that news of her landing reached him on April 16; and on April 24 he marched from Windsor in search of her army. He did not ascertain the Lancastrians' purpose to give him battle at Tewkesbury until May 3, though before leaving Windsor he was satisfied that they were not coming directly towards London, but were keeping to the north-west, in hope of gathering reinforcements from Wales and Lancashire.[1]

Act V. sc. iv.—The dramatist has disregarded his authority in making Queen Margaret address her confederates with such assurance of future triumph[2] (ll. 1-38); for Halle says (297) that, when news of Barnet field came,

[Warwick's
defeat over-
whelmed
Margaret.]
she, like a woman al dismaied for feare, fell to the ground, her harte was perced with scrowe, her speache was in maner passed, all her spirites were tormented with Malencoly.

Margaret would have deferred a battle, but she yielded to Somerset's advice that war should be renewed without delay (*Halle,* 298, 299).

Act V. sc. v.—In *The True Tragedie* this scene opens with the following stage direction: " Alarmes to the battell, Yorke flies, then the chambers be discharged. Then enter the King, Cla. & Glo. & the rest, & make a great shout, and crie, for Yorke, for Yorke, and then the Queene is taken, & the prince, & Oxf. & Som. and then sound and enter all againe." These instructions—which I print with the punctuation unaltered—show that a retreat and victorious re-entry of the Yorkists were exhibited on the stage. At Tewkesbury field, Richard—as we learn from Halle (300)—led the Yorkist vaward against that part of the entrenched Lancastrian camp which was defended by Somerset. Failing to carry the position by assault, Richard, "for a very politique purpose, wyth all hys men reculed backe." Somerset followed the Yorkists who, turning, discomfited their pursuers, and, supported by Edward's division, entered the camp. The Lancastrians who remained there were soon routed. "The Queene was founde in her Charriot almost deade for sorowe."[3] The Prince was "apprehended," and Somerset was " by force " taken prisoner.

---

[1] These particulars, with the dates of April 16, 24, and May 3, are given in *Arrival,* 22, 24, 25, and 28.

[2] Her speech just before the armies join battle (3 *Hen. VI.,* V. iv. 77-81) has a slight general resemblance to Warwick's oration when he was on the point of engaging Edward's troops at Barnet. The Earl told his men that " they fight not onely for the libertie of the countreye agaynste a tiraunte, which wrongfullye and againste all right had inuaded and subdued thys realme, but they fyght in the querel of a true and vndubitate king against a cruell man and a torcious vsurper ; in the cause of a Godly and a pitiful Prince against an abhominable manqueller and bloudy boutcher ; . . . In which cause beyng so good, so godly, & so iust, God of very iustice must nedes be their shilde and defence."—*Halle,* 295.

[3] On May 7 Edward heard that she had been found in "a powre religiows place " near Worcester, where she stayed during the battle.—*Arrival,* 31.

The victory won, Edward immediately disposes of two Lancastrian leaders (ll. 2, 3):

> Away with Oxford to Hames Castle straight!
> For Somerset, off with his guiltie Head!

Oxford shared the Lancastrians' defeat at Barnet, but he was not with them when they were vanquished at Tewkesbury, on May 4, 1471. It was not until February 15, 1474,[1] that

[*Hol.* iii. 693/2/20. *Halle*, 304.] Iohn earle of Oxford, which after Barnet field both manfullie and valiantlie kept saint Michaels mount in Cornewall, either for lacke of aid, or persuaded by his friends, gaue vp the mount, and yeelded himselfe to king Edward (his life onelie saued), which to him was granted. But, to be out of all doutfull imaginations, king Edward also sent him ouer the sea to the castell of Hammes, where, by the space of twelue yeeres, hee was in strong prison shut vp and warilie looked to.

The earls of Oxford [surrendered St. Michael's Mount, and was imprisoned in the castle of Hammes]. 1473 [1474]

On May 6, 1471,[2]

[*Halle*, 301.] was Edmond duke of Somerset . . . behedded in the market-place at Tewkesbury.

[Somerset beheaded.]

As Oxford and Somerset are led out, Edward asks (ll. 9, 10):

> Is Proclamation made, That who finds Edward
> Shall haue a high Reward, and he his Life?

Scarcely have these words been uttered when Prince Edward is seen approaching. The King thus addresses his rival (ll. 14-16):

> Edward, what satisfaction canst thou make
> For bearing Armes, for stirring vp my Subiects,
> And all the trouble thou hast turn'd me to?   16
>   *Prince.* Speake like a Subiect, prowd ambitious Yorke!
> Suppose that I am now my Fathers Mouth;
> Resigne thy Chayre, and, where I stand, kneele thou,
> Whil'st I propose the selfe-same words to thee,   20
> Which, Traytor, thou would'st haue me answer to!

---

[1] Escaping from the rout at Barnet, John Earl of Oxford went first to Scotland and afterwards to France.—*Warkw.*, 16, 26; *Arrival*, 20. On April 10, 1473, he was at Dieppe, purposing, as was supposed, to sail for Scotland.—*Paston*, iii. 88. He landed at St. Osyths in Essex on May 28, 1473, but soon reëmbarked.—*Paston*, iii. 92. On September 30, 1473, he took possession of St. Michael's Mount in Cornwall, which he defended against the royal forces until February 15, 1474, when the defection of his garrison obliged him to surrender. He was then brought as a prisoner to Edward, who immediately sent him to Hammes Castle (Calais).—*Warkw.*, 26, 27; *Polyd. Verg.*, 532/44. William of Worcester (*Itinerarium*, 123) and *Warkw.* differ as to the length of the siege, and the former gives Feb. 19 as the date of surrender.

[2] *Arrival*, 31. *Warkw.*, 19.

The Prince repeats his claim to sovereignty (ll. 33-37), and is forthwith murdered:

> *Edw.* Take that, thou [1] likenesse of this Rayler here!
> [*Stabs him.*
>
> *Rich.* Sprawl'st thou! take that, to end thy agonie!
> [*Rich. stabs him.*
>
> *Clar.* And ther's for twitting me with periurie!   40
> [*Clar. stabs him.*

The account of Prince Edward's death here dramatized is given by Holinshed, whose authority was Halle (301).

[*Hol.* iii. 688/2/7.] After the field was ended, proclamation was made, that whosoeuer could bring foorth prince Edward aliue or dead, should haue an annuitie of a hundred pounds during his life, and the princes life to be saued, if he were brought foorth aliue. Sir Richard Crofts [the Prince's captor], nothing mistrusting the kings promise, brought foorth his prisoner prince Edward, being a faire and well proportioned yoong gentleman; [2] whom when king Edward had well aduised, he demanded of him, how he durst so presumptuouslie enter into his realme with banner displaied?

Sir Richard Crofts deliuereth the prince in hope that his life should haue beene saued.

Wherevnto the prince boldlie answered, saieng: "To recouer "my fathers kingdome & heritage, from his father and grandfather "to him, and from him after him to me, lineallie descended." At which words king Edward said nothing, but with his hand thrust him from him, or (as some saie) stroke him with his gantlet; whom, incontinentlie, George duke of Clarence, Richard duke of Glocester, Thomas Greie marquesse Dorcet, and William lord Hastings, that stood by, suddenlie murthered: . . .

Prince Edward murthered.

Act V. sc. vi.—Having helped to slay Prince Edward, Richard posts off "to London on a serious matter" (V. v. 47). Scene vi. is laid at the Tower. Richard enters with Henry, whom, after some conference, he stabs to death (l. 57) with a sword (l. 63). Henry died on May 21 or 22, 1471.[3] He was

---

[1] 38. *thou*] Whole Contention (Q3). *the* 3 Hen. VI.

[2] *being a . . . gentleman*] Hol. *beynge a* good Femenine & a wel feautured *younge gentleman* Halle, 301. Edward apostrophizes him as "thou likenesse of this Rayler here" [Queen Margaret].

[3] *Warkw.* (21) says: "And the same nyghte that Kynge Edwarde came to Londone, Kynge Herry, beynge inwarde [? in ward] in presone in the Toure of Londone, was putt to dethe, the xxj. day of Maij, on a tywesday nyght, betwyx xj. and xij. of the cloke, beynge thenne at the Toure the Duke of Gloucetre, brothere to Kynge Edwarde, and many other"; . . . From a chronicle (MS. Arundel, Mus. Brit. 28, fol. 25, v°, cited in *Warkw.*, xiii.) we

[*Hol.* iii. 690/2/61.] in the Tower spoiled of his life, by Richard duke of Glocester, (as the constant fame ran,) who (to the intent that his brother king Edward might reigne in more suertie) murthered the said king Henrie with a dagger.

Illus. Halle [302]. *King Henrie the sixt murthered in the Tower.*

Edward is ignorant of Richard's sudden resolve to despatch Henry (l. 83). More—whose narrative I here give in Halle's words (343) —asserts that Richard

slewe in the towre kynge Henry the sixt; saiynge: "now is there "no heire male of kynge Edwarde the thirde but wee of the house "of Yorke!"[1] whyche murder was doen without kyng Edward his assent; which would haue appointed that bocherly office to [*too Halle*] some other rather then to hys owne brother.

Kyng Henry the .vi. slayn in the towar by Richard the iij.

Act V. sc. vii.—We may suppose this scene to be laid in the Palace at Westminster. There are present King Edward, Queen Elizabeth, Clarence, Gloucester, Hastings, and the infant Prince Edward, of whom a nurse has charge. Clarence demands (ll. 37-40):

> What will your Grace haue done with Margaret!
> Regnard, her Father, to the King of France
> Hath pawn'd the Sicils and Ierusalem,
> And hither haue they sent it for her ransome.   40
>   *King.* Away with her, and waft her hence to France!

An interval of more than four historic years elapsed between the dates of Margaret's ransom and the battle of Tewkesbury; though, according to dramatic time, the latter event is very recent. In 1475[2] the agreement was made by which

learn that Henry "*decessit*" on May 21. According to *Three Chronicles* (B. L. C.), 184, he died "*felicitæ*" on May 22. A fourth chronicle (MS. Laud, 674 (B. 23) fol. 11, r°, cited in *Warkw.*, xi.) records that Henry "*moriebatur*" on May 22. A fifth chronicle (MS. Bib. Reg. 2 B. xv. fol. 1, r°, cited in *Warkw.*, xi.) fixes the time of his death between ("inter") the 21st and 22nd of May. Finally, the Yorkist writer of *Arrival* (38) asserts that Henry died on May 23, "of pure displeasure, and melencoly."

[1] Glo. *The Tower, man, the Tower; Its root them out.*] T. T. Rich. [*The*] *Tower, the Tower.* 3 Hen. VI., V. v. 50. The words "now is . . . of Yorke" are in *Halle*, but not in *Hol*.

[2] The articles of this agreement—"aduisez par et entre Le Roy de France dune part Et messires Iehan seigneur de Hauart et Thomas seigneur de mongomery chevalers conseillers du Roy dangleterre Touchant le bail et deliurance de dame marguerit fille du Roy de Secille"—are dated October 2, 1475. Her ransom was 50,000 crowns of gold. The original articles, signed by Lewis's own hand, are preserved in the British Museum. An order, dated November 13, 1475, and addressed to Sir Thomas Montgomery, authorizes him to receive Margaret from Thomas Thwaytes and deliver her to Lewis or to such persons as shall be chosen by Lewis and Montgomery in Edward's name. —*Rymer*, xii. 22. Her ransom was to be paid within five years (*Rymer*, xii. 51); and, on March 21, 1480, Edward gave Lewis a full acquittance.—*Rymer*,

[René paid
Margaret's
ransom by
selling Lewis
XI. the two
Sicilies and
Provence.]

[*Halle*, 301.] King Reiner her father raunsomed her with money, which summe (as the French writers afferme) he borowed of kyng Lewes y⁰ xi. ; and, because he was not of power nor abilitie to repaye so greate a dutie, he solde to the French kyng & his heyres the kingdomes of Naples and both the Sciciles, wyth the countie of Prouince, . . .

There is another unhistorical personage in this play besides the dual "Somerset." "Westmerland" is a hot Lancastrian in 3 *Hen. VI.*, I. i., but the historical second Earl—son of Ralph Neville, the first Earl —kept aloof from civil strife.[1]

"Exeter," in the First and Third Parts of *Henry VI.*, is, I suspect, the same person ; though the historical Thomas Beaufort, Duke of Exeter, died in 1426, and, during the war of the Roses, this title was borne by Henry Holland. Holland was a staunch Lancastrian ; but the dramatic "Exeter" accepted the arrangement which reduced Henry VI. to the position of King by the grace of Richard Plantagenet.

French (*Shakspeareana Genealogica*, p. 199) conjectured that "Summerfield" (*T. T.*) or "Someruile" (3 *Hen. VI.*, V. i. 7-15) was meant for Sir Thomas Somerville, who died 16 Henry VII., 1500.

XII. RICHARD III.

THE Tragedy of Richard the Third [2] is not separated from *The third Part of Henry the Sixt* by a dramatic interval of one clear day. For although Clarence's arrest—the first incident of the former drama— occurred in 1477,[3] the action of sc. ii., Act I., takes us back to May

---

xii. 112. In consideration of the ransom, René agreed that Provence should be united to the French crown after his death, and Margaret confirmed the cession.—*Jean de Troyes*, 36, 37.

[1] The dramatist might have been misled by finding in *Halle* (255) or *Hol.* (iii. 665/1/27) that "the earles of Northumberland and Westmerland" were slain at Towton. John Lord Neville—a brother of Ralph Neville, second Earl of Westmoreland—was killed in this battle, fighting on the Lancastrian side. —*Rot. Parl.*, v. 477/2.

[2] I quote the text of F1.

[3] We do not know when Clarence was arrested, but a probable date is based on the following facts : On May 20, 1477, Burdett and Stacy, dependents of Clarence, were executed for constructive treason.—*D. K. Rep.* 3, appendix ii. p. 214. On May 21, Clarence came to the Council Chamber at Westminster, accompanied by a priest named Godard, who read before the Council the declarations of innocence made by Burdett and Stacy previous to execution. Resenting this interference, Edward summoned Clarence to appear "certo die" at the palace of Westminster, and there, in the presence of the civic dignitaries, vehemently censured him. The Duke was put "sub custodiâ," and remained a prisoner till his death.—*Cont. Croyl.*, 561, 562. Edward's privy seals show

23, 1471, when Henry's corse was conveyed to Chertsey (p. 345, n. 2, below).   Henry died on May 21 or 22 (p. 340, n. 3, above) ; but, even if we assume that May 21 was the date of his death, we can hardly refer the closing scene of 3 *Henry VI.* to the same day.   *The Tragedy of Richard the Third* ends with the battle of Bosworth, fought on August 22, 1485.[1]

Act I. sc. i.—Richard enters and soliloquizes.   Two serious obstacles may, he trusts, soon be removed from his path.

> Plots haue I laide, Inductions dangerous,
> By drunken Prophesies, Libels, and Dreames,
> To set my Brother Clarence and the King
> In deadly hate, the one against the other.—ll. 32-35.

News (ll. 136, 137) that

> The King is sickly, weake, and melancholly,
> And *his Physitians* feare him mightily,[2]

leads to further anticipations (ll. 145-152) :

> He cannot liue, I hope ; and must not dye
> Till George be pack'd with post-horse vp to Heauen.
> Ile in, to vrge his hatred more to Clarence,
> With Lyes well steel'd with weighty Arguments ;   148
> And, if I faile not in my deepe intent,
> Clarence hath not another day to liue :
> Which done, God take King Edward to his mercy,
> And leaue the world for me to bussle in !   152

"Some wise men " weened that Richard's

[*Hol.* iii. 712/2/28. *More*, 6/29.] drift, couertlie conueied, lacked not in helping foorth his brother of Clarence to his death : which he resisted openlie, howbeit somewhat (as men deemed) more faintlie than he that were hartilie minded to his wealth.

And they, that thus deeme, thinke that he long time in king Edwards life forethought to be king ; in case that the king his brother (whose life he looked that *euill diet*[3] should shorten) should

[Some beleeued that Richard couertly suggested Clarence's death, and had long looked forward to succeeding Edward.]

---

that on May 26 he was at Greenwich, on May 27 at Greenwich and West-minster, and on May 28 at Greenwich again.—*O. B.* May 27, then, is a date in accordance with the testimony of the Croyland continuator, who, as he tells us himself (*Cont. Croyl.*, 557, sidenote), was in 1471 or 1472 a member of the Council.   Clarence was attainted by the Parliament which met at Westminster on January 16, 1478.—*Rot. Parl.*, vi. 167/1 ; 193-195.

[1] *Fab.*, ii. 672.

[2] Edward perceived "that there was little hope of recouerie in the cunning of *his physicians* " (*Hol.* iii. 708/2/35. Not in *Halle*).

[3] Cp. what Richard says of Edward (I. i. 139, 140) :

> "O, he hath kept an *euill diet* long."

happen to deceasse (as in deed he did) while his children were
yoong. And they deeme, that for this intent he was glad of his
brothers death the duke of Clarence, whose life must needs haue
hindered him so intending ; whether the same duke of Clarence had
kept him true to his nephue the yoong king, or enterprised to be
king himselfe.

> If expectation fail not,
>> This day should Clarence closely be mew'd vp,
>> About a Prophesie, which sayes that G
>> Of Edwards heyres the murtherer shall be.—ll. 38-40.

And Clarence, entering on his road to the Tower, informs Richard
(ll. 55-59) that Edward

>> . . . from the Crosse-row pluckes the letter G,
>> And sayes a Wizard told him that by G   56
>> His issue disinherited should be ;
>> And, for my name of George begins with G,
>> It followes in his thought that I am he.

Rumour declared that Clarence's death

[The "G"
prophecy.]

Prophesies
diuelish
fantasies.

[*Hol.* iii. 703/1/46. *Halle*, 326.] rose of a foolish prophesie,
which was, that, after K. Edward, one should reigne, whose first
letter of his name should be a G. Wherewith the king and
queene were sore troubled, and began to conceiue a greeuous
grudge against this duke, and could not be in quiet till they had
brought him to his end. And, as the diuell is woont to incumber
the minds of men which delite in such diuelish fantasies, they said
afterward, that that prophesie lost not his effect, when, after king
Edward, Glocester vsurped his kingdome.

Richard accuses Queen Elizabeth of having sent Clarence to the
Tower (ll. 62-65). Another rumoured cause of Clarence's death was
his projected marriage to Mary Duchess of Burgundy, heiress of Charles
the Bold.

[The Queen
and her
kindred
hated
Edward's
lineage.]

[*Hol.* iii. 703/1/61. *Halle*, 326.] Which marriage king Edward
(enuieng the prosperitie of his brother) both gainesaid and disturbed, and thereby old malice reuiued betwixt them : which the
queene and hir bloud (euer mistrusting, and priuilie barking at the
kings linage) ceassed not to increase.

However,

[*Hol.* iii. 712/1/46. *More*, 5/13.] . . . were it by the queene and

lords of hir bloud, which highlie maligned the kings kinred, (as
women commonlie, not of malice, but of nature, hate them whome
their husbands loue,) or were it a proud appetite of the duke
himselfe, intending to be king; at the least wise hcinous treason
was there laid to his charge: . . .

I do not find that Hastings—who enters (l. 121) after his release
from the Tower—either actually suffered imprisonment through the
enmity of Queen Elizabeth and Rivers, or regained his liberty by
petitioning Mistress Shore (ll. 66-77). But the Queen disliked
Hastings, and he was once in great peril owing to the accusation of
Rivers. See p. 366 below.

Act L sc. ii.—" Enter the Coarse of Henrie the sixt with Halberds
to guard it, Lady Anne being the Mourner." The bier is set down for
a while till Lady Anne says (ll. 29, 30):

> Come now towards Chertsey with your holy Lode,
> Taken from Paules to be interrëd there ; . . .

Soon after Richard enters she cries to the guards (ll. 55, 56):

> Oh, Gentlemen, see, see ! dead Henries wounds
> Open their congeal'd mouthes and bleed afresh !

Holinshed (iii. 690/2/73) gives the following account of Henry's
funeral, and the bleeding of the corpse:

[*Hol.* iii. 690/2/73.] The dead corps, on the Ascension euen
[May 22, 1471], was conueied with billes and glancs pompouslie (if
[*p.* 691] you will call that a funerall pompe) from the Tower to
the church of saint Paule, and there, laid on a beire or coffen bare
faced, the same in presence of the beholders did bleed :[1] where it
rested the space of one whole daie. From thense he was caried
to the Blackfriers, and bled there likewise: and, on the next
daie[2] after, it was conueied in a boat, without priest or clerke,
torch or taper, singing or saieng, vnto the monasterie of Chertseie,
distant from London fifteene miles, and there was it first
buried : . . .

The nine and twentith of Maie. [A wrong date.]
[Henry's body was conveyed from the Tower to St. Pauls, and afterwards to Chertsey. It bled at St. Pauls and the Blackfriars.]

The historical Lady Anne did not attend Henry VI.'s funeral ; and
the dialogue between her and Richard (ll. 46-225) is imaginary. She

---

[1] This excerpt was partly derived from *Halle* (303), but he does not mention
the bleeding of Henry's corpse.

[2] Henry's body was conveyed to Chertsey on Ascension Day (May 23).—
Fab., ii. 662, and a London chronicle (Bibl. Cotton. Vitell. A. xvi. fol. 133, r°)
cited in *Warkw.*, xii. *Hol.* was wrong if the words " where it rested . . . next
daie after " mean that the body was conveyed to Chertsey on May 24.

married Richard in 1472.[1]   From Holinshed (iii. 751/1/45) Shakspere might have learnt that she was

[Anne,
Warwick's
younger
daughter,
married first
to Prince
Edward.]

[*Hol.* iii. 751/1/45.   *Halle,* 407.]   the same Anne, one of the daughters of the earle of Warwike, which, (as you haue heard before,) at the request of Lewes the French king, was maried to prince Edward, sonne to king Henrie the sixt.

Richard's entreaty that she would go to Crosby Place, and receive a visit from him there (ll. 213-217), was perhaps suggested by the mention (*Hol.* iii. 721/2/70) of his having "kept his houshold," as Protector, at "Crosbies in Bishops gates street."   A slip of the pen, or a compositor's error, may account for Richard's order that the body be taken to White-Friars, not to Chertsey (ll. 226, 227).   We have seen (p. 345 above) how Henry's corpse, after its removal from St. Pauls, rested at Black-Friars,[2] and was thence conveyed to Chertsey.

Act I. sc. iii.—Queen Elizabeth tells Rivers (ll. 11-13) that her son's

<blockquote>
minority
Is put vnto the trust of Richard Glouster,   12
A man that loues not me, nor none of you.
Riu. Is it concluded he shall be Protector ?
Qu. It is determin'd, not concluded yet :
But so it must be, if the King miscarry.   16
</blockquote>

Edward died on April 9, 1483,[3] and Richard was appointed Protector before the middle of May in the same year.[4]   When—on May 4, 1483[5]—Edward V. entered London,

[*Hol.* iii. 716/2/53.   *More,* 22/31.]   the duke of Glocester bare him in open sight so reuerentlie to the prince, with all semblance of lowlinesse, that, from the great obloquie in which he was so late before, he was suddenlie fallen in so great trust, that at the councell next assembled he was made the onelie man, chosen and

---

[1] In a letter written on February 17, 1472, Sir John Paston reports Clarence to have said "that he [Richard] may weell have my Ladye [Anne] hys [Clarence's] suster in lawe, butt they schall parte no lyvelod."—*Paston,* iii. 38. A petition for the reversal of the attainder of John Lord Neville was presented to the Parliament which met at Westminster on October 6, 1472, and was prorogued on November 30, 1472.   This petition contains a salvo that nothing asked for shall be prejudicial to "Richard Duke of Gloucestr' and Anne Duches of Gloucestr' his wyfe."—*Rot. Parl.,* vi. 25/1.   It appears, therefore, that Richard and Anne must have been married on some date between February 17 and November 30, 1472.

[2] *Halle* (303) does not mention the deposit of Henry's body at Blackfriars.

[3] *Cont. Croyl.,* 564.

[4] In commissions of the peace, dated May 14, he is styled Protector of England.—Rot. Pat. Edw. V. in dorso (cited in *Grants of Edward V.,* ed. J. G. Nichols, xiii., xxxi.).   If the entry on the Patent Roll can be trusted, he was Protector on April 21.—Gairdner's *Life of Richard III.,* ed. 2, p. 69.

[5] *Fab.,* 668.

thought most meet to be protector of the king and his realme; so that (were it destinie or were it follie) the lambe was betaken to the woolfe to keepe.

The dube of Glocester made protector.

The ensuing dialogue (ll. 17-319) is fictitious. Margaret—who is one of the speakers—left England soon after November 13, 1475, and died on August 25, 1482.[1] But as this scene cannot be historically dated before April 9, 1483, there is point in the rebuke (ll. 255-256) which she is made to give Dorset, who pronounced her to be "lunaticke."

> Peace, Master Marquesse, you are malapert!
> Your fire-new stampe of Honor is scarce currant.

Barely eight years had elapsed since Edward—on April 18, 1475[2]—

[*Hol.* iii. 702/2/8.] created the lord Thomas, marquesse Dorset, before dinner; and so in the habit of a marquesse aboue the habit of his knighthood he began the table of knights in saint Edwards chamber.

[Thomas Grey created Marquess Dorset.]

She calls Richard a "rooting Hogge" (l. 228). In the second year of Richard's reign (1484), William Collingborne published the couplet:

[*Hol.* iii. 746/2/10. *Halle,* 398.]

> The Cat, the Rat, and Louell our dog,
> Rule all England vnder an hog.

Meaning by the hog, the dreadfull wild boare, which was the kings cognisance. But, bicause the first line ended in dog, the metrician could not (obseruing the regiments of meeter) end the second verse in boare, but called the boare an hog.

[The wild boar— Richard's cognisance— called a hog.]

Although, as I have said, the dialogue of this scene is fictitious, Shakspere may have taken a hint for it from the following passage, in which Richard is accused of fomenting strife between the two factions at Court. The writer has been speaking of a man named Pottier, who, on hearing of Edward's death, straightway inferred that Richard would be King.

[*Hol.* iii. 712/2/68. *More,* 7/26.] And forsomuch as he [Richard]

---

[1] The date of Margaret's death is taken from *Anselme,* i. 233. Cp. Baudier's *History of the Calamities of Margaret of Anjou Queen of England,* 1737, pp. 191, 192. As to the date of Margaret's departure from England, see p. 341, n. 2, above.

[2] I take this date from *Stow* (713), *Hol.'s* authority for the passage in which Grey's elevation to the dignity of marquess is recorded.

[Before Edward's death, Richard had fostered enmity betwixt the kindred of the King and Queen.]
well wist and holpe to mainteine a long continued grudge and heart-burning betweene the queens kinred and the kings bloud, either partie enuieng others authoritie, he now thought that their diuision should be (as it was in deed) a furtherlie beginning to the pursuit of his intent.

[Afterwards he resolved to make their variance serve his ambition.]
Nay, he was resolued, that the same was a sure [*p.* 713] ground for the foundation of all his building, if he might first (vnder the pretext of reuenging of old displeasure) abuse the anger and ignorance of the tone partie to the destruction of the tother; and then win to his purpose as manie as he could, and those, that could not be woone, might be lost yer they looked therfore. For of one thing was he certeine, that, if his intent were perceiued, he should soone haue made peace betweene both the parties with his owne bloud.

Act I. sc. iv.—In this scene two murderers, sent by Richard, slay Clarence, though Edward's order for the Duke's death had been reversed (II. i. 86). The First Murderer exclaims, as he stabs Clarence (I. iv. 276, 277):

> Take that, and that! if all this will not do,
> Ile drowne you in the Malmesey-But within.

I quote a passage containing the only detail of sc. iv. which Shakspere did not invent. Edward's hatred of Clarence reached such a pitch

Anno Reg. 17 [18 *Stow*]. *George duke of Clarence drowned in a butt of malmsie.*
[*Hol.* iii. 703/1/40.] that finallie the duke was cast into the Tower, and therewith adiudged for a traitor, and priuilie drowned in a butt of malmesie, the eleuenth of March, in the beginning of the seuententh yeare of the kings reigne.[1]

Act II. sc. i.—Edward, who now daily expects death, has made, as he hopes, an "vnited League" between the two parties which divided his Court. Hastings exchanges assurance of friendship with Rivers[2]

---

[1] *Hol.* took this date (March 11) from *Stow* (717). The rest of the passage is derived from *Halle* (326). *Fab.* (666) says that Clarence was put to death on February 18, 1478 ; a date confirmed by *Inq. p. m.* 18 E. IV. 46 & 47 (O. B.). *More* (*Hol.*, iii. 712/1/54), *Fab.*, *Halle*, and *Stow*, agree that the Duke was drowned—or, as *Stow* puts it, "made his ende"—in a butt ("a vessell" *Stow*) of malmsey. Instead of "drowne you . . . within," the Qq. of *Rich. III.* read : "chop thee . . . But in the next roome."

[2] In F. (II. i. 7) Dorset and Rivers—who were not foes—are commanded by Edward to take each other's hand. In the Qq. the King gives this order to Rivers and Hastings. In both texts ll. 9-10 and 11 have the respective prefixes *Riu. Hast.*

and Dorset; and kisses Queen Elizabeth's hand, which she gives him as a sign of amity. Buckingham professes zealous regard for the Queen and her kindred (ll. 1-40).

Of this brief truce we have the following account:

[*Hol.* iii. 713/1/10. *More*, 8/15.] King Edward, in his life, albeit that this dissention betweene his freends somewhat irked him; yet in his good health he somewhat the lesse regarded it: bicause he thought, whatsoeuer businesse should fall betweene them, himselfe should alwaie be able to rule both the parties. *[While he was in good health Edward cared little for the strife of the two parties at his Court.]*

But, in his last sicknesse, when he perceiued his naturall strength so sore infeebled, that he despaired all recouerie, then he, considering the youth of his children, albeit he nothing lesse mistrusted than that that hapned, yet well foreseeing that manie harmes might grow by their debate, while the youth of his children should lacke discretion of themselues, & good counsell of their freends, of which either partie should counsell for their owne commoditie, & rather by plesant aduise to win themselues fauor, than by profitable aduertisement to doo the children good, he called some of them before him that were at variance, and in especiall the lord marquesse Dorset, the queenes sonne by hir first husband. *[But in his last sickness he tried to make peace between them.]*

So did he also William the lord Hastings, a noble man, then lord chamberleine, against whome the queene speciallie grudged, for the great fauour the king bare him: and also for that she thought him secretlie familiar with the king in wanton companie. Hir kinred also bare him sore, as well for that the king had made him capteine of Calis, (which office the lord Riuers, brother to the queene, clamed of the kings former promise,) as for diuerse other great gifts which he receiued, that they looked for. When these lords, with diuerse other of both the parties, were come in presence, the king, lifting vp himselfe, and vnderset with pillowes, as it is reported, on this wise said vnto them. [I omit "The oration of the king on his death-bed."] *[Hastings lord chamberleine maligned of the queene & hir kin.]*

[*Hol.* iii. 714/1/22. *More*, 11/30.] And therewithall the king, no longer induring to sit vp, laid him downe on his right side, his face towards them: and none was there present that could refraine from weeping.

But the lords, recomforting him with as good words as they could, and answering for the time as they thought to stand with his pleasure, there in his presence, as by their words appeared, ech forgane other, and ioined their hands togither ; when (as it after appeared by their deeds) their hearts were farre asunder.

A counterfet and pretended reconcilement.

When Buckingham has vowed peace, Richard enters and quickly seizes an opportunity to let Edward know that a royal order countermanding Clarence's death arrived too late (ll. 75-90).   Then comes the " Earle of Derby," [1] beseeching pardon for his servant, who has been guilty of homicide.   Edward exclaims (ll. 102-107) :

> Haue I a tongue to doome my Brothers death,
> And shall that tongue giue pardon to a slaue ?
> My Brother kill'd no man ; his fault was Thought,   104
> And yet his punishment was bitter death.
> Who sued to me for him ?   Who (in my wrath)
> Kneel'd at my feet, and bad [2] me be aduis'd ?

After Clarence's removal,

[*Hol.* iii. 703/1/66.   *Halle,* 326.]   although king Edward were consenting to his death, yet he much did both lament his infortunate chance, & repent his sudden execution : insomuch that, when anie person sued to him for the pardon of malefactors condemned to death, he would accustomablie saie, & openlie speake : "Oh infortunate brother, for whose life not one would make "sute ! "

[When a pardon was craved from Edward he would lament that no one had asked mercy for Clarence.]

Act II. sc. ii.—Shakspere might have learnt from Holinshed that " the old Dutchesse of Yorke " was grandmother to " the two children of Clarence," [3] with whom she enters in this scene. Holinshed has also an account (iii. 703/2/2) of the " two yoong infants " left by Clarence ; whose names were Edward [4] and Margaret.

The Duchess and her grandchildren speak of Clarence's death (February, 1478) as a recent event. Their talk is interrupted by the entrance of Queen Elizabeth, distracted with grief for the loss of King Edward (April 9, 1483). Rivers and Dorset accompany the Queen (l. 33). Soon the characters already assembled are joined by Richard, Buckingham, and Hastings (l. 100).

---

[1] In some other scenes of the Qq. and F. he is rightly called Stanley. Thomas Lord Stanley was created Earl of Derby by Henry VII., on October 27, 1485.—*Dugdale,* iii. 248/2.

[2] *Kneel'd at . . . and bad*] Q1.   *Kneel'd and . . . and bid* F1.

[3] " In this verie season [1495] departed to God Cicilie duchesse of Yorke, moother to king Edward the fourth."—*Hol.* iii. 780/1/1.

[4] In F. *Edw.* is prefixed to the first speech of Clarence's son. Afterwards —and throughout this scene in the Qq.—he is called *Boy.*

Buckingham reminds the lords present of their late reconciliation, and adds (ll. 120-122) :

Me seemeth good, that, with some little Traine,   120
Forthwith from Ludlow, the young Prince be fet
Hither to London, to be crown'd our King.
  Riuers. Why "with some little Traine," my Lord of Buckingham ?
  Buc. Marrie, my Lord, least, by a multitude,   124
The new-heal'd wound of Malice should breake out ;
Which would be so much the more dangerous,
By how much the estate is greene and yet vngouern'd : . . .

Rivers and Hastings accept Buckingham's advice (ll. 134-140).[1]
Richard says : " Then be it so " (l. 141).

The position of affairs at Edward's death, and Richard's intrigues to gain possession of the young King, are described in the following excerpts :

[*Hol.* iii. 714/1/36. *More,* 12/6.] As soone as the king was
departed, the noble prince his sonne drew toward London ; which
at the time of his deceasse kept his houshold at Ludlow in
Wales, . . .

[The Prince
kept his
houshold at
Ludlow.]

To the gouernance and ordering of this yoong prince, at his
sending thither, was there appointed sir Anthonie Wooduile, lord
Riuers, and brother vnto the queene ; a right honourable man, as
valiant of hand as politike in counsell. Adioined were there vnto
him other of the same partie ; and in effect euerie one as he was
neerest of kin vnto the queene, so was he planted next about the
prince. That drift by the queene not vnwiselie deuised, whereby
hir bloud might of youth be rooted into the princes fauour, the
duke of Glocester turned vnto their destruction ; and vpon that
ground set the foundation of all his vnhappie building. For
whome soeuer he perceiued either at variance with them, or bearing
himselfe their fauour, he brake vnto them, some by mouth, & some
by writing. . . .

Lord Riuers
[was his
governor].

The duke of
Glocesters
solicitations
[to the ene-
mies of the
Queen's
kindred].

[*Hol.* iii. 714/2/35. *More,* 14/6.] With these words and
writings, and such other, the duke of Glocester soone set on fire
them that were of themselues easie to kindle, &, in especiall,[2]
twaine, Henry[3] duke of Buckingham, and William lord Hastings,
then chamberleine ; both men of honour & of great power : the one

---

[1] 123-140. Riuers. *Why . . . say I*] F. Not in Qq.
[2] *in speciall*] More. *in especiallie* Hol.   [3] *Henry*] *Edward* Hol.

A consent
to worke
wickednesse
[betweene
Richard,
Bucking-
ham, and
Hastings.
They agreed
to remoue
the Queen's
friends from
the young
King.]
by long succession from his ancestrie, the other by his office and
the kings fauour.   These two, not bearing ech to other so much
loue, as hatred both vnto the queenes part, in this point accorded
togither with the duke of Glocester; that they would vtterlie
remoue from the kings companie all his mothers freends, vnder
the name of their enimies.

Upon this concluded the duke of Glocester, vnderstanding that
the lords, which at that time were about the king, intended to
bring him vp to his coronation accompanied with such power of
their freends, that it should be hard for him to bring his purpose
to passe, without the gathering and great assemblie of people and
in maner of open warre, whereof the end (he wist) was doubtfull;
and in which, the king being on their side, his part should haue the

[Richard
persuaded
the Queen
that her son
ought not to
have a large
escort.]
face and name of a rebellion: he secretlie therfore by diuers means
caused the queene[1] to be persuaded and brought in the mind, that
it neither were need, and also should be ieopardous, the king to
come vp strong.

For whereas now euerie lord loued other, and none other thing
studied vpon, but about the coronation and honor of the king; if
the lords of hir kindred should assemble in the kings name much
people, they should giue the lords, betwixt whome and them had
beene sometime debate, to feare and suspect, least they should
gather this people, not for the kings safegard, (whome no man
impugned,) but for their destruction; hauing more regard to their
old variance, than their new attonement.   For which cause they
should assemble on the other partie much people againe for their
defense, (whose power she wist well far stretched,) and thus should
all the realme fall on a rore.   And of all the hurt that thereof
should insue, (which was likelie [p. 715] not to be little, and the
most harme there like to fall where she least would,) all the world
would put hir and hir kindered in the wight, and saie that they
had vnwiselie and vntrulie also broken the amitie & peace, that
the king hir husband so prudentlie made, betweene his kin and

---

[1] In the play Queen Elizabeth is not asked to give her opinion about the
number of her son's escort. Richard merely requests her and his mother to
deliver their "censures" touching the persons who are to be sent post to
Ludlow (II. ii. 141-144).

hirs in his death bed, and which the other partie faithfullie obserued.

The queene, being in this wise persuaded, such word sent vnto hir sonne, and vnto hir brother, being about the king, and ouer that the duke of Glocester himselfe and other lords, the chiefe of his bend, wrote vnto the king so reuerentlie, and to the queenes freends there so louinglie, that they, nothing earthlie mistrusting, brought the king vp in great hast, not in good speed, with a sober companie. [So the King went from Ludlow with a small company.]

Act II. sc. iii.—Three London Citizens meet and discuss the news of Edward's death, which is not yet generally known (ll. 7, 8).   Before they go out, the Second Citizen remarks (ll. 38, 40):

> Truly, the *hearts* [1] of men are full of feare :
> You cannot reason almost with a man
> That lookes not heauily, and full of dread.   40
>   3 [*Cit.*].   *Before* the dayes of Change, still is it so :
> By a diuine *instinct mens* mindes mistrust
> Pursuing danger ; as, by proof, we see
> The Water *swell before a* boyst'rous storme.   44

These lines contain reminiscences of a passage describing public feeling in June, 1483 ; [2] when

[*Hol.* iii. 721/2/57. *More*, 43/19.] began there, here and there abouts, some maner of muttering among the people, as though all should not long be well, though they neither wist what they feared, nor wherefore : were it, that, *before* such great things, *mens hearts* of a secret *instinct* of nature misgiue them ; as the sea without wind *swell*eth of himselfe sometime *before a* tempest : [3] . . . [Men warned by a secret instinct of great political changes.]

Act II. sc. iv.—Thomas Rotherham, Archbishop of York, imparts to Queen Elizabeth news of her son's journey to London (ll. 1-3) :

> Last night, I heare, they lay at Northhampton ;
> At Stonistratford will they be to night :
> To morrow, or next day, they will be here.

In a previous scene (II. ii. 146-154) Richard and Buckingham resolved to leave London,[4] and meet the King on his way to the capital. My next excerpt concerns the two Dukes' arrival at Northampton.

---

[1] *hearts*] F. *soules* Qq.
[2] When the several councils were held (see p. 363 below).
[3] *as the sea . . . tempest*] Hol. *as the south wynde somtyme swelleth of hym selfe before a tempeste* Halle (358).
[4] On receiving news of Edward's death, Richard left York for London, and met the Duke of Buckingham at Northampton. Thence the two Dukes went

[*Hol.* iii. 715/1/15. *More*, 15/23.] Now was the king in his
waie to London gone from Northampton, when these dukes of

Glocester and Buckingham came thither; where remained behind
the lord Riuers the kings vncle, intending on the morrow to follow
the king, and to be with him at Stonie Stratford, certeine miles
thence, earlie, yer he departed.

I have quoted above the reading of the Quartos (Q1). The Folio
has (ll. 1-3):

> Last night I heard they lay at Stony Stratford;
> And at Northampton they do rest to night:
> To morrow, or next day, they will be heere.

London is nearer Stony Stratford than Northampton,[1] but the Folio
reading may be, perhaps, defended,[2] on the ground that Richard and
Buckingham, after arresting Rivers, Grey, and Vaughan, brought the
King back from Stony Stratford to Northampton.[3] These arrests made,

[*Hol.* iii. 715/2/51. *More*, 18/26.] the duke of Glocester tooke

vpon himselfe the order and gouernance of the yoong king, whome
with much honor and humble reuerence he conueied vpward

towards the citie. But, anon, the tidings of this matter came
hastilie to the queene a little before the midnight following, and
that in the sorest wise: that the king hir son was taken, hir
brother, hir sonne, & hir other freends arrested, and sent, no man
wist whither, to be doone with God wot what. . . .

Now came there one in likewise not long after midnight from
the lord chamberleine [Hastings], to doctor Rotheram the archbishop of Yorke, then chancellor of England, to his place not farre
from Westminster. And for that he shewed his seruants that he
had tidings of so great importance, that his maister gaue [*p.* 716]
him in charge, not to forbeare his rest, they letted not to wake
him, nor he to admit this messenger in, to his bed side. Of whom

he heard that these dukes were gone backe with the kings grace
from Stonie Stratford vnto Northampton. "Notwithstanding, sir"
(quoth he) "my lord sendeth your lordship word, that there is no

---

to Stony Stratford, where they found the King.—*Polyd. Verg.*, 539, 540.
Richard was appointed Lieutenant-General against the Scots, June 12, 1482.—
Rymer, xii. 157, 158.

[1] The difference is fourteen miles.—*Lewis.*

[2] This explanation is, however, inconsistent with the fact that Rotherham
is made to speak unconcernedly of the King's return to Northampton.

[3] *Hol.* iii. 715/1/48—2/30. *More*, 16/20—18/7.

"feare: for be assureth you that all shall be well." "I assure
"him" (quoth the archbishop) "be it as well as it will, it will
"neuer be so well as we haue seene it."

Thus, according to the historical narrative, Queen Elizabeth had
learnt all before Rotherham received his information, yet in the play
she accepts what he tells her as news.

The young Duke of York is entertaining the Queen and Duchess
with his waggish humour when a messenger [1] announces (ll. 42-45) that,
by "the mighty Dukes, Gloucester and Buckingham,"

> Lord Riuers and Lord Grey are sent to Pomfret,
> With [2] them Sir Thomas Vaughan, Prisoners.

Both Dukes took part in the arrests (*Hol.* iii. 715/1/61; 2/27.
More, 16/32; 18/4), but Richard alone

[*Hol.* iii. 715/2/46. *More*, 18/21.] sent the lord Riuers, and
the lord Richard, with sir Thomas Vaughan, into the north
countrie, into diuerse places to prison; and afterward all to
Pomfret, where they were in conclusion beheaded.

The death of the lord Riuers & other [at Pomfret].

Hoping to save her younger son from destruction, the Queen says
(l. 66):

> Come, come, my Boy; we will to Sanctuary. . . .
> Arch.   My gracious Lady, go;   68
> And thether beare your Treasure and your Goodes.
> For my part, Ile resigne vnto your Grace
> The Seale I keepe: and so betide to me
> As well I tender you and all of yours!   72
> Go, Ile conduct you to the Sanctuary.

On hearing what had befallen her elder son, Queen Elizabeth,

[*Hol.* iii. 715/2/60. *More*, 19/1.] in great fright & heauinesse,
bewailing hir childes reigne, hir freends mischance, and hir owne
infortune, damning the time that euer she dissuaded the gathering
of power about the king, gat hir selfe in all the hast possible with
hir yoonger sonne and hir daughters out of the palace of Westminster, (in which she then laie,) into the sanctuarie; lodging hir
selfe and hir companie there in the abbats place.

The queene takrth sanctuarie.

After the departure of Hasting's messenger, Rotherham

[*Hol.* iii. 716/1/11. *More*, 19/25.] caused in all the hast all
his seruants to be called vp, and so, with his owne houshold about
him, and euerie man weaponed, he tooke the great seale with him,
and came yet before daie vnto the queene. About whom he found

[The Arch-bishop went to West-minster, and

---

[1] In the Qq. Dorset is the bearer of these tidings.
[2] 43. *With them*] Q. *and with them* F.

much heauinesse, rumble, hast, and businesse; cariage and conueiance of hir stuffe into sanctuarie; chests, coffers, packs, fardels,
trussed all on mens backs; no man vnoccupied, some lading, some
going, some discharging, some comming for more, some breaking
downe the walles to bring in the next waie, and some yet drew to
them that holpe to carrie a wrong waie: . . .

The queene hir selfe sate alone alow on the rushes all desolate
and dismaid, whome the archbishop comforted in best manner he
could; shewing hir that he trusted the matter was nothing so sore
as she tooke it for, and that he was put in good hope and out
of feare by the message sent him from the lord chamberleine.
"Ah, wo woorth him!" (quoth she) "for he is one of them that
"laboreth to destroie me and my bloud." "Madame" (quoth he)
"be yee of good cheere, for I assure you, if they crowne anie other
"king than your sonne, whome they now haue with them, we shall
"on the morow crowne his brother, whome you haue here with
"you. And here is the great seale, which in likewise as that noble

"prince your husband deliuered it vnto me; so here I deliuer it
"vnto you, to the vse and behoofe of your sonne:" and therewith
he betooke hir the great seale, and departed home againe, yet in
the dawning of the daie.

Act III. sc. i.—After receiving the congratulations of Buckingham
and Richard upon his entrance into London, the young King says (l. 6):

I want more Vnkles [1] heere to welcome me.

Richard answers:

Those Vnkles which you want were dangerous;   12
Your Grace attended to their Sugred words,
But look'd not on the poyson of their hearts:
God keepe you from them, and from such false Friends!
   Prin. God keepe me from false Friends! but they were none.   16

Richard and Buckingham arrested Rivers before they left Northampton. At Stony Stratford they overtook the King, and arrested in
his presence Sir Richard Grey, whom they accused of plotting with
Rivers and Dorset to obtain supreme control of the realm.

[*Hol.* iii. 715/2/21. *More,* 17/31.] Vnto which words the king
answered: "What my brother marquesse hath doone I cannot

---

[1] Sir Richard Grey was the King's half-brother. See the excerpt quoted to
illustrate ll. 6; 12-16. Rivers, Grey, and Vaughan were arrested on April 30,
1483.—*Cont. Croyl.,* 565.

"saie, but in good faith I dare well answer for mine vncle Riuers
"and my brother here, that they be innocent of anie such matter.'
"Yea, my liege" (quoth the duke of Buckingham) "they haue
"kept their dealing in these matters farre fro the knowledge of
"your good grace."

The "Lord Maior" enters, and is introduced to the King by Richard (l. 17):

> My Lord, the Maior of London comes to greet you.

Edward V.'s reception by the Lord Mayor is thus described:

[*Hol.* iii. 716/2/46. *More*, 22/24.] When the king approched neere to the citie, Edmund Shaw, goldsmith, then maior, with William White, and Iohn Matthew, shiriffes, and all the other aldermen in scarlet, with fiue hundred horsse of the citizens, in violet, receiued him reuerentlie at Harnesie; and riding from thence accompanied him into the citie, which he entered the fourth daie of Maie, the first and last yeare of his reigne.

The King is chafing at the absence of his mother and brother when Hastings comes to announce (ll. 27, 28) that

> The Queene your Mother, and your Brother Yorke,
> Haue taken Sanctuarie: . . .

Addressing Rotherham,[1] and then turning to Hastings, Buckingham says (ll. 32-36):

> Lord Cardinall, will your Grace
> Perswade the Queene to send the Duke of Yorke
> Vnto his Princely Brother presently?—
> If she denie, Lord Hastings, goe with him,
> And from her iealous Armes pluck him perforce!

Rotherham promises to try the effect of his oratory upon the Queen; " but," he adds (ll. 39-43),

> if she be obdurate
> To milde entreaties, God in heauen [2] forbid   40
> We should infringe the holy Priuiledge
> Of blessed Sanctuarie! not for all this Land
> Would I be guiltie of so great a sinne.

---

[1] The prelate, who is sent to bring the Duke of York out of sanctuary, is styled a Cardinal in the Qq. and F. According to *More* (25/28), *Hol.'s* authority, the Cardinal who undertook this mission was Rotherham, Archbishop of York. Editors have adhered to *More* in deciding that the Cardinal (Qq.) or Archbishop (F.) of Act II. sc. iv. is Rotherham, but they have followed *Cont. Croyl.* (566), *Fab.* (668), *Polyd. Verg.* (542/11), or *Halle* (352), in making Bourchier, Archbishop of Canterbury, the Cardinal of Act III. sc. i. I agree with Mr. Daniel in doubting "whether the dramatist intended to present more than one personage."—*T.-A.*, 328, note.   [2] *in heauen*] Q. om. F.

Buckingham replies (ll. 48-56) that to seize the Duke of York
cannot be a breach of sanctuary :

> The benefit thereof is alwayes granted   48
> To those whose dealings haue deseru'd the place,
> And those who haue the wit to clayme the place :
> This Prince hath neyther claym'd it nor deseru'd it ;
> *And therefore,* in mine opinion, *cannot haue it :* [See p. 360 below.] 52
> Then, taking him from thence that is not there,
> You breake no Priuiledge nor Charter there.
> *Oft haue I heard of Sanctuarie men ;*
> *But Sanctuarie children ne're till now.* [See p. 360 below.]   56

These quotations (ll. 32-56) embody portions of speeches delivered
by Richard, Cardinal Rotherham, and the Duke of Buckingham, at a
council held on or about June 16, 1483.[1] Having pointed out what
evils might arise from the Duke of York's detention in sanctuary,
Richard concluded :

The lord cardinall thought the fittest man to deale with the queene for the sur-rendring of hir sonne.

[*Hol.* iii. 717/1/42. *More,* 24/25.] "Wherefore me thinketh it
"were not worst to send vnto the queene, for the redresse of this
"matter, some honorable trustie man, such as both tendereth the
"kings weale and the honour of his councell, and is also in fauour
"and credence with hir.   For all which considerations, none
"seemeth more meetlie, than our reuerend father here present,
"my lord cardinall, who may in this matter doo most good of anie
"man, if it please him to take the paine ; " . . .

[If she will not surren-der her son, let him be fetched out.]

"And if she be percase so obstinate, and so preciselie set vpon
"hir owne will, that neither his wise and faithfull aduertisement
"can not mooue hir, nor anie mans reason content hir ; then shall
"we, by mine aduise, by the kings authoritie, fetch him out of that
"prison, and bring him to his noble presence, in whose continuall
"companie he shall be so well cherished and so honorablie
"intreated, that all the world shall to our honour and hir reproch
"perceiue, that it was onelie malice, frowardnesse, or follie, that
"caused hir to keepe him there."

Rotherham

[Rotherham would vse argument, but could not assent to York's removal against the Queen's will.]

[*Hol.* iii. 717/2/8. *More,* 25/30.] tooke vpon him to mooue hir,
and therein to doo his vttermost deuoir.   Howbeit, if she could be
in no wise intreated with hir good will to deliuer him, then thought
he, and such other as were of the spiritualtie present, that it were
not in anie wise to be attempted to take him out against hir will.

---

[1] See p. 361, n. 1, below.

For it should be a thing that would turne to the great grudge Reasons [omitted] why it was not thought meet to fetch the queenes son out of sanctuarie. of all men, and high displeasure of God, if the priuilege of that holie place should now be broken, which had so manie yeares be [1] kept, . . .

He protested against the employment of force:

[*Hol.* iii. 717/2/28. *More,* 26/16.] "God forbid that anie man [God forbid that any man should violate sanctuary !] "should, for anie thing earthlie, enterprise to breake the immunitie "& libertie of the sacred sanctuarie, that hath beene the safegard "of so manie a good mans life. And I trust" (quoth he) "with "Gods grace, we shall not need it. But, for anie maner need, I "would not we should doo it."

A long reply from Buckingham on the abuse of sanctuary contains the following passages, which should be compared with ll. 48-56. Let sanctuaries, said he, be respected

[*Hol.* iii. 718/2/3. *More,* 30/5.] "as farre foorth as reason "will, which is not fullie so farre foorth, as may serue to let "vs of the fetching foorth of this noble man to his honor and "wealth, out of that place, in which he neither is, nor can be, a "sanctuarie man. . . .

"But where a man is by lawfull means in perill, there needeth "he the tuition of some speciall priuilege; which is the onelie "ground and cause of all sanctuaries.

"From which necessitie, this noble prince is farre, whose loue "to his king, nature and kinred prooueth; whose innocencie to all "the world, his tender youth prooueth; and so sanctuarie, as for [The Duke of York needs no sanctuary, and therefore cannot claim it.] "him, neither none he needeth, nor also none can haue. Men "come not to sanctuarie, as they come to baptisme, to require it "by their godfathers; he must aske it himselfe that must haue it. "And reason, sith no man hath cause to haue it, but whose con- "science of his owne fault maketh him fain need to require it. "What will then hath yonder babe, which, and if he had discretion [If he had discretion he would be angry with those who detain him.] "to require it, if need were, I dare say would now be right angrie [2] "with them that keepe him there? . . .

---

[1] *be,* been. *bee* More.

[2] Hastings tells the King (III. i. 29, 30) that York

"Would faine haue come with me to meet your Grace, But by his Mother was perforce with-held."

[I never heard of sanctuary childres.]

"And verelie, *I haue often heard of sanctuarie men, but* I *neuer* "heard earst of *sanctuarie children.*"[1]

During a subsequent conference with the Queen in the sanctuary, Rotherham warned her that there were "manie" who thought

[The Duke of York has neither will to ask, nor malice to deserve, sanctuary.]

[*Hol.* iii. 720/1/4. *More,* 36/2.] "he can haue no priuilege in "this place, which neither can haue will to aske it, nor malice to "deserue it. And therefore, they reckon no priuilege broken, "though they fetch him out; which, if yee finallie refuse to deliuer "him, I verelie thinke they will."

Replying, she contemptuously stated his argument before meeting it :

The queenes replie vpon the lord cardinall.

[*Hol.* iii. 720/1/20. *More,* 36/17.] "But my sonne can deserue "no sanctuarie, *and therefore* he *can not haue it.*"[2]

Rotherham yields to Buckingham's arguments, and goes out with Hastings (l. 60). Soon the two envoys return with the Duke of York (l. 94). Meanwhile Richard, in answer to the King's query (l. 62),

Where shall we soiourne till our Coronation ?

proposes the Tower, and obtains a reluctant assent from his victim (ll. 64, 65 ; 149, 150). More says that, after Buckingham's speech, the majority of the council

[Rotherham was sent to essay the removal of York with the Queen's good will.]

[*Hol.* iii. 719/1/2. *More,* 32/7.] condescended in effect, that, if he were not deliuered, he should be fetched. Howbeit, they thought it all best, in the auoiding of all maner of rumor, that the lord cardinall should first assaie to get him with hir good will.

Wherevpon all the councell came vnto the Starre chamber at Westminster ; and the lord cardinall, leauing the protector with the councell in the Starchamber, departed into the sanctuarie to the queene, with diuers other lords with him : . . .

[York brought to the Protector.]

[*Hol.* iii. 721/1/42. *More,* 41/2.] When the lord cardinall, and these other lords with him, had receiued this yoong duke, they brought him into the Star chamber, where the protector tooke him

O dissimulation.

in his armes and kissed him with these words : "Now welcome, my "lord, euen with all my verie heart!" And he said in that of likelihood as he thought. Therevpon, foorthwith they brought him

---

[1] Cp. III. i. 55, 56, p. 358 above.
[2] Cp. III. i. 52, p. 358 above.

vnto the king his brother into the bishops palace at Paules, and
from thense thorough the citie honourablie into the Tower,[1] out of
the which after that daie they neuer came abroad.

[The King
and York
conveyed to
the Tower.]

The King and his brother leave the stage (l. 150); followed by all
the persons present except Richard, Buckingham, and Catesby. At
some time preceding this scene,—perhaps, as Mr. Daniel conjectures,[2]
during the journey to London, and after the arrests had been effected,—
the dramatic Buckingham became aware of Richard's intention to usurp
the throne. (See III. i. 157—164.) But More—as my next excerpt
shows—believed that Buckingham was not apprized of Richard's
purpose until the young Princes were safely lodged in the Tower.

[*Hol.* iii. 721/1/52. *More*, 41/12.] When the protector had
both the children in his hands, he opened himselfe more boldlie,
both to certeine other men, and also cheeflie to the duke of
Buckingham. Although I know that manie thought that this
duke was priuie to all the protectors counsell, euen from the
beginning; and some of the protectors freends said, that the duke
was the first moouer of the protector to this matter; sending a
priuie messenger vnto him, streict after king Edwards death.

[Opinions
differed as
to whether
Buckingham
knew
Richard's
purpose
from the
first,

But others againe, which knew better the subtill wit of the
protector, denie that he euer opened his enterprise to the duke,
vntill he had brought to passe the things before rehearsed. But
when he had imprisoned the queenes kinsfolks, & gotten both hir
sonnes into his owne hands, then he opened the rest of his purpose
with lesse feare to them whome he thought meet for the matter,
and speciallie to the duke, who being woone to his purpose, he
thought his strength more than halfe increased.

[or was
ignorant of
it until the
Princes were
in the
Tower.]

Though Catesby is sure of Hastings's love for the young King,
Buckingham resolves to test this conviction, and therefore says
(ll. 169-171):

goe, gentle Catesby,
And, as it were *farre off*,[3] sound thou Lord Hastings,
How he doth stand affected to our purpose; . . .

---

[1] *More* erred in saying that the Duke of York was brought to the Bishop's
palace at St. Paul's. We learn from *Cont. Croyl.* (566) and Stallworthe's letter
(*Excerpta Historica*, 16, 17) that York left sanctuary on June 16, 1483, and
went thence to the Tower. A letter given under the King's signet shows that
Edward V. was in the Tower on May 19.—*Grants*, viii., 15.
[2] The "story" (II. ii. 149), therefore, concerned Richard's purposed
assumption of the protectorate.
[3] *a farre off*] Q.

We learn from More (45/3) that

[*Hol.* iii. 722/1/41.] the protector and the duke of Buckingham made verie good semblance vnto the lord Hastings, and kept him much in companie. And vndoubtedlie the protector loued him well, and loth was to haue lost him, sauing for feare least his life should haue quailed their purpose.

[Richard moued Catesby to sound Hastings.] For which cause he mooued Catesbie to prooue with some words cast out a *farre off*, whether he could thinke it possible to win the lord Hastings vnto their part.

Catesby having departed, Richard promises Buckingham a reward (ll. 194-196):

> And, looke, when I am King, clayme thou of me
> The Earledome of Hereford, and all the moueables
> Whereof the King my Brother was possest.

After the Princes had been conveyed to the Tower,

[*Hol.* iii. 721/2/31. *More*, 42/30.] it was agreed, that the protector should haue the dukes aid to make him king, . . . and [The rewards which Richard promised Buckingham.] that the protector should grant him the quiet possession of the earldome of Hereford, which he claimed as his inheritance, and could neuer obteine it in king Edwards time.

Besides these requests of the duke, the protector, of his owne mind, promised him a great quantitie of the kings treasure, and of his houshold stuffe.

Act III. sc. ii.—"Vpon the stroke of foure" (l. 5) in the morning of the dramatic day next after that on which the action of the last scene passes,—or at midnight of the historic June 12-13, 1483,—a message is brought to Hastings from Stanley, who "this Night"

> Dreamt the Bore had rasëd off his Helme:
> Besides, he sayes there are two Councels kept ;   12
> And that may be determin'd at the one,
> Which may make you and him to rue at th'other.
> Therefore he sends to know your Lordships pleasure,
> If you will presently take Horse with him,   16
> And with all speed post with him toward the North,
> To shun the danger that his Soule diuines.
>   *Hast.* Goe, fellow, goe, returne vnto thy Lord ;
> Bid him not feare the seperated Councells : [1]   20

---

[1] *councels*] Q.   *Councell* F.

His Honor and my selfe are at the one,
And at the other is my good friend [1] Catesby ;
Where nothing can proceede, that toucheth vs,
Whereof I shall not haue intelligence.   24

When Richard and Buckingham had come to terms,

[*Hol.* iii. 721/2/42. *More,* 43/6.] they went about to prepare
for the coronation of the yoong king, as they would haue it seeme.
And that they might turne both the eies and minds of men from
perceiuing of their drifts other-where, the lords, being sent for from
all parts of the realme, came thicke to that solemnitie. But the
protector and the duke, after that they had sent the lord cardinall
[Bouchier], the archbishop of Yorke, then lord chancellor, the
bishop of Elie, the lord Stanleie, and the lord Hastings, then lord
chamberleine, with manie other noble men, to common & deuise   [The
about the coronation in one place, as fast were they in an other   separate
place, contriuing the contrarie, and to make the protector king.   councils.]

To which councell . . . there were adhibited verie few, and
they were secret: . . .

The rumoured existence of a cabal produced general uneasiness, and
caused

[*Hol.* iii. 722/1/8. *More,* 44/8.] some lords eke to marke the
matter and muse thereon; so farre foorth that the lord Stanleie,
(that was after earle of Derbie,) wiselie mistrusted it, and said
vnto the lord Hastings, that he much misliked these two seuerall
councels. "For while we" (quoth he) "talke of one matter in   [Stanley
"the tone place, little wot we wherof they talke in the tother   disliked the
"place."   separate
                                                                   councils.]

"My lord" (quoth the lord Hastings) "on my life, neuer doubt   [Hastings
"you: for while one man is there, which is neuer thense, neuer   did not fear
"can there be thing once mooued, that should sound amisse   the secret
"toward me, but it should be in mine eares yer it were well out of   Catesby
"their mouths." This ment he by Catesbie, which was of his   attended it.
neere secret councell, and whome he verie familiarlie vsed, and in
his most weightie matters put no man in so speciall trust ; reckoning
himselfe to no man so liefe, sith he well wist there was no man so

---

[1] *good friend*] F. *seruant* Q. The Q reading perhaps better characterizes
the relative social positions of Hastings and Catesby.

*Catesbie
and his
conditions
described.* much to him beholden as was this Catesbie, which was a man well
learned in the lawes of this land, and, by the speciall fauour of the
lord chamberlaine, in good authoritie, and much rule bare in all
the countie of Leicester, where the lord chamberlains power
cheefelie laie.

But suerlie great pitie was it, that he had not had either more
truth, or lesse wit. For his dissimulation onelie kept all that
[Hastings
was betrayed
by Catesby.] mischeefe vp. In whome if the lord Hastings had not put so
speciall trust, the lord Stanleie & he had departed with diuerse
other lords, and broken all the danse; for manie ill signes that he
saw, which he now construes all to the best. So suerlie thought
he, that there could be none harm toward him in that councell
intended, where Catesbie was.

Having given a reason for not fearing "the seperated Councells,"
Hastings adverts to Stanley's dream (ll. 26-33):

> And for his Dreames, I wonder hee's so simple
> To trust the mock'ry of vnquiet slumbers:
> To flye the Bore, before the Bore pursues,　　　　　28
> Were to incense the Bore to follow vs,
> And make pursuit where he did meane no chase.
> Goe, bid thy Master rise and come to me;
> And we will both together to the Tower,　　　　　33
> Where, he shall see, the Bore will vse vs kindly.
> 　　*Mess.* Ile goe, my Lord, and tell him what you say.　　[*Exit.*

Hastings had a warning of his fate when, on

[*Hol.* iii. 723/1/35. *More*, 48/19.] the selfe night next before
his death, the lord Stanleie sent a trustie messenger vnto him at
midnight in all the hast, requiring him to rise and ride awaie with
him, for he was disposed vtterlie no longer to bide, he had so
*The lord
Stanleies
dreame.* fearfull a dreame; in which him thought that a boare with his
tuskes so rased them both by the heads, that the bloud ran about
both their shoulders. And, forsomuch as the protector gaue the
boare for his cognisance, this dreame made so fearefull an impression in his heart, that he was throughlie determined no longer to
tarie, but had his horsse readie, if the lord Hastings would go with
him, to ride so farre yet[1] the same night, that they should be out
of danger yer daie.

---

[1] *so far yet*] More. *yet so farre* Hol.

"Ha, good Lord!" (quoth the lord Hastings to this messenger) "leaneth my lord thy maister so much to such trifles, and hath [Hastings despised Stanley's dream.] "such faith in dreames, which either his owne feare fantasieth, or "doo rise in the nights rest by reason of his daies thought?   Tell "him it is plaine witchcraft to beleeue in such dreames, which if "they were tokens of things to come, why thinketh he not that we "might be as likelie to make them true by our going, if we were "caught & brought backe, as freends faile fliers; for then had the "boare a cause likelie to rase vs with his tusks, as folke that fled "for some falsehood. . . .   And therefore go to thy maister (man) "and commend me to him, & praie him be merie & haue no feare: "for I insure him I am as sure of the man that he woteth of, as I "am of mine owne hand."   "God send grace, sir!" (quoth the messenger) and went his waie.

Stanley's messenger gone, Catesby enters, and answers Hastings's demand for news " in this our tott'ring State," by saying (ll. 38-40):

> It is a reeling World indeed, my Lord;
> And, I beleeue, will neuer stand vpright,
> Till Richard weare the Garland of the Realme.

Hastings replies (ll. 43, 44):

> Ile haue this Crown of mine cut from my shoulders,
> Before Ile see the Crowne so foule mis-plac'd!

He is no mourner for the news—which Catesby brings from the Protector—of the impending execution of the Queen's kindred at Pomfret, on " this same very day ";

> But, that Ile giue my voice on Richards side,
> To barre my Masters Heires in true Descent,
> God knowes I will not doe it, to the death!

Catesby,—who had, as we have seen (p. 362 above), been charged to sound Hastings,—

[*Hol.* iii. 722/1/50. *More*, 45/11.]   whether he assaied him, or [Catesby reported Hastings's loyalty.] assaied him not, reported vnto them, that he found him so fast, and heard him speake so terrible words, that he durst no further breake.

Stanley now enters (l. 73), and, after being reassured by Hastings, departs with Catesby. As they are leaving the stage, a pursuivant enters, and is accosted by Hastings (l. 98):

> How now, Sirrha! how goes the World with thee?
> *Purs.* The better that your Lordship please to aske.
> *Hast.* I tell thee, man, 'tis better with me now,   100

Then when thou met'st me last where now we meet :
Then was I going Prisoner to the Tower,
By the suggestion of the Queenes Allyes ;
But now, I tell thee, (keepe it to thy selfe !)　　　　　104
This day those Enemies are put to death,
And I in better state then ere I was.

Of this incident we have the following account :

[*Hastings met a pursuivant of his own name.*]
[*Hol.* iii. 723/2/31. *More,* 50/9.] Upon the verie Tower wharfe, so neare the place where his head was off soone after, there met he with one Hastings,[1] a purseuant of his owne name. And, at their meeting in that place, he was put in remembrance of another time, in which it had happened them before to meet in like manner [*Hastings had once been in danger through an accusation of Rivers.*] togither in the same place. At which other time the lord chamberleine had beene accused vnto king Edward by the lord Riuers, the queenes brother, in such wise, as he was for the while (but it lasted not long) farre fallen into the kings indignation, & stood in great [*Hastings reminded the pursuivant of this.*] feare of himselfe. And, forsomuch as he now met this purseuant in the same place, that ieopardie so well passed, it gaue him great pleasure to talke with him thereof ; with whom he had before talked thereof in the same place, while he was therein.

And therefore he said : "Ha, Hastings ! art thou remembred "when I met thee here once with an heauie heart ?" "Yea, my "lord" (quoth he) "that remember I well, and thanked be God, "they gat no good, nor you no harme thereby." "Thou wouldest "say so" (quoth he) "if thou knewest as much as I know, which "few know else as yet, and mo shall shortlie." That meant he by [*The Queen's kindred were to be executed on that day.*] the lords of the queenes kinred that were taken before, and should that daie[2] be beheaded at Pomfret : which he well wist, but nothing ware that the ax hung ouer his owne head. "In faith, man"

---

[1] *Enter Hastin. a Pursuant.*] Q. *Enter a Pursuiuant.* F.

[2] Hastings was executed on June 13 (*Cont. Croyl.,* 566) ; but Rivers's will was made at Sheriff Hutton (Yorkshire), on June 23.—*Excerpta Historica,* 246. A Latin obituary calendar of saints (Cottonian MS. Faustina, B. VIII.), written in the 14th century, has later additions at the side. On leaf 4 back, at the side of "Iunij 25," is written, in a 16th or late 15th century hand, "Anthonij Ryvers"; an entry which probably means that the obit of Earl Rivers was kept on June 25. This calendar is cited in *Excerpta Historica,* 244. (Dr. Furnivall, who examined the MS., tells me that it is not, as was supposed, an obituary calendar belonging to St. Stephen's Chapel, Westminster.) Cp. also *York Records,* 156, note, and *Cont. Croyl.* (567), for proof that the execution of Rivers, Grey, and Vaughan took place after June 13.

(quoth he) "I was neuer so sorie, nor neuer stood in so great dread
"in my life, as I did when thou and I met here. And, lo, how
"the world is turned! now stand mine enimies in the danger, (as
"thou maiest hap to heare more hereafter,) and I neuer in my life [Hastings's
"so merrie, nor neuer in so great suertie!" joy and confidence.]

The pursuivant's departure is succeeded by the entry of a priest, in
whose ear Hastings is whispering [1] when Buckingham appears and
exclaims (ll. 114-116):

> What, talking with a Priest, Lord Chamberlaine?
> Your friends at Pomfret, they doe need the Priest;
> Your Honor hath no shriuing worke in hand.

In the morning of June 13, ere Hastings was up, there

[*Hol.* iii. 723/2/6. *More*, 49/26.] came a knight [2] vnto him, as it [In the
were of courtesie, to accompanie him to the councell, but of truth morning of June 13
sent by the protector to hast him thitherwards; with whome he Richard sent a knight for
was of secret confederacie in that purpose: a meane man at that Hastings.]
time, and now of great authoritie.

This knight (I say) when it happened the lord chamberleine by
the waie to staie his horsse, & common a while with a priest whom
he met in the Tower street, brake his tale, and said merilie to
him: "What, my lord, I pray you come on, whereto talke you so [The knight
"long with that priest? you haue no need of a priest yet": and jested at Hastings for stopping to
therwith he laughed vpon him, as though he would say, "Ye shall speak with a priest.]
"haue soone." But so little wist the tother what he ment, and
so little mistrusted, that he was neuer merier, nor neuer so full
of good hope in his life; which selfe thing is oft seene a signe of
change.

---

[1] *He whispers in his eare.*] Q (against l. 113). om. F.
[2] "ere he [Hastings] were vp from his bed . . . , there came to him Sir
Thomas Haward, sonne to the lorde Haward, (whyche lord was one of the
priueyest of the lord protectours counsaill and doyng,) as it were of curtesye
to accompaignye hym to the counsaile, but of truthe sent by the lorde protectour to hast him thetherward."—*Halle*, 361. Thomas Howard was knighted
at the child-marriage of Anne Mowbray and Richard Duke of York, second son
of Edward IV.—*Weever*, 555. The Duke of York was married on January 15,
1478.—*Sandford*, 415, 416. On June 28, 1483, Richard III. created Sir Thomas
Howard Earl of Surrey.—*Doyle*, ii. 589. On February 1, 1514, the dukedom
of Norfolk was conferred on Surrey by Henry VIII.—*Ibid.*, 590. Writing
about 1513 More might justly say that the "meane man" of Edward V.'s time
was "now of great authoritie"; for in the above-named year Surrey commanded
our army at Flodden.

As the scene closes Hastings and Buckingham go out on their way
to the Tower.

Act III. sc. iii.—"Enter Sir Richard Ratcliffe, with [1] Halberds,
carrying the Nobles to death at Pomfret." The historical date of
Rivers's execution could not have been earlier than June 23 (see p. 366
above, n. 2); but, according to dramatic time, Rivers and Hastings
were beheaded on the same day (June 13). Shakspere followed the
narrative which Holinshed took from More (55/25), who says :

[*Hol.* iii. 725/1/55. *More*, 55/25.] Now was it so deuised by
the protector and his councell, that the selfe daie, in which the
lord chamberleine was beheaded in the Tower of London, and
about the selfe same houre, was there (not without his assent)
beheaded at Pomfret, the foreremembred lords & knights that
were taken from the king at Northampton and Stonie Stratford.
Which thing was doone in the presence, and by the order, of sir
Richard Ratcliffe, knight; whose seruice the protector speciallie
vsed in that councell, and in the execution of such lawlesse
enterprises ; as a man that had beene long secret with him,
hauing experience of the world, and a shrewd wit, short & rude
in speech, rough and boisterous of behauiour, bold in mischiefe,
as far from pitie as from all feare of God.

Sir Richard Ratcliffe [described].

This knight bringing them out of the prison to the scaffold, and
shewing to the people about that they were traitors, (not suffering
them to declare & speake their innocencie, least their words might
haue inclined men to pitie them, and to hate the protector and
his part,) caused them hastilie, without iudgement, processe, or
maner of order to be beheaded ; and without other earthlie gilt,
but onelie that they were good men, too true to the king, and too
nigh to the queene.

The lord Rivers & other beheaded.

Act III. sc. iv.—The historical date of this scene is June 13, 1483.[2]

---

[1] *Enter . . . with the Lo. Rivers, Gray, and Vaughan, prisoners.*] Q.
Vaughan says (III. iii. 7): "You liue that shall cry woe for this heereafter";
and Rivers asks God to remember Margaret's curse upon Hastings, Buckingham, and Richard (ll. 17-19). *Halle* added to *More's* narrative a passage (364)
wherein Vaughan appeals Richard "'to the high tribunal of God for his wrong-
ful murther & our true innocencye.' And then Ratclyffe sayed : 'you haue
well apeled ; lay doune youre head.' 'Ye,' quod sir Thomas, 'I dye in right,
beware you dye not in wrong.'"

[2] Hastings was beheaded on Friday, June 13, 1483.—*Cont. Croyl.* 566.
Simon Stallworthe, writing on Saturday, June 21, to Sir William Stonor,
says: "on fryday last was the lord Chamberleyn [Hastings] hedded sone

In a room in the Tower are assembled Buckingham, Stanley, Hastings, the Bishop of Ely, Ratcliffe, and Lovel. Hastings says (ll. 1-3):

> Now, Noble Peeres, the cause why we are met
> Is, to determine of the Coronation.
> In Gods Name, speake! when is the Royall day?
> *Buck.* Are[1] all things ready for the Royall time?
> *Darb.* [*Stan.*] It is, and wants but nomination.
> *Ely.* To morrow, then, I iudge a happie day.

Discussion is prevented by Richard's entrance and greeting (ll. 23, 24):

> My Noble Lords, and Cousins all, good morrow!
> I haue beene long a sleeper: . . .

Soon he addresses the Bishop of Ely (ll. 33-35):

> When I was last in Holborne,
> I saw good Strawberries in your Garden there:
> I doe beseech you, send for some of them.
> *Ely.* Mary, and will, my Lord, with all my heart.   36
>   [*Exit Bishop.*

Taking Buckingham aside, Richard tells him of Catesby's failure to seduce Hastings (ll. 38-42). Richard and Buckingham then withdraw. Business is resumed by Stanley's proposal that the coronation be deferred until a later date than to-morrow (ll. 44-47). Whereupon the Bishop of Ely re-enters and asks (ll. 48, 49): "Where is my Lord the Duke of Gloster? I haue sent for these Strawberries."

> *Ha.* His Grace looks chearfully & smooth this morning;
> There's some conceit or other likes him well,
> When that he bids good morrow with such spirit.   52

Stanley distrusts Richard's cheerful mien. Hastings replies, but fails to convince his friend (Q.), and the Protector re-enters with Buckingham (ll. 56-60). Richard immediately demands (ll. 61-64):

> I pray you all, tell me what they deserue
> That doe conspire my death with diuellish Plots
> Of damnèd Witchcraft, and that haue preuail'd
> Vpon my Body with their Hellish Charmes?   64
> *Hast.* The tender loue I beare your Grace, my Lord,
> Makes me most forward in this Princely presence
> To doome th' Offendors: whosoe're they be,
> I say, my Lord, they haue deserued death.   68
> *Rich.* Then be your eyes the witnesse of their euill!
> Looke how I am bewitch'd; behold mine Arme

---

apons noon."—*Excerpta Historica*, 16. To reconcile this piece of news with the high authority of the Croyland continuator, we must suppose that Stallworthe meant Friday-week. *More*, although he gave no dates, made the execution of Hastings succeed York's removal from sanctuary, but according to *Cont. Croyl.* (566) the latter event took place on the Monday (June 16) following Hastings's death; a date confirmed by Stallworthe (see p. 361, n. 1, above), if we assume that "fryday last" = Friday-week.

[1] *Are*] Q. *Is* F.

Is, like a blasted Sapling, wither'd vp!
And this is Edwards Wife, that monstrous Witch,   72
Consorted with that Harlot Strumpet Shore,
That by their Witchcraft thus haue markēd me!
  Hast. If they haue done this deed, my Noble Lord,—
  Rich. "If"! thou Protector of this damnēd Strumpet!   76
Talk'st thou to me of "Ifs"! Thou art a Traytor!—
Off with his Head!—Now, by Saint Paul I sweare,
I will not dine vntill I see the same!—
Louell and Ratcliffe, looke that it be done :—   80
The rest, that loue me, rise and follow me.
  [*Exeunt. Mane[n]t Louell and Ratcliffe, with the Lord Hastings.*[1]

Soon after Catesby had sounded Hastings ;

[*Hol.* iii. 722/1/65. *More,* 45/24.] that is to wit, on the fridaie
[being the thirteenth of Iune],[2] manie lords assembled in the Tower,
and there sat in councell, deuising the honourable solemnitie of
the kings coronation ; of which the time appointed then so neere
approched, that the pageants and subtilties were in making daie
& night at Westminster, and much vittels killed therfore, that
afterward was cast awaie. These lords so sitting together com-

muning of this matter, the protector came in amongst them, first
about nine of the clocke, saluting them courteouslie, and excusing
himselfe that he had beene from them so long ; saieng merilie that
he had beene a sleeper that daie.

After a little talking with them, he said vnto the bishop of
Elie : "My lord, you haue verie good strawberies at your garden
"in Holborn, I require you let vs haue a messe of them."
"Gladlie, my lord" (quoth he) "would God I had some better
"thing as readie to your pleasure as that !" And therewithall in

_____

[1] *Exeunt . . . Hastings.*] F. *Exeunt. manet Cat. with Ha.* Q. Sc. iii.
Act III. accords with *More* (see p. 368 above) in making Ratcliffe supervise
the execution of Rivers, Grey, and Vaughan, at Pomfret ; and the same
authority is followed in assigning the deaths of Hastings and his enemies to
the same day. In the F. version of sc. v. Act III. (l. 13), Catesby enters with
the Lord Mayor, who was presumably sent for after Hastings's arrest. Then
(III. v. 21) Lovel and Ratcliffe enter, with Hastings's head. In the Q. version
of this scene no one accompanies the Lord Mayor, whose entry precedes the
appearance of Catesby bearing Hastings's head. In both versions, after the
Lord Mayor's entry, Richard bids Catesby "o'erlook the walls" (l. 17). Thus,
while the F. allows Ratcliffe to be present at Pomfret and London on the
same day, the Q. represents Catesby as being addressed while absent from the
stage.
[2] *friday the   day of   many*] More. The date (June 13), and the
brackets enclosing it, appear in *Hol.'s* reprint of *More.*

all the hast he sent his seruant for a messe of strawberies. The *The behauior of the lord protector in the assemblie of the lords [when he returned].* protector set the lords fast in communing, & therevpon, praieng them to spare him for a little while, departed thense. And soone after one houre, betweene ten & eleuen, he returned into the chamber amongst them, all changed, with a woonderfull soure angrie countenance, knitting the browes, frowning, and fretting [1] and gnawing on his lips : and so sat him downe in his place.

All the lords were much dismaid, and sore maruelled at this maner of sudden change, and what thing should him aile. Then, when he had sitten still a while, thus he began : " What were they *[Richard asked what should be done to those who imagined his death.]* "worthie to haue that compasse and imagine the destruction of "me, being so neere of bloud vnto the king, and protector of his "roiall person and his realme ? " At this question, all the lords sat sore astonied, musing much by whome this question should be meant, of which euerie man wist himselfe cleere. Then the lord chamberlaine (as he that for the loue betweene them thought he *[Hastings answered that they ought to be punished as traitors.]* might be boldest with him) [2] answered and said, that they were worthie to be punished as heinous traitors, whatsoeuer they were. And all the other affirmed the same. " That is " (quoth he) *[Richard accused the Queene and others.]* " yonder sorceresse my brothers wife, and other with hir " (meaning the queene.)

At these words manie of the other lords were greatlie abashed, that fauoured hir. But the lord Hastings was in his mind better content, that it was mooned by hir, than by anie other whome he loued better : albeit his heart somewhat grudged, that he was not afore made of councell in this matter, as he was of the taking of hir kinred, and of their putting to death, which were by his assent before deuised to be beheaded at Pomfret this selfe same daie ; in *[The Queen's kindred beheaded on that day.]* which he was not ware that it was by other deuised, that he him-selfe should be beheaded the same daie at London. Then said the protector : " Ye shall all see in what wise that sorceresse, and that " other witch of hir councell, Shores wife, with their affinitie, haue,

---

[1] *browes, frowning and froting and knowing*] More.

[2] Hastings proposes to give a proxy-vote for Richard in the matter of fixing a day for the King's coronation. Touching this offer Richard says (III. iv. 30, 31) :

> " Then my Lord Hastings no man might be bolder ;
> His Lordship knowes me well, and loues me well."

[Richard shewed his arm, withered (as he said) by the Queen and Shore's wife.]

"by their sorcerie and witchcraft, wasted my bodie." And therwith he plucked vp his dublet sleeue to his elbow, vpon his left arme, where he shewed a weerish withered arme, and small; as it was neuer other.

Herevpon euerie mans mind sore misgaue them, well perceiuing that this matter was but a quarell. For they well wist that the queene was too wise to go about anie such follie. And also, if she would, yet would she, of all folke least, make Shores wife of hir counsell; whome of all women she most hated, as that concubine whome the king hir husband had most loued. And also, no man was there present, but well knew that his arme was euer such since his birth. Naithlesse, the lord chamberlaine (which from the death

[Hastings kept Shore's wife.]

of king Edward kept Shores wife, on whome he somewhat doted in

[Hastings replied that they deserved punishment, if they had so heinously done.]

the kings life, sauing, as it is said, he that while forbare hir of reuerence toward the king, or else of a certeine kind of fidelitie to his freend) answered and said: "Certeinelie, my lord, if they haue "so heinouslie doone, they be worthie heinous punishment."

[Richard . cried out at Hastings's "ifs," and called him a traitor.]

"What" (quoth the protector) "thou seruest me, I weene, with "'ifs' and with 'ands': I tell thee they haue so doone, and that "I will make good on thy bodie, traitor!" and therewith, as in a

[Hastings arrested.]

great anger, he clapped his fist vpon the boord a great rap. At which token one cried, [*p. 723*] "Treason!" without the chamber. Therewith a doore clapped, and in come there rushing men in harnesse, as manie as the chamber might hold. And anon the protector said to the lord Hastings: "I arrest thee, traitor!" "What me, my lord?" (quoth he.) "Yea, thee, traitor!" quoth the protector. . . .

Then were they all quickelie bestowed in diuerse chambers, except the lord chamberleine, whome the protector bad speed and

[Richard would not dine till Hastings was beheaded.]

shriue him apace, "for, by saint Paule" (quoth he) "I will not to "dinner till I see thy head off!" It booted him not to aske whie, but beauilie he[1] tooke a priest at aduenture, and made *a short shrift:*[2] for a longer would not be suffered, the protector made so much

---

[1] *As*] More. om. Hol.

[2] "*Ra.* [*Cat.* Q.] Come, come, dispatch! the Duke would be at dinner: Make *a short Shrift;* he longs to see your Head."

—*Rich. III.,* III. iv. 96, 97.

hast to dinner, which he might not go to, vntill this were doone,
for sauing of his oth.

While Hastings lingers to muse on his sudden downfall, he recalls
an incident till now unheeded (ll. 86-88) :

> Three times to day my Foot-Cloth-Horse did stumble,
> And started, when he look'd vpon the Tower,
> As loth to beare me to the slaughter-house.

[*Hol.* iii. 723/1/71.   *More*, 49/18.]   Certeine is it also, that in
riding towards the Tower, the same morning in which he was
beheded, his horsse twise or thrise stumbled with him, almost to
the falling.

Fore tokens of imminent misfortune to the lord Hastings.

At the close of this scene Hastings is led out to execution.   I quote
a passage which gives particulars of his death :

[*Hol.* iii. 723/1/19.   *More*, 48/11.]   So was he brought foorth
to the greene beside the chappell within the Tower; and his head
laid downe vpon a long log of timber, and there striken off, . . .

Lord Hastings, lord chamberlaine, beheaded.

Act III. sc. v.—"Enter Richard and Buckingham, in rotten
Armour, maruellous ill-fauoured." [1]   They feign great timidity (ll. 14-
21).   Addressing the Lord Mayor,—who has been sent for to hear an
explanation of the step which they have taken,—Richard speaks thus
of Hastings (ll. 29-32) :

> So smooth he dawb'd his Vice with shew of Vertue,
> That, his apparant open Guilt omitted,
> (I meane, his Conuersation with Shores Wife,)
> He liu'd from all attainder of suspect. [2]   32

When Richard sent for "manie substantiall men out of the citie"
(see next page), he despatched to the city a herald with a proclamation (the same which the scrivener produces in sc. vi., Act III.),
giving particulars of the alleged conspiracy, and accusing Hastings of

[*Hol.* iii. 724/1/43.]   vicious liuing and inordinate abusion of his
bodie, both with manie other, and also speciallie with Shore's wife,
which was one also of his most secret counsell in this most heinous
treason; with whom he laie nightlie, and namelie the night last
past next before his death. [3]

[Hastings's "conuersa- tion" with Shore's wife.]

Buckingham asks the Mayor (ll. 35-39) :

> Would you imagine, or almost beleeue,
> (Wert not that, by great preseruation,   36

---

[1] *Enter Richard . . .*] F.   *Enter Duke of Glocester and Buckingham in armour.* Q.
[2] *suspect*] Q.   *suspects* F.
[3] *with whom . . . his death.*] Halle (362).   om. More.

We liue to tell it,) that the subtill Traytor
This day had plotted, in the Councell-House,
To murther me and my good Lord of Gloster!

The succeeding excerpt shows that Hastings was not represented to
have confessed his treason (ll. 57, 58). The "substantiall men" were,
however, outwardly as acquiescent as the credulous dramatic Mayor,
who answers Richard thus (ll. 62, 63):

But, my good Lord, your Graces word[1] shal serue,
As well as I had seene and heard him speake: . . .

[*Hol.* iii. 723/2/74. *More,* 51/14.] Now flew the fame of this
lords death [*p.* 724] swiftlie through the citie, and so foorth
further about, like a wind in euerie mans eare. But the protector,
immediatlie after dinner, intending to set some colour vpon the
matter, sent in all the hast for manie substantiall men out of the
citie into the Towre.

[The citizens, whom Richard sent for, found him and Buckingham arrayed "in old ill-faring briganders."]

Now, at their comming, himselfe with the duke of Buckingham
stood harnessed in old ill faring briganders, such as no man should
weene, that they would vouchsafe to haue put vpon their backs,
except that some sudden necessitie had constreined them. And
then the protector shewed them, that the lord chamberleine, and
other of his conspiracie, had contriued to haue suddenlie destroied

[Richard said that he and Buckingham had barely escaped death from a plot of Hastings.]

him, and the duke, there the same day in the councell. And what
they intended further, was as yet not well knowne. Of which their
treason he neuer had knowledge before ten of the clocke the same
forenoone; which sudden feare draue them to put on for their
defense such harnesse as came next to hand. And so had God
holpen them, that the mischiefe turned vpon them that would haue

[The citizens professed to believe this tale, which Richard desired them to report.]

doone it. And this he required them to report.

Euerie man answered him faire, as though no man mistrusted
the matter, which of truth no man beleeued.

Richard now bids Buckingham follow the Lord Mayor to Guildhall,
and there seize an opportunity of decrying Edward IV. in the citizens'
presence. As a proof of the late King's tyrannical humour Buckingham
is to

Tell them how Edward put to death a Citizen,   76
Onely for saying he would make his Sonne
Heire to the Crowne; meaning indeed his House,
Which, by the Signe thereof, was tearmëd so.

---

¹ *word*] Q. *words* F.

In a speech delivered at the Guildhall, on June 24, 1483,[1] Buckingham accused Edward of having turned "small trespasses into mispris[i]on, mispris[i]on into treason"; and, to prove his charge, cited the following case as being well known :

[*Hol.* iii. 728/2/35.   *More,* 67/26.]   Whereof (I thinke) no man looketh that we should remember you of examples by name, as though Burdet were forgotten, that was for a word spoken in hast *Burdet.* cruellie beheaded, by the miscontruing of the laws of this realme, for the princes pleasure.

Between the words "beheaded" and "by," Halle[2] inserted the subjoined parenthetical comment (369) :

This Burdet was a marchaunt dwellyng in Chepesyde at ye signe   [Burdet was a merchant dwelling at of ye croune, which now is ye signe of y^{e3} floure de luse, ouer agaynst   "The Crown" in soper lane. This man merely, in ye rufflyng time of king Edward   Cheapside.] y^e .iiij. his raign,[4] sayd to his owne sonne that he would make him

---

[1] According to *Fab.* (669) Shaw's sermon (see p. 379 below) was preached on June 15,—the Sunday following Hastings's execution on June 13,—and Buckingham's speech was delivered on Tuesday, June 17. These dates agree with More's order of events (cp. 56, 57, 63, 66). But Stallworthe—writing from London on Saturday, June 21, and mentioning, amongst other news, Hastings's execution—says not a word about Shaw's sermon (*Excerpta Historica,* 16, 17). Besides, as the sermon was a complete unveiling of Richard's purpose, we can hardly suppose that such a hazardous step would be taken before June 16, when the Duke of York was conveyed to the Tower.

[2] In *Grafton* (ii. 107) the same story is foisted into *More's* narrative. *Hol.* records, under the year 1476, that " Thomas Burdet, an esquier of Arrow in Warwikeshire, . . . was beheaded for a word spoken in this sort. King Edward in his progresse hunted in Thomas Burdets parke at Arrow, and slue manie of his deere, amongst the which was a white bucke, whereof Thomas Burdet made great account. And therefore when he vnderstood thereof, he wished the buckes head in his bellie that moued the king to kill it. Which tale being told to the king, Burdet was apprehended and accused of treason, for wishing the buckes head (hornes and all) in the kings bellie : he was condemned, drawne from the Tower of London to Tiburne, and there beheaded, and then buried in the Greie friers church at London."—*Hol.* iii. 703/1/6.

[3] y^e] Halle (1548). om. Halle (1550).

[4] *raign*] Ed. *rage* Halle. The six editions of *Halle* belonging to the British Museum have the wrong reading "rage." In one of these editions (6004, ed. 1548), a corrector has written n upon the e ; a change which substitutes the reading "ragn" (= *reign*) for "rage." Crotchets enclose "This Burdet . . . Chepesyde" in the edd. of (?) 1542, and 1548, but these words are not marked as a parenthesis in the edd. of 1550, or in *Grafton.* Part of *Halle's* addition was thus expanded by *Grafton* (ii. 107) : " This man merily, in the ruffling time, betwene king Edward the fourth, and king Henry the sixt, said to his owne sonne," . . . In *Halle* and *Grafton* a comma is placed after "spoken." In *More* and *Hol.* "spoken" is unpunctuated, and in *More* a comma follows "hast." *Hardyng-Grafton* has not *Halle's* addition. The punctuation of *More* was evidently changed to suit *Halle's* version of Burdet's offence.

inheritor of yᵉ croune, meaning his owne house, but these wordes
king Edward made to be misconstrued & interpreted that Burdet
meant the croune of yᵉ realme: wherfore, within lesse space [1] then
.iiij. houres, he was apprehended, iudged, drawen and quartered in
Chepesyde, by the misconstruynge of the lawes of the realme for
the princes pleasure, . . .

When Buckingham has departed, Richard says (ll. 103-105) :

> Goe, Louell, with all speed to Doctor Shaw ;
> [To Cate.] Goe thou to Fryer Penker ; bid them both   104
> Meet me within this houre at Baynards Castle.[2]

Among those whom Richard employed to advocate his right to the
throne were

[Hol. iii. 725/2/30. More, 57/4.] Iohn Shaw, clearke, brother
to the maior, and frier Penker, prouinciall of the Augustine friers ;
both doctors of diuinitie, both great preachers, both of more
learning than vertue, of more fame than learning.

Left alone, Richard mentions his resolve (ll. 108, 109)

> . . . to giue order, that no manner person
> Haue any time recourse vnto the Princes.

When Richard became King (June 26,[3] 1483),

[Hol. iii. 735/1/37. More, 83/16.] foorthwith was the prince
and his brother both shut vp, & all other remooued from them ;
onelie one (called Blacke Will, or William Slaughter) excepted, set
to serue them and see them sure.

Act III. sc. vi.—" Enter a Scrivener with a paper in his hand " (Q.
with . . . hand om. F.). He thus addresses the audience (ll. 1-9) :

> Here is the Indictment of the good Lord Hastings ;
> Which in a set Hand fairely is engross'd,
> That it may be to day read o're in Paules.
> And marke how well the sequell hangs together :
> Eleuen houres I haue spent to write it ouer,
> For yester-night by Catesby was it sent me ;
> The Precedent was full as long a doing :
> And yet within these fiue houres Hastings liu'd   8
> Vntainted, vnexamin'd, free, at libertie.

---

[1] space] Halle (1548). place Halle (1550).
[2] Ll. 103-105 are not in Q.
[3] The Memoranda Rolls of the Exchequer in Ireland contain a letter from
Richard III. to his Irish subjects, who were, it appears, uncertain about the
exact date of his accession. The King informs them that his reign began on
June 26, 1483.—Nicolas's Chronology of History, 326, 327. See also Cont.
Croyl., 566, and York Records, 157, note.

The proclamation of Hastings's treason and vicious life (see p. 373 above) was

[*Hol.* iii. 724/1/62. *More,* 52/31.] made within two houres after that he was beheaded, and it was so curiouslie indicted, & so faire written in parchment, *in* so well *a set hand,* and therewith of it selfe so long a processe, that euerie child might well perceiue that it was prepared before. For all the time, betweene his death and the proclaming, could scant haue sufficed vnto the bare writing alone, all had it bene but in paper, and scribled foorth in hast at aduenture. So that, vpon the proclaming thereof, one that was schoolemaister of Powles, of chance standing by, and comparing the shortnesse of the time with the length of the matter, said vnto them that stood about him: "Here is a gaie goodlie cast, foule "cast awaie for hast." And a merchant answered him, that it was written by prophesie.

[The procla-
mation was
prepared
before
Hastings's
death.]

[Jests of a
school-
master and a
merchant.]

Act III. sc. vii.—The scene is laid at Baynard's Castle. Since sc. v. closed Buckingham had harangued the citizens at Guildhall. Richard now asks (l. 4):

> Toucht you the Bastardie of Edwards Children?
>   *Buck.* I did; with his Contráct with Lady Lucy,
> And his Contráct by deputie in France;[1]
> Th'vnsatiate greedinesse of his desire,
> And his enforcement of the Citie Wiues;[2] . . .   8

Buckingham reminded the citizens at Guildhall how on Sunday (June 22) Dr. Shaw

[*Hol.* iii. 729/2/53. *More,* 70/21.] "groundlie made open vnto "you, the children of king Edward the fourth were neuer lawfullie "begotten; forsomuch as the king (leauing his verie wife dame "Elizabeth Lucie)[3] was neuer lawfullie maried vnto the queene their "mother," . . .

A slanderous
lie confirmed
[: that
Edward was
betrothed to
Lady Lucy.]

---

[1] We do not learn from *More* that Warwick's marriage-making embassy was noticed in Buckingham's speech at the Guildhall. The Shaksperian Buckingham refers to this matter again (III. vii. 179-182), together with Edward's supposed contract to Lady Lucy. Ll. 5, 6 (*his . . . France*), are not in Q.

[2] 8. *And . . . Wiues*] F. om. Q.

[3] The Parliament which met on January 23, 1484, ratified a petition—no doubt presented to the Protector at Baynard's Castle—setting forth reasons for Richard's assumption of the crown. One of the petitioners' objections to the validity of Edward IV.'s union with Elizabeth Grey was "that at the tyme of contract of the same pretensed Mariage, and bifore and longe tyme after, the

Buckingham also declared that

[*Hol.* iii. 720/1/58. *More,* 1557, pp. 62, 63.] "the kings [1] greedie "appetite was insatiable, and euerie where ouer all the realme "intollerable.

"For no woman was there anie where, yoong or old, rich or "poore, whome he set his eie vpon, in whome he anie thing liked, "either person or fauour, speech, pase, or countenance, but, with- "out anie feare of God, or respect of his honour, murmur or "grudge of the world, he would importunelie pursue his appetite, "and haue hir, to the great destruction of manie a good woman, "and great dolor to their husbands, . . . And all were it that, "with this and other importable dealing, the realme was in euerie

He directeth his speech to y[e] commun- altie of the citie [, who suffered most through Edward's lust.]

"part annoied, yet speciallie yee heere, the citizens of this noble "citie, as well for that amongest you is most plentie of all such "things as minister matter to such iniuries, as for that you were "neerest at hand; sith that neere heere abouts was commonlie "his most abiding."

Richard had prescribed Edward's illegitimacy as a topic for Buck- ingham's speech; adding, however (III. v. 93, 94):

Yet touch this sparingly, as 'twere farre off ;
Because, my Lord, you know my Mother liues.

Buckingham therefore reports (III. vii. 9-14) having drawn attention to Edward's

---

owne Bastardie,
As being got, your Father then in France,
And his resemblance, being not like the Duke :[1]
Withall I did inferre your *Lineaments*, [See next page.]   12
Being the right Idea of your Father,
Both in your forme and Noblenesse of Minde ;[2]

In his speech at the Guildhall, Buckingham alluded to

[*Hol.* iii. 729/2/69. *More*, 70/32.] other things which the said worshipfull doctor rather signified than fullie explaned, & which things shall not be spoken for me, as the thing wherein euerie man forbereth to say that he knoweth [*p.* 730]; in auoiding displeasure of my noble lord protector, bearing (as nature requireth) a filiall reuerence to the duchesse his mother.

[Edward IV.'s illegitimacy alluded to.]

Richard and his Council resolued that Dr. Shaw should broach Edward V.'s deposition

[*Hol.* iii. 725/2/53. *More*, 57/24.] in a sermon at Paules crosse; in which he should (by the authoritie of his preaching) incline the people to the protectors ghostlie purpose. But now was all the labor and studie in the deuise of some conuenient pretext, for which the people should be content to depose the prince, and accept the protector for king. In which diuerse things they deuised. But the cheefe thing & the weightiest of all that inuention rested in this, that they should alledge bastardie, either in king Edward himselfe, or in his children, or both. So that he should seeme disabled to inherit the crowne by the duke of Yorke, and the prince by him.

[The chiefest deuise to depose the prince [: to allege bastardy in Edward himself and his children.]

To laie bastardie in king Edward sounded openlie to the rebuke of the protectors owne mother, which was mother to them both ; for in that point could be no other color, but to pretend that his owne mother was an adultresse ; which, notwithstanding, to further this purpose, he letted not. But neuerthelesse he would that point should be lesse and more fauourablie handled : not euen fullie plaine and directlie, but that the matter should be touched aslope, craftilie ; as [*p.* 726] though men spared in that

[Shaw was to touch lightly on the first point, for reuerence of the protector's mother ; but the bastardy of Edward's children was to be fully declared.]

---

[1] 11. *And . . . Duke*] F. om. Q.
[2] " Layd open all your Victories in Scotland," is the next line. Buckingham's speech, in *More* and *Halle*, contains no allusion to these victories. Richard's Scottish campaign is related by *Hol.* iii. 705-708.

point to speake all the truth, for feare of his displeasure. But
the other point, concerning the bastardie that they deuised to
surmize in king Edwards children, that would he should be openlie
declared and inforced to the vttermost.

So instructed, Shaw, after denying the legitimacy of the late King's
children, told the people that

[Neither
Edward nor
Clarence
was deemed
to be cer-
tainly the
son of
Richard
Duke of
York.]
[*Hol.* iii. 727/2/50. *More*, 64/26.]   neither king Edward himselfe, nor the duke of Clarence, among those that were secret in
the houshold, were reckoned verie suerlie for the children of the
noble duke ; as those that by their fauours more resembled other
knowne men than him.   From whose vertuous conditions he said
also that the late king Edward was far off.

[The Pro-
tector was
the image of
York.]
But the lord protector, he said, the verie noble prince, the
speciall paterne of knightlie prowesse, as well in all princelie
behauiour, as in the *lineaments*[1] and fauour of his visage, represented
the verie face of the noble duke his father.   "This is " (quoth he)
"the fathers owne figure, this is his owne countenance, the verie
"print of his visage, the sure vndoubted image, the plaine expresse
"likenesse of that noble duke."

Buckingham thus concludes his report (ll. 20-41) :

> And, when my Oratorie drew toward end,
> I bid them, that did loue their Countries good,
> Cry, "God saue Richard, Englands Royall King ! "
>   *Rich.* And did they so ?
>   *Buck.* No, so God helpe me, they spake not a word ;   **24**
> But like dumbe Statuas,[2] or breathing Stones,
> Star'd each on other, and look'd deadly pale.
> Which when I saw, I reprehended them ;
> And asked the Maior what meant this wilfull silence :   **28**
> His answer was, the people were not vsed
> To be spoke to but by the Récorder.
> Then he was vrg'd to tell my Tale againe,
> "Thus sayth the Duke, thus hath the Duke inferr'd ;"   **32**
> But nothing spake[3] in warrant from himselfe.
> When he had done, some followers of mine owne,
> At lower end of the Hall, hurld vp their Caps,
> And some tenne voyces cry'd, "God saue King Richard ! "   **36**
> And thus I tooke the vantage of those few,
> "Thankes, gentle Citizens and friends," quoth I ;
> "This generall applause and chearefull showt,

---

[1] Cp. III. vii. 12, p. 379 above.
[2] *Statuas*] Steevens (Reed). *Statues.* Q. F.
[3] *spake*] Q. *spoke* F.

"Argues your wisdome, and your loue to Richard:"   40
And euen here brake off, and came away.

More's account of Buckingham's speech contains details which were
omitted by Shakspere.   The citizens' silence caused Buckingham—
"somewhat lowder"—to broach "the same matter againe in other
order, and other words."   Howbeit the people remained "as still as the
midnight."   After the Recorder's address, Buckingham whispered to
the Mayor,—"this is a maruellous obstinate silence" (cp. III. vii. 28),
—and then told his hearers that, though the lords, and the commons of
other parts, could do what was asked, yet regard for the citizens was a
motive for seeking their consent also.   Hence he required an answer.
Thereupon a whispering began among the people, "as it were the sound
of a swarme of bees," till at last were heard the shouts proceeding from
"an ambushment of the dukes seruants."

[*Hol.* iii. 730/1/71. *More,* 72/16.] When the duke had said,
and looked that the people, whome he hoped that the maior had
framed before, should, after this proposition made, haue cried,
"King Richard, king Richard!" all was husht and mute, and not   [The citizens
were silent.]
one word answered therevnto. . . .

When the maior saw this [the failure of Buckingham's second
speech], he with other partners of that councell drew about the
duke, and said that the people had not beene accustomed there to
be spoken vnto, but by the recorder, which is the mouth of the   [The Mayor
said that
they might
answer their
recorder.]
citie, and happilie to him they will answer.   With that the
recorder, called Fitz William, a sad man, & an honest, which was   *Fitz William,*
recorder
[, rehearsed
Bucking-
ham's
speech].
so new come into that office, that he neuer had spoken to the
people before, and loth was with that matter to begin, notwithstanding, thervnto commanded by the maior, made rehearsall to
the commons of that the duke had twise rehearsed to them
himselfe.

But the recorder so tempered his tale, that he showed euerie   [But Fitz-
William
spoke as
Bucking-
ham's
mouth-
piece.]
thing as the dukes words, and no part his owne.   But all this
nothing[1] no change made in the people, which alwaie after one   [Still the
citizens were
silent]
stood as they had beene men amazed. . . .

[When Buckingham demanded an answer] the people began   [when
Buckingham
demanded
an answer.]
to whisper among themselues secretly, that the voice was neither
lowd nor distinct, but as it were the sound of a swarme of bees;
till at the last, in the nether end of the hall, an ambushment of

---

[1] *nothing*] More.   *noting* Hol.   *thys no chaunge made* Halle.

the dukes seruants, and one Nashfield,[1] and other belonging to the protector, with some prentisses and lads that thrust into the hall

K. Richards election pre- ferred by voices of confederacie [; crying "King Richard, King Richard !"]

amongst the prease, began suddenlie at mens backes to crie out, as lowd as their throtes would giue: "King Richard, king "Richard !" and threw vp their caps in token of ioy. And they, that stood before, cast backe their heads, maruelling thereof, but nothing they said. Now when the duke and the maior saw this maner, they wiselie turned it to their purpose, and said it was a

[Bucking-ham affirmed that these shouts expressed the citisens' minds.]

goodlie crie, & a ioifull, to heare eueric man with one voice, no man saieng naie.

"Wherefore, friends" (quoth the duke) "sith we perceiue it "is all your whole minds to haue this noble man for your king, "(whereof we shall make his grace so effectuall report, that we "doubt not but it shall redound vnto your great weale and com- "moditie,) we [*p.* 731] require ye, that ye to morrow go with vs, and "we with you, vnto his noble grace, to make our humble request "vnto him in maner before remembred." And therewith the lords came downe, and the companie dissolued and departed, . . .

The historical date of the rest of this scene (ll. 45-247) is June 25, 1483.[2] The Lord Mayor is now at hand, so Richard departs in order to show himself presently on the leads of Baynard's Castle. When the Mayor and citizens enter they find Buckingham apparently waiting for an audience. Catesby then brings what purports to be the Protector's answer (ll. 59-64):

> He doth entreat your Grace, my Noble Lord,
> To visit him to morrow or next day :   60
> He is within, with two right reuerend Fathers,
> Diuinely bent to Meditation ;
> And in no Worldly suites would he be mou'd,
> To draw him from his holy Exercise.   64

Catesby is despatched to ask again for an audience, but Richard sends him back with another excuse (ll. 84-87):

> He wonders to what end you haue assembled
> Such troopes of Citizens to come to him,
> His Grace not being warn'd thereof before :
> He feares, my Lord, you meane no good to him.

---

[1] *and one Nashfeld (Nashfeelde)*] Halle. *and Nashfelds* Hol. *and Nashefeldes* More.
[2] The morrow of Buckingham's speech at the Guildhall. See p. 375, note 1, above. Scenes ii.-vii., Act III., make one dramatic day.—*T-A.*, 328-331.

Receiving Buckingham's profession of good faith, Catesby goes out, and thereupon Richard enters "aloft, betweene two Bishops"[1] (l. 94).

I must premise (1) that nothing said by More, or any other historical authority, supplied a hint even for the dramatic Richard's refusal of an audience on the ground of preoccupation with "holy Exercise" : (2) the words "with a byshop on euery hand of him"—which I have placed between square brackets—were added by Halle or Grafton to More's text.

I resume More's narrative at the point when, "on the morrow after" Buckingham's speech,

[*Hol.* iii. 731/1/11. *More,* 74/27.]   the maior with all the aldermen,[2] and chiefe commoners of the citie, in their best maner apparelled, assembling themselues togither, resorted vnto Bainards castell, where the protector laie.   To which place repaired also, (according to their appointment,) the duke of Buckingham, and diuerse noble men with him, beside manie knights and other gentlemen. And therevpon the duke sent word vnto the lord protector, of the being there of a great and honourable companie, to mooue a great matter vnto his grace. Wherevpon the protector made difficultie to come out vnto them, but if he first knew some part of their errand, as though he doubted and partlie mistrusted the comming of such a number vnto him so suddenlie, without anie warning, or knowledge whether they came for good or harme.

Then the duke, when he had shewed this to the maior and other, that they might thereby see how little the protector looked for this matter, they sent vnto him by the messenger such louing message againe, and therewith so humblie besought him, to vouchsafe that they might resort to his presence to propose their intent, of which they would vnto none other person anie part disclose ; that at the last he came foorth of his chamber, and yet not downe vnto them, but stood aboue in a gallerie ouer them [with a byshop on euery hand of him], where they might see him, and speake to him, as though he would not yet come too neere them till he wist what they ment.

The maior comming to Bainards castell, vnto the lord protector.

[Buckingham sent word to Richard that a great company desired an audience on an important matter.]

[Richard declined to come till he knew something of their business.]

[After another message he came forth and stood in a gallery.]

---

[1] 94. *Enter Richard aloft, . . . Bishops.*] F. *Enter Rich. with two bishops aloft (a loste* Q1).] Q.   Richard's summons of Shaw and Penker to meet him at Baynard's Castle (III. v. 103-105) is not in the Qq. See p. 376 above.
[2] In the F. version of III. vii. 66, "the Maior and Aldermen" desire a conference with Richard. The Q. reads: "the Maior and Cittizens;" and F. has (l. 55): "Enter the Maior, and Citizens."

Speaking on behalf of the Mayor and citizens, Buckingham thus
addresses Richard (ll. 100-103) :

> Famous Plantagenet, most gracious Prince,
> Lend fauourable eare to our requests ;
> And pardon vs the interruption
> Of thy Deuotion and right Christian Zeale.

Richard asks "what is your Graces pleasure ?" and Buckingham
answering (ll. 109, 110),

> Euen that (I hope) which pleaseth God aboue,
> And all good men of this vngouern'd Ile ;

proceeds, after some flattery, to make known their suit (ll. 130-136) :

>   we heartily solicite
> Your gracious selfe to take on you the charge
> And Kingly Gouernment of this your Land ;   **132**
> Not as Protector, Steward, Substitute,
> Or lowly Factor for anothers gaine ;
> But as successiuely, from Blood to Blood,
> Your Right of Birth, your Empyrie, your owne.   **136**

Richard's answer (ll. 141-173) contains nothing resembling the
speech attributed to him by More, save in ll. 148-150; 171. With
these lines compare the passage, "Notwithstanding, he not onlie . . .
to the prince." If, says Richard, I elect to keep silence, you might
deem that I consented ;

> If to reproue you for this suit of yours,   **148**
> (So season'd with your faithfull loue to me,)
> Then, on the other side, I check'd my friends.[1] . . .
> On him [Edward V.] I lay that you would lay on me, . . . 171

[*Hol.* iii. 731/1/39.   *More*, 75/20.] And thervpon the duke of
Buckingham first made humble petition vnto him on the behalfe

[Buckingham craued Richard's pardon beforehand for the intent of their comming.] of them all, that his grace would pardon them, and licence them
to propose vnto his grace the intent of their comming, without his
displeasure; without which pardon obteined, they durst not be
bold to mooue him of that matter.

In which albeit they ment as much honor to his grace, as
wealth to all the realme beside, yet were they not sure how his
grace would take it; whome they would in no wise offend. Then
the protector (as he was veric gentle of himselfe, and also longed
[Richard gaue Buckingham leaue to speak.] sore to wit what they ment) gaue him leaue to propose what him
liked ; verelie trusting (for the good mind that he bare them all)
none of them anie thing would intend vnto himward, wherewith he
ought to bee greeued. When the duke had this leaue and pardon
to speake, then waxed he bold to shew him their intent and

---

[1] 148-150. *If . . . friends*] F. om. Q.

purpose, with all the causes mooning them therevnto (as ye before
haue heard); and finallie to beseech his grace, that it would like
him, of his accustomed goodness and zeale vnto the realme, now
with his eie of pitie to behold the long continued distresse and
decaie of the same, and to set his gratious hands to redresse and
amendment thereof.

[Richard
entreated to
assume the
soueraignty
of this
distressed
realm.]

All which he might well doo, by taking vpon him the crowne
and gouernance of this realme, according to his right and title
lawfullie descended vnto him; and to the laud of God, profit of
the land, & vnto his noble grace so much the more honour, and
lesse paine, in that, that neuer prince reigned vpon anie people,
that were so glad to liue vnder his obeisance, as the people of this
realme vnder his.   When the protector had heard the proposition,
he looked verie strangelie thereat, and answered: that all were it
that he partlie knew the things by them alledged to be true, yet
such entire loue he bare vnto king Edward and his children, &[1]
so much more regarded his honour in other realmes about, than
the crowne of anie one, (of which he was neuer desirous,) that
he could not find in his hart in this point to incline to their
desire. . . .

O singular
dissimula-
tion of king
Richard [, in
refusing
Bucking-
ham's offer !]

Notwithstanding, he not onlie pardoned them the motion that
they made him, but also thanked them for the loue and hartie
fauour they bare him; praieng them for his sake to giue and beare
the same to the prince, . . .

K. Richard
spake other-
wise than he
meant
[, when he
prayed them
transfer
their love to
his nephew].

Buckingham replies[2] by urging the illegitimacy of Edward IV.'s
children (ll. 177-180):

> You say that Edward is your Brothers Sonne:
> So say we too, but not by Edwards Wife;
> For first was he contráct to Lady Lucie,
> (Your Mother liues a Witnesse to his Vow,) . . .

When Edward IV. made known his betrothal to Lady Grey, the
Duchess of York

---

[1] & so much] Halle.   that so much Hol. (More).

[2] In this speech (III. vii. 189) Buckingham says that Edward was seduced,
by a fancy for Lady Grey, "To base declension and loath'd Bigamie." The
Duchess of York told Edward that Lady Grey's widowhood should be a
sufficient deterrent, for it was "a verie blemish and high disparagement to the
sacred maiestie of a prince, that ought as nigh to approch priesthood in clean-
nesse as he dooth in dignitie, to be defiled with bigamie in his first mariage.'
—Hol. iii. 726/2/21.   More, 60/12.

Elisabeth
Lucie (was—
so the
Duchess of
York
asserted—
betrothed to
Edward).
[*Hol.* iii. 727/1/16. *More,* 61/31.] openlie obiected against his
mariage, (as it were in discharge of hir conscience,) that the king
was sure to dame Elizabeth Lucie and hir husband before God.

As Richard still affects to hesitate, the petitioner uses a final
argument (ll. 214-217):

> Yet whether[1] you accept our suit or no,
> Your Brothers Sonne shall neuer reigne our King;
> But we will plant some other in the Throne,   216
> To the disgrace and downe-fall of your House: . . .

Richard yields; declining all responsibility for his acquiescence
(ll. 227-236). Buckingham exclaims (ll. 239, 240):

> Then I salute you with this Royall Title:
> Long liue King Richard, Englands worthie King!

The following passages illustrate the rest of this scene:

[*Hol.* iii. 731/2/30. *More,* 77/11.] Upon this answer giuen, the
duke, by the protectors licence, a little rowned aswell with other
noble men about him, as with the maior and recorder of London.
And after that (vpon like pardon desired & obteined) he shewed
alowd vnto the protector for a[2] finall conclusion: that the realme

[Bucking-
ham's reply:
They would
not suffer
Edward's
line to
reign.]
was appointed K. Edwards line should not anie longer reigne vpon
them, both for that they had so farre gone, that it was now no
suertie to retreat, as for that they thought it for the weale
vniuersall to take that waie, although they had not yet begun it.
Wherefore, if it would like his grace to take the crowne vpon him,
they would humblie beseech him therevnto. If he would giue

[If Richard
refused their
offer, they
should seek
for some
other noble
who would
accept it.]
them a resolute answer to the contrarie, (which they would be loth
to heare,) then must they needs seeke and should not faile to find
some other noble man that would. . . .

[A shout:
"King
Richard,
King
Richard!"]
[When Richard accepted the crown] there was a great shout,
crieng: "King Richard, king Richard!"

Act IV. sc. i.—Queen Elizabeth, the Duchess of York,[3] the Marquess of Dorset, Anne Duchess of Gloucester, and Lady Margaret
Plantagenet (Clarence's daughter), meet before the Tower; purposing
to visit the Princes. They are informed by the Lieutenant of the

---

[1] *yet whether*] Q. *yet know, where* F.
[2] *for a*] Halle. *that for a* Hol. (More).
[3] As this scene closes the Duchess of York says (l. 96):

> "Eightie odde yeeres of sorrow haue I seene," . . .

The historical Duchess was born on May 3, 1415 (*Wyrc.,* 453); and was therefore about eighty years of age when she died in 1495 (see p. 350, n. 3, above).

Tower that Richard will not suffer their visit (ll. 15-17 ; cp. p. 376 above). In the previous scene (III. vii. 242-244) Richard's coronation was appointed for to-morrow. Stanley now enters, and, addressing Anne, says (ll. 32, 33) :

> Come, Madame, you must straight to Westminster,
> There to be crownèd Richards Royall Queene.

On July 6, 1483,[1]—nearly a fortnight after the election at Baynard's Castle,—Richard and Anne ascended their thrones in Westminster Abbey,

[*Hol.* iii. 734/1/3. *Halle*, 376.] where the cardinall of Cantur-burie, & other bishops them crowned according to the custome of the realme, . . . *The king & queens crowned.*

Queen Elizabeth then bids Dorset begone (ll. 42, 43) :

> If thou wilt out-strip Death, goe crosse the Seas,
> And liue with Richmond, from the reach of Hell : . . .

Dorset went with Queen Elizabeth into sanctuary at Westminster,[2] and left it to join the rebellion raised by Buckingham in October, 1483.[3] Buckingham, before his capture, hoped either to collect a new army, " or else shortlie to saile into Britaine to the earle of Richmond " (*Hol.* iii. 743/2/56. *Halle*, 394). Dorset, more fortunate, was one of those who " fled by sea," and " arriued safelie in the duchie of Britaine " (*Hol.* iii. 743/2/68. *Halle*, 394). When Richmond returned to Brittany, after his fruitless attempt to succour the rebellion,

[*Hol.* iii. 745/1/55. *Halle*, 396.] he was certified by credible information, that the duke of Buckingham had lost his head ; and that the marquesse Dorset, and a great number of noble men of England, had a little before inquired and searched for him there, and were now returned to Vannes. . . . *[Dorset in Brittany, searching for Richmond.]*

When they knew that he was safelie returned into Britaine, Lord, how they reioised I for before that time they missed him, and knew not in what part of the world to make inquirie or search for him. For they doubted and no lesse feared least he had taken land in England, & fallen into the hands of king Richard, in whose person they knew well was neither mercie nor compassion. *[Dorset and the Lancastrians rejoiced to hear of Richmond's safety.]*

Wherefore in all speedie maner they galoped toward him, and him reuerentlie saluted. *[Their meeting with Richmond.]*

Act IV. sc. ii.—Richard enters " crownd " (Q.) ; attended by Buck-ingham, Catesby, a Page, and others. The King requires Buckingham's " consent " that the young Princes shall die (l. 23). Buckingham

---

[1] *Cont. Croyl.*, 567. [2] *Polyd. Verg.*, 540/39.
[3] *Hol.* iii. 743/1/59 (*Halle*, 393).

craves "some litle breath, some pawse," ere he can "positively speake
in this" (ll. 24, 25); and goes out. Angered by Buckingham's
hesitation, Richard calls the Page and asks (ll. 34, 35) :

> Know'st thou not any whom corrupting Gold
> Will tempt vnto a close exploit of Death !
>   *Page.* I know a discontented Gentleman,   36
> Whose humble meanes match not his haughtie spirit :
> Gold were as good as twentie Orators,
> And will (no doubt) tempt him to any thing.
>   *Rich.* What is his Name !
>   *Page.*   His Name, my Lord, is Tirrell. 40
>   *Rich.* I partly know the man : goe, call him hither, Boy.

After the Page's exit, Richard hears from Stanley of Dorset's flight.
The King then says (ll. 51-53) :

> Come hither, Catesby : rumor it abroad
> That Anne, my Wife, is very grieuous sicke ;[1]
> I will take order for her keeping close.

In March, 1485,[2] Richard

*A rumour
spred abroad
of the queenes
death : at
the procure-
ment of king
Richard.*   [*Hol.* iii. 751/1/18. *Halle,* 407.] procured a common rumor
(but he would not haue the author knowne) to be published and
spred abroad among the common people, that the queene was
dead ; to the intent that she, taking some conceit of this strange
fame, should fall into some sudden sicknesse or greeuous maladie :
and to procue, if afterwards she should fortune by that or anie
other waies to lease hir life, whether the people would impute hir
death to the thought or sicknesse, or thereof would laie the blame
to him.

Catesby departs, and Richard communes with himself (ll. 61, 62) :

> I must be married to my *Brothers Daughter*,
> Or else my Kingdome stands on brittle Glasse.

In 1485, Richmond heard that Richard

  [*Hol.* iii. 752/2/47. *Halle,* 409.] intended shortlie to marie the
ladie Elizabeth, his *brothers daughter ;* . . .

The Page now returns with Tyrrel, who at once undertakes to
despatch the Princes (ll. 78-81).

> Let me haue open meanes to come to them,
> And soone Ile rid you from the feare of them.
>   *Rich.* Thou sing'st sweet Musique. Hearke, come hither, Tyrrel :
> Goe, by this token : rise, and lend thine Eare : . . .   80
>   [*Whispers.*

---

[1] *is sicke and like to die*] Q.   [2] See p. 396, n. 3, below.

Tyrrel's work is to be done "straight" (F.), or before Richard
sleeps (Q.).

The ensuing excerpts form the source of ll. 8-41 ; 66-85.

[*Hol.* iii. 734/2/38. *More*, 81/15.]   King Richard, after his
coronation, taking his waie to Glocester to visit (in his new honour)
the towne of which he bare the name of his old, deuised (as he
rode) to fulfill the thing which he before had intended.   And forsomuch as his mind gaue him, that, his nephues liuing, men would
not reckon that he could haue right to the realme, he thought
therefore without delaie to rid them ; as though the killing of his
kinsmen could amend his cause, and make him a kindlie king.
Wherupon he sent one Iohn Greene (whom he speciallie trusted)
vnto sir Robert Brakenberie, constable of the Tower; with a letter
and credence also, that the same sir Robert should in anie wise
put the two children to death.

This Iohn Greene did his errand vnto Brakenberie, kneeling
before our ladie [1] in the Tower.   Who plainelie answered, that he
would neuer put them to death to die therefore.   With which
answer Iohn Greene returning, recounted the same to king Richard
at Warwike, yet in his waie.   Wherewith he tooke such displeasure
& thought, that the same night he said vnto a secret page of his:
"Ah! whom shall a man trust?   Those that I haue brought vp
"myselfe, those that I had weent would most suerlie serue me, euen
"those faile me, and at my commandement will doo nothing for
"me."   "Sir" (quoth his page) "there lieth one on your pallet
"without, that I dare well saie, to doo your grace pleasure, the
"thing were right hard that he would refuse."   Meaning this by
sir Iames Tirrell, which was a man of right goodlie personage, and
for natures gifts worthie to haue serued a much better prince ; if
he had well serued God, and by grace obteined as much truth and
good will as he had strength and wit.

The man had an high heart, & sore longed vpward, not rising
yet so fast as he had hoped, being hindered & kept vnder by the
meanes of sir Richard Ratcliffe, [*p.* 735] and sir William Catesbie,
which, (longing for no mo partoners of the princes fauour ; and,

*[Richard
determined
to have his
nephews
slain.]*

*Iohn Greene
[sent to
sound]
Robert
Braken-
berie, con-
stable of the
Tower.*

*The murther
of the two
yoong
princes set
abroch.*

*Sir Iames
Tirrell
described.*

*Authoritie
loueth no
partners
[: Ratcliffe
and Catesby
kept Tyrrel
out of em-
ployment].*

---

[1] Kneeling in prayer before an image of our Lady.

namelie, not for him, whose pride they wist would beare no peere,)
kept him by secret drifts out of all secret trust: which thing this page
well had marked and knowne.   Wherefore, this occasion offered, of
verie speciall friendship he tooke his time to put him forward, and
by such wise doo him good, that all the enimies he had (except the
deuill) could neuer haue doone him so much hurt.   For vpon this
pages words king Richard arose, (for this communication had he
sitting at the draught, a conuenient carpet for such a councell,) and
came out into the pallet chamber, on which he found in bed sir
Iames and sir Thomas Tirrels, of person like, and brethren of
blond, but nothing of kin in conditions.

[Richard
easily gained
Tyrrel's
consent.]
The constable
of the Tower
deliuereth
the keies to
sir Iames
Tyrrell vpon
the kings
commande-
ment.

Then said the king merilie to them: "What, sirs, be ye in bed
"so soone?"   And calling vp sir Iames, brake to him secretlie his
mind in this mischeeuous matter.   In which he found him nothing
strange.   Wherefore on the morow he sent him to Brakenberie
with a letter, by which he was commanded to deliuer sir Iames all
the keies[1] of the Tower for one night; to the end he might there
accomplish the kings pleasure, in such things as he had giuen him
commandement.   After which letter deliuered, & the keies receiued,
sir Iames appointed the night next insuing to destroie them;
deuising before and preparing the meanes.[2]

When Tyrrel is gone, Buckingham re-enters and makes a demand
(ll. 91-94):

> My Lord, I clayme the gift, my due by promise,
> For which your Honor and your Faith is pawn'd;   92

---

[1] The men sent to murder Clarence have a commission addressed to
Brakenbury, who, after reading it, delivers to them the keys.—*Rich. III.*, I.
iv. 90-96.

[2] Assuming this account to be true, the Princes were murdered about the
middle of August, 1483.   Richard III.'s privy seals show that he was at
Warwick from August 8 to August 14.   On August 15 he was at Coventry
(*H. S.*).   At Warwick Grene reported Brakenbury's answer (*More*, 81/33).   On
the day following Grene's arrival at Warwick, Tyrrel was despatched to take
the keys of the Tower from Brakenbury (*More*, 82/2, 83/2).   The deed was
done on "the night nexte ensuing" the delivery of the keys to Tyrrel (*More*,
83/6).   Warwick is 90 miles distant by road from London.—*Lewis.*   In
Richard's reign messengers could post 100 miles a day.—*Cont. Croyl.*, 571.   If
Tyrrel were sent from Warwick, the latest date for his departure must have
been August 14, and he could reach London the same day.   When Buckingham's rebellion began (October), there was a rumour that the Princes were
dead.—*Cont. Croyl.*, 568.

Th'Earledome of Herford,[1] and the moueables,
Which you haue promisëd I shall possesse.

While carrying out a purpose of contemptuously ignoring Buckingham's demand, Richard, vouchsafing no response, addresses Stanley (ll. 95, 96):

Stanley, looke to your Wife : if she conuey
Letters to Richmond, you shall answer it.

In 1484,[2]

[*Hol.* iii. 746/1/56. *Halle*, 398.] nothing was more maruelled at, than that the lord Stanleie had not beene taken and reputed as an enimie to the king; considering the working of the ladie Margaret his wife, moother to the earle of Richmond. But, forsomuch as the enterprise of a woman was of him reputed of no regard or estimation, and that the lord Thomas hir husband had purged himselfe sufficientlie to be innocent of all dooings and attempts by hir perpetrated and committed ; it was giuen him in charge to keepe hir in some secret place at home, without hauing anie seruant or companie: so that from thense foorth she should neuer send letter or messenger vnto hir sonne, nor anie of his freends or confederats, by the which the king might be molested or troubled, or anie hurt or preiudice might be attempted against his realme and communaltie.

King Richard chargeth the lord Stanleie to keepe his wife in some secret place from dealing against him.

Still apparently unmindful of Buckingham, Richard soliloquizes about Henry VI.'s prophecy that Richmond should be King (see p. 329 above), which leads to a reflection on the prophet's unforeseen death,[3] and is followed by a disagreeable reminiscence (ll. 106-110):

Richmond ! When last I was at Exeter,
The Maior in curtesie showd me the Castle,
And called it Ruge-mount : at which name I started,   108
Because a Bard of Ireland told me once,
I should not liue long after I saw Richmond.[4]

---

[1] *Herford*] Q. *Hertford* F. *erle of Herfordes landes* Halle (382), but (387) *Earle of Hartfordes landes.* See p. 450, n. 2, below.

[2] This general feeling of surprise at Stanley's freedom is spoken of by *Halle* (397, 398) as having been prevalent about the time when Richard's sole Parliament was sitting. The session opened on January 23, 1484.—*Rot. Parl.,* vi. 237/1.

[3]   " How chance the prophet could not at that time
     Haue told me, I being by, that I should kill him ?" (Q. om. F.)
The dramatic Richard of 3 *Hen. VI.* was, like the historic character, absent from England during Henry's brief restoration.

[4] 106-110. *Richmond ! . . . Richmond.*] Q. om. F.

In November, 1483,[1] *Exeter* was visited by Richard,

[*Hol.* iii. 746/1/1.] whome the maior & his brethren in the best maner they could did receiue, and then presented to him in a purse two hundred nobles; which he thankefullie accepted. And during his abode here he went about the citie, & viewed the seat of the same, & at length he came to the castell; and, when he vnderstood that it was called Rugemont, suddenlie he fell into a dumpe, and

(as one astonied) said: "Well, I see my daies be not long." He spake this of a prophesie told him, that, when he came once to Richmond, he should not long liue after: which fell out in the end to be true; not in respect of this castle, but in respect of Henrie earle of Richmond, who the next [*i. e.* second] yeare following met him at Bosworth field, where he was slaine.

Buckingham again solicits attention to his demand for the promised earldom (114, 115). He supported Richard at Northampton in April, 1483;

[*Hol.* iii. 736/1/21. *More,* 86/29.] and from thense still continued with him partner of all his deuises; till that, after his coronation, they departed (as it seemed) verie great freends at Glocester. From whense as soone as the duke came home, he so lightlie turned from him, and so highlie conspired against him, that a man would maruell whereof the change grew. And, suerlie, the occasion of their variance is of diuerse men diuerselie reported.

Some haue I heard say, that the duke, a little before his coronation, among other things, required of the protector the erle[2] of Herefords lands, to the which he pretended himselfe inst inheritor. And, forsomuch as the title, which he claimed by inheritance, was somwhat interlaced with the title to the crowne by the line of king

Henrie before depriued, the protector conceiued such indignation, that he reiected the dukes request with manie spitefull and minatorie words. Which so wounded his heart with hatred and mistrust, that he neuer after could indure to looke aright on king Richard, but euer feared his owne life; . . .

---

[1] Buckingham was beheaded on November 2, 1483 (see p. 410 below). On the following day Richard left Salisbury and marched westwards till he reached Exeter.—*Cont. Croyl.*, 568. About the end of November the King returned to London.—*Cont. Croyl.*, 570.

[2] *erle*] Halle. *duke* Hol. (More).

Richard rejects his former ally's demand with studied insult; and
all leave the stage save Buckingham, who lingers a moment to muse
(ll. 123-126):

> And is it thus? repayes he my deepe seruice
> With such contempt? made I him King for this?
> O, let me thinke on Hastings, and be gone
> To Brecnock, while my fearefull Head is on!

In the Summer of 1483, "soone after" Buckingham's

[*Hol.* iii. 736/2/3. *More,* 88/12] comming home to Brecknocke,
hauing there in his custodie, by the commandement of king
Richard, doctor Morton, bishop of Elie, . . . [Buckingham] waxed
with him familiar; whose wisedome abused his pride to his owne
deliuerance, and the dukes destruction.

[Bucking-
ham re-
turned to
Brecknock,
and became
friendly with
Dr. Morton.]

Halle's Chronicle contains (387) what professes to be an account of
this matter given by Buckingham himself to Dr. Morton, during the
time of the Bishop's detention at Brecknock Castle. When, said
Buckingham, Richard

[*Hol.* iii. 739/1/74.] was once crowned king, and in full possession of the whole realme, he cast awaie his old conditions as the
adder dooth hir skin, verifieng the old prouerbe, "Honours change
manners," as the parish preest remembreth that he was neuer[1]
parish clearke. For when I my selfe sued vnto him for my part
of the earle of Herefords lands, which his brother king Edward
wrongfullie deteined and withheld from me; and also required to
haue the office of the high constableship of England, as diuerse of
my noble ancestors before this time haue had, and in long descent
continued: in this my first sute shewing his good mind toward
me, he did not onelie first delaie me, and afterward denaie me,
but gaue me such vnkind words, with such tawnts & retawnts, ye,
in manner checke and checkemate, to the vttermost proofe of my
patience: as though I had neuer furthered him, but hindered him;
as though I had put him downe, and not set him vp. . . .

The princi-
pall cause
why the duke
of Bucking-
ham obtained
such inward
grudge
against king
Richard [was
Richard's
scornful
rejection of
the Duke's
claim to the
Earl of
Hereford's
lands, and
the Con-
stableship of
England.]

But when I was crediblie informed of the death of the two
yoong innocents, his owne naturall nephues, contrarie to his faith
and promise; to the which (God be my iudge!) I neuer agreed, nor
condescended; O Lord, how my veines panted, how my bodie
trembled, and how my heart inwardlie grudged! insomuch that I
so abhorred the sight, and much more the companie, of him, that

[When
Buckingham
heard of the
Princes'
murder, (to
which he
never
agreed,)

---

[1] (?) never remembreth that he was euer.

he left
Richard's
Court.]

I could no longer abide in his court, except I should be openlie
reuenged : the end whereof was doubtfull.

Act IV. sc. iii.—The Princes have been smothered while abed by
Dighton and Forrest, at the instance of Tyrrel, who now enters and
describes his agents' remorse (ll. 3-21). Richard, entering, learns from
Tyrrel that " the thing " commanded " is done "; and asks (l. 27) :

> But did'st thou see them dead ?
>
> *Tir.* I did, my Lord.
> *Rich.*   And buried, gentle Tirrell !   28
> *Tir.* The Chaplaine of the Tower hath buried them ;
> But where (to say the truth)[1] I do not know.

Having undertaken to make away with the Princes,

The two
murtherers
of the two
princes
appointed.

[*Hol.* iii. 735/1/45. *More,* 83/23.] sir Iames Tirrell deuised,
that they should be murthered in their beds. To the execution
whereof, he appointed Miles Forrest, one of the foure that kept
them, a fellow *fleshed*[2] in murther before time. To him he ioined
one Iohn Dighton, his owne horssekeeper, a big, broad, square, and
strong knaue.

The yoong
K. and his
brother mur-
thered in
their beds at
midnight in
the Tower.

Then, all the other being remooued from them, this Miles
Forrest, and Iohn Dighton, about midnight, (the seelie children
lieng in their beds,) came into the chamber, &, suddenlie lapping
them vp among the clothes, so to bewrapped them and intangled
them, keeping downe by force the fether-bed and pillowes hard
vnto their mouths, that, within a while, smothered and stifled,
their breath failing, they gaue vp to God their innocent soules into
the ioies of heauen ; leaning to the tormentors their bodies dead in
the bed. Which after that the wretches perceiued, first by the
strugling with the paines of death, and after long lieng still, to be
thoroughlie dead, they laid their bodies naked out vpon the bed,
and fetched sir Iames to see them ; which, vpon the sight of them,
caused those murtherers to burie them at the staire foot, meetlie
deepe in the ground, vnder a great heape of stones.

[Richard
gaue Tyrrel
great thanks
(cp. ll. 83,
84).]

Then rode sir Iames in great hast to king Richard, and shewed
him all the maner of the murther; who gaue him great thanks,
and (as some saie) there made him knight. But he allowed not
(as I haue heard) the burieng in so vile a corner; saieng, that he

---

[1] *where (to say the truth)*] F. *how or in what place* Q.
[2] Tyrrel calls both the murderers "*flesht* Villaines" (IV. iii. 6).

would haue them buried in a better place, bicause they were a
kings sonnes. . . . Whervpon, they saie that a priest of sir
Robert Brakenberies tooke vp the bodies againe, and secretlie [The
interred them in such place, as, by the occasion of his death, which Princes'
                                                                     bodies never
onelie knew it, could neuer since come to light.   found.]

When he is alone Richard recounts what has happened since the
close of sc. ii., Act IV. He had purposed (III. v. 107) secretly

> To draw the Brats of Clarence out of sight.

Afterwards he remarked (IV. ii. 56):

> The Boy is foolish, and I feare not him.

Now (IV. iii. 36) he says:

> The Sonne of Clarence haue I pent vp close.

Edward Plantagenet, Earl of Warwick, son of George Duke of
Clarence, was executed in November 1499, for having shared Perkin
Warbeck's plot to escape from the Tower.[1] Warwick

[*Hol.* iii. 787/2/15. *Halle*, 490.] had beene kept in prison *Edward*
                                                                    Plantagenet,
within the Tower almost from his tender yeares; that is to saie,   *earle of*
                                                                    Warwike, a
from the first yeare of the king [Henry VII.], to this fifteenth   *verie*
                                                                    innocent.
yeare, out of all companie of men & sight of beasts; insomuch
that he could not discerne a goose from a capon, . . .

Within a day or two after the battle of Bosworth, Henry VII. sent

[*Hol.* iii. 762/1/6. *Halle*, 422.] sir Robert Willoughbie, knight,
to the manour of Sheriffehuton in the countie of Yorke, for Edward
Plantagenet, earle of Warwike, sonne and heire to George duke of
Clarence; then being of the age of fifteene yeares: whome king [Warwick
                                                                 imprisoned
Richard had kept there as prisoner during the time of his vsurped at Sheriff
                                                                   Hutton by
reigne.[2]   Richard.]

A few dramatic hours have elapsed since Catesby departed, at
Richard's bidding, to

> Inquire me out some meane poore Gentleman,
> Whom I will marry straight to Clarence Daughter.—IV. ii. 54, 55.

Both obstacles are now removed. Clarence's son is "pent vp close";

> His daughter meanly haue I matcht in marriage.—IV. iii. 37.

---

[1] *Halle*, 491.
[2] Richard was at York in September, 1483 (*York Records*, 171-173); and
there knighted the young Earl of Warwick (*Rows Rol*, 60).

Margaret Plantagenet, Countess of Salisbury, Clarence's daughter,
was about twelve years of age at the time of Richard's death.[1] She
married Sir Richard Pole, Chief Gentleman of the Bed-Chamber to
Prince Arthur.[2] The Dramatist has, apparently, confounded her
with her first cousin. In 1485, the rumour that Richard would
marry his niece was accompanied by a report that he meant also

[*Hol.* iii. 752/2/48. *Halle,* 409.] to prefer the ladie Cicilie
hir sister to a man found in a cloud, and of an vnknowne linage
and familie.

Richard proceeds (ll. 38, 39):

> The Sonnes of Edward sleepe in Abrahams bosome,
> And Anne my wife hath bid this world good night.

Richard was, as we have seen (p. 388 above), accused of spreading a
false report of Anne's death. Hearing of this rumour, she feared that
Richard "had iudged hir worthie to die," and so

[*Hol.* iii. 751/1/40. *Halle,* 407.] either by inward thought and
pensiuenesse of hart, or by infection of poison (which is affirmed
to be most likelie), within few daies after the queene departed out
of this transitorie life.[3]

Richard's meditations are interrupted by the entrance of Ratcliffe
(*Catesby* Q.), announcing (l. 46),

> Bad news, my Lord : Mourton is fled to Richmond.

John Morton, Bishop of Ely, though he became a confidant of his
jailor Buckingham's plots against Richard,

[*Hol.* iii. 741/1/71. *Halle,* 390.] did not tarrie till the dukes

---

[1] She was born in August, 1473.—*Rows Rol,* 61.
[2] " Margaret Plantagenet . . . became the Wife of Sir Richard Pole Kt.
(Son of Sir Jeffrey Pole Kt. descended from a Family of ancient Gentry in
Wales) who having valiantly served King Henry the Seventh, in his Wars of
Scotland [? in 1497 : see Bacon's *Henry VII.,* 158/2], and being a Person much
accomplished, was made chief Gentleman of the Bed-Chamber to Prince
Arthur, and Kt. of the Garter; whereupon attending him into Wales, he
receiv'd Command to Govern in those Parts."—*Sandford,* 441. As her son
Henry Pole had livery of his lands on July 5, 1513 (*Calendar, Hen. VIII.,*
I. 4325), the year of her marriage could not have been later than 1492.
[3] The writer of *Cont. Croyl.* (572) says that Queen Anne's death occurred
about the middle of March, 1485 ; "in die magnae ecclipsis solis." The Rev.
S. J. Johnson, Vicar of Melplash, Dorset, wrote thus in response to my enquiry
anent the precise date of this eclipse : "The eclipse to which you refer took
place on 16 March 1485. On making a rough calculation of it some years ago,
I found 9 digits or three-fourths of the Sun would be eclipsed at London
about half-past three in the afternoon. In the Mediterranean it would be
total." *Stow* (782) gives March 16, 1485, as the date of Anne's death.

companie were assembled, but, secretlie disguised, in a night *The bishop of Elie saileth into Flanders to the earle of Richmond.* departed, (to the dukes great displeasure,) and came to his see of Elie; where he found monie and freends; and so sailed into Flanders, where he did the earle of Richmond good seruice.[1]

Ratcliffe continues (ll. 47, 48):

> And Buckingham, backt with the hardy Welshmen,
> Is in the field, and still his power encreaseth.

Buckingham was

[*Hol.* iii. 743/2/10. *Halle*, 394.] accompanied with a great *The duke of Buckinghas power of wild Welshmen (falsehartes) doo faile him.* power of wild Welshmen, whom he (being a man of great courage and sharpe speech) in maner against their willes had rather thereto inforced and compelled by lordlie and strcit commandement, than by liberall wages and gentle demenour; which thing was the verie occasion why they left him desolate, & cowardlie forsooke him. The duke, with all his power, marched through the forrest of Deane, intending to haue passed the riuer Seuerne at Glocester, & there to haue ioined his armie with the Courtneis, and other westerne men of his confederacie and affinitie.   Which if he had doone, no doubt but king Richard had beene in great ieopardie, either of priuation of his realme, or losse of his life, or both.

Richard orders Ratcliffe to "muster men" (l. 56) for immediate action, and the scene closes.

Buckingham's revolt was seconded by simultaneous risings in different parts of England,[2] but

[*Hol.* iii. 743/1/70. *Halle*, 393.] king Richard, (who in the *K. Richards drift in the disposing of his armie.* meane time had gotten togither a great strength and puissance,) thinking it not most for his part beneficiall, to disperse and diuide his great armie into small branches, and particularlie to persecute anie one of the coniuration by himselfe, determined (all other *[Richard determined to march against Buckingham.]* things being set aside) with his whole puissance to set on the chiefe head, which was the duke of Buckingham.

Act IV. sc. iv.—Richard's forces have been mustered, and he enters "marching, with Drummes and Trumpets" (Q.).   He is met by the

---

[1] Richard says (IV. iii. 49, 50):

> " Ely with Richmond troubles me more neere,
>   Then Buckingham and his rash leuied Strength."

[2] See p. 403 below.

Duchess of York and Queen Elizabeth. His mother goes out, laying
her "most greeuous Curse" upon him ; but he detains his sister-in-law,
and sues for the hand of his niece the Princess Elizabeth.   In pleading
his cause, he says (ll. 311-314) :

> Dorset your Sonne, that, with a fearfull soule,
> Leads discontented steppes in Forraine soyle,   312
> This faire Alliance quickly shall call home
> To high Promotions, and great Dignity.

After long railing at him the Queen is so far appeased by his fair
words as to ask (l. 426) :

> Shall I go win my daughter to thy will ?
> *Rich.* And be a happy Mother by the deed.
> *Qu.* I go.   Write to me very shortly,   428
> And you shal vnderstand from me her mind.
> *Rich.* Beare her my true loues kisse ; and so, farewell !
>
> $\qquad\qquad\qquad\qquad\qquad\qquad$ [*Exit* Q[*ueen*].

Earlier in the eventful dramatic day which embraces scenes ii.—v.,
Act IV., Richard sent Catesby to spread a rumour of Anne's mortal
sickness.   Soon we hear from him of her death, and he adds (IV. iii.
40-43) :

> Now, for I know the Britaine Richmond aymes
> At yong Elizabeth, my brothers daughter,
> And, by that knot, lookes proudly on the Crowne,
> To her go I, a iolly thriuing wooer.

In the Autumn of 1483 the Countess of Richmond and Queen
Elizabeth communicated through the agency of Lewis, the Countess's
physician, whose profession afforded him a convenient pretext for
visiting the sanctuary at Westminster, where the Queen still abode.
Acting under instructions obtained from the Countess, Lewis broached
to Queen Elizabeth a proposal—which was accepted—for uniting the
rival Houses : [1]

---

[1] *Polyd. Verg.*, 550/9. Richard III.'s privy seals show that he was at
Gloucester on August 2-4, 1483 (*H. S.*) ; and there Buckingham left him
(*More*, 88/11).   Thence Buckingham went to Brecknock Castle, where he had
the custody of John Morton, Bishop of Ely.—*More*, 87/21—88/15. The
result of a conference at Brecknock between Buckingham and Morton was
that the former promised to aid Henry Earl of Richmond in obtaining the
crown, if the Earl agreed to marry Elizabeth, eldest daughter of Edward IV.
By Morton's invitation, Reginald Bray, one of the household of Margaret
Countess of Derby, Richmond's mother, came from Lancashire—where she
was then residing—to Brecknock ; and, after conferring with Buckingham,
returned to the Countess and informed her of the Duke's promise.—*Hardyng-
Grafton*, 526 ; Halle, 390.   Thereupon she sent her physician Lewis to the
Queen Dowager, who was then in the sanctuary at Westminster ; instructing
him to propose the matrimonial alliance as though it were an idea of his own.
—*Hardyng-Grafton*, 526 ; *Halle*, 390, 391. Allowing time for the journies
and previous negotiations, we may fairly refer Lewis's share in the latter to
the early autumn of 1483. Before October 12, 1483, Buckingham had rebelled,
and Richard was marching against him.—*Ellis*, II. i. 159, 160.

[*Hol.* iii. 742/1/1. *Halle*, 391.] "You know verie well, *The conjunc-*
"madame, that, of the house of Lancaster, the earle of Richmond *tion of the*
two families
"is next of bloud, (who is liuing, and a lustic yoong batcheler,) and *moued to*
the Q. by the
"to the house of Yorke your daughters now are beires. If you *physician.*
"could agree and inuent the meane how to couple your eldest
"daughter with the yoong earle of Richmond in matrimonie, no
"doubt but the vsurper of the realme should be shortlie deposed,
"and your heire againe to hir right restored."

On Christmas Day, 1483, Richmond was at Rennes, where he swore
to marry the Princess Elizabeth after his accession to the throne, and
received oaths of fidelity from the refugees who had espoused his cause.[1]
Early in the year 1484,[2]

[*Hol.* iii. 750/1/27. *Halle*, 406.] king Richard was crediblie
aduertised, what promises and oths the earle and his confederates
had made and sworn togither at Rennes,[3] and how by the earles
means all the Englishmen were passed out of Britaine into France.
Wherefore, being sore dismaid, and in a maner desperate, bicause
his craftie chieuance[4] tooke none effect in Britaine, he imagined & *K. Richards*
deuise to
deuised how to infringe and disturbe the earles purpose by an *infringe and*
defeat the
other meane ; so that, by the marriage of ladie Elizabeth his neece, *earle of*
Richmonds
he should pretend no claime nor title to the crowne. . . . *purpose.*

[Richard therefore] determined to reconcile to his fauour his
brothers wife queene Elizabeth, either by faire words, or liberall
promises ; firmelie beleeuing, hir fauour once obteined, that she
would not sticke to commit (and louinglie credit) to him the rule *A subtill and*
lewd practise
and gouernance both of hir and hir daughters ; and so by that *of king*
Richard to
meanes the earle of Richmond of the affinitie of his neece should *beguile the*
earle of
be vtterlie defrauded and beguiled. . . . *Richmond.*

[Richard] would rather take to wife his cousine and neece the

---

[1] *Polyd. Verg.* 553/44.
[2] On March 1, 1484, Richard took a solemn oath—peers spiritual and
temporal with the Lord Mayor and aldermen of London being present—to
ensure the personal safety and welfare of his nieces if they, leaving sanctuary,
would commit themselves to his care.—*Ellis*, II. i. 149. Before Richard
opened the negotiations with the Queen which placed her daughters in his
power, he had considered the expediency, if he should become a widower, of
marrying the Princess Elizabeth and thus forestalling Richmond.—*Polyd.
Verg.* 556/2.
[3] *Rennes*] *Renes* Halle. *Reimes* Hol.
[4] To detain Richmond in Brittany.

[Richard's motive for marrying Elizabeth.]

ladie Elizabeth,[1] than for lacke of that affinitie the whole realme should run to ruine; as who said, that, if he once fell from his estate and dignitie, the ruine of the relme must needs shortlie insue and follow.[2] Wherefore he sent to the queene (being in sanctuarie) diuerse and often messengers, which first should excuse and purge him of all things before against hir attempted or procured, and after should so largelie promise promotions innumerable, and benefits, not onelie to hir, but also to hir sonne lord Thomas, Marquesse Dorset, that they should bring hir (if it were possible) into some wanhope, or (as men saie) into a fooles paradise.

[Richard sent messengers to the Queen, excusing past injuries and making promises to her and Dorset.]

The messengers, being men both of wit and grauitie, so persuaded the queene with great and pregnant reasons, & with[3] faire and large promises, that she began somewhat to relent, and to giue to them no deafe eare; insomuch that she faithfullie promised to submit and yeeld hir selfe fullie and frankelie to the kings will and pleasure. . . .

Queene Elizabeth allureth hir sonne the marquesse Dorset home out of France.

After she sent letters to the marquesse hir sonne, (being then at Paris with the earle of Richmond,) willing him in anie wise to leaue the earle, and without delaie to repaire into England, where for him were prouided great honours, aud honourable promotions; asserteining him further, that all offenses on both parts were forgotten and forgiuen, and both he and she highlie incorporated in the kings heart.

After Anne's death, in March, 1485, the

---

[1] There can be no doubt that rumour attributed this purpose to Richard. A little before Easter, 1485 (Easter fell on April 3), at the Priory of St. John of Jerusalem, Clerkenwell, in the presence of the Mayor and citizens of London, the King absolutely repudiated the design of marriage with his niece Elizabeth.—*Cont. Croyl.*, 572. In a letter to the Mayor and Aldermen of York, dated April 5 (1485), Richard spoke of various ways by which "sedicious and evil disposed personnes" sowed "sede of noise and disclaundre agaynest our persone"; and added: "for remedie wherof, and to thentent the troth opinlye declared shuld represse all suche false and contrived invencions, we now of late called before us the Maire and Aldermen of our Citie of London, togidder with the moste sadde and discrete persones of the same Citie in grete nombre, being present many of the lordes spirituel and temporel of our land, and the substance of all our housland, to whome we largely showed our true entent and mynd in all suche thinges as the said noise and disclaundre renne upon in suche wise as we doubt not all wel disposed personnes were and be therwith right wele content"; . . .—*York Records*, 209.

[2] Cp. *Rich. III.*, IV. iv. 406-411.

[3] *with*] Halle. *what with* Hol.

[*Hol.* iii. 751/1/49.   *Halle*, 407.]   king thus (according to his *K. Richard casteth his*
long desire) lo[o]sed out of the bonds of matrimonie, began to cast *love on his neece, pur-*
a foolish fantasie to ladie Elisabeth his neece ; making much sute *posing to marie hir.*
to haue hir ioined with him in lawfull matrimonie.

Queen Elizabeth's exit is followed by the entrance of Ratcliffe with
the announcement (ll. 433-439) that

on the Westerne Coast

Rideth a puissant Nauie ; . . .
'Tis thought that Richmond is their Admirall ;   437
And there they hull, expecting but the aide
Of Buckingham to welcome them ashore.

Richard gives Catesby a message for the Duke of Norfolk (ll. 448-
450) :

bid him leuie straight

The greatest strength and power that he can make,
And meet me suddenly at Salisbury.

Starting from London, Richard

[*Hol.* iii. 743/2/5.   *Halle*, 394.]   tooke his iournie toward *[Richard marched toward Salisbury.]*
Salisburie, to the intent that in his iournie he might set on the
dukes [Buckingham's] armie, if he might know him in anie place
incamped, or in order of battell arraied.

While Ratcliffe is speaking historic time has not advanced beyond
October, 1483, but, were it not for the rendezvous appointed, we might
suspect that the message with which Catesby is charged should be dated
August, 1485 ; when, on hearing of Richmond's landing, Richard

[*Hol.* iii. 754/1/53.   *Halle*, 412.]   sent to Iohn duke of Norffolke, *The king sendeth to*
Henrie earle of Northumberland, Thomas earle of Surrie, and to *his friends for a chosen*
other of his especiall & trustie friends of the nobilitie, which he *power of men.*
iudged more to preferre and esteeme his wealth and honour, than
their owne riches and priuate commoditie ; willing them to muster
and view all their seruants and tenants, and to elect and choose
the most couragious and actiue persons of the whole number, and
with them to repaire to his presence with all speed and diligence.

Ratcliffe's news is confirmed by Stanley, who pretends to know
merely " by guesse " that Richmond

. . . makes for England, here to clayme the Crowne (l. 469).

The rebellion of Buckingham and his adherents began on October
18, 1483.[1]   They were to be supported by Richmond, who had

---

[1] This is the date given in the attainder of Buckingham and his confederates.—*Rot. Parl.*, vi. 245/1, &c.   But Norfolk, writing from London on

[*Hol.* iii. 744/2/48. *Halle*, 395.]   prepared an armie of fiue
thousand manlie Britons, and fortie well furnished ships. When
all things were prepared in a readinesse, and the daie of departing
and setting forward was appointed, which was the twelfe daie of
the moneth of October [1483], the whole armie went on shipbord,
and halsed vp their sailes, and with a prosperous wind tooke
the sea.

Richard taunts Stanley with a design of joining Richmond (ll. 476-
478).   Stanley asks permission to depart and collect men for the King's
service (488-490).   Richard yields a conditional assent (ll. 496-498) :

> Goe, then, and muster men ; but leaue behind
> Your Sonne George Stanley : looke your heart be firme,
> Or else his Heads assurance is but fraile.

Holinshed copied from Halle (408) a passage whence we learn that,
among those whom Richard

[*Hol.* iii. 751/2/5.]   most mistrusted, these were the principall :
Thomas lord Stanleie, sir William Stanleie his brother, Gilbert
Talbot, and six hundred other : of whose purposes although king
Richard were ignorant,[1] yet he gaue neither confidence nor credence to anie one of them ; and least of all to the lord Stanleie,
bicause he was ioined in matrimonie with the ladie Margaret,
mother to the earle of Richmond, as afterward apparantlie yee
may perceiue.   For when the said lord Stanleie would haue
departed into his countrie to visit his familie, and to recreate and
refresh his spirits, (as he openlie said, but the truth was, to the
intent to be in a perfect readinesse to receiue the earle of Richmond
at his first arriuall in England,) the king in no wise would suffer
him to depart, before he had left as an hostage in the court George
Stanleie, lord Strange, his first begotten sonne and heire.

When Stanley is gone, four messengers enter successively with news
of the revolt.   The first messenger announces (ll. 500-504) a rising in
Devonshire, headed by

> Sir Edward Courtney, and the haughtie Prelate
> Bishop of Exeter, his brother there,[2] . . .

The "Guilfords," a second messenger reports (ll. 505-507), have

---

October 10, 1483, tells John Paston, "that the Kentysshmen be up in the
weld, and sey that they wol come and robbe the cite, which I shall lett yf I
may."—*Paston*, iii. 308.

[1] *were ignoraunt*] Halle.   *were not ignorant* Hol.
[2] *brother there*] Q.   *elder Brother* F.

taken up arms in Kent.   A fourth messenger brings tidings of another
outbreak (ll. 520, 521):

> Sir Thomas Louell and Lord Marquesse Dorset,
> 'Tis said, my Liege, in Yorkeshire are in Armes.

The rebellion was well-concerted, for Buckingham had

[*Hol.* iii. 743/1/56. *Halle*, 393.]   persuaded all his complices
and partakers, that euerie man in his quarter, with all diligence,
should raise vp people & make a commotion.   And by this means,
almost in one moment, Thomas marques Dorset came out of
sanctuarie, (where since the begin[n]ing of K. Richards daies he had
continued, whose life by the onelie helpe of sir Thomas Louell[1]
was preserued from all danger & perill in this troublous world,) [Risings in
[and] gathered together a great band of men in Yorkeshire.   Yorkshire,

Sir Edward Courtneie, and Peter his brother,[2] bishop of
Excester, raised an other a[r]mie in Deuonshire and Cornewall. [Devonshire,
In Kent, Richard Gilford and other gentlemen collected a great   Cornwall,
companie of souldiers, and openlie began warre.   and Kent.]

The news of a third messenger

> Is, that by sudden Floods and fall of Waters,   512
> Buckinghams Armie is dispers'd and scatter'd ;
> And he himselfe wandred away alone,
> No man knowes whither.

Buckingham meant to cross the Severn, and effect a junction with
his allies in the west (p. 397 above), but before

[*Hol.* iii. 743/2/25. *Halle*, 394.] he could atteine to Seuerne *A sore floud,*
side, by force of continuall raine and moisture, the riuer rose so   *or high*
high that it ouerflowed all the countrie adioining ; insomuch that   *water,*
men were drowned in their beds, and houses with the extreame   *doeing much*
                                                                 harme, called
violence were ouerturned, children were caried about the fields *the duke of*
                                                                 Buckinghams
swimming in cradels, beasts were drowned on hilles.   Which rage *great water.*
of water lasted continuallie ten daies, insomuch that in the countrie
adioining they call it to this daie,[3] "The great water"; or, "the
duke of Buckinghams great water."   By this floud the passages
were so closed, that neither the duke could come ouer Seuern to

---

[1] The translator of this passage from *Polyd. Verg.* (551/45) substituted
"sir Thomas louell esquyer" for plain Thomas Rowell (" Rouell ").

[2] Cousin.—*French*, 248.

[3] The account of this flood was added to the translation of *Polyd. Verg.*
(552) in *Halle*.

[The Welsh-
men de-
parted.] his adherents, nor they to him. During the which time, the
Welshmen, lingring idelie, and without monie, vittels, or wages,
suddenlie scattered and departed: and, for all the dukes faire
promises, threatnings, and inforcements, would in no wise either
go further nor abide.

[Bucking-
ham fled.] The duke (being thus left almost post alone) was of necessitie
compelled to flie, . . .

[Bucking-
ham's adher-
ents fled
when they
heard that
he could not
be found.] Now when it was knowne to his adherents, (which were redie to
giue battell,) that his host was scatred, and had left him almost
alone, and [he] was fled, & could not be found, they were suddenlie amazed & striken with a sudden feare, that euery man like
persons desperate shifted for himselfe & fled.

Richard asks (ll. 517, 518):

> Hath any well-aduiséd friend proclaym'd
> Reward to him that brings the Traytor in!
> *Mess.* Such Proclamation hath been made, my Lord.

From Leicester, on October 23, 1483,[1] Richard

A proclama-
tion for the
apprehen-
sion of the
duke of
Buckingha,
with large
rewards to
the appre-
hendor. [*Hol.* iii. 744/1/21. *Halle*, 394.] made proclamation, that what
person could shew and reneale where the duke of Buckingham
was, should be highlie rewarded: if he were a bondman, he should
be infranchised and set at libertie; if he were of free bloud, he
should haue a generall pardon, and be rewarded with a thousand
pounds.

The fourth messenger's doubtful report of Dorset's appearance in
arms is counterbalanced by better and certain news (ll. 523-529):

> The Brittaine Nauie is dispers'd by Tempest:[2]
> Richmond, in Dorsetshire, sent out a Boat   524
> Vnto the shore, to aske those on the Banks,
> If they were his Assistants, yea or no!
> Who answer'd him, they came from Buckingham
> Vpon his partie: he, mistrusting them,   528
> Hoys'd sayle and made his course againe for Brittaine.

On October 12, 1483, Richmond put to sea "with a prosperous
wind" (p. 402 above):

[*Hol.* iii. 744/2/55. *Halle*, 396.] But toward night the wind
changed, and the weather turned, and so huge and terrible a

---

[1] I take the date from *Rymer*, xii. 204, where the proclamation is printed.
[2] *by Tempest*] F. om. Q.

tempest so suddenlie arose, that, with the verie power and strength His ships disparkled by tempest.
of the storme, the ships were disparkled, seuered & separated
asunder: some by force were driuen into Normandie, some were
compelled to returne againe into Britaine. The ship wherein the
earle of Richmond was, associat onelie with one other barke, was
all night tossed and turmoiled.

In the morning after, (when the rage of the furious tempest was
asswaged, and the ire of blustering wind was some deale appeased,)
about the houre of noone the same daie, the earle approched to
the south part of the realme of England, euen at the mouth of the He seeth all the sea banks furnished with souldiers.
hauen of Pole, in the countie of Dorset; where he might plainelie
percciue all the sea bankes & shores garnished and furnished with
men of warre and souldiers, appointed and deputed there to defend
his arriuall and landing. . . . Wherefore he gaue streict charge,
and sore commandement, [*p.* 745] that no person should once presume to take land, and go to shore, vntill such time as the whole
nauie were assembled and come togither. And, while he taried and He sendeth to know whether they were with him or against him.
lingered, he sent out a shipboate toward the land side, to know
whether they, which stood there in such a number, and so well
furnished in apparell defensiue, were his foes and enimies, or else
his freends and comfortors.

They, that were sent to inquire, were instantlie desired of the
men of warre keeping the coast, (which thereof were before
instructed & admonished,) to descend and take land; affirming that A forged tale to intrap the earles messengers.
they were appointed by the duke of Buckingham there to await
and tarie for the arriuall and landing of the earle of Richmond,
and to conduct him safelie into the campe, where the duke, not far
of[f], laie incamped with a mightie armie, and an host of great
strength and power, to the intent that the duke and the earle,
ioining in puissances and forces togither, might prosecute and
chase king Richard being destitute of men, and in maner desperate;
and so, by that meanes, and their owne labours, to obteine the end
of their enterprise which they had before begun.

The earle of Richmond, suspecting their flattering request to be [Richmond distrusted the invitation to land, and sailed away.]
but a fraud (as it was in deed), after he perceiued none of his ships
to appeare in sight, he weied vp his anchors, halsed vp his sailes,
&, hauing a prosperous and streinable wind, and a fresh gale sent

euen by God to deliuer him from that perill and ieopardie, arriued
safe and in all securitie in the duchie of Normandie ; where he (to

*The earle
arriueth in
Normandie
& passeth by
land into
Britaine
againe.*
refresh and solace his soldiers and people) tooke his recreation by
the space of three daies, and cleerelie determined with part of his
companie to passe all by land againe into Britaine.

Catesby—whom Richard had despatched (IV. iv. 444-450) to
summon the Duke of Norfolk to Salisbury—now re-enters with the
latest advices (ll. 533-536):

> My Liege, the Duke of Buckingham is taken ;
> That is the best newes : that the Earle of Richmond
> Is, with a mighty power, landed at Milford,
> Is colder tidings[1], but yet they must be told.

Here Shakspere annihilates the historical time which intervened
between Buckingham's luckless rebellion and Richmond's victorious
enterprise. Buckingham was captured in October, 1483. Richmond,

[*Hol.* iii. 753/1/23. *Halle*, 410.] being accompanied onelie
with two thousand men, and a small number of ships, weied vp his
anchors, and halsed vp his sailes in the moneth of August [1485],
and sailed from Harfleet with so prosperous a wind, that, the

*The earle
arriueth at
Milford
hauen.*
seuenth daie[2] after his departure, he arriued in Wales in the
enening, at a place called Milford hauen, and incontinent tooke
land, . . .

Act IV. sc. v.—Stanley enters with Christopher Urswick, to whom
he says (ll. 1-5):

> Sir Christopher, tell Richmond this from me :
> That, in the stye of the most deadly Bore,
> My Sonne George Stanley is frankt vp in hold :
> If I reuolt, off goes yong Georges head ;
> The feare of that holds off my present ayde.

In August, 1485, "a daie or two before" Richmond sojourned at
Lichfield,

[*Hol.* iii. 753/2/73. *Halle*, 411.] the lord Stanleie, hauing in his
band almost fiue thousand men, lodged in the [p. 754] same towne.

*The lord
Stanleies
denies to*
But, hearing that the erle of Richmond was marching thitherward,
gaue to him place, dislodging him and his, and repaired to a

---

[1] *tidings*] Q. *Newes* F.
[2] *Polyd. Verg.* says (559/45) that Richmond sailed from the mouth of the
Seine on August 1 ("Calend. Augusti"), and reached Milford Haven seven
days after his departure, about sunset. According to *Cont. Croyl.* (573) August
1 was the date of Richmond's arrival at Milford Haven. *Rous* (218) gives
August 6 as the date on which Richmond arrived at Milford Haven.

towne called Aderstone; the reabiding the comming of the earle. *auoid suspicion of K.
Richard and
to saus his
sonnes lift.*
And this wilie fox did this act, to auoid all suspicion on king
Richards part.

For the lord Stanleie was afraid, least, if he should seeme
openlie to be a fautor or aider to the earle his sonne in law, before
the day of the battell, that king Richard, (which yet vtterlie did not
put in him diffidence and mistrust,) would put to some cruell death
his sonne and heire apparant, George lord Strange, whome king
Richard (as you haue heard before) kept with him as a pledge or
hostage, to the intent that the lord Stanleie his father should
attempt nothing preiudiciall to him.

Until the day before the battle of Bosworth, Richmond

[*Hol.* iii. 754/2/54.   *Halle*, 413.]   could in no wise be assured
of his father in law Thomas lord Stanleie, which, for feare of the [Fear for his
son made
Stanley hold
back to the
last.]
destruction of the lord Strange his sonne (as you haue heard), as
yet inclined to neither partie.   For, if he had gone to the earle,
and that notified to king Richard, his sonne had beene shortlie
executed.

Stanley also asks (l. 6) :

> But, tell me, where is Princely Richmond now ?
>   *Chri.* At Penbroke, or at Harford-west,[1] in Wales.
>   *Stan.* What men of Name resort to him ?
>   *Chri.* Sir Walter Herbert, a renownëd Souldier ;
> Sir Gilbert Talbot, Sir William Stanley ;
> Oxford, redoubted Pembroke, Sir Iames Blunt,
> And Rice ap Thomas, with a valiant Crew ;   12
> And many other of great name and worth :
> And toward London do they bend their power,
> If by the way they be not fought withall.[2]

The Earls of Oxford and Pembroke sailed with Richmond from
Normandy.   On the day after his arrival at Milford Haven, Richmond,
"at the sunne rising, remooued to Hereford west " (*Hol.* iii. 753/1/33.
Halle, 410).   While there he received a

[*Hol.* iii. 753/1/44.   *Halle*, 410.] message from the inhabitants [A message
from the
inhabitants
of Pem-
broke.]
of the towne of Penbroke, . . . that the Penbrochians were readie
to serue and giue their attendance on their naturall and immediat
lord Iasper earle of Penbroke.

---

[1] *Harford-west*] Q.   *Hertford West* F.
[2] 6-15. *At . . . withall.*   I have taken these lines in the order of the Qq.

Advancing farther, Richmond

[*Hol.* iii. 753/2/10.   *Halle*, 411.] was by his espials ascerteined,

that sir Walter Herbert, and Rice ap Thomas were in harnesse
before him; readie to incounter with his armie, and to stop their
passage.   Wherefore, like a valiant capteine, he first determined to
set on them, and either to destroie or to take them into his fauour;
and after, with all his power and puissance, to giue battell to his
mortall enimie king Richard.   But, to the intent his freends should
know in what readinesse he was, and how he proceeded forward,
he sent of his most secret and faithfull seruants with letters and
instructions to the ladie Margaret his mother, to the lord Stanleie
and his brother [Sir William Stanley], to sir Gilbert Talbot, and to
other his trustie freends; declaring to them that he, being succoured
and holpen with the aid and reliefe of his freends, intended to
passe ouer the riuer of Seuerne at Shrewesburie, and so to passe
directlie to the citie of London.

Wherefore he required them, (as his speciall trust and confidence was fixed in the hope of their fidelitie,) that they would
meet him by the waie with all diligent preparation; to the intent
that he and they, at time and place conuenient, might communicate
togither the deepnesse of all his doubtfull and weightie businesse.
When the messengers were dispatched with these commandements
and admonitions, he marched forward towards Shrewesburie: and,
in his passing, there met and saluted him Rice ap Thomas,
with a goodlie band of Welshmen; which, making an oth and
promise to the earle, submitted himselfe wholie to his order and
commandement.

In the evening of the day on which Richmond encamped near
Newport,

[*Hol.* iii. 753/2/59.   *Halle*, 411.] came to him sir Gilbert
Talbot, with the whole power of the yoong earle of Shrewesburie,
then being in ward; which were accounted to the number of two
thousand men.   And thus, his power increasing, he arriued at the
towne of Stafford, and there paused.

There also came sir William Stanleie accompanied with a few
persons.

In 1484,[1]

[*Hol.* iii. 749/1/17. *Halle*, 405.] Iohn Vere, earle of Oxford, which (as you haue heard before) was by king Edward kept in prison within the castell of Hammes, so persuaded Iames Blunt, capteine of the same fortresse, and sir Iohn Fortescue, porter of the towne of Calis, that he himselfe was not onelie dismissed and set at libertie, but they also, abandoning and leauing their fruitfull offices, did condescend to go with him into France to the earle of Richmond, and to take his part.

The historic date of this scene must be August, 1485, but Stanley gives Urswick a message relating to a matter which had been settled in 1483 (p. 399 above):

> Retourne vnto thy Lord ; commend me to him :
> Tell him, the Queene hath hartelie consented
> He shall espouse Elizabeth her daughter.—ll. 16-18. (Q1).

When the marriage between Richmond and the Princess Elizabeth had been arranged,

[*Hol.* iii. 742/1/58. *Halle*, 392.] the countesse of Richmond tooke into hir seruice Christopher Urswike, an honest and wise priest, and (after an oth of him for to be secret taken and sworne) she vttered to him all hir mind and counsell ; adhibiting to him the more confidence and truth, that he all his life had fauoured and taken part with king Henrie the sixt, and as a speciall iewell put to hir seruice by sir Lewes hir physician. So the mother, studious for the prosperitie of hir son, appointed this Christopher Urswike to saile into Britaine to the earle of Richmond, and to declare and reueale to him all pacts and agreements betweene hir & the queene agreed and concluded.

Act V. sc. i.—When sc. iv., Act IV., closed, Richard was setting out toward Salisbury, whither he commanded that Buckingham should be brought. Buckingham now enters on his way to execution. He asks the sheriff (l. 1) :

---

[1] Oxford probably joined Richmond in October, 1484. We learn from the minutes of Charles VIII.'s Council, sitting at Montargis, that Richmond had left Brittany before October 11, 1484.—*Séances du Conseil de Charles VIII.*, 128. The Council remained at Montargis until October 25, 1484.—*Ibid.*, 142. According to *Polyd. Verg.* (556/13), Richmond, after escaping from Brittany, went to Angers and thence to Montargis, where Oxford, Blunt, and Fortescue came to him.

Will not King Richard let me speake with him?
  Sher. No, my good Lord ; therefore be patient.

Assured, in answer to his enquiry, that it is All Souls' Day, the
Duke says (l. 12) :

  Why, then Al-soules day is my bodies doomsday.

Buckingham,

The duke of Buckingham beheaded without arreignment or iudgement [; on All Souls' Day].

[*Hol.* iii. 744/2/13. *Halle*, 395.] vpon All soules daie, without
arreigment or iudgement, . . . was at Salisburie, in the open
market place, on a new scaffold, beheaded and put to death.

Act V. sc. ii.—Richmond and his adherents enter. One of the
stages of his march was "the towne of Tamworth" (*Hol.* iii. 754/2/32.
Halle, 413) ; and scene ii. is laid in or near that place (l. 13). Blunt
depreciates Richard's strength (ll. 20, 21) :

  He hath no friends but what are friends for fear,
  Which in his deerest neede will flye from him.

Holinshed copied Halle's mention (413) of some who joined Richmond during the march between Lichfield and Tamworth ; but altered
the sense of the next passage.[1] I quote this latter passage as it stands
in Holinshed :

[Some who hated Richard came to him through fear.]

[*Hol.* iii. 754/2/42. *Halle*, 413] Diuerse other noble personages, which inwardlie hated king Richard woorse than a tode or
a serpent, did likewise resort to him with all their power and
strength, wishing and working his destruction; who otherwise
would haue beene the instrument of their casting away.

On the day of battle,

[Traitors in Richard's army.]

[*Hol.* iii. 757/1/26. *Halle*, 416.] such as were present (more
for dread than loue) kissed them openlie, whome they inwardlie
hated. Other sware outwardlie to take part with such whose
death they secretlie compassed, and inwardlie imagined. Other
promised to inuade the kings enimies, which fled and fought with
fierce courage against the king. Other stood still and looked on,
intending to take part with the victors and ouercommers.

Act V. sc. iii.—Richard enters with his partisans, and says (l. 1) :
  Here pitch our tentes,[2] euen here in Bosworth field.

On August 21, 1485,[3]

---

[1] "Diuerse . . . strength" is *Halle's* translation of *Polyd. Verg.* (561/45,
46). *Hol.*, not perceiuing that "him" refers to Richmond, added the words
"wishing . . . away."   [2] *tentes*] Q. *Tent* F.
[3] I take the date from *Cont. Croyl.*, 573.

[*Hol.* iii. 755/1/36. *Halle*, 413.] king Richard, which was
appointed now to finish his last labor by the very diuine iustice &
prouidence of God, (which called him to condigne punishment for
his mischiefous deserts,) marched to a place meet for two battels to
incounter, by a village called Bosworth, not farre from Leicester: [Richard
encamped
near
Bosworth.]
and there he pitched his field on a hill called Anne Beame,
refreshed his souldiers, and tooke his rest.

Norfolk is among those who are in attendance. Richard asks (l. 9):

> Who hath descried the number of the Traitors !
> *Nor.* Six or seuen thousand is their vtmost power.
> *Rich.* Why, our Battalia [1] trebbles that account: . . .

When the two armies were drawn up for action, Richmond's

[*Hol.* iii. 755/2/57. *Halle*, 414.] whole number exceeded not [Richmond
was out-
numbered
by more
than two to
one.]
fiue thousand men, beside the power of the Stanleies, wherof three
thousand were in the field, vnder the standard of sir William
Stanleie. The kings number was double so much and more.

Richard returns from surveying "the vantage of the ground" (V.
iii. 15), and takes up his quarters in the royal tent. He gives some
orders ; one being (l. 64):

> Saddle white Surrey for the Field to morrow.

On or about August 19, 1485,[2]

[*Hol.* iii. 754/2/20. *Halle*, 412.] he, (inuironed with his gard,) [Richard's
white
courser.]
with a frowning countenance and cruell visage, mounted on a great
white courser, . . . entered the towne of Leicester after the sunne
set, . . .

Richard then demands of Ratcliffe (l. 68):

---

[1] *battalion* Q.
[2] After Richmond's arrival at Lichfield, Richard left Nottingham for
Leicester.—*Polyd. Verg.*, 561/11-39. The King proposed leaving Nottingham
on August 16 (*Paston*, iii. 320) ; but a messenger—who was at York on
August 19—found Richard at Bestwood (*York Records*, 216). Bestwood is
four miles north of Nottingham.—*Bartholomew*. This messenger might have
ridden as swiftly as one who seems to have been at Bosworth field on August
22, and, on the following day, brought news of the battle to York.—*York
Records*, 218. Such a feat was surpassed by Bernard Calvert, who, on July
17, 1619, rode—with relays of horses—140 miles in 9 hours.—Stow's *Annales*,
ed. 1631, p. 1032, col. 2. In Richard's reign messengers could, within two
days, ride post for 200 miles.—*Cont. Croyl.*, 571. The distance between
Nottingham and Leicester is twenty-two miles in a straight line. Richard, as
we have seen, departed from Leicester on August 21. (In regard to Mr.
Davies's conjecture, *York Records*, 216, note, that for Bestwood we should read
Prestwould, see Mr. Gairdner's *Richard III.*, p. 294, note.)

> Saw'st thou the melancholly Lord Northumberland ?
> *Rat.* Thomas the Earle of Surrey, and himselfe,
> Much about Cockshut time, from Troope to Troope
> Went through the Army, chearing vp the Souldiers.

Here Malone quoted the following passage, prefacing it with the explanation that " Richard calls him [Northumberland] *melancholy*, because he did not join heartily in his cause."—*Var. Sh.*, xix. 213. Among those who submitted to Richmond after the battle

[*Hol.* iii. 759/2/43. *Halle*, 419.] was Henrie the fourth earle of Northumberland, which (whether it was by the commandement of king Richard, putting diffidence in him; or he did it for the *[Northumberland took no part in the battle.]* loue and fauour that he bare vnto the earle) stood still with a great companie, and intermitted not in the battell, . . .

It is now " darke night " (l. 80). Richmond is in his tent, which has been pitched at the other side of the field. He is secretly visited by Stanley, who promises, " in this doubtfull shocke of Armes," such aid as may not endanger George Stanley (ll. 91-96). Stanley then says (ll. 97-100):

> Farewell ! the leysure and the fearfull time
> Cuts off the ceremonious Vowes of Loue,
> And ample enterchange of sweet Discourse,
> Which so long sundred Friends should dwell vpon ;

and goes out with the lords who have the charge of conducting him to his " Regiment." Richmond, left alone, prays and sleeps (ll. 108-117). On or about August 20, 1485,[1] in the daytime, Richmond went

[The lord Stanleie, the earle of Richmond, & others meet, embrace, and consult.] [*Hol.* iii. 755/1/17. *Halle*, 413.] to the towne of Aderston, where the lord Stanleie and sir William his brother with their bands were abiding. There the erle came first to his father in law, in a litle close, where he saluted him, and sir William his brother : and after diuerse and freendlie imbracings, each reioised of the state of other, and suddenlie were surprised with great ioy, comfort, and hope of fortunate successe in all their affaires and dooings. Afterward they consulted togither how to giue battell to king Richard if he would abide, whome they knew not to be farre off with an huge host. . . .

[*Hol.* iii. 755/2/22. *Halle*, 414.] After that the earle of Richmond was departed from the communication of his freends (as you haue heard before) he began to be of a better stomach,

---

[1] *Polyd. Verg.*, 562/16, 24, 42.

and of a more valiant courage, and with all diligence pitched his
field iust by the campe of his enimies, and there he lodged that
night. [Richmond encamped neer Richard.]

Richard and Richmond sleep, each in his tent. Their dreams bring
before them Prince Edward, Henry VI., Clarence, Rivers, Grey, and
Vaughan, Hastings, the young Princes, Anne, and Buckingham, who—
visible and audible to those present at the play—enter successively the
space between the armies. While promising victory to Richmond, the
ghosts bid their murderer despair and die. When Buckingham
vanishes, "Richard starts out of his dreame" (l. 176).

Richard encamped near the village of Bosworth on August 21,
1485 (p. 410 above).

[*Hol.* iii. 755/1/45. *Halle*, 414.] The fame went, that he had
the same night a dreadfull and terrible dreame: for it seemed to
him being asleepe, that he did see diuerse images like terrible
dinels, which pulled and haled him, not suffering him to take anie
quiet or rest. The which strange vision not so suddenlie strake
his heart with a sudden feare, but it stuffed his head and troubled
his mind with manie busie and dreadfull imaginations. For incontinent after, his heart being almost damped, he prognosticated
before the doubtfull chance of the battell to come; *not* vsing the
alacritie and mirth *of mind* [1] and countenance as he *was* accustomed
to doo before he came toward the battell. And least that it might
be suspected that he was abashed for feare of his enimies, and for
that cause looked so pitiouslie; he recited and declared to his
familiar freends in the morning his wonderfull vision and fearefull
dreame. [The dreame of king Richard the third, fore-telling him of his end.] [Richard was dejected by his dream.]

The night is past. "Enter the Lords to Richmond, sitting in his
Tent" (l. 222). He asks (l. 234):

How farre into the Morning is it, Lords?
Lor. Vpon the stroke of foure.
Rich. Why, then 'tis time to Arme, and giue direction.

Richmond's procedure before the battle is thus described:

[*Hol.* iii. 755/2/27. *Halle*, 414.] In the morning betimes, he
caused his men to put on their armour, and apparell themselues
readie to fight and giue battell; . . . [Richmond's soldiers armed themselues betimes.]

---

[1] Before he sleeps Richard says (V. iii. 73, 74):

"I haue *not* that *Alacrity* of Spirit,
Nor cheere *of Minde* that I *was* wont to haue."

" His Oration to his Souldiers" ensues (ll. 237-270) :

God, and our good *cause, fight* vpon our side ; . . .   240
Richard except, those whom we fight against   243
Had *rather* haue vs win then him they follow :
For what is he they follow ? Truly, Gentlemen,
A bloudy Tyrant and *a Homicide* ; . . .
One that made meanes to come by what he hath,   248
And slaughter'd those that were the meanes to help him ; . . .
If you do *sweats* [1] to put a Tyrant downe,   255
You sleepe in peace, the Tyrant being slaine ;
If you do fight against your Countries Foes,
Your Countries Fat shall pay *your paines* the hyre ; . . .
Then, *in the name of God* and all these rights,   263
Aduance your *Standards*, draw your willing Swords!
For me, the ransome of my bold attempt
Shall be this cold Corpes *on the* earth's *cold* face ; . . .
God *and Saint George!* Richmond and Victory !   270

I give excerpts from " The oration of king Henrie the Seauenth to
his armie," [2] for comparison with V. iii. 240-270 :

[*Hol.* iii. 757/2/14. *Halle,* 416.] I doubt not, but *God* will
rather aid vs (yea and *fight* for vs) than see vs vanquished and
ouerthrowne by such as neither feare him nor his lawes, nor yet
regard iustice or honestie.

*The earles
cause iust
and right, &
therefore
libells of
good
successe.*

Our *cause* is so iust, that no enterprise can be of more vertue,
both by the lawes diuine & ciuill. *For what* can be a more honest,
goodlie, or godlie quarrell, than to fight against a capteine, being
an *homicide* and murtherer of his owne bloud or progenie, an
extreame destroier of his nobilitie, and to his and our countrie and
the poore snbiects of the same a deadlie mallet, a firie brand, and
a burthen intollerable ? . . .

[Richard
cannot trust
his soldiers.]

[*Hol.* iii. 757/2/49. *Halle,* 417.] Beside this, I assure you,
that there be yonder in the great battell, men brought thither for
feare, and not for loue ; souldiers by force compelled, and not with
good will assembled ; persons which desire *rather* the destruction
than saluation of their maister and capteine : . . .

[Richard
slew his
friends.]

[*Hol.* iii. 758/1/7. *Halle,* 417.] What mercie is in him that
sleieth his trustie freends as well as his extreame enimies ? . . .

[*Hol.* iii. 758/1/59. *Halle,* 417.] Therefore labour for your
gaine, & *sweat* for your right. While we were in Britaine, we had

---

[1] *sweats*] Q. *sweare* F.   [2] *The . . . armie.*] Hol. om. Halle.

small liuings and little plentie of wealth or welfare, now is the [The reward of victory.]
time come to get aboundance of riches, and copie of profit; which
is the reward of your seruice, and merit of *your paines.* . . .

[*Hol.* iii. 758/2/23. *Halle,* 418.] And this one thing I assure [Richmond preferred death to captivity.]
you, that in so iust and good a cause, and so notable a quarrell,
you *shall* find me this daie rather a dead carrion vp*on the cold*
ground, than a free prisoner on a carpet in a ladies chamber. . . .

[*Hol.* iii. 758/2/50. *Halle,* 418.] And therefore, *in the name of* [God and S. George?]
God and S. George, let cuerie man couragiouslie *aduance* foorth his
standard!

In the opposite camp Norfolk enters exclaiming (l. 288):

Arme, arme, my Lord! the foe vaunts in the field!

Richard thereupon declares how the royal troops are to be marshalled
(ll. 291-300):

I will leade forth my Soldiers to the plaine,	
And thus my Battell shal be orderëd :	292
My Foreward shall be drawne out all [1] in length,	
Consisting equally of Horse and Foot ;	
Our Archers shall be placëd in the mid'st :	
Iohn Duke of Norfolke, Thomas Earle of Surrey,	296
Shall haue the leading of the Foot and Horse.	
They thus directed, we will follow	
In the maine Battell, whose puissance on either side	
Shall be well-wingëd with our cheefest Horse.	300

On August 22, 1485,

[*Hol.* iii. 755/2/7. *Halle,* 414.] king Richard, being furnished King Richard bringeth all his men into the plaine.
with men & all ablements of warre, bringing all his men out of
their campe into the plaine, ordered his fore-ward in a maruellous
length, in which he appointed both horsmen and footmen, to the
intent to imprint, in the hearts of them that looked a farre off, a
sudden terror and deadlie feare, for the great multitude of the
armed souldiers : and in the fore-front he placed the archers like a
strong fortified trench or bulworke. Ouer this battell was capteine,
Iohn duke of Norffolke, with whome was Thomas earle of Surrie, The duke of Norffolke and the earle of Surrie on K. Richards side.
his sonne. After this long vant-gard, followed king Richard him-
selfe with a strong companie of chosen and approued men of warre,
hauing horssemen for wings on both sides of his battell.

---

[1] *out all*] Q1. The rest omit.

Norfolk shows the King a paper, saying (l. 303):

> This found I on my Tent this Morning.

The paper contains the ensuing couplet (ll. 304, 305):

> Iockey of Norfolke, be not too bold,[1]
> For Dickon thy maister is bought and sold.

From Halle (419) Holinshed copied a story that Norfolk

[*Hol.* iii. 759/2/3.] was warned by diuerse to refrain from the field, in so much that the night before he should set forward toward the king, one wrote this rime vpon his gate:

> Iacke of Norffolke be not too bold,
> For *Dikon thy maister is bought and sold.

Yet all this notwithstanding, he regarded more his oth, his honor, and promise made to king Richard, like a gentleman; and, as a faithfull subiect to his prince, absented not himselfe from his maister; but as he faithfullie liued vnder him, so he manfullie died with him, to his great fame and laud.

Soon Richard's "*Oration to his army*"[2] is delivered. From this speech (ll. 314-341) I give the following extracts:

> Remember whom you are to cope withall;　　　　　315
> A sort of Vagabonds, Rascals, *and Run-awayes*,
> A scum of *Brittaines*, and base Lackey Pezants, . . .
> You hauing Lands, and blest with beauteous *wiues*,　321
> They would restraine the one, distaine the other.
> And who doth leade them but a paltry Fellow,　　　323
> Long kept *in Britaine* at our *Mothers* cost ?
> A *Milke-sop*, . . .
> If we be conquered, let men conquer vs,　　　　　332
> And not these bastard *Britaines*; whom *our* Fathers
> Haue, in their owne Land, beaten, bobb'd, and thump'd,
> And, on Record, left them the heires of shame.

"The *oration* of king Richard the third *to* the chiefteins of *his armie*" contains the subioined passages, which should be compared with the lines quoted above:

[*Hol.* iii. 756/1/60. *Halle*, 415.] Ye see . . . , how a companie of traitors, theeues, outlawes, *and runnagates* of our owne nation, be aiders and partakers of his [Richmond's] feat and enterprise, readie at hand to ouercome and oppresse vs.

You see also, what a number of beggerlie *Britans* and faint-

---

[1] *too*] Capell. *to* Qq. 6-8. *so* Qq. 1-5 Ff.
[2] *His . . . army*.] Hol. om. Halle.

hearted Frenchmen be with him arriued to destroie vs, our *wiues* and children. . . .

[*Hol.* iii. 756/2/17. *Halle*, 415.] And to begin with the erle of Richmond, capteine of this rebellion, he is *a* Welsh *milksop*, a man of small courage, and of lesse experience in martiall acts and feats of warre; brought vp by my *moothers*[1] meanes, and mine, like a captiue in a close cage, *in* the court of Francis duke of *Britaine;* . . .

[*Hol.* iii. 756/2/43. *Halle*, 415.] And as for the Frenchmen and *Britans*, their valiantnesse is such, that *our* noble progenitors, and your valiant *parents*[2] haue them oftener vanquished and ouercome in one moneth, than they in the beginning imagined possible to compasse and finish in a whole yeare.

Almost immediately after Norfolk's last entrance, Richard sent for Stanley's contingent (l. 290).   The King demands of a messenger who now enters (l. 341):

> What sayes Lord Stanley? will he bring his power?
> *Mes.* My Lord, he doth deny to come.
> *King.* Off with his sonne Georges head!   344
> *Nor.* My Lord, the Enemy is past the Marsh:
> After the battaile let George Stanley dye.

Halle, Holinshed's authority, says:

[*Hol.* iii. 760/1/59. *Halle*, 420.] When king Richard was come to Bosworth, he sent a purseuant to the lord Stanleie, commanding him to aduance forward with his companie, and to come to his presence; which thing if he refused to doo, he sware, by Christes passion, that he would strike off his sonnes head before he dined. The lord Stanleie answered the purseuant that, if the king did so, he had more sonnes aliue; and, as to come to him, he was not then so determined.   When king Richard heard this answer, he commanded the lord Strange incontinent to be beheaded: which was at that verie same season, when both the armies had sight ech of other.   But the councellors of king Richard pondered the time and cause, (knowing also the lord Strange to be innocent of his fathers offense,) & persuaded the king that it was now time to fight, & no time to execute.

---

[1] *moothers*] Hol. (ed. 2).   *brothers* Halle.   Hol. (ed. 1).
[2] *parents*] Hol. ed. 1.   *parts* Hol. ed. 2.

Besides that, they aduised him to keepe the lord Strange as prisoner till the battell were ended, and then at leisure his pleasure might be accomplished. So (as God would) king Richard brake his holie oth, and the lord was deliuered to the keepers of the kings tents, to be kept as prisoner.

Richard attacked as soon as Richmond's right flank was no longer protected by the marsh of which Norfolk speaks.

[The marsh on Richmond's right flank.]

[*Hol.* iii. 758/2/65. *Halle*, 418.]   Betweene both armies there was a great marish then (but at this present, by reason of diches cast, it is growne to be firme ground) [1] which the earle of Richmond left on his right hand; for this intent, that it should be on that side a defense for his part, and in so dooing he had the sunne at his backe, and in the faces of his enimies. When king Richard saw the earles companie was passed the marish, he did command with all hast to set vpon them.

The policie of the earle. [Richmond was attacked when he had passed the marsh.]

Accepting Norfolk's counsel Richard cries (ll. 348-350):

> Aduance our Standards, set vpon our Foes ;
> Our Ancient word of Courage, faire *S. George*,
> Inspire vs with the spleene of fiery Dragons !

Compare some closing words in the speech attributed by Halle to Richard, from which I have given excerpts above (pp. 416, 417).

[*Hol.* iii. 757/1/16. *Halle*, 416.]   Now *saint George* to borow, let vs *set* forward, . . .

Act V. sc. iv.—Fortune has turned against Richard, and, when the King enters calling for a horse, Catesby answers (l. 8) :

> Withdraw, my Lord ; Ile helpe you to a Horse.
> *Rich.* Slaue, I haue set my life vpon a cast,
> And I will stand the hazard of the Dye !

Richard might have fled, for

[A swift horse was brought to him.]

[*Hol.* iii. 759/2/73. *Halle*, 419.]   when the losse of the battell was imminent and apparant, they brought to him a [p. 760] swift and a light horsse, to conuoie him awaie. He which was not ignorant of the grudge and ill will that the common people bare toward him, casting awaie all hope of fortunate successe and happie chance to come, answered (as men saie) that on that daie he would make an end of all battels, or else there finish his life.

[He refused to fly.]

Act V. sc. v.—In V. iv. 1-6, Catesby appealed to Norfolk for rescue :

---

[1] *then . . . ground*] Not in *Polyd. Verg.*, 563/19.

Rescue, my Lord of Norfolk, rescue, rescue!
The King enacts more wonders then a man,
Daring an opposite to euery danger:
His horse is slaine, and all on foot he fights,
Seeking for Richmond in the throat of death.
Rescue, faire Lord, or else the day is lost!

The entry of scene v. (F) runs thus: "Alarum.   Enter Richard and
Richmond; they fight.   Richard is slaine."   While the vanguards of
the two armies were hotly engaged,

[*Hol.* iii. 759/1/26.   *Halle*, 418.] king Richard was admonished
by his explorators and espials, that the earle of Richmond (accompanied with a small number of men of armes) was not far off.
And, as he approched and marched toward him, he perfectlie knew
his personage by certeine demonstrations and tokens, which he
had learned and knowen of others that were able to giue him full
information.   Now, being inflamed with ire, and vexed with out- *[Richard ran with spear in rest toward Richmond.]*
ragious malice, he put his spurres to his horsse, and rode out of
the side of the range of his battell, leauing the vant-gard fighting;
and like a hungrie lion ran with speare in rest toward him.   The *The earle of Richmond profferth to incounter K. Richard bodie to bodie.*
earle of Richmond perceiued well the king furiouslie comming
toward him, and, bicause the whole hope of his wealth and purpose
was to be determined by battell, he gladlie proffered to incounter
with him bodie to bodie, and man to man.

King Richard set on so sharplie at the first brunt, that he *Sir William Brandon slaine.*
ouerthrew the earles standard, and slue sir William Brandon[1] his
standard-bearer, (which was father to sir Charles Brandon, by king
Henrie the eight created duke of Suffolke,) and matched hand to
hand with sir Iohn Cheinie, a man of great force and strength,
which would haue resisted him: but the said Iohn was by him *[Richmond kept Richard at the sword's point longer than might have been expected.*
manfullie ouerthrowen.   And so, he making open passage by dint
of sword as he went forward, the earle of Richmond withstood his
violence, and kept him at the swords point, without aduantage,
longer than his companions either thought or iudged: which, being *[Richmond's army rein- forced by Sir William Stanley.]*
almost in despaire of victorie, were suddenlie recomforted by sir

---

[1] Sir William Brandon was not slain at Bosworth.   *Polyd. Verg.* (563/38)
merely says that Richard overthrew both standard and standard-bearer.   A
petition presented by Brandon in the first Parliament of Henry VII. (November,
1485) shows that fear of Richard obliged him to keep sanctuary at Gloucester
from Michaelmas 1484 "unto youre comeing into this Reame, Soveraine
Lord."—*Rot. Parl.*, vi. 291/2.

The kings
armie fleeth
[Richard
slain].
William Stanleie, which came to his succors with three thousand
tall men.   At which verie instant, king Richards men were driuen
backe and fled, & he himselfe, manfullie fighting in the middle of
his enimies, was slaine; and (as he worthilie had deserued) came to
a bloudie death, as he had lead a bloudie life.

A "Retreat and Flourish" precede the re-entry of Richmond, who
went out after slaying Richard.   Stanley follows "bearing the
Crowne," which he offers to Richmond (ll. 4-7):

> Loe, heere, this long vsurpèd roialtie,[1]
> From the dead Temples of this bloudy Wretch
> Haue I pluck'd off, to grace thy Browes withall:
> Weare it, enioy it,[2] and make much of it !

Richmond's extemporaneous coronation was the last event of the
day.   At the close of his second speech to his army (see next page),

[*Hol.* iii. 760/1/42. *Halle*, 420.] the people reioised, and clapped
their hands, crieng vp to heauen, "King Henrie, king Henrie !"

The lord
Stanleie
setteth ye
crowne on
king Henrias
head.
When the lord Stanleie saw the good will and gladnesse of the
people, he tooke the crowne of king Richard, (which was found
amongst the spoile in the field,) and set it on the earles head; as
though he had beene elected king by the voice of the people, as in
ancient times past in diuerse realmes it hath beene accustomed; . . .

After his coronation Richmond asks (L. 9):

> But, tell me, is yong George Stanley liuing !
> *Der.* [*Stan.*] He is, my Lord, and safe in Leicester Towne ;
> Whither, if it please you, we may now withdraw vs.[3]

George Stanley, Lord Strange, was, as we have seen (p. 418 above),
" deliuered to the keepers of the kings tents, to be kept as prisoner."

Proclama-
tion made to
bring in the
lord Strange.
[*Hol.* iii. 760/2/6. *Halle*, 420.] Which, when the field was
doone, and their maister slaine, and proclamation made to know
where the child was, they submitted themselues as prisoners to the
lord Strange, and he gentlie receiued them, and brought them to
the new proclamed king; where, of him and of his father, he was
receiued with great ioy.   After this the whole campe remooued
with bag and baggage.

[Henry
entered
Leicester on
the evening
after the
battle.]
The same night, in the euening, king Henrie with great pompe
came to the towne of Leicester; . . .

---

1 *this . . . roialtie*] Q. *these . . . Royalties* F.
2 *enioy it*] Q. 1, 2.   The rest omit.
3 *if it please you we may now withdraw vs*] Q.   (*if you please*) *we may*
withdraw vs F.

To Richmond's enquiry (l. 12),

What men *of name* are *slaine on* either *side ?* [see sidenote to 759/2/1].

Stanley replies :

    Iohn Duke of Norfolke, Walter Lord Ferrers,[1]
    Sir Robert Brakenbury,[2] and Sir William Brandon.[3]

Halle (419) and Holinshed record that

[*Hol.* iii. 759/2/1.]   of the nobilitie were slaine Iohn duke of Norffolke, . . . *Duke of Norffolke slaine in the field.*

There were slaine beside him, Walter lord Ferrers of Chartleie, sir Richard Radcliffe, and Robert Brakenberie, lieutenant of the Tower, and not manie gentleman more. *What persons of name were slaine on king Richards side.*

The play ends with a speech of Richmond, which represents in a measure his address to his soldiers before Stanley placed the crown on his head (p. 420 above). I quote two excerpts partly illustrating the commencement of the dramatic oration (ll. 15-17):

    Interre their Bodies as become their Births :
    Proclaime a pardon to the Soldiers fled,
    That in submission will returne to vs : . . .

The victory won, Richmond

[*Hol.* iii. 760/1/35. *Halle,* 420.] ascended vp to the top of a little mounteine, where he not onelie praised and lauded his valiant souldiers, but also gaue vnto them his hartie thanks, with promise of condigne recompense for their fidelitie and valiant facts ; willing and commanding all the hurt and wounded persons to be cured, and the dead carcasses to be deliuered to the sepulture. [Richmond praised his soldiers, and commanded that the slain should be delivered to sepulture.]

[*Hol.* iii. 759/2/32. *Halle,* 419.] Of captiues and prisoners there were a great number. For, after the death of king Richard was knowne and published, euerie man, in manner vnarming himselfe, & casting awaie his abiliments of warre, meekelie submitted themselues to the obeisance and rule of the earle of Richmond : of the which the more part had gladlie so doone in the beginning, if they might haue conuenientlie escaped from king Richards espials, which, hauing as cleere eies as Lynx, and open eares as Midas, ranged & searched in euerie quarter.[4] [After their master's death Richard's soldiers submitted to Richmond.]

---

[1] *Ferrers*] Capell. *Ferris* Qq. Ff.
[2] *Brackenbury*] F4. *Brokenbury* Qq. 3—8. Ff. 1—3.
[3] Brandon was not slain. See p. 419, n. 1, above.
[4] In V. iii. 221, 222, Richard goes out with Ratcliffe ; saying,
    "Vnder our Tents Ile play the eaves-dropper [F4. *Ease-dropper* F.],
    To heare if any meane to shrinke from me."

Lastly I quote passages describing the characters and personal traits
of Edward IV., George Duke of Clarence, Richard III., and Richmond.
Edward

*Description
of Edward
the fourth.*
*[His
character.]*

[*Hol.* iii. 711/1/46. *More,* 2/17.] was a goodlie personage, and
princelie to behold, of heart couragious, politike in counsell, in
aduersitie nothing abashed, in prosperitie rather ioifull than proud,
in peace iust and mercifull, in warre sharpe and fierce, in the field
bold and hardie, and natheles no further (than wisdome would)
aduenturous; whose warres who so well considered, he shall no
lesse commend his wisedome where he voided, than his manhood
*[Personal
appearance.]*
where he vanquished. He was of visage louelie, of bodie mightie,
strong, and cleane made: howbeit, in his latter daies, with ouer
*[Over liberal
diet in his
latter days.]*
liberall diet,[1] somewhat corpulent and boorelie, and nathelesse
*[Fleshly
wantonness
in youth.]*
not vncomelie. He was of youth greatlie giuen to fleshlie
wantonnesse:[2] . . .

*George duke
of Clarence.*

[*Hol.* iii. 712/1/41. *More,* 5/9.] George duke of Clarence was
a goodlie noble prince, and at all times fortunate, if either his
owne ambition had not set him against his brother, or the enuie of
* *had not set* his enimies * his brother against him.

*The descrip-
tion of
Richard the
third.*
*[Personal
appearance.]*

[*Hol.* iii. 712/1/59. *More,* 5/25.] Richard, the third sonne, of
whome we now intreat, was in wit and courage equall with either
of them, in bodie and prowesse farre vnder them both; litle of
stature, ill featured of limmes, crooke backed, his left shoulder
much higher than his right,[3] *hard fauoured* of visage,[4] and such as
*[Malicious,
wrathful,
and
envious.]*
is in states called warlie, in other men otherwise; he was malicious,
wrathfull, enuious, and from afore his birth euer froward. It is for
truth reported, that the duchesse his mother had so much adoo in
*[His
portentous
birth.]*
hir trauell, that she could not be deliuered of him vncut; and that
he came into the world with the feet forward, as men be borne
outward, and (as the fame runneth also) not vntoothed.[5] . . .

[1] Cp. *Rich. III.,* I. i. 139-141.
[2] Cp. 3 *Hen. VI.,* II. i. 41, 42; and the asides of Clarence and Richard in
3 *Hen. VI.,* III. ii.
[3] Cp. 3 *Hen. VI.,* III. ii. 153-162; *Rich. III.,* I. i. 14-23.
[4] "*Hard fauor'd* Richard" (3 *Hen. VI.,* V. v. 78).
[5] Cp. 3 *Hen. VI.,* V. vi. 49-54, 70-75; *Rich. III.,* II. iv. 27-29; IV. iv.
162—168.

None euill capteine was he in the warre, as to which his dis- *[A good general.]*
position was more meetly than for peace. Sundrie victories had
he, & sometimes ouerthrowes; but neuer on default as for his
owne person, either of hardinesse or politike order. Free was he *[Liberal in expenditure.]*
called of dispense, and somewhat aboue his power liberall: with
large gifts he gat him vnstedfast freendship, for which he was
faine to pill and spoile in other places, and got him stedfast hatred.
He was close and secret, a deepe dissembler, lowlie of countenance, *[A dissembler.]*
arrogant of heart, outwardlie companiable where he inwardlie
bated, not letting to kisse whome he thought to kill: despitious *[Ambition made him cruell]*
and cruell, not for euill will alway, but ofter for ambition, and
either for the suertie or increase of his estate.

Friend and fo was much what indifferent, where his aduantage *[and un-scrupulous.]*
grew; he spared no mans death whose life withstoode his purpose.

Holinshed also contains the subjoined description of Richard,
which was freely translated by Halle from Polydore Vergil (*Angl.
Hist.*, 565/3):

[*Hol.* iii. 760/2/52. *Halle*, 421.] As he was small and little of *The descrip-tion of king Richard.*
stature, so was he of bodie greatlie deformed; the one shoulder *[Personal appearance.]*
higher than the other; his face was small, but his countenance
cruell, and such, that at the first aspect a man would iudge it to
sauour and smell of malice, fraud, and deceit. When he stood *[Was wont to bite his lip while musing.]*
musing, he would bite and chaw busilie his nether lip;[1] as who
said, that his fierce nature in his cruell bodie alwaies chafed,
stirred, and was euer vnquiet: beside that, the dagger which he
ware, he would (when he studied) with his hand plucke vp &
downe in the sheath to the midst, neuer drawing it fullie out: he
was of a readie, pregnant, and quicke wit, wilie to feine, and apt *[Character.]*
to dissemble: he had a proud mind, and an arrogant stomach, the
which accompanied him euen to his death; rather choosing to suffer
the same by dint of sword, than, being forsaken and left helplesse *[Would not save his life by flight.]*
of his vnfaithfull companions, to preserue by cowardlie flight such
a fraile and vncerteine life, which by malice, sicknesse, or condigne
punishment was like shortlie to come to confusion.

Richard's remorse for his nephews' murder is thus pictured:

---

[1] Cp. *Rich. III.*, IV. ii. 27. See p. 371 above.

[*Hol.* iii. 735/2/39. *More,* 85/19.] I haue heard by credible

report of such as were secret with his chamberleine, that, after this
abhominable deed doone, he neuer had a quiet mind. . . .

He neuer thought himselfe sure. Where he went abroad, his
eies whirled about, his bodie priuilie fensed,[1] his hand euer vpon
his dagger, his countenance and maner like one alwaies readie to
strike againe; he tooke ill rest a nights, laie long waking and
musing, sore wearied with care and watch, rather slumbered than

slept, troubled with fearefull dreames, suddenlie sometime start
vp, lept out of his bed, and ran [2] about the chamber;[3] . . .

Richmond

[*Hol.* iii. 757/1/53. *Halle,* 416.] was a man of no great
stature, but so formed and decorated with all gifts and lineaments
of nature, that he seemed more an angelicall creature, than a
terrestriall personage. His countenance and aspect was cheerefull
and couragious, his haire yellow like the burnished gold, his eies
graie, shining, and quicke : prompt and readie in answering, but of
such sobrietie, that it could neuer be iudged whether he were more
dull than quicke in speaking (such was his temperance.)

XIII. HENRY VIII.

THE meeting of Henry and Francis—June, 1520 [4]—is a recent event
when *The Famous History of the Life of King Henry the Eight* opens.
The action is brought to an end on September 10, 1533, the day of
Elizabeth's christening ;[5] but Cranmer's appearance before the Council
—July, 1544—is dramatized in a preceding scene (Act V. sc. iii.).

Act I. sc. i.—Enter Norfolk, Buckingham, and Abergavenny.
Buckingham says (ll. 4-7):

>   An vntimely Ague
> Staid me a Prisoner in my Chamber when
> Those Sunnes of Glory, those *too* Lights of Men,
> *Met in the vale of Andren.*
>   *Nor.*   'Twixt Guynes and Arde :
> I was then present, saw them salute on Horsebacke;

8

---

[1] *fensed*] Hol. (More). *feinted* Halle.
[2] *ran*] Hol. (More). *loked* Halle.
[3] Cp. *Rich. III.,* V. iii. 159, 160.
[4] June 7, 1520, was the date of their first meeting (*Halle,* 608) ; and they
took leave of each other on June 24 (*Halle,* 620).   [5] *Halle,* 805.

Beheld them, when they lighted, how they clung
In their Embracement, as they grew together ; . . .

On June 7, 1520,

[*Hol.* iii. 858/1/33. *Halle,* 608.] the *two* kings *met in the vale* *The inter-*
of Andren, accompanied with such a number of the nobilitie of
both realmes, so richlie appointed in apparell, and costlie iewels,
as chaines, collars of S S, & other the like ornaments to set foorth
their degrees and estates, that a woonder it was to behold and
view them in their order and roomes, which euerie man kept
according to his appointment.

The two kings meeting in the field, either saluted other in
most louing wise, first on horssebacke, and after alighting on foot
eftsoones imbraced with courteous words, to the great reioising of
the beholders : and, after they had thus saluted ech other, they
went both togither into a rich tent of cloath of gold, there set vp
for the purpose, in the which they passed the time in pleasant
talke, banketting, and louing deuises, till it drew toward the
euening, and then departed for that night, the one to Guisnes, the
other to Ard.

The historical Buckingham was not his "Chambers Prisoner"
(l. 13) on June 17, 1520 ; for on that day,—after Francis had taken
leave of Queen Katharine and her ladies,—

[*Hol.* iii. 860/2/64. *Halle,* 616.] The lord cardinall, in statelie
attire, accompanied with the duke of Buckingham, and other great
lords, conducted forward the French king, and in their way they
incountered and met the king of England and his companie right
in the vallie of Anderne, apparelled in their masking apparell ;
which gladded the French king.

But Thomas Howard, second Duke of Norfolk, was in England[1]
while Henry and Francis were displaying the magnificence which the
dramatic "Norfolk" saw and describes (ll. 16-38).

Though Buckingham asks who arranged the pageantry, he is able,
on learning that Wolsey ordered all (ll. 45-51), to give the following
proof of the Cardinal's absolute control therein (ll. 72-80) :

Buc.   Why the Diuell,   72
Vpon this French going out, tookeyhe vpon him
(Without the priuity o'th'King) t'appoint'

---

[1] *Calendar (Hen. VIII.),* III. i. 873, 895.

Who should attend on him !   He makes vp the File
Of all the Gentry ; for the most part such   76
To whom as great a Charge, as little Honor
He meant to lay vpon : and his owne Letter
(The Honourable Board of Councell out)
Must fetch him in the Papers.

I quote passages illustrating Buckingham's words, and noticing his
hatred of Wolsey :

[The nobles
were dis-
pleased at
being sum-
moned to
attend
Henry with-
out the
council's
sanction.]
[*Hol.* iii. 855/2/1.   *Polyd. Verg.* 659/3.] The peeres of the
realme (receiuing letters to prepare themselues to attend the king
in this iournie, and no apparant necessarie cause expressed, why
nor wherefore) seemed to grudge, that such a costlie iournie
should be taken in hand to their importunate charges and
expenses, without consent of the whole boord of the councell.
But namelie the duke of Buckingham (being a man of a loftie

[Bucking-
ham was
especially
aggrieved.]
courage, but not most liberall) sore repined that he should be at
so great charges for his furniture foorth at this time, saieng: that
he knew not for what cause so much monie should be spent about
the sight of a vaine talke to be had, and communication to be
ministred of things of no importance.   Wherefore he sticked not
to saie, that it was an intollerable matter to obeie such a vile and
importunate person.[1]

*Great hatred
betweene the
cardinall,
and the duke
of Bucking-
ham.*
The duke indeed could not abide the cardinall, and speciallie
he had of late conceiued an inward malice against him for sir
William Bulmer's cause, whose trouble was onelie procured by the
cardinall ; who first caused him to be cast in prison.[2]   Now
such greeuous words, as the duke thus vttered against him, came to
the cardinalls eare ; wherevpon he cast before hand all waies possible
to haue him in a trip, that he might cause him to leape headlesse.

In response to Norfolk's opinion that the peace is of little worth
(ll. 87-89), Buckingham says (ll. 89-94) :

Euery man,
After the hideous storme that follow'd, was

---

[1] *Halle* merely says (600) that the project of an interview "was often
tymes hard and litle regarded, but yet by the meanes of the Cardinall at the
last, in the ende of February [1520] it was agreed that the kyng in person
should passe the sea to his castell and lordshyp of Guisnes, & there in Maie
next comming, betwene Guisnes and Arde, the kyng and the Frenche kyng
should mete."

[2] See p. 438, n. 1, below.

> A thing Inspir'd ; and, not consulting, broke
> Into a generall Prophesie : That this Tempest, 92
> Dashing the Garment of this Peace, aboaded
> The sodaine breach on't.

This supposed portent occurred about a week before the final leave-taking of Henry and Francis.

[*Hol.* iii. 860/2/74. *Halle*, 616.] On mondaie, the eighteenth *A great and tempestuous* of Iune, was such an hideous storme of wind and weather, that *wind prognosticating* manie coniectured it did prognosticate trouble and hatred shortlie *trouble.* after to follow betweene princes.

" Which," adds Norfolk, referring to the portent,

> is budded out;
> For France hath flaw'd the League, and hath attach'd
> Our Merchants goods at Burdeux.
> *Abur.*   Is it therefore 96
> Th'Ambassador is silenc'd ?
> *Nor.*   Marry, is't.

The historic Edward Stafford, Duke of Buckingham, was beheaded on May 17, 1521 ; some ten months before the event here spoken of. On March 6, 1522,

[*Hol.* iii. 872/2/47. *Halle*, 632.] the French king commanded *The French K. attacheth* all Englishmens goods, being in Burdeaux, to be attached and put *the English-mens goods* vnder arrest, . . . [*Halle*, 633.] The Merchauntes of England, *in Burdeux.* that had factors at Burdeaux, complayned to the King of England, and shewed hym how the French king, contrary to his league and his safeconduyte vnder hys seal, by hys people, had taken their goodes, and emprisoned their factors and frendes, and can haue no remedy.[1]

This outrage was met by retaliatory measures ; and the French

[*Halle*, 634.] Ambassador was commaunded to kepe his house *[The French* in silence,[2] and not to come in presence till he was sent for, . . . *ambassador silenced.]*

Wolsey crosses the stage ; and, "in his passage, fixeth his eye on Buckingham, and Buckingham on him, both full of disdaine " (l. 114). Fearing that the Cardinal is gone to Henry for some malicious purpose, Buckingham is about to follow, but Norfolk detains the angry Duke, who then asserts (ll. 163-167) that Wolsey

---

[1] The substance of this excerpt from *Halle* and the words "league" and "merchants" are in *Hol.'s* epitome (872/2/73) of *Halle* 633, but not in one passage.
[2] *in silence*] Halle. om. Hol.

Only to shew his pompe, as well in France
As here at home, suggests the King our Master
To this last costly Treaty, th'enteruiew,
That swallowed so much treasure, and like a glasse
Did breake i'th'wrenching.
    Norf.   Faith, and so it did.
    Buck.   Pray giue me fauour, Sir! This cunning Cardinall, 168
The *Articles* o'th'Combination drew
As himselfe pleas'd ; . . .

According to Polydore Vergil (658/34), whom Holinshed translated,
Francis,

[*Hol.* iii. 853/1/11.] desirous to continue the friendship latelie
begun betwixt him and the king of England, made meanes vnto
the cardinall, that they might in some conuenient place come to
an interuiew togither, that he might haue further knowledge of

[Wolsey's
love of pomp
made him
desire to
bring about
the Inter-
view of
Henry and
Francis.]

Note the
ambitious
humor of the
cardinal of
yorke.

king Henrie, and likewise king Henrie of him. But the fame
went that the cardinall desired greatlie, of himselfe, that the two
kings might meet ; who, mesuring by his will what was conuenient,
thought it should make much with his glorie, if in France also, at
some high assemblie of noble men, he should be seene in his vaine
pompe and shew of dignitie : hee therefore breaketh with the king
of that matter, declaring how honourable, necessarie, and conuenient it should be for him to gratifie his friend therein ; and thus

[Henry was
persuaded
by Wolsey
to meet
Francis.]

with his persuasions the K. began to conceiue an earnest desire to
see the French king, and thereupon appointed to go ouer to Calis,
and so in the marches of Guisnes to meet with him.

It having been

The whole
manner of the
interview
committed
to the
cardinall.

[*Hol.* iii. 853/2/10. *Halle,* 601.] concluded, that the kings of
England and France should meet (as yee haue heard), then both
the kings committed the order and manner of their meeting, and
how manie daies the same should continue, & what preheminence
each should giue to other, vnto the cardinall of Yorke, which, to
set all things in a certeintie, made an instrument,[1] conteining an
order and direction concerning the premisses by him deuised and
appointed.

---

[1] In the instrument Wolsey uses these worde: "we haue made, declared,
and ordeined certaine *articles* accepted & approoued by the same princes
respectiuelie," &c.—*Hol.* iii. 853/2/64. *Halle,* 601.

After attributing the costly and useless interview to Wolsey's love
of ostentation, Buckingham makes a more serious charge (ll. 176-190):

Charles the Emperour,   176
Vnder pretence *to see the Queens his Aunt*,
(For 'twas indeed his colour, but he came
To whisper Wolsey,) here makes visitation:
His feares were, that the Interview betwixt   180
England and France might, through their amity,
Breed him some preiudice; for from this League
Peep'd harmes that menac'd him: he[1] priuily
Deales with our Cardinal; and, as I troa,—   184
Which I doe well; for, I am sure, the Emperour
Paid ere he promis'd; whereby his Suit was granted
Ere it was ask'd;—but, when the way was made
And pau'd with gold, the Emperor thus desir'd: 188
That he would please to alter the Kings course,
And breake the foresaid peace.   Let the King know
(As soone he shall by me) that thus the Cardinall
Does buy and sell his Honour as he pleases,   192
And for his owne aduantage.

On the Eve of Whit Sunday (May 26, 1520) Charles landed at
Dover, where, on the following day, Henry met him.

[*Hol.* iii. 856/1/51.   *Halle*, 604.]   On Whitsundaie, earlie in *The emperor and K.*
the morning, they tooke their horsses, and rode to the citie of *Henrie keeps*
Canturburie, the more to keepe solemne the feast of Pentecost, *whitsuntide at Cantur-*
but speciallie *to see the queene* of England *his aunt* was the *burie.*
emperour his intent; of whome ye may be sure he was most *[Charles wished to see the Queen, his aunt.]*
ioifullie receiued and welcomed. . . .

[*Hol.* iii. 856/1/70.   *Polyd. Verg.* 660/45.]   The chiefe cause,
that mooued the emperour to come thus on land at this time, was
to persuade that by word of mouth, which he had before done
most earnestlie by letters; which was, that the king should not
meet with the French king at anie interuiew: for he doubted least,
if the king of England & the French king should grow into some
great friendship and faithfull bond of amitie, it might turne him to
displeasure.

But, now that he perceiued how the king was forward on his *The emperor*
iournie, he did what he could to procure that no trust should be *labourth to hinder the*
committed to the faire words of the Frenchmen: and that, if it *purposed interuiew.*
were possible, the great friendship, that was now in breeding
betwixt the two kings, might be dissolued.   And, forsomuch as he

---

[1] he] F2. om. F1.

[Wolsey insisted that the interview should go forward, but accepted Charles's bribe to dissolve the friendship of Henry and Francis.]

knew the lord cardinall to be woone with rewards, as a fish with a bait, he bestowed on him great gifts, and promised him much more; so that hee would be his friend, and helpe to bring his purpose to passe. The cardinall (not able to susteine the least assault by force of such rewards as he presentlie receiued, and of such large promises as on the emperours behalfe were made to him) promised to the emperour, that he would so vse the matter, as his purpose should be sped: onelie he required him not to disalow the kings intent for interuiew to be had; which he desired in anie wise to go forward, that he might shew his high magnificence in France, according to his first intention.

An officer named Brandon[1] now enters (l. 197), preceded by "a Sergeant at Armes" and "two or three of the Guard." At Brandon's bidding Buckingham and Abergavenny are arrested; it being Henry's pleasure that they shall both to the Tower (ll. 198-214). Brandon also (ll. 217—221) shows a warrant from

The King, t'attach Lord Mountacute; and the Bodies
Of the Dukes Confessor, Iohn de la Car,
One Gilbert Pecke, his chancellor,[2]—
    Buck.   So, so;
These are the limbs o'th'Plot: no more, I hope.   **220**
    Bra.   A Monke o'th'Chartreux.
    Buck.   O! Nicholas Hopkins![3]
    Bra.   He.

Buckingham having been accused of treasonable designs

Edw. Hall [, 623].

[*Hol.* iii. 863/1/21.] was sent for vp to London, &, at his comming thither, was streightwaies attached, and brought to the Tower by sir Henrie Marneie, capteine of the gard, the sixteenth of Aprill [, 1521]. There was also attached the . . . Chartreux monke [, Nicholas Hopkins], maister Iohn de la Car *alias* de la Court, the dukes confessor, and sir Gilbert Perke, priest, the dukes chancellor.

[Arrest of Buckingham, Hopkins, Delacourt, and Perke.]

Anno Reg. 13.

After the apprehension of the duke, inquisitions were taken in diuerse shires of England of him; so that, by the knights and

---

[1] Perhaps "sir Thomas Brandon, master of the kings horse," who appeared in the royal train on the day before Henry VIII.'s coronation.—*Hol.* iii. 801/2/1. *Halle,* 508.
[2] *chancellor*] Pope, ed. 2 (Theobald). *Councellour* F. It appears from Buckingham's indictment that the chancellor's name was Robert Gilbert. By *Halle* (623) he was named Gylbert Perke.
[3] *Nicholas*] Pope, ed. 2 (Theobald). *Michaell* F.

gentlemen, he was indicted of high treason, for certeine words
spoken . . . by the same duke at Blechinglie, to the lord of
Aburgauennie [1] and therewith was the same lord attached for
concelement, and so likewise was the lord Montacute, and both led
to the Tower.

*The duke of Buckingham indicted of treason.
[Lords Abergavenny and Montague attached and sent to the Tower.]*

Act I. sc. ii.—Henry enters, "leaning on the Cardinals shoulder,"
whom he thanks for detecting Buckingham's treason (ll. 1-4). The
King wishes to hear in person the evidence which Buckingham's surveyor has laid before Wolsey (ll. 4-8); but at this moment Queen
Katharine enters, ushered by the Dukes of Norfolk and Suffolk. She
is a petitioner for Henry's subjects, who

> Are in great grieuance : there haue beene Commissions   20
> Sent downe among 'em, which hath flaw'd the heart
> Of all their Loyalties : wherein, although,
> My good Lord Cardinall, they vent reproches
> Most bitterly on you, as putter on   24
> Of these exactions, yet the King, our Maister,
> (Whose Honor Heauen shield from soile !) euen he escapes not
> Language vnmannerly, yea, such which breakes
> The sides of loyalty, and almost appeares   28
> In lowd Rebellion.
>   *Norf.*   Not "almost appeares,"
> It doth appeare ; for, vpon these Taxations,
> The Clothiers all, not able to maintaine
> The many to them longing, haue put off   32
> The Spinsters, Carders, Fullers, Weauers, who,
> Vnfit for other life, compeld by hunger
> And lack of other meanes, in desperate manner
> Daring th'euent to th'teeth, are all in vprore,   36
> And danger serues among them.

Resuming her petition Queen Katharine explains (ll. 56-60) that

>   The Subiects griefe   56
> Comes through Commissions, which compels from each
> The sixt part of his Substance, to be leuied
> Without delay ; and the pretence for this
> Is nam'd, your warres in France : . . .

Previous to her entry historic time has not reached the date of
Buckingham's trial (May 13, 1521),[2] but as soon as she begins to speak
we are transported to the historic year 1525,[3] when Henry,

[*Hol.* iii. 891/1/31. *Halle,* 694.] being determined . . . to
make wars in France, & to passe the sea himselfe in person, his
councell considered that aboue all things great treasure and
plentie of monie must needes be prouided. Wherfore, by the

---

[1] See pp. 434, 435, below.   [2] *Stow,* 862.   [3] *Halle,* 694.

cardinall there was deuised strange commissions, and sent in the
end of March into euerie shire, and commissioners appointed, and
priuie instructions sent to them how they should proceed in their
sittings, and order the people to bring them to their purpose:
which was, that the sixt part of euerie mans substance should be
paid in monie or plate to the king without delaie, for the furniture
of his war. Hereof followed such cursing, weeping, and exclamation against both king & cardinall, that pitie it was to heare. . . .

[*Hol.* iii. 891/1/70. *Halle*, 697.] The cardinall trauelled
earnestlie with the maior and aldermen of London, about the aid
of monie to be granted, and likewise the commissioners, appointed
in the shires of the realme, sat vpon the same: but the burthen
was so greeuous, that it was generallie denied, and the commons
in euerie place so mooned, that it was like to grow to rebellion. . . .

[*Hol.* iii. 891/2/8. *Halle*, 699.] The duke of Suffolke, sitting
in commission about this subsidie in Suffolke, persuaded by
courteous meanes the rich clothiers to assent therto: but, when
they came home, and went about to discharge and put from them
their spinners, carders, fullers, weauers, and other artificers, (which
they kept in worke afore time,) the people began to assemble in
companies. . . . And herewith there assembled togither, after the
maner of rebels, foure thousand men of Lanam [Lavenham],
Sudberie, Hadleie, and other townes thereabouts; which put
themselues in harnesse, and rang the bels alarme, and began still
to assemble in great number. . . .

The duke of Norffolke,[1] being therof aduertised, gathered a
great power in Norffolke, and came towards the commons, &,
sending to them to know their intent, receiued answer, that they
would liue and die in the kings causes, and be to him obedient.
Herevpon he came himselfe to talke with them, and, willing to
know who was their capteine, that he might answer for them all,
it was told him by one Iohn Greene, a man of fiftie yeares of age,
that Pouertie was their capteine, the which, with his cousin
Necessitie, had brought them to that dooing.

Henry exclaims (ll. 67, 68):

---

[1] The third Duke. The second Duke died in June, 1524.—*Halle*, 697.

[He annulled the commissions by letter, and pardoned those who had refused to pay the tax.]

[Wolsey spread a report that this grace was due to his intercession.]

spiritualtie and temporaltie. Therefore he would no more of that trouble, but caused letters to be sent into all shires, that the matter should no further be talked of: & he pardoned all them that had denied the demand openlie or secretlie. The cardinall, to deliuer himselfe of the euill will of the commons, purchased by procuring & aduancing of this demand, affirmed, and caused it to be bruted abrode,[1] that through his intercession the king had pardoned and released all things.

Historic time runs back to the year 1521 when Charles Knyvet, Buckingham's surveyor, enters, and, at Henry's command, proceeds to give evidence of the Duke's treason:

> *Sur.* First, it was vsuall with him, euery day   132
> It would infect his Speech, that *if the King*
> Should *without issue dye,* hee'l carry it so
> To make the Scepter his : these very words
> I'ue heard him vtter to his Sonne in Law,   136
> Lord Aburgany ; to whom by oth he menac'd
> Reuenge vpon the Cardinall. . . .
> *Kin.*   Speake on !
> How grounded hee his Title to the Crowne,   144
> Vpon our faile ? to this poynt hast thou heard him
> At any time speake ought ?
> *Sur.*   He was *brought* to this
> By a vaine *Prophesie* of *Nicholas Henton.*
> *Kin.* What was that Henton ?
> *Sur.*   Sir, a Chartreux Fryer,   148
> His Confessor, who fed him euery minute
> With words of Soueraignty.

On the authority of Polydore Vergil (665/11) Holinshed relates that

The cardinall deuiseth the destruction of the duke of Bucking-ham (, by meanes of Knyvet)

[*Hol.* iii. 862/2/53.] the cardinall, boiling in hatred against the duke of Buckingham, & thirsting for his blond, deuised to make Charles Kneuet (that had beene the dukes surueior, and put from him[2] . . .) an instrument to bring the duke to destruction. This Kneuet, being had in examination before the cardinall, disclosed

---

[1] *Halle* says (701) that "letters were sent to all commissioners to cease, with instruccions how to declare the kynges pardon. In whiche declaracion was shewed that the Cardinal neuer assented to the first demaunde [for a sixth. Henry afterwards asked for what his subjects would willingly giue him.—*Halle,* 697] ; and in the instruccions was comprehended that the lordes and the Iudges, and other of the kynges counsaill, diuised the same demaunde, and that the Cardinall folowed the mynd of the whole counsaill : these two poyntes were contrary one to another, whiche were well marked. And farther the instruccions were that, at the humble peticion and supplicacion of the Cardinall, the saied greate sommes, whiche were demaunded by the kyng, auctho-ritie royall, were clerely pardoned and remitted," . . .   [2] See p. 437 below.

all the dukes life. And first he vttered, that the duke was
accustomed, by waie of talke, to saie how he meant so to vse the [Buckingham talked of succeeding to the crown if Henry died without issue.]
matter, that he would atteine to the crowne, *if king* Henrie
chanced to *die without issue:* & that he had talke and conference
of that matter on a time with George Neuill, lord of Aburgauennie, vnto whome he had giuen his daughter in marriage;
and also that he threatned to punish the cardinall for his manifold
misdooings, being without cause his mortall enimie.

The cardinall, hauing gotten that which he sought for, incour- *The cardinall imboldeneth Kneuet against the duke.*
aged, comforted, and procured Kneuet, with manie comfortable
words and great promises, that he should with a bold spirit and
countenance obiect and laie these things to the dukes charge, with
more if he knew it when time required. Then Kneuet [*p.* 863],
partlie prouoked with desire to be reuenged, and partlie mooned [Buckingham was influenced by a prophecy of Nicholas Hopkins.]
with hope of reward, openlie confessed, that the duke had once
fullie determined to deuise meanes how to make the king away,
being *brought* into a full hope that he should be king, *by a vaine
prophesie* which one *Nicholas* Hopkins, a monke of an house of the
Chartreux order beside Bristow, called *Henton*, sometime his
confessor, had opened vnto him.

The cardinall, hauing thus taken the examination of Kneuet, *The cardinall accuseth the duke of Buckingham to the king.*
went vnto the king, and declared vnto him, that his person was in
danger by such traitorous purpose, as the duke of Buckingham
had conceiued in his heart, and shewed how that now there is
manifest tokens of his wicked pretense: wherefore, he exhorted
the king to prouide for his owne suertie with speed. The king,
hearing the accusation, inforced to the vttermost by the cardinall,
made this answer: "If the duke haue deserued to be punished,
"let him haue according to his deserts."

Knyvet then explains how he knew of Nicholas Hopkins's prophecy
(ll. 151-171):

> *Sur.* Not long before your Highnesse sped to France,
> *The Duke* being at *the Rose, within the Parish*   152
> *Saint Laurence Poultney*, did *of* me *demand*
> *What was the* speech *among the* Londoners,
> *Concerning the* French *Iourney:* I replide,
> Men fear'd [1] *the French* would proue perfidious,   156

---

[1] *fear'd*] Pope. *feare* F.

To the Kings danger. Presently, the Duke
Said, 'twas the feare, indeed ; and that he doubted
'Twould proue the verity of certaine *words*
Spoke by *a holy Monke; "that* oft," sayes he,   160
" *Hath sent to me,* wishing *me* to permit
" *Iohn de la Car, my Chaplaine,* a choyce howre
" To heare from him a matter of some moment :
" *Whom* after, vnder the Confessions [1] Seale,   164
" *He* sollemnly *had sworne,* that, *what* he spoke,
" My Chaplaine to *no Creature liuing,* but
" *To me,* should vtter, with demure Confidence
" This pausingly ensu'de : ' *Neither the King, nor's Heyres*   168
' (Tell you the Duke) shall *prosper :* bid him striue
' To gain [2] *the* loue *o'th'Commonalty : the Duke*
' Shall gouerne England.' "
       One of the charges in Buckingham's [3] indictment [4] was that

[Bucking-
ham asked
Knyvet
what the
Londoners
said of
Henry's
journey.]
[*Hol.* iii. 864/2/12. *Stow,* 861.] *the* same *duke,* the tenth of
Maie, in the twelfe yeare of the kings reigne [1520], at London in
a place called *the Rose, within the parish* of *saint Laurence Poultnie*
in Canwike street ward, *demanded of* the said Charles Kneuet
esquier, *what was the* talke amongest *the Londoners concerning the*

[Knyvet's
answer.]
kings *iourneie* beyond the seas ? And the said Charles told him,
that manie stood in doubt of that iourneie, least *the French*men

*The duke
discouereth
the secrecie
of all the
matter to
his owne
vndoing.*
meant some deceit towards the king. Whereto the duke answered,
that it was to be feared least it would come to passe according
to the *words* of *a* certeine *holie moonke :* " For there is " (saith he)
" a Chartreux moonke, *that* diuerse times *hath sent to me,* willing
" *me* to send vnto him my chancellor : and I did send vnto him
" *Iohn de la Court my chapleine,* vnto *whome he* would not declare
" anie thing, till de la Court *had sworne* vnto him to keepe all
" things secret, and to tell *no creature liuing what* hee should
" heare of him, except it were *to me.*

---

[1] *Confessions*] Theobald. *Commissions* F. Theobald justified his emend-
ation by quoting *Hol.* iii. 863/2/52: " The duke in talke told the monke
[Hopkins]that he had doone verie well to bind his chapleine Iohn de la Court,
vnder the seale of confession, to keepe secret such matter " : . . .
[2] *gain*] F4. om. F. Malone supported this insertion by quoting " that
I should indeuor my selfe to purchase the good wils of the communaltie of
England " (see close of next excerpt).
[3] On July 20, 1517, Hopkins prophesied " that before Christmas next there
should be a change, & that the duke should haue the rule and gouernement of
all England."—*Hol.* iii. 864/1/31. *Stow,* 860.
[4] The indictment, as it appears in *Stow,* is prefaced by the remark that he
had " seen and read " it (859).

"And then the said moonke told de la Court, that *neither the*
"*king nor his heires* should *prosper*, and that I should indeuour my
"selfe to purchase *the* good wils *of the communaltie* of England;
"for I *the* same *duke* and my bloud should prosper, and haue the
"rule of the realme of *England*."

At this point Queen Katharine interposes with an appeal to
Knyvet's conscience (ll. 171-175):

> If I know you well,
> You were the Dukes Surueyor, and lost your Office   172
> On the complaint o'th'Tenants : take good heed
> You charge not in your spleene a Noble person,
> And spoyle your nobler Soule !

In 1520

[*Hol.* iii. 856/1/7. *Polyd. Verg.* 660/33.] it chanced that the
duke, comming to London with his traine of men, to attend the
king into France, went before into Kent vnto a manor place which
he had there. And, whilest he staid in that countrie till the king
set forward, greeuous complaints were exhibited to him by his
farmars and tenants against Charles Kneuet his surueiour, for such
bribing as he had vsed there amongest them. Wherevpon the
duke tooke such displeasure against him, that he depriued him of
his office; not knowing how that in so dooing he procured his owne
destruction, as after appeared.[1]

Resuming his evidence Knyvet says (ll. 178-186):

> I told my Lord the Duke, by *th'Diuels illusions*
> *The Monke* might *be deceiu'd* ; and that 'twas dangerous for him [2]
> To ruminate on this so farre, vntill   180
> It forg'd him some designe, which, being beleeu'd,
> It was much like to doe: he answer'd, "Tush !
> " It can doe me no damage "; adding further,
> *That, had the King in his last Sicknesse* faild,   184
> *The Cardinals* and *Sir Thomas Louels heads*
> Should *haue* gone *off*.

To illustrate these lines I quote the rest of the charge concerning
Buckingham's talk with Knyvet on May 10, 1520:

---

[1] The excerpt " it chanced . . . appeared" is preceded by the following
passage : " Now in this meane while [Spring of 1520], the cardinall ceassed not
to bring the duke out of the kings fauour by such forged tales and contriued
surmises as he dailie put into the kings head : insomuch that (through the
infelicitie of his fate) diuerse accidents fell out to the aduantage of the
cardinall ; which he not omitting, atchiued the thing whereat he so studiouslie
(for the satisfieng of his canckered & malicious stomach) laid full aime."—
Hol. iii. 855/2/73.   [2] *him*] Rowe. *this* F.

[Knyvet said that Hopkins might be deceived by the devil.]

But the end of that ioy [of Buckingham] was fearfulness [: though he said that the prophecy could do him no harm].

[If Henry had died, Buckingham would have chopped off the heads of Wolsey and Lovel.]

[*Hol.* iii. 864/2/37. *Stow*, 862.] Then said Charles Kneuet: "*The moonke* maie *be deceiued* through *the diuels illusion:*" and that it was euill to meddle with such matters. "Well" (said the duke) "it cannot hurt me;" and so (saith the indictment) the duke seemed to reioise in the moonks woords. And further, at the same time, the duke told the said Charles, *that*, if *the king had* miscaried now *in his last sicknesse*, he would *haue* chopped *off* the heads of *the cardinall*, of *sir Thomas Louell* knight, and of others; and also said, that he had rather die for it, than to be vsed as he had beene.

Questioned by Henry, Knyvet gives an instance of Buckingham's truculent mood:

    Sur.   Being *at Greenwich*,   188
After your Highnesse *had reprou'd the Duke*
About *Sir William Bulmer*,[1]—
    Kin.   I remember
Of such a time: being my sworn seruant,
The Duke *retein'd* him his. But on! what hence!   192
    Sur. "*If*" (quoth he) "I for this had *beene committed*,
"*As, to the Tower*, I thought, I *would haue plaid*
"*The Part* my *Father* meant to act vpon
"Th'Vsurper *Richard*; *who*, being *at Salsbury*,   196
"*Made suit to come* in's *presence*; *which if* granted,
"(*As he made semblance* of his duty,) *would*
"*Haue* put his *knife into* him."
    Kin.   A Gyant Traytor!
    Card. Now, Madam, may his Highnes liue in freedome, 200
And this man out of Prison!
    Queen.   God mend all!
    Kin. Ther's somthing more would out of thee; what say'st!
    Sur. After "the Duke his Father," with "the knife,"
He stretch'd him, and, with one *hand on his dagger*,   204
Another spread on's breast, mounting his eyes,
He did discharge a horrible Oath; whose tenor
Was, *were he euill vs'd, he would* outgoe
His Father, by as much as a performance   208
Do's an irresolute *purpose.*

In his indictment Buckingham was accused of having,

[Henry reproved Buckingham for retaining Sir William Bulmer.]

[*Hol.* iii. 864/1/64. *Stow*, 861.] on the fourth of Nouember, in the eleuenth yere of the kings reigne [1519], *at* east *Greenwich* in the countie of Kent, said vnto one Charles Kneuet esquier, (*after* that the king *had reprooued the duke* for *reteining William Bulmer*, knight, into his seruice,[2]) that, *if* he had perceiued that he

---

[1] *Bulmer*] Hol. *Blumer* F.
[2] In November, 1519, "the king speciallie rebuked sir William Bulmer,

should haue *beene committed to the Tower* (as he doubted hee should haue beene), hee would haue so wrought, that the principall docers therein should not haue had cause of great reioising : for he *would haue plaied the part* which his *father* intended to haue put in practise against king *Richard* the third *at Salisburie; who made* earnest *sute to haue come* vnto the *presence* of the same king Richard : *which* sute *if* he might haue obteined, he hauing a *knife* secretlie about him, *would haue* thrust it *into* the bodie of king Richard, *as he* had *made semblance* to kneele downe before him. And, in speaking these words, *he* maliciouslie laid his *hand* vpon *his dagger,* and said, that, if *he were* so *euill vsed, he would* doo his best to accomplish his pretensed *purpose ;* swearing to confirme his word by the bloud of our Lord.

[Buckingham expected to be committed to the Tower.]

See the historie of Richard the third, pag. 744.

[He would then have done to the king what Henry duke of Buckingham meant to do to Richard III.

Act I. sc. iii.—The Lord Chamberlain and Lord Sandys censure the Gallic airs of those courtiers who went to France with Henry in 1520. The Lord Chamberlain says (ll. 5-10) :

> As farre as I see, all the good our English
> Haue got by the late Voyage, is but meerely
> A fit or two o'th' face ; (but they are shrewd ones ;)
> For when they hold 'em, you would sweare directly,   8
> Their very noses had been Councellours
> To Pepin or Clotharius, they keepe State so.

Sir Thomas Lovell entering brings tidings of a

new Proclamation
That's clapt vpon the Court Gate.
> *L. Cham.*   What is't for ?
> *Lou.* The *reformation* of our trauel'd Gallants,
> That fill the Court with quarrels, talke, and Taylors.   20
> *L. Cham.* I'm glad 'tis there : now I would pray our Monsieurs
> To thinke an English Courtier may be wise,
> And neuer see the Louure.

Mr. Boyle supposes the "trauel'd Gallants" of James I.'s reign to be ridiculed in this scene (*Henry VIII.* in *New Sh. Soc.'s Trans.*, 1885-86, p. 461), but the following excerpt shows that they had their predecessors. When, in 1519,[1] "diuerse yoong gentlemen of England," who resided awhile at the French Court,

[*Hol.* iii. 850/1/17. *Halle,* 597.] came againe into England,

---

knight, bicause he, *being his seruant scorne,* refused the kings seruice, and became seruant to the Duke of Buckingham."—*Hol.* iii. 852/2/72. *Halle,* 599.

[1] After recording our surrender of Tournay on February 8, 1519, *Halle* describes the conduct of these young gentlemen at Paris, "during this time" ; and then speaks of their behaviour when they returned to England (597).

they were all French, in eating, drinking, and apparell, yea, and
in French vices and brags, so that all the estates of England were
by them laughed at, the ladies and gentlewomen were dispraised ;
so that nothing by them was praised, but if it were after the

French turne ; which after turned them to displesure, as you shall
heare.

In May 1519 Henry's Council complained to him of "certeine
yoong men in his priuie chamber," who, "not regarding his estate or
degree, were so familiar and homelie with him, that they forgat
themselues."

[*Hol.* iii. 852/2/7. *Halle*, 598.] To whome the king answered,
that he had chosen them of his conncell, both for the maintenance
of his honour, and for the defense of all things that might blemish
the same : wherefore, if they saw anie about him misuse them-

selues, he committed it vnto their *reformation.* Then the kings
councell caused the lord chamberleine to call before them diucrse
of the priuie chamber, (which had beene in the French court,) and
banished them the court for diuerse considerations ; laieng nothing
particularlie to their charges, & they that had offices were commanded to go to their offices. Which discharge out of court
greeued sore the hearts of these yoong men, which were called the
kings minions.

In a passage omitted by Holinshed, Halle adds (598) :

These young minions, which was thus seuered from the kyng,
had bene in Fraunce, and so highly praised the Frenche kyng and
his courte, that in a maner they thought litle of the kyng and his
court in comparison of the other, they were so high in loue with
the Frenche court ; wherefore their fall was litle moned emong
wise men.

Act I. sc. iv.—Towards the close of sc. iii., Act I., the Lord
Chamberlain remembers an invitation of Wolsey :

> This night he makes a Supper, and a great one,   52
> To many Lords and Ladies ; there will be
> The Beauty of this Kingdome, Ile assure you.

While going out to his barge, accompanied by Lord Sandys, the
Lord Chamberlain says (ll. 66, 67) :

> For I was spoke to, with Sir Henry Guilford,
> This night to be Comptrollers.

Sc. iv., Act I., opens thus:

"Hoboies. A small Table vnder a State for the Cardinall, a longer
Table for the Guests. Then Enter Anne Bullen, and diuers
other Ladies, & Gentlemen, as Guests, at one Doore; at an other
Doore, enter Sir Henry Guilford."

After l. 34: "Hoboyes. Enter Cardinall Wolsey, and takes his
State."

The historical date of sc. iv. was January 3, 1527.[1] The excerpts
illustrating sc. iv. were taken by Stow from Cavendish's *Life of Wolsey*,
and transferred from Stow to the pages of Holinshed. Cavendish—
who was present when Henry came disguised to Wolsey's banquet—
thus describes the ceremony observed:

[*Hol.* iii. 922/1/1. *Stow*, 845.] First, yee shall vnderstand that
the tables were set in the chamber of presence banquetwise couered,[2]
& the lord cardinall sitting vnder the cloth of estate, there hauing
all his seruice alone: and then was there set a ladie with a noble
man, or a gentleman and a gentlewoman, throughout all the tables[3]
in the chamber on the one side, which were made and ioined as it
were but one table: all which order and deuise was doone by the

*The car-
dinals stat-
lie sitting at
table like a
prince.*

[Lord
Sandys and
Sir Henry
Guildford

---

[1] This banquet is noticed by *Halle* (719), who tells us that, on the night of
January 3, 1527, "the kyng and many young gentelmen with hym came to
Bridewell, & there put hym and xv. other all in Maskyng apparell, and then
toke his Barge, and rowed to the Cardinalles place, where wer at supper a
great compaignie of lordes and ladies; and then the Maskers daunced, and
made goodly pastyme, and, when they had well danced, the Ladies plucked
away their visors, and so they were all knowen, and to the kyng was made a
great banket." Gasparo Spinelli, Venetian Secretary in London, writing to
his brother Ludovico on January 4, 1527, says: "Last evening I was present
at a very sumptuous supper given by Cardinal Wolsey, there being amongst
the guests the Papal, French, and Venetian ambassadors, and the chief nobility
of the English Court . . . During the supper the King arrived, with a gallant
company of masqueraders, and his Majesty, after presenting himself to the
Cardinal, threw a main at dice and then unmasked, as did all his companions;
whereupon he withdrew to sup in one of the Cardinal's chambers, the rest of
the guests continuing their repast, with such variety of the choicest viands and
wines as to be marvellous." After supper the *Menaechmei* was acted in
another hall, and Latin verses were recited to Henry by the actors. "Having
listened to them all, the King betook himself with the rest of the guests to the
hall where they had all supped, the tables (at which they seated themselves in
the same order as before) being spread with every sort of confection, whereof
they partook." A pageant was then displayed, in which six damsels appeared,
each of whom was subsequently "taken by the hand by her lover, and to the
sound of trumpets they performed a very beautiful dance. On its termination
the King and his favourites commenced another with the ladies there present,
and with this the entertainment and the night ended, for it was already
day-break."—*Ven. State PP.*, IV. 4.

[2] *banquetwise couered*] Cavendish. *iust couered* Hol. and Stow.

[3] The Lord Chamberlain to Lord Sandys (I. iv. 22, 24):

"Two women, plac'd together, makes cold weather: . . .
Pray, sit betweene these Ladies."

[regulated
Wolsey's
banquet.] lord Sandes, then lord chamberleine to the king, and by sir Henrie
Gilford, comptrollor of the kings maiesties house.

Soon after Wolsey's entrance comes the stage direction: "Drum
and Trumpet, Chambers dischargd" (l. 49). Attendants leave the
stage in obedience to the Lord Chamberlain's command, "Looke out
there, some of ye"; and one of them, re-entering, announces

A noble troupe of *Strangers* ;
For so *they seeme* : th'haue left their Barge and landed,
And hither make, *as great Embassadors*
From forraigne Princes.
    Card.   Good Lord Chamberlaine,   **56**
Go, giue 'em welcome! *you can speake* the *French* tongue ;
And, pray, *receiue 'em* Nobly, *and conduct 'em*
Into our presence, *where* this heauen of beauty
Shall shine at full vpon them.—Some attend him!   **60**
  [Exit Chamberlain, attended.] [All rise, and Tables remou'd.
—You haue now a broken Banket ; but wee'l mend it.
A good digestion to you all ! and once more
I showre a welcome on yee ; welcome all !

  Hoboyes. Enter *King* and others, as *Maskers*, habited *like*
    Shepheards, vsher'd by the Lord Chamberlaine. *They passe*
    directly before the Cardinall, and gracefully *salute him.*
A noble Company! what are their pleasures ?   **64**
  Cham. Because *they speak* no *English*, thus they praid
To tell your Grace : *That, hauing* heard by fame
Of this so Noble and so faire assembly,
This night to meet heere, *they could doe no lesse,*   **68**
(Out of the great respect they beare to *beauty*,)
But leaue their Flockes ; and, *vnder your* faire Conduct,
Craue leaue *to view* these Ladies, and entreat
An houre of Reuels *with* 'em.
    Card.   Say, Lord Chamberlaine,   **72**
They haue done my poore house grace ; for which I pay 'em
A thousand thankes, and pray 'em take their pleasures !

  Wolsey's

The car-
dinals house
like a princes
court for all
kind of
braucrie and
sumptuous-
nesse. [*Hol.* iii. 921/2/45. *Stow*, 844.] house was resorted to with
noblemen and gentlemen, feasting and banketting ambassadors
diuerse times, and all other right noblie. And when it pleased
the king for his recreation to repaire to the cardinals house, (as he
did diuerse times in the yeare,) there wanted no preparations or
furniture : bankets were set foorth with maskes and mummeries,
in so gorgeous a sort and costlie maner, that it was an heauen to
behold. There wanted no dames or damosels meet or apt to
danse with the maskers, or to garnish the place for the time : then

was there all kind of musike and harmonie, with fine voices both
of men and children.

On a time the *king* came suddenlie thither [1] in a maske, with a
dozen *maskers* all in garments *like sheepheards*, made of fine cloth
of gold, and crimosin sattin paned, & caps of the same, with
visards of good physnomie, their haires & beards either of fine
goldwire silke, or blacke silke ; hauing sixteene torch-bearers,
besides their drums and other persons with visards, all clothed
in sattin of the same color. And, before his entring into the hall,
he came by water to the water gate without anie noise ; where
were laid diuerse chambers and guns charged with shot, and at his
landing they were shot off, which made such a rumble in the aire,
that it was like thunder : it made all the noblemen, gentlemen,
ladies, and gentlewomen, to muse what it should meane, comming
so suddenlie, they sitting quiet at a solemne banket, . . .

[*Hol.* iii. 922/1/11. *Stow*, 845.] Then immediatlie after, the
great chamberleine and the said comptrollor [were] sent to looke
what it should meane (as though they knew nothing of the matter) ;
who, looking out of the windowes into the Thames, returned againe
and shewed him, that it *seemed they* were noblemen and *strangers*
that arriued at his bridge, comming *as ambassadours from* some
forren prince.

With that, quoth the cardinall, "I desire you, bicause *you*
"*can speake French*, to take the paines to go into the hall, there to
"*receiue* them according to their estates, *and to conduct* them *into*
"this chamber, *where* they *shall* see vs, and all these noble person-
"ages being merie at our banket ; desiring them to sit downe with
"vs, and to take part of our fare." Then went he incontinent
downe into the hall, whereas they receiued them with twentie new
torches, and conueied them vp into the chamber, with such a noise
of drums and flutes, as seldome had beene heard the like. At
their entring into the chamber, two and two togither, *they* went
directlie before the cardinall, where he sate, *and saluted him*
reuerentlie.

*A maske and
banket, the
king in
person
present at
the cardinals
house.*

[Chambers
shot off.]

*The car-
dinall knew
not that the
king was in
the number.*

[They were
received by
the Lord
Chamber-
laín.]

---

[1] *On . . . thither*] Hol. (Stow). *I haue seen the king suddenly come in
thither* Cavendish, i. 49.

To whom the lord chamberleine for them said: "Sir, for as
"much as *they* be strangers, and can not *speake English*, they haue
"desired me *to* declare vnto you, *that* they, *hauing* vnderstanding
"*of this* your triumphant banket, where was assembled such a
"number of excellent dames, *they could doo no lesse, vnder* support
"*of your* grace, *but* to repaire hither, *to view* as well their incom-
"parable *beautie,* as for to accompanie them at mum-chance, and
"then to danse *with them:* and, sir, they require of your grace
"licence to accomplish the said cause of their comming." To
whom the cardinall said he was verie well content they should
so doo.

The masquers "choose Ladies." Henry takes Anne Boleyn's hand
(l. 75). "Musicke, Dance" is the next stage direction. Then Wolsey
addresses the Lord Chamberlain (ll. 77-81):

> *Card.* My Lord!
> *Cham.*   Your Grace!
> *Card.*   Pray tell 'em thus much from me:
> *There should be* one *amongst 'em,* by his person,
> *More* worthy *this place then* my selfe ; *to whom*
> (*If I* but *knew him*) with *my* loue and *duty*   80
> *I would surrender it.*
> *Cham.*   I will, my Lord.   Whisper[s the Maskers.]
> *Card.* What say they!
> *Cham.*   Such a one, *they* all *confesse,*
> *There is* indeed ; which they would haue *your Grace*
> Find *out,* and *he* will take it.
> *Card.*   Let me see, then.—   84
> By all your good leaues, Gentlemen ; heere Ile make
> My royall choyce.
> *Kin.*   Ye haue found him, Cardinall : . . .

Having played at mumchance with the guests, the masquers poured
out what coin they had before Wolsey, who won it all by a single cast
of the dice.

[*Hol.* iii. 922/1/57.   *Stow,* 846.] Then quoth the cardinall to
the lord chamberleine, "I praie you" (quoth he) "that you would
"shew them, that me seemeth *there should be* a nobleman *amongst*
"them, who is *more* meet to occupie *this* seat and *place than* I am ;
"*to whome I would* most gladlie *surrender* the same according to
"*my dutie, if I knew him.*"

Then spake the lord chamberleine to them in French, and they
rounding him in the eare, the lord chamberlein said to my lord

cardinall: "Sir" (quoth he) "*they confesse*, that among them *there* [Wolsey was desired to point him out.]
"*is* such a noble personage, whome, if *your grace* can appoint him
"*out* from the rest, *he* is content to disclose himselfe, and to
"accept your place." With that the cardinall taking good aduisement among them, at the last (quoth he) "me seemeth, the gentle-
"man with the blacke beard should be euen hee":[1] and with that
he arose out of his chaire, and offered the same to the gentleman
in the blacke beard, with his cap in his hand. The person to *He taketh his marke amiss and is deceiued.*
whom he offered the chaire was sir Edward Neuill, a comelie
knight, that much more resembled the kings person in that maske
than anie other.

The king, perceiuing the cardinall so deceiued, could not for- *The king disclaundeth his face and is verie pleasant.*
beare laughing, but pulled downe his visar and master Neuels also,
and dashed out such a pleasant countenance and cheere, that all
the noble estates there assembled, perceiuing the king to be there
among them, reioised verie much.

Henry learns that his partner is the daughter of Thomas Boleyn,
"Viscount Rochford" (l. 93). The King kisses her and demands a
health; whereupon Wolsey speaks (ll. 98, 99):

        Sir Thomas Louell, is the Banket ready
I'th' Priuy Chamber?
  Lou.   Yes, my Lord.
  Card.   Your Grace
I feare, with dancing, is a little heated.   100
  Kin. I feare, too much.
  Card.   There's fresher ayre, my Lord,
In the next Chamber.

Henry proposes to drink the healths of the ladies, and dance again
(ll. 105-107). Then they all go out, "with Trumpets."
The historical Wolsey, after failing to detect the King,

[*Hol.* iii. 922/2/11. *Stow*, 846.] eftsoons desired his highnesse [Henry withdrew to change his apparel.]
to take the place of estate. To whom the king answered, that he
would go first and shift his apparell, and so departed into my lord
cardinals chamber, and there new apparelled him: in which time
the dishes of the banket were cleane taken vp, and the tables
spred againe with new cleane perfumed cloths; euerie man and
woman sitting still, vntill the king with all his maskers came
among them againe all new apparelled.

---

[1] *hee*] Stow. *be* Hol.

A new banket vpon the sudden of 200 dishes, brought in when Henry returned.

Then the king tooke his seat vnder the cloth of estate, commanding euerie person to sit still as they did before: in came a new banket before the king, and to all the rest throughout all the tables, wherein were serued two hundred diuerse dishes, of costlie deuises and subtilties. Thus passed they foorth the night with banketting, dansing, and other triumphs, to the great comfort of the king, and pleasant regard of the nobilitie there assembled.

Act II. sc. i.—Two gentlemen enter, one of whom (Sec. Gent.) is on his way to Westminster Hall. There—as he learns from the other gentleman (First Gent.)—Buckingham has already been tried and condemned (ll. 1-8). The First Gentleman gives a brief account of the trial, at which he was present (ll. 11-22):

> *The great Duke*
> Came *to the Bar ;* where, *to his* accusations,   12
> He *pleaded* still, *not guilty, and alleadged*
> Many sharpe *reasons* to defeat the Law.
> *The Kings Atturney,* on the contrary,
> Vrg'd on *the Examinations, proofes, confessions*   16
> *Of* diuers *witnesses ;* which *the Duke desir'd*
> To haue[1] *brought,* viua voce, to his face :
> At which appear'd against *him,* his Surueyor ;
> Sir Gilbert Pecke his Chancellour ; and Iohn Car,   20
> Confessor to him ; with that Diuell *Monke,*
> *Hopkins,* that made this mischiefe.
>   2.   That was hee
> That fed him *with his Prophecies ?*
>   1.   The same.
> All these accus'd *him* strongly ; *which he faine*   24
> *Would haue* flung from him, but, indeed, he could not :
> And so his Peeres, vpon this euidence,
> Haue *found* him *guilty of high Treason.* Much
> He spoke, and learnedly, for life ; but all   28
> Was either pittied in him, or forgotten.
>   2. After all this, how did he beare himselfe ?
>   1. When he *was brought* agen *to th' Bar,* (to heare
> His Knell rung out, his Iudgment,) he was stir'd   32
> With such an Agony, he *sweat* extreamly,
> And somthing spoke in choller, ill, and hasty :
> But he fell to himselfe againe, and, sweetly,
> In all the rest shew'd a most Noble patience.   36

The judges appointed to try Buckingham met at Westminster Hall on May 13, 1521.[2] Their president was Thomas Howard, second Duke of Norfolk.

---

[1] *haue*] F4. *him* F.
[2] The date from *Stow,* 862. The other particulars from *Halle,* 623.

[*Hol.* iii. 865/1/20. *Halls,* 623.]   When the lords had taken
their place, *the duke* was brought *to the barrs,* and, vpon *his*
arreignement, *pleaded not guiltie,* and put himselfe vpon his peeres.
Then was his indictment read, which the duke denied to be true,
and (as he was an eloquent man) [1] *alledged reasons* to falsifie the
indictment; pleading the matter for his owne iustification verie
pithilie and earnestlie. *The kings attourncie,* against the dukes
reasons, alledged *the examinations, confessions,* and *proofes of witnesses.*

 The duke desired that the witnesses might bee *brought* foorth.
And then came before *him* Charles Kneuet, Perke, De la Court,
& *Hopkins* the *monke* of the priorie of the Charterhouse beside
Bath, which like a false hypocrite had induced the duke to the
treason *with his* false forged *prophesies.*   Diuerse presumptions and
accusations were laid vnto *him* by Charles Kneuet; *which he would
faine haue* couered.   The depositions were read, & the deponents
deliuered as prisoners to the officers of the Tower.   Then spake
the duke of Norffolke, and said: "My lord, the king our souereigne
"lord hath commanded that you shall haue his lawes ministred
"with fauour and right to you. [2]   Wherefore, if you haue anie other
"thing to say for your selfe, you shall be heard."   Then he was
commanded to withdraw him, and so was led into Paradise, a
house so named.   The lords went to councell a great while, and
after tooke their places.

 Then said the duke of Norffolke to the duke of Suffolke:
"What say you of sir Edward duke of Buckingham, touching the
"high treasons?"   The duke of Suffolke answered: "He is giltie":
& so said the marques [of Dorset] and all the other earles and lords.
Thus was this prince, duke of Buckingham, *found giltie of high
treason,* by a duke, a marques, seuen earles, & twelue barons. [3]   The

[Buckingham pleaded not guilty, and made an eloquent defence.]

Polydor. Edw. Hall.
[The king's attorney alleged the evidence against him.]

[The witnesses whom Buckingham desired to be brought forth.]

Edw. Hall. in H. 8. fol. lxxxvj.

The duke of Buckingham convinced of high treason.

---

[1] "he . . . man."—*Polyd. Verg.,* 665/34.   In I. ii. 111, Henry says of
Buckingham:

  "The Gentleman is Learn'd, and a most rare Speaker"; . . .
 [2] Cp. Henry's last words anent Buckingham (I. ii. 211, 212):
       "if he may
    Finde mercy in the Law, 'tis his"; . . .
 [3] Cp. Buckingham's admission (II. i. 118, 119):
    "I had my Tryall,
    And, must needs say, a Noble one"; . . .

duke *was brought to the barre* sore chafing, and *most* maruellouslie ;
&, after he had made his reuerence, he paused a while. The duke of
Norffolke, as iudge, said : "Sir Edward, you haue heard how you
"be indicted of high treason; you pleaded thereto not giltie,
"putting your selfe to the peeres of the realme, which haue found
"you giltie."

The Second Gentleman's remark—(l. 40) "the Cardinall is the end
of this"—may be compared with the words of Holinshed, who,
declining to examine the truth or falsehood of Buckingham's
indictment, adds :

[Wolsey
believed
to have
procured
Bucking-
ham's
death.]

[*Hol.* iii. 864/2/68.] Sauing that (I trust) I maie without
offense saie, that (as the rumour then went) the cardinall chieflie
procured the death of this noble man, no lesse fauoured and
beloued of the people of this realme in that season, than the
cardinall himselfe was hated and enuied. Which thing caused the
dukes fall the more to be pitied and lamented, sith he was the
man of all [*p.* 865] other that chieflie went about to crosse the
cardinall in his lordlie demeanor, & headie proceedings.

In response to the Second Gentleman's positive assertion that
Wolsey was "the end of this," the First Gentleman says (ll. 40-44) :

1.   Tis likely,   40
By all coniectures : first, Kildares Attendure,
Then Depu of Ireland ; who remou'd,
Earle Surrey was sent thither, and in hast too,
Least he should helpe his Father.

On the authority of Polydore Vergil (659/20) Holinshed relates
that Wolsey, enraged by Buckingham's "greeuous words" (see p. 426
above), sought the Duke's destruction, but

[Wolsey
resolved to
send Surrey
out of the
way.]

[Enmity
between
Wolsey and
Surrey.]

[*Hol.* iii. 855/2/25.] bicause he doubted his freends, kinnesmen,
and alies, and cheeflie the earle of Surrie, lord admerall, (which
had married the dukes daughter,) he thought good first to send
him some whither out of the waie, least he might cast a trumpe in
his waie. There was great enimitie betwixt the cardinall and the
earle,[1] for that, on a time, when the cardinall tooke vpon him to
checke the earle, he had like to haue thrust his dagger into the
cardinall.

---

[1] Afterwards (1524) 3rd Duke of Norfolk. In III. ii. 275-277, the dramatic
"Surrey" (see p. 474, n. 1, below) professes to be deterred by naught save
Wolsey's priesthood from answering the Cardinal's rebuke with the sword.

At length there was occasion offered him to compasse his purpose, by occasion of the earle of Kildare his comming out of Ireland. For the cardinall, knowing he was well prouided of monie, sought occasion to fleece him of part thereof. The earle of Kildare, being vnmarried, was desirous to haue an English woman to wife ; and, for that he was a suter to a widow, contrarie to the cardinals mind, he accused him to the king, of that he had not borne himselfe vprightlie in his office in Ireland, where he was the kings lieutenant. Such accusations were framed against him, when no bribes would come, that he was committed to prison, and then by the cardinals good preferment the earle of Surrie was sent into Ireland as the kings deputie, in lieu of the said earle of Kildare ; there to remaine rather as an exile than as lieutenant to the king, euen at the cardinals pleasure, as he himselfe well perceiued.[1]

[Kildare's visit to England.]

The earle of Kildare committed to ward [; and Surrey sent to Ireland as deputy].

[Surrey knew that he was exiled by Wolsey.]

The two gentlemen's converse is interrupted by the entrance of " Buckingham from his Arraignment ; Tipstaues before him ; the Axe with the edge towards him ; Halberds on each side : accompanied with Sir Thomas Louell, Sir Nicholas Vaux, Sir William[2] Sands, and common people, &c." Addressing those who are following him the Duke says (II. i.) :

I haue this day receiu'd a Traitors iudgement,
And by that name must dye : yet, Heauen beare witnes,
(And if I haue a Conscience, let it sincke me
Euen as the Axe falls,) if I be not faithfull !   60
The Law I beare no mallice for my death ;
T'has done, vpon the premises, but Iustice :
But those that sought it I could wish more Christians :   64
Be what they will, I heartily forgiue 'em : . . .
For further life in this world I ne're hope,
Nor will I sue, although the King haue mercies
More then I dare make faults. You few that lou'd me,
And dare be bold to weepe for Buckingham,   72
His Noble Friends and Fellowes, whom to leaue
Is only bitter to him, only dying,
Goe with me, like good Angels, to my end ;
And, as the long diuorce of Steele fals on me,   76
Make of your Prayers one sweet Sacrifice,
And lift my Soule to Heauen !

---

[1] In III. ii. 260-264, " Surrey " accuses Wolsey of this.
[2] *William*] Theobald. *Walter* F. Created Lord Sandys on April 27, 1523. — *Stow*, 874. In Act I., scenes iii. and iv., he appears as Lord Sandys.

A speech to this effect was made by Buckingham [1] on May 13, after Norfolk had pronounced sentence of death.

[Bucking-
ham's speech
after
sentence.]

[*Hol.* iii. 865/1/68. *Halle,* 624.] The duke of Buckingham said, "My lord of Norffolke, you haue said as a traitor should be "said vnto, but I was neuer anie : but, my lords, I nothing maligne "for that you haue doone to me, but the eternall God forgiue you "my death, and I doo. I shall neuer sue to the king for life, how- "beit he is a gratious prince, and more grace may come from him

[The edge of
the axe was
turned
towards
him.]

"than I desire. I desire you, my lords, and all my fellowes, to "pray for me." Then was the edge of the axe turned towards him, and he led into a barge.

Sir Thomas Lovell resigns the custody of Buckingham (ll. 95-97) :

> To th' water side I must conduct your Grace ;
> Then giue my Charge vp to Sir Nicholas Vaux,   96
> Who vndertakes you to your end.
> *Vaux.*   Prepare there,
> The Duke is comming : see the Barge be ready ;
> And fit it with such furniture as suites
> The Greatnesse of his Person.
> *Buck.*   *Nay,* Sir Nicholas,   100
> Let it alone ; my State now will but mocke me.
> *When I* came hither, *I was* Lord High Constable
> And *Duke of Buckingham ; now,* poore *Edward Bohun :* . . .

When Buckingham was "led into a barge"

[Bucking-
ham said :
"Now I am
but Edward
Bohun."
He was
received at
the Temple
stairs by
Vaux and
Sandys.
He desired
the people to
pray for
him.]

[*Hol.* iii. 865/2/4. *Halle,* 624.] Sir Thomas Louell desired him to sit on the cushins and carpet ordeined for him. He said, "nay ; for *when I* went to Westminster *I was duke of Buckingham ;* "*now* I am but *Edward Bohune,* [2] the most caitife of the world." Thus they landed at the Temple, where receiued him sir Nicholas Vawse & sir William Sands, baronets, and led him through the citie ; who desired euer the people to pray for him, . . .

---

[1] He was beheaded on May 17, 1521.—*Halle,* 624. As the "last houre" of the dramatic Buckingham has come in this scene (II. i. 132), it is evident that the dates of his sentence and execution have been unified.

[2] Buckingham's surname was Stafford. His descent from the Bohuns is thus traced by Francis Thynne : "Humfrie de Bohune, the eight [seventh] & last erle of Hereford of that surname of Bohune, . . . had issue two daughters and heires, Eleanor the eldest, maried to Thomas of Woodstocke ; and Marie the second, married to Henrie of Bollingbrooke, after king of England, . . . He [Thomas] had issue [by his marriage with Eleanor de Bohun] . . . foure daughters : . . . The foure daughters, heires to Thomas of Woodstocke, . . . were Anne the eldest, married to Edmund Stafford erle Stafford," . . . *Hol.* iii. 867/2/25. Edward Stafford, Duke of Buckingham, was the great-great-grandson of Edmund Earl Stafford.—*Collins,* ii. 37-40.

Buckingham compares his lot with that of his father Henry, who was also betrayed by a servant, but was not, like the speaker, tried by his peers (II. i. 107-111 ; 118-123).

After the desertion of his troops (p. 404 above), Henry Duke of Buckingham

[*Hol.* iii. 743/2/49. *Halle*, 394.] conueied himselfe into the house of Humfreie Banaster, his seruant, beside Shrewesburie ; whome he had tenderlie brought vp, and whome he aboue all men loued, fauóured, and trusted : now not doubting but that in his extreame necessitie he should find him faithfull, secret, and trustie ; . . .

[*Hol.* iii. 744/1/50. *Halle*, 395.] Humfreie Banaster (were it more for feare of life and losse of goods, or allured & prouoked by the auaricious desire of the thousand pounds) [1] . . . bewraied his guest and maister to Iohn Mitton, then shiriffe of Shropshire ; . . .

Contrasting his treatment by his late sovereign and present King, Buckingham notes that Henry VII. had restored him to his honours, but Henry VIII. deprived him of life and all which belonged to it (ll. 112-118).

In the first Parliament of Henry VII. (November, 1485),

[*Hol.* iii. 763/1/25. *Halle*, 424.] Edward Stafford, eldest sonne to Henrie late duke of Buckingham, he [Henry VII.] restored to his name, dignitie, & possessions, which by king Richard were confiscat and atteinted.

When Buckingham and his Train have departed, the two gentlemen resume their discourse.   The Second Gentleman asks (ll. 147-149) :

> Did you not of late dayes heare
> A buzzing, of a Separatiön   148
> Betweene the King and Katherine ?
>   1.   Yes, but it held not :
> For when the King once heard it, out of anger
> He sent command to the Lord Mayor straight
> To stop the rumor, and allay those tongues   152
> That durst disperse it.

In the Summer of 1527 [2]

---

[1] See p. 404 above.
[2] On June 2, 1527, news of the sacking of Rome reached Windsor. On July 3, Wolsey, who had been appointed ambassador to France, passed through London.—*Halle*, 727, 728. Between these dates occurs mention in *Halle* (728) of the rumour touching Henry's marriage, prefaced by the words : " This season began a fame in London that the kinges confessor," &c.

[*Hol.* iii. 897/1/65. *Halle*, 728.] rose a secret brute in London
that the kings confessor, doctor Longland, and diuerse other great

The kings marriage brought in question.

clerks, had told the king that the marriage betweene him and the
ladie Katharine, late wife to his brother prince Arthur, was not
lawfull: wherevpon the king should sue a diuorse, and marrie the
duchesse of Alanson, sister to the French king, at the towne of
Calis, this summer: and that the vicount Rochford had brought

[Henry bade the Mayor preuent people from talking of the marriage.]

with him the picture of the said ladie. The king was offended
with those tales, and sent for sir Thomas Seimor, maior of the
citie of London, secretlie charging him to see that the people
ceassed from such talke.

The Second Gentleman replies (ll. 153-161):

2.   But that slander, Sir,
Is found a truth now: for it growes agen
Fresher than e're it was; and held for certaine
The King will venture at it. Either the Cardinall,   156
Or some about him neere, haue, out of malice
To the good Queene, possest him with a scruple
That will vndoe her: to confirme this too,
Cardinall Campeius is arriu'd, and lately;   160
As all thinke, for this busines.
1.   Tis the Cardinall;
And meerely to reuenge him on the Emperour,
For not bestowing on him, at his asking,
The Archbishopricke of Toledo, this is purpos'd.   164

In the first of the ensuing paragraphs Holinshed records—as though
it were a suspicion generally entertained—Polydore Vergil's unfounded
assertion (685/9) that Wolsey was the author of Henry's matrimonial
scruple:

[*Hol.* iii. 906/2/24.] Ye haue heard how the people talked a
little before the cardinals going ouer into France, the last yeare,

Doctor Long-land, bishop of Lincolne [, denied the legality of Henry's marriage].

that the king was told by doctor Longland, bishop of Lincolne, and
others, that his marriage with queene Katharine could not be
good nor lawfull. The truth is, that, whether this doubt was first
mooued by the cardinall, or by the said Longland, being the kings
confessor, the king was not onelie brought in doubt, whether it
was a lawfull marriage or no; but also determined to haue the
case examined, cleered, and adiudged by learning, law, and

Why the car-dinall was suspected to

sufficient authoritie. The cardinall verelie was put in most blame
for this scruple now cast into the kings conscience, for the hate he

bare to the emperor, bicause he would not grant to him the arch- *be against the marriage.*
bishoprike of Toledo, for the which he was a suter. And therefore
he did not onelie procure the king of England to ioine in freendship with the French king, but also sought a diuorse betwixt the *[Wolsey wished*
king and the queene,[1] that the king might haue had in marriage *Henry to marry the*
the duchesse of Alanson, sister vnto the French king: and (as *Duchess of Alençon.]*
some haue thought) he trauelled in that matter with the French *Polydor.*
king at Amiens, but the duchesse would not giue eare therevnto.[2]

But howsoeuer it came about that the king was thus troubled *Edw. Hall. [. 755].*
in conscience concerning his mariage, this followed, that, like a
wise & sage · prince, to haue the doubt cleerelie remooued, he
called togither the best learned of the realme; which were of *The king is desirous to be*
seuerall opinions. Wherfore he thought to know the truth by *resolued by the opinions*
indifferent iudges, least peraduenture the Spaniards, and other *of the learned touching his*
also in fauour of the queene, would saie, that his owne subiects *marriage.*
were not indifferent iudges in this behalfe. And therefore he
wrote his cause to Rome, and also sent to all the vniuersities in
Italie and France, and to the great clearkes of all christendome,
to know their opinions, and desired the court of Rome to send
into his realme a legat, which should be indifferent, and of a
great and profound iudgement, to heare the cause debated.
At whose request the whole consistorie of the college of *Cardinall*
Rome sent thither Laurence Campeius, a preest cardinall, a *Campeius sent vnto*
man of great wit and experience,[3] . . . and with him was *England.*

---

[1] *Polyd. Verg.* does not say that Wolsey's revenge was to counsel Henry's
divorce, but asserts that the Cardinal wanted a Queen whose disposition
resembled his own, since Katharine, although she had done him no harm,
"eius . . . malos oderat mores, quos ut continentia emendaret, identidem
benignè monebat."—685/12.

[2] Wolsey was ambassador to France in July—September, 1527.—*Halle*,
728-733. Margaret Duchess of Alençon married Henry King of Navarre in
January, 1527.—*Ven. State PP.*, IV. 7, 17. These dates are irreconcilable
with *Polyd. Verg.*'s supposition (687/1) that Wolsey endeavoured while at
Amiens to arrange a marriage between Henry and Margaret.

[3] Cp. Wolsey's praise of the course which Henry took in regard to
Katharine (II. ii. 90-97):

> "The Spaniard, tide by blood and fauour to her,
> Must now confesse, if they haue any goodnesse,
> The Tryall iust and Noble. All the Clerkes
> (I meane the learnèd ones) in Christian Kingdomes
> Haue their free voyces: Rome, the Nurse of Iudgement,
> Inuited by your Noble selfe, hath sent

ioined in commission the cardinall of Yorke and legat of
England.[1]

This cardinall came to London in October,[2] and did intimate
both to the king & queene the cause of his comming: which
being knowne, great talke was had thereof.

Act II. sc. ii.—I find no historical authority for the letter (ll. 1—10)
which the Lord Chamberlain is reading as he enters. After l. 73 the
Cardinals enter and have a private audience of Henry. Wolsey
assumes that Katharine is not to be denied what

> A Woman of lesse Place might aske by Law :　　　　112
> Schollers allow'd freely to argue for her.
> *Kin.* I, and the best she shall haue ; and my fauour
> To him that does best : God forbid els ! . . .

We learn from Halle (756) that, after Christmas 1528, and till
Easter 1529, "was none other thing commoned of but onely of the
kinges mariage."

[Henry
wished
Katharine
to have the
best clerks
for her
counsel.] [*Hol.* iii. 907/1/2. *Halle,* 756.] And bicause the king meant
nothing but vprightlie therein, and knew well that the queene
was somewhat wedded to hir owne opinion, and wished that she
should do nothing without counsell, he bad hir choose the best
clearks of his realme to be of hir counsell, and licenced them to
doo the best on hir part that they could, according to the truth.

Addressing Wolsey, Henry says (ll. 115-117) :

> 　　　　　　　　　　　　　　　Cardinall,
> Prethee call Gardiner to me, my new Secretary:
> I find him a fit fellow.

Henry and Gardiner go aside and converse in whispers. Drawing
Wolsey's attention to the King's new secretary, Campeggio asks (ll.
122, 123) :

> *Camp.* My Lord of Yorke, was not one Doctor Pace
> In this mans place before him ?

> One generall Tongue vnto vs, this good man,
> This iust and learnèd Priest, Cardnall Campeius "; . . .

With "the Clerkes . . . Christian Kingdomes" cp. "profound clerkes . . .
all christendome" (p. 479 below).

　　[1] In II. ii. 104-107, Campeggio tenders to Henry the

> . . . "Commission ; by whose vertue,
> The Court of Rome commanding, you, my Lord
> Cardinall of Yorke, are ioyn'd with me their Seruant
> In the vnpartiall iudging of this Businesse."

　　[2] Campeggio had his first audience of Henry on October 22, 1528.—*Calendar*
(*Hen. VIII.*), IV. ii. p. 2100 (op. no. 4879, p. 2111).

Wol.   Yes, he was.
Camp. Was he not held a learnëd man ?
Wol.   Yes, surely.   124
Camp. Beleeue me, there's an ill opinion spread, then,
Euen of your selfe, Lord Cardinall.
Wol.   How ! of me ?
Camp. They will not sticke to say, you enuide him ;
And, fearing he would rise, (he was so vertuous,)   128
Kept him a forraigne man still ; which so greeu'd him,
That he ran mad, and dide.

About the year 1529,[1]

[*Hol.* iii. 907/1/20. *Polyd. Verg.* 687/20.] the king receiued
into fauour doctor Stephan Gardiner, whose seruice he vsed in
matters of great secrecie and weight, admitting him in the roome
of doctor Pace, the which, being continuallie abroad in ambassages,
and the same oftentimes not much necessarie, by the cardinals
appointment,[2] at length he tooke such greefe therewith, that he
fell out of his right wits.

Doctor
Stephå
Gardiner.
1529
———
Doctor Pace
falleth out of
his wits.

Act II. sc. iii.—In this scene the Lord Chamberlain announces to
Anne Boleyn that

　　　　　　　　the Kings Maiesty   60
Commends his good opinion of you to you ;[3] and
Doe's purpose honour to you no lesse flowing
Then Marchionesse of Pembrooke ; to which Title,
A Thousand pound a yeare, Annuall support,   64
Out of his Grace he addes.

Halle (790) was Holinshed's authority for the following passage :

[*Hol.* iii. 928/2/30.] On the first of September [, 1532,] being
sundaie, the K., being come to Windsor, created the ladie Anne
Bullongne marchionesse of Penbroke, and gaue to hir one
thousand pounds land by the yeare.

The ladie
Anne
Bullongne
created
marchiones
of Penbroke.

Act II. sc. iv.—In Act II., sc. ii., ll. 138-141, Henry directs that
the trial of his marriage shall be held at Black-Friars, and he bids

---

[1] After November 17, 1529, Gardiner is spoken of as Henry's "newly made
Secretary."—*Halle*, 760.

[2] *Foxe* says (ii. 963/1) : "But as the laude, and the renowmed prayse of
men, for their worthy prowesse, commonly in this world neuer go vnaccom-
panyed without some priuye canker of enuy & disdayne folowyng after, so the
singular industry of Pacie, as it wanne much commendation with many, so it
could not auoyde the secret stynge of some Serpentes. For the conceaued
hatred of this Cardinall so kyndled against him that he neuer ceassed till first
he brought him out of the kynges fauour, and at last also, out of his perfect
wittes."

[3] *of you, to you*] F. *to you* Pope. *of you* Capell.

Wolsey see that the place be "furnish'd." Scene iv. opens with the
ensuing stage direction :

> Trumpets, Sennet, and Cornets.
>
> Enter two Vergers, with short siluer wands ; next them, two Scribes,
> in the habite of Doctors ; after them, the Bishop of Canterbury
> alone ; after him, the Bishops of Lincolne, Ely, Rochester, and
> S. Asaph : Next them, with some small distance, followes a
> Gentleman bearing the Purse, with the great Seale, and a
> Cardinals Hat : Then two Priests, bearing each a Siluer Crosse :
> Then a Gentleman Vsher bareheaded, accompanyed with a
> Sergeant at Armes, bearing a Siluer Mace : Then two Gentlemen
> bearing two great Siluer Pillers : After them, side by side, the
> two Cardinals ; two Noblemen, with the Sword and Mace.
> The King takes place vnder the Cloth of State. The two
> Cardinalls sit vnder him as Iudges. The Queene takes place
> some distance from the King. The Bishops place themselues on
> each side the Court, in manner of a Consistory ; Below them,
> the Scribes. The Lords sit next the Bishops. The rest of the
> Attendants stand in conuenient order about the Stage.

The arrangements made for the trial are thus described :

Anno Reg.
21.
Edw. Hall
[. 751].

[A hall at
Black-Friars
furnished
for the
trial.]

Abr. Fl. ex.
I. S. pag.
959.

The maner of
the session,
euerie
personage of
account in
his place.

[*Hol.* iii. 907/1/27.] The place where the cardinals should sit,
to heare the cause of matrimonie betwixt the king and the queene,
was ordeined to be at the Blacke friers in London ; where in the
great hall was preparation made of seats, tables, and other furniture, according to such a solemne session and roiall apparance.
The [1] court was platted in tables and benches *in manner of a consistorie*, one seat raised higher for the iudges to sit in. Then as
it were in the midst of the said iudges, aloft, aboue them three
degrees high, was a *cloth of estate* hanged, with a chaire roiall
vnder the same, wherein sat the king ; and, besides him, *some
distance from* him sat *the queene*, and vnder the iudges feet sat
the scribes and other officers : the cheefe scribe was doctor
Steeuens,[2] and the caller of the court was one Cooke of
Winchester.

Then before the king and the iudges, within the court, sat the

---

[1] *The . . . furnished* (pp. 456, 457).] Stow, 912 (Cavendish, i. 147).

[2] Stephen Gardiner. "The chief scribe there was Dr. Stephens, (who was
after Bishop of Winchester) ; " . . . —*Cavendish*, i. 147. As to Gardiner being
known as Stevens or Steven, see a note in *Cavendish* (loc. cit.). Brewer says
(ii. 245, note 1) : " Gardiner always writes his own name Steven Gardiner, but
Wolsey and others call him by his Christian name Stevens (i. e. Stephanus),
Steven or Stevens being the same name."

archbishop of Canturburie, Warham, and all the other bishops.
Then stood at both ends within, the counsellors learned in the
spirituall laws, as well the kings as the queenes. The doctors of
law for the king . . . had their *conuenient* roomes. Thus was the
court furnished.

In obedience to Henry's command, that she should "choose the
best clearks of his realme to be of hir counsell" (p. 454 above), Katharine

[*Hol.* iii. 907/1/9. *Halle*, 756.] elected William Warham,
archbishop of Canturburie, and Nicholas West, bishop of Elie,
doctors of the laws; and Iohn Fisher, bishop of Rochester, and
Henrie Standish, bishop of St. Assaph, doctors of diuinitie; and
manie other doctors and well learned men, which for suertie, like
men of great learning, defended hir cause, as farre as learning
might mainteine and hold it vp.

The queene chooseth lawyers for hir part.

Part of the stage direction—"a Gentleman bearing . . . great
Siluer Pillers"—is taken from a description of Wolsey's "order in
going to Westminster hall dailie in the tearme."

[*Hol.* iii. 921/1/63. *Stow*, 844.] Before him was borne, first
the broad seale of England, and his cardinals hat, by a lord, or
some gentleman of worship, right solemnlie: &, as soone as he
was once entered into his chamber of presence, his two great
crosses were there attending to be borne before him: then cried
the gentlemen vshers, going before him bare headed, and said:
"On before, my lords and maisters, on before; make waie for
"my lords grace!" Thus went he downe through the hall with
a sergeant of armes before him, bearing a great mace of siluer,
and two gentlemen carieing two great pillers of siluer.

The tokens and marks of his dignities borne before him.

After Wolsey had been appointed legate,

[*Hol.* iii. 920/1/14. *Stow*, 841.] had he his two great crosses
of siluer, the one of his archbishoprike, the other of his legacie,
borne before him whither soeuer he went or rode, by two of the
tallest priests that he could get within the realme.

[Wolsey's cross-bearers.]

When all who have entered are in their places, Wolsey says (II. iv.
1—10):

Car. *Whil'st our commission from Rome is read,*
Let silence be commanded!
King. What's the need!
It hath already publiquely bene read,

And on all sides th'Authority allow'd ;
You may, then, spare that time.
    Car.   Bee't so.—Proceed !
    Sori. Say, " *Henry, K. of England, come into the Court !* "
    Crier. " *Henry, King of England,* " &c.
    King. *Heere !*
    Scribe. Say, " *Katharine, Queene of England, come into the Court !* "
    Crier. " *Katharine, Queene of England,* " &c.
      [The Queene makes *no answer,* rises *out of her Chaire,* goes
        about *the Court,* comes *to the King, and kneeles at his*
        Feete ; then speakes.

On June 21, 1529, Henry and Katharine appeared personally before
the Court.[1]

[*Hol.* iii. 907/1/50. *Stow,* 912.] The iudges *commanded silence*
whilest their *commission* was *read,* both to the court and to the
people assembled. That doone the scribes commanded the crier

The king and queene called into the court.

to call the king by the name of " *king Henrie of England, come*
" *into the court,* " &c. With that the king answered and said,
" *Heere !* " Then called he the queene by the name of " *Katharine,*
queene of England, come into the court, " &c. Who made *no answer,*
but rose *out of hir chaire.*

[Katharine knelt at Henry's feet.]

And, bicause shee could not come to the king directlie, for
the distance seuered betweene them, shee went *about by the court,*
and came *to the king, kneeling* downe *at his feet,* to whome she
said in effect as followeth :[2]

I exhibit in parallel columns Katharine's speech as it appears in
Holinshed, and the version of it given in *Henry VIII.,* Act II. sc. iv.
ll. 13-57 :

Queene Katharines lamentable

[*Hol.* iii. 907/1/63. *Stow,* 912.]	*Sir, I desire you do me Right and*
" *Sir* " (quoth she) " *I desire you*	*Iustice ;*
" *to doo me iustice and right, and*	*And to bestow your pitty on me : for*
	I am a most poore Woman, and a
	Stranger,

---

[1] The Court met for the first time on June 18, 1529, and adjourned to the
21st. Katharine was present on the 18th, but Henry was on that day represented by proxies.—*Calendar (Hen. VIII.),* IV. iii. 5694, 5707.

[2] This speech was taken by *Stow* from *Cavendish* (i. 149-152). According
to *Halle* (757), " the Quene departed without any thing saiyng." We learn,
however, from a letter of Campeggio that on June 21—the day on which he
was writing—Katharine " interposed a very full appeal and supplication to the
Pope and withdrew ; but first she knelt there before the seat of judgment,
although the King twice raised her up, asked permission of the King that, as
it was a question which concerned the honour and conscience of herself and of
the house of Spain, he would grant her full permission to write and send
messengers to [the Emperor] and to his Holiness," . . .—*Brewer,* ii. 491.

"take some *pitie* vpon *me, for I*
"am a poore *woman, and a stranger,*
"*borne out of your dominion;*
"*hauing heere no indifferent* coun-
"sell, & lesse *assurance of freend-*
"*ship. Alas, sir,* [in] *what haue I*
"*offended you,* or *what* occasion of
"*displeasure* haue I shewed you;
"intending *thus to put me* from
"you after this sort? I take God
"to my iudge, *I haue beene to you*
"*a true & humble wife,* euer con-
"*formable to your will* and pleasure;
"that neuer contraried or gaine-
"said any thing thereof, and, being
"alwaies contented with all things
"wherein you had any delight,
"whether little or much, without
"grudge or displeasure, I loued
"for your sake all them whome
"you loued, whether they were
"my freends or enimies.

"*I haue beene your wife* these
"*twentie yeares* and more, & you
"*haue* had *by* me diuerse children.
"*If* there be anie iust cause that
"*you can* alleage against me,
"either of dishonestie, or matter
"lawfull to put me from you, I
"am content to depart to my
"shame and rebuke: and if there
"be none, then I praie you to let
"me haue iustice at your hand.
"*The king your father was* in his
"*time of excellent wit,* and the
"*king of Spaine, my father, Fer-*
"*dinando, was reckoned one of the*
"*wisest princes that reigned in*
"Spaine *manie yeares before. It*
"*is not to be* doubted, but *that they*
"*had gathered as wise* counsellors
"*vnto them of euerie realme,* as to
"their wisedoms they thought
"meet, *who deemed the marriage*.

Borne out of your Dominions; hauing 16
heere
No Iudge *indifferent,* nor no more
assurance
Of equall *Friendship* and Proceeding.
Alas, Sir,
In *what haue I offended you?* what
cause
Hath my behauiour giuen to your 20
displeasure,
That *thus* you should proceede *to put*
me off,
And take your good Grace from me?
Heauen witnesse,
I *haue bene to you a true and humble*
Wife,
At all times *to your will conformable;* 24
Euer in feare to kindle your Dislike,
Yea, subiect to your Countenance;
Glad, or sorry,
As I saw it inclin'd! When was the
houre
I euer contradicted your Desire,   28
Or made it not mine too? Or which
of your Friends
Haue I not stroue to loue, although
I knew
He were mine Enemy? what Friend
of mine,
That had to him deriu'd your Anger, 32
did I
Continue in my Liking? nay, gaue
notice
He was from thence discharg'd? Sir,
call to minde,
That *I haue beene your Wife,* in this
Obedience,
Vpward of *twenty yeares, and haue* 36
bene blest
With many *Children by* you: *if,* in
the course
And processe of this time, *you can*
report,
And proue it too, against mine
Honor aught,
My bond to Wedlocke, or my Loue 40
and Dutie,
Against your Sacred Person, in God's
name
Turne me away! and let the fowl'st
Contempt
Shut doore vpon me, and so giue me vp
To the sharp'st kinde of Iustice! 44
Please you, Sir,
The King, your Father, was reputed
for
A Prince most Prudent, *of an excellent*
And vnmatch'd *Wit,* and Iudgement:
Ferdinand,
My Father. King of Spaine, was 48
reckon'd one
The wisest Prince, that there had
reign'd, by many

and *pithie*
speech in
presence of
the court.

[I desire you
to do me
iustice.
How have I
offended
you?]

[I have been
a dutiful
wife.]

[We have
been married
these twenty
years.]

[If there be
a real cause
for my
divorce, I
will submit;
if not, let
me have
iustice.]

The queene
iustifieth the
marriage
[: Our
fathers were
wise men,
and they
deemed our
marriage
lawful.]

[I desire a
respite till
I can have
counsel from
my friends
in Spain.]

"betweene you and me good and
"*lawfull*, &c. *Wherefore, I hum-*
"*blie* desire *you to spare me, vntill*
"*I may* know what counsell *my*
"*freends in Spaine* will aduertise
"me to take, and, *if* you will *not*,
"then *your pleasure be fulfilled*."

A *yeare before: it is not to be
question'd,
That they had gather'd a wise Councell
to them
Of every Realme*, that did debate this 52
Businesse,
*Who deem'd our Marriage lawfull.
Wherefore I humbly
Beseech you, Sir, to spare me, till I may*
Be, by *my Friends in Spaine*, aduis'd;
whose Counsaile
I will implore. *If not*, i'th'name of God, 56
Your pleasure be fulfill'd!

Wolsey and Campeggio object to a delay of the trial (ll. 57-68).
Katharine [1] then brings an accusation against Wolsey (ll. 75-84):

        I do beleeue

(Induc'd by potent Circumstances) that   76
You are mine Enemy; and make my Challenge,
You shall not be my Judge: for it is you
Haue blowne this Coale betwixt my Lord, and me;
(Which Gods dew quench!) Therefore, I say againe,   80
I *vtterly abhorre*, yea, from my Soule,
Refuse you for my *Iudge;* whom, yet once more,
I hold my *most malicious* Foe, and thinke not
At all a Friend to truth!

Wolsey denies the charge (ll. 84-105); but Katharine is unmoved
(ll. 118-121):

I do refuse you for my Iudge; and heere,
Before you all, *Appeale vnto the Pope*,
To bring my *whole Cause* 'fore his Holinesse,   120
And *to be iudg'd* by *him!*

The source of this part of scene iv. (ll. 68-121) is the following
passage, derived by Holinshed from Polydore Vergil (688/4):

---

[1] In November, 1528, the two legates visited Katharine at Bridewell, and
told her that they had been appointed judges of the legality of her marriage.
After maintaining its lawfulness, she said : "'But of thys trouble I onely may
thanke you, my lorde Cardinall of Yorke; for because I haue wondered at
your hygh pride & vainglory, and abhorre your volupteous life and abhominable Lechery, and litle regard your presumpteous power and tiranny, therfore
of malice you haue kindled thys fyre and set thys matter a broche; & in
especial for y* great malice that you beare to my nephew the Emperour, whom
I perfectly know you hate worse then a Scorpion, because he would not satisfie
your ambicion and make you Pope by force; and therfore you haue sayed
more then once that you would trouble him and hys frendes, and you haue
kept hym true promyse, for, of al hys warres and vexacions, he only may
thanke you, and as for me, hys poore aunte and kynswoman, what trouble you
put me to by this new found doubt, God knoweth, to whom I commyt my
cause according to the truth.' The cardinall of Yorke excused himself, saying,
that he was not the begynner nor the mouer of the doubte, & that it was sore
agaynst hys wyl that euer y* mariage should come in question; but he sayd
that, by his superior, the Bishop of Rome, he was deputed as a Iudge to heare

[*Hol.* iii. 908/1/35.] Heere is to be noted, that the queene in presence of the whole court most greeuouslie accused the cardinall of vntruth, deceit, wickednesse, & malice ; which had sowne dissention betwixt hir and the king hir husband: and therefore openlie protested, that she did *vtterlie abhorre, refuse,* and forsake such a *judge,* as was not onelie a *most malicious* enimie to hir, but also a manifest aduersarie to all right and iustice ; and therewith did she *appeale vnto the pope,* committing hir *whole cause to be judged* of *him.*

Katharine's refusal of Wolsey as her judge (ll. 118-121) is succeeded by this stage direction : "She Curtsies to the King, and offers to depart." Campeggio draws attention to her movement, whereupon Henry cries (l. 125) :

> Kin.   *Call her againe !*
> Crier. *Katherine Q. of England, come into the Court !*
> Gent. Ush. *Madam, you are cald backe.*
> *Que.* What need you note it ? pray you, keep *your way :*
> When you are cald, returne ! (Now the Lord helpe,
> They vexe me past my patience !) Pray you, passe on !
> *I will not tarry;* no, nor euer more
> Vpon this businesse my appearance make
> *In any of their Courts !*
>   [Exeunt Queene, and her **Attendants.**

In the play Katharine's departure is preceded by her dispute with Wolsey (ll. 68-121), but, after Cavendish's report of her speech to Henry, the passage which forms my next excerpt immediately ensues :

[*Hol.* iii. 907/2/21. *Stow,* 913.] With that she arose vp, making a lowe curtesie to the king, and departed from thence.

The king, being aduertised that shee was readie to go out of the house, commanded the crier to *call hir againe;* who called hir by these words : "*Katharine, queene of England, come into the* "*court !*" With that quoth maister Griffith,[1] "*Madame, you be* "*called* againe." "On, on" (quoth she) "it maketh no matter, *I* "*will not tarrie,* go on *your waies !*" And thus she departed,

---

the cause, which he sware on his professyon to heare indifferently ; but, whatsoeuer was said, she beleued hym not, and so the Legates toke their leaue of her & departed. These wordes were spoken in Frenche, and written by Cardinall Campeius secretary, (which was present,) and by me translated as nere as I could."—*Halle,* 755.

[1] *Cavendish* says (i. 152) that Katharine "took her way straight out of the house, leaning (as she was wont always to do) upon the arm of her General Receiver, called Master Griffith."

without anie further answer at that time, or anie other, and neuer
would appeare after *in anie court.*

When Katharine is gone Henry closes a speech in her praise by
saying (ll. 141-143) :

> *Shee's Noble borne;*
> And, like her true Nobility, she ha's
> Carried her selfe towards me.

Wolsey then addresses Henry (ll. 143-149) :

> *Wol.*   Most gracious *Sir,*
> In humblest manner *I require your Highnes,*   **144**
> That it shall please you *to declare,* in hearing
> Of all these eares, (for where I am rob'd and bound,
> There must I be vnloos'd, although not there
> At once and fully satisfide,) *whether* euer *I*   **148**
> Did broach *this* busines *to your* Highnesse ; . . .

I continue to quote excerpts derived by Holinshed from Stow's
paraphrase of Cavendish :

[*Hol.* iii. 907/2/33. *Stow,* 913.] The king, perceiuing she was
departed, said these words in effect : "For as much" (quoth he)
"as the queene is gone, I will in hir absence declare to you all,
"that shee hath beene to me as true, as obedient, and as conform-
"able a wife, as I would wish or desire. She hath all the vertuous
"qualities that ought to be in a woman of hir dignitie, or in anie
"other of a baser estate ; *she is* also surelie a *noble* woman *borne ;*
"hir conditions will well declare the same."[1]

With that quoth Wolseie the cardinall : "*Sir,* I most humblie
"*require your highnesse, to declare* before all this audience, *whether*
"*I* haue beene the cheefe and first moouer of *this* matter *vnto your*
"maiestie or no, for I am greatlie suspected heerein."

Henry's oration (ll. 155-209 ; 217-230) and the intervening answer
of Longland Bishop of Lincoln (ll. 211-217) follow Wolsey's request :

> Kin.   *My Lord Cardinall,*
> *I* doe *excuse you ;* yea, vpon mine Honour,   **156**

---

[1] On November 8, 1528, at Bridewell, Henry spoke thus of Katharine to
an assemblage of nobles, judges, counsellors, and others whose attendance had
been commanded : "I assure you all that, beside her noble parentage of the
whiche she is discended, (as you wel know,) she is a woman of moste *gentlenes,*
of moste humilitie and buxumnes ; yea, and of al good qualities apperteignynge
to nobilitie she is wythoute comparyson, as I this .xx. yeres almoste haue had
the true experiment ; so that yf I were to mary agayne, if the mariage myght
be good, I would surely chose her aboue al other women."—*Halle,* 755. In
II. iv. 137-139, Henry praises her "sweet *gentlenesse,*" meekness, and obedience.

I free you from't ; . . .
But will you be more iustifi'de ? You euer
Haue wish'd the sleeping of this busines ; . . .
My Conscience first receiu'd a tendernes,
Scruple, and pricke, *on certaines* Speeches vtter'd
By *th'Bishop of Bayon*, then *French Embassador* ;   172
Who had beene hither sent on the debating
A [1] *Marriage* 'twixt *the Duke of Orleance, and*
Our Daughter Mary : i'th'Progresse of this busines,
Ere a determinate resolution, *hee*   176
(I meane the Bishop) did require a *respite* ;
Wherein he might *the King his* Lord *aduértise,*
Whether our Daughter were *legitimate,*
Respecting *this* our *Marriage with* the Dowager,   180
Sometimes our *Brothers Wife*. This "respite" shooke
The bosome [2] *of my Conscience,* enter'd me,
Yea, with a splitting [3] power, and made to tremble
The region of my Breast ; which forc'd such way,   184
That many maz'd considerings did throng,
And prest in with this Caution.   First, me *thought*
I stood not in the smile of Heauen ; who had
Commanded Nature, that my Ladies wombe,   188
If it conceiu'd a male-child by me, should
Doe no more Offices of life to't then
The Graue does to th' dead : for her *Male Issue*
Or *di'de* where they were made, or shortly *after*   192
This *world* had ayr'd them.   Hence I tooke a thought,
This was a Iudgement on me ; that my Kingdome
(Well worthy the best Heyre o'th' World) should not
Be gladded in't by me : then followes, that   196
I weigh'd *the danger* which my *Realmes stood in*
By this my issues faile ; and that gaue to me
Many a groaning throw.   Thus hulling in
The wild Sea of my Conscience, I did steere   200
Toward this remedy, whereupon we are
Now present heere together ; that's to say,
I meant to rectifie *my Conscience* (which
I then did feele full sicke, and yet not well)   204
By all the Reuerend Fathers of the Land,
And Doctors learn'd.—First, I began in priuate
With *you, my Lord of Lincolne ;* you remember
How vnder my oppression I did reeke,   208
When I first mou'd you.
　　　B. Lin.　　　　　　　Very well, my Liedge.
　　　Kin. I haue spoke long : be pleas'd your selfe to say
How farre you satisfide me.
　　　Lin.　　　　　　　So please your Highnes,
The question did at first so stagger me,   212

---

[1] *A*] Rowe (ed. 2). *And* F.
[2] *bottom*] Theobald. Cp. next excerpt from *Hol.* [3] *splitting*] F2. *spitting* F.

(Bearing a State of mighty moment in't,
And consequence of dread,) that I committed
The daringst Counsaile which I had, to *doubt* ;
And did entreate your Highnes to this course,　　216
Which you are running heere.
　　Kin.　　　　　　　　*I* then *mou'd you,*
My Lord of Canterbury ; and got your leaue
To make this present Summons : vnsolicited
I left no Reuerend Person in this Court ;　　220
But by particular consent proceeded
Vnder your hands and *Seales :* therefore, goe on ;
For no dislike i'th' world against *the person*
Of the good Queene, but the sharpe thorny points　　224
Of my alleadgèd reasons, driue'[1] this forward :
Proue but *our Marriage* lawfull, by my Life
And Kingly Dignity, we are *contented*
To weare our mortall State to come with her,　　228
(Katherine our Queene,) before the primest Creature
That's Parragon'd o'th' World !

With these lines compare the speeches of Henry and Longland, as they appear in Holinshed :

[Wolsey did not wish the lawfulness of Henry's marriage to be examined.]

[*Hol.* iii. 907/2/46.　*Stow,* 914.]　"*My lord cardinall*" (quoth the king) "*I* can well *excuse you* in this matter, marrie" (quoth he) "you haue beene rather against me in the tempting heereof, than "a setter forward or moouer of the same.　The speciall cause, that "mooued me vnto this matter, was a certeine scrupulositie that "pricked *my conscience,* vpon *certeine* words spoken at a time "*by the bishop*[2] *of Baion,* the *French ambassador,*[3] *who had beene* "*hither sent,* vpon *the debating* of *a marriage* to be concluded "betweene *our daughter* the ladie *Marie,* and *the duke of Orleance,* "second son to the king of France.

"Upon the resolution and determination whereof, *he* desired "*respit* to *aduertise the king his* maister thereof, *whether our* "*daughter* Marie should be *legitimate* in respect of *this* my "*marriage with* this woman, being *sometimes* my *brothers wife.* "Which words, once conceiued within *the* secret bottome *of my* "*conscience,* ingendered such a scrupulous doubt, that my con-

[The Princess Mary's legitimacy questioned.]
The king confesseth that the sting of conscience

---

[1] *driue*] Pope.　*driues* F.
[2] *time by the bishop*] Cavendish.　*time when it was, by the bishop* Hol. and Stow.
[3] A mistake.　The ambassador to whom these words were officially attributed was Gabriel de Grammont, Bishop of Tarbes.

"science was incontinentlie accombred, vexed, and disquieted; *made him*
"whereby I *thought* my selfe to be greatlie in danger of God's *mislike this marriage.*
"indignation. Which appeared to be (as me seemed) the rather,
"for that he sent vs no issue male, and all such *issues male*, as my said
"wife had by me, *died* incontinent *after* they came into the *world;* [He had no male issue.]
"so that I doubted the great displeasure of God in that behalfe.

"Thus, *my conscience* being tossed in the waues of a scrupulous
"mind, and partlie in despaire to haue [*p.* 908] anie other issue than
"I had alredie by this ladie now my wife, it behooued me further to
"consider the state of this *realme*, and *the danger* it *stood in* for [His realm was in
"lacke of a prince to succeed me. *I* thought it good in release of danger for lack of a
"the weightie burthen of *my* weake *conscience*, . . . to attempt the prince to succeed
"law therin, whether I may lawfullie take another wife more him.]
"lawfullie, . . . not for anie displeasure or misliking of *the*
"queenes *person* and age; with whome I would be as well *contented*
"*to* continue, if *our mariage* may stand with the laws of God, as
"with anie woman aliue.

"In this point consisteth all this doubt that we go about now
"to trie by the learning, wisedome, and iudgement of you our
"prelats and pastors of all this our realme and dominions, now
"heere assembled for that purpose; . . . Wherein, after that I
"perceiued my conscience so doubtfull, I mooued it in confession
"to *you, my Lord of Lincolne,* then ghostlie father. And, for so [He moved
"much as then you your selfe were in some *doubt,* you mooued me in confession to Long-
"to aske the counsell of all these my lords: wherevpon *I mooued* land; and obtained
"*you, my lord of Canturburie,* first to haue your licence, in as much licence to try it from
"as you were metropolitane, to put this matter in question, and Warham and the other
"so I did of all you, my lords: to which you granted *vnder your* bishops.]
"*seales,* heere to be shewed."

At the close of Henry's speech Campeggio says (ll. 230-235):

    Camp.   So please your Highnes,
The Queene being absent, 'tis a needfull fitnesse,
That we *adiourne* this *Court till* further *day;*   232
Meane while must be an earnest motion
Made to *the Queene, to call backe her Appeale*
She intends vnto his Holinesse.

Holinshed omitted a dispute between Warham and Fisher, which
succeeded the royal speech, and was silenced by Henry.

[*Hol.* iii. 908/1/33. *Stow,* 915.] After that the king rose [The court adjourned.]
vp, and the *court* was *adiourned vntill* another *daie.*

Notwithstanding Katharine's appeal,

[*Hol.* iii. 908/1/45.   *Polyd. Verg.*, 688/11.] the legats sat
weekelie, and euerie daie were arguments brought in on both
parts, and proofes alleaged for the vnderstanding of the case, and
still they assaied if they could by anie meanes procure *the queene*
to call backe hir appeale, which she vtterlie refused to doo.

[Katharine
urged to call
back her
appeal.]

Campeggio's proposal to adjourn is accepted by Henry (l. 240), but
not without an aside (ll. 235-237) :

> *Kin.*   I may perceiue
> These Cardinals trifle with me : I abhorre   235
> This dilatory sloth, and trickes of Rome.

Holinshed copied Polydore Vergil's remark (688/14) that the

The king
mistrusteth
the legats of
making
delaies.

[*Hol.* iii. 908/1/50.] king would gladlie haue had an end in
the matter, but, when the legats draue time, and determined vpon
no certeine point, he conceiued a suspicion that this was doone
of purpose, that their dooings might draw to none effect or
conclusion.

Act III. sc. i.—"Enter Queene and her Women, as at worke."   A
Gentleman announces that

> > the two great Cardinals   16
> Wait in the presence.
> *Queen.*   Would they speake with me ?
> *Gent.* They wil'd me say so, Madam.

Katharine bids her Gentleman invite them to "come neere" (l. 19) ;
and presently the Cardinals enter.

The court at Black-Friars closed its sessions in the latter part of
July, 1529.[1] It was opened, as we have seen (p. 458, n. 1, above) on June
18. Time passed in fruitless discussion, until one day, after the court
had adjourned, Henry's impatience obliged Wolsey and Campeggio to
make a direct appeal to Katharine.[2]

> *Wol.*   Peace to your Highnesse !
> *Queen.* Your Graces find me heere part of a Houswife :   24
> I would be all, against the worst may happen.
> *What are your pleasures with me*, reuerent Lords ?
> *Wol.* May *it please* you, Noble Madam, *to* withdraw
> *Into your* priuate *Chamber, we* shall giue *you*   28
> *The* full *cause of our comming.*
> *Queen.*   *Speake it* heere :
> There's nothing I haue done yet, o' my Conscience,
> Deserues a Corner : would all other Women

---

[1] "Cardinall Campeius sayd y[t] they myght not syt after Iuly, tyll October,
all whyche season was a vacacyon in the Courte of Rome, and their court
beynge a member of the Courte of Rome, they must nedes do the same."—
Halle, 758.   [2] *Cauendish*, i. 160, 161.

Could speake this with as free a Soule as I doe !   32
My Lords, I care not, (so much I am happy
Aboue a number,) if my actions
Were tri'de by eu'ry tongue, eu'ry eye saw 'em,
Enuy and base opinion set against 'em,   36
I know my life so euen. . . .
Out with it boldly ! . . .
   Card. [*Wol.*] Tanta est erga te mentis integritas, Regina
serenissima,—   41
   Queen. O, *good my Lord,* no Latin ! . . .
Pray, *speake in English !*

Wolsey replies (ll. 54-61) :

We come not by the way of Accusation,
To taint that honour euery good Tongue blesses,
Nor to betray you any way to sorrow ;   56
(You haue too much, good Lady !) but *to know*
How you stand minded *in* the waighty difference
Betweene the King and you ; and to deliuer,
Like free and honest men, *our* iust *opinions,*   60
And comforts to your [1] cause.
   Camp.   Most honour'd Madam,
My Lord of Yorke, (out of his Noble nature,
Zeale and obedience he still bore *your Grace,*)
Forgetting, like a good man, your late Censure   64
Both of his truth and him, which was too farre,
Offers, as I doe, in a signe of peace,
His Seruice and his Counsell.

"To betray me," Katharine murmurs. Then she addresses the
Cardinals (ll. 68-80) :

My Lords, I thanke you both *for your good wills ;*
Ye speake like honest men ; (pray God, ye proue so !)
But how *to make ye sodainly an Answere,*
In such a poynt of weight, so neere mine Honour,
(More neere my Life, I feare,) with my weake wit,   72
And to such men of grauity and learning,
In truth, I know not. *I was set at worke*
Among my Maids ; full little (God knowes) looking
Either for such men, or *such* businesse.   76
For her sake that I haue beene, (for I feele   ·
The last fit of my Greatnesse,) good your Graces,
Let me haue time and Councell for my Cause.
Alas, I am a Woman frendlesse, hopelesse !   80
   Wol. Madam, you wrong the Kings loue with these feares :
Your hopes and friends are infinite.
   Queen.   In England
But little *for my profit :* can *you thinke, Lords,*
That *any English* man dare giue *me* Councell ?   84

---

[1] *your*] F2. om. F1.

Or be a knowne *friend*, *'gainst* his Highnes *pleasure*,
(Though he be growne so desperate to be honest,)
And liue a *Subiect* ! *Nay*, *forsooth*, my Friends,
They that must weigh out my *afflictions*,
They that my *trust* must grow to, liue *not heere* :
They are (as all my other *comforts*) far hence,
In mine owne Countrey, Lords.

88

*Queene
Katharine
and the
cardinals
haue com-
munication
in hir priuie
chamber
[; but at
first she
required
them to
speak in her
Presence
Chamber].*

[*Hol.* iii. 908/2/2. *Stow*, 916.] The cardinals being in the
queenes chamber of presence, the gentleman usher aduertised the
queene that the cardinals were come to speake with hir. With
that she rose vp, &, with a skeine of white thred about hir necke,
came into hir chamber of presence, where the cardinals were
attending. At whose comming quoth she, "*What is your pleasure*
"*with me* !" "If *it please* your grace" (quoth cardinall Wolseie)
"*to go into your* priuie *chamber*, *we* will shew *you the cause of our*
"*comming*." "My lord" (quoth she) "if yee haue anie thing to
"saie, *speake it* openlie before all these folke ; for I feare nothing
"that yee can saie against me, but that I would all the world
"should heare and see it, and therefore speake your mind." Then

[Wolsey
addressed
her in
Latin.]

[He and
Campeggio
desired to
know her
mind in
regard to the
marriage
question,
and to
counsel her.]

*The queene
refuseth to
make sudden
answer in so
weightie a
matter as the
diuorse*
[: she had
just come
from work-
ing with her
maids].

[She said
that no

began the cardinall to speake to hir in Latine. "Naie, *good my*
"*lord*" (quoth she) "*speake* to me *in English*."[1]

"Forsooth" (quoth the cardinall) "good madame, if it please
"you, *we come* both *to know* your mind *how you* are disposed to
"doo *in* this matter *betweene the king and you*, *and* also *to* declare
"secretlie *our opinions and* counsell vnto you : which we doo
"onelie for verie *zeale and obedience* we beare vnto *your grace*."
"*My lord*" (quoth she) "*I thanke you for your good will* ; *but to*
"*make* you *answer* in your request I cannot so *suddenlie*, for *I was*
"set *among my maids at workes*, thinking *full little* of anie *such*
"matter, wherein there needeth a longer deliberation, and a better
"head than mine to make answer : for I need counsell in this case
"which toucheth me so neere, & for anie counsell or freendship
"that I can find *in England*, they are not *for my profit*. What,
"*thinks you*, my lords, will *anie Englishman* counsell me, or be

---

[1] *speake to me in English, for I can (I thanks God) both speake and understand English, although I vnderstand some latin.*] Stow., om. Hol. Cp. Katharine's words (III. i. 42, 44) :

"I am not such a Truant since my comming,
   As not to know the Language I haue liu'd in" : . . .

"*freend* to me *against* the K[ings] *pleasure* that is his *subiect !*
" *Naie, forsooth.*   And as for my counsell in whom I will put *my*
" *trust, they be not here, they* be in Spaine *in my owne countrie.*

"And, my lords, I am a poore woman, lacking wit, to answer
"to anie such noble persons of wisedome as you be, in so weightie
"a matter, therefore I praie you be good to me, poore woman,
"destitute of freends here in a forren region," . . .

Campeggio responds by offering his counsel (ll. 93-97):

> Put your maine cause into the King's protection ;
> Hee's louing and most gracious : 'twill *be much*
> Both for your *Honour better*, and your Cause ;
> For, if *the tryall of* the *Law* o'retake ye,   96
> You'l part away disgrac'd.

The object of the Cardinals' mission to Katharine was

[*Hol.* iii. 908/1/70. *Stow,* 916.]   to persuade with hir by their
wisdoms, and to aduise hir to surrender the whole matter into the
kings hands by hir owne consent & will, which should *be much*
better to hir *honour*, than to stand to *the triall of law*, and thereby
to be condemned, which should seeme much to hir dishonour.

Katharine's anger is roused by this perfidious advice, but, growing
calm at last, she says, as the scene ends (ll. 181, 182):

> Come, reuerend Fathers,
> Bestow *your Councels* on me !

We are not told by Cavendish how Katharine received the legates'
proposition.[1]   After her appeal,—"I praie you be good to me, poore
woman, destitute of freends here in a forren region,"—she added :

[*Hol.* iii. 908/2/41. *Stow,* 917.]   "and *your counsell* also I will be
"glad to heare."   And therewith she tooke the cardinall [Wolsey]
by the hand, and led him into hir priuie chamber with the other
cardinall, where they tarried a season talking with the queene.

Act III. sc. ii.—Norfolk, Suffolk, "Surrey," and the Lord Chamberlain enter.   Norfolk says (ll. 1-3):

> If you will now vnite in your Complaints,
> And force them with a Constancy, the Cardinall
> Cannot stand vnder them : . . .

Suffolk explains how Wolsey has forfeited Henry's favour (ll.
30-36):

---

[1] *Cavendish* says (i. 164) that "we, in the other chamber, might sometime
hear the queen speak very loud, but what it was we could not understand."

The Cardinals Letters to the Pope miscarried,
And came to th'eye o'th'King : wherein was read,
How that the Cardinall did intreat his Holinesse   32
To stay the Iudgement o'th'Diuorce ; for if
It did take place, " I do " (quoth he) " perceiue
" My King is tangled in affection to
" A Creature of the Queenes, Lady Anne Bullen."   36

After a while Wolsey enters and soliloquizes upon his intention of
uniting Henry to the Duchess of Alençon,[1] for the purpose of preventing
the King's marriage to Anne Boleyn (ll. 85-101). Soon Henry
enters and elicits from Wolsey great professions of loyalty, which the
King brings to a close by giving the Cardinal two papers, with these
words (ll. 201-203) :

                                      Read o're this ;
And after, this [the Letter to the Pope] ; and then to Breakfast with
What appetite you haue !
                    [Exit King, frowning vpon the Cardinall : the Nobles
                          throng after him, smiling and whispering.

Polydore Vergil (688/16) was the original authority for part of my
next excerpt, down to the sentence ending, " honor and dignitie." He
asserts that, while the lawfulness of Henry's marriage was being
debated at Black-Friars,

The kings
affection and
good will to
the ladie
Anne
Bullen.

[*Hol.* iii. 908/2/70.] the cardinall of Yorke was aduised that
the king had set his affection vpon a yoong gentlewoman named
Anne, the daughter of Sir Thomas Bullen, vicount Rochford, which
did wait vpon the queene. This was a [p. 909] great griefe vnto

[If Henry
were
divorced he
would marry
Anne
Boleyn.]

the cardinall, as he that perceiued aforehand, that the king would
marie the said gentlewoman, if the diuorse tooke place. Wherfore
he began with all diligence to disappoint that match, which, by
reason of the misliking that he had to the woman, he iudged

The secret
working and
dissimula-
tion of
cardinall
Wolsie [to
hinder the
divorce].

ought to be auoided more than present death. While the matter
stood in this state, and that the cause of the queene was to be
heard and iudged at Rome, by reason of the appeale which by hir
was put in, the cardinall required the pope by letters and secret
messengers, that in anie wise he should defer the iudgement of
the diuorse, till he might frame the kings mind to his purpose.

The king ob-
cerueth dis-
pleasure
against the
cardinall
[on this
account].

Howbeit he went about nothing so secretlie, but that the same
came to the kings knowledge, who tooke so high displeasure
with such his cloked dissimulation, that he determined to abase
his degree, sith as an vnthankefull person he forgot himselfe and

---

[1] An anachronism. See p. 453, n. 2, above.

his dutie towards him that had so highlie aduanced him to all
honor and dignitie. When the nobles of the realme perceiued the
cardinall to be in displeasure, they began to accuse him of such
offenses as they knew might be proued against him, and thereof
they made a booke conteining certeine articles, to which diuerse
of the kings councell set their hands.

Hol. Hall
[L 759].

Articles
exhibited
against the
cardinall
[by the
nobles].

Before Wolsey entered, Suffolk mentioned (ll. 56-60) a circumstance
which would be sure to confirm the resentment felt by Henry on
discovering the letter to the Pope.

> Cardinall Campeius
> Is stolne away to Rome ; hath ta'ne no leaue ;
> Ha's left the cause o'th'King vnhandled ; and
> Is posted, as the Agent of our Cardinall,
> To second all his plot.

When the day came for the Legates' judgment to be delivered,
Campeggio thus addressed the Court assembled at Black-Friars : [1]

[*Hol.* iii. 908/2/57. *Stow*, 917.] "I will not giue iudgement
"till I haue made relation to the pope of all our proceedings;
"whose counsell and commandement in this case I will obserue :
"the case is verie doubtfull, and also the partie defendant will
"make no answer here, but dooth rather appeale from vs, suppos-
"ing that we be not indifferent. Wherfore I will adiourne this
"court for this time, according to the order of the court of Rome."
And with that the court was dissolued, and no more doone. This
protracting of the conclusion of the matter, king Henrie tooke
verie displeasantlie. Then cardinall Campeius tooke his leaue of
the king [2] and nobilitie, and returned towards Rome.

Cardinall
Campeius
refuseth
to giue
iudgement.

[The Court
was dis-
solved, and
Campeggio
returned to
Rome.]

From my last excerpt it appears that Campeggio took leave of Henry
before returning to Rome. The Legate's clandestine departure was
perhaps inferred by the dramatist from the somewhat misleading expressions used by Foxe,[3] who says (ii. 967/2) that Campeggio

---

[1] On July 23 Campeggio prorogued the Court to October 1, 1529.—*Calendar*
(*Hen. VIII.*), IV. iii. p. 2589.

[2] Campeggio took leave of Henry at Grafton Regis, on September 20, 1529.
—Alward to Cromwell (*Ellis*, I. i. 309). *Cavendish*, i. 179. The testimony of
Alward and Cavendish—both of whom accompanied Wolsey to Grafton—does
not differ save in regard to the time of the day when Campeggio and Wolsey
took leave of Henry.

[3] At the end of the paragraph which contains my quotation, *Foxe* gives as
a reference, "Ex Hallo." *Halle* (759) records Campeggio's farewell of
Henry.

[Campeggio
left Henry's
cause un-
determined.]
craftily shifted hym self out of the realme before the day came
appoynted for determination, leauing his suttle felow behynd hym
to wey with the king in the meane time, while the matter might
be brought vp to the court of Rome.

In a subsequent reference to the same subject Foxe adds (ii. 1023/1)
that, when the Legates obserued the dangerous tendency of the question
which they were expected to decide,

[Henry had
a liking for
Anne
Boleyn, who
was a
Lutheran.]
Cardinall
Campeius
slippeth
frō the kyng.
& especially because the Cardinall of Yorke perceaued the kyng
to cast fauour to the Lady Anne, whom he knew to be *a Lutheran*,[1]
they thought best to winde them selues out of that brake by tyme,
& so Cardinal Campeius, dissemblyng the matter, conueyed himselfe home to Rome agayne, . . .

While Wolsey was musing, Henry entered "reading of a Scedule"
(l. 106). Showing it to Norfolk and Suffolk the King said, with
reference to Wolsey (ll. 120-128):

> This morning,   120
> Papers of State he sent me to peruse,
> As I requir'd: and wot you what I found
> There, (on my Conscience, put vnwittingly?)
> Forsooth, an Inuentory, thus importing,   124
> The seuerall parcels of his Plate, his Treasure,
> Rich Stuffes, and Ornaments of Houshold, which
> I finde at such proud Rate, that it out-speakes
> Possession of a Subiect.

Steevens pointed out (*Var. Sh.*, xix. 412) that a somewhat similar
mischance befel Thomas Ruthal, Bishop of Durham, who had two books
precisely like in outward appearance, one describing "the whole estate
of the kingdome," the other containing an account of his private means.
Henry VIII. sent Wolsey for the former book, and Ruthal inadvert-
ently gave the private volume

[*Hol.* iii. 796/2/60.]   to the cardinall to beare vnto the king.

---

[1] When Wolsey is soliloquizing on the necessity of preventing Anne Boleyn
from becoming Queen, he says (III. ii. 97-101):

> "What though I know her *vertuous*
> And well deseruing? yet I know her for
> A spleeny *Lutheran*; and not wholsome to
> Our cause, that she should lye i' th' bosome of
> Our hard rul'd King."

Elsewhere (ii. 1066/1) *Foxe* speaks thus of Anne Boleyn: "But because
touchyng the memorable vertues of this worthy Queene, partly we haue sayd
some thyng before, partly because more also is promised to be declared of her
vertuous life (the Lord so permittyng) by other who then were about her, I
will cease in this matter further to proceede."   I find no mention in *Halle* or
Hol. of her Lutheranism.

The cardinall, hauing the booke, went from the bishop, and after (in his studie by himselfe) vnderstanding the contents thereof, he greatlie reioised; hauing now occasion (which he long sought for) offered vnto him to bring the bishop into the king's disgrace.

Wherefore he went foorthwith to the king, deliuered the booke into his hands, and breefelie informed the king of the contents thereof; putting further into the kings head, that if at anie time he were destitute of a masse of monie, he should not need to seeke further therefore than to the cofers of the bishop, who by the tenor of his owne booke had accompted his proper riches and substance to the value of a hundred thousand pounds. *The bishops owne books disaduantageable to himself.*

The "Scedule," which Henry entered reading, is the first of the two papers examined by Wolsey when the King and Nobles are gone. It proves to be

th'Accompt
Of all that world of Wealth I haue drawne together
For mine owne ends ; indeed, to gaine the Popedome,   212
And fee my Friends in Rome.

In February, 1529, false news of the Pope's death reached England.[1] Wolsey aspired after the Papacy, and therefore wrote to Gardiner,

[*Foxe,* ii. 963/2.] willing hym to sticke for no coste, so farre as sixe or seuen thousand poundes woulde stretche : for more he sayd he would not geue for the triple crowne.[2] *[Wolsey's bid for the triple crown.]*

Finding the second paper to be the letter to the Pope, Wolsey despairs of regaining Henry's confidence (ll. 220-227). Then re-enter

---

[1] *Calendar (Hen. VIII.),* IV. iii. 5269.

[2] Gardiner was journeying towards Rome in January, 1529.—*Calendar (Hen. VIII.),* IV. iii. 5237. He reached it on February 15, 1529.—*Calendar (Hen. VIII.),* IV. iii. 5294. In February, 1529, Henry, believing Clement to be dead, sent instructions to Gardiner and others that they should, if necessary, endeavour to procure Wolsey's election as Pope by "promises of spiritual promotions, offices, dignities, rewards of money, and other things, to show them what Wolsey will give up if he enters into this dangerous storm and troublous tempest for the relief of the Church ; all of which benefices shall be given to the King's friends, besides other large rewards."—*Calendar (Hen. VIII.),* IV. iii. 5270. *Foxe,* ii. 965/2. Henry hoped thus to be divorced from Katharine by Papal sanction, which Wolsey would grant.—*Ibid. Foxe* printed a letter from Wolsey to Gardiner (ii. 964/1. *Calendar (Hen. VIII.),* IV. iii. 5272) in which general directions to make promises are given, but no specific sum of money is named. I suspect *Foxe's* 6000 or 7000 pounds for the Popedom to be the 6000 or 6000 ducats offered by Wolsey for bulls to hold Winchester.—*Wolsey to Sir Gregory Casale and Peter Vannes,* Feb. 20, 1529 (*Calendar (Hen. VIII.),* IV. iii. 5313).

(III. ii.) " the Dukes of Norfolke and Suffolke, the Earle of Surrey,[1] and the Lord Chamberlaine."

Nor. Heare *the King's pleasure*, Cardinall : who commands you
To *render vp the Great Seale* presently
Into our *hands;* and to Confine your selfe
To *Asher-house*, my Lord *of Winchesters*,[2]
Till you heare further from his Highnesse.

Car.   Stay :   232
Where's your *Commission*, Lords ! words cannot carrie
Authority so weighty.

Suf.   Who dare crosse 'em,
Bearing *the Kings* will from his *mouth* expressely !

Car. Till I finde more then will or words to do it,   236
(I meane your malice,) know, Officious Lords,
I dare, and must deny it. . . .

                That Seale,
You aske with such a Violence, the King,
(Mine and your Master,) with his owne hand, gaue me ;
Bad me *enioy* it, with the Place and Honors,   248
During my *life ;* and, to confirme his Goodnesse,
Ti'de it by *Letters Patents :* . . .

On October 16 (?), 1529,

<table>
<tr><td>*The card-inall is loth to part from the great seale.*</td><td>[*Hol.* iii. 909/1/39. *Stow,* 918.] the king sent the two dukes of Norfolke and Suffolke to the cardinals place at Westminster,</td></tr>
</table>

The card-inall is loth to part from the great seale.

who went as they were commanded, and, finding the cardinall

[He was ordered to depart to Asher.]
there, they declared that *the kings pleasure* was that he should surrender vp the great seale into their hands, and to depart simplie

[He de-manded the dukes' authority.]
vnto *Asher*, which was an house situat nigh vnto Hampton court, belonging to the bishoprike *of Winchester.* The cardinall de-manded of them their *commission* that gaue them such *authoritie ;* who answered againe, that they were sufficient commissioners, and had authoritie to doo no lesse by *the kings mouth.* Notwithstand-

[And refused to surrender the Great Seal, which Henry had given him for life.]
ing, he would in no wise agree in that behalfe, without further knowledge of their authoritie, saieng : that the great seale was deliuered him by the kings person, to *inioy* the ministration thereof, with the roome of the chancellor for the terme of his *life,* whereof for his suertie he had the kings *letters patents.*

---

[1] Norfolk and "Surrey" are historically one ; the dramatic twain form-ing the historical third Duke of Norfolk, whose " Father-in-law " was " Noble Buckingham " (III. ii. 256).
[2] The Bishopric of Winchester became vacant by the death of Richard Foxe in 1528.—*Godwin,* 246. Wolsey afterwards held the see *in commendam,* and was succeeded by Stephen Gardiner.—*Ibid.,* 247. Gardiner is, perhaps, the dramatist's "Lord of Winchester."

[7]   *Suf.   That*, out of meere Ambition, you haue *caus'd*   **324**
       Your Holy-*Hat to be* stampt *on the Kings Coine.*
[9]   *Sur.* Then, *That* you haue *sent innumerable substance*
       (By what meanes got, I leaue to your owne conscience)
       To furnish *Rome*, and to prepare the wayes   **328**
       You haue for *Dignities ; to the* meere vndooing
       Of all *the* Kingdome. *Many more* there are ;
       Which, since they are of you, and odious,
       I will not taint my mouth with.   **332**

In December, 1529,[1]

[*Hol.* iii. 912/2/15.   *Halle*, 767.] was brought downe to the
commons the booke of articles, which the lords had put to the
king against the cardinall ;[2] the chiefe wherof were these :

*Articles
exhibited
against the
cardinall of
Yorke.*

   1   *First, that* he *without the kings assent* had procured *to be a
legat*, by reason whereof he tooke awaie the right *of all bishops* and
spirituall persons.

   2   Item, *in all* writings which he wrote *to Rome, or* anie other
foreign prince, he wrote *Ego & rex meus*, I and my king: as who
would saie that *the king* were his *seruant.*[2] . . .

   4   Item, he *without* the kings assent carried *the* kings *great seale*
with him *into Flanders, when* he was sent *ambassador to the emperour.*

   5   *Item*, he, without the kings assent, *sent a commission to* sir
Gregorie de Cassado,[4] knight, *to conclude a league betweene* the king
& the duke of *Ferrar, without the kings* knowledge. . . .

   7   Item, *that* he *caused* the cardinals *hat to be* put *on the kings
coine.* . . .

   9   Item, *that* he had *sent innumerable substance to Rome*, for the
obteining of his *dignities ; to the* great impouerishment *of the realme.*

These articles, with *manie more*, read in the common house,
and signed with the cardinals hand, was [*sic*] confessed by him.

Before the nobles leaue Wolsey, Suffolk adds (ll. 337-344) :

   Suf. Lord Cardinall, the Kings further pleasure is,
    (Because *all those things* you haue *done* of late,

---

[1] December 1 is the date of the Articles.—*Calendar* (*Hen. VIII.*), IV. iii.
p. 2714. Parliament was prorogued on December 17.—*Halle*, 768.
[2] See p. 471 above.
[3] Halle has misquoted this article. Wolsey was accused (4) of "having in
divers letters and instructions to foreign parts used the expression, ' the King
and I,' . . . using himself more like a fellow to your Highness than a
subject."—*Calendar* (*Hen. VIII.*), IV. iii. p. 2712.
[4] Sir Gregory Casale.

> By your *power Legatine*,[1] *within this* Kingdome,
> Fall *into th'*compasse *of* a *Premunire*,)   340
> That therefore such a *Writ* be sued *against* you ;
> *To forfeit all* your *Goods, Lands, Tenements,*
> *Catalles*,[2] and whatsoeuer, *and to be*
> *Out of the Kings protection.* This is my Charge.   344

In October, 1529,[3]

[*Hol.* iii. 909/1/32. *Halle,* 760.] the king (being informed
that *all those things,* that the cardinall had *doone by* his *power*
legatine[4] *within this* realme, were *in the* case *of* the *premunire* and
prouision) caused his atturneie Christopher Hales to sue out *a writ*
of premunire *against* him ; in the which he licenced him to make
his atturneie.

The card-
inall sued
in a pre-
munire.

After Wolsey's retirement to Esher,

[*Hol.* iii. 909/2/43. *Halle,* 760.] in the kings bench, his
matter for the premunire, being called vpon, two atturneis, which
he had authorised by his warrant signed with his owne hand, confessed the action ;[5] and so had iudgement *to forfeit all* his *lands,*
tenements, goods, and *cattels, and to be out of the kings protection :* . . .

Iohn Scute,
and Edmund
Iennie
[. Wolsey's
attornies].
The card-
inall con-
demned in a
premunire.

Wolsey's soliloquy on his fall (ll. 351-372) succeeds the nobles'
departure.   Then Thomas Cromwell enters ; and, in response to
Wolsey's question, "What Newes abroad ? " answers (ll. 393, 394)

> that Sir Thomas Moore is chosen
Lord Chancellor in your place.

On October 25, 1529,[6]

[*Hol.* iii. 910/2/6. *Halle,* 761.] was sir Thomas Moore made
lord chancellor.

Sir Thomas
Moore lord
chancellor.

At the close of the trial-scene (II. iv. 238-240) Henry muttered :

> My learn'd and welbeloued Seruant, Cranmer,
> Prethee, returne : with thy approch, I know,
> My comfort comes along.

In this scene (III. ii. 64-67) Suffolk told Norfolk that Cranmer

> is return'd in his Opinions ; which   64
> Haue satisfied the King for his Diuorce,

---

[1] *Legatine*] Rowe (ed. 2). *Legatius* F.
[2] *Catalles*] Halle. *Castles* F. *Chattels* Theobald.
[3] October 9 is the date of the bill of indictment preferred by Hales against
Wolsey.—*Calendar (Hen. VIII.),* IV. iii. 6035.
[4] *legatine*] *legantine* Hol.
[5] On October 30, 1529.—*Calendar (Hen. VIII.),* IV. iii. 6035.
[6] *Calendar (Hen. VIII.),* IV. iii. 6025.

Together with all famous Colledges
Almost in Christendome : . . .

Suffolk then (l. 74) declared that Cranmer's services were to be
rewarded with an archbishopric ; and now (ll. 401, 402) Cromwell
answers Wolsey's request for more news by the information

That Cranmer is return'd with welcome ;   400
Install'd Lord Arch-byshop of Canterbury.

We learn from Foxe (ii. 1754/1) that Cranmer was employed by
Henry to write a book in defence of

[The ques-
tion of the
King's mar-
riage was dis-
puted in the
universities
abroad and
at home.]

The kings
marriage
found by
Gods word
unlawfull.

Doctour
Cranmer
with other
sent to
Rome
Ambassa-
dour to the
Pope.

his [Cranmer's] opinion, whiche was this : that the Bishop of Rome
had no suche authoritie as whereby he might dispence with the
word of God and the Scripture. . . . And thus, by meanes
of D. Cranmers handlyng of this matter with the Kyng, not
onely certane learned men were sent abroade to the most part
of the vniuersities in Christendome, to dispute the question,
but also the same beyng by Commission disputed by the diuines
in both the vniuersities of Cambridge and Oxforde, it was
there concluded that no suche matrimonie was by the word
of God lawfull. Whereupon a solemne ambassage was then prepared and sent to the Bishop of Rome, then [March, 1530][1] beyng
at Bonony, wherin went the Earle of Wiltshiere, D. Cranmer, D.
Stokesley, D. Carne, D. Benet, and diuers other learned men
& gentlemen.

When the embassy returned to England, Cranmer went to Germany,
and discussed the question of Henry's marriage with "diuers learned
men" of that nation ;

[Cranmer
satisfied the
doubts of
the German
divines
touching
Henry's
cause.]

[*Foxe*, ii. 1754/2.] who, verye ambiguouslye heretofore con-
ceiuyng the cause, were fully resolued and satisfied by hym.

This matter thus prosperyng on Doct. Cranmers behalfe, aswell touchyng the kinges question as concernyng the inualiditie of
the bishop of Romes authoritie, Bishop Warrham, then Archbishop
of Canterbury, departed this transitory life, wherby that dignity,
then beyng in the kynges gift and disposition, was immediatly
giuen to Doctour Cranmer,[2] as worthy, for his trauaile, of suche
a promotion.

Doctour
Cranmer
made Arch-
bishop of
Cant.

---

[1] *Halle*, 769.
[2] Cranmer was consecrated Archbishop of Canterbury on March 30, 1533.
—*Reg. Sacr. Angl.*, 76.

Suffolk, as we have seen (p. 478 above), speaks of the sanction given to Henry's divorce by "famous Colledges" abroad. These "determinations" were made known to the Commons on March 30, 1531, by Sir Thomas More, Lord Chancellor, who, after reminding the House of the doubtful legality of Henry's marriage, proceeded thus :

[*Hol.* iii. 923/2/28. *Halle*, 775.]   "Wherefore the king, like a "vertuous prince, willing to be satisfied in his conscience, & also "for the suertie of his realme, hath, with great deliberation, con- "sulted with profound clerkes, & hath sent my lord of London "here present, to the chiefe vniuersities of all christendome, to "know their opinion and iudgement in that behalfe.   And "although that the vniuersities of Cambridge and Oxford had "beene sufficient to discusse the cause, yet, bicause they be in his "realme, and to auoid all suspicion of parcialitie, he hath sent "into the realme of France, Italie, the popes dominions, and "Venecians, to know their iudgement in that behalfe, which haue "concluded, written, and sealed their determinations according as "you shall heare read."

Namelie, Edmund Bonner [John Stokesley. See p. 487, below].

Before Wolsey's entrance the Lord Chamberlain asserted that Henry had "already" married Anne Boleyn (III. ii. 41, 42).   Suffolk believed that "shortly" the King's

second Marriage shall be publishd, and   68
Her Coronation. *Katherine no more*
Shall *be call'd Queene, but Princesse Dowager,*
And *Widdow to Prince Arthur.*

The last piece of news which Cromwell tells Wolsey is

that the Lady *Anne,*
Whom the King hath in secrecie long married,
This day was view'd in open as his Queene,   404
Going to Chappell ; and the voyce is now
Onely about her Corronatiŏn.

The exact date of Anne Boleyn's marriage cannot be ascertained.[1]

---

[1] Cranmer—writing on June 17, 1533, to our ambassador at the Emperor's Court—says : "But nowe Sir you may nott ymagyn that this Coronacion [Anne Boleyn's coronation, described in a previous part of the letter] was before her mariege, for she was maried muche about sainte Paules daye last [January 25, 1533], as the condicion therof dothe well appere by reason she ys nowe sumwhat bygg with chylde. Notwithstandyng yt hath byn reported thorowte a greate parte of the realme that I maried her ; whiche was playnly false, for I myself knewe not therof a fortenyght after yt was donne."—*Ellis,* I. ii. 39. According to *Stow* (946) Henry was privately married to Anne Boleyn on January 25, 1533. On April 9, 1533, Norfolk told the Imperial ambassador, Eustace Chapuys, that Henry had married Anne more than two

According to Halle, Henry, after taking leave of Francis on October 30, 1532,

> [*Hol.* iii. 929/1/56. *Halle*, 794.] staied at Calis for a con-
> uenient wind till tuesdaie the twelfth[1] of Nouember at midnight,
> and then taking his ship, landed at Douer the next daie about fiue
> of the clocke in the morning.   And herewith vpon his returne, he
> married priuilie the ladie Anne Bullongne the same daie, being the
> fourteenth daie of Nouember, and the feast daie of saint Erken-
> wald ; which marriage was kept so secret, that verie few knew it
> till Easter next insuing, when it was perceiued that she was with
> child.

The king returneth into England. He marrieth the lady Anne Bullongne.

On April 12 (Easter Eve), 1533, Anne Boleyn

> [*Hol.* iii. 929/2/40. *Halle*, 795.] went to hir closet openlie as
> queene ; and then the king appointed the daie of hir coronation to
> be kept on Whitsundaie next following : . . .

Queene Annd's coronation day appointed].

In 1533,[2] it was enacted by Parliament

> [*Hol.* iii. 929/2/29. *Halle*, 795.] that queene *Katharine* should
> *no more be called queene, but princesse Dowager,* as the *widow* of
> *prince Arthur.*

Queene Katharine to be named princesse Dowager.

Dismissing Cromwell, Wolsey says :

>   Seeke the King ;
> (That Sun, I pray, may neuer set !) I haue told him
> What, and how true, thou art : he will aduance thee ; . . . 416

Cromwell answers :

> Beare witnesse, all that haue not hearts of Iron,   424
> With what a sorrow Cromwel leaues his Lord !
> The King shall haue my seruice ; but my prayres,
> For euer and for euer, shall be yours.

---

months ago.—Friedmann's *Anne Boleyn,* ii., appendix, note D, p. 239 (citing
Vienna Archives, P.C. 228, i. fol. 41). On May 10, 1533, Chapuys wrote that
the marriage was generally believed to have taken place on January 25.—*Ibid.*
(citing Vienna Archives, P.C. 228, i. fol. 61).

[1] *thirteenth*] Hol. Tuesday was November 12. *Hol.* was misled by a mistake in *Halle* (794), whereby we read that Henry "landed at Douer the
morowe after [Tuesday], beyng the .xiiii. daie of Nouember." As November
14 is the feast of S. Erkenwald, *Hol.* was betrayed into the further error of
assigning Henry's landing and marriage to "the same daie." *Halle* says (794) :
"The kyng, after his returne, maried priuily the lady Anne Bulleyn, on saint
Erkenwaldes daie," . . .

[2] *Halle,* 795. The act is 25 Hen. VIII. c. 23 (*Statutes,* iii. 472).

Cromwell was in Wolsey's service [1] for

[*Foxe*, ii. 1150/2.] a certayne space of yeares, growing vp *Cromwell*
in office and authoritie, till at length he was preferred to be *to the*
sollicitour to the Cardinall.   *Cardinall.*

In Lent, 1530,[2] "diuerse" of Wolsey's

[*Hol.* iii. 913/2/17. *Halle*, 769.] seruants departed from him *Thomas*
to the kings seruice, and in especiall Thomas Crumwell, one of his *Crumwell*
chiefe counsell, and chiefe dooer for him in the suppression of   *advanced to*
abbeies.   *service.*

Having obtained a seat in the Parliament which met on November
3, 1529, Cromwell answered every charge made against Wolsey in the
Commons; and thus, for his

[*Stow*, 926. *Cavendish*, i. 208.] behauior in his Masters cause,
he grew into such estimation in euerie mans opinion, that hee was
esteemed to be the most [3] faithfull seruaunt to his Master of all *[Cromwell*
other; wherein hee was greatlie of all men commended.   *praised for*
                                                                  his fidelity
                                                                  to Wolsey.]
From the same source (*Stow*, 930; *Cavendish*, i. 229) we learn
that Cromwell was esteemed not only for his ability, but also for his

true and faithfull demeanor towards his lord and master.

After again commending Cromwell to Henry's service, Wolsey says:

> prythee, leade me in:
> There take an Inuentory of all I haue,
> To the last peny; 'tis the Kings: . . .   452

On October 17, 1529, when Norfolk and Suffolk had departed with
the Great Seal, Wolsey

[*Hol.* iii. 909/1/69. *Stow*, 919.] called all his officers before *The cardi-*
him, and tooke accompt of them for all such stuffe, whereof they *nall call-*
had charge. And in his gallerie were set diuerse tables, where- *eth all his*
vpon laie a great number of goodlie rich stuffe, as whole peeces of *officers to*
                                                                  accounts.

---

[1] A petition placed after the grants of December 1524 is addressed to
"Master Cromwell, councillor to the lorde Legate."—*Calendar (Hen. VIII.)*,
IV. i. 979. There are earlier papers in Cromwell's handwriting relating to
Wolsey's public business; for example, a draft of a petition dated September
22, 1524.—*Calendar (Hen. VIII.)*, IV. i. 681.

[2] In Lent, 1530, Wolsey was ordered by Henry to reside in the province of
York.—*Halle*, 769. Cromwell then left Wolsey and became Henry's servant.
—*Ibid.* Wolsey set forth on his journey northwards in the beginning of
Passion Week (April 11, 1530.)—*Cavendish*, i. 241.

[3] *cause, he grew . . . the most*] Cavendish. *cause, grew so in euerie mans
opinion, how that hee was the most* Hol. and Stow.

silke of all colours, veluet, sattin, damaske, taffata, grograine, and other things. Also, there laie a thousand peeces of fine Holland cloth.

[Inventories of Wolsey's stuff.]

There was laid on euerie table, bookes reporting the contents of the same, and so was there inuentaries of all things in order against the kings comming. . . .

[Wolsey's officers were to account to Henry for the stuff in their charge.]

Thus were all things prepared, [Wolsey] giuing charge of the delivery thereof unto the king, to every officer within his office: for the order[1] was such, that euerie officer was charged with the receipt of the stuffe belonging to his office by indenture.

Wolsey's reflections on his fall close with these memorable words:

> O Cromwel, Cromwel !
> *Had I* but *seru'd my God* with halfe the Zeale
> *I* seru'd my *King, he would not in* mine Age   456
> *Haue* left *us* naked to mine Enemies !

On November 29, 1530, when Wolsey was dying, he said to Sir William Kingston, Constable of the Tower :

The cardinall ascribeth his fall to the iust iudgement of God.

[*Hol.* iii. 917/1/45. *Stow*, 940.]   "I see the matter how it is "framed;[2] but if *I had serued God* as diligentlie as *I* haue doone "the *king, he would not haue* giuen *me* ouer *in* my greie haires : "but it is the iust reward that I must receiue for the diligent "paines and studie that I haue had to doo him seruice ; not "regarding my seruice to God, but onelie to satisfie his pleasure."

Act IV. sc. i.—The two Gentlemen, who appeared in Act II. sc. i., meet again. Their "last encounter" was when Buckingham "came from his Triall" (ll. 4, 5). They now take their stand to see Anne Boleyn "passe from her Corronation" (ll. 2, 3). Between these events a historic interval of more than twelve years elapsed.

The First Gentleman has in his hand a list

> Of those that claime their Offices this day,
> By custome of the Coronatiön.   18
> The Duke of Suffolke is the first, and claimes
> To be High Steward ; next, the Duke of Norfolke,
> He to be Earle Marshall : you may reade the rest.

Proclamation for the

[*Hol.* iii. 930/1/35. *Halle*, 798.]   In the beginning of Maie [1533], the king caused open proclamations to be made, that all

---

[1] *charge of . . . for the order*] Cavendish. *charge of all the said stuffe, with all other remaining in euerie office, to be deliuered to the king, to make answer to their charge : for the order* Hol. and Stow.

[2] Wolsey presaged the truth ; which was, that Kingston had been sent to convey him to the Tower.—*Cavendish*, i. 304, &c. The date of Wolsey's death is given by *Cavendish* (i. 319).

men that cláimed to doo anie seruice, or execute anie office at the solemne feast of the coronation by the waie of tenure, grant, or prescription, should put their grant three weekes after Easter in the Starrechamber before Charles duke of Suffolke, for that time high steward of England, and the lord chancellor, and other com- missioners. The duke of Norffolke claimed to be erle marshall, and to exercise his office at that feast ; . . .

> The Second Gentleman asks :
>
>> But, I beseech you, what's become of Katherine,
>> The Princesse Dowager ?   How goes her businesse ?
>> 1 That I can tell you too. *The Árchbishop*   24
>> *Of Canterbury, accompanied with* other
>> *Learnëd* and Reuerend Fathers of his Order,
>> Held a late Court at *Dunstable, sixe miles* off
>> *From Ampthill, where the Princesse lay ;* to which   28
>> *She was* often *cyted by* them, but *appear'd not :*
>> *And,* to be short, *for* not *Appearance, and*
>> The Kings late Scruple, *by the* maine *assent*
>> *Of all* these *Learnëd men* she *was diuorc'd,*   32
>> *And the* late *Marriage* made *of none effect :* . . .

The Parliament which reassembled, after prorogation, on February 4, 1533, passed an act forbidding appeals to Rome ;[1]

[*Hol.* iii. 929/2/58. *Halle,* 796.] for that in ancient councels it had beene determined, that a cause rising in one prouince should be determined in the same.

This matter was opened with all the circumstances to the ladie Katharine Dowager (for so was she then called), the which per- sisted still in hir former opinion, and would reuoke by no meanes hir appeale to the court of Rome. Wherevpon *the archbishop of Canturburie, accompanied with* the bishops of London, Winchester, Bath, Lincolne, and diuers other *learned* men in great number, rode to *Dunstable,* which is *six miles from Ampthill, where the princesse* Dowager *laie;* and there *by* one Doctor Lee *she was cited* to appeare before the said archbishop in cause of matrimonie in the said towne of Dunstable, and at the daie of appearance she appeared *not,* but made default; and so she was called peremptori[li]e [*p.* 930] euerie daie fifteene daies togither, *and,* at the last, *for*

---

[1] *Halle,* 789, 795. The act is 25 Hen. VIII., c. 22 (*Statutes,* iii. 472, 473).

Cranmer's
court at
Dunstable,
and divorced
for non-
appearance]. lacke of *appearance, by the assent of all* the *learned men* there present, *she was divorced* [1] from the king, *and the mariage* declared to be void and *of none effect.*

The trumpets now sound, and the procession enters in the manner set forth by the following stage direction:

The Order of the Coronation.

1 A liuely Flourish of Trumpets.
2 Then, two *Iudges.*
3 *Lord Chancellor,* with Purse and Mace before him.
4 Quirristers, *singing.*   Musicke.
5 *Maior* of *London,* bearing the *Mace.* Then *Garter, in his Coate of Armes,* and on his head he wore a Gilt Copper Crowne. [2]
6 *Marquesse Dorset,* bearing a *Scepter of Gold,* on his head a Demy Coronall of Gold. With him, *the Earle of* Surrey, bearing *the Rod of* Siluer *with the Doue,* Crowned with an Earles Coronet. Collars of Essex.
7 *Duke of Suffolke, in his Robe of Estate,* his Coronet on his head, bearing *a long white* Wand, as *High Steward.* With him, *the* Duke of Norfolke, *with the Rod of Marshalship,* a Coronet on his head. Collars of Essex.
8 A *Canopy borne by foure of the* Cinque-Ports ; vnder it, *the Queene* in her *Robe; in her haire* richly adorned with Pearle, Crowned. On each side her, *the Bishops of London and Winchester.*
9 *The Olde Dutchesse of Norfolke,* in a Coronall of Gold, wrought with Flowers, bearing *the Queenes Traine.*
10 Certaine *Ladies* or Countesses, with plaine Circlets of Gold without Flowers. [3]

Anne Boleyn was crowned on June 1, 1533. [4] In the morning of that day a procession was formed which escorted her from Westminster Hall to a throne placed between the choir and high altar of the Abbey.

The comelie
order & araie
kept on the
coronation
daie of euerie
attendant in
his degree. [*Hol.* iii. 933/1/1. *Halle,* 802.] First went gentlemen, then esquiers, then knights, then the aldermen of the citie in their cloks of scarlet, after them the *iudges* in their mantels of scarlet and coiffes. Then followed the knights of the bath being no lords, euerie man hauing a white lace on his left sleeue; then followed

---

[1] On May 23, 1533, as we learn from Cranmer's letter (cited at p. 479, n. 1, above).—*Ellis,* I. ii. 36.
[2] Before the procession returned to Westminster Hall, "euerie king of armes put on a crowne of coper and guilt."—*Hol.* iii. 933/1/70. *Halle,* 802.
[3] When the kings of arms put on crowns of copper gilt, "euerie countesse [donned] a plaine circlet of gold without flowers."—*Hol.* iii. 933/1/69. *Halle,* 803. These crowns and circlets "were worne till night."—*Ibid.*
[4] *Hulle,* 802.

barons and vicounts in their parlement robes of scarlet. After [The Judges.] them came earls, marquesses, and dukes in their robes of estate of crimsin veluet furred with ermine, poudered according to their degrees. After them came the *lord chancellor* in a robe of scarlet [The Lord Chancellor.] open before, bordered with lettise; after him came the kings [The King's chapell and the moonks solemnelie *singing* with procession, then chapel, singing.] came abbats and bishops mitered, then sargeants and officers of armes; then after them went the *maior of London* with his *mace*, [The Mayor of London.] and *garter in his cote of armes;* then went the *marquesse Dorset* in [Garter.] a robe of estate, which bare the *sceptre of gold;* and *the earle of* [Marquess Dorset.] Arundell, which bare *the rod of* iuorie *with the doue;* both togither.

Then went alone the earle of Oxford, high chamberleine of [The Duke of Suffolk, England, which bare the crowne; after him went the *duke of Suffolke* Lord William *in his robe of estate* also, for that daie being *high steward* of England, Howard, representing hauing *a long white* rod in his hand; and *the* lord William Howard[1] the Duke of *with the rod of* the *marshalship;* and euerie knight of the garter had Norfolk.] on his collar of the order. Then proceeded foorth *the queene in* a *The queens circot* and *robe* of purple veluet furred with ermine, *in hir here,* under a canopie coiffe, and circlet as she had the saturdaie; and ouer hir was *borne* borne by foure of the the *canopie by foure of the* fiue *ports,* all crimsin with points of blue cinque ports. and red hanging on their sleeues; and *the bishops of London and* [The Bishops of London *Winchester* bare vp the laps of the queenes robe. *The queenes* and Winchester.] *traine,* which was verie long, was borne by *the old duches of* [The old Duchess of *Norffolke;* after hir folowed *ladies* being lords wiues. Norfolk.] [Ladies being Lords' wives.]

The procession passes over the stage, and goes out with a great flourish of trumpets. An interval is supposed to elapse before a Third Gentleman enters, and, joining the twain who have hitherto played chorus, gives them an account of the coronation:

> The rich streame
> Of Lords and Ladies, hauing *brought* the Queene
> *To* a prepar'd *place in the Quire,* fell off   64
> A distance from her; while her Grace sate downe
> To *rest a while,* some halfe an houre or so,
> *In a rich Chaire* of State, . . .
> At length, her Grace rose, and with modest paces
> Came to the Altar; where she kneel'd, and, Saint-like,

---

[1] In the Queen's procession from the Tower to Westminster Hall, on May 31, "rode the lord William Howard with the marshalles rod, deputie to his brother the duke of Norffolk, marshall of England; which was ambassador then in France."—*Hol.* 931/2/40. *Halle,* 800. *Hol.* has this sidenote: "The two dukes of Norffolke and Suffolke in their offices."

Cast her faire eyes to Heauen, and pray'd deuoutly :   84
Then rose againe, and bow'd her to the people :
When, by *the Arch-byshop of Canterbury*,
She had all the Royall makings of a Queene ;
As, holy Oyle, *Edward* Confessors *Crowns*,   88
The Rod, and Bird of Peace, and all such Emblemes,
Laid Nobly on her : which perform'd, *the Quire*,
With all the choysest Musicke of the Kingdome,
Together *sung* " *Te Deum.*" So she parted,   92
And with *the same* full State pac'd backe againe
To Yorke-Place, where the Feast is held.

The ceremony subsequent to the procession is thus described :

The maner of the corona-tis as it was then vsed.
[*Hol.* iii. 933/1/47. *Halle*, 803.] When she was thus *brought to* the high *place* made *in the* middest of the church, betweene the *queere* and the high altar, she was set *in a rich chaire*. And after that she had *rested a while*, she descended downe to the high altar, and there prostrate hir selfe while *the archbishop of Canturburie* [Anne Boleyn anointed and crowned by Cran-mer.] said certeine collects : *then* she *rose*, and the bishop annointed hir on the head and on the brest, and then she was led vp againe : where, after diuerse orisons said, the archbishop set the *crowne* of saint *Edward* on hir head, and then deliuered hir the scepter of gold in hir right hand, and *the rod* of iuorie with the doue in the [The quire sang Te Deum.] left hand ; and then all *the queere soong Te Deum*, &c. . . .

The queene and the ladies in their pompe [return to Westminster Hall].
When the queene had a little reposed hir, the companie returned in *the same* order that they set foorth ; and the queene went crowned, and so did the ladies aforesaid. . . . Now when she was out of the sanctuarie and appeered within the palace, the trumpets plaied maruellouslie freshlie ; then she was brought to Westminster hall, & so to hir withdrawing chamber : . . .

The last speaker's wrong designation of Henry's new palace is corrected by the First Gentleman :

                                                    Sir,
You must *no more* call it *Yorke-Place*, that's past ;
For, since the Cardinall fell, that Title's lost :   96
'Tis now the Kings, and call'd White-Hall.

In January, 1531,[1] Henry

[*Hol.* iii. 923/1/11. *Halle*, 774.] came to his manour of West-minster, which before was called Yorke place : for after that the

---

[1] After keeping Twelfth Night, 1531, at Greenwich.—*Halle*, 774.

cardinall was attainted in the premunire, & was gone northward,
he made a feoffement of the same place to the king, and the
chapiter of the cathedrall church of Yorke by their writing confirmed the same feoffement; & then the king changed the name
and called it the kings manor of Westminster,[1] and *no more Yorke*
place.

The Second Gentleman asks :

What two Reuerend Byshops
Were those that went on each side of the Queene ?   100
 3 Stokesley and Gardiner ; the one of Winchester,
Newly preferr'd from the Kings Secretary ;
The other, London.

Gardiner was consecrated Bishop of Winchester on December 3,
1531.[2] In 1530 the bishopric of London

[*Hol.* iii. 909/2/55. *Halle*, 761.] was bestowed on doctor
Stokesleie,[3] then ambassadour to the vniuersities beyond the sea for
the kings mariage.

The Second Gentleman remarks upon Gardiner's dislike to Cranmer.
The Third Gentleman answers that Cranmer will find an ally in

Thomas Cromwell ;   108
A man in much esteeme with th'King, and truly
A worthy Friend. The King ha's made him Master
O'th'Iewell House,
And one, already, of the Priuy Councell.

After Anne Boleyn's coronation had been ordained to take place on
Whit Sunday, 1533, the assessment of fines payable by those who
should refuse knighthood

[*Hol.* iii. 929/2/46. *Halle*, 795.] was appointed to Thomas
Cromwell, maister of the kings iewell house,[4] & councellor to the
king, a man newlie receiued into high fauour.

Act IV. sc. ii.—In Act IV. sc. i. the First Gentleman, after relating
the circumstances of Katharine's divorce, added (ll. 34, 35) :

---

[1] By the Act 28 Hen. VIII., cap. 12 (*Statutes*, iii. 668) this former residence
of the Archbishops of York was annexed to the old palace of Westminster, and
the whole was to be known as "the Kynges Paleys at Westmynster." The
index to *Halle* has : "York Place called now whyt hall." In 1530 a petition
is spoken of as having been made to Wolsey "when he lay at the White Hall,
then called York's Place."—*Calendar (Hen. VIII.)*, IV. iii. p. 2969.

[2] *Reg. Sacr. Angl.*, 76.

[3] Stokesley was consecrated Bishop of London on November 27, 1530.—
Reg. Sacr. Angl., 76.

[4] Cromwell was made Master of the Jewel House on April 14, 1532.—*Pat.*
23 H. VIII., p. 2, m. 36 (H. S.).

Since which, she was remou'd to Kymmalton,
Where she remaines now sicke.

The second scene of Act IV. opens with the following stage
direction :

Enter Katherine, Dowager, sicke; lead [led] betweene
Griffith, her Gentleman Vsher, and Patience, her
Woman.

About the middle of the scene a messenger announces to Katharine
(L 106),

A Gentleman, sent from the King, to see you.

Griffith goes out and re-enters with Eustace Chapuys, the Imperial
ambassador, whom Katharine thus addresses :

If my sight faile not,   108
You should be Lord Ambassador from the Emperor,
My Royall Nephew, and your name Capuchius.

Chapuys's reasons for presenting himself at Kimbolton are :

First, mine owne seruice to your Grace ; the next,
The Kings request that I would visit you ;   116
Who greeues much for your weaknesse, and by me
Sends you his Princely Commendatiõns,
And heartily entreats you take good comfort.

Before dismissing the ambassador, Katharine says to her woman :

Patience, is that Letter,
I caus'd you write, yet sent away ?
   Pat.   No, Madam.   128
   Kath. Sir, I most humbly pray you to deliuer
This to my Lord the King.
   Cap.   Most willing, Madam.
   Kath. In which I haue commended to his goodnesse
The Modell of our chaste loues, his yong daughter, 132
(The dewes of Heauen fall thicke in Blessings on her !)
Beseeching him to giue her vertuous breeding ;
(She is yong, and of a Noble modest Nature ;
I hope she will deserue well ;) and a little   136
To loue her for her Mothers sake, that lou'd him,
Heauen knowes how deerely ! My next poore Petition   .
Is, that his Noble Grace would haue some pittie
Vpon my wretched women, that so long   140
Have follow'd both my Fortunes faithfully :
Of which there is not one, I dare auow,
(And now I should not lye,) but will deserue,
For Vertue, and true Beautie of the Soule,   144
For honestie, and decent Carriäge,
A right good Husband, let him be a Noble :
And, sure, those men are happy that shall haue 'em.
The last is, for my men ; (they are the poorest, 148
But pouerty could neuer draw 'em from me ;)
That they may haue their wages duly paid 'em,

ensuing excerpt.   On December 17, 1533,[1] Henry sent to Katharine the
Duke of Suffolk, who

[*Höl.* iii. 936/2/7.   *Halls,* 808.]   discharged a great sort of hir
houshold seruants, and yet left a conuenient number to serue hir
like a princesse; which were sworne to serue hir not as queene, but
as princesse Dowager.   Such as tooke that oth she vtterlie refused,
and would none of their seruice; so that she remained with the
lesse number of seruants about hir.

[Katharine
rejected
servants
who did not
serve her as
Queen.]

Before she entered Katharine had learnt from Griffith that Wolsey
was dead (ll. 5-7).   To her question how the Cardinal died Griffith
answered:

Well, the voyce goes, Madam:
For after the stout Earle Northumberland   12
Arrested him at Yorke, and brought him forward
(As a man sorely tainted) to his Answer,
He fell *sicke* sodainly, and grew so ill
He could not sit *his Mule.*
   Kath.   Alas, poore man!   16
   Grif. At last, with easie Rodes, *he came to Leicester,*
Lodg'd in the Abbey; *where the* reuerend *Abbot,*
With all his Couent, honourably receiu'd him;
To whom he gaue these words, "O, *Father Abbot,*   20
"An old man, broken with the stormes of State,
"Is *come to lay* his weary *bones among* ye;
"Giue him a little earth for Charity!"
So *went to bed :* where eagerly his sicknesse   24
Pursu'd him still; and, three nights after this,
About the houre of eight, (which he himselfe
Foretold should be his last,) full of Repentance,
Continuall Meditations, Teares, and Sorrowes,   28
He gaue his Honors to the world agen,
His blessëd part to Heauen, and slept in peace.

On November 4, 1530, Wolsey was arrested at Cawood Castle
(Yorkshire), by Henry Percy, Earl of Northumberland.[2]   The Cardinal
left Cawood, under arrest, on November 6,[3] and on November 8
reached Sheffield Park, where for a fortnight he enjoyed the hos-
pitality of George Talbot, Earl of Shrewsbury.[4]   On November 22
Sir William Kingston, Constable of the Tower, arrived at Sheffield
Park, charged with the duty of conveying Wolsey to London.   On the
same day—but before he knew of Kingston's arrival—Wolsey was
seized with a sudden illness.[5]

---

[1] *Calendar* (*Hen. VIII.*), VI. 1541.   [2] *Cavendish,* i. 268, 275-280.
[3] *Cavendish,* 283, 284, 288.   [4] *Cavendish,* 293, 299.
[5] *Cavendish,* 299-302.   As to this date cp. 310, 311, 313-319.

Though his disorder increased he began his journey to London, and, on November 26, rode from Nottingham [1]

[*Hol.* iii. 917/1/10. *Stow*, 940.] to Leicester abbeie, and by the waie waxed so *sicke* that *he* was almost fallen from *his mule;* so that it was night before *he came to* the abbeie of *Leicester, where* at his comming in at the gates, *the abbat with all his conuent* met him with diuerse torches light; whom they *honorablie receiued* and welcomed.

To whom the cardinall said: "*Father abbat,* I am *come* hither "*to lay* my *bones among* you"; riding so still vntill he came to the staires of the chamber, where he allighted from his mule, and master Kingston led him vp the staires, and as soone as he was in his chamber he *went to bed.* This was on the saturday at night; and then increased he sicker and sicker, vntill mondaie, that all men thought he would haue died: so on tuesdaie, saint Andrewes euen, master Kingston came to him and bad him good morrow, (for it was about six of the clocke,) and asked him how he did?

In less than two hours after Kingston's morning salutation, Wolsey was at the point of death:

[*Hol.* iii. 917/1/65. *Stow*, 940.] & incontinent the clocke stroke eight, and then he gaue vp the ghost, and departed this present life: which caused some to call to remembrance how he said the daie before, that at eight of the clocke they should loose their master. [Wolsey died at eight in the morning, as he had predicted.]

Having heard how Wolsey died, Katharine says:

So may he rest; his Faults lye gently on him!
Yet thus farre, Griffith, giue me leaue to speake him,   32
And yet with Charity. He *was* a man
Of an vnbounded *stomacke,* euer ranking
Himselfe with Princes; one that, *by suggestion,*
Ty'de all the Kingdome: *Symonie* was faire play;   36
His owne Opinion was his Law: *i'th'presence*
He would say vntruths; and be euer *double*
Both in his words *and meaning:* he *was* neuer
(But where he meant to Ruine) *pittifull:*   40
His Promises were, as he then was, Mighty;
But his performance, as he is now, Nothing:

---

[1] *Cavendish,* i. 311-313.

Of his owne body he was ill, *and gaue*
The Clergy ill example.

With Katharine's leave, Griffith thus proceeded to "speake"
Wolsey's "good":

48

This Cardinall,
Though from an humble Stocke, *vndoubtedly*
Was fashion'd *to* much *Honor* from his Cradle.
He was a Scholler, and *a ripe* and good one ;

52

Exceeding wise, faire spoken, and perswading :
Lofty and sowre *to* them that lou'd him not ;
But, *to those* men that *sought* him, sweet as Summer.
And though he were vnsatisfied in *getting*,

56

(Which was a sinne,) yet *in bestowing,* Madam,
He was most *Princely* : euer witnesse for him
Those twinnes of Learning, that he rais'd in you,
Ipewich and *Oxford !* one of which fell with him,

60

Vnwilling to out-liue the good that did it ;
The other (though *vnfinish'd*) *yet* so Famous,
So excellent in Art, and still so rising,
That *Christendome* shall euer speake his Vertue.

64

His Ouerthrow heap'd Happinesse vpon him ;
For then, and not till then, he felte himselfe,
And found the Blessednesse of being little :
And, to adde greater Honors to his Age

68

Then man could giue him, he dy'de fearing God.

For comparison with Katharine's unfavourable judgment of Wolsey
I quote the following passage, taken by Holinshed from Halle (774) :

[*Hol.* iii. 922/2/48.] This cardinall . . . *was of a great stomach*,
for he compted *himselfe* equall *with princes*, & *by craftie suggestion*
gat into his hands innumerable treasure : he forced little on
simonie, and *was* not *pittifull*, and stood affectionate in *his owne*
opinion: in open *presence he would* lie and *saie vntruth, and was*
double both in speach *and meaning:* he would promise much &
performe little : *he was* vicious *of his bodie, & gaue the clergie euill*
example: . . .

Griffith's defence should be compared with another estimate of
Wolsey, which forms my next quotation :

[*Hol.* iii. 917/2/20.] *This cardinall* (as Edmund Campian in
his historie of Ireland [1] describeth him) *was* a man *vndoubtedly* borne
to honor: I thinke (saith he) some princes bastard, no butchers

---

[1] In the dedication of an account of Ireland (*Hol.* ii.), Raphael Holinshed
acknowledged his obligation to Campian's "two bookes of the Irish histories."

sonne ; *exceeding wise ; faire spoken ;* high minded ; full of reuenge ; [Edmund Campian.]
vitious of his bodie ; *loftie to* his enimies, were they neuer so big ;
to those that accepted and *sought* his freendship woonderfull
courteous ; *a ripe* schooleman ; thrall to affections ; brought a bed
with flatterie ; insatiable to *get,* and more *princelie in bestowing,* as
appeareth by his two colleges at *Ipswich and Oxenford,* the one [Wolsey's colleges at Ipswich and Oxford.]
ouerthrowne with his fall, *the other vnfinished,* and *yet,* as it lieth
for an house of students, considering all the appurtenances, incomparable thorough *Christendome ;* whereof Henrie the eight is now
called founder, bicause he let it stand. He held and inioied at [His benefices.]
once the bishopriks of Yorke, Duresme, & Winchester, the dignities of lord cardinall, legat, & chancellor, the abbeie of saint
Albons, diuerse priories, sundrie fat benefices "In commendam:"[1] [His character (continued).]
a great preferrer of his seruants, an aduancer of learning, stout in
euerie quarell, neuer happie till this *his ouerthrow.* Wherein he
shewed such moderation, and ended so perfectlie, that the houre of [His exemplary death.]
his death did him more honor than all the pompe of his life passed.

Act V. sc. i.—Gardiner and Lovell meet. Hearing from Lovell
that Queen Anne is in labour and in great extremity, Gardiner wishes
that she, together with Cranmer and Cromwell, were dead. "As for
Cromwell," answers Lovell, he

> Beside that of the Iewell-House [2] is made Master
> O'th'Rolles, and the Kings Secretary ; . . .

[*Hol.* iii. 938/1/6. *Stow,* 962.] The one and twentith of Sep- [Cromwell made Master of the Rolls.]
tember [1534], doctor Tailor, master of the rolles, was discharged
of that office ; and Thomas Cromwell sworne in his place, the
nineteenth of October.[3]

In Holinshed, iii. 940/1/15 (Stow, 964), "Thomas Cromwell secretarie" is mentioned as being one of the four persons who brought
Anne Boleyn to the Tower on May 2, 1536 ; but I find no record
of his appointment in Halle, Holinshed, Stow, or Foxe.[4]

---

[1] I have substituted quotation commas for the original italics of *In commendam.*

[2] See p. 487, n. 4, above.

[3] Cromwell was made Master of the Rolls on October 8, 1534.—*Pat.* 26 H. VIII. p. 2, m. 1 (H. S.).

[4] A letter from Henry Marquis of Exeter to Cromwell, dated April 7, 1534, is addressed : "Master Secretary."—*Calendar (Hen. VIII.),* VII. 446. In a document dated April 12, 1534, appointing Cromwell to be one of the pleni-potentiaries for concluding peace with Scotland, he is called " Primarius Secretarius noster."—*Rymer,* xiv. 536.

"Th' Árchbyshop," adds Lovell,

> Is the Kings hand and tongue; and who dare speak
> One syllable against him!

Touching the folly of those persons who hoped to ruin Cranmer through the conspiracy which is dramatized in sc. iii. Act V., Foxe remarks (ii. 1760/1):

And it was muche to be marueiled that they would goe so farre with hym, thus to seeke his vndoyng, this well vnderstandyng before, that the kyng moste entirely loued him, and alwaies would stande in his defence, who soeuer spake againste hym: as many other tymes the kynges pacience was, by sinister informations, against hym tried.

Gardiner replies that there are some who dare accuse Cranmer;

> and I my selfe haue ventur'd　　　　　　　40
> To speake my minde of him: and, indeed, this day,
> (Sir, I may tell it you,) I thinke I haue
> Incenst the Lords o'th'Councell, that he is
> (For so I know he is, they know he is)　　　44
> A most Arch-Heretique, a Pestilence
> That does infect the Land: with which they moued,
> Haue broken with the King; who . . .
> 　　　　　　　　　　　hath commanded,
> To morrow Morning to the Councell Boord
> He be conuented.　　　　　　　　52

In (?) 1544,[1]

[Foxe, ii. 1759/1.] certaine of the Counsaile, whose names neede not to bee repeated, by the entisement and prouocation of his [Cranmer's] auncient enemy the Bishop of Winchester, and other of the same secte, attempted the Kyng againste hym; declaryng plainely that the realme was so infected with heresies and heretickes, that it was daungerous for his highnesse farther

---

[1] According to Foxe (ii. 1759/1) these counsellors attacked Cranmer "not long after" the time when Cromwell was in the Tower. Cromwell was committed to the Tower on June 10, 1540 (Lords' Journals, i. 143/2), and remained there until he was beheaded on the 28th of July.—Halle, 839. But the attempt to ruin Cranmer is placed under the year 1544 by Strype, who, in regard to the latter date, says: "I leave Fox to follow [Ralph] Morice, the Archbishop's secretary, in his manuscript declaration of the said Archbishop."—Strype's Cranmer, i. 176. Of the authority cited Strype speaks thus: "There is an original writing of this Morice's hand, preserved in the Benet-library [the library of Corpus Christi, Cambridge], entitled, A declaration, &c., which he drew out for the use, and by the command, of Archbishop Parker."—Strype's Cranmer, i. 615.

to permit it vnreformed, . . . [1759/2]. The **kyng, perceiuyng** the spread of heresy ought to be checked.] their importune sute against the Archebishoppe, (but yet meanyng [Henry consented that Cranmer should be committed to the Tower.] not to haue hym wronged, and vtterly giuen ouer vnto their handes,) graunted to them that they should, the nexte daie, committe hym to the Tower for his triall.

Gardiner goes out and Henry enters with Suffolk (l. 55). Suffolk's exit is followed by the entrance of Sir Anthony Denny, who thus addresses the King (ll. 80, 81):

> Sir, I haue brought my Lord the Arch-byshop,
> As you commanded me.

As Henry desires Cranmer's immediate presence, Denny goes out and re-enters with the Archbishop. The King then bids Lovell and Denny "Auoyd the Gallery." When they are gone Henry says to Cranmer, who has knelt:

>   Pray you, arise,
> *My good and gracious Lord of Canterburie.*   92
> Come, you and I must walke a turne together;
> *I* haue *Newes* to *tell you* : . . .
> I haue, and most vnwillingly, of late
> Heard many greeuous, I do say, my Lord,
> Greeuous complaints of you; which, being consider'd,
> Haue mou'd Vs and our Councell, that you shall   100
> This Morning come before vs; where, I know,
> You cannot with such freedome purge your selfe,
> But that, till further Trial in those Charges
> Which will require your Answer, you must take   104
> Your patience to you, and be well contented
> To make your house our Towre : *you a* Brother of vs,
> It fits we thus proceed, *or else no witnesse*
> Would *come* against you.
> *Cran.*   I humbly thanke your Highnesse; 108
> And am right glad to catch this good occasion
> Most throughly to be winnowed, where my Chaffe
> And Corne shall flye asunder : for, I know,
> There's none stands vnder more calumnious tongues,   112
> Then I my selfe, poore man !
> *King.*   Stand vp, good Canterbury :
> Thy Truth and thy Integrity is rooted
> In vs, thy Friend. Giue me thy hand, stand vp :
> Prythee, let's walke. Now, by my Holydame,   116
> *What manner of man* are *you ?* My Lord, *I* look'd
> *You would haue* giuen me your *Petition*, that
> I should haue *tane* some *paines to* bring *together*
> Your selfe *and your Accusers ;* and to haue heard you, 120
> *Without indurance*, further. . . .
>   *Know you not*
> How your *state* stands *i'*th'world, *with the whole world ?*

Your *Enemies* are *many*, and not small ; their practises 128
Must beare the same proportion ; and not euer
The Iustice and the Truth o'th'question carries
The dew o'th'Verdict with it : at *what* ease
Might corrupt mindes *procure Knaues* as corrupt 132
To sweare *against you !* such things haue bene done.
You are Potently oppos'd ; and with a Malice
Of as great Size.   Weene *you* of *better lucke*,
(I meane, in periur'd Witnesse,) *then your Master*, 136
(Whose Minister you are,) whiles heere he liu'd
Vpon this naughty Earth !   Go to, go to :
You take a Precepit for no leape of danger,
And wooe your owne destruction. . . . 140
                                      Be of good cheere ;
They *shall* no more *preuaile* then we giue way to.
Keepe comfort to you ; and this Morning see 144
You do appeare before *them* : *if they* shall chance,
In charging you with matters, to *commit you*,
The best *perswasions* to the contrary
Faile not to *vse*, and with what vehemencie 148
Th'occasion shall instruct you : *if intreaties*
Will render you no remedy, *this Ring*
Deliuer them, and your Appeale to vs
There make before them. (Looke, the good man weeps ! 152
He's honest, on mine Honor.   Gods blest Mother !
I sweare he is true-hearted ; and a soule
None better in my Kingdome !)   Get you gone,
And do as I haue bid you.   [Exit Cranmer. 156

I resume my historical excerpts from the point where we learn that
Cranmer's enemies had obtained permission to "committe hym to the
Tower for his triall" (p. 495 above).

The King
sent Syr
Antony
Deny at mid-
night for the
Archbyshop.

[*Foxe*, ii. 1759/2.]   When Nighte came, the Kyng sent Sir
Anthonie Denie, aboute Midnight, to Lambeth, to the Archbishop,
willyng hym forthwith to resorte vnto hym at the Courte.   The
message doen, the Archbishop speedily addressed hym self to
the Court, and commyng into the Galerie where the kyng walked,
and taried for hym, his highnesse saied : "Ah, *my Lorde of*

[Henry and
the Council
intended to
commit
Cranmer
to the
Tower.]

"*Canterburie, I* can *tell you newes.*   For diuers waightie consider-
"ations it is determined by me and the Counsaile, that you to
"morrowe at nine of the clocke shall bee committed to the
"Tower, . . . the Counsail haue requested me . . . to suffer
"them to commit you to the Tower, *or els no* man dare *come*
"forthe, as *witnesse* in these matters, *you* beyng *a* Counsellour."
When the kyng had said his minde, the Archbishop kneeled

doune, and saied: "I am content, if it please your grace, with all
"my harte, to go thether at your highnes commaundemente; and
"I moste humbly thanke your Maiestie that I maie come to my
"triall, for there bee that haue many waies sclaundered me, and
"nowe this waie I hope to trie my self not worthy of suche
"report."

The Arch-byshope answere to the King.

　　The Kyng, perceiuyng the mannes vprightnesse, ioyned with suche
simplicitie, saied: "Oh Lorde, *what maner a man* be *you!* What
"simplicitie is in you! *I* had thought that *you would* rather *haue*
"sued to vs to haue *taken* the *paines to* haue heard you *and your*
"*acousers together,* for your triall, *without* any suche *indurance.*
"Doe *not you knowe* what *state* you bee *in with the whole worlde,*
"and how *many greate enemies* you haue? Doe you not consider
"*what* an easie thyng it is to *procure* three or fower false *knaues*
"*to* witnesse *againste you?* Thinke *you* to haue *better lucke* that
"waie *then your Maister* Christe had? I see by it, you will runne
"headlonge to your vndoyng, if I would suffer you. Your enemies
"*shall* not so *preuaile* against you, for I haue otherwise deuised
"with my selfe, to keepe you out of their handes. Yet, notwith-
"standing, to morrowe, when the Counsaile shall sitte, and sende
"for you, resort vnto *them,* and *if, in chargyng you with* this
"*matter, they* doe *commit you* to the Tower,[1] . . . *vse* for your selfe
"as good *perswasions* . . . as you maie deuise, and, *if* no *intreatie*
"or reasonable request will serue, then *deliuer* vnto *them this* my
"*ryng;*" (whiche then the Kyng deliuered vnto the Archbishoppe;)
. . . "for," (saied the Kyng then vnto the Archbishoppe,) "so
"sone as thei shall see this my ryng, thei knowe it so wel that
"they shall vnderstande that I haue resumed the whole cause
"into myne owne handes and determination, and that I haue
"discharged them thereof."

[Henry was astonished at Cranmer's simplicity.]

The Kinges fauorable care & consideration toward y' Arch-byshop of Canterbury.

The King sendeth his signet in the behalfe of the Arch-bishop of Canterbury.

　　The Archebishoppe, perceiuyng the kynges benignite so muche
to him wardes, had muche a doe to forbeare teares. "Well," saied
the kyng, "goe your waies, my Lorde, and doe as I haue bidden
"you." My Lorde, humblyng hym self with thankes, tooke his
leaue of the kynges highnesse for that night.

[Cranmer " had muche a doe to forbeare teares."]

[He thanked Henry, and departed.]

---

[1] See p. 500, n. 1, below.

An "Olde Lady"—who appeared with Anne Boleyn in sc. iii.,
Act II.—now enters and tells Henry that a daughter has been born to
him (V. i. 158-165).

The birth of Elizabeth is thus recorded :

[Birth of
Elizabeth.]   [*Hol.* iii. 934/2/1. *Halle*, 805.] The seuenth of September
[1533], being sundaie, betweene three & foure of the clocke in the
afternoone, the queene was deliuered of a faire yoong ladie, . . .

Act V. sc. ii.—Cranmer is discovered at the door of the Council
Chamber. He says (ll. 1-4) :

> I hope I am not too late ; and yet the Gentleman,
> That was sent to me from the Councell, pray'd me
> To make great hast.—All fast ! What meanes this ?—Hoa !
> Who waites there ? Sure, you know me !
>   Enter [Door-]Keeper.
> *Keep.*   Yes, my Lord ;
> But yet I cannot helpe you.
> *Cran.* Why ?
> *Keep.* Your Grace must waight till you be call'd for.

Dr. Butts enters, and, witnessing the affront offered to Cranmer,
murmurs to himself :

> This is a Peece [1] of Malice. I am glad   8
> I came this way so happily : the King
> Shall vnderstand it presently.   [Exit Butts.
>   *Cran.* [*aside*]   'Tis *Butts*,
> *The Kings Physitian* : . . .

Butts re-enters with the King, "at a Windowe aboue," and says :

> *Butts.* Ile shew your Grace the strangest sight—
> *King.*   What's that, Butts ?   20
> *Butts.* I thinke your Highnesse saw this many a day.
> *Kin.* Body a me ! where is it ?
> *Butts.*   There, my Lord :
> The high promotion of his Grace of Canterbury ;
> Who holds his State at dore, 'mongst Purseuants,   24
> Pages, and Foot-boyes !
> *Kin.*   Ha ! 'Tis he, indeed.
> Is this the Honour they doe one another ?
> 'Tis well there's one aboue 'em yet. I had thought
> They had parted so much honesty among 'em,   28
> (At least, good manners,) as not thus to suffer
> A man of his Place, and so neere our favour,
> To dance attendance on their Lordships pleasures,
> And at the dore too, like a Post with Packets.   32
> By holy Mary, Butts, there's knauery :
> *Let 'em alone*, and draw the Curtaine close :
> *We shall heare more* anon.

---

[1] *Peece*] *Peere* F.

The incident here dramatized is thus related by Foxe (ii. 1759/2) :

On the morowe, about ix. of the clock before noone, the Coun- *The Arch-*
saile sent a gentleman Husher for the Archebishop, who, when he *byshop, being one*
came to the Counsail chamber dore, could not bee let in, but of *of the Counsel, made to*
purpose (as it seemed) was [1760/1] compelled there to waite *stand at the Counsail*
among the Pages, Lackeis, and seruyng men, all alone. Doctor *chamber dore, wayting.*
Buttes, the kynges Phisition, resortyng that waie, and espiyng howe
my Lorde of Canterburie was handled, went to the kynges highnesse
and saied : "My lorde of Canterbury, if it please your grace, is *Doctor Buttes, yᵉ*
"well promoted : for nowe he is become a lackey or a seruyng *kinges Phi- sition, a*
"man ; for yonder he standeth this halfe hower, without the *friend of the Arch-*
"Counsail chamber doore, amongest them."   "It is not so," *quoth* *byshops [, told Henry*
the kyng, "I trowe ; nor the Counsaile hath not so little dis- *how Cran- mer was*
"cretion as to vse the Metropolitane of the Realme in that sort, *treated].*
"specially beyng one of their owne number : but *let* them *alone*" *[Henry resolved not*
(saied the kyng) "and *we shall heare more* sone." *to interfere for a while.]*

Act V. sc. iii.—The scene is laid in the Council-Chamber. When
the counsellors are seated, " Norfolk " addresses the door-keeper :

                                        Who waits there ?
Keep.   Without, my Noble Lords ?
Gard.   Yes.
Keep.   My Lord Archbishop ;
And ha's done halfe an houre to know your pleasures.
Chan. Let him come in.
Keep. [*To Cran.*]   Your Grace may enter now.
Cranmer [enters and] approches the Councell Table.

The Lord Chancellor then censures Cranmer, because

                        you, that best should teach vs,
Haue misdemean'd your selfe, and not a little,
Toward the King first, then his Lawes, in filling
The whole Realme, by your teaching & your *Chaplaines,*   16
(For so we are inform'd,) with new opinions,
Diuers and dangerous ; which are *Heresies,*
And, not reform'd, may proue *pernicious.*

Gardiner adds :

                        . . . If we suffer   24
(Out of our easinesse and childish pitty
To one mans Honour) this contagious sicknesse,
Farewell all Physicke ! and what followes then ?
Commotions, vprores, with a generall Taint   28
Of the whole State : as, of late dayes, our neighbours,

The vpper *Germany*, can deerely witnesse,
Yet freshly pittied in our memories.

When Cranmer's enemies drew Henry's attention to the spread
of heresy in England, they urged (see pp. 494, 495 above) "that it
was daungerous for his highnesse farther to permit it"

[*Foxe*, ii. 1759/1.] vnreformed, lest peraduenture, by long
sufferyng, suche contention should arise and ensue in the realme

among his subiectes, that thereby might spryng horrible *commotions*
and *vprores*, like as in some partes of *Germanie* it did not long
agoe: the enormitie whereof they could not impute to any so
muche as to the Archbishop of Canterburie, who, *by his own*
preachyng *and* his *Chapleins*, had filled *the whole realme* full of
diuers *pernicious heresies*.

Cranmer's speech in answer to this charge closes with the request

> That, in this case of Iustice, my Accusers,
> Be what they will, may stand forth face to face,
> And freely vrge against me ! [1]
> *Suff.*   Nay, my Lord,   48
> That cannot be : you are a *Counsellor*,
> And, by that vertue, *no man* dare *accuse* you.
>   *Gard.* My Lord, because we haue busines of more moment,
> We will be short with you.   'Tis *his Highnesse* pleasure,   52
> And our consent, for better tryall of you,
> From hence you be *committed to the Tower* ;
> Where, being but a priuate man againe,
> You shall know many dare accuse you boldly,   56
> More then (I feare) you are prouided for.

Having been informed that Cranmer " had filled the whole realme
full of diuers pernicious heresies," Henry "would needes knowe" the
Archbishop's

[*Foxe*, ii. 1759/2.] accusers. Thei [Cranmer's enemies]
answered that, forasmuche as he was a *Counseller, no man* durst
take vpon hym to *accuse* him ; but, if it would please *his highnesse*
to *committe* hym *to the Tower* for a tyme, there would bee
accusations and proofes enough agaiuste him ; for otherwise iuste
testimonie and witnesse against hym would not appeere ; "and

----

[1] During their private conference, Henry said to Cranmer (see p. 497 above):
" if, in chargyng you with this matter, they [the Council] doe commit you to
the Tower, require of them, because you are one of them a Counseller, that
you maie haue your accusers brought before them, and that you maie aunswere
their accusations before them, without any further induraunce, and vse for your
selfe as good perswasions that waie, as you maie deuise," . . .

"therefore your highnesse" (saied they) "muste needes giue vs the
"Counsaill libertie and leaue to commit hym to duraunce."

Cranmer's committal to the Tower is delayed through an altercation.
Angered by Cromwell's mild censure for being "a little too sharpe"
with the Archbishop, Gardiner retorts :

Doe not I know you for a Fauourer   80
Of this new Sect? ye are not sound.
   Crom.   Not sound!
Gard. Not sound, I say.
   Crom.   Would you were halfe so honest!
Mens prayers then would seeke you, not their feares.

Foxe says of Cromwell (ii. 1159/2) :

In this worthy and noble person, besides diuers other eminent
vertues, iij. thinges especially are to bee considered, to wytte,
florishyng authoritie, excellyng wysedome, and feruent zeale to
Christ & to his Gospell.[1] First as touching his feruent zeale in
settyng forward the sinceritie of Christen fayth, . . . more can
not almost be wyshed in a noble man, and scarse the lyke hath
bene sene in any.

[1160/2] Thus, . . . as he was labouring in the common wealth,
and doyng good to the poore afflicted Saintes, helpyng them out
of trouble, the malice of his enemies so wrought, continuallye
huntyng for matter agaynst hym, that they neuer ceased till in the
end they, by false traynes and crafty surmises, brought him out
of the kinges fauour.

The chiefe and principal enemie against him was Steuen
Gardiner, Byshop of Winchester, . . .

Foxe gives the following description of Gardiner (ii. 1679/1) :

He was of a proude stomake and high minded, in his owne
opinion and conceite flatteryng hym selfe to muche ; in wit craftie
and subtile ; toward his superiour flattering and faire spoken ;[2]
to his inferiours fierce ; against his equal stout and enuious,
namely if in iudgement and sentence hee any thyng withstode him:

---

[1] "This Cromwell was at that tyme [1538] the chief frend of the Gos-
pellers."—*Foxe*, 1097/2.
[2] Cp. the rebuke addressed by Henry to Gardiner (V. iii. 126, 127):
   "To me you cannot reach, you play the Spaniell,
   And thinke with wagging of your tongue to win me;" . . .

*Three
thinges in
the L.
Cromwell.
1. Zeale.
2. Wisdome.
3. Author-
itie.*

*Ste. Gar-
diner chiefe
enemie to
the L.
Cromwell.*

*[Character
of Gardiner.]*

[He and Cromwell were stout opponents.]

as appered betwene the good Lord Cromwell and hym in the reigne of king Henry, beyng of like hautines of stomacke, . . .

Cromwell's taunt—"would you were halfe so honest"—may be illustrated by a passage (ii. 1679/1) in which Foxe pointed out the apparent contradictions of Gardiner's teaching :

And as touching diuinitie, he was so variable waueryng with tyme, that no constant censure can be geuen what to make of hym. If

[Either Gardiner held contradictory opinions or he was a time-server.]

his doyngs & writynges were accordyng to his conscience, no man can rightlye say whether he was a right protestant or Papist. If he wrote otherwise then he thought, for feare, or to beare with time, then was he a double depe dissembler before God and man, to say & vnsay, to write & vnwrite, to sweare and forsweare, so as he did.

The Lords of the Council agree that Cranmer shall be sent to the Tower (ll. 87-92). He asks :

Is there no other way of mercy,
But I must needs to th' Tower, my Lords ?

The Bishop of Winchester answers slightingly, and calls for the Guard, to whom he commits Cranmer. Cranmer then replies :

Stay, good *my Lords,*
I haue a little yet to say. Looke there, my Lords ;
By vertue of that Ring, *I* take *my cause*
Out of the gripes of cruell men, *and* giue it   100
To a most Noble Iudge, the King my Maister.

At their interview on the night before the council-meeting, Henry bade Cranmer, "if no intreatie or reasonable request will serue, then deliuer vnto them this my ryng" (p. 497 above) ;

[Cranmer was to appeal from the Councell to the King.]

[*Foxe,* ii. 1759/2.] and saie vnto them : "if there be no "remedie, *my Lordes,* but that I must needes goe to the Tower, "then *I* reuoke *my cause* from you, *and* appeale *to* the Kynges "owne persone, by this his token vnto you all," . . .

Henry had foreseen what would happen. After waiting a "halfe hower" (see p. 499 above),

[The Archbyshop called before the Counsaile. The Counsaile being sette against ye Archbishop, hee sheweth the kynges ring & appealeth from them.]

[*Foxe,* ii. 1760/1] the Archbishop was called into the Counsaill Chamber : to whom was alledged, as before is rehearsed. The Archbishop aunswered in like sort as the kyng had aduised hym : & in the ende, when he perceiued that no maner of perswasion or intreatie could serue, he deliuered to them the Kynges rynge, reuoking his cause into the Kynges handes.

Recognizing the ring, Suffolk exclaims :

'Tis the right Ring, by Heau'n ┃   *I told* ye all,
When we *first* put *this* dangerous stone a rowling   104
'T*wold* fall vpon our selues.
    Norf.   *Doe you thinke*, my Lords,
The King will suffer but the little finger
Of *this man* to be vex'd ┃
    Cham.   'Tis now too certaine :
How *much more* is *his Life* in value with him ┃   108
Would I were fairely out on't ┃
    Crom.   My mind gaue me
In seeking *tales and* Informations
Against this man, . . .
Ye blew the fire that burnes ye : . . .

Foxe relates (ii. 1760/1) that, Cranmer having delivered to them
Henry's ring, and the

whole Counsaile beyng thereat somewhat amased, the Erle of
Bedford, with a loude voice, confirmyng his woordes with a solemne
othe, saied : "*when* you *first* began *this* matter, my Lordes, *I tolde*
"you what *would* come of it. *Doe you thinke* that *the Kyng will*
"*suffer this mannes finger to* ake ┃ *muche more* (I warrant you)
"wil he defende *his life* against brablyng varlettes. You doe but
"comber your selues to heare *tales &* fables *against* hym."

[The Earl of Bedford reminded the Council that he had warned them not to seek witness against Cranmer.]

Immediately after Cromwell's speech (l. 113) Henry enters,
"frowning on them, takes his Seate." The King sternly answers
(ll. 122-129) a flattering address from Gardiner (ll. 114-121), reassures
Cranmer (ll. 130-133), and then says :

I had *thought I had had men* of some vnderstanding
And wisedome *of my Councell ;* but *I finde* none.   136
Was it *discretion,* Lords, to let this man,
This good man, (few of you deserue that Title,)
This honest man, *wait* like a lowsie Foot-boy
At Chamber dore ┃ and one as great as *you* are ┃   140
Why, what a shame was this ┃ Did my *Commission*
Bid ye so farre forget your selues ┃ *I* gaue ye
Power, *as* he was *a Counsellour,* to *try him,*
Not as a Groome : there's *some of* ye, *I* see,   144
More out of Malice then Integrity,
Would trye him to the vtmost, had ye meane ;
Which ye shall neuer haue while I liue.
    Chan.   Thus farre,
My most dread Soueraigne, may it like your Grace,   148
To let my tongue excuse all. What was purpos'd
Concerning his Imprisonment, *was rather*
(If there be faith in men) *meant for his Tryall,*
And faire *purgation* to the world, *then malice,*   152
I'm sure, in me ┃
    Kin.   *Well, well, my Lords,* respect him ;

Take him, and vse him well, hee's worthy of it.
I will say thus much for him, *if a Prince*
May be beholding to a Subiect, I
Am, for his loue and seruice, so to him.
Make me no more adoe, but all embrace him.

After recording the Earl of Bedford's speech, Foxe proceeds thus (ii. 1760/1) :

[The Council surrendered Cranmer's matter to Henry's decision.]

And so, incontinently vpon the receipt of the kynges token, thei al rose, and caried to the king his ring; surrendering that matter, as the order and vse was, into his own handes.

The kinges wordes to the counsaile in defence of the Arch-bishop.

When thei wer all come to the kynges presence, his highnes, with a seuere countenaunce, said vnto them : "Ah, my lordes, *I* "*thought I had had* wiser *men of my counsaile* then now *I finde* "you. What *discretion was* this in you, thus to make the Primate "of the Realme, & one of you in office, to *waite at* the Counsail "*chamber dore* amongest seruyng men! You might haue con-"sidered that he was a Counseller as well as you, and you had no "suche *commission* of me so to handle hym. *I* was content that "you should *trie him as a Counseller*, and *not as a* meane subiect. "But now *I* well perceiue that things be doen against him "maliciously, and, if *some of* you might haue had your minds, you "*would* haue *tried him to the vttermost.* But I do you all to wit, "and protest, that *if a Prince maie bee beholdyng vnto his subiecte*"; and so (solem[n]ly laiyng his hande vpon his breaste) saied : "by "the faithe I owe to God, I take this man here, my Lorde of "Canterburie, to be of al other a moste faithfull subiecte vnto vs, "and one to whom we are muche beholding": giuyng hym greate

[The excuse offered by "one or twoo of the chiefest of the Counsaile."]

commendations otherwise. And with that one or twoo of the chiefest of the Counsaile, making their excuse, declared, that, in requesting his induraunce, it *was rather meante for his triall, and* his *purgation* against the common fame and sclaunder of the worlde, *then* for any *malice* conceiued against him : " *Well, well,* "*my Lordes,*" quoth the kyng, "*take hym and well vse hym,* as

The Lordes of the Coun-saile glad to bee friendes againe with the Arch-bishop.

"*he is worthie* to be, and *make no more ado.*" And with that euery man caught hym by the hand, and made faire weather of altogethers, whiche might easely be doen with that man.

Henry "once more" bids Gardiner embrace Cranmer; and, observing, as this command is obeyed, the Archbishop's "ioyfull teares," remarks (ll. 176-178):

> The *common* voyce, I see, is verified
> Of thee, which sayes thus : " *Doe my Lord of Canterbury*
> " *A shrewd turne, and* hee's *your friend* for euer."

According to Foxe (ii. 1756/1) Cranmer's forgiving disposition was so notorious

that it came into a *common* prouerbe : " *Do* vnto *my Lord of Canter-* "*bury* displeasure or *a shrewd turne, and* then you may be sure " to haue him *your frend* whiles he lyueth." [Cranmer's gentle nature renowned in a prouerb.]

Act V. sc. v.—In sc. iii., Act V., Henry desired Cranmer to be the godfather of " a faire young Maid that yet wants Baptisme" (l. 162); adding : "You shall haue two noble Partners with you; the old " Duchesse of Norfolke, and Lady Marquesse Dorset :" . . .

The return of the christening party to the Palace is set forth in the following stage direction, with which sc. v. opens :

> Enter Trumpets, sounding: Then two Aldermen, L. Maior, Garter, Cranmer, Duke of Norfolke with his Marshals Staffe, Duke of Suffolke, two Noblemen bearing great standing Bowles for the Christening Guifts: Then foure Noblemen bearing a Canopy, vnder which the Dutchesse of Norfolke, Godmother, bearing the Childe richly habited in a Mantle, &c., Traine borne by a Lady : Then followes the Marchionesse Dorset, the other Godmother, and Ladies. The Troope passe once about the Stage, and Garter speakes.

> *Gart.* Heauen, from thy endlesse *goodnesse, send prosperous life, long,* and euer happie, *to the high and Mighty Princesse of England, Elizabeth !*

> Flourish.   Enter King and Guard.

Addressing the godparents, Henry says (ll. 13-15) :

> My Noble Gossips, y'haue beene too Prodigall :
> I thanke ye *heartily ;* so shall this Lady,
> When she ha's so much English.

The christening

[*Hol.* iii. 934/2/5.   *Halle,* 805, 806.] was appointed on the wednesdaie next following [Elizabeth's birth on Sunday, Sept. 7, 1533]; and was accordinglie accomplished on the same daie, with all such solemne ceremonies as were thought conuenient. The god-father at the font was the lord archbishop of Canturburie, the god-mothers, the old dutches of Norffolke, & the old marchionesse [Date of Elizabeth's christening.] [Her godparents.]

Dorset, widowes;[1] and at the confirmation the ladie marchionesse
of Excester was godmother: the child was named Elizabeth.

*Hw. Hall.
Ox. vij.* [806.]
[The Lord
Mayor and
Aldermen
of London
present at
her christen-
ing.]
Upon the daie of the christening, the maior, sir Stephan
Peacocke, in a gowne of crimsin veluet, with his collar of S S, and
all the aldermen in scarlet, with collars and chaines, and all the
councell of the citie with them, tooke their barge after dinner, at
one of the clocke, and the citizens had another barge; and so
rowed to Greenwich, where were manie lords, knights, and gentlemen assembled.

When the procession to the church was formed

[The old
Duchess of
Norfolk
and the
Dukes of
Norfolk and
Suffolk were
in the pro-
cession to
the church.]
[*Hol.* iii. 934/2/47. *Halle,* 805, 806.] the old dutches of Norffolke bare the child in a mantell of purple veluet, with a long traine
furred with ermine. The duke of Norffolke with his marshall rod
went on the right hand of the said dutches, and the duke of
Suffolke on the left hand, and before them went the officers of
armes. The countesse of Kent bare the long traine of the childs
mantell; and betweene the countesse of Kent and the child went
the earle of Wilshire on the right hand, and the earle of Darbie
on the left hand, supporting the said traine: in the middest, ouer

*A canopie
borne ouer
the yoong
princesse.*
the said child, was borne a canopie by the lord Rochford, the
lord Husee, the lord William Howard, and by the lord Thomas
Howard the elder; after the child followed manie ladies and
gentlewomen. . . .

When the ceremonies and christening were ended, Garter,
[Garter's
proclama-
tion.]
cheefe king of armes, cried alowd, "God of his infinite *goodnesse*
"*send prosperous life & long to the high and mightie princesse of*
"*England, Elizabeth:*" & then the trumpets blew. Then the
*Rich gifts
giuen to the
princesse.*
archbishop of Canturburie gaue to the princesse a standing cup
of gold: the dutches of Norffolke gaue to hir a standing cup of
gold, fretted with pearle: the marchionesse of Dorset gaue three
gilt bolles, pounced, with a couer: and the marchionesse of
Excester gaue three standing bolles, grauen, all gilt, with a
[The pro-
cession
returned in
the same
order.]
couer. . . . [*Hol.* iii. 935/1/3. *Halle,* 806.] Then they set for-
wards, the trumpets going before in the same order towards the
kings palace, as they did when they came thitherwards, sauing

---

[1] *widowes*] Halle. *widow* Hol.

that the gifts that the godfather and the godmothers gaue were
borne before the child by foure persons, that is to saie: First, sir
Iohn Dudleie bare the gift of the ladie of Excester, the lord
Thomas Howard the yoonger bare the gift of the ladie of Dorset,
the lord Fitzwater bare the gift of the ladie of Norffolke,
and the earle of Worcester bare the gift of the archbishop of
Canturburie, . . .

Who bare the gifts presented to the princesse.

In this order they brought the princesse to the Q[ueen's]
chamber, & tarried there a while with the maior & his brethren
the aldermen, and at the last the dukes of Norffolke & Suffolke
came out from the K., thanking them *hartilie;* who commanded
them to giue thanks in his name: which being doone, with other
courtesies, they departed, & so went to their barges.

[Norfolk and Suffolk thanked the Lord Mayor and Aldermen in Henry's name.]

INDEX.

ABERGAVENNY, George Neville, Baron (1491—1535), arrested, 431

"ablements," habiliments, 415

"abrayded," started, 163

"accustomablie," habitually, 350

"adoption," acquiring, xiv.

Africa (Mahadiah), Tunis, 112

Aganippus, a prince of Gallia. *See* France, King of

Albany, Duke of (Maglanus), marries Gonorilla, 3; half of Britain bequeathed to him, *ib.*; rebels against Lear, and assigns him a portion to live on, 4; defeated and slain, 5

——, Robert Steward, Duke of, father of Murdach Steward, 132, 133

Albemarle (Aumerle), Edward Duke of (1397-99), becomes bail for Bolingbroke, 78; sent by Richard to make peace between Bolingbroke and Norfolk, 79; spent money in Richard's service, 81; officiates as high constable in the lists at Coventry; 86—88; retires to King's Langley, 92; brings reinforcements to Ireland, 99; his loyalty doubted, *ib.*; persuades Richard to linger in Ireland, 100, 102 n 2; returns with Richard, 106; deserts him, 109 n 1; accused by Bagot, 111; accepts Fitz-Walter's challenge, *ib.*; challenges Norfolk, 112; his mother, 121 n 1; deprived of his dukedom, 121, 122; reprobated by the commons, 130. *See* Rutland, Edward Earl of

Albergati, Nicholas, Cardinal of Santa Croce, counsels "a godlie peace," 234. (*Cp.* 1 *Hen. VI.,* V. i. 5)

Albret, Charles d'. *See* Constable of France

Alençon, John I., Duke of (1404-15), gives advice for the defence of France, 179; promises battle to Henry V., 184 n 2; encounters Henry, 195; slain, 195, 196

——, John II., Duke of (1415-76), relieves Orleans, 215, 216; present at Margaret's espousals, 243

Alexander the Mason denies the pope's authority in temporal matters, 56 n 3

"alongst," along, 98

"alow," low down, 356

"altogethers" = altogether, 504

"ands," ifs, 372

Angers (Angiers) delivered to Arthur, 46; taken

by Eleanor, 51; taken by John, *ib.*; Constance and Arthur flee to, 53; restored to John, *ib.*

Angus, George Douglas, Earl of, taken prisoner at Homildon, 132, 133

Anjou yields allegiance to Arthur, 46; Arthur's homage for, 52; possession of, demanded for Arthur, *ib.*; recovered by John, 59; ravaged by York and Somerset, 230; ceded to René, 244; a key of Normandy, 245

——, René, Duke of (1434-80), 182 n 4; his daughter Margaret's marriage arranged, 238; his kingly style, 241; present at Margaret's espousals, 243; could not pay for her journey to England, 245; advises her to discard Gloucester's authority, 260; visited by her, 312 n 1; ransoms her, 342

Anne (Neville), wife of Richard III., married to Edward (Lancastrian) Prince of Wales, 318, 346; date of her marriage to Richard, 345, 346; crowned, 387; rumour of her death spread by Richard, 388; dies, 396; eclipse of the sun at her death, 396 n 3

"antecessors," ancestors, 309

Antelope, Henry V.'s pursuivant, sent to Charles VI., 178

"apert, in," openly, 293

Apollo, Lear's oath by, 5 n 1

"appaire," deteriorate, 249

"appent," belonged, 129 n 2

Armagnac, John IV., Count of, proffers his daughter in marriage to Henry VI., 235

Armourer, an, appeached of treason by his servant, 248; who overcomes him in a judicial duel, 260, 261; his servant was perjured, 261 n 1

Arras, representatives of England and France meet at, 226; and are exhorted to make peace, 234; terms proposed at, 240

Arthur. *See* Britany, Arthur Duke of

Articles devised by the Percies, 135; which win approval but no help, 136; presented to Henry IV., 144

Arundel, Richard Fitz-Alan, Earl of (1376-97), rebels against Richard II., 94; careful in choosing soldiers, 143

——, Thomas Fitz-Alan, Earl of (1400-15), joins Bolingbroke's invasion, 96; "broke

ARU

from the Duke of Exeter," 97; goes with
Bolingbroke to meet York, 102; "let sacke"
a man ordained to murder Prince Henry, 213
Arundel, William Fitz-Alan, Earl of (1524—44),
in the coronation procession of Anne Boleyn,
485. (His place is filled by the dramatic
"Surrey")
—— (or Fitz-Alan), Thomas, Archbishop of
Canterbury, persuades Bolingbroke to dethrone Richard II., 96; joins Bolingbroke's
invasion, ib.; goes with Bolingbroke to meet
York, 102; meets Richard at Flint Castle,
109 n 1; scroll of Richard's abdication delivered to, 114; places Bolingbroke in "the
regall throne," 115; lends money to Henry
IV., 159 n 1
Arviragus, son of the legendary Cymbeline, 7;
a British prince named A., 7 n 3; Spenser
made A. a brother of Cymbeline, 10 n 1
Ascension Day (May 27, 1199), date of John's
coronation, 45; prophecy that John would
not be king on, in 1213 ("quod non foret
rex in die Dominica Ascensionis."—M. Paris,
ii. 535), 62
"aslope," indirectly, 379
Aspall, Robert, tries to save Rutland, 297, 298
"assaie, take the," taste the food, 126
"assayled," assoiled, 188
Athol, Walter Steward, Earl of, taken prisoner
at Homildon, 132
Audley, Sir Thomas, 485. See Chancellor, Lord
Augustus knights the legendary Cymbeline, 7,
8; prepares to invade the Britons, who refused tribute, 7; turns his arms against the
Pannonians and Dalmatians, 8; the British
princes seek his amity, 9; sends an ambassador
to Cymbeline, ib.
Aumerle. See Albemarle, Rutland, and York
Aurelius Ambrosius borne to battle in a litter,
226. See Uter
Aurora Borealis, (?) appearance of, 61 n 1. Cp.
137
"Austria," a composite character, 53 n 1. See
Limoges, 48

Bagot, Sir William, talks with Norfolk about
Gloucester's death, 83; his tower a lodging
for Richard II., 86; farms England, 90;
gives advice for resisting Bolingbroke, 98;
flees to Ireland, 100; accuses Aumerle, 110,
111; hated by the commons, 130
Baker, John, reports Cardinal Beaufort's last
words, 269
Baldud (Bladud), father of Leir, 1
Ball, John, exhorts the villeins at Blackheath,
272
Banaster, Humphrey (Ralph), betrays Henry
Duke of Buckingham, 451
Bangor, Archdeacon or Dean of (David Daron),
tripartite division of England framed at his
house, 138
"banquetwise," as for a banquet, 441
Banquo, thane of Lochaber, a fictitious person,
xiii.; supposed ancestor of the Stewards, 19,

BED

35; wounded by rebels, 19; complains to Duncan, ib.; sent against Macdowald, 20; commands the rear in the war with Sueno, 21;
defeats the Danes sent by Canute, 22; meets
the weird sisters, 23, 24; jests with Macbeth
about their prophecy, 24, 25; connives at
Duncan's murder, 25; murdered by Macbeth's
order, 33
Bar, Edward Duke of, promises battle to Henry
V., 184 n 2; slain, 196
Bardolf, Thomas Bardolf, Baron, conspires
against Henry IV., 151; invades England
and is defeated, 157
"bare him sore," had a grudge against him,
349
Barkloughly (Q1 and F1. Barclowlie Hol.
Harlech Williams conj.), Richard II. lands
there, 106
Barons form a league against John at Bury St.
Edmunds, 66, 67; excommunicated by Innocent, 68; offer the English crown to Lewis,
69 (cp. 67, 68); their ruin plotted by Lewis,
72; become averse to Lewis, 72, 73; give
allegiance to Henry III., 75, 76
"baste," bastardly, 269
"Battes" (clubs), Parliament of, 221
Bay trees wither, 103
Bayly beheaded for knowing Cade's base lineage,
276
Bayonne, Bishop of. See Gabriel de Grammont,
464 n 3
Beaufort, Henry, Bishop of Lincoln (1398—
1405), Winchester (1405—1447), and Cardinal
(1427), returns with Richard II. from Ireland,
106; informs parliament of Henry V.'s projected war with France, 168 n 2; appointed
guardian of Henry VI., 209; accused by
Gloucester of plotting Henry's abduction, ib.;
dissension betwixt him and Gloucester, 212;
orders the Tower to be kept against Gloucester,
212, 213; who accuses him of plotting Prince
Henry's murder, 213; and obstructing London
bridge, 220, 221; truce between, and Gloucester, 222; godfather to Henry VI., 224;
crowns Henry VI. at Paris, 228; made a
cardinal, 235, 236; conspires against Gloucester, 246; accused of selling offices, 250;
his character, 269; last words, 269, 270
"Beaumont," Earl of, slain at Agincourt, 196.
Not in Monstrelet's lists or in Harleian MS.,
782. (See "Fois" and "Lestrake") Perhaps Henri II., Comte de Blamont, is meant
(Mons. iii. 349)
Beaumont, Henry Beaumont, Baron, joins
Bolingbroke, 98
——, John Beaumont, Viscount, arrests
Gloucester, 264
Bedford, John Duke of, not at Agincourt, 197;
at the siege of Melun, 201 n 1; secures the
Normans' allegiance to Henry VI., 206 n 1;
at Henry V.'s death-bed, 208; appointed
Regent of France, ib.; appoints Suffolk to
besiege Orleans, 214; petition to, from Eleanor
Mortimer, 219 n 5; godfather to Henry VI.,

Bri

52; reconciled to John, *ib.*; flees from John, 53; does homage to John, and returns with Philip, 54; takes Mirabeau, 58; captured by John, 59; demands possession of Richard's dominions, *ib.*; imprisoned, *ib.*; persuades Hubert de Burgh to save him from blinding, 60; his blinding and death rumoured, 61; rumour of his death contradicted, 63; various accounts of his death, *ib.*; his murder attributed to John, 70 (cp. 61 *n* 1)

Brittany, Constance Duchess of, entrusts Arthur to Philip, 47; repudiates her second husband and marries Guy de Thouars, 53; dies, 61 *n* 1; accused John of Arthur's murder, *ib.*

——, John V., Duke of (1364–99), Brest surrendered to, 84, 95; aids Bolingbroke, 96

——, John VI., Duke of (1399—1442), at the council summoned after Henry V. crossed the Somme, 182

——, Francis I., Duke of (1442-50), present at Margaret of Anjou's espousals, 243

——, Francis II., Duke of (1458-88), receives the earls of Pembroke and Richmond, 329, 330; Richmond brought up in his court, 417

Brocas, Sir Leonard, conspirator against Henry IV., beheaded, 127

"broch," *sb.*, spit, 23

Buckingham, Humphrey Stafford, Duke of (1444-60), conspires against Gloucester, 246; when made duke, 246 *n* 3; present at Gloucester's arrest, 264; sent to York before the battle of St. Albans, 284 *n* 1; wounded at St. Albans, 290

——, Henry Stafford, Duke of (1460-83), aids Gloucester in removing the queen's friends from Edward V., 351, 352; aids Gloucester to get possession of Edward at Stony Stratford, 354; asserts that York needed no sanctuary, 359, 360; was he in Richard's confidence from the first? 361; courts Hastings, 362; promises made him by Richard, *ib.*; takes part in Richard's secret council, 363; his speech at the Guildhall on Richard's claim to the crown, 377—379; was received with silence, 381; accepts packed applause as an answer, 382; invites Richard to assume the crown, 383—385; vainly demands the earldom of Hereford, 392 (cp. 362, 450 *n* 2); relates his wrongs to Morton, 393; rebels, 397; promised to support Richmond, 398 *n* 1; stopped by a flood, 403; his army deserts him, 404; beheaded, 410; meant to have stabbed Richard, 439; betrayed by Banaster, 451

——, Edward Stafford, Duke of (1486—1521), escorts Francis I. in the vale of Andren, 425; grudged the charges of attending the kings' interview, 426; hated Wolsey, *ib.*; arrested, 430; Knyvet's evidence against, 436—439; had dismissed Knyvet, 437; tried and found guilty, 447, 448; Wolsey blamed for his death, 448; denies that he was a traitor, 450; the edge of the axe turned towards him, *ib.*; says that he is now "but Edward Bohune,"

Cae

ib.; his dukedom restored by Henry VII., 451

Balmer, Sir William, his imprisonment by Wolsey, 426; Buckingham's threat in connection therewith, 433, 439

Burdett, Thomas, executed, 342 *n* 3; and why, 375, 375 *n* 2

Burgundy, John the Fearless, Duke of (1404-19), murders Lewis Duke of Orleans, 48; murdered, 199 *n* 3; conferred with Henry V. at Meulan, 200; was the "let" of Henry's desires, *ib.*

——, Philip the Good, Duke of (1419-67), offers peace to Henry V., 199; concludes a truce with Henry, *ib.*; accompanies Henry's ambassadors to Troyes, 200; swears to observe the treaty of Troyes, 203; makes peace with Charles VII., 226; besieged Calais, 226 *n* 1; obtains Orleans's release, and why, 227, 228; his excuse for deserting Henry VI., 229; receives the Duchess of York's sons, 303

——, Charles the Bold (*le téméraire*), Duke of 1467-77), secretly aids Edward IV.'s restoration, 330

Bushy, Sir John, spokesman for Richard II. regarding Bolingbroke's appeal, 79; announces the decision to settle Bolingbroke's appeal by battle, 82; reads the sentences of Bolingbroke and Norfolk, 88; farms England, 90; gives advice for resisting Bolingbroke, 98; flees to Bristol, 100; beheaded there, 104; his character, 129; flatters Richard II. 130; hated by the commons, *ib.*

"buskling," bustling, noise, 28

Butler, Dame Eleanor, betrothed to Edward IV., 377 *n* 3

Buttes, Dr. William, tells Henry that Cranmer waits outside the council-chamber, 499

"by," about, concerning, 363, 371, 389

Cade (*alias* Mend-all), John, date of his rebellion, 265; called himself Mortimer, 266; a feeler for York, 266, 282 *n* 2; defeats the Staffords, 273; dons Sir H. Stafford's brigandine, *ib.*; releases prisoners, *ib.*; sends a supplication to Henry, 273, 274; confers with Henry's messengers, 274; lodges at the White Hart in Southwark, *ib.*; robs, 275 *n* 1; enters London unopposed, 276 *n* 2; strikes his sword on London stone, 276; kills those who knew his base lineage, *ib.*; tries to seize London bridge, 276, 277; the dramatic C. and Wat Tyler, 277, 278; proposes to abolish fifteenths, 278; puts to death Lord Saye and Sir James Cromer, 278, 279; makes their heads kiss, 279; his followers disperse and he flies, 280, 281; reward offered for him, 281, 284; date of his death, 283; slain by Iden, 284

Caesar, C. Julius, imposes a tribute on Britain, 9 *n* 2; calls Britain "another world," 11; his ships wrecked, 12; his good luck fails him in Britain, 12 *n* 1; the British account of his invasions, 12, 13; loses his sword, 13

CLE

eses, 319; marries Isabel, elder daughter of Warwick, 320; invades England with Warwick, 322 n 3; aids Warwick in capturing Edward, 323; releases Henry from the Tower, 326; made governor of England and heir to the crown in remainder, 327; urges Warwick to make peace with Edward, 334; his reconciliation with his brothers, 335, 336; had been urged not to supplant his own lineage, 336; helps to murder Prince Edward, 340; probable date of his arrest, 342 n 3; the "G" prophecy a rumoured cause of his death, 344; his marriage to Mary of Burgundy opposed by Edward, ib.; hated by the queen's kindred, 344, 345; put to death, 346; his fortune, 422

"clepyd," named, 221

Clifford, Thomas Clifford, Baron (1422–55), "old Clifford," 289 n 2; slain at St. Albans, 290

——, John Clifford, Baron (1455–61), at Wakefield, 296; kills Rutland, 298; insults York's corpse, 299; defeats the Yorkists at Ferrybridge, 305; slain, 307

Clifton, Sir John, slain at Shrewsbury, 147

Cobham, Edward Brooke, Baron, a supporter of York's claim, 283; joins the Yorkist lords, 296

——, Eleanor. See Gloucester, Eleanor Duchess of

—— of Sterborough, Reginald Cobham, Baron, joins Bolingbroke's invasion, 96

"Coinacke," Cognac, 48

Coint, Francis, joins Bolingbroke's invasion, 96

Colchester, William. See Westminster, Abbot of

Colevile of the Dale, Sir John, beheaded for rebelling against Henry IV., 155; in arms at Topcliffe, 155 n 2

Collingbourne, William, ridicules Richard III. in a couplet, 347

"Colon," Cologne, 254

Constable of France, the (Charles d'Albret), fortifies towns against Henry V., 179; promises battle to Henry, 184 n 2; encamps at Agincourt, 185; slain, 196

Constance. See Brittany, Constance Duchess of

Copeland, John, captures David II., 172

Cordeilla's answer to Lear, 3; disinherited by him, ib.; marries Aganippus, 4; receives Lear kindly, 5; made his sole heiress, and returns with him to Britain, ib.; succeeds Lear, 6; her nephews rebel against her, ib.; she slays herself, ib.

Cordelia, the name so spelt in the Faerie Queene, 2 n 1

Cornwall, Duke of (Henninus), marries Regan, 3; half of Britain bequeathed to him, ib.; rebels against Lear and assigns him a portion to live on, 4; defeated and slain, 5

"counterpane," counterpart of a deed, 124

Courtenay, Edward Courtenay, Baron, aids Buckingham's rebellion, 403

——, Peter, Bishop of Exeter, aids Buckingham's rebellion, 403

DES

Courtiers return from France with French predilections, 439, 440

Cranmer, Thomas, Archbishop of Canterbury, in favour of Henry's divorce, 478; made archbishop, ib.; on the date of Anne Boleyn's marriage, 479 n 1; divorces Katharine, 483, 484; crowns Anne Boleyn, 486; beloved by Henry, 494; accused to Henry of spreading heresy, 494, 495, 500; his committal to the Tower urged, and licensed by Henry, 496, 500, 501; instructed by Henry how to meet his foes, 496, 497, 502; obliged to wait outside the council-chamber, 499; shows Henry's ring to the council, 502; and justifies Bedford's warning, 503; his placable temper was proverbial, 505; godfather to the princess Elizabeth, 505

Crema, John of, legate, taken with a strumpet, 475 n 3

"Croces mors," name of Cæsar's sword, 13 n 2

Cromer, Sir James, beheaded and his head borne on a pole, 279

Cromwell, Thomas, in Wolsey's service, 481; enters Henry's service, ib.; faithful to Wolsey, ib.; made master of the jewel house, 487; master of the rolls and Henry's secretary, 493; favoured the Protestants, 501; his chief enemy was Gardiner, ib.

"cullions," testicles, 148

Cymbeline, authentic particulars concerning, 6; the legendary C. knighted by Augustus, 7, 8; who sends an ambassador to him, 9; refuses tribute to the Romans, 10 n 1

Cymbeline, names in Hol. occurring there, 17, 18

"damnific," injure, 385

"damning," censuring, 355

Danes, the, defeated at Loncarty, 16, 17; drugged with "mekilwoort," 21 n 2; their dead buried at Inchcolm, 22; make peace with the Scots, 23

Daron, David. See Bangor, Archdeacon of, 138

Dauphin, Guichard, seigneur de Jaligny, Grand Master of the King's Household, ("Souverain Maitre de l'Hotel du Roi."—Anselme, viii. 346), confounded by Shakspere with the Dauphin, 183 n 1; slain, 196

David II., King of Scots, taken prisoner at Neville's Cross, 172

Davy, John, armourer's servant, appeaches his master of treason, 248 n 3

Delacourt, John, arrested, 430; hears Hopkins's prophecy, 436, 437; brought forth at Buckingham's trial, 447

Denny, Sir Anthony, requires Cranmer's attendance on Henry, 496

Derby, Henry Earl of, joins a conspiracy against Richard II., 82; was a crusader in Prussia, not in Barbary, 112, 113; anti-clerical in youth, 122; made a pilgrimage to Jerusalem, 160 n 1. See Hereford, Henry Duke of

Despencer, Thomas Despencer, Baron, conspires

ELI

Constance, 47; takes Angers, 51; scandal about her, ib.; besieged in Mirabeau, 58; dies, 61
Elizabeth (widow of Sir John Grey, afterwards married to Edward IV.), a suitor to Edward, 310; refuses to be his paramour, 311; is betrothed to him, 312; her son Edward born in sanctuary, 324; troubled by the "G" prophecy, 344; hated Edward's kindred, 344, 345; persuaded to lessen her son's escort to London, 352, 353; hears that his journey had been interrupted, 354; takes sanctuary with her children, 355; receives the great seal from Rotherham, 355, 356; answers his advice to part with York, 360; suffers York to go, ib.; accused of witchcraft by Gloucester, 371; union between Richmond and her daughter proposed to her, 398, 399; beguiled by Richard III.'s promises, 400
——, eldest daughter of Edward IV., project for her marriage to Richard III., 388, 399, 400, 401; Richmond swears to marry her, 399
——, daughter of Henry VIII., born, 498; her god-parents, 505, 506; bearers of her canopy in her christening procession, 506 (Baron Rochford, ? Baron Hussey of Sleford, Baron Howard of Effingham, and Lord Thomas Howard); bearer of her train, ib. (Anne, Countess of Kent); her proclamation, ib.; gifts to, ib.
Ely, Bishop of, 167 n 1 (John Fordham)
English, the, given to gormandizing, 42; paid for food on the march to Calais, 184; can't fight on an empty stomach, 185 n 3; their camp and the Romans' compared, 186; their demeanour on the eve of Agincourt, 187; silent when marching to their camping-ground, ib.; number of, at Agincourt, 189; search for wounded French after the battle, 195; number of, slain at Agincourt, 196; repulse Dunois's sally from Orleans, 210; adopt French habits, 439, 440
Ermengarde of Lorraine (170), ancestress of Lewis IX. through Alix of Namur, whose grand-daughter Isabelle married Philip II., King of France
Erpingham, Sir Thomas, joins Bolingbroke's invasion, 96; begins the battle of Agincourt, 187
"Esperance! Percy!" (battle-cry of the Percies), 145
"Everwyk," York, 152 n 2
Exeter, John Holland, Duke of (1397-99), had the custody of Thomas Fitz-Alan, 97; returns with Richard II. from Ireland, 106; accompanies Richard to Conway, 107; deprived of his dukedom, 121, 122; reprobated by the commons, 130. See Huntingdon
——, Thomas Beaufort (Earl of Dorset, 1412-16; Duke of Exeter, 1416-26), ambassador to France, 178 (see Bouratier, 179); captain of Harfleur, 181; a negotiator of the treaty of Troyes, 200; (?) present at Henry V.'s betrothal to Katharine, 201 n 1; attends on Henry V.'s funeral, 205 n 4; appointed guardian of Henry VI., 209

FOI

Exeter, Henry Holland, Duke of (1447-78), his ship intercepts Suffolk, 270; advises Margaret to oppose York, 294, 295; at Wakefield, 298; flees from Towton, 306 n 2; with Warwick at Barnet, 335
"Exeter," the dramatic, 342
Exton, Sir Piers of, moved by Bolingbroke's words to slay Richard, 125; murders Richard, 126; his remorse, ib.

"facundious," eloquent, 247 n 2
Famine, one of Bellona's handmaidens, 166
"fastely," stedfastly, 254
Fastolfe, Sir John, lieutenant of Harfleur, 181; withdraws from the battle of Patay, 207, 208; a K.G., 208; joined with others in the siege of Orleans, 214; the Garter restored to, 229
Fauconberg, the bastard (son of William Neville, Baron Fauconberg, afterwards Earl of Kent), made vice-admiral, 294
Faulconbridge, Philip, collects money from the clergy, 47; his inheritance claimed by his younger brother, 48; chooses to be called Richard's bastard, ib.; historic parallels of his choice, 48—60
——, Sir Robert, (?) ambassador to the Emperor, 50
Fauquembergue, Waleran Count of, holds his men together at Agincourt, 193; defeated and slain, ib., 196
"faytoure," rogue, 254
"feare," terrify, 218
"fensed," (?) was protected by a mail-coat, or "feinted," flinched, 424
Ferrers of Chartley, Walter Devereux, Baron, slain at Bosworth field, 421
Fife, Murdoch Steward, Earl of, taken prisoner at Homildon, 132, 133; wrongly called "eldest son to" Douglas, 132 n 1; was Earl of Menteith, 132 n 3; delivered to Henry IV. by the Percies, 133
Fire, one of Bellona's handmaidens, 166
Fisher, John, Bishop of Rochester, Katharine's counsel, 457
Fitz-Alans, they and the Stewards descended from Alan (temp. Hen. I.), 35 n 2
Fitz-Walter, Walter Fitz-Walter, Baron, appeals Aumerle of treason, 111; challenged by Surrey, ib.; replies to Surrey, 112
Fitzwilliam, Thomas, recorder of London, rehearses Buckingham's speech, 381; present at Baynard's Castle, 386
Fleance, son of Banquo, a fictitious person, xiii; escapes Macbeth's plot, and flees to Wales, 33; in the genealogy of the Stewards, 35
"flix," flux, dysentery, 182
"flyttand Wod," Birnam Wood, 42 n 1
"Fois" (Foyes F.), Earl of, slain at Agincourt, 193. No Comte de Foix is mentioned in Monstrelet's lists (iii. 348—356). The list given in Harleian MS. 782, fol. 48 verso, col. 2 (quoted in Nicolas's Agincourt, ed. 2, p. 367), places "The Countie de fois" among the slain

GOD

V., 346, 347; fosters strife in his brother's court, 347, 348; intrigues with Buckingham and Hastings to remove the queen's friends from Edward V., 351—353; gets possession of Edward at Stony Stratford, 354; asks Rotherham to bring York from sanctuary, 356; receives York joyfully, 360; was Buckingham in his confidence from the first? 361; seeks to win Hastings, 362; his promises to Buckingham, ib.; held secret councils, 363; calls Hastings to the coronation council, 367; asks for strawberries and leaves the council, 370, 371; returns and denounces Hastings, 371, 372; tells the Londoners that Hastings had plotted his death, 374; was the image of his father, 380; invited to assume the crown, 383—385; his answer, 385; accepts the crown, 386. See Richard III.

"Gods blessed ladie, by," Edward IV.'s oath, 312

Gonorilla, her answer to Lear, 3; marries Maglanus, ib.; diminishes Lear's retinue, 4

Gough (or Goche), Matthew, obtains news of the French in Le Mans, 216, 217; appointed to assist the Londoners against Cade, 275; slain, 277; his military renown, ib.

Grammont, Gabriel de, Bishop of Tarbes, questioned the Princess Mary's legitimacy, 464 n 3

Grand-Pré, Edward Count of, slain at Agincourt, 196

Great Chamber, the, in Westminster Palace, Prince Henry's peril there, 213. See addition, p. xxiii

Greene, John, brings Brakenbury an order to murder Richard III.'s nephews, 389; reports Brakenbury's refusal to Richard, ib. Cp. 390 n 2

——, Sir Henry, farms England, 90; gives advice for resisting Bolingbroke, 98; flees to Bristol, 100; beheaded there, 104; hated by the commons, 130

Grey of Ruthin, Reginald, Baron, warred upon by Glendower, 105; defeated by Glendower, 137; and imprisoned, 258; confounded with Sir Edmund Mortimer, ib. See correction, p. xxiii

Grey, Sir Richard, arrested by Gloucester and Buckingham, 354, 356; sent to Pomfret and beheaded, 355

——, Sir Thomas, treason of, made public, 173 n 3; found guilty, ib.; his conspiracy detected, 174; led to doom himself, 174 n 1; was of the privy council, 175; says that he was bribed by France, 176; doomed by Henry, 176, 177

Griffith (Griffin Richardes), leads Katharine out of the court at Black-Friars, 461

"Grimbaut briga," Grimbald Bridge, 157

"groundlie," solidly, 377

Gruoch, Macbeth's wife, gives Kirkness to the Culdees, xiii

Gualo (Walo) tries to prevent Lewis from invading England, 69; visits John, 70; present at the conclusion of peace with Lewis, 75; a party to the treaty of peace with Lewis, 77

HEN

Guiderius, son of the legendary Cymbeline, rebels against the Romans, 10

Guildford, Richard, aids Buckingham's rebellion, 403

——, Sir Henry, regulated Wolsey's banquets, 441, 442

"Gun-stones," cannon-balls, 173 n 1

"hails," pavilions, 192

"Haliwell" (Holy Well, afterwards Sadler's Wells), 280

Harlech Castle, 106 n 1. Richard II. landed near? See Barkloughly

"Harnesie," Hornsey, 367

Hastings, a pursuivant, meets Lord Hastings on Tower wharf, 366

Hastings, William Hastings, Baron (1461—83), flees with Edward IV. from England, 235, 326; helps to murder Prince Edward, 340; his reconciliation with the queen's friends, 349; aids Gloucester in removing the queen's friends from Edward V., 351, 352; takes part in the coronation council, 363; served not the secret council while Catesby attended it, ib.; trusted and advanced Catesby, 363, 364; despises Stanley's dream, 365; refuses to make Richard king, ib.; had been endangered by Rivers's accusation, 366; of which he cheerily reminds a pursuivant, 366, 367; sent for by Gloucester, 367; talks with a priest on his way to the Tower, ib.; kept Jane Shore, 372; denounced by Gloucester and beheaded, 372, 373 (see 368 n 2); omen of his fate, 373; a proclamation of his virtuous life, ib.; prepared before his death, 377

——, Edward Hastings, Baron (1497—1506), married the heiress of Lord Hungerford, 319 n 2

Hay and his sons check the Scots' flight at Loncarty, 16

Henninus. See Cornwall, Duke of

Henry IV., his first expedition against Glendower, 105; his coronation-day, 119; the crown entailed upon his heirs, ib.; the abbot of Westminster's conspiracy against, 122—124; is revealed to him by Rutland, 124; complains of peril from Richard, 125; flees from Windsor, 127; present at Richard's funeral, 128; demands the Percies' Scottish prisoners, 133; refuses to ransom Sir Edmund Mortimer, 134; threatens Henry Percy, 134 n 5; ignorant of the Percies' conspiracy, 135; why he would not ransom the Earl of March (i. e. Sir Edmund Mortimer), 135, 136; his second and third expedition against Glendower, 138; his realm partitioned, 138, 139; prophesied of as the moldwarp, 139; distrusts his son Henry, but is reassured, 140; disgraces Prince Henry, 141; his rapid advance against Hotspur, 142; offers terms to the Percies, 143; reads the Percies' articles and offers battle, 144; relieves his men at Shrewsbury, 146; withdrawn from the main attack at Shrewsbury, ib.; breaks the enemy's ranks, 147; felled by Douglas, ib.; again

Hen

valiantly, *ib.* ; takes Warkworth, 149, 150; Scrope and Mowbray brought as prisoners to him, 155 ; struck with leprosy, 155 *n* 3 (*cp.* 160); loses consciousness, *ib.* ; vexed with sickness, 156 ; fears dissension between Prince Henry and Clarence, *ib.* ; his crown removed by Prince Henry, 158 ; dies, 159 ; his preparations for a crusade, 159, 160, 160 *n* 1; for an expedition to France, 159 *n* 1 ; his death caused by apoplexy, 160 ; taken with his last sickness at Edward the Confessor's shrine, *ib.* ; died in the Jerusalem Chamber, *ib.* ; had made a pilgrimage to Jerusalem, 160 *n* 1; his person and character, 164 (*cp.* 142, last sentence of excerpt); bill for disendowing the clergy in his reign, 167 ; enjoined by the Pope to have prayer made for Richard II.'s soul, 188

Henry V., chooses wise counsellors after his coronation, 161 ; calls his first parliament, 163, 164; his coronation, 164 ; banishes his former misleaders, *ib.* ; besieges Rouen, 165; his answer to an orator's plea for Rouen, 166 (*cp.* 165 *n* 3); summons parliament to Leicester, 167 ; advised to claim the crown of France, 168—172; his dying declaration that his war with France was lawful, 168 *n* 3; promised a large subsidy from the clergy, 171, 172 ; advised to conquer Scotland, 172 ; receives tennis-balls from the Dauphin, 173 ; conspiracy against, detected, 174 ; dooms the traitors, 176, 177; encourages his lords, 177 ; lands near Harfleur, 177, 178; urges Charles VI. to resign France peaceably, 178; gives audience to the French proposals for peace, 179 ; grants a truce to Harfleur, 180 ; Harfleur surrendered to, 181 ; sacks Harfleur, *ib.* ; makes Exeter (Dorset) captain of Harfleur, *ib.* ; colonizes Harfleur with English folk, 181 *n* 1 ; resolves on a march to Calais, 181, 182 ; crosses the Somme, 182 ; was to be borne captive in a chariot, 182, 183; crosses the Ternoise, 183 ; executes a soldier for stealing a pyx, 184 ; forbids theft and violence, *ib.* ; pays for food, *ib.* ; answers Montjoy's defiance, 185 ; orders silence on the march to the camping-ground, 187 ; removes Richard II.'s body to Westminster, 188 ; gives alms and founds chantries on Richard's behalf, *ib.* ; speech before the battle attributed to, 190 ; refuses to fix his ransom, 191 ; overthrows the French rearward, 192 ; his camp robbed, *ib.* ; orders his men to slay their prisoners, 192, 193 ; his men renew the battle, 193 ; bids the lingering French fight or decamp, 194 ; questions Montjoy, *ib.* ; names the battle, *ib.* ; date of the battle, 195 ; grants burial to the French dead, *ib.* ; encounters Alençon, *ib.* ; gives thanks to God for his victory, 196, 197; reaches Calais, 197 ; his return to France in 1417, *ib.* ; lands at Dover after a rough passage, 197, 198 ; his welcome at Blackheath, 198 ; his humility, *ib.* ; peace offered to him by Philip the Good, 199 ; concludes a truce

Hen

with Philip, *ib.* ; sends ambassadors to Troyes, 199, 200 ; his marriage with Katharine arranged, 200 ; made heir of France, *ib.*; conference with, at Meulan, *ib.* ; snubs the "let" of his desires (John the Fearless), 200, 201 ; at Troyes when the treaty was revised, 201 ; falls in love with Katharine at Meulan, 201 *n* 3 ; styled heir of France, 202 ; affianced to Katharine, *ib.* ; date of his marriage, 202 *n* 3 ; swears to observe the treaty of Troyes, 203 ; his bodily powers, and character, 203, 204 ; military skill, 204 ; aspect and speech, 205 ; an example to princes, *ib.* ; his funeral, 205 *n* 4 ; his dying injunctions and advice, 208, 209 ; prophecy touching his son, 224

Henry VI., guardians of, 209 ; knights Richard Duke of York, 223 (*cp. n* 2) ; birth of, at Windsor, 223, 224 ; his godparents, 224 ; prophecy about, *ib.* ; crowned at Paris, 228 ; deserted by Burgundy, 229 ; loses Paris, 237 (*cp.* 205 *n* 5); his marriage to Margaret arranged, 238 ; espoused to her by Suffolk, 243 ; his character, 249 ; date of his coronation at Westminster, 259 *n* 4 ; begins to govern, *ib.* ; banishes Suffolk, 268, 269 ; receives a supplication from Cade, 273, 274 ; marches against him, 274 ; retires to Kenilworth, *ib.* ; tries Cade's followers, 281, 282 ; marches against York, 285 ; sends envoys to York, *ib.* ; becomes insane, 286 *n* 1, 290 ; defeated at St. Albans, 288, 289 ; reconciles the Yorkist and Lancastrian parties, 290 ; defeated at Northampton, *ib.* ; in custody of Norfolk and Warwick, 295, 302 ; released by the Yorkists' defeat at St. Albans, 302, 303 ; knights his son, 303 ; his presence brought defeat, 304 ; flees from Towton, 306 ; justified his right to reign, 309 ; returns secretly to England, *ib.* ; arrested and sent to the Tower, *ib.* ; had been in Scotland, 312 ; his regnal years, 313, 314 ; deposed by popular vote, 315 ; restored, 326, 327 ; his parliament attaints Edward and makes Clarence heir in remainder, 327 ; prophesies that Richmond shall be king, 329 ; again imprisoned, 333 ; date of his death, 340 *n* 3 ; his murderer supposed to be Gloucester, 341 ; his corpse bled at his funeral, 345

—— VII. restored the dukedom to Buckingham, 451

—— VIII. meets Francis I. in the vale of Andren, 425 ; silences the French ambassador, 427 ; tax of a sixth demanded for him, 431, 432 ; repudiates the tax, 433, 434 ; his answer to Wolsey's accusations of Buckingham, 435 (*cp. Hen. VIII.* I. ii. 211—213) ; a rumour that his marriage was unlawful, 452 ; bids the lord mayor silence such talk, *ib.* ; takes steps to have the matter sifted, 452—454 ; desires that Katharine should have the best counsel, 454 ; called into court, 458 ; Katharine's appeal to, 458—460; commends her, 462 ; his reasons for submitting the lawfulness of his marriage to trial, 464, 465 ; suspects that the legates mean to do nothing,

466; sends them to Katharine, *ib.*; in love with Anne Boleyn, 470; angered by Wolsey's secret opposition to his divorce, 470, 471; by chance sees Ruthal's private accounts, 472, 473; sends to Wolsey for the great seal, 474; marries Anne Boleyn, 479, 480; changes the name of York Place, 486, 487; attached to Cranmer, 494; is told that Cranmer spreads heresy, 494, 495, 500; licenses Cranmer's committal to the Tower, 495; instructs Cranmer how to meet the accusers, 496, 497, 502; hears that Cranmer waits outside the council-chamber, 499; rebukes the council for insulting Cranmer, 504; to whom he is much beholden, *ib.*; bids the counsellors be friends with Cranmer, *ib.*; sends thanks to the lord mayor for attending Elizabeth's christening, 507

Herbert, Sir Walter, in arms for Richard III., 408

Hereford, Henry, Duke of (1397–99), appeals Norfolk of treason, 78; bail taken for him, *ib.*; refuses to make peace with Norfolk, 79, 81; his specific charges against Norfolk, 80; casts down his gage, 81; day and place of battle appointed him, 82; date of his exile, 82 *n* 1; takes leave of Richard II. near Coventry, 86; arms for the battle, *ib.*; enters the lists, 87; his spear delivered to him by Surrey, 88; sets forward against Norfolk, *ib.*; banished for ten years, *ib.*; swears that he will keep apart from Norfolk, 89; his exile reduced to six years, *ib.*; goes to France, *ib.*; beloved of the people, *ib.* *See* Lancaster

Hertlowli (Barkloughly), Richard II. landed near the castle of, 106 *n* 1

"heuyncasse," displeasure, 262

Holinshed, Raphael, his will, ix; 2nd ed. of his chronicles the source of some plays, ix, x; used unauthentic materials, xii; names in *Cymb.* occurring in his chronicles, 17, 18

Hopkins, Nicholas, arrested, 430; lived at Henton, 435; his prophecy about Buckingham, 437; brought forth at Buckingham's trial, 447

Horses eat their own flesh, 31; immersed in blood, 187

"hosto" (*hostia*), victim, 333

Howard, John Howard, Baron, one of Gloucester's trustiest counsellors, 367 *n* 2. *See* Norfolk, John Duke of

——, Lord Thomas, son of Thomas 2nd Duke of Norfolk, and Agnes Tilney ("the old dutches of Norffolke"), bearer of the princess Elizabeth's canopy, 506

—— of Effingham, William Howard, Baron (1554–73), deputy in the coronation procession of Anne Boleyn, 485; bearer of the princess Elizabeth's canopy, 506

——, Sir Thomas, laughs at Hastings for lingering with a priest, 367; when knighted, 367 *n* 2. *See* Surrey, Thomas Earl of, *and* Norfolk, 2nd Duke of

Hubert, difference between the dramatic and historic H., 77. *See* Kent for the historic Hubert

Hume (or Hun), John, accused of sorcery, 253; pardoned, 259; was the Duchess of Gloucester's chaplain, 259 *n* 1

Hungerford, Sir Walter (afterwards Baron Hungerford), wishes for more soldiers at Agincourt, 190 *n* 3; taken prisoner at Patay, 207

——, Thomas (son of Robert 3rd Baron Hungerford), his heiress married Lord Hastings, 319 *n* 2

Huntingdon, John Holland, Earl of (1387–1400), misled Richard II., 86; conspires against Henry IV., 122, 123; devises Henry's death at a justs, 123; requests Henry to be present, *ib.*; raises men and joins his confederates, 124. *See* Exeter, John Holland

——, John Holland, Earl of (1416–48), present at Henry V.'s betrothal to Katharine, 201; at the siege of Melun, 201 *n*; attends Henry VI.'s coronation at Paris, 238

"hurlynge," strife, 141 *n* 1

Hussey of Sleford, John Hussey, Baron, (?) bearer of the princess Elizabeth's canopy, 506

Iden (or Eden) slays Cade, 264 (*cp.* 263 *n* 3)

"importable," intolerable, 375

"imposteme," aposteme, abscess, 266

Ina, King of Wessex, his daughters' answers touching their love for him, 2 *n* 2

"incensed," insensed, instructed, 249

Innocent III. causes Langton to be chosen Archbishop of Canterbury, 55; threatens John with an interdict, *ib.*; sends Pandulph to John, 56; deposes John, 57; commands Philip to make war on John, *ib.*; John does homage to, 65; sides with John against the English barons, 68; tries to prevent Lewis from invading England, 69; defends John's title, 70, 71

"insane Root," the, possibly "mekllweert," 21 *n* 2

"intreatie," conference, 317, 318

Irish, the, war with the Britons 8 *n* 2; invade the English pale, 89; attached to York, 248, 282 *n* 1, 296; and Rutland, 296

Isabel, daughter of Pedro the Cruel, was Aumerle's mother, 121 *n* 1

Isabelle of Bavaria, wife of Charles VI., receives Henry V.'s ambassadors at Troyes, 200; present at the conference of Meulan, *ib.*; at Troyes when Katharine was married, 201 *n* 1; brought Katharine to Meulan, 201 *n* 3

—— of Flanders. *See* Ermengarde

—— of Valois, second wife of Richard II., her marriage mentioned, 81; her residence, 110 *n* 1; leaves London 120

"Isoldune," Issoudun, 54

James, titular king of Majorca, was Richard II.'s godfather, 118. *See* correction, p. xxiii

Jeanne Darc brought to Charles VII., 210; date of her first audience, 210 *n* 2; her surname, 210 *n* 5; parentage and condition, 210, 211; person and character, 211; journey to Charles, *ib.*; sword, *ib.*; ensign, *ib.*; first talk with Charles, *ib.*; an army appointed her by

JOH

Charles, 212; her exploits and death, *ib.*;
raises the siege of Orleans, 215, 216; the
dramatic Jeanne takes Rouen, 224, 225;
historic date of her capture, 237; examined
by Cauchon, 238; called "the Pucelle," 238
n 3; relapses, 239; burnt, *ib.*; her visions, *ib.*
John, Richard II., baptized as, 118
"John Baptist, by St.," Richard II.'s oath, 81
John, King of England, his regnal years computed from Ascension Day, 45 *n* 3; proclaimed
king, 46; Chinon and Saumur delivered to,
ib.; owed his crown chiefly to Eleanor, *ib.*;
exacted money from the clergy, 47, 48;
takes Angers, 51; England bequeathed to,
52; rejects Philip II.'s terms, *ib.*; reconciled to Arthur, *ib.*; cedes and regains
territory, 53, 54; does homage to Philip and
receives Arthur's homage, 54; returns to
England, *ib.*; refuses to confirm Langton's
election, 55; gives audience to Pandulph, 56;
formally deposed by Innocent, 57; refuses to
surrender his transmarine dominions to
Arthur, 57 *n* 3; recaptures Mirabeau, 58, 59;
takes Arthur prisoner, and offers friendship
to him, 59; imprisons Arthur, *ib.*; recrowned,
59, 60; orders the blinding of Arthur, 60;
accused by Constance of Arthur's murder, 61
n 1; his deposition prophesied, 62; imprisons
and hangs Peter of Pomfret, *ib.*; glad to hear
that Arthur was not blinded, 63; suspected
of being Arthur's murderer, *ib.*; prepares to
resist Philip's invasion, *ib.*; receives a message from Pandulph, 64; confers with Pandulph and yields to Innocent, 64, 65; delivers
his crown to Pandulph, 65; blamed for hanging Peter, *ib.*; influenced by Peter's prophecy,
65, 66; his forces defeated by Philip at Bouvines, 66; fails to recover Poitou and Brittany,
ib.; league against him formed by his barons,
66, 67; retreats from Lewis, 67, 68; repudiates
the Great Charter, 68; his crown offered to
Lewis, 69; his procurators oppose Lewis's
claim, 70; receives Gualo, *ib.*; loses his
baggage in the Wash, 73; sickens and dies,
ib.; said to have been poisoned, 74; buried
in Worcester Cathedral, *ib.*; his person and
character, 76; quarreled with the clergy, *ib.*;
hated by his subjects for pinching their
purses, 76, 77
—— of Lancaster, 3rd son of Henry IV., concerned with a riot in Eastcheap, 141 *n* 1;
marches against Archbishop Scrope, 152;
receives the submission of Scrope and Mowbray, 154. *See* Bedford, John Duke of
"Iolie," joyful, 204
Jourdain, Margery, accused of sorcery, 253;
executed, 259

Katharine of Arragon visited by Charles V.,
429; rumour that her marriage was unlawful,
452; the best clerks were to be her counsel,
454; their names, 457; called into court,
458; her appeal to Henry, 458—460; accuses
Wolsey, 461; leaves the court, 461, 462; will

LAN

not recall her appeal to the pope, 466, 483;
visited by the two cardinals, 468, 469; who
advise her to surrender her cause to Henry's
decision, 469; styled princess dowager, 480;
divorced, 483, 484; visited by Chapuys,
489; her letter to Henry, *ib.*; dies, *ib.*;
would be served as a queen, 490
Katharine of Valois, her marriage to Henry V.
broached, 178; her dowry offered, 179;
receives Henry's ambassadors at Troyes, 200;
her marriage with Henry arranged, *ib.*;
present at the conference of Meulan, *ib.*;
affianced to Henry, 202; date of her marriage,
202 *n* 3; grant to, of house inherited by
York, 223 *n* 2; her son born, 223, 224
Kenneth III., King of Scots, defeats the Danes
at Loncarty, 16, 17; reproached by a noctur-
nal voice for the murder of Malcolm Duff, 30
Kent, Anne (born Blennerhasset), Countess of,
bears the train of the princess Elizabeth, 506
——, Hubert de Burgh, Earl of, would not
blind Arthur, 60; yet gives out that Arthur
was blinded and was dead, 61; holds Dover
Castle against Lewis, 68, 77; assists in
defeating Lewis's reinforcements, 71, 72; a
party to the treaty of peace with Lewis, 77
——, Thomas Holland, 2nd Earl of, his
daughter married York, 121 *n* 1; story of his
dog Maths, 124 *n* 3
——, 3rd Earl of, conspires against Henry
IV., 122, 123; beheaded, 127. *See* Surrey,
Thomas Holland
Kentishmen were Yorkists, 296
"kiffe," kith, 2 *n* 2
Kikelie (*Kelly* F.), Sir Richard, slain at Agincourt, 196. "Le S' de Richard Kykelley,"
Harleian MS. 782, fol. 49, col. 1 (quoted in
Nicolas's *Agincourt*, ed. 2, p. 369)
Kildare, Gerald Fitzgerald, 9th Earl of, committed to prison, 449
Knyvet, Charles, Buckingham's surveyor, procured by Wolsey to accuse Buckingham, 434,
435; his evidence, 436—439; had been dis-
missed by Buckingham, 48'; brought forth
at Buckingham's trial, 447

Lady, a, bearing the train of the princess
Elizabeth, 506. (Anne, Countess of Kent)
Lady Macbeth (Gruoch), xiii
"Laford," Sleaford, 73
Lancaster, John of Gaunt, Duke of, becomes
bail for Bolingbroke, 78; ambush laid against
him by Norfolk, 81; excuses Gloucester to
Richard II., 84; reproves Gloucester, and
leaves the court, 85; comes to London with a
power, *ib.*; forgives Gloucester's death, 86;
dies, 91; his third marriage disliked by Gloucester, 129; his house (the Savoy) burnt by the
villains, 277; his Spanish expedition, 313
——, Henry of Bolingbroke, Duke of, his
inheritance confiscated, 91, 102; his marriage prevented, 92; invited to dethrone
Richard II., 96; sails from Brittany, *ib.*;
delays landing in England, 96, 97;

York's levies will not resist him, 98, 101; lands at Ravenspur, 98; joyfully received, *ib.*; his oath to the lords at Doncaster, 101; marches to Berkeley and meets York, 101, 102; adherents flock to him, 102; Richard's favourites brought before him at Bristol, 104; goes to Flint, 107, 108; meets Richard there, 109; rides with him to London, *ib.*; present at Richard's abdication, 114, 118; claims the crown, 114, 115; his claim confirmed by parliament, 115; ring put on his finger by Richard, 117, 118; the crown delivered to him by Richard, 118; was joyfully received by the Londoners, 120, 121; followed by Richard's greyhound, 124 *n* 3. *See* Henry IV.

"Lancastriall," Lancastrian, 312

Lane, the long, at Loncarty, 16

Langton, Stephen, chosen Archbishop of Canterbury, 55; rejected by John, *ib.*; goes with Pandulph to Philip II., 57

"laund," *ib.* plain, 33

"leame," *ib.* light, 15 *n* 2

Lear (Leir), sources for the story of, 1; madness of, *ib.*; built Leicester, 2; his daughter's answers touching their love for him, 2, 3; gives his elder daughters in marriage, and makes their husbands his heirs, but disinherits Cordelia, 3; deposed, and his retinue diminished, 4; flees to Cordelia and is kindly received, 5; makes her his sole heiress, *ib.*; restored to the throne by Aganippus, *ib.*; dies, *ib.*; swears by Apollo, 5 *n* 1; compares himself to a dragon, *ib.*

"legacie," legateship, 457

Leicester, Abbot of (Richard Pexal), receives Wolsey as his guest, 491

"Lestrake" (*Lestrale* F.), Earl of, slain at Agincourt, 196. No similar title occurs in Monstrelet's lists (iii. 348—356). The list given in Harleian MS. 782, fol. 48 verso, col. 2 (quoted in Nicolas's *Agincourt*, ed. 2, p. 367), places "The Countie de Lestrake" among the slain

"lettise," grey fur, 485

Leuenox, Lennox, 45

"lewdeate," most illiterate, 270 *n* 2

Lewis, son of Philip II., King of France, betrothed to Blanch of Castile, 53; invades England, 67; many Englishmen do homage to him, 67, 68; he makes them large promises, 68; his procurators defend his title to the crown of England, 69, 70; his army defeated at Lincoln, 71; the reinforcements sent him destroyed, 71, 72; his plot against the English barons, 72; makes peace with Henry III., and leaves England, 74, 75

——, Dauphin of France, eldest son of Charles VI., sends tennis-balls to Henry V., 165, 173; seeks advice for the defence of France, 178, 179; refuses succour to Harfleur, 181; prevented by his father from being at Agincourt, 183; at Agincourt according to the F. text of *Hen. V.*, 183 *n* 1

Lewis XI., King of France, refuses to deface Bedford's tomb, 232, 233; favours the Lancastrians, 312; assents that Bona shall marry Edward IV., 313; leagues with the Lancastrians, 317, 318; lends René money to ransom Margaret, 342 (*op.* 341 *n* 2)

Lewis, the Countess of Richmond's physician, proposes to Queen Elizabeth an alliance of Lancaster and York, 398, 399

Limoges, Widomar Viscount of, slain by Richard L.'s bastard, 48. *See* Austria, 53 *n* 1

Lingard, fictitious ancestress of Hugh Capet, 170

Lisle, John Talbot, Viscount, refuses to desert his father, 231, 232

Lists not to be touched, 87

"lode-starre in honour," Henry V. a, 205

London, Mayor of, in 1 *Hen. VI.* (John Coventre), prevents rioting, 213. *See also* Sir Edmund Shaw *and* Sir Stephen Peacock

London, rejoicing there to celebrate Caesar's defeat, 14; took its name from Lud, *ib.*; temple there—afterwards St. Paul's—built by Lud, 14 *n* 1; Lewis (son of Philip II.) there, 68; the citizens of, sorry for Gloucester's death, 85; joyful reception of Bolingbroke there, 120, 121; balls, Henry V.'s, 173; mayor of, welcomes Henry V., 196; troubled by the strife of Gloucester and Winchester, 222; mayor of, asks for help against Cade, 275; bridge, conflict on, with Cade, 276, 277, 279 *n* 1, 280; favours the Yorkists, 292; Edward IV.'s chief residence, 378

Longland, John, Bishop of Lincoln, asserts that Henry's marriage was unlawful, 452

"Lovell, Sir Thomas," 403 *n* 1. *See* Rewell, Thomas

——, Sir Thomas, attends Buckingham to the Temple stairs, 450

Lucy, Dame Elizabeth, her alleged betrothal to Edward IV., 377

Lud, King of Britain, much esteemed London, 14; which took its name from him, *ib.*; built a temple there, turned to St. Paul's church, 14 *n* 1

Lynx, Lynceus the Argonaut, 36, 421. But *op.* a marg. note in *Halle* (54): "Lynx is a beast like to a wolfe, whose sighte dooeth perce all thinges"

Macbeth probably not regarded as an usurper, xii; stories about, xiii; his wife's name was Gruoch, *ib.*; temporarily dethroned, xiii *n* 1; rebellion against, *ib.*; his parentage, 18; character, *ib.*; blames Duncan's leniency, 20; sent against Macdowald, whom he defeats, *ib.*; sends Macdowald's head to Duncan, 21; commands the van in the war with Sueno, *ib.*; defeats the Danes sent by Canute, 22; grants burial to their dead, *ib.*; meets the weird sisters, 23, 24 (*op.* xiii); jests with Banquo about their prophecy, 24; made thane of Cawdor, *ib.*; resolves to seize the kingdom, 25; urged thereto by his wife, *ib.*; murders Duncan, *ib.*; is made king,

MAC

26 ; rules well for ten years, 32 ; his laws, *ib.* ; causes Banquo to be murdered, 33 ; becomes a cruel tyrant, 34 ; builds a castle on Dunsinane, 34, 35; is angered by Macduff's refusal to visit Dunsinane, 35 ; warned to beware of Macduff, 36 ; trusts in a witch's prophecies, 36, 41 ; keeps spies in his nobles' houses, 36; slays Macduff's wife and children, 37 ; tries to entrap Malcolm, 38, 40 ; some of his nobles take part with Malcolm, 41 ; retires to Dunsinane, *ib.* ; his friends' advice, *ib.* ; sees the approach of Birnam Wood, 42 (*cp* xiii); flies from Dunsinane, *ib.* ; slain by Macduff in 1057 (*cp.* xiii), 43 ; length of his reign, xiii, 43 ; escapes from the battle with Siward, 44 *n* 1

Macdowald (Macdonwald *Macb.*) rebels against Duncan, 19 ; obtains men from the western isles, 20 ; defeats Duncan's people, *ib.* ; defeated by Macbeth, and slays himself, *ib.* ; his head sent to Duncan, 21

Macduff, thane of Fife, refuses to visit Dunsinane, 35 ; destined to slay Macbeth, 36 (*cp.* xiii) ; resolves to join Malcolm Canmore in England, *ib.* ; his wife and children slain by Macbeth, 37 ; acquaints Malcolm with Macbeth's cruelty, *ib.* ; urges Malcolm to attempt Macbeth's overthrow, 38 ; answers Malcolm's self-accusations, 38, 39 ; despairs when he hears of Malcolm's dissimulation, 39 ; is undeceived by Malcolm, 40 ; requires the Scottish nobles to support Malcolm, 40, 41 ; pursues Macbeth to Lumphanan, 42 ; was ripped from his mother's womb, 43 ; slays Macbeth, *ib.* ; made earl of Fife, 45

Maglanus, Duke of Albania. *See* Albany, Duke of

Maine yields allegiance to Arthur, 46 ; Arthur's homage for, 52 ; possession of, demanded for Arthur, *ib.* ; ceded to René of Anjou, 244 ; a key of Normandy, 245

"mainpernour," surety, 124

Malcolm III. (Canmore) made prince of Cumberland, 25 ; takes refuge with Eadward the Confessor, 31 ; hears from Macduff of Macbeth's cruelty, 37 ; tests Macduff's sincerity by accusing himself of vices, 38, 39 ; his piety, 39 *n* 1 ; undeceives Macduff, 40 ; obtains the assistance of Siward, 41 ; attached to English habits, *ib.* (*cp.* xii); his soldiers take branches from Birnam Wood, 42 ; is presented with Macbeth's head, 43 ; crowned at Scone, 44 ; calls a parliament at Forfar, 45 ; gives earldoms to his thanes, *ib.*

March, Edmund Mortimer, fifth Earl of (1398—1425), confounded with his uncle Edmund, 131 *n* 1, 134 *n* 4, 257, 258 ; reveals Cambridge's conspiracy to Henry V., 174 *n* 1 ; date of his death, 218 ; charge of, entrusted to Prince Henry, 219 ; not a state prisoner, *ib.* ; his offices, *ib.* ; Halle's obituary notice of, *ib.* ; (?) confounded with Sir John Mortimer, 219 *n* 5

MOR

March, Edward Plantagenet, Earl of. *See* Edward IV.

——, George de Dunbar, Earl of ("Lord Mortimer of Scotland "), defeats the Scots at Homildon, 131—133 ; urges Henry IV. to attack Hotspur without delay, 142 ; engages to become Henry's subject, 142 *n* 1 ; withdraws Henry from the main attack at Shrewsbury, 146

Margaret of Anjou, her intrigue with Suffolk a fiction, xiii, xiv ; her marriage to Henry VI. arranged, 238 ; her character, 242 ; her espousals, 243 ; conveyed to England, *ib.* ; crowned, 244 ; was dowerless, *ib.* (*cp.* 246) ; favours the conspiracy against Gloucester, 246 ; deprives him of power, 260 ; ruined by his death, 264, 265 ; tries to screen Suffolk, 267, 268 ; sends the Staffords against Cade, 273 ; releases Somerset from ward, 286, 287 ; refuses to join Henry, and raises an army, 294, 295 ; York's head presented to, 299 ; withdraws to the north, 301, 304 ; defeated the Yorkists at St. Albans, 302 ; reunited to Henry, 302, 303 ; fortunate in two battles, 304 ; defamed, *ib.* ; seeks help from Lewis XI., 312 ; visits René, 312 *n* 1 ; leagues with Warwick, 317, 318 ; her return to England delayed by weather, 328 ; met Somerset at Cerne Abbey, 334 *n* 3 ; landed at Weymouth, 337 ; her despair after Warwick's defeat, 338 ; a prisoner after Tewkesbury field, *ib.* ; ransomed, 341 *n* 2, 342 ; date of her death, 347

Marle, Robert de Bar, Count of, holds his men together at Agincourt, 193 ; defeated and slain, *ib.*, 196

Mathe, Richard II.'s greyhound, story of, 12 *n* 3

"mawmet," puppet, 139 *n* 2

"meane stature," middle height, 164

Melun, Adam, Viscount of, confesses Lewis's plot against the English barons, 72 ; his confession averts them from Lewis, 72, 73

Merlin likens Utherpendragon to a dragon's head, 5 *n* 1 ; his prophecy about the moldwarp, 139 *n* 2

"messe, a," four persons' share, 370

"mewe, in," encaged, concealed, 259 *n* 4

Minions, the king's, courtiers who had been in France, 440

"mirrour of magnificence," Henry V. a, 205

Montague, Henry Pole, Baron, arrested, 431

——, John Neville, Baron and afterwards Marquess, 290 *n* 2 ; loth to revolt from Edward, 321, 322 ; with Warwick at Barnet, 335 ; slain, 337

Montgomery, Sir Thomas, obliges Edward IV. to proclaim himself king, 332

Montjoy, Herald of France, sent to defy Henry V., 182 ; sent to Aire, 184 *n* 2 ; receives Henry's answer to his defiance, 185 ; craves burial for the dead, 194 ; answers Henry's questions, *ib.*

Moons, five seen at once in John's reign, 62

Moray, Thomas Dunbar, Earl of, taken prisoner at Homildon, 132

Lightning Source UK Ltd.
Milton Keynes UK
UKOW04f1533020118
315266UK00007BC/787/P